KT-196-454

# Human Resource Management

## MANAGEMENT, ORGANIZATIONS AND BUSINESS SERIES

*Series Editor: John Storey*

This wide-ranging series of texts, surveys and readers sets out to define the study of the management of people and organizations. Designed for both postgraduate and undergraduate students of business and management, it will draw on the leading authors from the various contributing disciplines, including organizational psychology, sociology and labour economics. A distinctive characteristic of the Series is that these subject specialists will make their work available to the general business and management student in a highly accessible way.

### Forthcoming titles in the Series:

*Motivation and Performance*, David Guest

*Analyzing Labour Markets*, Marion Whitaker

*Management Development*, Andrew Thomson, John Storey, Christopher Mabey and Colin Gray

# Human Resource Management

## A Strategic Introduction

*Second Edition*

Christopher Mabey, Graeme Salaman and John Storey

BLACKWELL
Business

Copyright © Christopher Mabey, Graeme Salaman and John Storey 1998

The right of Christopher Mabey to be identified as author of this work has been asserted in accordance with the Copyright, Designs and Patents Act 1988.

First published 1998

Reprinted 1999 (twice), 2000

Blackwell Publishers Ltd
108 Cowley Road
Oxford OX4 1JF, UK

Blackwell Publishers Inc
350 Main Street
Malden, Massachusetts 02148, USA

All rights reserved. Except for the quotation of short passages for the purposes of criticism and review, no part of this publication may be reproduced, stored in a retrieval system, or transmitted, in any form or by any means, electronic, mechanical, photocopying, recording or otherwise, without the prior permission of the publisher.

Except in the United States of America, this book is sold subject to the condition that it shall not, by way of trade or otherwise, be lent, re-sold, hired out, or otherwise circulated without the publisher's prior consent in any form of binding or cover other than that in which it is published and without a similar condition including this condition being imposed on the subsequent purchaser.

*British Library Cataloguing in Publication Data*
A CIP catalogue record for this book is available from the British Library

*Library of Congress Cataloging in Publication Data has been applied for*

ISBN 0–631–21145–4 (hbk) — ISBN 0–631–20823–2 (pbk)

*Commissioning Editor:* Catriona King
*Desk Editor:* Tony Grahame
*Production Controller:* Rhonda Pearce
*Text Designer:* Rhonda Pearce

Typeset in 10 on 12pt Book Antiqua
by Grahame & Grahame Editorial, Brighton
Printed and bound in Great Britain
by T. J. International Limited, Padstow, Cornwall

This book is printed on acid-free paper

# Contents

# Acknowledgements

The authors and publisher gratefully acknowledge the following for permission to reproduce copyright material:

Figure 2.2 HRM responses: contrasting responses in the changing world of computing: P. Sparrow and A. Pettigrew, *Personnel Management*, February 1988 (reproduced by courtesy of Personnel Publications, London and P. Sparrow); Figure 6.1 Stages of European HRD, *International Journal of HRM*, 3 3, 1992 (Routledge, London, 1992); Figure 6.2 A framework, fig 8.3, A.W. Harzing and van Ruysseveldt, *International Human Resource Management* (Sage Publications, London, 1995); Figure 10.2 The energy-flow model, M. Pedler, T. Boydell and J. Burgoyne, *The Learning Company* (McGraw-Hill Publishing Co., London, 1988); Figure 11.4 Five development, A.M. Jones and C. Hendry, *The Learning Organisation: a review of literature and practice* (HRD Partnership, London, 1994, Institute of Personnel and Development, London); Figure 14.1 The relationship between change context and decision-making/control modes, fig 2.10, R. Stacey, *Strategic Management and Organisational Dynamics* (Pitman, London, 1996, © Financial Times Management); Figure 14.2 How individuals typically cope with personal life changes, C. Carnall, *Managing Change* (Routledge, London, 1991, © International Thomson Publishing).

The publishers apologize for any errors or omissions in the above list and would be grateful to be notified of any corrections that should be incorporated in the next edition or reprint of this book.

# List of Figures

# List of Tables

# Preface

Since the publication of the first edition of this text, there have been a number of important changes in the field of Human Resources. There is now a greater self-confidence about the potential benefit of intangible assets, notably human resources, contributing to the strategic success of organizations. We weigh these claims more fully in this edition, and partly for this reason subtitle the book 'A strategic introduction'. Changes to the design of, and relationships within, organizations are becoming ever more complex, and to assess this shifting architecture we include a totally new section on managing organizational structures. Updated with the fruits of research and case material where pertinent, the text is now organized around six parts, each intended to provide readers with a different route into the subject matter depending on their primary interest. The HR literature has continued to burgeon, and the realities of organization, of power, of market, of priorities and politics which lie behind the management of human resources, continue to be disguised by some of the language in the field. Importantly, by being disguised, they are also served by this language. Hence the need for a new edition of this book to reflect the concern with rhetoric and reality, and to keep pace with the persistent discrepancies between them.

While we must take responsibility for the final product, this text has been significantly enriched by the work and contribution of a number of colleagues, not least Greg Clark for the original generation of chapter 4 and Paul Iles for the original version of chapters 3 and 6. Finally, we are indebted once again to the Blackwell team, especially Catriona King and Bridget Jennings, for keeping the project on track.

*Christopher Mabey*
*Graeme Salaman*
*John Storey*

# Introduction

Strategic Human Resource Management (SHRM) is big business; it promises a great deal; and these promises are seductive. But while it is true that 'huge resources have been committed in the last four decades or so to managerial activities often designed by consultants, or academics with consulting aspirations, aimed at improving managerial effectiveness, 'all too often this has a transitory nature which seems to proceed from deep disillusionment with one panacea that has run its course to high enthusiasm for the next' (Gill and Whittle 1992: 282). There is a noticeable and striking pattern apparent in the history of approaches to organization change and improvement: high enthusiasm, extravagant promises, followed by failure, deep disillusionment and rejection. And then silence, as if it had never happened. Until the next time; for oddly, despite the frequency of this pattern – this triumph of hope over experience – it doesn't seem to disturb or reduce enthusiasm for the next solution, the next panacea.

SHRM places great emphasis on the capacity – indeed the possibility – of organizational learning: learning about an organization's environment, about its performance, its objectives, its capability, and in the light of this, its capacity to learn from the change. Capability in SHRM is not simply capability to achieve a given strategy, important as this is; it is also, and primarily, capability to develop, and re-develop, strategy in the first place, and thus to design and oversee the necessary systemic change. But there may be a paradox here. This was spotted a long time ago by Argyris: 'One might say that participants in organizations are encouraged to learn to perform as long as the learning does not question the fundamental design, goals and activities of their organizations . . . [The] high degree of consonance between learning acculturation and the kind of limitations placed on learning within groups and organizations result in processes that limit exploration and information and so help provide stability but also inhibit learning in fundamental organizational issues' (Argyris 1976: 367).

How far does SHRM really intend what it often promises: an emphasis on valuing and developing the organization's 'human resources'? And how far does the focus of SHRM on structures, systems and cultures, mask a concern to retain certain fundamental priorities and values: namely short-termism and boardroom privilege?

Can we, who need these SHRM solutions, and who are disturbed by the failure of our organizations and the principles on which they are built – can we, who are part of the problem, escape the assumptions and habits we wish to reject. How can we think anew? Is SHRM actually possible?

## The Distinctiveness of this Text

These are not the only potential limitations to the possibility of SHRM – there are many others, discussed within this volume: how far does SHRM *really* question the basic (and possibly limiting and damaging) assumptions of senior management? How far are the objectives actually pursued by SHRM initiatives sensible and productive, in the long term? Is SHRM essentially a guide to corporate cost-cutting, in another guise? Or does it really represent, at least potentially, a way out of the habits and mind sets and values that very clearly are hampering the full flowering of organizational, and indeed national potential?

This book will explore these extremes: we believe that there is a great deal that is exciting and interesting in SHRM – and we will describe these developments and try to excite and enthuse you. We also believe that SHRM is important and powerful and therefore needs to be taken very seriously, and understood. We will show how and why SHRM is having such a dramatic effect on the way senior managers think and talk about, and act on, issues of organizational change. But we also believe that some features of SHRM need serious and radical critical attention because they are based on unacceptable and flawed assumptions. We will show where they are contradictory and ill-considered. The book is a mixture of description, analysis and critique; of excitement, moderation and concern: possibly a difficult mixture, but we hope an interesting and stimulating one, and we believe that to offer anything less than this would be to do you, the reader, a disservice.

We believe that this combination of elements makes the volume distinctive. There are already books that offer critiques – but that is all they do. And there are many books that offer SHRM recommendations and prescriptions; but that too is all they do. This book not only tries to do both, it tries to assess the implications of critique for prescription, and to point the way, out of an assessment of strengths and weaknesses, towards some suggestions that are of use to the practitioner. We see our duty in this volume not simply to warn, but also to be of real practical assistance to someone who needs advice on what to do and how to do it.

There is another distinctive strength of this volume which arises out of its origins in an MBA programme for mature students of management. This book is the set text for one of the largest MBA programmes in Europe. A consequence of this provenance is that the book is designed not simply as an adjunct to teaching – although we think and hope that it will play this role admirably – but as the centrepiece of a course on SHRM. It is in order to support the book in playing this role that we have added learning objectives, boxes with mini-cases and research results, summaries, and discussion questions. Those who use this volume as a basis for teaching will have access to a tutor's guide which will offer suggestions for the structure and content of teaching activities and inputs based on the book.

Another major benefit is that these materials and this book's structure have been developed over a number of years in the course of teaching the research, and endless discussions among the authors and between the authors and colleagues and students. As teaching materials at least, they have been developed through and from experience – sometimes painfully.

The book not only contains a variety of approaches and angles – descriptive, analytic and evaluative – it also contains a mixture of levels of analysis and presentation. We believe that a major and proper purpose of a book like this is to describe what is happening and to describe the relevant literature along with its constituent debates and themes: training, performance, culture, the learning organization, and so on. So, one objective of the book is to map the field.

But another purpose is to identify, to make explicit and to engage with the theory underpinning SHRM. Very frequently this theory is implicit and submerged. We will try to bring it to the surface. If we are to assess the value of an argument of prescription it is crucial to know the theoretical underpinnings on which it is based, and to assess these. This is one major way in which we may escape the sad cycle, mentioned earlier, of fashionable panacea being greeted with (unjustified) rapture and being followed by disappointment and rejection. Theory is important in any attempt to think about or plan organizational change, for such activities are inevitably based on theoretical assumptions about what organizations are, how they work, and how they can be changed.

## Part 1: SHRM: A New Way of Managing?

When characterized stereotypically it is not difficult to establish qualitative differences between personnel management and human resource strategies. But this is not comparing like with like. Rather it is distinguishing personnel management practice from the normative ideals of human resource management. One of the themes of this book is *choice* between human resource strategies: the selection of appropriate cultural, structural and behavioural strategies to redress the organizational inertia and facilitate competitive success. Part 1 examines the nature of these contingencies through a differentiation between open and closed approaches to SHRM.

By tracing some of the historical antecedents to the SHRM approach and resisting the notion of a standard set of pre-packaged human resource strategy solutions, we attempt to distil the conceptual and practical essence of SHRM. At a planning level, human resource policies will be integrated with the strategic objectives of an organization. Human resources will be viewed as vital to the achievement of these objectives, so investments will be made in the appropriate knowledge, competences and attitudes of the work force. The psychological contract between employer and employee is thus based on commitment rather than on compliance. There will be a coherence between the various human resource policies and practices chosen to bring about this commitment, with a heavy reliance on the involvement of the line manager and his or her ownership of the process. Typical hallmarks would be devolved responsibility and decision making, and flexibility leading to organizational adaptability. Nevertheless, while such attractive features of SHRM can be described, they remain normative and over-simplified.

Firstly, such descriptions tend to assume a rational conception and implementation of the organization's overall strategy; that this can be readily interpreted without distortion or political connivance; that suitable HR interventions can be found to 'fit' the strategy; that a 'package' of HR strategies can be pursued without internal contradiction; and that varying interest groups within the organization will subscribe implicitly to the goals and values advocated. Secondly, such descriptions seem to imply that – given its 'self-evident' benefits – there is widespread adoption of strategic HR policy and practice. But what indication is there that organizations are implementing human resource strategies in such a manner? Focusing on large, diversified, multinational companies in Britain, Purcell (1989) points to the structural and attitudinal constraints put on the development of integrated human resource initiatives. He argues that the pressure of 'second-order' strategies on unit managers to achieve short-run rates of return on investment and to maintain improvements to profit margins inhibits any attempt to build long-term, socially responsible human resource policies.

Looking further afield, cross-national research (Brewster and Hegewisch 1994) seems to indicate a slow and undramatic uptake of human resource strategies in the companies they surveyed in ten European countries. Despite this pessimistic picture, we refer to case studies and case extracts which suggest that organizations are at least attempting to reorientate their human resource planning processes and to choose human resource policies in a strategic manner in an effort to achieve the organizational outcomes they promise. Which brings us to the final and perhaps clinching set of questions for this section. When organizations endeavour to manage their human resources strategically in this way, are they then successful? Do they perform better than those who do not? Do the benefits of adopting human resource strategies outweigh their inherent costs? Having critically assessed the theory and the practice, the claims and the reality, the cogency and the contradictions of SHRM, we leave it to subsequent chapters to answer the crucial questions raised by this opening section.

## Part 2: Managing Performance

Managing performance is an intrinsic ingredient in all human resource strategies. Indeed, the very notion of first segmenting activities such as formal performance review, appraisal, staff development, team building and reward strategies from each other, and secondly, isolating them from the all pervasive, on-going aspects of the management role is indicative of piecemeal personnel practice rather than inherent human resource strategy. However, it is because performance management is such a core thread running through so many other strategically-oriented HR activities that we believe it deserves special attention. There are assumptions underlying the way performance is managed in organizations that unless surfaced and tested may introduce an incipient weakness into every other HR policy and practice.

Training has always been a favoured human resource response to individual and organizational performance issues, and is an essential, arguably a central, tool of SHRM. Certainly, the way development activities are conducted and co-ordinated is a telling index of how an organization views and values its staff: as commodities to be maximized at minimum cost at one extreme, or as resources to be developed-to-potential, at the other. Here we take the rational model of training provision to address skill performance gaps as its starting point. For instance, it is suggested that successful training is grounded in a careful diagnosis of not just present but also of future strategic requirements which takes account of the current and projected skills available or trainable within the company and in the external labour market. We examine the assumptions frequently made by HR and line managers about what different types of training can realistically achieve and suggest a model which facilitates an informed match between the learning theories that underlie different training methods and the developmental activities chosen to address them.

Undoubtedly an international approach to SHRM is something few organizations can afford to ignore legislatively, demographically, culturally, and politically even if – competitively – they do not inhabit a global or international marketplace themselves. In Part 2 we consider the impact of the world system on, for example, the international division of labour, and we draw upon cross-cultural research to understand better the implications upon country-level SHRM. Here we take an organizational perspective in order to analyse what might be learnt about recruiting, training, teamworking and rewarding across international boundaries, and how human resource development initiatives might be used to heighten awareness of national diversity and optimize the advantages of employing an increasingly multicultural workforce. While there is some evidence to suggest that organizations are achieving success in these areas, the effort and investment needed to support such strategic change – both structural and attitudinal – is high and not without instances of ethnocentric insensitivity.

## Part 3: Managing Structures

Part 3 describes and assesses the fundamental changes which are occurring in both structures and relationships. The first two chapters in the section focus on the various ways in which organizations are being restructured, and the third chapter examines the newly-emerging forms of employment relations. In all three chapters a managerial choice perspective is adopted and the meaning, implications, strengths and limits of such a perspective are explored.

The two chapters on organizational structuring and restructuring are built around a new analytical framework which for the first time places the myriad new forms within a conceptual order. Such an analytical framework is overdue and urgently required in the light of the bewildering array of forms. Mergers and take-overs are reported alongside demergers and corporate break-ups. Decentralization appears to be a perpetual process – a phenomenon only made possible by the resilient pull of (often hidden) recentralization. These two chapters also examine in some detail the more exotic developments in network and virtual organizations. The chapters are distinctive in that the treatment of organizational structuring and restructuring is undertaken with the strategic human resource management dimensions very much to the fore. Chapter 7 focuses mainly on restructuring occurring within conventional organizational boundaries, whereas chapter 8 attends to the novel forms of restructuring which extend well beyond and challenge these boundaries.

Chapter 9 turns to a review and assessment of employment relations. To a certain extent this chapter marks a departure from the perspectives which conventionally prevail in human resource management. Many of the concepts and ideas belong to a very different tradition. Indeed, some commentators conceptualize a progression *from* industrial/employment relations *to* human resource management. The employment relations tradition is rather more alert to issues of power and conflicts of interest than is normally the case within HRM and HRD. In this chapter we attend to these issues. It examines the nature of the employment relationship, the parties who have a stake in it, the institutions which have been designed to govern it, the processes which constitute it, and the key issues which make it vital and contentious. The central parts of the chapter examine the degree and nature of the changes re-shaping employment relations in so many countries and makes links back to the implications arising from the organizational restructurings covered in the preceding two chapters. The chapter is also distinctive in addressing in some detail employment relations in small firms and in non-union workplaces.

## Part 4: Managing Learning

The importance of learning is linked to the current pressures for change facing most if not all organizations. Within a stable, unpressured environment, the need for organizational learning on a major scale is seen as unnecessary. In fact, of course, there were never stable, unpressured environments; just environments which were *perceived* as unthreatening, where organizations failed to detect the small signs of emerging change and threat, or reacted to them confidently in terms of established ways of doing things which required no change or replacement. Here we argue that it is precisely the capacity of organizations to be so structured and organized that they are able to perceive accurately and to react appropriately to internal and external signals, which facilitates organizational learning. But what is it that distinguishes this kind of natural, incremental and necessary learning from the so-called 'learning organization'? Part of the answer lies in the ability of all members of the organization to question established habits and methods, to think the unthought of or unthinkable, and to discuss the undiscussable. Challenging their own and other's assumptions in this way paves the way to double-loop, even triple-loop learning at times when such creative leaps are commercially necessary: here the object of enquiry is error in the learning process itself.

Despite the evident virtue in this kind of approach, it is perhaps surprising to find so few firms getting beyond short-term problem-solving. In Part 4 we explore why it is that development activities often fail to 'deliver' the knowledge, skills and attitudes intended, why the fruits of learning at an individual level – when this does occur – are so infrequently garnered corporately, and why it is that organizations have an in-built defensiveness against new insights. We also discuss the central paradox of whether learning can be managed. This is a key issue for SHRM, because by definition the term suggests focused, integrated and organizationally productive outcomes. And yet, learning theory tells us that learning is most likely to occur when unfettered from external controls and undistorted by others' agendas. Once again, in our consideration of SHRM, we find ourselves in ethical territory: learning is not a neutral, apolitical activity. Learning is constantly taking place, whether deliberately constructed and reflected upon or not. However, the motives may be enthusiastic but 'suspect', the outcomes may be valid but 'negative', the lessons may be real but 'mistakes', the applications may be well-intentioned but 'wrong'. It all depends, of course, on who is asking the questions, for what reason and the degree to which yardsticks of learning are consensually derived. In short, the learning organization is probably more to do with a shared culture than procedural contrivance.

## Part 5: Managing Change

Change is now endemic to even the most mature and traditional of industries. The question is, to what extent can the opportunities, crises and conflicts of change be managed in a purposeful manner? Incremental change is constant but largely calculable and undisruptive. However, change associated with SHRM is typically transitional and in some cases transformational for the company concerned: people at all levels and with as many agendas are involved, the resources required are less determinate, the repercussions less easy to control, and the outcomes – possibly many months, even years hence – almost impossible to predict with any kind of precision. In these circumstances, how can HR interventions be meaningfully planned, how can support be won from those holding the budget, and how can the fine line between organizational control and individual creativity be maintained? Some of the main options are discussed in this volume. Whether to cultivate the change process through grass-roots support, via a successful pilot project nurtured quietly but credibly in some corner of the organization or whether to rely on a top-down 'cascade'; whether to use SHRM to primarily target skills and behaviours, or the way jobs are configured, roles and responsibilities are assigned, or – most ambitious of all – to attempt to shift the cultural centre of gravity in the organization. Each implies a very different mix of HR measures, some more broad in their scope and desired effects than others. Other choices concern the style of the change management process (indeed some would argue that this 'gameplan' is almost as important as the content of the HR package itself), the degree to which broad ownership of the HR schemes are sought prior to their implementation (which is frequently dictated by commercial urgency and/or top team predisposition), and the type of change agency called upon to steer the SHRM through the organization.

Conceptually, the notion of a unified and malleable culture seriously underestimates the systemic conflict inherent in most organizations, the unequal power structures and the heterogeneity of employee groupings. It also seriously overestimates the capacity and wit of managers to influence differentiated cultures and sub-cultures in anything approaching a predetermined manner. This is not to say cultures cannot change, or be changed. However, caution needs to be exercised about the level of change that is being attempted and for whose ends. At a time when the devolving of decision making to autonomous groups of employees and the empowering of staff are much in vogue as HR strategies, it is important to distinguish consensus from control, commitment from compliance, behavioural changes from attitudinal (or even values) change, and the genuine migration of cultural norms from the superficial manipulation of meanings and symbols, mission statements and corporate logos.

## Part 6: Managing Meaning

Having made a detailed examination of several key ingredients of, and themes within SHRM (Parts 2–5) we return in Part 6 to a more searching analysis of the propositions that underlie the concept of strategic human resource management itself. Many of these issues were raised in the opening section, others have become apparent in our discussion of specific HR strategies; collectively they comprise a set of highly pertinent and provocative questions. How, for instance, at a conceptual level, can the following contradictions within HRS be reconciled: the need for greater central control at the same time as devolved decision-making and greater autonomy for staff groups; the exhortation to align HR policies with strategic objectives in a financial context that urges short-term profitability; the delayering, downsizing and redundancies of competitive restructuring (associated with 'hard' SHRM) alongside the empowering, commitment-generating, developmental policies typical of 'soft' SHRM; the encouragement of teamworking and collective responsibility for quality in a context of individualistic performance-related reward strategies and personal contracts? These are just some of the on-going contradictions in SHRM (Storey 1992). At an implementation level there are further inherent difficulties with HR strategies as advocated: even if issues of vertical, horizontal and sub-unit integration can be overcome, do managers actually have the capacity to discern and design HR initiatives which 'fit' the external demands and internal capabilities of the organization? And, even if fit were achieved, how long would the chosen strategies be appropriate before market exigencies rendered them outmoded or redundant? For example, the harsh competitive climate of the 1990s led to many European enterprises adopting HR measures which overruled the previously favoured soft SHRM approach.

Having considered difficulties with HRS from conceptual and implementation perspectives, Part 6 goes on to examine two further and possibly more fundamental flaws in the more celebratory claims of SHRM. The first concerns the way decisions are made and enacted in organizations. Too often it is assumed that strategies – including HR strategies – are conceived and delivered in a political vacuum, where the correctness of the proposed policies will be self-evident, where consensus is both achievable and sustainable, and where appropriate cultural and structural levers can be pulled in concert to bring about the desired outcomes. A number of inhibiting factors are discussed which interfere with the rationality of these processes – including the in-built inefficiencies, indifference, ignorance, defensiveness and learned helplessness of managers and senior management teams. The final concern we raise takes us from the inevitability of delusion in organizational strategy-making to the possibility of knowing deceit on the part of those arguing the SHRM case. We suggest that, for all the personal and corporate benefits arising from the renewed interest in the more enlightened management of human resources, there is a real risk that the rhetoric of SHRM has been and will be used to usher in old forms of managerial control; that the changes proposed in the name of SHRM, with their developmental appeal and espoused valuing of the individual – resonating as this does with wider cultural and political agendas of free markets, personal performance and corporate excellence – actually serves the agendas of organizational leaders most conveniently; and that the language of SHRM sometimes has more to do with defining the meaning of work and securing commitment from a workforce who are no less oppressed and no more emancipated than they traditionally have been.

## References

Argyris C. (1976) 'Single-loop and double-loop models in research on decision-making', *Administrative Science Quarterly*, vol. 21, 363–75.

Brewster, C. and Hegewisch, A. (1994) (eds) *Policy and practice in European HRM: the evidence and analysis from the Price Waterhouse Cranfield Study*, London: Routledge.

Cohen, M. and March, J. (1974) *Leadership and Ambiguity*, New York: McGraw-Hill.

Gill, J. and Whittle, S. (1992) 'Management by Panacea', *Journal of Management studies*, vol. 30, no. 2, 281–98.

Guest, D. (1987) 'Human resource management and industrial relations', *Journal of Management Studies*, vol. 24, no. 5, 503–21.

Purcell, J. (1989) 'The impact of corporate strategy on human resource management', in J. Storey, (ed.) *New perspectives on human resource management*, London: Routledge.

Storey, J. (1992) *Developments in the Management of human resources*, Oxford: Blackwell.

part 1

# SHRM: A New Way of Managing?

chapter 1

# The Nature, Origins and Implications of SHRM

CHAPTER OUTLINE

## Learning Objectives

After reading this introductory chapter you will be more aware of what Strategic Human Resource Management (SHRM) is and of the variety of current developments which may constitute SHRM in practice. Discussions of definitions can be tiresome and appear indulgent or unnecessary. But in this case they are crucial. The term SHRM has been used in a number of different ways to mean a variety of very different things. We need to be clear about the ways people are using the expression if we are to explore if it is happening in practice or indeed if it is possible to achieve it in practice. Chapters 3–16 present and discuss a comprehensive wealth of research findings, generalization and analyses with respect to the purpose and content of discrete specific SHRM initiatives in different areas. They offer research materials on the occurrence and impact of SHRM. But for these to make sense, and to contribute incrementally to an overall understanding of what SHRM is, and its impact and implications, it is necessary that you are able to locate these more detailed analyses in the context of a broad overview of SHRM, its background, origins and key features.

By the end of this chapter you will also be aware of where SHRM came from and so understand the intellectual and practical origins of SHRM theory and practice. As a result you will be able to make informed, and when necessary, critical and questioning analyses of SHRM ideas and recommendations. By enabling you to understand the nature, origins and implications of SHRM the chapter will equip you to recognize some of the tensions and questions that surround SHRM projects.

Specifically you will:

- Recognize the types of current organizational changes that are widely seen as indicative of SHRM.
- Be able to recognize the extent to which these changes do or do not constitute SHRM-type change.
- Know what SHRM is, in its various forms. This chapter identifies some of the key ideas inherent in SHRM approaches. The following chapter explores variations in types of, or definitions of, SHRM.
- Be aware of the background to SHRM and its underlying ideas. The ideas are not new yet there is something distinctive about SHRM, not simply as a set of practices, but as a body of ideas and associations, powerfully packaged and influential in their implications.

# Introduction

This book is intended both to be descriptive of SHRM and its key constituent ideas and to be analytical of the approach and its ideas. It will present, describe, analyse and critique. It is intended that the reader leaves the volume not only better informed about what SHRM is, but better able to evaluate SHRM and to understand it. These goals require us to consider the concept or approach of SHRM carefully and critically; not to tear it apart for the sake of it, but to assess how robust and impressive it is in terms of its constituent ideas and assumptions. This activity however, which starts in this chapter, is not easy. This is partly because SHRM is an 'elusive target, characterised by a diversity of meanings and ambiguous conceptual status' (Hales 1994: 51) Therefore we must spend some time looking at how SHRM has been defined and how it has been employed. But this is also difficult because SHRM may be not only diverse and ambiguous, it may also be contradictory – it may contain elements, or depend on assumptions, which are themselves inconsistent, pulling in different directions.

If this is the case it is important to identify and isolate these contrary impulses. Adam Smith, whose celebration of the nature and role of the market in *The Wealth of Nations* in 1776 inspires today's executives and politicians, once remarked that, 'The pretence that corporations are necessary for the better government of the trade, is without any foundation' (Smith 1937: 129). Is it then the case that there is an essential opposition between protecting managers' 'right to manage' in pursuit of maximum profitability, and the sorts of organizational structures, employee relations and job design principles associated with SHRM? Is SHRM possible within a market place which is inherently cyclical and chaotic?

Part of the answer to these questions depends on how SHRM is defined. From the chapters in Part I it will be apparent there is no single entity of SHRM, but a variety of different definitions and approaches. Furthermore, SHRM as an approach has much in common with other approaches to organizational restructuring, such as a focus on internal marketing (see Hales 1994). Because of the variety and complexity of approaches to SHRM, it is important to have some understanding of how SHRM is defined and used. It might seem that a discussion of the nature and merits and provenance of the ideas and assumptions inherent in approaches to organizational restructuring such as SHRM is simply academic. After all if it works, why worry? But, as we shall see, it isn't easy to know whether or not it *is* working; and anyway what do we mean by *working*? Working for whom, over what time-scale? And even if SHRM is working (by whatever measure) what costs are involved, and what costs are we prepared to pay, or to suffer? (We return to these questions in chapter 18.) And if SHRM is not working or is working partially and incompletely, is this because it is not being implemented properly or because the constituent ideas or even the basic approach itself is flawed?

So, thorough discussion of SHRM, even from the most hard-nosed, practical point of view, requires some analysis of the ideas and assumptions inherent in the approach. All activity on which we embark in which we seek to achieve some objective (of which SHRM is a good example) is ultimately theory-based, whatever the protestations of the people involved. Programmes of change intended to make organizations more effective or more efficient rely on the change-agent's theories of how organizations work and how they can be changed to make them work better (whatever that means). These assumptions and theories are often implicit, even subconscious – which is a pity because it means that they do not get the attention they merit and require. But they exist none the less and they significantly inform the practices derived from them. That is why they merit attention.

In this book we seek to make them explicit. After all, if a theory is ill-developed or unsustainable, the actions based on it will fail. It may be, for example, that one of the reason for the lack of take up of SHRM, or its lack of success, is that the approach is flawed by fundamental contradictions and confusions: that it doesn't make sense as a collection of ideas. For example, does SHRM assume a conception of group relations within the organization – that all groups and parties share the same goals, values and objectives? And if there are such unitarist assumptions, how realistic and secure are they? And does SHRM thinking and practice in some cases move from assumptions (about how organizations are, and how they work, however precarious) to facts – to claims that they actually conform with these assumptions: does SHRM 'drift from proclaiming the idea of organisations as harmonious teams, in which there is a congruence of values and interests among members as a *desideratum*, to asserting such congruence as fact' (Hales 1994: 62). If such an elision of hope and reality occurs then when conflict does occur it will be seen in terms of management failure to communicate effectively with staff, or to ensure that staff are brought round to management's viewpoint. The possibility that organizational structures and reward systems and experiences might generate a fundamental plurality of interests or inevitability of conflict is never entertained (Hales 1994: 62).

There is another ominous possibility – that SHRM ideas are essentially sensible but that market pressures make them unrealistic in practice.

SHRM ideas are attractive and powerful; they largely define the agenda of organizational change and restructuring. But for some commentators their attractiveness does not necessarily reflect their practical value: in fact their appeal may owe as much to their resonance with larger, social values as to their practical realism. In other words is SHRM so attractive, so appealing – so obviously 'right' – simply because it fits so well with pervasive current assumptions which because they are popular we think *must* be true? Like the ideas of Reagan and Thatcher (under whose auspices SHRM developed) SHRM presents as inevitable and necessary organizational strategies which may in fact be political choices aimed at displacing the costs of organizational decline to the less advantaged members of the organization, while presenting these policies as inevitable and neutral. The magic of SHRM is that it does this by trying to induce a sort of hypnotic trance wherein senior members of the organization become convinced of the unassailability and inevitability of ideas and policies which serve political purposes while denying their possible origin in powerful sectional interests and faddishness. Indeed is SHRM essentially a formula for managing decline, down-sizing, retrenchment, or genuinely, as it claims, a formula for unleashing, focusing and enhancing organizational creativity and capability?

After all, while SHRM has become the major approach to organizational restructuring, and is clearly extremely attractive to senior managers – so much so that this approach dominates current thinking on organizations and change – it has also been criticized on a number of fundamental fronts, most of them concerned with the status and value of SHRM thinking and SHRM ideas. It has, for example, been accused of assuming a naively optimistic view of internal organizational relations which is either ill-informed, or cynically manipulative. It has been accused of encouraging but masking control, exploitation and manipulation under the guise of a rhetoric of consensus, mutuality and empowerment. It has been held to consist of contradictory ideas – for example, simultaneously stressing individualism (in pay schemes) *and* co-operation; employee commitment *and* managerial flexibility exemplified in employment practices which enable management to turn labour on and off like a tap depending on demand for products or services; or strong corporate cultures *and* changeability and adaptability.

Nevertheless SHRM has also been seen as a ray of hope in the analysis and intervention in organization – as a genuinely new way of organizing and managing which could represent a break with the features traditionally associated with the structure and dynamics of large organizations: internal conflict, external inefficiencies and poor quality, and employee alienation. At a meeting of senior executives in 1993 from 25 leading UK companies, concerned to identify the key features of 'Tomorrow's Company', one of the central conclusions was the 'strong correlation between the companies with the highest emphasis on individualism and the poorest economic performance over the last ten years' (RSA, 1995, quoted in Clark 1995: 239). This was contrasted with the high levels of commercial success of companies adopting a team approach, particularly through collaboration between managers and employees, and companies and their investors, suppliers, customers and host communities (Clark 1995: 239–40). This is, essentially, the message of SHRM. Ghoshal and Bartlett, for example, see SHRM in these terms – as a radical new approach to organization, management and employee relations – and indeed to the relationship between firms and their host societies and to each other. They advocate a view of corporate strategy which moves away from the classical economic model of firms scrapping for their share of a limited market, maximizing the extraction of value from customers, and from staff. They note that the traditional approach to staff mirrors the traditional approach to suppliers – it is exploitative. And for this reason it fails. Instead they advocate a strategy towards human resources in which employees are developed and made employable – and this keeps the employer honest. Because staff are now more marketable, they will only stay with an employer that gives them a job they want to do (Ghoshal and Bartlett 1997).

There is also some evidence that these basic assumptions of SHRM do (or can) work. It is this contradictory terrain – of questionable assumptions and doubtful promises and exciting possibilities and the chance for real radical change – that constitutes the subject matter of this chapter, and which reverberates throughout the book as a whole.

Specifically this chapter is concerned with the following issues:

- The organizational changes which are widely seen as indicative of SHRM.
- The key arguments or ideas inherent in SHRM approaches.
- The background to SHRM – where it came from. Few of the ideas in SHRM

are new, as this sections shows. Yet there *is* something important and distinctive about SHRM, not simply as a set of practices, but as a body of powerful ideas and associations, powerfully packaged, and influential in its implications.

# The Nature of SHRM

It is now a cliché of those who work in and write about organizations that something new is happening with respect to the nature and speed of change in and around organizations. But this is a cliché that has some basis in reality. Probably there has been more change in organizations during the last 15 years than occurred in the previous 80 years. These days organizational structures are changing, work processes are changing, employment conditions and arrangements are changing, organizational values and cultures are changing. For many people this change is a personal reality: jobs change, careers change, labour markets change, organizational systems change, work technologies, products, relevant legal frameworks change.

Let's start with some typical and key views. In box 1.1 are some descriptions of SHRM projects. The descriptions differ markedly in what they describe and in the implied evaluation of what is described. Clearly SHRM involves not only inherent differences in the thing itself but differences in evaluations of the impact of these change projects.

## *What's going on?*

*On the one hand,* we have people exhorting the need for change, advocating change of a particular sort, claiming that such changes are possible and desirable, and insisting that these changes are occurring. Clark (1995) for example, describes in fascinating detail how Pirelli Cables deliberately set out, in the 1980s, to design a factory that represented the realization of many core SHRM ideas – notably a highly-skilled, flexible workforce with a single-union agreement, a flat organization structure, a large number of common employment conditions (holidays, pensions, work hours) and facilities, an emphasis on training and communications. These initiatives represented a major and deliberate break with past practices. Some years later the researcher and the senior manager who initiated and sponsored the experiment assessed its performance. Their conclusions are interesting. In many respects the factory had not succeeded in terms of its financial targets; but it had met production efficiency measures, customer satisfaction measures and personnel measures. The financial performance was affected by external environmental developments and specifically the recession of the early 1990s and its impact on the factory's customers in the construction industry. Furthermore the organizational environment of the Pirelli group also changed drastically during this period: factories were reduced from 102 to 80 between 1980 and 1992, and the workforce was reduced from 50,000 to 40,000. So the impact of

## BOX 1.1 DIFFERING CONCEPTIONS OF SHRM

First, some classics from the early days of SHRM – accounts which establish the essence of accounts of SHRM. The Personnel Director of Nissan UK writes:

> 'In the United States Pratt and Whitney has examined its 60-year-old culture. The company concluded that it was product-oriented, achieved quality through inspection, saw its people as an expendable resource, believed in management by control and used one-way communication. Now the value system has changed to one where the customer is the centre of the universe, quality is built in and people are regarded as the single most important part of the organisation and its only appreciable asset. The purpose of management is to facilitate and thus recognise that the largest single repository of ideas is the workforce, so "two-way communication" is of paramount importance.' (Wickens 1987: 183)

Or consider these remarks, about the then chairman of BP – Robert Horton's efforts to change the company in the late 1980s. This project includes the key elements of SHRM projects – achieving flexibility in response to clients and the market but also maintaining if not tightening central monitoring (and control) over performance, changing the corporate culture so that managers and staff want to do what the senior management want them to do, replacing obedience with initiative:

> 'Horton wants to reinforce its (BP's) strengths as a corporation while allowing its constituent businesses much greater flexibility and speed of response in the market place; achieving this "tight-loose" balancing act, . . . is one of the most difficult tasks facing multinationals today. In a phrase Horton's task is the complete stream-lining of BP: not just of its complex, costly, committee-ridden and over controlled formal organisation but also of the way managers behave within it . . . In place of the existing culture of bureaucracy, constant second-guessing and extreme distrust, Horton wants to create what last autumn he called "the corporate equivalent of perestroika and glasnost" . . . a structure with the minimum of controls and the maximum of delegation of responsibility, plus a supporting culture of openness, informal communication and verve. In other words rather than establish a shallower, flatter, more efficient pyramid, he wants to develop an organisation that works, thinks and feels entirely differently.' (Lorenz 1992a, b, c and d: 6)

Some research suggests that if SHRM can be achieved, if management are genuinely prepared to install SHRM initiatives, then it can work. These are big *ifs* . . .

Investigating the link between company performance and staff attitudes, one study claims that job satisfaction and employee commitment accounts for around 10 per cent of variations in profitability and 20 per cent of productivity (ESRC 1997). The more satisfied the staff, the better the company's performance. Altogether SHRM type practices account for 19 per cent of variations in performance – i.e. for improvements – and 18 per cent in productivity improvements. In contrast, quality programmes, business strategy and new technology accounted for far smaller percentage variations in performance or productivity. The study concludes that employee commitment and a positive conception of the psychological contract between employer and employee are fundamental to performance. But the authors make another point: that despite its potential impact, emphasis on HRM is one of the most neglected areas of management practice.

But some authors still find the whole notion of SHRM puzzling and contradictory, and note the contrast between the espoused claims of senior managers and their actions. For them, much (if not all) SHRM is, in practice, manipulative and hypocritical:

> 'The litany of innovative HRM social practices . . . should be regarded as cultural constructions fabricated through Government policy and corporate administrative fiat. They are self-conscious attempts not merely to change social behaviour but to transform the norms and values guiding social behaviour. As such, in the majority of cases, their introduction and implementation has been based on a fairly simplistic set of psychologistic behavioural assumptions: the structural context of social interaction is changed while, at the same time, attempts are made to engineer change in the interpretative frameworks of social action. We have seen the techniques of advertising, marketing and proselytising enlisted to propagate new images of organizational "reality" (Berg, 1986). The imposition of this new social order has been mediated by the "market" and massaged with management exhortation to induce not merely the acceptance of a negotiated order but, ultimately, individual normative commitment . . . The HRM "movement", a self-seeking cultural product, has been installed to manufacture, mediate and administer cultural transformation in an environment softened up by recession and unemployment. Fear is a great catalyst; but what is being constructed to replace it?' (Keenoy and Anthony 1992: 235–6)

the SHRM initiatives was strongly affected not by the logic of the initiative themselves but by their location within what the author calls 'the extraordinarily turbulent internal and external environments with which managers and staff at all levels had to cope while at the same time engaging with the design and implementation of a large-scale and highly innovative experiment' (Clark 1995: 237).

*On the other hand,* there are people claiming that all these proposed changes are inherently flawed in terms of their assumptions, that they wouldn't work anyway, or if they do work that they represent a glib attempt to exploit the current weaknesses and insecurity of employees and to manipulate employees' ways of thinking and values. It is this complex, messy and contentious area that this chapter attempts to clarify and map.

| | *Austin Rover* | *British Rail* | *Bradford Council* | *Eaton Ltd* | *Ford* | *ICI* | *Jaguar* | *Lucas* | *Massey Ferguson* | *NHS* | *Peugeot-Talbot* | *Plessey* | *Rolls-Royce* | *Smith & Nephew* | *Whitbread* | *Total* ✓ |
|---|---|---|---|---|---|---|---|---|---|---|---|---|---|---|---|---|
| *Beliefs and assumptions* | | | | | | | | | | | | | | | | |
| 'Business need' is prime guide to action | ✓ | ✓ | ✓ | ● | ✓ | ✓ | ✓ | ✓ | ✓ | ● | ✓ | ✓ | ✓ | ✓ | ✓ | 13 |
| Aim to go 'beyond contract' | ✓ | ● | ✓ | ✓ | ✓ | ✓ | ✓ | ✓ | ✓ | ✓ | ● | ✓ | ● | ● | ✓ | 11 |
| Values/mission | ✓ | ● | ✓ | ✓ | ✓ | ✓ | ✓ | ✓ | ✓ | ✓ | ✓ | ● | ● | ● | ✓ | 11 |
| Impatience with rules | ✓ | ✓ | ✓ | ✓ | ● | ✓ | ✓ | ✓ | ✓ | ● | ● | ✓ | ● | ● | ✓ | 10 |
| Standardization/parity not emphasized | ✓ | ● | ✓ | ✓ | ● | ✓ | ● | ✓ | ✓ | ✗ | ● | ✓ | ✗ | ✗ | ✓ | 8 |
| Conflict de-emphasized rather then institutionalized | ✓ | ● | ✓ | ● | ● | ✓ | ● | ✗ | ● | ● | ● | ✓ | ✗ | ● | ✓ | 5 |
| Unitarist relations | ● | ● | ✗ | ✗ | ✗ | ● | ● | ✗ | ● | ✗ | ✗ | ✓ | ✗ | ✗ | ✓ | 2 |
| Nurturing orientation | ● | ✗ | ● | ● | ● | ● | ● | ● | ● | ● | ● | ● | ● | ● | ● | 0 |
| *Strategic aspects* | | | | | | | | | | | | | | | | |
| Customer-orientation to fore | ✓ | ✓ | ✓ | ✗ | ● | ✓ | ✓ | ✓ | ✓ | ● | ● | ✓ | ✓ | ✓ | ✓ | 11 |
| Integrated initiatives | ✓ | ✗ | ✓ | ✗ | ● | ● | ● | ● | ● | ● | ● | ✗ | ✗ | ✗ | ✓ | 3 |
| Corporate plan central | ✓ | ● | ✓ | ✗ | ● | ● | ● | ● | ● | ✗ | ● | ✗ | ● | ● | ✓ | 3 |
| Speedy decision-making | ✓ | ✗ | ● | ✗ | ● | ● | ● | ● | ● | ✗ | ✗ | ● | ✗ | ✗ | ✓ | 2 |
| *Line managers* | | | | | | | | | | | | | | | | |
| General/business/line managers to fore | ✓ | ✓ | ✓ | ✓ | ✓ | ✓ | ✓ | ✓ | ✓ | ✓ | ✓ | ✓ | ✓ | ✓ | ✓ | 15 |
| Facilitation is prized skill | ✓ | ✓ | ✓ | ✓ | ✓ | ✓ | ✓ | ● | ✓ | ● | ● | ● | ✗ | ● | ✓ | 9 |
| Transformational leadership | ✓ | ✗ | ● | ● | ● | ● | ● | ✓ | ✓ | ✓ | ● | ● | ● | ● | ● | 4 |
| *Key levers* | | | | | | | | | | | | | | | | |
| Increased flow of communication | ✓ | ✓ | ✓ | ✓ | ✓ | ✓ | ✓ | ✓ | ✓ | ✓ | ✓ | ✓ | ✓ | ✓ | ✓ | 15 |
| Selection is integrated key task | ✓ | ✓ | ✓ | ✓ | ✓ | ✓ | ✓ | ✓ | ✓ | ● | ✓ | ✓ | ● | ✗ | ✓ | 12 |
| Wide ranging cultural, structural and personnel strategies | ✓ | ✓ | ✓ | ● | ✓ | ✓ | ✓ | ✓ | ✓ | ✓ | ✓ | ✓ | ● | ● | ✓ | 12 |
| Teamworking | ● | ● | ✓ | ✓ | ✓ | ✓ | ✓ | ✓ | ✓ | ✓ | ● | ✓ | ✓ | ● | ✓ | 11 |
| Conflict reduction through culture change | ✓ | ● | ✓ | ✓ | ✓ | ✓ | ✓ | ✓ | ✓ | ✓ | ● | ✓ | ● | ● | ✓ | 11 |
| Marginalization of stewards | ✓ | ● | ● | ● | ✗ | ● | ✓ | ✓ | ✓ | ✓ | ✓ | ✓ | ● | ● | ✓ | 8 |
| Learning companies/heavy emphasis on training | ✓ | ● | ✓ | ✗ | ● | ● | ✓ | ✓ | ✓ | ● | ● | ● | ✓ | ● | ● | 6 |
| Move to individual contracts | ● | ✓ | ● | ✗ | ✗ | ✗ | ● | ● | ● | ● | ● | ✓ | ● | ✗ | ✓ | 3 |
| Performance-related pay, few grades | ✓ | ● | ● | ● | ✗ | ✗ | ✗ | ● | ● | ● | ● | ● | ✗ | ● | ● | 1 |
| Harmonization | ✓ | ● | ● | ✗ | ✗ | ✗ | ● | ✗ | ✗ | ✗ | ● | ● | ✗ | ✗ | ● | 1 |

*Key:* ✓ = yes (existed or were significant moves towards); ✗ = no; ● = in parts

**Figure 1.1** Take-up of key SHRM characteristics
*Source:* Storey and Sisson (1993: 20–1)

We can start with some broad area of agreement. It certainly appears to be the case that, as Karen Legge has remarked, companies and organizations in the UK and USA have been 'confronted by Japanese competition and employment stereotypes, struggled with recession and searched for excellence, so the vocabulary for managing their workforces has tended to change. "Personnel management" is giving way to "human resource management", or, better still to "strategic human resource management" ' (Legge 1989: 19).

Note how in this passage, Legge draws attention to environmental pressures of a business nature – 'Japanese competition', and to pressure of a moral, or ideological sort – 'Japanese employment stereotypes', 'excellence'. It is exactly this mix of identified business challenges and the seductive offer of ways of meeting these challenges that constitute the attraction of the SHRM approach. SHRM diagnoses illnesses for which it has, uncannily, the perfect remedy. And it is this relationship between 'environmental challenges' and 'organizational responses', which constitutes the central plank of the SHRM argument. For example, Hendry and Pettigrew, argue that in the mid-1980s, 'changes in the political, economic and business environment over the past few years have cued many organisations to rethink their business strategy and at the same time the content and style of their human resource policies' (Hendry and Pettigrew 1986: 3).

But is there any reality to all of this? Is anyone actually taking these claims and exhortations seriously? Is it actually *possible* to achieve all these goals, however desirable they may be? A number of years ago, at the beginnings of the SHRM movement, Severance and Passino noted that 'recent studies of Fortune 1000 CEOs document strategic planning and implementation to be the area of greatest concern to chief executive officers. It is also the area to which they currently allocate the greatest amount of their time and the one to which they feel that even more of their attention should go' (1986: 1). This US survey concluded that the dominant manufacturing strategy of the 1980s was one of dramatic quality improvements coupled with significant cost reduction achieved through the elimination of inventories and the slashing of direct labour content. The most obvious marketing strategy has been the attempt to increase current market share while offering new products into the market. Strategy implementation has been punctuated by a replacement of the management team and characterized by substantial investments in plant, equipment, R&D, and manufacturing control systems (Pettigrew 1988: 2).

These examples of SHRM have been going on for almost 20 years. A survey in the UK by Thomson, Pettigrew and Rubashow in 1985 exposed the classic SHRM formula: this survey of 1000 middle and senior executives and directors in 190 companies enquired about changes made since 1979. Over 30 per cent of the managers reported 'radical changes', with 56 per cent acknowledging 'some change' and 10 per cent indicating little or no change. Factors influencing changes in strategy most notably included the general recession and changing markets (Pettigrew 1988: 1–2).

However do these developments add up to SHRM? Storey (1992: 82) has distinguished some key differences between SHRM and traditional industrial relations. Storey and Sisson assess the extent to which these 25 key dimensions of

SHRM have been implemented in a number of UK firms. The results of the study are presented in figure 1.1. The ticks represent the researcher's own assessment of what was going on, based on 'multiple sources of information'. This evidence would seem to suggest that at least to some extent, SHRM is occurring. The authors note that the table shows 'extensive take-up of HRM-style approaches in the British mainstream organisations. Two-thirds of the companies recorded a definite tick scoring on at least 11 of the dimensions' (Storey and Sisson 1993: 19). Clearly, then, there is a lot going on – there is considerable evidence of pervasive organizational change of a sort which can legitimately be regarded as typical of SHRM.

The authors also sound an important warning. If a critical test of SHRM is an explicit and deliberate connection between HR strategy and corporate strategy, or evidence of a clear, people-focused strategy, then these results do *not* support pervasive SHRM: 'apart from an insistence on a customer orientation, most cases failed to show much in the way of an integrated approach to employment management, and still less was there evidence of strategic integration with the corporate plan. This finding lends some support to the view that the HRM model is not itself a coherent, integrated phenomenon. Many of the initiatives . . . arose for diverse reasons, . . . [this] might indicate the true nature of the HRM phenomenon – i.e. that it is in reality a symbolic label behind which lurk multifarious practices' (Storey and Sisson 1993: 22–3).

Similar results are reported by, Guest who, summarizing a 1985 study by the Bureau of National Affairs in the USA, notes that this research found that 44 per cent of employers had installed some sort of employee involvement programme to improve productivity; 24 per cent had installed quality circles, and 44 per cent flexitime. Job enrichment and job enlargement had been introduced by 27 and 28 per cent respectively (Guest 1990: 385). However, as Guest notes, evidence of take up of these measures in itself is not enough to indicate commitment to SHRM.

## *Key elements of SHRM thinking*

However if there are many current projects of organizational change which can, arguably, be seen as evidence of or as constitutive of SHRM type change, it is necessary to identify the key features that enable us to characterize these changes as typically SHRM. What are the key defining elements of the SHRM approach? What are the criteria that we should use to decide if a process or organizational change constitutes a case of SHRM change?

At the most general level, there are three key elements. First, that internal processes of organizational change are caused or necessitated by processes of external, environmental change. This argument projects ultimate responsibility for SHRM and the consequences of SHRM action, outside the organization, away from management, and onto the environment. And it justifies all SHRM initiatives in terms of rational, productivity benefits.

Secondly, that under these new environmental pressures (competition, technology, clients' demands, and so on) management must develop new and appropriate strategies to defend or advance corporate interests. So environmental challenge *requires strategic response*.

Finally, this strategic response in turn requires organizational response. If the organization is to be capable of achieving or delivering the new strategy it will be necessary to design and implement changes in any or all aspects of the Human Resource structures and systems – which can be variously defined but would (or should) include all aspects of the organization which impact on how employees behave. Thus SHRM is represented as developing corporate capability to deliver new organizational strategies.

However, the argument that environmental cues *require* strategic responses and that senior managers are responsible for identifying these cues and developing the appropriate responses overlooks two important issues. First, the definition of environmental cues and developments as strategic issues is a matter of judgement. Strategic issues are developments that managers label as strategic: 'no issue is inherently strategic . . . an issue becomes strategic when top management believes that it has relevance for organisational performance' (Dutton and Ashford 1993: 397). It is necessary therefore to understand the processes whereby senior managers identify environmental issues as strategic, and obviously one influence on this process is the arguments of the pervasive SHRM literature itself. Thus although the SHRM literature presents itself as a commentary on the role of environmental factors, in reality it contributes to the recognition and evaluation of these factors by sensitizing senior managers. There is a risk therefore that SHRM becomes a self-fulfilling prophecy.

Secondly, the SHRM approach argues that managers, recognizing external threat and opportunities, design programmes of organizational change in response to these perceived needs. This raises a number of difficulties. It, first of all, assumes that managers 'see' the environmental threats. As we shall note later in this volume, some aspects of organizational structures and culture militate against managers recognizing such environmental developments; they fail to see that these structures need to be changed. It also assumes that managers, when they see the need for change, will know how to change their organization to make it more effective. This is questionable. Why should managers suddenly know how to design organizations? The very fact that they have to change the organization now suggests that their predecessors were not entirely adept at designing organizations. Why should this generation be different?

Finally, the SHRM approach assumes that organizational change is driven by managers' perceptive and informed understanding of the need for, and the principles of, organizational change. This, too, is arguable. Much change is probably driven as much by the attractiveness of fashionable solutions and fashions as it is by the analysis of problems; and much organizational change is a response not to internal needs but to external standards and norms which define what modern organizations should look like.

## Environmental challenges and organizational responses

We need to look more closely at these core elements of the SHRM project. Within SHRM thinking, processes and programmes of organizational change are attributed to challenges and pressures in organizations' environments which make such change necessary. A direct connection is posited between identified environmental developments and organizational adjustments, which are mediated by the business strategy which is a response to environmental challenge, but which requires organizational adjustment for the strategy to be delivered.

Organizational environments are defined as rapidly changing, and they are changing in new ways. The key environmental changes are characterized as: the decline of the traditional industries of mature capitalism (steel, coal, shipbuilding etc.); the drastic increase in competitive pressures, particularly from the newer industrialized economies; and the increase in environmental pressures from deregulation and from political, consumer and environmental lobbies. Within the UK, the decline of the manufacturing industry and the transformation of what remains has been accompanied by the imposition, in the still very considerable public sector (over 25 per cent of the workforce employed), of politically-derived pressures for performance measurements and improvement. Changes in energy costs, resources, inflation, employment legislation and new technology are also important challenges.

We need to reiterate our earlier warning here: this argument, although highly persuasive and pervasive, represents a highly managerialist and rationalist point of view. It assumes that all SHRM initiatives are necessary, and right; that they are designed solely to improve performance; and that they are inevitable, unavoidable and well-designed – namely, management knows best. Some commentators (and some employees) have taken a different stance. They might see SHRM also as a legitimatory device to establish tighter control over employees and to enhance the status of HR specialists (including academics and consultants who advise on, or write about, SHRM matters). In this view SHRM, despite its claims for introducing radically new ways of managing labour to avoid the old adversarial type of relations, is actually a way of masking new forms of traditional attempts to tighten control. Or they might claim that SHRM-type change is driven more by fashion than by rigorous analysis. Or they may claim that SHRM is not happening at all.

There is no doubt that at one time the rise of highly competitive economies in Southeast Asia using new technology, relatively cheap labour and new organizational principles seemed to pose a major threat to established western and European businesses; as did the emergence of a genuinely international market – a world economy – through computer-based communications and the emergence of multinationals operating at a global level. Yet also crucial is the changed nature of international competition – the decline and fragmentation of hitherto mass markets, resulting in the need for customized products: 'there are no non-niche markets any more' (Peters, 1989: 28). We discuss this in more detail in chapter 3.

Under 'economic' environmental changes SHRM writers would include changes in markets, or market segments, changes in competition (new entries, takeovers, decline), changes in the national or local economy in terms of inflation rates, unemployment, interest rates and balance of trade. Political changes would include the single European market in 1992, legal and political deregulation, the European Social Charter, levels of Government or local authority spending, privatization/public ownership, the end of the Cold War, the Green movement and energy issues. Technological changes include the likely or current form of technological developments, and the costs and implications of such developments. Social changes refer to factors which affect people as consumers/users of an organization's goods or services through influencing attitudes, life-styles, values, expectations, or which affect people as employees. Of obvious importance here are demographic trends which bring about staff and skill shortages.

As we have noted, the argument that these changes *require* or *cause* organizational change, and organizational change of a certain sort, with definite implications for all aspects of organizational structures, systems and skills, is a crucial element in SHRM approaches, but a contentious one. This view has some obvious advantages, one of which is that it attributes the trigger for organizational change, with all its implications for skills, careers and jobs, outside the organization itself. Senior managers, according to this approach, are not responsible for initiating organizational change; they simply respond to the need for change. They would be *irresponsible* if they did not change it in line with the requirements of the environment. Thus those who design and implement processes of organizational change become mere cyphers – relays in the connections between environment and organizational dynamics and structure, both neutral and innocent.

But organizational realities are rather different. It is clear that much pressure for change – and many of the suggestions for the nature of change – arise not from the business environment per se but from the values and expectation of the larger society. As two researchers of processes of organizational change have put it: Organizational problems are not in themselves enough to trigger organizational change. 'A supply of ideas for solutions is also needed: more specifically, ideas for administrative solutions which deal with organizational structures, processes and ideologies and which differ from current solutions. Solutions can exert an attraction on reformers and reformees. *Like problems, solutions can provide incentives to reform*' (Brunsson and Olsen 1993: 36; our emphasis). This phenomenon can occur internally too. BP's early enthusiasm for classic SHRM-type change (discussed in box 1.2) was driven by pressures for change from within BP not least from the chairman and his enthusiasm for 'solutions', and the processes of review he initiated such as the surveying of 4000 members of staff. The BP case illustrates that organizational change can be clearly driven as much by managers' enthusiasm to apply what seems to them right and appealing fashionable solutions as by any independently generated, problem-based analysis of possible forms and directions of organizational change.

Equally, the initiation of, even the recognition of the need for, necessary processes of organizational change can be actively obstructed by senior management if the culture of the organization or the dynamics of top team decision-making allow complacency or discourage radical change to cherished organizational values. In both cases the point is the same: while in theory SHRM starts with an objective analysis by senior management of the organization's environments, in practice existing organizational arrangements, cultures and senior managers' mind sets may well obstruct this process. This is also shown by the BP case.

## Strategic responses and the links with environmental changes

Nevertheless within SHRM, environmental pressures are typically seen as associated with a series of strategic responses. In this section a variety of key, strategic SHRM responses are identified and considered.

Child's (1987) analysis is typical of many commentators who have attempted to identify classified developments in the environment with classified responses from the organization. The attempt to track relationships between environments and organization, and the argument that the environment is the ultimate source of organizational changes, are fundamental to SHRM thinking.

Child argues that environmental and competitive pressures produce three types of strategic challenge.

- The first is *demand risk*, that is, a reduction in the market and/or an increase in levels of competition. This brings the risk of sharply fluctuating demand or demand collapse. It follows recession, increased global competition, and/or entry of new competitors to the market, and is compounded by variations in product specifications. It leads to a need for flexibility and responsiveness and improved quality.
- The second strategic challenge derives from *innovation risk* – the failure to match competitors' technological innovations. To counter this organizations need to retrieve or develop the capacity to innovate.
- The third is the strategic risk of inefficiency – *inability to match competitors' costs*. This leads to a drive to cut costs. These three strategies – innovation, quality and cost – may all occur within one multi-product/service organization.

Each of these environmental challenges, it is argued, is *met* by an organizational response. Child argues that the complexity of current forms of organization, with particular reference to the nature of relationships (or transactions) between elements of the organization (departments, sub-units, suppliers, agents, head office etc.), has implications for such responses. For example, a common response to the need for flexibility in the face of demand risk is to move to looser internal organizational relationships in order to encourage innovative capacity, in the shape of new ideas and concepts, within a context of commercial and production support. 'The organisational contribution here turns on the integration of inputs to innovation from a range of sources (some external to the enterprise) and the facilitation of speedy implementation attuned to commercial needs' (Child 1987: 34). On the other hand, pulling in the opposite direction is the need to counter inefficiency and risk, which requires increased control over operations,

### BOX 1.2 STRATEGIC HUMAN RESOURCE CHANGE AT BP

This case describes an early and classic attempt to initiate radical organizational change which was 'inspired' by SHRM approaches. The chairman of BP – at that time – tried to apply the theories of Tom Peters.

In 1989 BP went through a fundamental and radical process of organizational restructuring – Project 1990. This project and the thinking and negotiations that lay behind it, are described by Lorenz in a series of articles (Lorenz 1990a, b and c). Work on the change proposals was carried out by a team hand-picked by the chairman of the time – Robert Horton. This group regarded no aspect of the company as sacred and was apparently guided by an upswell of concern at all levels of the company. BP had recently gone through a massive divestment programme, withdrawing to core businesses. Lorenz describes Horton's ambitions in the language of Peters and Waterman. He notes that Horton wanted to reinforce BP's strengths. That while allowing BP's businesses much greater flexibility and speed of response in the market place, his goal is a complete stream-lining of BP: not only of its complex, costly, committee-ridden and over controlled formal organization but also of the way managers behave. He wishes to replace the existing culture of bureaucracy, constant second-guessing and extreme distrust, with a structure with the minimum of controls and the maximum delegation of responsibility, with a culture of open-ness and informality. Horton and his team want: clear vision, continuous innovation, open communication, empowered people, deep trust, team accountability, when the current reality is the opposite of these qualities.

Lorenz describes a 'burning impatience for change on all fronts – structure, process and culture' which was evident right across the company and evidence for this was gathered through 4,000 questionnaires distributed to staff. Yet despite the claims of the change champions that change was necessary and that the proposed changes would successfully impact on BP's performance, there were still a number of senior managers who found it hard to fully comprehend the proposals, or who doubted their efficacy, indeed even their practical possibility. Of these people, Horton himself remarked that he was not prepared: 'to let the long shadows of conservatism loom around to foul up the process.'

Central to the changes were changes in organizational structures: regional structures were redefined on a regional and business mix; businesses, wherever they may be located, now report to their respective international business heads, with consequent implications for reductions in numbers of regional co-ordinators jobs. In the head office staff will no longer work in large formal hierarchies but in small, flexible cross-functional teams. But these changes were seen as inextricably associated with changes in management style and culture (away from centralization, control and authoritarianism towards greater trust and delegation), and with changes in personnel systems and procedures – especially appraisal systems which focused unhelpfully on individual rather than team performance. Fundamental to the success of the change was the behaviour of Horton himself, the chairman. Senior managers noted that Horton would himself have to model the new style, and to overcome his naturally autocratic style. His position was also closely associated with the success and survival of the change programme.

Horton is no longer with BP.

inventories and so on. It also requires tight control and co-ordination of outside suppliers. A number of commentators have noted this classic SHRM contradiction, in various forms: while SHRM stresses the importance and benefits of being able to ensure staff comply rigorously with managerial intentions and requirements (quality programmes, JIT systems and customer-care programmes), at the same time SHRM frequently advocates the importance of empowerment, staff 'ownership' and involvement which are aimed to achieve staff commitment and participation. The only solution to this contradiction is if SHRM managers ensure that staff commit themselves freely and energetically to precisely those behaviours and standards management wish them to support. This is clearly unlikely. However, some commentators have claimed that this is precisely what HRM achieves – that it creates a situation 'which motivates the employee to respond favourably to management's demands' (Gronroos 1990: 43, quoted in Hales 1994: 65). Less optimistically, the tension between control and commitment may account for the charge that SHRM is 'employee manipulation dressed up as mutuality' (Fowler 1987). It may also explain the focus on symbols as much as substance in many SHRM initiatives.

To return to Child, however, it is interesting that Child not only uses a classification of strategic pressures, thus asserting a hypothesized connection between environmental and organizational structures, but also argues that these threats *require different sorts of organizational solutions*. This is very important. Child is here offering one important version of the SHRM model: i.e. that organizational structures change (are changed/should change) in line with environmental challenges and demands, an argument which is fundamental to SHRM. However, the BP case suggests that the SHRM 'response' to change pressures may be influenced as much by fashions of organizational change as by the identification of SHRM appropriate to business strategies.

We shall return to this relationship in the discussion of strategy/SHRM interconnections, in the next chapter. But Child also makes another key point – he notes how organizational responses to one threat (flexibility, delegation) might conflict with other responses (the increased control necessary for reduced costs) – i.e., that SHRM in practice and indeed in theory might involve irreconcilable contradictions. This too will be discussed later.

Like a number of other writers, Child offers a map of the relationship between a set of strategic risks and a number of organizational 'responses'. However what is central in this form of analysis are the processes whereby environmental 'challenges/threats' are perceived, defined, recognized – and the processes whereby *suitable* strategic responses are discussed, selected and implemented. Also crucial is the nature of the relationship between strategic response and the design and implementation of a Human Resource strategy. These are all social and human processes, so they can go wrong. They will not be neutral. And being organizational processes they will be influenced by existing structures of power, interests and values. We shall argue later that one of a number of fundamental weaknesses of the SHRM approach is its simplistic approach to processes of organizational decision-making about SHRM matters.

Of course, change champions within organizations always justify the change in terms of its positive impact on some desired outcome, and explain it in terms of the pressures and threats of the environment. And it is a fundamental feature of SHRM as a body of ideas that it asserts a critical relationship between 'environment', strategy and human resource strategies. But no environmental development can have any effect within an organization, indeed produce any 'response' at all, unless it is identified and interpreted by managers, who then seek to change the organization in terms of their theory of what needs to be done. It is precisely one of the critical features of SHRM that it offers a conception of, and the necessity for, and nature of, environmental–strategy–SHRM connections. Since such ideas are powerful in their consequences it is important to assess where this appeal lies. In other words SHRM thinking and writing play a significant role in the definition and construction of the very 'forces' which it claims to handle.

This is not to deny that distinctive relationships between environments, strategies and SHRM *are* apparent. Cappelli and McKersie (1987), for example, argue on the basis of their research that management may initiate a programme of what Sisson calls 'asset management': 'Shifting the firm's capital away from the high-cost/low-profit businesses to those that are more profitable: in the extreme case it means selling all or part of the business and transferring the assets to an alternative line of business in the same or another country' (Sisson 1989: 23). This may well result in divestment or acquisition, organic growth along established policy parameters, or joint ventures.

An alternative approach involves the attempt to improve the 'value added' by each employee – attempting to change employees' behaviour through modifying systems, structures, training etc., in the areas of activity where that value is added.

There is evidence that UK companies have pursued both these strategies. With respect to the second, organizations have frequently attempted to cut costs, to reduce payroll numbers, to reduce stocks and inventories. Frequently staff reductions have necessarily been accompanied by the introduction of new production methods, new forms of work organization and new technology, particularly information technology. Elsewhere Hendry et al. have described a set of 'generic strategic responses' to environmental challenge and change: competitive restructuring, decentralization, internationalization, acquisition and merger, quality improvement, technological change, and new concepts of service provision and distribution (Hendry et al. 1988). These strategic responses to environmental change may themselves occasion further change: diversification will require internal change, new structures, systems and cultures.

## SHRM responses

It has been argued that during the 1980s management has increasingly reacted to the environmental developments described earlier by attempting to improve organizational, performance both by increasing the efficiency of organizational operations in terms of processes and costs and by improving organizational effectiveness in terms of their strategic objectives – for example customer satisfaction, quality, innovation etc. It is these various organizational measures that are frequently identified as the component elements of SHRM.

Organizations have made and are making a number of different types of changes in HR systems and structures, which are commonly identified as aspects of SHRM (see, for example, the discussion of the work of Storey and Sisson, above). These changes are commonly aimed at the efficiency, performance, quality and flexibility of labour.

In the early days of SHRM, management efforts centred on increasing flexibility; they have recently moved to increasing work output through re-engineering and downsizing, but flexibility remains a valued objective. A recent analysis of manufacturing organizations within the UK, for example, argues that 'such things as trends in the use of technology, work organization and job design, training and payment systems, can be seen to be part of a new distinctive pattern for the organisation of manufacture. This distinctive configuration of plants we designate the new flexible firm.' This study used 12 indices of SHRM including TQM, JIT, empowerment, BPR, supply-chain management and teamwork (ESRC 1997).

A number of different characteristics are covered by the expression flexibility: numerical flexibility, which is the ability to adjust the number of employees in response to varying demand; functional flexibility, which is the ability to use the skills of the work force in varying ways in response to demand; and financial flexibility, which means adjusting wages to demand and to performance. The notion of the 'flexible firm', developed by Atkinson (1985) at the Institute of Manpower Studies, offers one view of the elements seen as necessary to be able to adjust quickly and readily to market changes. The flexible firm, which exhibits the three sorts of flexibility described above, may also operate flexible employment practices whereby workers are divided into 'core' or full-time, reasonably secure workers and 'pheripheral' or part-time workers with less advantageous conditions.

However a major problem with the flexibility thesis (which characterizes much SHRM thinking) concerns the *status* of the argument. Is Atkinson describing actual practices or supplying a framework for analysis of change (without making any assumptions about the extent of such changes)? Is he talking about what management wants and is trying to do, or what it should do? That is, is he describing management thinking or management practice? In fact, in the case of the flexibility debate, Atkinson argues that while 'flexibility has become an important theme in emerging corporate thinking' (1985: 26), in reality 'relatively few UK firms have explicitly and comprehensively reorganised their labour force on this basis' (ibid.: 28). Certainly there have been significant examples of numerical, functional and financial flexibility, yet the scope and significance of these changes remains unclear.

Recently it has been argued that while many typical SHRM initiatives are indeed concerned with achieving flexibility, this does not imply the upgrading of skills nor investment in technology. Flexibility can be and has been achieved by the flexible use of relatively unskilled labour and the use of external resources ('outsourcing') and the deployment of semi-autonomous business units operating as profit-centres.

Part of the problem of the nature and implications of organizational efforts to achieve flexibility, when these have taken place, occurs because of confusion about the meaning of the term and ambiguity about the reasons for flexibility initiatives. Pollert's remarks about flexibility could apply equally to a great deal of SHRM writing and prescription. She notes: 'The concept of flexibility is highly amorphous; it obscures changes in the management of labour, such as job enlargement, effort intensification and cost controls, by conflating them into flexibility . . . the use of the new orthodoxy of "flexibility" in descriptions of changing employment and work organization has caused enormous confusion by imposing a single typology on a diversity of social realities' (Pollert 1988: 1). Pollert notes that the importance of flexibility is less as a useful way of classifying a large variety of changes in the organization and employment of labour over the last decade (for these changes are more varied than similar), and more as an extraordinarily powerful idea which is used to describe the 'emergence of a new era' of work and organization. The real question, as Pollert notes, is why is this idea so powerful and attractive? In making this point about flexibility and its role as an idea as well as (or indeed even *instead of*) a set of practices, Pollert introduces us to an important and much discussed aspect of SHRM and its constituent practices: the possiblity that SHRM is important and significant, not simply in terms of its existence as a series of events and programmes and changes (which gives rise to discussion about whether or not SHRM is really happening, as discussed earlier); but that it is also important as a way of thinking about and understanding organizations and their employees.

Nevertheless there is no doubt that over the last decade there has been a very considerable interest in flexibility, if not necessarily through the means identified by Atkinson but more through the deployment of semi-skilled labour working in teams, competing with sub-contracted or outsourced labour and employed in profit centred business units. Lane notes that many UK firms claim to be seeking to improve functional flexibility, yet surveys also show that progress had been slow: 'for the vast majority of companies flexible working consists of slow change over a number of years' (Lane 1989: 182). Studies show evidence of continuity of employment practices, as well as some change towards flexibility. With respect to task flexibility, Elger summarizes the evidence thus: 'The most striking feature of the findings on functional flexibility . . . is actually the modesty of rather than the radicalism of the changes involved, and the centrality of reduced manning levels rather than upskilling' (Elger 1991: 50). There is evidence of 'mundane' change, but little sign of a serious move towards multi-skilling.

This is important because the issue with flexibility, and much SHRM-type change, is not simply *what* is happening, but the *meaning* of what is happening – the motives and intentions of management; the consequences for workers' skills and commitment. Are these apparent flexibility initiatives truly strategic? A number of writers have offered classifications of different approaches to flexibility. Blyton and Morris distinguish between *strategic* and *ad hoc* approaches: the former seeking to use flexibility initiatives to further long-term business purpose; the latter being limited, piece-meal, opportunistic, aimed at increasing control. Elger's review of current research of flexibility suggests that these initiatives typically represent the reassertion of managerial control over job mobility allied to work intensification (Elger 1991: 56). Not surprisingly, such moves have been related to the increase in productivity during recent years. But this should be seen not as indicating a radical shift to a new-style human resource approach to the management of labour, nor as revealing the benefits of the new approach. It simply shows the efficacy of the old patterns of management – at least in the short term: 'recent productivity gains do not step from a fundamental reorganisation of the forces of production in Britain but . . . are the product of a series of step-by-step changes' premised upon a 'new and intrinsically fragile, power shift arising from the exceptionally brutal crisis conditions of the early 1990s' (Nolan 1989: 101, quoted in Elger 1991: 58).

Also of importance are work changes which, again borrowing from the Japanese, attempt to overcome the classic disadvantage of the traditional, scientific management forms of work organization: low levels of worker motivation and commitment resulting in poor-quality work and insignificant creativity, and poor balance of the flow of work through the assembly process. The Japanese shop-floor system of work organization, through quality circle programmes, 'empowers' workers so that, in groups, they become involved in aspects of management decision-making such as quality and problem-solving, and in management decisions on tools, materials handling layout and improvements. This system seeks to make every worker a quality inspector, to be responsible for continuous change and improvement, and through 'just-in-time' production methods and improved supplier–end-user relations seeks to balance the assembly process. These methods, particularly just-in-time material flow systems, quality circles and team working, have been applied in the UK and hailed as a revolutionary break with previous practice, and a crucial stage in the achievement of competitive levels of quality and efficiency.

Another significant area of change, which also reflects the pursuit of flexibility but on an organizational level rather than at the level of work design, is the move among many organizations towards types of structure which achieve the twin goals of accountability of management decision-making and sufficient management control over delegated decision-making. This is attempted by decentralization, reduction of bureaucracy, reduction of layers of management and thus the separation of parts of the business into separate, accountable business units, autonomous within a structure of financial controls and corporate policy. These developments have not only occurred within the private sector. The Post Office and the National Health Service have also been exposed to decentralization and division into profit-responsible divisions. These developments represent an effort to achieve an optimum relationship between the corporate centre and operating companies. Goold and Campbell (1986), in a study of 17 multi-divisional UK firms, identify three types of centre–operating company relationship, each of which is empirically apparent and each of which solves some problems and raises others (see Storey and Sisson 1993: 80–6).

A similar sort of development is the move towards formal and explicit service level agreements between service departments and their internal customers. For example, within local authorities discrete divisions may now be required to install service agreements formally specifying what each division agrees to supply to its internal customers. For external services they are required to arrange for competitive tendering as usual. Interestingly, one result of this move is to increase the quantity of bureaucratic paperwork, with the details of each interdepartmental relationship being formally specified.

For some years it has been widely maintained that an important element in organizational change – possibly the most important element – is an organization's culture. This refers to the symbolic, normative aspect of organizational life which, culture proponents argue, is a fundamental determinant of employees' behaviour and attitudes, and specifically of their sense of commitment and enthusiasm. Culture can be defined as: 'the taken for granted assumptions, beliefs, meanings and values enacted and shared by organizational members' (Gowler and Legge 1986: 19). The concept of culture is to draw attention to role and importance of the irrational within organizations, seeing the organization as a source of primary social relations and as a significant shaper of fundamental social values (see chapters 15 and 16).

Changes have also occurred in the traditional areas of personnel: selection, assessment, payments systems and training. A study by the Institute of Personnel Management reported that nearly 20 per cent of the organizations studied had a formal performance management programme, three-quarters said they had performance-related pay, and a third Total Quality programmes (Bevan and Thompson 1992: 15, quoted in Storey and Sisson 1993: 135). Yet here, too, the evidence is inconclusive. Follow-up studies suggested that many of the performance management claims were unjustified. Studies have, however, confirmed the growth of performance-related pay schemes (Storey and Sisson 1993: 136). (For a useful overview of SHRM type developments on many personnel dimensions see Storey and Sisson 1993.)

There is evidence of a revitalized interest in assessment centres, in the design of reward systems, and in their relationship to performance, often defined in terms of the growing interest in management competences. Performance-related payment allied to measured performance is not only to be found among the major private sector companies within the UK, it is also characteristic of the once-traditional financial sector, local authorities and even the National Health Service.

However, although there are three key elements of SHRM thinking: environmental challenge, which then requires strategic response(s), which in turn require a series of internal organizational changes designed to improve organizational capability. Our interest in this volume is primarily with the third element of this causal chain – changes in organizational capability (SHRM) and their relationship with organizational strategies. In the following section we will consider some of the main assumptions and ideas that underpin current attempts to improve organizational effectiveness and efficiency.

It is crucial that we recognize that designing and implementing organizational change is neither obvious nor easy. Although management consultants and writers may seek to persuade us of the obviousness of the currently fashionable formulae of organizational change (anti-bureaucracy, BPR, TQM, The Business Excellence model, Investors in People etc.) the fact remains that history is littered with many such discarded formulae. It is easy to design organizational change but much harder to implement it; but as we shall see later in this volume it is also easier to promise the benefits of the planned change than to demonstrate them. 'It is not difficult to find . . . better solutions when designing reforms: current practice seldom appears as attractive as novel solutions; unlike current solutions, reforms promise to overcome both current and future problems, (Brunsson and Olsen 1993: 36). If we are to be able thoroughly to assess the promises of those who urge programmes of organizational change it will help to be able to unpack and unravel the premises and assumptions on which these changes programmes are built. As Brunsson and Olsen drily note of much organizational change – it is facilitated not by organizational learning but by organizational forgetfulness: by 'mechanisms that cause the organisation to forget previous reforms . . . Forgetfulness ensures that experience will not interfere with reform: it prevents the past from disturbing the future' (ibid.: 41). The following section explores the past precisely in order to enable us to analyse the nature and merits of promises about the future.

## The Origins of Key SHRM Ideas

The elements – and values – of SHRM are not new. But their combination, and the power of their combination, which arises from their capacity to manipulate the meanings attached to programmes of organizational change, as much as to achieve performance outputs, is new. The power of SHRM resides in the *combination* of old elements in a new package, which resonates with key extra-organizational values and frames of reference. In this section we will identify some major contributions to the core ideas of SHRM.

Hendry and Pettigrew note that many of the academics who supported the value of radical organizational change were highly prescriptive and normative, stressing: 'commitment' (Walton and Lawrence 1985), 'mutuality' (Beer et al. 1985), and 'communitarianism' (Lodge 1985). Essentially these authors were offering an indictment of American organizations, as structures that destroy commitment, which produce deskilled and oppressed staff, and therefore destroy any chance of developing the qualities that are seen as fundamental to corporate success (most borrowed from Japan): loyalty, commitment, responsibility, intelligence.

In his review of critics of the American SHRM literature Beaumont notes some important points. First, that many of the key messages of the SHRM movement (and indeed of HR) are not new: Human relations has long preached the relationship between job satisfaction and productivity; socio-technical systems theory emphasized the need to integrate technology human systems; and many years ago Burns and Stalker (1961) presciently asserted the importance of flexible organizational and work forms in organizations facing competitive, uncertain and unstable environments. But this misses the point: these ideas may have been around before, but they were never so powerful. The important point about SHRM is not the quality of the ideas but their *power*. Senior managers are now taking these issues seriously.

Hendry and Pettigrew note the origin of SHRM in the crisis of confidence in American economic performance initiated by the perceived failure of American manufacturers in the face of Japanese competition, and most obviously propounded in the work of Abernathy et al. This crisis produced a widespread concern to address many aspects of organizational functioning, including organizational cultures, and thus moved beyond the traditional focus of Organizational Development (OD) or Quality of Working Life (QWL) programmes.

The British emergence of a human resources approach was also centred around a concern for declining competitiveness, but was also associated with the organizational implications of Thatcherism, with particular reference to entrepreneurism and client focus, (see Du Gay and Salaman 1992). The decline of trade union power allowed an opportunity for drastic organizational change, not least in work design, the personnel management function itself increasingly saw a chance to integrate its function with corporate objectives: 'What HRM did . . . was to provide a label to wrap around some of the observable changes while providing a focus for challenging deficiencies – in attitudes, scope, coherence and direction – of existing personnel management' (p. 19).

As a body of ideas SHRM did not arrive fully formed: many of the values, assumptions and arguments of SHRM have been around for some time, although they have not previously been fused together as they are now. Hendry and Pettigrew (1990), in their review of the origins and history of SHRM, argue that a concern with the organizational benefits of an emphasis of the development of 'human resources' goes back at least in management writing to Drucker (1954) and has been evident in the argument that a well-trained and co-operative workforce is likely to contribute positively to organizational and economic development. Some writers have applied this argument to organizational structures, others to employment policies, or to job design principles.

What is new about SHRM, however, is the amalgamation of a number of ideas, the strength of the essential argument about the relationship between structures and strategy, and the widespread awareness that organizational change is necessary to achieve the required degree of 'fit' – that is, the appropriateness of an organization's structures and systems for the objectives, or strategy it is pursuing. The work of organization theorists known as the Aston School, for example, noted that organizational structures or profiles on a number of measured dimensions varied with the sort of work the organization was doing. Other writers argued a relationship between structures and aspects of the production process. If structures vary with activities connected to organizational purposes it is a small step to argue that structures fit, or are more or less appropriate to, these purposes.

For example, the argument that different organizational structures are likely to encourage or suppress creativity and flexibility, which has a number of sociological antecedents, proposes that aspects of structure have implications for organizational capabilities that may be relevant to the organization's strategy. It has also long been argued by organizational researchers that bureaucracy as a set of structural principles may have limitations, and that different forms of organizational structure might be more appropriate for different forms of organization and/or for different tasks or environments. Burns and Stalker, for example, argue that organization structures differed in their capacity to produce innovation, and that innovative structures were less controlling and allowed more autonomy (Burns and Stalker 1961).

## *Some key sources: theories of work design*

A major source of SHRM ideas and assumptions is the concern to enhance organizational performance by two sorts of (potentially conflicting) performance improvement measures: measures that increase employee involvement and commitment, and measures that improve organizational efficiencies (i.e. the output/input ratio).

Much SHRM literature, and arguably some SHRM activity, is concerned with improving not simply the quantity but also the quality of employees' efforts – to achieve a movement from employee compliance to employee commitment. Williamson argues that organizational performance is improved when 'perfunctory co-operation' is replaced by 'consumate cooperation', i.e. when employees stop merely fulfilling the basic formal contractual requirements and start showing mutual loyalty and commitment to the enterprise and its goals. Concern with improving the nature of employees' attitude and commitment to their employing organization has a long history in management thinking. Indeed it is probably the oldest and most basic management concern – inevitably, since management attempts to control and direct and maximize the work and output of employees, SHRM has always been recognized as having significant implications for employees' attitudes. The link between work design and employee attitude and behaviour has been the focus of considerable research and management attention.

A long tradition of analysis of job design principles and their implications has a number of key elements which are fundamental to much SHRM thinking. First, the notion that shop floor staff would produce better quality work and be more committed to their employer if their jobs were designed to allow greater skill and autonomy has a long pedigree, for example, in the Quality of Working Life Movement (QWLM) and in job enrichment programmes. Even during the period when bureaucracy and Taylorism were widely regarded as the twin pillars of industrial organization – principles which had much in common in their emphasis on regulation, specification and control – there were those who argued against them, sometimes on moral grounds, sometimes on the basis of efficiency. Henry Ford himself noted that the principles of work design implemented by, and made notorious through, the Ford plants achieved high levels of control over the process of production but totally failed to achieve a similar level of control over the work force. Indeed, the approach actively undermines such control by subjecting employees to a regime which is so insufferable that they become alienated from the work process, the product and the employer. It thus achieves some types of control, over work speeds and output for example, but sacrifices others, over quality and employees' attitudes and commitment. Ford wrote: 'Machines do not give us mass production. Mass production is achieved by both machines and man. And while we have gone a long way toward perfecting our mechanical operations, we have not successfully written into our equations whatever complex factors represent Man, the human element' (Ford, quoted in Littler and Salaman 1986: 91).

The costs of this approach were quickly appreciated. But employers, noting them and attempting to develop solutions, were unable to escape from the limited thinking which produced the initial problem. Davis et al., on the basis of a survey of job design, found practices were consistent with the principles of scientific management – minimizing the dependence of the organization on the individual and minimizing the contribution of the individual to the organization. By adhering to the very narrow and limited criteria of minimizing immediate cost or maximizing immediate productivity, it (scientific management) designs jobs based entirely on the principles of specialization, repetitiveness, low skill content and minimum impact of the worker on the production process. Management then frequently spend large sums of money and prodigious effort on many programmes that attempt to:

1 counteract the effects of job designs,
2 provide satisfaction, necessarily outside the job, which the job cannot provide; and
3 build on the satisfaction and importance of the individual which the job has diminished. (Davis et al. 1972: 81)

But others saw that a better solution was to design jobs in ways which allowed inherent satisfaction, and which thus encouraged creativity and commitment (the QWLM). This approach is a major forerunner of the principles of current SHRM. Those who argued against bureaucracy and against Taylorism/Fordism argued that both were wrong, not because they were stifling and inhumane (although many thought this), but because they were inefficient, either absolutely, or at least under conditions where quality, responsiveness, flexibility and innovation were important.

The SHRM movement – at least the 'soft', humanistic approach – includes values and assumptions derived from writers who questioned the efficacy and morality of Taylorist work forms. But, as Guest has noted, the use of these 'psychological growth theories' underpinning SHRM tend to 'sit comfortably' with the 'individualist, anti-union stance of employers, combining to provide a coherent anti-union or at least non-union strategy' (Guest 1990: 388). Also while some SHRM thinking stresses the importance of maximizing the commitment of employees to their organization, there has been relatively little attention paid to the precise means whereby such commitment might be achieved, except by reference to the mobilization of 'culture change' programmes.

The second theme of work design analysis concerns the importance of relationships at work. Within SHRM, work and employment are frequently seen as a major focus of social relationships and personal identification. This is particularly obvious in the emphasis on team working and on organizations as sources of meaningful work-based cultures. This emphasis on the social aspect of work – on work as a source of social relationships – derives largely from the 'human relations' movement, whose approach, based on the famous studies undertaken by the Western Electric Company at the Hawthorne Works in Chicago from the 1920s to the early 1940s, concluded that work attitudes (satisfaction, frustration, tolerance of supervision etc.) were strongly influenced by social relationships at work, particularly by the existence, membership and culture of the work group. This 'social man' was discovered to supplant the 'economic man' of Taylorism. Human relations proponents argued that within work-based social relationships or groups, worker behaviour, particularly productivity or co-operativeness with management, was thought to be shaped and constrained by the worker's role and status in a group. Other informal sets of relationships might spring up within the formal organization as a whole, modifying or overriding the official structure of the factory, which was based on purely technical criteria such as the division of labour (Rose 1988: 104).

The human relations movement bequeathed to SHRM the suggestion that workers had significant social needs that could be satisfied at work, and the idea that if satisfied, these needs could be used to influence the workers' attitudes and behaviour. This has had a major impact on the importance attached to team work in SHRM thinking. The two key advantages of team work from a management perspective are that it encourages the flexible use of labour with team members covering for and replacing each other; and that it replaces management discipline with peer pressure – loyalty to one's colleagues.

The third element concerns the role and possibility of choice of work and organizational structures – a key SHRM idea. SHRM and the QWLM on which it draws have both been influenced by the work of the Tavistock Institute. The researchers there identified the advantages, in terms of output and morale, of self-managing groups with a degree of autonomy. The Tavistock studies have been used to argue that work design principles are not determined, but can be chosen, and that achieving the right form of work design (enhanced work-group autonomy and responsibility) increases benefits for the organization and the employees. This finding underpins much of the empowerment literature. It suggests that it is possible for management to allow a degree of autonomy, and under the right conditions for workers to use their autonomy 'responsibly' in the services of their contribution to the organization's goals.

This leads us to the fourth element of job design studies that is influential in SHRM: the conceptualization of the nature of the relationship between organizations and their employees. Taylorism, and to a lesser degree bureaucracy, define the relationship between employee and organization explicitly in terms of a clear contract of wages paid in return for measured effort or output. Taylorism thus represents the managerial equivalent of the instrumental worker who defines work entirely in terms of financial rewards. An obvious outcome of this approach is that both parties have an interest in minimizing their part of the exchange and maximizing the contribution of the other side. This view thus leads to, or reflects, a notion of the employment relationship as inherently competitive or conflictive. However, approaches to work design that argue the importance of allowing employees discretion and responsibility, and insist that staff will react to greater trust by increased commitment, and will react positively to enriched jobs and empowered roles, assume, at least implicitly, a high degree of shared interest between employer and employee. They argue that what is good for the employee is good for the organization; that conflict, if it occurs, is pathological and deviant – i.e., that there is little if any need for trade unions to mediate between staff and employer. Furthermore, they not only assume this, they assert it.

The distinction between the consensus and conflict view of employee/organization relations is important because clearly the workplace is a place of co-operation and commitment, of conflict and consensus. And while the SHRM movement on the whole, if not exclusively, argues that organizations and their staff share interests (so that to benefit staff is to benefit the organization and vice versa), it is obvious that major grounds for conflict between employers and employees exist and are inherent in the fact that organizations are hierarchical and inegalitarian. This has a number of implications. SHRM may offer more effective ways of organizing staff and structuring jobs but it will not eliminate conflicts within employing organizations, which may surface in ways that disrupt SHRM initiatives. Also, if SHRM is based upon a consensus view of essential harmony it will be vulnerable when competitive pressures force decisions on wage increases, redundancies or increased output which run counter to this message. Another possibility is that within a conflict scenario some staff may regard typical SHRM pronouncements as manipulative and ideological rather than as signalling a real change of approach (see box 1.3).

**BOX 1.3 ASSESSING THE IMPACT OF QUALITY PROGRAMMES**

Quality consultants and writers claim that the superior route to sustainable competitive advantage is not via the traditional paths of products characteristics or price because these are easily emulated. The best way is via something that is hard to copy: superior quality as perceived and valued by the customer. Critical academic commentators are quick to question the efficacy of the various means of achieving this quality through employee's commitment and capacity to achieve quality. They note that employees may be unwilling to accept management's invitation to participate in management values and goals, and argue that quality programmes, although using the rhetoric of empowerment, increased discretion, employee autonomy, in fact rely on increased surveillance and are probably simply a way of intensifying work by increasing the amount of work extracted from staff. Methods of achieving quality that rely on changes in the attitudes and orientations of employees – the culture of quality – are also questioned by many commentators who define such efforts as ideological attempts to manage meaning for employees. 'Quality management has been . . . characterised as ideological, . . . as an attempt by management to create new forms for controlling subordinate staff that establish hegemonic control of their thoughts and so substitute consent for coercion' (Rosenthal et al. 1997: 485). However, a recent study into the actual impact of quality programmes found that despite the scepticism of the critical observers, empowerment (discretion and participation) did in fact increase; work was not seen to have intensified in the effort required; staff did feel freer to be themselves and less constrained by regulation. The research report concludes: 'This investigation provides no support for the view that, if a company's objectives of improving service quality are realised, they are achieved through some combination of sham empowerment, work intensification and increased surveillance . . . a large majority of employees strongly endorse Service Excellence, and there is a substantial level of support for the values and concepts of service quality and internalisation of the programme . . . half of the staff say that they engage in the sort of customer-oriented behaviours that the programme is seeking to elicit' (Rosenthal et al. 1997: 497).

## *Some key sources: the Japanese example*

Many of the key ideas of SHRM derive from a long-standing tradition in the North American and British organizational research into the impact of work design forms and principles on worker attitudes. However, a further and highly significant boost to SHRM thinking came from what was seen and presented – in numerous popular management and academic texts as the threat (and example)

## BOX 1.4 HIGH-CONTEXT CORPORATE CULTURE

Japanese corporate cultures have been seen as contributing to the performance of Japanese organizations. They have been described as 'high context' cultures, in contrast to 'low context' corporate cultures (Hall 1977). 'Context' refers to the framework within which communications make sense.

To communicate properly and meaningfully, it is necessary to understand the context of communications, to pay attention to the right things. According to Hall, Japan, unlike the US, is a high context culture (Hall 1977: 45). In this sense, Japanese socialize meaning and experience into a deep value structure which can form the context of particular events or situations. Social relationships and communications in Japan reflect the way Japanese use uncertainty and interdependence in subtle ways, and in what appear to be ambiguous communication signals. What this reflects in reality, however, is the high context culture wherein contextual factors provide meaning and value to social relations (McMillan 1985: 35).

The two culture types differ with respect to four dimensions: characteristics of business; characteristics of communication within the organization; characteristics of rules within the organization; and a category of general distinguishing characteristics.

With respect to business, high context cultures are characterized by: low pressure sales, long sales cycles, high customer and employee involvement, the avoidance of protagonist/antagonist relations and acceptance of ambiguity. The low context culture features the reverse of these: high pressure sales, us and them attitudes, and so on. With respect to communications, within the high context culture communications are indirect, economical, expect a great deal of interpretation from the listener, depend very much on the form of the communication and are difficult to change. Within the low context culture on the other hand, communications are once again characterized by the reverse of these features and are to the point, explanative, content-focused etc. Rules within high context cultures are holistic and integrated and cannot be manipulated. Generally the two types of culture differ with respect to the way in which the high context focuses on covert knowledge, rather than on legalistic and specified relationships and data, and emphasizes responsibility for organizational employees.

As McMillan notes, the important point of Hall's argument is the suggestion that the key features of the Japanese management system lies not so much in the uniquely Japanese elements of Japanese social culture, but in the broad characteristic of these elements – characteristics which could occur outside Japan. McMillan himself argues that a number of non-Japanese organizations display high context cultures: for example, the Jesuits, IBM, Michelin.

– posed by Japanese organizations. The Japanese threat is important in understanding the origins and development of SHRM because senior managers in the West are faced not only by vigorous Japanese competition; they are also faced by what they see as a management approach which threatens what they do and how they do it. Of course lessons can be drawn from aspects of the Japanese model, and the 'excellence' literature draws selectively from it. The SHRM approach is heavily influenced by some key elements drawn from western perceptions of the Japanese model – for example the Japanese corporation's 'high context' culture (see box 1.4).

The point of Hall's analysis is that it argues the superiority, in human resource terms, of the 'high context' type cultures over 'low context' ones, because in the former, organizational meanings and values are transmitted not only through direct forms of communication but also through symbols and values. Furthermore, high context cultures' relationships, both external with customers, banks and suppliers, and internal with employees, are long term and supportive, in contrast to the view of these relationships in low context cultures, which defines them in oppositional, contractual terms. Hall does not argue that there is anything necessarily essentially Japanese about high context cultures; western organizations such as the Jesuits and IBM are examples of such cultures. Undoubtedly, interest in Japanese-type corporate cultures has contributed significantly to the emphasis on culture in SHRM writings and consultancy.

Of obvious imporant to western approaches to SHRM is the Japanese attitude towards staff. Employees of large Japanese organizations are clearly seen as a resource which must be cherished and made best use of. The pattern of employment relations in large firms means effectively that staff will not be laid off: they are a fixed cost, not a variable one. The system of life-time employment, allied to the Nenko system of wages tied to age and length of service, creates a major opportunity and a major need for large-scale staff development. In this context it is possible to describe employees as a corporate resource to be developed and used. SHRM borrows this language. It may not always borrow the institutional framework within which it is located in Japan.

Finally, SHRM borrows many ideas from Japanese production methods. There are three main elements. The first is 'just-in-time' (JIT) production, which aims to produce the right materials or products in the necessary quantities and quality at the appropriate time. It reduces stocks, reduces scrap, highlights inefficiences, and forces them to be addressed. It also reduces lead times. The other two elements are cellular working and total quality control (TQC), both associated with JIT. Cellular working groups combine processes and machines with a multi-skilled work force to enhance flexibility. TQC attempts to locate responsibility for quality in the manufacturing process by making it the responsibility of the operator. SHRM schemes borrow many of these ideas, some of which, it has been suggested, originated in the West anyhow and were recognized early on by Japanese industrialists as ways of avoiding some of the inefficiencies and pathologies of western methods (Dore 1973).

But there is need for caution when borrowing from Japan. Thompson and McHugh (1990) note the power of the Japanese model for western business leaders concerned about declining competitiveness. These authors note the importance of JIT, flexibility, quality programmes etc., but argue that the main focus has been on management skills, attitudes and values, including a commitment to the management of human resources. However, these authors argue that this 'culturalist' emphasis (advocated by many seminal writers such as Ouchi 1981; Pascale and Athos 1982) underestimates the importance of other Japanese elements, notably the nature of industrial organization and production expertise. They note, for example, how the JIT system with all its advantages depends upon 'flexible labour utilisation and harmonising of tacit skills, close managerial involvement in production, multi-purpose machinery and reductions in set-up times . . . Such a system also frequently depends on a set of relations between large corporations and suppliers' (Thompson and McHugh 1990: 202).

The 'culturalist' explanations also seriously underestimate the role and importance of state intervention and support in Japan, with the Japanese state historically playing an active part in shaping domestic markets, overseeing the supply of long-term cheap credit and supporting technological development. The role of culture as a determinant of organizational performance is discussed in chapter 15.

## *Some key sources: the consultancy and 'Excellence' literatures*

Some prescriptive management literature variously claims to have identified the necessary structural/behavioural features of the organization of the future, or of the successful ('excellent') organization. Thus Handy describes three future types of organization: the federal organization with marked decentralization; the contractual organization in which there is a substitution of fees for wages; and the professional organization where the number of experts and professionals is increased (Handy 1984: 78–89). The Prospect Centre, a management consultancy, argues: 'Turning outwards to face an increasingly turbulent environment, successful companies have developed strategies based on quality, innovation and responsiveness to their customers' (Prospect Centre 1988: 1). Wickens, on the basis of his study of a Nissan plant in the UK, talks of the three key elements of corporate success: team working, quality and flexibility (Wickens 1987). Peters, whose contributions to this literature are highly significant, stresses the importance of 'new products, new markets, new competition and new thinking' (Peters 1989: 27). Against new environmental demands, he argues, organizations must achieve quality design and service, and must be flexible in responding to customer requirements; large corporations must learn to behave in new ways; new organizational configurations other than the traditional (but inflexible) hierarchical bureaucracy must be developed; big may no longer be best; single organizations will be replaced by co-operative networks; and the ordinary member of staff will necessarily be committed to improvement and retraining (Peters 1989: 28–9).

Wood (1989) points out that many 'Excellence' texts focus on the need for continuous change, for achieving a form of organizational structure which is consistently capable of responding to changing circumstances: 'learning to love change' as Peters puts it. The need for change follows the fact that environmental change – changes in markets, producers, competitors – is now constant and endemic. Structural responses are not adequate: they over-complicate and produce rigidity. Organizational responsiveness, opportunism arise from unleashing the creativity and enthusiasm of staff. Peters and Waterman have urged companies to adopt the eight claimed attributes of 'excellence' companies: A bias for action; Close to the customer; Autonomy and entrepreneurship; Productivity through people; Hands-on, value driven; Stick to the knitting; Simple form, lean staff; Simultaneous loose–tight properties.

Central to the 'excellence' literature, Wood notes, is not just that environments are changing and that organizations must change in line with the broadly anti-bureaucratic direction described, but that these changes must be produced by changes in culture: 'Culture is paramount as it structures the way people think, make decisions and act in organisations' (Wood 1989: 385).

The shared message of these writers moves beyond their anti-bureaucracy, pro-flexibility stance and coheres around a strongly culturalist perspective: change it is argued, can only come from changed attitudes and outlook, not from systems and structures. One reason for this, as will be seen in chapter 15, is that the process of decision making is seen as excessively rational, logical and systematic, not as it is: fumbling, gradual and messy. For this reason, a strong culture of innovation and risk-taking is more likely to produce appropriate outcomes than mere structure or systems. The excellence/consultancy literature differs from more analytical writing not only in its preference for broad-ranging prescription, but also in its neglect of issues of power, authority and conflict, and the political processes to which these give rise (Wood 1989: 381). Organizations, of whatever sort, are houses of power. Power is the blood that supports the system: it is a reward and a resource, and is inherent in any structure having co-ordination and direction. Because power is inherent it will affect the potential of a human resource strategy and its direction. We return to these issues in the final two chapters.

## Conclusions and Summary

This chapter has explored some of the basic questions that arise in any consideration of SHRM – namely, what are the empirical developments that have been seen to constitute the phenomenon, what are the key elements of these developments that make them essential to SHRM and, finally the ideas which inform SHRM and their origins. The chapter has charted a journey from actual developments in the world of organizations, to structures and systems of ideas inherent in the approach to organizational restructuring known as SHRM, to the key relationships between environment, strategy and organizational capability, and finally to explore the origins of the key theoretical ideas and assumptions on which SHRM approaches are built.

One of the key points of the chapter is to establish that there is an important relationship between these three issues – developments in organizations, the key ideas implicit in SHRM, and the ideas which inform SHRM recommendations. We have seen that these relationships are not simple and straightforward. SHRM is not a thing that we can all accept and recognize. Definitions of SHRM vary, and the events in the world that can be regarded as evidence of, or constitutive of SHRM, vary with the definitions being employed – which is why these definitions are important and are treated in the following chapter. But there is a further complexity – definitions of SHRM and of the core ideas inherent within SHRM are developed and maintained, and promulgated and employed, by people within organizations who are in positions of power; and therefore their views and definitions carry weight and authority – not least for those who work within organizations. That is why issues of definition and the analysis of the ideas within the SHRM model are important. The issue is not simply the sense or reasonableness of the way the expression SHRM is used, but the power and reality of the way it and its constituent ideas and assumptions are used.

## Key Points

- Organizations are currently changing, sometimes fundamentally and drastically. These changes are often described – and justified – as SHRM changes. It is therefore important to know what SHRM is, and whether these changes constitute genuine examples of this ambitious approach to organizational change; an approach which seeks to align organizational systems structures and skills with organizational strategies in order to improve organizational effectiveness.
- These changes are usually seen as associated with changes in organizations' environments. The changes themselves occur on a number of levels: structures, cultures, job design (flexibility) and elsewhere.
- However, it is far from clear that these changes are always examples of genuine SHRM – i.e. that they are systematically integrated with each other and related to the organization's overall strategy.
- Part of this difficulty is due to the various ways in which SHRM is defined. Understanding these differences helps to interpret the success, or otherwise, of SHRM.
- SHRM is new but it consists of a powerful combination of ideas, which carry their own historic assumptions and purposes. These constituent ideas and their intellectual origins are important in accounting for the appeal of SHRM. That is why they need to be thoroughly identified and dismantled.

## Discussion Questions

1 What current changes occurring within organizations are typically claimed to be examples of SHRM?
2 In the light of current definitions of SHRM, can these developments be seen as genuine examples of SHRM-type change?
3 What are the key sources of SHRM ideas and themes, and what are their implications for the SHRM approach and its assumptions?

## References

Aberthany, W., Clark, K. B., and Kantrow, A. M. (1981) 'The new industrial competition', *Harvard Business Review*, October, 69–77.

Atkinson, J. (1985) 'Flexibility: Planning for an uncertain future', *Manpower Policy and Practice*, no. 1, Summer.

Beaumont, P. B. (1992) 'The US human resource management literature', in G. Salaman et al. (eds) *Human Resource Strategies*, London: Sage.

Beaumont, P. B. (1993) *Human Resource Management*, London: Sage, 20–38.

Beer, M. and Spector, B. (eds) (1985) *Readings in Human Resource Management*, New York: Free Press.

Beer, M. et al. (1985) *Human Resources Management: A general manager's perspective*, New York: Free Press.

Blyton, P. and Turnbull, P. (eds) (1992) *Reassessing Human Resource Strategies*, London: Sage.

Blyton, P. and Turnbull, P. (1992) 'HRM: debates, dilemmas and contradiction', in P. Blyton and P. Turnbull (eds) *Reassessing Human Resource Management*, London: Sage, 1–15.

—— and Morris, (1992) 'HRM and the limits of flexibility', in P. Blyton and P. Turnbull (eds) *Reassessing Human Resource Management*, London: Sage, 116–30

Brewster, C. J., Hegewisch, A., Holden, L., and Lockhart, T. (1990) 'Trends in human resource management in Europe 1990', Cranfield, Beds: Price Waterhouse Cranfield Project working paper.

Brunsson, N. and Olsen, J. (1993) *The Reforming Organisation*, London: Routledge.

Buchanan, D. A. (1992) 'High Performance: new boundaries of acceptability in worker control', in G. Salaman et al. (eds) *Human Resource Strategies*, London: Sage, 138–55.

Burns, T. and Stalker, G. M. (1961) *The Management of Innovation*, London: Tavistock.

Cappelli, P. and McKersie, R. B. (1987) 'Management strategy and the redesign of work rules', *Journal of Management Studies*, vol. 24, no. 24, 441–62.

Child, J. (1972) 'Organisational structure, environment and performance: The role of strategic choice', *Sociology*, vol. 6, no. 1, 1–22.

—— (1987) 'Information technology, organization and response to strategic challenges', *California Management Review*, vol. 30, no. 1, 33–50.

Clark, J. (1995) *Managing Innovation and Change*, London: Sage.

Cressey, P. and Jones, B. (1992) 'Business strategy and human resource', *B884 Human Resource Strategies, Supplementary Readings 1*, Milton Keynes: Open University, 61–74.

Davis, L., Canter, R. and Hoffman, J. (1972) 'Current work design criteria', in L. Davis and J. Taylor (eds) *Design of Jobs*, Harmondsworth: Penguin.

Dore, R. (1973) *British Factory – Japanese Factory*, London: Allen and Unwin.

Drucker, P. F. (1954) *The Practice of Management*, New York: Harper.
Du Gay, P. and Salaman, G. (1992) 'The cult(ure) of the customer', *Journal of Management Studies*, vol. 29, no. 5, 615–33.
Dutton, J. and Ashford, S. (1993) 'Selling issues to top management', *Academy of Management Review*, vol. 18, no. 3, 397–428.
Elger, T. (1991) 'Task flexibility and the intensification of labour in UK manufacturing', in A. Pollert (ed.) *Farewell to Flexibility?* Oxford: Blackwell, 46–66.
ESRC Centre for Organisation and Innovation (1997) *The Use and Effectiveness of Modern Manufacturing Techniques in the UK*, Institute of Work Psychology, University of Sheffield.
Fiat (1988) *Facts and Figures*.
Fombrun, C. J., Tichy, N. M., and Devanna, M. A. (1984) *Strategic Human Resource Management*, New York: John Wiley.
Fowler, A. (1987) 'When chief executives discover HRM', *Personnel Management*, January, 3.
Ghoshal, S. and Bartlett, C. (1997) *The Individualised Corporation*, London: Heinemann.
Goold, M. and Campbell, A. (1986) *Strategies and Styles: The role of the centre in managing diversified corporations*, Oxford: Blackwell.
Gowler, D. and Legge, K. (1986) 'Images of employees in company reports – Do company chairmen view their most valuable asset as valuable?', *Personnel Review*, vol. 15, no. 5, 9–18.
Gronroos, C. (1990) 'Internal marketing – theory and practice', in T. Bloch, G. Upah and V. Zeithaml (eds) *Services Marketing in a Changing Environment*, Chicago, IL: American Marketing Association.
Guest, D. E. (1987) 'Human resource management and industrial relations', *Journal of Mangement Studies*, vol. 24, no. 5, 503–21.
—— (1989) 'Human resource management: Its implications for industrial relations and trade unions' in J. Storey (ed.) *New Perspectives on Human Resource Management*, London: Routledge, 41–55.
Guest, D. (1990) 'Human resource management and the American dream', *Journal of Management Studies*, vol. 27, no. 4, 377–97.
Hales, C. (1994) 'Internal marketing as an approach to human resource management', *Journal of Management Studies*, vol. 5, no. 1, 50–71.
Hall, E. T. (1977) *Beyond Culture*, New York: Doubleday.
Handy, C. (1984) *The Future of Work*, Oxford: Basil Blackwell.
Hendry, C. and Pettigrew, A. (1986) 'The practice of strategic human resource management', *Personnel Review*, vol. 15, no. 5, 3–8.
——, ——, and Sparrow, P. (1988) 'Changing patterns of human resource management', *Personnel Management*, 37–41.
—— and —— (1990) 'Human resource management: An agenda for the 1990s', *International Journal of Human Resource Management*, vol. 1, no. 1, 17–43.
Keenoy, T. and Anthony, P. (1992) 'HRM: metaphor, meaning and morality', in P. Blyton and P. Turnbull (eds) *Reassessing Human Resource Management*, London: Sage, 233–55.
Lane, C. (1989) 'New technology and changes in work organisation', in C. Lane (ed.) *Management and Labour in Europe*, Aldershot: Edward Elgar, 163–95.
Legge, K. (1988) 'Personnel management in recession and recovery', *Personnel Review*, vol. 17, no. 2.
—— (1989) 'Human resource management: A critical analysis', in J. Storey (ed.) *New Perspectives on Human Resource Management*, London: Routledge, 19–40.
Littler, C. and Salaman, G. (1986) *Class at Work*, London: Batsford.

Lodge, G. C. (1985) 'Ideological implications of changes in human resource management' in R. E. Walton and P. R. Lawrence (eds) *HRM Trends and Challenges*, Boston, MA: Harvard Business School Press.
Lorenz, C. (1992a) 'A drama behind closed doors that paved the way for a corporate metamorphosis', *B884 Human Resource Strategies*, Milton Keynes: Open University, 5–7.
—— (1992b) 'Re-appraising the power of regional barons', *B884 Human Resource Strategies*, Milton Keynes: Open University, 9–10. (All first published in the *Financial Times*, 1990).
—— (1992c), 'A cultural revolution that sets out to supplant hierarchy with informality', *B884 Human Resource Strategies*, Milton Keynes: Open University, 11–12.
—— (1992d) 'Countdown to a consultative revolution', *B884 Human Resource Strategies*, Milton Keynes: Open University, 8.
McMillan, C. J. (1985) *The Japanese Industrial System*, New York: de Gruyter.
Morris, J. (1974) 'Developing resourceful managers' in B. Taylor and G. L. Lippitt (eds) *Management Development and Training Handbook*, New York: McGraw-Hill.
Mueller, F. (1996) 'Human resources as strategic assets: an evolutionary resource-based theory', vol. 33, no. 6, 757–85.
Nolan, P. (1989) 'The productivity miracle?' in F. Green (ed.) *The Restructuring of the UK Economy*, Hemel Hampstead: Harvester.
Ouchi, W. (1981) *Theory Z*, Reading, MA: Addison-Wesley.
Pascale, R. T. and Athos, A. G. (1981) *The Art of Japanese Management*, New York: Simon and Schuster (Penguin edn, 1982).
Peters, T. J. and Waterman, R. H. (1982) *In Search of Excellence: Lessons from America's best-run companies*, New York: Harper & Row.
Peters, T. (1987) *Thriving on Chaos*, Basingstoke: Macmillan.
—— (1989) 'New products, new markets, new competition, new thinking', *The Economist*, March 4.
Pettigrew, A. (1988) 'Introduction: Researching strategic change' in A. Pettigrew (ed.) *The Management of Strategic Change*, Oxford: Blackwell, 1–14.
Pollert, A. (1988) 'The "flexible firm": Fixation or fact?', *Work Employment and Society*, vol. 2, no. 3, 281–316.
Prospect Centre (1988) *Strategies and People*, Kingston: Prospect Centre.
Rose, M. (1988) *Industrial Behaviour*, Harmondsworth: Penguin.
Rosenthal, P., Hill, S., and Peccei, R. (1997) 'Checking out service: evaluating excellence, HRM and TQM in retailing', *Work, Employment and Society*, 481–503.
Salaman, G., Cameron, S., Hamblin, H., Iles, P., Mabey C., and Thompson K. (eds) (1992) *Human Resource Strategies*, London: Sage.
Severance, D. G. and Passino. J. H. (1986) *Senior Management Attitudes toward Strategic Change in US Manufacturing Companies*, Ann Arbor, MI: University of Michigan Press.
Sisson, K. (1989) 'Personnel management in transition' in K. Sisson (ed.) *Personnel Management in Britain*, Oxford: Blackwell, 23–54.
Smith, A. (1937) *The Wealth of Nations*, New York: Random House.
Sparrow, P. and Pettigrew, A. (1988) 'Contrasting HRM responses in the changing world of computing', *Personnel Management*, February, 40–5.
Storey, J. (1992) *Developments in the Management of Human Resources*, Oxford: Blackwell.
—— and Sisson , K. (1993) *Managing Human Resources and Industrial Relations*, Buckingham: Open University Press.
Thompson, P. and McHugh, D. (1990) *Work Organisations: A critical introduction*, Basingstoke and London: Macmillan Education.
Thomson, A., Pettigrew, A. M. and Rubashow, N. (1985) 'British management and strategic change', *European Management Journal*, vol. 3, no. 3, 165–73.

Walton, R. E. and Lawrence, P. R. (eds) (1985) *HRM Trends and Challenges*, Boston, MA: Harvard Business School Press.
Wickens, P. (1987) *The road to Nissan: Flexibility, quality, teamwork*, London: Macmillan.
Wood, S. (1989) 'New wave management?' *Work, Employment and Society*, vol. 3, no. 3, 379–402.

chapter 2

# Linking Organizational and Human Resource Strategies

CHAPTER OUTLINE

## Learning Objectives

This chapter looks at the different ways in which the approach to organizational re-structuring known as SHRM, introduced in the previous chapter, is defined and conceptualized.

Specifically this chapter will:

- Introduce you to the various major approaches to SHRM so that you are aware of the potentially very different ways in which the expression can be used.
- Enable you to understand the implications, content, assumptions and prerequisites of each approach.
- Help you recognize the advantages and limitations of the different approaches to SHRM.

# Introduction

As the previous chapter indicated, while acknowledging the reality of the various organizational changes that have been seen as constituting SHRM, debate nevertheless continues on a major question: the significance of such changes. Do these changes indicate the reality of SHRM? Is there a major and qualitative change in the design of work and the structuring of work organizations, and the design of key personnel processes, which signifies a comprehensive programme of radical, *strategically-driven* organizational change? Consultants love to quote the crowning words of Japanese Industrialist Konoke Matsushita, spoken in 1978 to a group of American business people: 'We are going to win and the industrialised West is going to lose out . . . the reasons for your failure are within yourselves. With your bosses doing the thinking the workers wield the screwdrivers, you are convinced deep down that this is the right way to do business. For you the essence of management is getting the ideas out of the heads of the bosses and into the hands of labour . . .' (quoted in Clark 1995: 240). But Matsushita's challenge goes to the heart of the SHRM project and the debate around it. For at its best, the SHRM movement claims to represent a break with this traditional, Taylorite conception of the workplace; alternatively, it could be argued that these developments are so piecemeal, uneven and variable in their implementation, or so driven by opportunism and a traditional concern for tightened management control, that they cannot possibly be seen as indicating any major strategic transformation? Furthermore, do these changes work? Do they deliver the changes in employee behaviour, and thus ultimately in organizational performance, that is promised?

These are simple questions but it is difficult and complex to answer them – not necessarily because of insufficient empirical data, but because the questions are not actually as simple as they appear. For example, the very terms of the questions themselves require further elaboration, and some of the implications of the questions can themselves be questioned. For example, the definitions of strategic HR may be such that it is unlikely that the behaviour of actual managers in practice would satisfy such criteria. The definition of organizational effectiveness used by SHRM writers and by those who initiate SHRM change may vary and may be open to critique; and indeed the notions of 'strategy' and 'capability' and 'fit', which play such a major part in all definitions of SHRM, may require considerable further attention. For example, many approaches to SHRM employ a highly rationalistic view of strategy and of the processes whereby business strategies are developed and formulated – seeing this as a distinctly rational, analytical logic and carefully-planned process resulting in intended strategies which in turn (and with appropriate SHRM modifications when necessary) become actual achieved strategies. The same sort of rationalistic approach is frequently employed in discussions of HR strategy formulation: where it is assumed that HR strategies are also developed in a logical and rational and carefully planned manner, in response to strategic developments. Yet both processes of strategy development may be incremental, ad hoc social, cultural and political affairs where numerous cognitive, information limitations – allied to cultural ways of thinking, and political loyalties, and historic relationships and interests – play major roles in structuring how managers think and what they think about.

To some extent this entire book is a response to, and a debate with, these questions about the nature and implications of SHRM. So by the time you finish your work on this book you will be well equipped to come to your own conclusions. This chapter aims to equip you to begin an informed consideration of these issues through an analysis of different definitions of, and approaches, to SHRM. We shall return to these questions in the final chapter.

## What is SHRM?

Box 2.1 reveals the complexity of SHRM. It is an elusive target: a set of exhortations, a metaphor, a set of substantive propositions, a mess of contradictions? SHRM is not any single thing but a variety of differently conceptualized approaches. In what follows we will try to make some sense of the different definitions of the term by offering some maps to the rather confused terrain of SHRM. It is important and useful to have a general understanding of how the approaches to SHRM differ, because this allows us to evaluate the approaches on offer, and to understand the prescriptions and assumptions that are inherent in each approach.

### *Some useful definitions*

We start with some basic issues of definition. What is SHRM? What do people mean by the term? The issues here are not trivial. Different definitions carry different assumptions, assert different causal relationships, even seek different

## BOX 2.1 THE DIFFICULTY OF IMITATING SHRM

While the speed of information diffusion and emulation between firms has increased, excellent SHRM practices appear to be confined to a few selected and persistently successful corporations. How can this be true? 'How can increased inter-firm diffusion of information coexist with persisting heterogeneity of firms HR practices and business performances?' (Mueller 1996: 758). One solution to this puzzle may be that the extent of real diffusion of SHRM models is more apparent than real: that it reflects management wishful thinking about their SHRM practices and not the reality of their organizational situation.

'The belief that planned and formalised HRM practices are "strategic", rational answers to specific problems and likely to lead to enhanced business performance, may be partly due to managerial rationalisations . . . Through ex-post rationalisations, managers often impute a strategic quality to changes which did not exist at the time of the event' (Ibid.: 769).

In reality, strategic advantage through SHRM factors may be the result not of short term, codified, consultant packages of SHRM measures (which are frequently applied by the competition anyway) but may grow in a 'slow, incremental, highly uncertain evolutionary process that requires patience and stamina to sustain the long drawn out process. 'This suggests that it is misplaced to have any expectations of a quick fix through HRM or quick return on investment' (ibid.: 771). The conclusion is striking: that for SHRM initiatives to work, they need to be consistent with and supportive of, 'forms of spontaneous co-operation that are embedded into daily operational routines. This means that while HRM policies cannot substitute for the potential that resides within established patterns of co-operation, they can help exploit this "hidden reservoir" ' (ibid.: 774).

Another study, which reviews and classifies the forms of SHRM initiatives, argues that these SHRM systems can be grouped into two broad categories: cost reducers (control) and commitment maximizers. These are seen to represent two distinct approaches to shaping employee behaviour and attitudes at work.

'The goal of control human resource systems is to reduce direct labour costs, or improve efficiency, by enforcing employee compliance with specified rules and procedures and basing employee rewards on some measurable output criteria. . . . In contrast, commitment human resource systems shape desired employee behaviours and attitudes by forging psychological links between organisational and employee goals' (Arthur 1994: 672).

goals. However, if we are to be able to explore the differences between views and definitions of SHRM, we first need to identify the general characteristics of the field. Sisson (1989) proposes four features associated with SHRM:

1 a stress on the integration of personnel policies both with one another and with business planning more generally;

2 the locus of responsibility for personnel managers no longer resides with specialist managers, but is now assumed by senior line management;

3 the focus shifts from management–trade union relations to management–employee relations, from collectivism to individualism: and

4 there is stress on commitment and the exercise of initiative, with managers now donning the role of 'enabler', 'empowerer' and 'facilitator' (Storey 1990: 5; quoted in Blyton and Turnbull 1992a: 3).

Hendry and Pettigrew (1986) argue that the strategic aspect of SHRM consists of four key elements:

1 the use of planning;

2 a coherent approach to the design and management of personnel systems based on an employment policy and manpower strategy, and often underpinned by a 'philosophy';

3 matching HRM activities and policies to some explicit strategy;

4 seeing the people of the organization as a 'strategic resource' for achieving 'competitive advantage'.

These authors point to a minimal specification of SHRM as a degree of dual integration: coherence of HR practices with each other, and of all SHRM practices with the organization's strategy. This is a key element of many SHRM definitions. A recent overview has noted: 'Two forms of match that were seen as conditions for competitive advantage were distinguished first as the match between SHRM policies themselves, and secondly as the match between SHRM policies and the business strategy pursued by the company . . . The theme of simultaneously maximising internal and external fit has been explored by a number of authors' (Mueller 1996: 761).

These various summaries have common themes. At its simplest, the overlap has been described by Beaumont in these terms: 'the key message of the HRM literature is the need to establish a close, two-way relationship between business strategy or planning and SHRM strategy or planning' (Beaumont 1992: 40). Note three points here. First, the common emphasis on strategic integration – that organizational and personnel structures and systems should be designed to support, or 'fit', the strategy of the organization; secondly, the insistence that staff should be managed and treated so that they are committed to the organization and its goals; and thirdly, that by achieving the first of these, there will be real tangible benefits for the organization in terms of critical outputs of quality, performance, and so on. Thus the second of these (which will rely on a variety of

## BOX 2.2 SHRM CHANGE AT FIAT

Cressey and Jones have studied programmes of SHRM-type change in Fiat. They note that while aspects of SHRM are being introduced quite widely, this is not necessarily associated with the management explicitly espousing or claiming a commitment to SHRM principles.

Reorganization within Fiat has involved recruitment, retraining and changes in jobs – skills, authority and specialisms. Efforts have been made to engage the ordinary worker in the quality upgrading of the product which is, as the authors note, a typical SHRM initiative, and for some writers is a fundamental tenet of SHRM. Work roles have been redesigned and operating systems changed to further this goal. Job changes were associated with efforts to change workers' attitudes and values – the organizational culture – in order to enhance employee commitment. The authors note that the Fiat programme involved a series of inter-connected changes: integrating Personnel, IR and business policies; culture change and employee commitment programmes; individualized reward and appraisal schemes; downgrading the role of unions and enhanced consultation.

The authors also note that the specific human resource policies evident in the case of Fiat occurred 'downstream' of major strategic and investment decision-making: 'Human resources are the last link in the chain of policy development and implementation. Often policies from HRM will not be adopted as the most desirable foundations in the architecture of the business but as solutions to glaring inadequacies in existing programmes by specific transplants of HRM-style practices' (Cressey and Jones 1992: 62). The main focus of the change programme at Fiat is summarized by a quotation from an official Fiat publication: 'The cornerstone of all Fiat's plans and operations is the maximisation of the vital resource constituted by the ideas, experience and team spirit possessed by its employees at all levels' (Fiat 1988).

At the heart of Fiat's programme is the construction of a key new job. Gianni Agnelli took over as chairman of Fiat in 1966, and worked to decentralize the group, which had previously been highly centralized. By the late 1960s Fiat was being squeezed by falling demand and increasing worker unrest. By the 1970s Fiat was a loss maker. Management adopted a policy of concession towards the highly unionized and militant workforce, (which exercised a significant degree of shopfloor control), allied to an inflation linked bargaining system. Performance suffered and by the end of the 1970s leftist activity involved violence and arson. In 1980 Agnelli left to be replaced by Cesare Romiti as sole managing director. Faced with what amounted to the imminent collapse of managerial authority, Romiti reacted by announcing several thousand redundancies. This resulted in factory occupation and strikes. But in response to these, middle managers and clerical workers mounted a massive demonstration which ended the strike.

With militancy reversed, Romiti mounted a programme of investment focused on robotics and new technology, allied to a centralized system of business administration and the elimination of many union negotiating processes. The change programme reduced labour costs significantly, possibly by as much as 47 per cent of jobs over seven years, through technology and rationalization. By the end of the 1980s Fiat was at the top of the European sales league, together with Volkswagen.

However, Fiat had also to improve the flexibility of its product, productivity through employee commitment to a number of corporate goals, and quality of organization, services and product. Although automation and new technology are central to the achievement of these goals, it became clear that the use of technology was inadequate without the redesign of some key jobs since minor disruptions or failures now placed a great burden on workers' initiative and commitment. Cressey and Jones note that 'By the mid 1980s individual managers were already aware that the basic quantitative gains from computer-programmed automation would need complementing by an expansion of production workers' responsibilities to cover both quality enhancement and the optimisation of machine time' (Cressey and Jones 1992: 65–6).

The solution to this was the identification and creation of a key new job, and therefore a new worker: the *conduttore* or line controller. This work role was designed to enable individuals to inter-face between three system elements of the new computerized production process: materials, supply of units and control of operations on the units. 'The advantages of this new work role are that the *conduttore* has his or her own video terminal for making operating changes to the control systems, [and] can undertake simple maintenance tasks that might otherwise involve the complex reallocation of maintenance specialists' (Cressey and Jones 1992: 66).

This new role required a significant change of culture, a process which also aimed to 'sell' the new role to middle managers and union officials. *Conduttore* also required training – a total of 12 months, 10 months of which was formal class room format. The new role was justifiably regarded as a fundamental change. Workers below the *conduttore* and managers above it saw the new role as a threat to identity and authority, and as a source of resentment. The *conduttore* was a sign of a larger process of organizational change. Romiti stressed the importance of a move towards greater co-operation, and the importance of achieving employee participation in the business and in change, on a wider front (Cressey and Jones 1992: 61–74).

organizational measures and changes) 'is seen as a method of releasing untapped reserves of "human resourcefulness" by increasing employee commitment, participation and involvement'. While the third feature ensures the value of these achievements: 'maximising the economic return from the labour resource by integrating HRM into business strategy' (Blyton and Turnbull 1992b: 4). The clearest and most explicit statement of this causal relationship has been offered by Guest (see below), who has argued that only when organizations pursue a clear and coherent policy aimed at achieving four specific goals will the identified performance benefits be achieved. Box 2.2 illustrates some of these elements and outcomes of SHRM.

The definitions presented so far show us some of the key ideas and some of the similarities and differences in approaches to SHRM. These issues require further attention.

## Two classic approaches

We will begin our analysis of different approaches to SHRM with a bit of history. It is common to distinguish two seminal and influential American schools of SHRM. These are represented by two key texts from two institutions: Harvard and Michigan. The books are *Strategic Human Resource Management* (Fombrun, Tichy and Devanna 1984), and *Human Resources Management: A General Manager's Perspective* (Beer et al. 1986). The first book, as Hendry and Pettigrew remark, focuses on strategic management; the second book focuses on human relations (see also Blyton and Turnbull 1992b: 4).

The Michigan group developed the notion of strategic SHRM which entailed the interconnection of business strategies, organizational structures and SHRM (which meant, in this context, key personnel systems: selection, appraisal, rewards and development). SHRM systems were best designed to support the implementation of corporate strategy. Some key contributors have argued in a classic statement that: 'just as firms will be faced with inefficiencies when they try to implement new strategies with outmoded structures, so they will also face problems of implementation when they attempt to effect new strategies with inappropriate HR systems. The critical management task is to align the formal structure and the HR systems so that they drive the strategic objective of the organisation' (Fombrun, Tichy and Devanna 1984: 37).

At the heart of the Harvard approach (Beer et al. 1984) was the responsibility and capacity of managers to make decisions about the relationship between the organization and its employees such as to maximize the organizational outcomes for key stakeholders. This approach tends to adopt a particular approach to workplace relations: emphasizing unitary, integrative, individualistic systems. It also undermines workforce organization or collectivist values, seeing them as outcomes of management choices about the key SHRM levers affecting workforce-organization relations. This approach focuses on managers responsibility to manage four key SHRM policy areas: employee influence (participation); human resource flow; reward system; and work systems (work organization). Beer and Spector define this approach as follows:

> A business enterprise has an external strategy: a chosen way of competing in the market place. It also needs an internal strategy: a strategy for how its internal resources are to be developed, deployed, motivated and controlled . . . external and internal strategies must be linked. (Beer and Spector 1985:6)

The concept of strategy in these definitions draws on that of the Harvard Business School in the 1950s. Corporate strategy is the establishment of a company's long-term goals, policies and plans, and the adoption of courses of action to achieve these goals. The notion of strategy, as its military origins suggest, means choosing means and resources to achieved selected objectives. But business strategy involves two key elements: formulating strategies and implementing them. Furthermore, establishing the proper link between HR strategy and corporate strategy may prove to be difficult, as we shall see.

One important issue that is raised here is the excessively rationalist notion of strategy. Experience suggests that strategic decision-making – either corporate or HR – is incremental, piece-meal, ad-hoc, incomplete, and negotiated and only partly rational. Both the two cases discussed so far – BP and Fiat – demonstrate this. In the case of BP, the pressure for change was based on a formal survey of employees initiated by those who were convinced of the need for change; the SHRM change programme itself was clearly derived from the classic consultancy texts of the period – especially the 'Excellence' literature. The Fiat case suggests that the pressure for SHRM-type change came from a business strategy (flexibility, productivity and quality) and from the recognized need to establish a new interface role to handle the requirements of new technology systems, which were themselves key elements of the business strategy and the restructuring process.

The Harvard notion of strategy tends to focus on the role of external, market pressures. These can clearly be very important, yet internal issues and resources (politics, culture, relationships) are also important in establishing the need for, and the form of, successful HR strategies. Bailey and Johnson (1992) usefully plot the various ways in which strategy formulation has been approached and analysed: logical incrementalism, political, cultural, visionary, natural selection, and planning. While the planning perspective may be the most traditional view of how strategies are developed within organizations its popularity is probably due as much to its attractiveness as to its practical feasibility.

## Overviews of the relationship between strategies and structures

Useful overviews of the relationship between strategy and Human Resource Strategies have been offered by Beaumont (1992), Hendry and Pettigrew (1990), and Storey and Sisson (1993). Beaumont traces a broadly similar development of the SHRM approach to that offered by Hendry and Pettigrew (1990): competitive pressure, the Japanese model etc. His analysis focuses on various conceptualizations of the relationship between types of corporate strategy and types of human resource strategy. Like other authors, he notes that three bases of classification have been employed: stages in the business or product cycle; different types of business strategy as identified by Porter; and connections between strategy and structure in terms of types and numbers of products.

These studies, most of which are American, tend to use a limited sense of SHRM, which they call human resource management (HRM) and which refers broadly to elements of conventional personnel policies and activity: selection, assessment, training, appraisal, and so on. That is, HRM does not refer to cultural or structural dimensions. Nevertheless, a number of studies have attempted to plot the connections between aspects of SHRM (or HRM) and aspects of organizational strategy. This requires the classification of such business strategies.

Some researchers, following Chandler's (1962) emphasis on growth strategies that lead to structural modifications in organizations, have used a classification of types of strategy based on variations in product focus and have related this to aspects of HRM. Consider by way of illustration table 2.1, which is drawn from such analysis and which correlates aspects of personnel strategy (HRM) with organizational characteristics as defined by numbers and types of products.

From within another tradition, Beer and Spector have noted when discussing their Harvard approach, that, for example, 'A competitive strategy based on becoming the low-cost producer may indicate different approaches to compensation and employment security than a competitive strategy that depends on product innovation. The very idea of an internal Human Resource strategy implies there is consistency among all the specific tactics or activities that affect human resources' (Beer and Spector 1985: 5–6).

The work of Schuler and Jackson (1987) also argues that three discrete business strategies – innovation, quality enhancement and cost reduction – are associated with distinctive variations in key aspects of SHRM as defined by the Harvard approach.

In table 2.2, from Kochan and Barocci (1985), variations in four key human resource functions are related to variations in the life-cycle stages of businesses – growth, maturity and decline. Table 2.1 argues that there is – or should be – a temporal dimension of HRM and business development. It suggests that different aspects or dimensions of an organization's SHRM system, i.e. what we would call the personnel systems dimension of SHRM, are of particular salience at different stages of the product life-cycle.

These authors, who have attempted to identify and analyse the relationships – desired or actual – between business strategies and HR strategies, focus on the key component, and the key promise, of the SHRM project: that it is possible to identify the relevant HR elements for different strategies and having identified these, to install them in organizations so that employees behave as the strategy requires. This promise is the subject of this chapter.

There are a number of obvious problems or limitations with attempts to relate aspects of business strategy to appropriate forms of HR strategies. The first is that it is not, as we shall see, by any means obvious or straightforward to translate business strategies into SHRM or SHRM elements. We cannot assume that management is always serious and genuine in its concern to redesign HR structures and systems. Radical thinking and action on organizational issues may require a type of thinking and learning which is uncommon in organizations; this is because it threatens existing relationships and hierarchies and the deeply entrenched and established ways of non-learning associated with them. Argyris has argued that many typical SHRM projects, which appear to be concerned with achieving serious and radical change – such as TQM, or Continuous Improvement

**Table 2.1** Human resource management links to strategy and structure

| | | Human resource management | | | |
|---|---|---|---|---|---|
| *Strategy* | *Structure* | *Selection* | *Appraisal* | *Rewards* | *Development* |
| 1 Single product | Functional | Functionally oriented: subjective criteria used | Subjective: measure via personal contact | Unsystematic and allocated in a paternalistic manner | Unsystematic, largely through job experiences: single function focus |
| 2 Single product (vertically integrated) | Functional | Functionally oriented: standardized criteria used | Impersonal: based on cost and productivity data | Related to performance and productivity | Functional specialists with some generalists: largely through job rotation |
| 3 Growth by acquisition (holding company) of unrelated businesses | Separate, self-contained businesses | Functionally oriented, but varies from business to business in terms of how systematic | Impersonal: based on return on investment and profitability | Formula-based and includes return on investment and profitability | Cross-functional but not cross-business |
| 4 Related diversification of product lines through internal growth and acquisition | Multi-divisional | Functionally and generalist oriented: systematic criteria used | Impersonal: based on return on investment, productivity, and subjective assessment of contribution to overall company | Large bonuses: based on profitability and subjective assessment of contribution to overall company | Cross-functional, cross-divisional, and cross-corporate/divisional: formal |
| 5 Multiple products in multiple countries | Global organization (geographic centre and world-wide) | Functionally and generalist oriented: systematic criteria used | Impersonal: based on multiple goals such as return on investment, profit tailored to product and country | Bonuses: based on multiple planned goals with moderate top management discretion | Cross-divisional and cross-subsidiary to corporate: formal and systematic |

*Source:* Fombrum et al. (1984), p. 53, adapted from Galbraith and Nathanson (1978).

**Table 2.2** Critical human resource activities at different organizational or business unit stages

| *Human resource functions* | *Introduction* | *Life-cycle stages* | | |
|---|---|---|---|---|
| | | *Growth* | *Maturity* | *Decline* |
| Recruitment, selection and staffing | Attract best technical/ professional talent | Recruit adequate numbers and mix of qualified workers; management succession planning; manage rapid internal labour market movements | Encourage sufficient turnover to minimize lay-offs and provide new openings; encourage mobility as reorganizations shift jobs around | Plan and implement workforce reductions and re-allocation |
| Compensation and benefits | Meet or exceed labour market rates to attract needed talent | Meet external market but consider internal equity effects; establish formal compensation structures | Control compensation | Tighter cost control |
| Employee training and development | Define future skill requirements and begin establishing career ladders | Mould effective management team through management development and organizational development | Maintain flexibility and skills of an ageing workforce | Implement retraining and career consulting services |
| Labour–employee relations | Set basic employee relations philosophy and organization | Maintain labour peace and employee motivation and morale | Control labour costs and maintain labour peace; improve productivity | Improve productivity and achieve flexibility in work rules; negotiate job security and employment adjustment policies |

*Source:* Kochan and Barocci (1985).

– actually reinforce the organization's existing ways of working and thinking. Such projects may also inhibit the sort of radical thinking that real change requires by using existing relationships and defensive routines which prevent managers from getting at the kind of deep and threatening information and awareness change requires. Furthermore, even if we assume that management thinking on

HR issues is logical and consistent and fully knowledgeable about all possible options and their implications (which is highly unlikely), the problem with the design of appropriate SHRM elements is that it is not easy to identify the SHRM ingredients that generate the desired form of employee behaviour. For example, if you wanted to build an organization that encouraged employee commitment, or innovation, what HR systems and structures would you use?

There are also difficulties of implementation. It is easier to design change in organization than to achieve it. But the even more basic difficulty is that the links between HR structures and systems and business strategies themselves are complex and multi-faceted. How do HR strategies relate to business strategies? And what are management seeking to achieve when they design new HR strategies? These are the issues of this chapter.

We need to consider to what extent the logical connections between SHRM and business strategies identified by the researchers discussed earlier in this chapter are apparent, or possible, in reality. And we need to identify some of the various ways in which HR strategies and business strategies could inter-relate. We suggest that we hold to the overall definition offered by Beaumont presented earlier: 'the key message of the HRM literature is the need to establish a close, two-way relationship between business strategy or planning and HRM strategy or planning' (Beaumont 1992: 40). However it is important to consider just what this 'two-way relationship' between strategy might mean. What forms might this relationship take? Let us broaden the definition even more and say that at the heart of definitions of SHRM is the notion of a connection between strategy and corporate capability – the ability of the organization to act. If we accept this, then two obvious questions arise. First, what do we mean by 'capability'? And secondly, what sorts of relationship between capability and strategy are possible and significant? These are the key questions. There are four possibilities, and they vary precisely in the different senses of capability on which they focus, and the different relationship they posit between strategy and capability.

1. *SHRM as the enhancement of corporate capability to deliver and achieve corporate strategy.* This is the essential, classic view of SHRM which focuses on the 'fit' between strategies and structures. This approach comes in at least two major forms (see below), which are sometimes conflated. In this case structures and systems and cultures follow, and support, strategies.
2. *SHRM as the identification, development and deployment of corporate capabilities which are used as the basis for strategy development.* Here strategy follows structures. This is the resource-based view of SHRM.
3. *SHRM as the enhancement of strategy development.* The classic approach to SHRM assumes that the strategy around which the new HR strategy is developed is sensible and well-considered. But what if the organization's capability to develop strategies is itself under-developed? This is SHRM as the enhancement of the capability for strategy development. Clearly it is likely to be insufficient in itself and to require either 1 or 2 as well.

4 *SHRM as the enhancement of the organization's capability to learn and change.* Much SHRM activity requires extensive and sometimes radical programmes of organizational change – for example see 1, above, where the organization's structures and systems are changed to bring them into line with new strategies. But this assumes that the organization will be capable of effectively designing and implementing programmes of organizational change. The success of the change will depend on the organization's capability to design and manage change and to recognize, on an on-going basis, the need for change, and to change alertly and effectively. But such a capability cannot be assumed; and some approaches to SHRM regard the enhancement of this capability as the essence of SHRM.

Not all of these approaches to SHRM will be covered in this chapter. Here our concern is mainly with the first and to a lesser degree the second relationship between strategy and capability: i.e. SHRM as fitting structures to strategies, and strategies to structures (capabilities). However, in the book as a whole we cover all four approaches. Chapter 17 covers the enhancement of strategy formulation; and chapters 13 and 14 address SHRM as the management of change.

We will continue our analysis in this chapter with the classic, conventional approach which we have already considered earlier. This views SHRM as achieving consistency or 'fit' between the organization's systems and structures and its strategies, ensuring that the way the organization is structured, its culture and personnel systems, support the achievement of its strategy.

This equates SHRM with capability enhancement. We find, however, that within this approach there are two significantly different points of view. These differences have already been apparent in the earlier discussion.

## Structures Follow Strategies

### *The open and closed approaches*

As described above, and the classic approaches to SHRM which involve ensuring 'appropriate' organizational structures and systems, share one important feature. They all assert that the suitable form of SHRM will (or should) vary with the type of business strategy. There is no one best way. These approaches are *open* or *contingent* with respect to the characteristics of the 'appropriate' HR strategy, and do not seek to impose one particular package of measures in every case. These approaches do not say what a particular HR strategy should be like; for this is a matter that can only be solved with reference to particular circumstances and particular strategies. The view of Hendry and Pettigrew, for example, is entirely open: it says nothing about what a coherent, planned, contingent strategy would be like in any particular case. It would simply be 'appropriate'.

This is, however, what Fombrun et al., and Schuler and Jackson, and others, try to do. Their definitions argue that for a particular business strategy there is a single HR strategy, or a very limited range of HR strategy options. They attempt to describe what a particular HR strategy would be like for a particular business strategy – noting that it would be contingent.

Thus a cost reduction strategy would have different implications for SHRM than an innovation strategy. This is important because we shall find that for many SHRM writers, the essence of SHRM lies in the application of a specific and limited range of policies in every situation. As such, they are also closed views. These state that *regardless of the nature of the business, or the business strategy at a stage in the product life-cycle, one HR Strategy is appropriate*. It will be noted below that some definitions of SHRM define it not in terms of achieving a suitable human resource strategy, but in terms of installing certain fixed elements, or in terms of certain fixed goals, regardless of business strategy.

For example, Guest has argued that the key elements of SHRM are:

> Integration of relevant employee activities into general organizational strategies and policies;
>
> Fluid and adaptive organizational structure;
>
> High quality staff and internal practices to achieve high quality products;
>
> Optimal employee commitment to enterprise goals and practices. (Guest 1987)

Presumably the argument here is that these goals are necessary and valuable in every case, for every strategy and every set of conditions.

Obviously these open and closed views cannot live happily together. There will be difficulties in reconciling the proposition that SHRM strategies should be integrated with, and supportive of, the business strategy (whatever this is), with the proposition that all HR strategies should consist of the same elements (see Peters and Waterman 1982) regardless of the business strategy pursued.

There are, then, two broadly different types of SHRM. They share some features, notably that there should be a close, supportive and mutual relationship between organizational strategy and HR strategy. But one school then leaves the content of this relationship open, arguing that the only test of any HR strategy is its *appropriateness* or fit to the strategy.

This is the open, or contingent, approach. The other approach is more closed. It too asserts the importance of the connection between strategy and SHRM, but sees the *essential* SHRM as consisting of the implementation of some or all of the policy goals listed by Guest and others; namely, participation, quality, flexibility, and so on.

Some writers try to have it both ways. Beaumont, for example, argues that:

> The key messages . . . in the human resource management literature are a strategic focus, the need for human resource policies and practices to be consistent with overall business strategy, and the need for individual components of a human resource management package to reinforce each other, *while the individual components of the package should particularly emphasise teamwork, flexibility, employee involvement and organisational commitment*. (Beaumont 1993: 25, our emphasis)

Poole takes a similar view but adds a moral (or moralistic element). He defines SHRM as follows:

> Human resource management is viewed as strategic; it involves all managerial personnel . . . it regards people as the most important single asset of the organisation; it is proactive in its relationship with people; and it seeks to enhance company performance, employee 'needs' and societal well being. (Poole 1990: 3)

On the other hand, the open, general sense of SHRM is as follows. We present it in diagrammatic form in figure 2.1.

This model starts with an analysis of the environment within which organizations exist, and which they seek to control or survive in through certain strategies. These strategies, once defined, in turn require certain sorts of desired behaviours if they are to be achieved. If, for example, a bank is planning to move to a more customer-focused, sales-driven approach, and away from an emphasis on regulations and procedures and central bureaucratic control, then the attitudes, skills and behaviour of staff will have to change. These desired behaviours will be produced by certain sorts of human resource strategies (and not by others). People have to know what to do, want to do it, and be able to do it. To stick with our bank example, this change will probably require changes in training (for customer-care skills, and others), in job descriptions (which will now specify business and performance targets), in management style (greater discretion) and direction (towards new business), in internal assessment procedures (possibly the use of assessment centres), in organizational structures (more decentralized

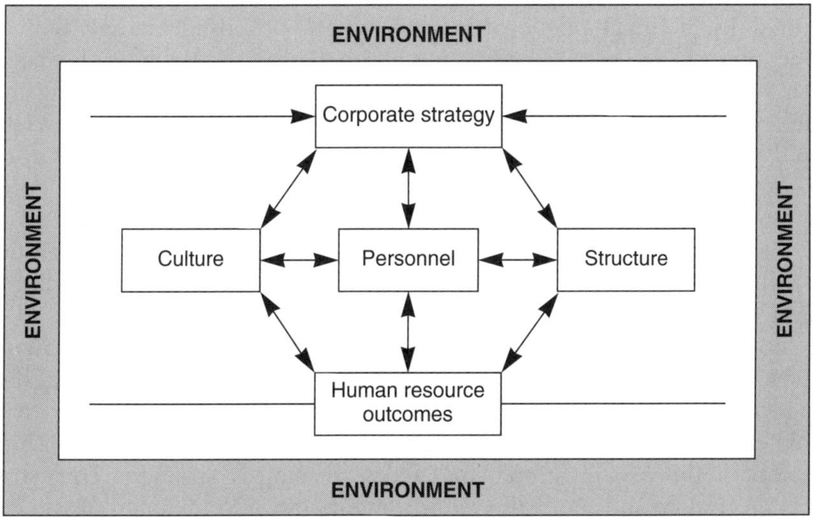


Figure 2.1 The 'open' approach to HRS

structures), in culture (away from rule-compliance, towards a more commercial, entrepreneurial approach), and so on.

As can be seen from figure 2.1, this open approach to SHRM has three key SHRM components, three constituent strategies which are intended to subsume all aspects of organization which have an impact on employees' behaviour: structural, cultural and personnel, and one fundamental conceptual assumption – that of 'integration', or appropriateness. If these are 'appropriate', they will produce the desired behaviours, at least to some degree. This proviso is important because a possible human resource strategy would be to accept that a given strategy might be somewhat beyond the current capacities of systems, structures and staff, and that therefore they have to 'stretch' to achieve it. Ultimately, however, if integration of SHRM and strategy is not seen as necessary to the achievement of strategy, the effort to achieve integration is seen as a necessary dynamic behind organizational pursuit of strategic objectives.

The degree of fit achieved will affect the relationship between behaviour and strategy, and will affect the level of achievement of organizational goals. The degree of success of the SHRM components in supporting the achievement of corporate strategies must be monitored and evaluated. This is a fantastically idealized picture: in reality achieving it is extremely rare, and the risk in these rarefied discussions of the abstract principles of SHRM is that people begin to believe that the world is actually like this. It is not. And it is crucial that we recognize the many ways in which reality differs from these models.

At the same time, the objectives of SHRM – ensuring that the organizational system (with all its constituent elements) supports the achievement of the overall strategy, i.e. that staff are clear about, willing, able and motivated to do what is necessary to achieve the organization's goals – is obvious good sense. But numerous factors will interrupt these processes: every stage is complex and subject to pressures which will discourage cool, detached, systematic analysis and implementation. The possibility of rational analysis within organizations is limited by political phenomena, and where proposed change will affect existing interests and established values and power-bases, the interplay between these interests will have an impact on SHRM decision-making. Achieving change within organizations is difficult, particularly when change occurs within a context of rapid and urgent environmental challenges. Also the world in which organizations actually exist is highly unstable and dynamic; the normality of constant change means that the situation will change even during the change process, requiring adjustment to some on-going process, delay in others, acceleration to others, new ones, and so on. Many of these problems and limitations are discussed in chapter 17.

The open, contingent, SHRM model is in principle dynamic (and idealized): it involves a series of active relationships, many of which are reciprocal. Senior managers define the business the organization is in. This then frames a particular organizational environment, including a market or market segment. Within this environment the organization's managers develop a strategy. This strategy reflects an understanding of the environment, and a knowledge of the organization's human resource strengths. The achievement of the strategy requires certain sorts of behaviours. These will be produced by the appropriate choice of structural, cultural and personnel strategies. And these must in turn be integrated so that they mutually support each other. Once in place these strategies will produce human resource outcomes, and will thus support or influence the achievement of the organizational strategy. But their effect will only be known through constant evaluation and monitoring, which very likely will result in modification to the SHRM plans, or how they are implemented, or to the organizational strategy itself.

The basic argument is that competitive advantage will accrue to those organizations best able to exploit environmental opportunities and avoid or survive threats; and that the strategic management of human resources will assist organizations in this by encouraging and generating the appropriate sorts of behaviours, attitudes and competencies from employees. As noted, human resource strategies involve an attempt to produce a match between key strategic priorities and the organizational processes, which in turn, will produce the behaviours necessary for their achievement. This 'integration' has two aspects.

The separate constituent elements of SHRM – payments systems, training programmes, appraisal procedures, management communications, attempts to manipulate organizational culture etc. – must be integrated such that they mutually support each other. There must be internal consistency. There is no point in recruiting qualified, ambitious, enthusiastic staff to fill repetitive, dead-end jobs, or in starting graduate selection without a graduate/management development scheme, or in 'empowering' supervisors without first ensuring that they are capable of taking on the increased responsibilities. Similarly, there is little value in launching a culture change programme emphasizing customer-care values when reward systems and management systems fail to reward, and possibly even demoralize, key staff. You can probably think of your own examples here – occasions when one aspect of organizational structure or policy seems to work against other priorities.

Schein, for example, argues that, 'The major problem with existing HRPD (Human Resource Planning and Development) systems is that they are fragmented, incomplete, and sometimes built up on faulty assumptions about human or organisational growth' (Schein 1987: 29). Schein argues that successful organizations are those which are able to match organizational needs with individual needs, thus achieving organizational growth along with individual development, commitment, creativity etc.

For Schein, SHRM (or HRPD) involves the fulfilment of *both* individual and organizational needs. This is a 'soft' view of SHRM and one which is typified by ideas not only about how organizations and individuals learn – they learn and develop together – but also about how employees and employers should, and do, interrelate. Like many writers in this field, Schein's view of SHRM is not only highly prescriptive, it is highly normative and value-laden. It describes how he would prefer people and organizations to interact.

Note then that the development of this idealized model of SHRM involves four discrete stages. These are cyclical and continuous. They are also highly demanding.

- The formulation of an organizational strategy.
- The identification of the key behaviours necessary to achieve strategic objectives.
- The identification and implementation of the organizational processes required to generate these behaviours.
- The monitoring of the effectiveness and success of the change programme.

For example, if a major strategic objective is the achievement of competitive advantage through greater responsiveness to customers and reduced lead time, then this objective requires staff to be willing and able to identify and respond to customer requirements, and able to control the production process. This in turn may require delegation of authority, change in job skills, more 'flexible' working practices, a change of attitude, new staff in key positions etc. But this

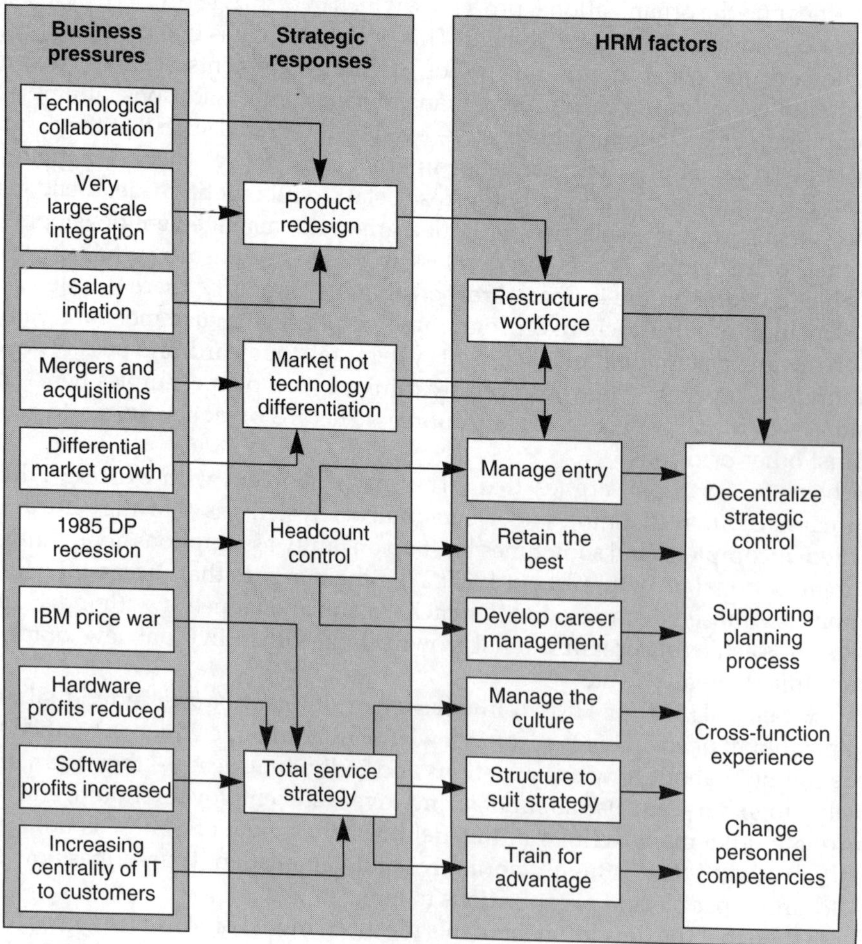


**Figure 2.2** HRM responses to a changing environment
*Source:* Sparrow and Pettigrew (1988: 42)

process also assumes that senior management have been able to scan the organization's environment thoroughly; have picked up the key signals in time, have analysed these sensibly and thoroughly and understood their implications for the fortunes of the organization; have developed an appropriate strategy to handle and exploit these developments; and have in turn been able and willing to restructure the organization to ensure its capability to support the new strategy. This is a daunting and demanding list of prerequisite steps for any group of senior managers.

Figure 2.2, which describes SHRM developments in the computer industry, illustrates these relationships. The figure depicts, in the cases of the companies studied, the SHRM factors developed in response to business strategies, which in turn were responses to business pressures. The details of each column need not concern us here; the interesting point is the clear establishment, by the researchers, of connections *across* the various levels: between SHRM elements, business strategies and business pressures.

## Achieving fit between strategies and structures

Discussions so far of SHRM models may allow the impression that the achievement of an appropriate 'fit' between business strategy and HR strategy is

### BOX 2.3 INNOVATION AT PIRELLI

The study of innovation in Pirelli (Clark 1995) illustrates the importance and complexity of achieving 'fit'. Clark reports that although the original plan was to achieve an innovative plant on one site:

'What became abundantly clear as the project progressed was that what may have appeared at the outset to be a major innovation in one aspect of the organisation – technology – proved to have major implications for virtually all other aspects of the organisation too. For example, the high degree of computer-integrated production at Aberdare would not have been possible without the innovations which were made – incrementally – in site location, building and factory layout. The same is true for the innovations – some planned from the beginning, others elaborated more incrementally as they went along – in organisation culture, organisation design and human resource management. One of the most important "lessons" of the Aberdare story is the extent to which technical, production, distribution, human resource, financial and commercial activities are inter-related. Ensuring their conceptual and practical "fit" was a highly complex and never-ending task, crucial to the realisation of wider corporate, business and operational strategies' (Clark 1995: 239).

relatively uncomplicated. This is far from the case. It is the most demanding aspect of the SHRM project (see box 2.3).

Formulating and implementing strategic human resource strategies is complex and difficult. This may be one reason why there seems to be relatively few cases of successfully implemented SHRM. Many writers have argued that little SHRM is occurring at all; while much change is occurring, little can be called true, SHRM change. And furthermore, much change is unsuccessful (Storey and Sisson 1993). Beaumont notes that there 'has been relatively little systematic empirical research designed to identify the nature and determinants of the human resource management policy mix of individual organisations. Some potentially useful conceptional discussions of the issue have put forward a number of general and specific hypotheses but these have rarely been taken up and tested' (Beaumont 1993: 19).

Storey and Sisson (1993) note that much of the work attempting to match business to HR strategies is vulnerable for two reasons: because of a simplistic notion of strategy, and of the connections between the two types of strategy; and because of limitations on managers' willingness and ability to formulate appropriate HR strategies. Much work on the relationship between HR and corporate strategies assumes a rational, consensual, explicit and unilinear process of strategic decision-making, of both sorts. The reality, however, is not like this. This means that strategies may not always be easy to discern, that the processes of decision making may be implicit, incremental, negotiated and compromised. In Europe, a study by researchers at Cranfield of SHRM developments in France, the UK, Germany, Spain and Sweden defined SHRM in terms of three key variables:

- Coherent, planned and evaluated policies on all aspects of personnel management that are developed with respect to corporate strategies.
- A move from collective to individual employee relations.
- An increase in line management responsibility for personnel management and a corresponding change in the role of the personnel function.

Now this definition of SHRM, which is concerned with personnel activities and the location of the personnel function may seem a little odd, and this may be due to the need to define SHRM in terms that were relatively easily measurable. But the application of these criteria to a number of European organizations produces an interesting and familiar conclusion: '. . . there appears to be a relatively high level of acceptance of certain tenets of HRM policies across all countries (although to varying degrees), with far less evidence that this formal acceptance is carried through into coherent planned and evaluated policies' (Brewster et al. 1990).

## A Resource-Based Approach to SHRM

Hendry and Pettigrew note that efforts to match these frameworks to identity SHRM requirements have not proved very illuminating, although this exercise is valuable in principle. The lack of empirical data has led to 'prescriptive theorising and the armchair exercise of matching strategy to HR practices – a game easy to indulge in since there was little empirical backing for these formulations' (Hendry and Pettigrew 1990: 34). The authors point out the need for empirical analysis of the connections between SHRM and corporate strategies, and the need to employ a conception of strategy as an incremental process (Hendry and Pettigrew 1990: 35).

These authors identify a number of key points with respect to the relationship between strategies and structures. They are:

1 That strategy should not be seen as a ready-formed output to which human resource strategies are moulded.

2 The structure and culture change can precede strategy.

3 That Human Resource strategy developments need not be simply reactive to strategy but 'can contribute to it through and development of culture, as well as to the frames of reference of these managers who make strategy.'

4 That the rationality of strategic and SHRM thinking is inevitably, within an organizational context, limited.

In effect these authors are usefully raising questions about the nature and direction of the links between the two sorts of strategy (business strategy and HR strategy). The approach discussed in the previous section clearly argues that structures (and systems and personnel processes etc.) must be brought into line with – made to 'fit' – organizational strategies, which are themselves based on market developments threats and opportunities. But what if a better solution is to fit strategy to structures – to develop a strategy which builds on the particular and distinctive strengths and resources of the organization, or to develop organizational abilities constantly, and quickly to develop and implement strategies ahead of the completion?

## Organizational capabilities

In this view of SHRM, the focus is less on laboriously and often radically changing the organization to fit strategies for which it is not historically equipped to handle, and more on developing or identifying and nurturing the organization's distinctive resources, including organizational capability to develop and implement strategies. As Prahalad and Hamel remark: 'A few companies have proven themselves adept at inventing new markets, quickly entering emerging markets, and dramatically shifting patterns of customer choice in established markets. These are the ones to emulate. The critical task for management is to create an organisation capable of infusing products with irresistible functionality or, better yet, creating products that customers need but have not yet even imagined' (Prahalad and Hamel 1990: 80).

By the 1970s British writers were beginning to make a distinction between hard and soft versions of SHRM: between what Morris calls 'human resources' and 'resourceful humans' (Morris 1974: 110). The former represents the strategy of treating staff as a resource like any other to be exploited and controlled; the latter represents attempts to develop and utilize the creativity and resourcefulness of staff for benefit to employer and individual. The point made by Prahalad and Hamel and others is that the effective matching of SHRM and organizational strategies need not mean manipulating personnel activities, organizational culture etc., to match and support corporate strategy, but that the relationship could well work the other way around. 'Firms that engage in a strategy formulation process that systematically and reciprocally considers human resources and competitive strategy will perform better – over the long term – than firms that manage human resources primarily as a means to solve competitive strategy issues' (Lengnick-Hall and Lengnick-Hall 1988: 468).

According to this view, human resource strategies must be integrated with organizational strategy in the sense that they must be mutually supportive. And while the classic, conventional view of this relationship is that SHRM must be designed to achieve organizational strategies, it is also possible that organizational strategies might be chosen in the light of existing human resource strengths and experience. As Hendry and Pettigrew note:

> HRM [has] a role in creating competitive advantage, in which the skills and motivation of a company's people and the way they are deployed can be a major source of competitive advantage. A company can methodically identify wherein its HR strengths lie and gear its HRM policies and business strategies towards utilising and developing these advantages. The HR skills that will be crucial for the future in its industry can be identified, and [the company] can take steps to acquire these. (Hendry and Pettigrew 1986: 7)

This is the resource-based view of SHRM, where 'the firm is seen as a bundle of tangible and intangible resources and capabilities required for product/market competition' (Kamoche 1996: 214). A number of definitions of resources and capabilities have been used; that offered by Kamoche on the basis of a thorough overview is useful: 'the accumulated stock of knowledge, skills, and abilities that the individuals possess, which the firm has built up over time into an identifiable expertise. The effectiveness with which organisational activities are achieved through HRCs (Human Resource Capabilities) is both a measure of the firm's ability to link its human resources to its strategic objectives and a behavioural manifestation of expertise' (Kamoche 1996: 216).

It is important to recognize that the resource-based view emphasizes not simply competitively valuable human skills and knowledge and aptitudes, nor easily imitated SHRM techniques and projects (payments systems, TQM etc.), but historic organizational systems (cultures, structures, relationships) which attract, retain, motivate, develop and deploy these competitively advantageous and hard to imitate skills and resources. Kamoche notes the importance in this respect of the firm's ability to generate the stock of knowledge and collective learning that enables it to provide core product/services (Kamoche 1996: 219).

For some contributors, the resource-based approach emphasizes the ability of the organization to manage the 'appropriability' of employees' skills and knowledge. Appropriability refers to the differing capacity of organizations to benefit from the utilization of their resources and capabilities – attracting and retaining relevant personnel; building and developing their expertise through development and learning systems and relationships; rewarding and sharing expertise and learning. Appropriability refers to more than the capacities of employees: it refers to the ability of the organization to develop and deploy these skills. Amit and Schoenmaker describe these organizational capabilities as 'based on developing, carrying and exchanging information through the firm's human capital' (Amit and Schoenmaker 1993: 35). One author has described this organizational capability to manage appropriability effectively as 'social architecture', which refers to forms of spontaneous co-operation that are embedded into daily routines. One interesting and important implication of this argument is that it is these 'social architectures', with their historic and deeply embedded patterns of skill formation, of knowledge accumulation and learning, (which comprise tacit knowledge and skills, the historic patterns of co-operative relationships, the deep capacity of the organization to attract develop and employ skills, attitudes and enterprise) that it is these rather than the formulaic packages of SHRM consultants that distinguish successful organizations from the others. 'Thus corporate prosperity not seldom rests in the social architecture that has emerged slowly and incrementally over time and may even predate the tenure of current senior management' (Mueller 1996: 757). We shall return to this point in chapter 18 when we consider the evidence for the impact of SHRM.

## Core competencies

However, although some contributors to the resource-based approach stress the ability of the organization to attract, develop, retain, deploy etc. the skills and aptitudes of its staff, others take a slightly different view, stressing the ways in which organizations differ in their historic and collective learning about and around key organizational activities – production skills, R&D, design, supplier management etc. For Prahalad and Hamel, these are the organization's 'core competencies' which: 'are the collective learning in the organization, especially how to co-ordinate diverse production skills, and integrate multiple streams of technologies' (Prahalad and Hamel 1990: 82). They offer Sony's miniaturization capacity and Philips' optical-media expertise as examples.

Core competencies involve more than merely deep layers of skill; they also involve the ways in which people work together, communicate, co-operate and encourage each other, often across boundaries and organizational demarcations. Core competencies are about how the organization as a whole works, which is why they are hard to develop and hard to emulate: 'The skills that together constitute core competences must coalesce around individuals whose efforts are not so narrowly focused that they cannot recognise the opportunities for blending their functional expertise with those of others in new and interesting ways' (Prahalad and Hamel 1990: 82). This raises an important point to which we will return: if these core competencies are the potential source of real organizational advantage then how, if at all, are these developed by currently popular HR packages? Is it possible indeed that some current HR approaches – the emphasis on profit centres and on SBUs, for example – might actively discourage the sort of cross-functional thinking and working regarded by Prahalad and Hamel as so important?

## Business processes

Stalk et al. take this focus on organizational process at potential sources of strategic advantage a step further by arguing that organizational capabilities are the ultimate source of advantage. By this they are emphasizing the importance of the effective management of business processes such that an organization is aware of its key processes and that it ensures that it is competitively superior at managing them: 'A capability is a set of business processes strategically understood. Every company has business processes that deliver value to the customer. But few think of them as the primary object of strategy. Capabilities-based competitors identify their key business processes, manage them centrally and invest in them heavily, looking for long-term payback' (Stalk et al. 1992: 62). Whereas the core competencies approach emphasizes technological and production expertise, Stalk et al.'s emphasis on capabilities is used to emphasize organizations' variable ability to manage all aspects of the value chain as a total process.

One of the interesting aspects of the resource-based approach is that in some measure it includes a number of ways in which SHRM could be useful. You will remember that earlier in this chapter four different senses of SHRM were identified, two of which have received little attention so far – SHRM as enhanced organizational capacity for change and SHRM as enhanced strategy development capability. Both of these are given attention in the resource-based approach. Stalk et al. clearly define their organizational capabilities in terms of strategy development and change management – being able to track the environment, respond to customers' demands, analyse possibilities, explore options, make decisions, exploit possibilities, *faster and better than others*.

However, it is important to recognize, as many contributors to this literature have stressed, the key distinction between necessary and sufficient strategically relevant resources or core competencies – that is, key organizational resources must be evaluated against the competition, 'because only a competitively unique and superior competence can be a source of economic value' (Kamoche 1996: 215). Prahalad and Hamel offer three 'tests' for core competencies: first, they must offer access to a number of markets. If an organization has a competitive advantage in some area of activity, there are enormous benefits if it can find other markets in which to exploit this ability. If it cannot, then there is little benefit to be gained from this particular skill. Secondly, core competencies must be perceived by, and seen as valuable by, customers. Many organizations make the mistake of assuming that the activities at which they excel and of which they are proud are core competencies. They are not unless they are also valued by the customers who recognize them, value them and, crucially, are prepared to pay for them. Thirdly, a core competence must be difficult for competitors to imitate. Again many organizations think that if they are good at some process which customers recognize and value, then this is a core competence. It is not if the competitors are – or can quickly become – good at this activity. In this case competence becomes simply a qualifying feature – something that major players in this industry must be competent at.

This discussion of the resource-based approach to SHRM raises a number of important points, particularly when seen in contrast to the conventional approach to SHRM outlined earlier. First, in many ways the two approaches are in opposition, at least in their extreme forms. The conventional approach focuses on market analysis, to discern market dynamics, threats, opportunities etc.; this is followed by strategy development, which in turn is followed by whatever organizational restructuring is required to change the original organization into the sort of organization required to deliver the new strategy. The resource-based approach starts with the organization as it is, and having identified its particular strengths, develops a strategy to exploit these (as, for example, core competencies). The conventional approach is likely to require radical programmes of change; the resource-based approach will place more emphasis on stability, and conserving and developing the traditional and historic strengths of the organization. Furthermore for some authors there are other possible areas of difference, even conflict, between the two approaches. Prahalad and Hamel, for example, argue that many of the elements of current SHRM packages – performance-related pay (PRP), the move to small business units (SBUs) etc. – are directly inimical to the development or retention of the ways of working required for core competencies. They note that the move to SBUs in a number of ways stresses intra-firm competition, blocks necessary co-operation, and stresses short-term returns rather than building competencies. They stress the value of a view of the firm not as a portfolio of businesses but as a portfolio of competencies: 'When the organisation is conceived of as a multiplicity of SBUs, no single business may feel responsible for maintaining a viable position in core products nor be able to justify the investment required to build world leadership in some core competence' (Prahalad and Hamel 1990: 87).

Finally, it may be the case that in some respects the relationship between the two approaches is closer than might appear. First, for many of the contributors to analysis of the resource-based approach, the key to competitively advantageous organizational resources or capabilities lies in the way the organization works – the way appropriability is managed, the way collective learning is encouraged and cherished, the way in which employees co-operate and communicate. These are ultimately HR processes. And it could well be the case that the most effective form of HR intervention is not one that consists of readily available and pervasive, fashionable packages (TQM, IiP, Continuous Improvement, BPR, and so on, whose effectiveness anyway is highly doubtful), but those SHRM interventions which seek to identify and nurture precisely the sorts of relationships and patterns of co-operations and mechanisms of process enhancement and appropriation noted as critical by the resource-based writers. Ironically it may be the case that many common HR packages not only fail to create organizational architectures and collective learning but threaten them.

This is indeed the assessment of one recent researcher who has written: 'SHRM . . . can lead to competitive advantage only under those conditions described by an evolutionary resource-based approach, . . . truly valuable strategic assets are unlikely to result from senior management's codified policies alone. Rather, what is truly valuable is the "social architecture" that results from ongoing skills formation activities, incidental or informal learning, forms of spontaneous co-operation, the tacit knowledge that accumulates as the . . . side effects of intentional corporate behaviour' (Mueller 1996: 777).

## Conclusions and Summary

Organizations are changing and they are changing in new ways and with new intensities. Many of these changes seem dramatic and certainly attract much attention. Whether or not these changes add up to SHRM-type change is another matter. It partly depends on the view you take of what SHRM is, and in this chapter we have noted that definitions of SHRM differ markedly. But it also depends upon the extent to which current programmes of organizational change are, behind all the claims, actually concerned with enhancing and focusing organizational capability for growth and performance; or façades which disguise and justify cost cutting, downsizing, attacks on unions, and increased control and surveillance of 'flexible' and frequently de-skilled staff. After you study the substantive chapters in this book – Parts II–IV – you will be able to come to your own conclusions on these issues.

Parallel with these changes, and inspiring or legitimating them, exists a body of ideas, of a various and complex nature, known as SHRM. These ideas promise much, and the management dream-makers and purveyors of promises ensure that the promises are publicized and amplified. But closer analysis suggests some conceptual, logical problems with these dreams. The issue is not simply their inefficiency and that managers may be disappointed. It is whether anyone really believed them in the first place. Is SHRM a promise that is not yet fully fulfilled, or a disturbed dream. Is it a failed promise that could never work, or a dream that is most powerful in disguising and distorting the realities it advocates? Or does it, at least potentially, offer a radically new way of structuring organizational work and employment – thus representing a way out of the historic 'iron cage' of bureaucracy and Taylorism?

The ideas in SHRM thinking are not new. But their combination is new, and their resonance with extra-organizational socio-political values is new, and is crucial to their power and appeal. The importance of SHRM lies as much in management of meaning as in the management of staff: indeed it collapses this distinction between words actions itself. SHRM means the attempt to manage staff by managing meanings as much as by managing systems and structures, for not only does it involve the re-definition of why and how these are being changed, but in many cases it also entails systematic attempts to manipulate employees' values and attitudes.

This chapter paid particular attention to issues of definition. By now we hope that the importance and indeed relevance of this discussion should be clear. Although our starting point has been different definitions of SHRM we very quickly began to address critical issues of the value and implications of these definitions, through considering such questions as the feasibility and logic of the various approaches. Definitions matter not because they are right or wrong but because they carry implications and make assumptions which we can test against reality. For example, the classic view of SHRM argues the importance of 'fit' of two sorts. But is such 'fit', however attractive as an idea, practical in reality? And both this approach and the resource-based view adopt a certain view of what strategies are like and how they are developed. Are these views of strategy realistic?

We have left some issues under-developed and incomplete. By focusing on different definitions of SHRM we have contributed to the analysis of the effectiveness of SHRM (for such an assessment requires an understanding of the different things SHRM is, or could be) but we have not completed this assessment. The more detailed and specific discussions of SHRM initiatives of various sorts that make up the main body of this book (Parts II–V) will develop and flesh out these preliminary analyses of variants of SHRM. And we have noted that two views of SHRM would see it in terms of the capability to develop strategy and in terms of the management of change. Both of these are emphasized by the resource-based approach, which we shall return to later.

## Key Points

- Definitions of SHRM vary widely and these differences in definition matter since they assert different views of how business strategies and organizational structures and systems should be – and can be – inter-related. Definitions are not right or wrong: they simply vary in their utility and, in as much as they point to causal connections between structures and strategies, in their feasibility.
- Discussions of SHRM must, however, acknowledge two critical and complex elements in many SHRM models: the notion of strategy on which they depend, and the notion of 'fit' or consistency. Both these elements are much more complex and uncertain in reality than they are in many SHRM models.
- Four basic approaches to the link between strategies and structures have been identified, covering the major approaches to SHRM: structures changes to support strategies; strategies built around organizational capabilities and resources; SHRM as the enhancement of strategy formulation capability; and SHRM as the improved management of change. All of these are important. Conventionally some get more attention than others. Politically some are more sensitive than others.
- Within the classic approach to SHRM, the open and closed versions were identified.

- Within the resource-based approach, different conceptions of 'resource' were identified, and some possible connections between this approach and the classic approach discussed.

## Discussion Questions

1 Identify some of the major ways in which definitions of (or approaches to) SHRM differ?
2 Discuss the significance of the concept of 'fit' to definitions of SHRM.
3 What are the four major approaches to SHRM and how can they support or conflict with each other?
4 What is the difference between 'open' and 'closed' approaches to SHRM?

## References


Amit, R. and Shoemaker, P. J. H. (1993) 'Strategic assets and organisational rent', *Strategic Management Journal*, vol. 14, 33–46.

Arthur, J. (1994) 'Effects of human resource systems on manufacturing performance and turnover', *Academy of Management Journal*, vol. 37, no. 3, 670–87.

Bailey, A. and Johnson, G. (1992) 'How strategies develop in organisations', in D. Faulkner and G. Johnson (eds) *The Challenge of Strategic Management*, London: Kogan Page, 147–77.

Beaumont, P. B. (1992) 'The US human resource management literature', in G. Salaman et al. (eds) *Human Resource Strategies*, London: Sage.

Beaumont, P. B. (1993) *Human Resource Management*, London: Sage.

Beer, M. and Spector, B. (eds) (1985) *Readings in Human Resource Management*, New York: Free Press.

Beer, M. et al. (1985) *Human Resources Management: A general manager's perspective*, New York: Free Press.

Blyton, P. and Morris, J. (1992) 'HRM and the limits of flexibility', in P. Blyton and P. Turnbull (eds) *Reassessing Human Resource Management*, London: Sage, 116–30.

—— and Turnbull, P. (eds) (1992a) *Reassessing Human Resource Strategies*, London: Sage.

—— and —— (eds) (1992b) 'HRM: debates, dilemmas and contradiction', *Reassessing Human Resource Management*, London: Sage, 1–15.

Brewster, C. J., Hegewisch, A., Holden, L., and Lockhart, T. (1990) 'Trends in human resource management in Europe 1990', Cranfield, Beds: Price Waterhouse Cranfield Project working paper.

Chandler, A. D. (1962) *Strategy and Structure*, Cambridge, MA: MIT Press.

Clark, J. (1995) *Managing Innovation and Change*, London: Sage.

Cressey, P. and Jones, B. (1992) 'Business strategy and human resource', *B884 Human Resource Strategies, Supplementary Readings 1*, Milton Keynes: Open University, 61–74.

Dyer, L. and Reeves, T. (1995) 'Human resource strategies and firm performance: What do we know and where do we need to go?', *International Journal of Human Resource Management*, vol. 6, no. 3, 656–70.

Fiat (1988) *Facts and Figures*.

Fombrun, C. J. (1983) 'Strategic management: integrating the human resource systems into strategic planning', *Advances in Strategic Management*, vol. 2, Greenwich, CT: JAI Press.

——, Tichy, N. M., and Devanna, M. A. (1984) *Strategic Human Resource Management*, New York: John Wiley.

Galbraith, J. R. and Nathanson, D. A. (1978) *Strategy Implementation: the role of structure and process*, St Paul, MN: West Publishing.

Goold, M. and Campbell, A. (1987) *Strategies and Styles: The role of the centre in managing diversified corporations*, Oxford: Blackwell.

Gowler, D. and Legge, K. (1986) 'Images of employees in company reports – do company chairmen view their most valuable asset as valuable?', *Personnel Review*, vol. 15, no. 5, 9–18.

Guest, D. E. (1987) 'Human resource management and industrial relations', *Journal of Management Studies*, vol. 24, no. 5, 503–21.

—— (1989) 'Human resource management: Its implications for industrial relations and trade unions' in J. Storey (ed.) *New Perspectives on Human Resource Management*, London: Routledge, 41–55.

—— (1990) 'Human resource management and the American dream', *Journal of Management Studies*, vol. 27, no. 4, 377–97.

Hendry, C. and Pettigrew, A. (1986) 'The practice of strategic human resource management', *Personnel Review*, vol. 15, no. 5, 3–8.

——, ——, and Sparrow, P. (1988) 'Changing patterns of human resource management', *Personnel Management*, 37–41.

—— and —— (1990) 'Human resource management: An agenda for the 1990's', *International Journal of Human Resource Management*, vol. 1, no. 1, 17–43.

Kamoche, K. (1996) 'Strategic human resource management within a resource-capability view of the firm', *Journal of Management Studies*, 213–31.

Keenoy, T. and Anthony, P. (1992), 'HRM: metaphor, meaning and morality', in P. Blyton and P. Turnbull (eds) *Reassessing Human Resource Management*, London: Sage, 233–55.

Kochan, T. A. and Barocci, T. A. (1985) *Human Resource Management and Industrial Relations*, Boston, MA: Little Brown.

Lengnick-Hall, C. and Lengnick-Hall, M. (1988) 'Strategic human resources management: a review of the literature and a proposed typology', *Academy of Management Review*, vol. 13, No. 3, 454–70.

Lodge, G. C. (1985) 'Ideological implications of changes in human resource management' in R. E. Walton and P. R. Lawrence (eds) *HRM Trends and Challenges*, Boston, MA: Harvard Business School Press.

Morris, J. (1974) 'Developing resourceful managers' in B. Taylor and G. L. Lippitt (eds) *Management Development and Training Handbook*, New York: McGraw-Hill.

Mueller, F. (1996) 'Human resources as strategic assets: an evolutionary resource-based theory', *Journal of Management Studies*, vol. 33, no. 6, 757–85.

Peters, T. and Waterman, R. H. (1982) *In Search of Excellence*, New York: Harper and Row.

Pettigrew, A. (1988) 'Introduction: Researching strategic change' in A. Pettigrew (ed.) *The Management of Strategic Change*, Oxford: Blackwell, 1–14.

Poole, M. (1990) 'Human resource management in an international perspective', *International Journal of Human Resource Management*, vol. 1, no. 1, 1–5.

Prahalad, C. K. and Hamel, G. (1990) 'The core competences of the corporation', *Harvard Business Review*, May/June, 79–91.

Purcell, J. (1989) 'The impact of corporate strategy on human resource management', in J.

Storey (ed.) *New Perspectives on Human Resource Management*, London: Routledge, 67–91.
Salaman, G., Cameron, S., Hamblin, H., Iles, P., Mabey C., and Thompson, K. (eds) (1992) *Human Resource Strategies*, London: Sage.
Schein, E. (1987) 'Increasing organisational effectiveness through better human resource planning and development', in E. Schein (ed.) *The Art of Managing Human Resources*, New York: Oxford University Press, 25–45.
Schuler, R. S. and Jackson S. E. (1987) 'Linking competitive strategies with human resource management practices', *Academy of Management Executive*, vol. 1, no. 3, 207–19.
Sisson, K. (1989) 'Personnel management in transition', in K. Sisson (ed.) *Personnel Management in Britain*, Oxford: Blackwell, 23–54.
Sparrow, P. and Pettigrew, A. (1988) 'Contrasting HRM responses in the changing world of computing', *Personnel Management*, February, 40–5.
Stalk, G., Evans, P., and Shulman, L. (1992) 'Competing on capabilities: the new rules of corporate strategy', *Harvard Business Review*, March/April, 57–69.
Storey, J. (1992) *Developments in the Management of Human Resources*, Oxford: Blackwell.
—— and Sisson, K. (1993) *Managing Human Resources and Industrial Relations*, Buckingham: Open University Press.
Tichy, N., Fombrun, C., and Devanna, M. A. (1982) 'Strategic human resource management', *Sloan Management Review*, Winter, 47–61.
Walton, R. E. and Lawrence, P. R. (eds) (1985) *HRM Trends and Challenges*, Boston, MA: Harvard Business School Press.

chapter 3

# SHRM in a Global Context

CHAPTER OUTLINE



*This chapter was contributed by Paul Iles*

## Learning Objectives

At the end of the chapter you will be able to:

- Recognize that decisions of multi-national and international organizations – particularly decisions about the siting of work activities – occur within a global context, and have definite and highly significant SHRM implications.
- Appreciate the importance of analysing international human resource strategies at the global, industry, regional/national and enterprise levels.
- Critically analyse the modernization and the new international division of labour at the global level.
- Evaluate the adequacy of both perspectives in the light of the evidence drawn from the textiles, electronics and software industries.
- Describe the relevance of differences in national business systems and regional and national cultures for international HRS.
- Critically evaluate the evidence for a distinctively 'European' model of SHRM.
- Identify differences between domestic and international SHRM systems.

# Introduction

Approaches to international SHRM differ radically – and these differences are themselves national in nature. Most treatments of international strategic human resource management, especially those from the USA, focus on very local issues – the problems that multinational companies (MNCs) and other transnational organizations have had in recruiting, selecting, training, appraising and rewarding expatriates. More recently they have begun to include staffing issues associated with joint ventures and other forms of transnational strategic alliances. Both foci of interest appear to be driven by practical parochial problems that seem particularly American: the apparently high and costly 'failure rate' experienced by American expatriates in comparison with their European and Japanese equivalents, and an apparent belief that their companies have been somehow deskilled and 'hollowed out' when entering alliances with Japanese, Korean and Taiwanese firms in particular.

In contrast, European treatments of international SHRM have examined issues of strategic control and co-ordination of multi-national corporations (MNCs) and the contribution that SHRM can play; focused at a regional level on what appears to be a European model of SHRM as compared to a North American or Japanese model; and have explored differences between countries or clusters of countries within Europe in terms of SHRM practices and their links with national culture and with national legal, political and social institutions.

Both the North American and European treatments appear to be driven by particular political and economic agendas. In the case of the European approach, the perspectives adopted appear to be influenced by the developing nature of European integration and especially the creation of the Single European Market. The concern is partly to enhance the competitiveness of European industry in relation to its continental rivals; partly to explore what makes (or should make) Europe distinctive in terms of economic and social policy; and partly to map out existing intra-European differences either as possible brakes or barriers to European integration and the harmonization of employment policies, or as possible 'building blocks' with which to construct a distinctively European model of SHRM.

Our concerns in this chapter are somewhat different. At one level we wish to broaden our analysis of SHRM beyond the rather limited definitions used in existing American and European accounts. We will introduce a wider global perspective by including the Asia-Pacific region, in addition to Japan, within our focus. We also wish to place our analysis of international SHRM within a broader examination of the globalization process; in particular, to look at changes within the international division of labour and its relation to some of the broader SHRM themes treated elsewhere in the book (flexibility, Fordism, integration, open vs. closed models of SHRM etc.). In locating our analysis within the context of global developments we are making a point often overlooked by conventional treatments of 'International SHRM' – that a global perspective reveals a number of critically important patterns concerning the nature and role of the international division of labour, and decisions about the location of production, which have a fundamental significance for all the organization's employees and consumers, yet which are frequently not regarded as essentially SHRM-type decisions. In this sense, much SHRM literature is guilty of socially structured silences on issues which would seem, prima facie to be unquestionably SHRM matters; for example, decisions about the location of production or work administration, since they are frequently based on assessments about issues such as the cost of local labour, the existence, strength and role of unions, the attitudes of local governments etc., are critical SHRM decisions. But they are not always seen as such.

Consequently this chapter will be organized around an exploration of international SHRM at three analytical levels:

1 The global level, especially in terms of the international division of labour.

2 The industry level, exploring the globalization process in selected industries.

3 The regional/national level, examining the differences between European, Japanese and North American approaches to HRS and exploring some of the differences in HR practice between countries or clusters of countries.

Chapter 6 will continue the analysis of this chapter through a focus on the enterprise level. That discussion will, however, be located within the context of the three levels treated here, which constitute and contribute to the complexity and diversity of the environment faced by the international enterprise.

# Human Resource Strategies at the Global Level

Advances in technology, transport and communication have contributed to a 'shrinking world' where inter-organizational relationships now transcend national or regional boundaries so that 'events, decisions and activities in one part of the world can come to have significant consequences for individuals and communities in quite distant parts of the globe' (McGrew 1992: 65–6). The jobs and conditions of Scottish electronics workers, for example, may be more dependent on decisions taken in the USA than by local management. This sense of global interconnectedness is well brought out by Hall (1992: 299), who uses the term globalization to refer to 'those processes operating on a global scale which cut across national boundaries, integrating and connecting communities and organisations in new space–time combinations, making the world in reality and experience more interconnected'. These processes have crucial implications for SHRM decisions.

Giddens (1990; 1992) also emphasizes the separation and compression of time and space, in globalization, arguing that: 'in the current era global processes impinge upon the most local and personal aspects of social life; conversely, individual actions and localised social interaction contribute to globally ordered systems' (1992: 1). Such a perspective also applies to organizational life and to HRS. Although it may be true that capitalism always had a global reach, it is undoubtedly the case that the scope and pace of global integration has greatly increased in recent years, and that the multinational or transnational company is one of the major agents of such globalization processes. Production, trade, finance and employment are increasingly organized on a transnational basis, making it less and less defensible to think of purely domestic or national economies, organizations or strategies, including HR strategies.

Yet whilst global integration is increasingly a major theme in strategic management, it is also the case that 'globalising influences do not work exclusively towards integration; globalisation also divides, marginalises and excludes' (Hall 1992: 1). An important feature of these influences is that they reveal the play of power relations – the 'power geometry' of globalization – particularly as displayed in the rise of the new international division of labour, which is a central feature of globalization. This interplay between the global and the local is central: 'globalisation (in the form of flexible specialisation and "niche" marketing) actually exploits local differentiation' (Hall 1992: 304).

## *Modernization theory, development and globalization*

In order to be able to understand and explore the ramifications of globalization, and its power geometry for SHRM decisions and processes, it will be useful to consider different theoretical approaches to the relationship between industrial and industrializing, or developed and developing, societies and economies.

'Modernization theory' proposes that social and economic development in what is usually termed the Third World (or developing/less developed countries, or increasingly the 'South') can occur through the application of western capitalist methods. It asserts the need for southern countries to modernize their political, social and economic institutions along similar lines (such as an emphasis on enterprise, achievement, rationality and progress) to the nature and thrust of the Industrial Revolutions in the West. Modernization theory has had significant influence on western development policies and such transnational organizations as the World Bank and the International Monetary Fund. This theory envisages development as a unilinear process which moves through a serious of clear stages from traditional societies to the early stages of industrialization; then, as a sort of critical mass of mutually sustaining industrial activity is achieved, the society progresses to a final stage of high consumption. The theory displays an evolutionary, unilinear and Eurocentric bias, projecting the western experience onto developing countries.

## Dependency theory, global capitalism and the classical international division of labour

Dependency theory, on the other hand, which originated in attempts to understand the relationship between the Third World and western capitalism, has different concerns from the conventional SHRM literature – and rather different theoretical perspectives. Nevertheless, it raises important questions about, and offers useful insights into, the nature of international SHRM. Dependency theory views the relationship between the West and the Third World in terms of relations of power and exploitation. An obvious corollary therefore is that organizations' decisions *vis-à-vis* the Third World, whether they concern location decisions, or recruitment or investment decisions, can also be seen in this light.

Dependency theory views the Third World as a subsidiary and dependent part of western capitalism as it spreads throughout the globe in the period of western colonial expansion. Accordingly, the capitalist system is less an engine of Third World development than a brake on its development. Wallerstein points out that capitalism 'was from the beginning an affair of the world economy and not of nation states – capital has never allowed its aspirations to be determined by national boundaries' (Wallerstein 1974: 19). He also emphasizes the unequal structure of capitalism's global scope, viewing the capitalist world economy as divided into *core* (Japan, North America and Western Europe), *semi-peripheral* (Southern Europe and Eastern Europe) and *peripheral* (the Third World) regions. Such terminology is reminiscent of earlier analyses of the division of labour at the level of the domestic economy (e.g. core vs. peripheral workers, primary and secondary labour markets) and reminds us that globalization, whatever the modernization theorists might say, is a process that is unevenly distributed both between different sections of the population within nations, and between regions and nations.

Massey (1991) refers to this as globalization's 'power geometry' to draw attention to the unequal distribution of power and decision making within the globalization process – a point stressed by dependency theory. As Sklair (1991: 6) puts it: 'the global system is marked by a very great asymmetry. The most important economic, political and cultural-ideological goods that circle around the globe tend to be owned or controlled by small groups in a relatively small number of countries.'

These writers draw attention to the inequalities present in the often bland assertions of 'globalization'. They also note the international nature of the contemporary division of labour. Traditionally, this took the form of Europe and North America (and later Japan) becoming the manufacturers of finished products and the Third World simultaneously acting as an exporter of raw materials and cash crop agricultural products, and an importer of relatively high-priced western products in a process of unequal exchange. We shall refer to this as the classical international division of labour in contrast to the 'new' international division of labour.

## The new international division of labour

The development of flexible production technologies, and IT systems in particular, have facilitated a process of decentralization of production and the de-domiciling of capital, with multinational companies moving parts of their production or servicing process outside the home countries, especially to the 'newly industrializing countries' of the Asia-Pacific region. The pursuit of low-cost, disciplined and less-organized labour to work in routinized, labour-intensive production has often been ascribed to the multinationals' search for low-cost competitive advantage and crisis conditions in the *core* countries. Jameson (1992: 319) describes 'the global reconstruction of production and the introduction of radically new technologies – that have flung workers in archaic factories out of work, displaced new kinds of industry to unexpected parts of the world, and recruited workforces different from the traditional ones in a variety of features, from gender to skill and nationality'. For Fröbel et al. (1980: 12), 'the old or classical international division of labour is now open for replacement . . . developing countries have increasingly become sites for manufacturing – producing manufactured goods which are competitive in the world market . . . this means that any company almost irrespective of its size which wishes to survive is now forced to initiate a transnational reorganisation of production.'

This relocation of deskilled and routinized jobs seems particularly characteristic of the garment and electronics sectors, explored further in the next section. The West German garment and textile industries, for example, have used North African subsidiaries, working under Taylorist rather than Fordist conditions. Since employment is seen as essentially unskilled, technology transfer is minimal, and there are few links between such enclaves and the rest of the economy. Hence the new international division of labour is seen as deepening historical underdevelopment, not as reversing it.

In this version of the international division of labour (IDL) the world market for manufacturing or services is becoming fragmented and work activities located wherever the most profitable combination of capital and labour can be obtained. However, IDL does not refer only to work moving to cheap labour but also cheap labour moving to where the work is located, across national borders, or indeed to the segmentation of national labour markets. For example, women and migrant labour are commonly employed to perform many of the less desirable, less rewarded and dirtier jobs of advanced industrial economies, whether Mexicans in the USA, Moroccans in France, Indonesians in the Netherlands, or Turks in Germany (the lines of migration often following old colonial, imperial networks). British firms in the 1980s often subcontracted production to the inner city, with secondary sector firms making heavy use of minority ethnic labour as well as relocating production overseas. Women workers are often preferred by multinational companies, being seen not only as cheaper but also as subordinated by their domestic role and beliefs about their 'suitability' for routine, fragmented and repetitive work. Pearson (1988; 1994), refers to the dominant image of nimble-fingered young women working in a South-East Asian electronics factory, and points out that female productivity in such conditions is often higher than male productivity. However, she also challenges any undifferentiated view of women's work in the new international division of labour, noting that location decisions are not just about lowest costs but also about other incentives.

In one sense the new international division of labour goes hand in hand with a new sexual division of labour, notably in manufacturing; but also in services, agriculture and the informal sector. Bangladeshi women, for instance, seemed to have flocked to work in the clothing industry, but this may be due to a lack of other options. As Elson (1994: 205) puts it: 'while jobs in the clothing factories improve the terms on which young women are able to negotiate the social relations that subordinate them the structures of gender inequality are not thereby dissolved.'

However Hoogvelt (1987) points out that whereas the Third World in general has made significant advances in terms of structural transformation and the contribution of manufacturing output to gross domestic product (GDP), the process has been uneven, rendering the relevance of the term 'Third World' questionable (even more so now, given the collapse of the Second World). At one extreme, eight newly industrialized countries are now virtually comparable with the First World, whereas in almost 50 countries industrialization has hardly begun. At the same time, de-industrialization, especially in terms of employment but also in terms of output relative to GDP, has been steadily taking place in the *core* countries. Whilst the Third World's share of exports has grown rapidly, this has been extremely sporadic, suggesting that the original thesis as it stands is too sweeping.

The New International Division of Labour (NIDL) thesis may exaggerate the scale of relocation to Third World sites. Multinational companies may relocate not simply in pursuit of cheap labour, but also to establish market position. Reducing direct labour costs is only one route to competitive advantage; increasing labour productivity through, for example, technical innovation or flexible specialization is another. Pearson (1994) argues that relocation is limited and concentrated in a narrow range of goods in specified countries and regions, particularly textiles and garments from East Asia and Latin America and electronics components/ assembly of consumer electronics goods from South-East Asia. There has also been an erosion in some sectors of the comparative advantage of relocation, due to computerization and automation, and neo-protectionist measures to restrict imports from the developing world in particular industries have contributed to relocation back to the North.

Having analysed the trends and implications of these shifting patterns of employment at the level of the global system as a whole, we now turn our attention to the industry level, exploring three sectors in particular, two of which (textiles/clothing and electronics) played an important part in the original NIDL thesis. The software industry, which became important in the 1990s, played no part in the original thesis, but illustrates some emerging trends.

## International SHRM at the Industry Level

This discussion of the IDL is relevant to our broader interest in SHRM because of course IDL refers to employers' decisions about where to locate work activities, and these decisions have implications for – and are determined by – issues such as availability of labour, cost of labour, employment law, working conditions etc. But these decisions may not concern national boundaries. Within western national boundaries, the existence of migrant labour allows the development of a segmented labour market whereby some workers – women, ethnic minorities, migrants – tend to be employed on employment terms that are markedly inferior to those of traditional, skilled workers. The Conservative Governments of the 1980s/1990s in the UK encouraged the use, and size, of this 'flexible' cadre of workers. Employers' strategic (i.e. cost-cutting) use of this 'secondary' labour market also reveals a localized international dimension. Many firms in 'core' countries have responded to intensifying international competition through a range of measures, many of which have been discussed in earlier chapters, including closures, rationalizations, mergers and acquisitions, restructuring of relationships with suppliers and contractors, and the introduction of post-Fordist (or neo-Fordist) flexible working practices. They have also shifted production to low-cost areas overseas and engaged in a variety of transnational strategic alliances. This restructuring of employment relationships on a global scale is not always considered as a SHRM matter; our argument in this chapter is that it should be.

In the two following sections we will consider the implications of globalization and IDL in a specific industry.

### *Globalized production in the textile industry*

Globalization is not a new phenomenon in the textile industry. As Elson (1994: 189) puts it: 'the production, distribution and consumption of textiles and clothing has epitomised the uneven development of the world economy since the very beginning of industrial capitalism in the eighteenth century, when the high quality, handicraft-based Indian textile industry was destroyed by the output of Lancashire's mills. In its turn, Lancashire gave way to the United States, Germany and Japan, while today South Korea, Taiwan, Hong Kong and, latterly, China, challenge the older established locations.'

Nor are flexibility or subcontracting strategies recent innovations. Nation states have always attempted to regulate the global development and patterns of labour utilization in the textile industry. Since the 1970s, the proportion of global production in the South has grown from around 18 per cent in 1975 to over 31 per cent in 1993 (Elson 1994), and not just in the low-tech areas. Despite restrictive measures such as the Multi-Fibre Arrangement, an increasing share of global exports has also come from the South, especially from a few East Asian countries. In contrast to the NIDL thesis, off-shore assembly by Northern MNCs for re-export to the North is not a feature of fibre and fabric production; nor is foreign direct investment (FDI), except by Japanese companies, an important dynamic. Networks or 'commodity chains' of small- and medium-sized firms, including developing country firms owned by citizens of such countries, are much more characteristic. Western MNCs have played only a small role, for example, in the South Korean and Bangladeshi industries, although Japanese companies have been active. The state in many East Asian nations has often sought to stimulate production and export activities through export processing zones, subsidies and other measures.

As the leading role of textile companies in the industrialization of South Korea, for example, has declined under lower-cost competition from China and Indonesia, South Korean companies have looked for locations in countries like Bangladesh. Although jobs have been shed on a massive scale in the North, this is not just the result of job transfer to the South, but also due to growth in productivity and changes in demand. In general, wages and conditions in the South

## BOX 3.1 THE INTERNATIONALIZATION OF TOOTAL

'One of the three leading British textile/clothing MNCs, Tootal's drive to internationalization and its reduction of its British labour force seems to owe more to a desire to access East Asian markets than a search for cheap labour. Offering design, technical, marketing and financial expertise to a variety of Southern partners, it attempted to reposition itself as a service company. Production factories in Asia were rarely wholly-owned export platforms for the UK market, although they were integrated into its global sourcing network. Cloth imported into the UK was printed with batik designs and re-exported to West Africa as "traditional costume". In the 1980s, the over-valuation of sterling reduced its competitiveness and left it vulnerable to takeover from Coates-Viyella.' (Elson 1994) seem better in larger, export-oriented factories and in MNCs than in local firms. Given that the North does retain its leading role in new technology, the South continues to feel pressures to invest in new technologies and in training.

Box 3.1 shows the experience of one British textile MNC, Tootal. Its development shows the limitations of the NIDL thesis in its focus on low-cost assembly as the driving force behind the globalization of production.

## *Regional division of labour in the electronics industry*

The electronics industry is second only to garments and textiles as a source of manufacturing employment in the South. Southern states have seen it as an attractive, capital- and knowledge-intensive industry, able to deliver higher value-added and faster economic growth. Its ability to stimulate demand for engineers and scientists, specialized supplies, components and services, and fuel pressures for investment in education and training, have also made it attractive (Henderson 1994). However, the realization of this potential has been largely limited to the Asian and Latin American NICs, and only Korea and Taiwan compete directly with the dominant core industries, leaving most of the others foreign-owned and at the labour intensive, low value-added end of the spectrum. As Henderson (1994: 263) puts it, 'the largely US and, more recently, Japanese companies responsible for FDI developed a global production system which, until the late 1970s, was perhaps the supreme example of an industry organized according to the principles of the new international division of labour thesis.' Control, R&D, and capital- and technology-intensive parts of the production process remained firmly in the North.

However, 'by the mid to late 1980s, the international division of labour as represented by semi-conductor production had already been transformed' (Henderson 1994: 263). There had been extensive investment in high-skill, high-technology processes in Singapore and Hong Kong in particular; the Singapore government forced up labour costs in a successful attempt to encourage MNCs to emphasize high-technology operations, with both countries emerging as regional headquarters. The more peripheral Asian economies then became subjected to a secondary layer of control and dependency from Hong Kong and Singapore, creating a regionally segmented division of labour as the peripheral economies became increasingly integrated into the production systems of the Asian NICs. The whole region became subject to substantial FDI by Japanese companies driven not just by the search for lower labour costs, but by the demands for localized production to serve just-in-time systems.

A particular feature of note is that the electronics industry in the Latin American and Asian NICs owes much of its origin and development to *state* industrial policy, in contrast to many of the free market/organizational autonomy arguments often associated with HRS. Linkages with the local economy, the upgrading of personnel and genuine technology transfer have been mainly limited to Singapore, Korea and Taiwan (which are also among the most egalitarian of NICs). However, changing market conditions, declining demand in the North, the need for technological upgrading and the dependent nature of many production systems on Original Equipment Manufacture, all pose problems for the continued development of the NICs.

In general, it seems as if the NIDL is giving way to commodity chains and interfirm relationships where peripheral economies are becoming subject to the technical and managerial control of intermediary economies like Taiwan and Korea, as well as core economies like Japan. FDI from the North to the South, except for that going to the Asian and Latin American NICs and near NICs and China, has collapsed, making it unlikely that other Southern countries can create viable electronics industries.

The original NIDL thesis focused on static technologies and standardized mass production. Fears of job transfers to the South have, however, recently been voiced even in the software industry, as highly skilled but low-paid employees in India, China and Eastern Europe can now communicate with western mainframe computers directly by satellite.

## *International SHRM in a borderless world*

The NIDL thesis, with its vision of footloose multinationals with no specific ties, constantly on the move to close down unnecessary locations and continually seeking new investment opportunities in search of lower labour costs, is curiously paralleled by authors more clearly located in the 'modernization' camp, who trumpet the 'globalization of markets' and propose that international business is becoming increasingly 'borderless' and international corporations increasingly 'placeless'.

### BOX 3.2 IT OPERATIONS MIGRATING SOUTH?

'The entry of the previously closed Indian, Chinese and Eastern European economies into the global capitalist system, the return of US-trained software graduates, and a well-educated labour force (often female) prepared to work for relatively low wages has stimulated the electronics industry in the South. Lufthansa and Swissair, for example, have outsourced all or part of their IT operations to India through subsidiaries or contract partners, whilst BA has established a satellite ticket reservation processing facility in Delhi. Other companies have established joint ventures, whilst some Indian software houses have exported directly to the North. However, growth areas like "object oriented" systems and the selling of "total solutions" remain in Western hands.'
(Crabb 1995)

For example, Levitt (1983) has argued that all markets are becoming global and that the globalization of operations is becoming a requirement for all companies. Whilst 'internationalization' is seen as referring to the geographical dispersal of operations across national boundaries, 'globalization' is seen as a qualitatively different process, involving the *functional integration* of such internationally dispersed operations. For example, Reilly and Campbell (1990, quoted in Barnett 1990: 7) define globalization as: 'The integration of business activities across geographical and organisational boundaries. It is the freedom to conceive, design, buy, produce, distribute and sell products and services in a manner which offers maximum benefit to the firm without regard to the consequences for individual geographic locations or organisational units – the global firm is not constrained by national boundaries as it searches for ideas, talent, capital and other resources required for its success. In short, the global firm operates with few – if any – self imposed geographical or organisational constraints on where or how it conducts its business operations.'

For Levitt (1983), technological change and the 'proletarianization' of communications, transport and travel have caused consumer tastes across the world to converge. This has required companies to develop globally standardized products that are advanced, reliable, functional and low-priced, and able to deliver what *everyone* is said to want – the alleviation of life's burdens and the expansion of discretionary time and spending power. The global corporation will increasingly operate 'as if the entire world (or major regions of it) were a single entity; it sells the same things in the same way everywhere' (Levitt 1983: 92–3).

This reference to 'major regions' already introduces one qualification to the argument – Levitt is primarily concerned with what Ohmae (1985) refers to as the 'Triad' of North America, Europe and Asia-Pacific. Ohmae (1989) also stresses the key role of information in creating a 'borderless world', although he also acknowledges the continued importance of distinctive national tastes and cultures. For Ohmae (1989: 94), talking about the global firm, 'Country of origin does not matter. Location of headquarters does not matter. The products for which you are responsible and the company you serve have become denationalised.' Reich (1991), US Secretary of Labour at the time of writing, has also asserted that, in the future, there will be no more 'national' corporations. For routine production workers, there will be a constant shifting of jobs to ever-lower-paying locations – just as the NIDL theorists predicted! Routine personal service workers will also find their wages depressed. However, knowledge workers will gain, finding a larger and larger market for their services. The importance of education, training, skill and high technology will continue to grow, making international SHRM of even greater significance.

In the 1970s, modernization theorists locked horns with dependency theorists over whether capitalism had developed or could develop the South; yet both remained imprisoned within similar technological/teleological, deterministic, evolutionary and Eurocentric frameworks, allowing little space for diversity. In the 1990s, new international division of labour theorists spar with globalization theorists about the benefits of the emerging stateless, placeless, footloose multinational constantly driven to reduce its labour costs.

Simultaneously, management consultants and academics try to convert the corporations of the industrialized West to the structures and cultures of the Asian Tiger economies (see box 3.3). It is clear that the kind of global, geocentric, standardized low-cost strategy championed by Levitt (1983) is only one possible global strategy. Many transnational companies have adopted other successful SHRM strategies, focusing on innovation, differentiation or quality; have focused on regions through 'regiocentric' strategies; and focused on different domestic markets, through polycentric or multidomestic strategies. Adopting a 'global perspective' does not mean always adopting a product-driven, standardized strategy; customer needs and interests remain diverse, even within nations. Indeed Hall (1992) has pointed out that globalization may also stimulate differentiation and the creation of diverse identities (e.g. companies in Cataluña now have to advertize in Catalan as well as in Spanish). It does not seem to be the case that price rather than variety or quality of service is becoming increasingly important, and flexible specialization appears to be undermining the advantages of standardization in many instances. For example, the standardized, low-cost approach of Zanussi, highly successful up to the 1970s, was undermined within Europe by niche operators and firms operating more diverse, multi-domestic strategies, leaving Zanussi to be acquired by Electrolux. The bases of global competition are dynamic – some markets may well be truly global, others may

## BOX 3.3 THE ILLUSION OF GREENER GRASS ELSEWHERE

Until the late 1990s management writers maintained that if only western corporations could emulate the cultures, structures, work philosophies, production technologies, qualities processes, of organizations in Japan and the tiger economies of East Asia, their success would be assured. But recently the scandals and bankruptcies of Japanese financial institutions, and the collapse of the Korean economy, have raised doubts about the wisdom of constantly looking abroad for models of salvation. There has been a long tradition of this 'grass is greener' thinking. In the 1950s UK firms were encouraged to emulate American Fordism; in the 1960s they were told to copy Volvo's team philosophy; in the 1970s, German worker participation models. But there have been few magic solutions to be drawn from the management and organizational philosophies of other countries. Despite the exhortations of the management writers, the causes of success in national economies are usually highly complex and dependent on a variety of inter-locking national factors which are hard to emulate and which are often due to the time when industrialization occurred and the fact that newly industrializing economies have done in a few generations what the West achieved in centuries, and with the benefits of a fresh start with modern technology.

well be local, others regional. In a later section, we will explore the role of HRS in supporting such differentiated corporate strategies.

Rebutting Ohmae (1989) and Reich (1991), it will be noted that most MNCs remain embedded in particular national and cultural milieux and carry with them features of their parent-country environment, as well as taking on some of the characteristics of their host-country environment. MNCs continue to have most of their assets located in particular states, continue to look to particular countries for legal and diplomatic protection, continue to be at least potentially taxable on global earnings in particular nations, and continue to employ parent-company nationals, both in senior positions at headquarters (usually in the home country) and to run foreign subsidiaries. However, while this requires us to abandon the wilder claims of the globalization thesis, it does not weaken the argument of the new international division of labour theorists that MNCs are increasingly taking a global perspective when considering such key matters as location of their activities, and this is the most significant of all international SHRM decisions and strategies.

However we must recognize that location decisions by no means exhaust all international SHRM issues, and in order to address these we need to focus on a different level of analysis: international SHRM not at the global and industry levels, but at the national and regional levels. We will begin by exploring the role of the state in setting the context for SHRM and then briefly explore the role of regional groupings and blocs. Both analyses confirm the importance of geographical dispersion and cultural diversity to our conception of international SHRM.

## International SHRM at Regional and National Levels

A particular focus in the 1990s has been the growing acceptance in the North that it must avoid pricing itself out of world markets and pay particular attention to labour costs (an emphasis common to many of the globalization and 'new international division of labour' arguments). As Table 3.1 shows, differences in labour costs in the manufacturing sector are very considerable, even within Europe, but differ even more when other countries are taken into consideration. Of course, these figures disguise differences within each country – especially the different terms, conditions, wage rates, training, career possibilities, etc., of 'primary' and 'secondary' labour categories. While remaining within a single country employers can strategically exploit significant differences in wage rates and employment conditions by decisions on the location of activities, or the employment conditions to prevail.

Clearly, high wages do not necessarily imply high unit labour costs, or low wages low unit labour costs. The efficiency with which labour is utilized – itself a function of HRS – can be much more important, and social welfare costs can also affect overall costs considerably. Governments, however, do seek to influence

**Table 3.1** Contribution of labour to manufacturing costs – a cross-country comparison 1991 (average US $ per hour)

| *Country* | *Pay for time worker* | *Holiday pay and bonuses* | *Non-wage labour costs (A)* | *Total labour costs (B)* | *(A) as a per cent of (B)* |
|---|---|---|---|---|---|
| *EC average* | 9.92 | 2.95 | 4.08 | 16.95 | 24.1 |
| Germany | 12.67 | 4.63 | 4.87 | 22.17 | 22.0 |
| Italy | 8.66 | 3.04 | 5.48 | 17.18 | 31.9 |
| France | 8.34 | 2.56 | 4.36 | 15.26 | 28.6 |
| UK | 9.88 | 1.60 | 1.94 | 13.42 | 14.5 |
| Spain | 9.03 | | 3.62 | 12.65 | 28.6 |
| *Non EC countries* | | | | | |
| US | 11.33 | 1.00 | 3.12 | 15.45 | 20.2 |
| Japan | 8.38 | 4.14 | 1.89 | 14.41 | 13.1 |
| Asian countries | 3.82 | | 0.38 | 4.21 | 9.0 |

wage costs, inflation rates and internal relativities, as well as the external value of the currency against others so as to affect relative labour costs. Governments also seek to influence non-wage costs, such as welfare benefits, and to influence tax rates. Legal regulations are often seen by companies as adding to their costs – an argument made strongly by the UK government (and some UK companies) in relation to the 'social costs' perceived as inherent in much European legislation concerned with employee protection (e.g. equal opportunity, health and safety, hiring and firing regulations). Governments also seek to use education and training to create a more productive labour force, although even here there are competing calls, and some governments (such as the British government) have sought to push much of the cost onto individuals or private companies, not all of whom have fully taken up this responsibility. Education and training not only enhance skills, but also affects discipline and motivation, allowing a high-wage country like Germany, with a highly skilled and educated labour force, to successfully compete with countries offering much lower wages.

## The role of regional trade groupings

National governments and international governments groupings and agencies play an increasingly powerful role in establishing the context of SHRM and international SHRM decisions (for example trade areas, tariff agreements), and indeed in intervening directly in SHRM matters through employment law, benefits and compensation standards, safety legislation, minimum wage levels etc. Although the rhetoric of much SHRM thinking – particularly in the USA and the UK – has been to celebrate market forces as the only possible arbiter of corporate decision-making the reality is increasing levels of political structuring of markets, for labour and for products. (Many of the economies western organizations are encouraged to emulate have of course been markedly averse to the play of market forces.)

The political structuring of trade areas is important. For Ohmae (1989), successful globalization requires that companies compete in the three regions (or Triad) of North America, Europe and Asia-Pacific. In recent years, the North American Free Trade Association (NAFTA) has been ratified in Canada, the USA and Mexico, whilst the Asia-Pacific Economic Council has emerged as a looser association, centred on Japan. Neither, as yet, have gone as far down the road to both economic and political integration as the European Union, but SHRM policies and practices are increasingly likely to be influenced by such emerging trade blocs. The development of the Single European Market in particular means that the 'domestic market' for national firms no longer stops at national borders. Wage levels, jobs, inflation rates and interest rates are increasingly influenced by pan-European decisions, and HRS is no longer able to address purely local or national issues. In addition, European social policy, as embodied in the Treaty of Rome, and amended by the Single European Act of 1986, is having an increasing impact on a range of HRM issues by creating principles which fall within the jurisdiction of the European Court of Justice and which domestic legislation in a whole range of areas needs to take into account (see box 3.4). Such issues include

## BOX 3.4 IMPLICATIONS OF THE EUROPEAN SOCIAL CHARTER

The Social Charter, a developing framework initiated in 1988 and ratified as the Social Chapter in 1991 at the Maastricht Council, is also becoming increasingly important to HRS. Though not legally binding, the implementing directives that will be developed from it will have legal force. These principles cover such areas as equal treatment, free movement, working conditions, social protection, freedom of association and collective bargaining, vocational training, equal opportunity, health and safety, the protection of young children, young people and the elderly and the disabled, and the right to information, consultation and participation. Under the Delors presidency, the Commission has pursued the idea of 'l'éspace sociale' to accompany the 'economic space' created by the Single Market, in part to avoid 'social dumping', where companies move jobs within the EU from the richer North, with its high social costs, to the poorer South, with lower social costs (critics and NIDL theorists, of course, would point out that such companies could transfer jobs out of Europe altogether). Large multinational companies in Europe were required to set up European Works Councils for information and consultation by 1996. European legislation is having an increasing impact on British employment adopted by British companies like United Biscuits, Coates-Viyella and ICI, with an Institute of Directors survey reporting that 80 per cent of UK multinationals were preparing to set one up (Bassett 1995). Over 300 UK companies may be affected – more than in any other European country.

the right to freedom of movement, to equal treatment, to employee participation, and to equal pay and benefits.

Within the UK, the pursuit of harmonization and the role of European law has become embroiled in wider arguments about a common currency, defence policy and eventual political integration. Some have argued that the UK government has deliberately sought to lower labour costs to attract Japanese and Korean inward investment, although there may be other reasons why such investment has continued to flow (e.g. the English language infrastructure, market position). Similar arguments have occurred within NAFTA over whether US jobs would be exported to Mexico, or whether wages would converge closer to the Mexican level rather than the US level. It is clear that, even if the 'strong' version of the NIDL thesis and the placelessness and footlooseness of MNCs is rejected, MNCs will continue to assess alternative investment opportunities within the various regional blocs, and that unit labour costs will be a major consideration. Other factors, however, will come into play, such as cultural factors and the kind of HRM systems in existence in the various blocs, and the nation states that make them up. And it is to these aspects of comparative SHRM that we now turn.

## *Culture and international SHRM at regional and national levels*

Traditional questions (e.g. Kidger 1991) raised in connection with the relationship between culture and international SHRM include:

- Are SHRM practices culture bound or culture free?
- Can we introduce a successful SHRM practice from one national setting to another?
- Are policies and practices universally applicable or must they be adapted to fit the local culture?
- Are national and corporate culture potentially antagonistic forces in the MNC?
- What are the implications of this for developing a global workforce?
- Should an international company pursue different strategies in different countries or follow global strategies?

The major analyses of cultural differences between managers from different parts of the world have generally surveyed attitudes using questionnaires. On the basis of a massive survey of IBM employees, Hofstede (1980) found statistically significant differences between national groups of managers on four discrete dimensions: Power Distance, Uncertainty Avoidance, Individualism–Collectivism and Masculinity–Femininity. Managers from the same society were, of course, not uniform in their views, but tended to be more similar than managers in other societies. However, the common conflation of nation and culture is inexact – not only can countries be clustered into regional groups (e.g. within western Europe a Nordic, Germanic, Anglo-Saxon and Latin group), but regions within countries can show considerable cultural differences (e.g. between French-speaking Wallonia/Walloons and Dutch-speaking Flanders in Belgium). Later studies by Hofstede and Bond (e.g. Hofstede and Bond 1988), perhaps following the logic of their own position to its conclusion, have argued that such dimensions did not fully capture the dynamics of East Asia. Using Asian scholars, they developed a scale termed 'Confucian Dynamism' (forward looking, persevering, thrifty, long-term, work and family oriented etc.). This scale seemed, in particular, to distinguish such societies, although it was also applicable to other countries (e.g. the UK appeared very short-term compared to the Netherlands). It is, of course, tempting to argue that such a value-orientation is associated with the recent economic success of those East Asian countries historically influenced by Confucian thought.

Other approaches in this area have also used attitude survey methods. For example, Laurent (1983; 1986) compared the attitudes of different groups of managers to organizational authority structure and success, finding that whereas German managers emphasized technical expertise and knowledge, French managers emphasized identification as in high potentials and political connections. British managers emphasized self-presentation, negotiation and communication. Trompenaars (1993) has used a 57-item questionnaire given to managers in around 50 countries and followed it up with workshops presenting managers and others with a series of scenarios or dilemmas. He has identified six dimensions on which cultures differ:

- universalism vs. particularism.
- individualism vs. collectivism.
- affectivity vs. affective neutrality.
- specificity vs. diffuseness.
- achievement vs. ascription.
- internality vs. externality.

Hofstede (1980) has also shown that it is possible to 'cluster' countries together on the basis of similarities and differences in their scores on the four dimensions. Within Europe, there emerges a Germanic group, characterized by high masculinity and low power distance; a Scandinavian group, including the Netherlands, characterized by low masculinity and low power distance; an Anglo-Saxon group, characterized by high individualism and masculinity, and low power distance and uncertainty avoidance; and a Latin group, showing high uncertainty avoidance and high power distance.

However, the use of 'culture' in this sense (and particularly its association with the generating of organizational commitment) is problematic (see chapters 15 and 16). In an MNC, for example, local employees may adjust their behaviour to head office 'corporate culture' requirements at a superficial level, whilst deeper-rooted societal cultural values may affect the meaning given to actions. In this sense corporate culture may be merely complied with rather than internalized. One suggestion is to develop policies which are not uniform and universal, but can accommodate multiple value systems, cultural diversity and different interests. This challenge for international SHRM of responding to cultural diversity is taken up later in this chapter. One key implication is that underlying cultural beliefs about relationships to nature and to others may affect the acceptability and effectiveness of SHRM practices, such as recruitment and selection, performance management and socialization. However, culture is only one of the elements that constitute a national or regional 'business system' and it is to such a comparative analysis of business systems that we now turn.

## Comparative business systems and international SHRM

One important sense of international SHRM is to consider the internationalization – or globalization – of key SHRM decisions, particularly around decisions about the location of corporate activities, but also around global products and markets. However, another important aspect of international SHRM concerns the possibility that there are national variations in typical SHRM styles or patterns, raising the possibility that an international approach to SHRM might (a) move beyond national styles and limitations, and (b) that globally distributed production might vary according to the 'local' SHRM style, or even (c) that truly international SHRM somehow rises above local variations.

Originally, most theories of international business focused on the *country* level, and sought to explain why countries traded with each other. Mercantilist views, emphasizing the need for trade surpluses, gave way in the eighteenth century to theories of absolute and comparative advantage in production, generating an international division of labour. 'Factor endowments', like land, labour and capital, were held to be particularly significant. However, the rise of the 'third world multinational' and the recognition that trade does not occur on a fair and equal basis have cast doubt on such 'traditional' explanations of foreign trade. Despite the assertions of Ohmae (1989) and Reich (1991), recent 'orthodox' theories have recognized the importance of 'place'. Porter (1990), in his analysis of the 'competitiveness of nations', has argued that national competitiveness and firm competitiveness are interlinked, and that the determinants of national advantage form a 'diamond' or playing field. The home market (such as the existence of internationally competitive suppliers and related industries) has great significance for international business – close, collaborative and competitive relationships with suppliers and domestic rivals, such as those in the Italian footwear and fashion industries or Japanese automobile industries. And this can stimulate innovation and enterprise. This suggests that *domestic* SHRM can act as a level or springboard for *international* SHRM (e.g. Hendry 1993), a contention given further weight by Porter's (1990) suggestion that one of the major 'factor conditions' in the diamond of national advantage is the presence of skilled labour, knowledge resources and infrastructures. These, which have clear relationships with SHRM, are influenced by cultural characteristics.

SHRM at the company level in an international enterprise is influenced both by the parent or home country context from which it originated, and the host country context in which it operates. We therefore need, in order to make sense of the complexity and diversity of the environment in which international enterprises operate, to develop a framework for analysing the SHRM systems of nations and regions. Begin (1992: 380) defines SHRM systems as 'all HRM structures, processes, policies and policy effects at the societal and organisational levels of a particular country that comprise the operation of internal and external labour markets'. Particular constellations of institutional components may mould domestic businesses and their SHRM strategies. Whitley's (1992: 6) analysis of comparative business systems sees these as 'particular arrangements of hierarchy–market relations which have become institutionalised and relatively successful in particular contexts.' The three broad components, shown in table 3.2

**Table 3.2** The components of comparative business systems

| |
|---|
| **1 The nature of the firm** |
| • The degree to which private managerial hierarchies co-ordinate economic activities. |
| • The degree of managerial discretion from owners. |
| • Specialization of managerial capabilities and activities within authority hierarchies. |
| • The degree to which growth is discontinuous and involves radical changes in skills and activities. |
| • The extent to which risks are managed through mutual dependence with business partners and employees. |
| **2 Market organization** |
| • The extent of long-term co-operative relations between firms within and between sectors. |
| • The significance of intermediaries in the co-ordination of market transaction. |
| • Stability, integration and scope of business groups. |
| • Dependence of co-operative relations on personal ties and trusts. |
| **3 Authoritative co-ordination and control systems** |
| • Integration and interdependence of economic activities. |
| • Impersonality of authority and subordination relations. |
| • Task, skill and role specialization and individualization. |
| • Differentiation of authority roles and expertise. |
| • Decentralization of operational control and level of work-group autonomy. |
| • Distance and superiority of managers. |
| • Extent of employer–employee commitment and organization-based employment system. |

*Source:* Whitley (1992).

are the nature of the firm, market organization, and authoritative co-ordination and control systems.

For Whitley (1992: 6), 'these differences can be seen as alternative responses to three fundamental issues. First, how are economic activities and resources to be co-ordinated and controlled? Second, how are market connections between authoritatively co-ordinated economic activities in firms to be organized? Third, how are activities and skills within firms to be organized and directed through authority relations?' The coherence and stability of such institutions and their dissimilarity across nation states is seen to determine the extent to which business systems are distinctive, integrated and nationally differentiated. We need to focus more closely on national and regional differences in SHRM practice as one key element in the analysis of comparative business systems.

## Comparative SHRM practices: convergence or divergence?

Some general empirical studies of comparative SHRM practices and policies demonstrate the existence of regional 'clusters' sharing SHRM systems in common and marked off, to some extent, from other regional clusters. Kanter (1991), for example, presents a global survey of management practices and expectations drawn from 1200 managers. This distinguishes 'cultural allies' such as the US, the UK and Australia from 'cultural islands' such as Korea and Japan, which represent unique HR systems. She also found a 'North European' cluster of Germany and the Nordic countries, and a 'Latin' cluster of southern European countries and Latin America.

Another study reanalysing IBM–Towers Perrin data drawn from a global survey of CEOs and HR directors in 12 countries found a similar pattern, but also revealed some interesting differences. Using cluster analysis on 15 dimensions of HR practice and policy, Sparrow et al. (1994) identified several regional clusters and also several 'islands'. In one cluster they placed an Anglo-Saxon group of Australia, the US, Canada and Australia with Germany and Italy; in another, the Latin American countries (but not Italy); in another and on its own, France; in another, Japan; and in another, Korea. In some ways, their results support culturalist explanations such as those by Hofstede (1983) and Trompenaars (1993) – the Anglo Saxon countries tended to emphasize empowerment, equality, diversity and flexibility; France and Korea were less interested in these dimensions of HRS and more interested in centralization and hierarchy; Latin America was less interested in flexibility and more interested in managing outflows.

As the authors themselves note, their study methodology has limitations in sampling only large organizations judged internationally competitive and in assuming that the items had the same meaning for all the respondents. Sparrow et al. (1994) reported that respondents in all countries rated all SHRM items higher for the year 2000 than they did in 1991, the year they completed the survey. This suggests that SHRM is becoming increasingly important to strategy. Firms in all clusters were placing increasing emphasis on empowerment, diversity and equality, as well as on other dimensions, suggesting some 'convergence' of SHRM policy.

## Convergence vs. divergence

This theme of 'convergence or divergence' has also been taken up by authors with a particular interest in European SHRM. In part, this focus is driven by the apparently essentially American origin and nature of the classic SHRM model (e.g. Guest 1992). This raises the question of whether such a model, with its individualistic, task-oriented view of human 'resources' to be 'managed' is applicable to

### BOX 3.5 A EUROPEAN MODEL OF SHRM?

Clearly influenced by developments over the 'Social Chapter or Social Charter', Thurley (1990) and Thurley and Widenius (1990), identify four principles they regard as essential building blocks for a 'European model', distinct from both the American and Japanese models of SHRM:

- dialogue between social partners.
- multicultural organizations.
- participation in decision-making.
- continuous learning.

This stress on a supposedly distinctive European 'social market' model, with its emphasis on social partnership and social responsibilities (and fears over its vulnerability to intensifying global competition), is also reflected in the studies based on interviews with 51 chief executives and others from 40 major European multinationals associated with the European Round-Table of Industrialists and ESC Lyon (Bloom et al. 1994). This project identified the following characteristics of an emerging 'European management model':

- a focus on managing international diversity.
- an emphasis on social responsibility.
- an orientation towards people.
- a stress on internal and external negotiation between stakeholders and partners.
- less reliance on formal systems.
- a product orientation.
- management between the US and Japanese extremes, especially over time frames and the relationship between the individual and the collective.

Europe. In part, this is a view driven by a concern, often stemming from the European Commission itself, to strengthen and improve the competitive position of 'Europe' (in practice, the European Union). Some studies have sought to identify whether a distinctive 'European model' of SHRM exists or is emerging (see box 3.5).

Not only does the model in box 3.5 represent something of an idealized 'wish list', it also obscures much of the diversity within Europe, even the geographically and culturally limited Europe under study. The interviewees themselves showed some ambivalence towards the UK, recognizing that in some respects its model of SHRM seems closer to the USA or lay perhaps mid-way between 'Europe' and 'North America'. This transatlantic/mid-Atlantic perception of the UK has probably been reinforced by the experience of the long years of Conservative rule, with their idolization of the market, the dominance of the City and shareholders to the exclusion of other stakeholders, and the emphasis given to deregulation and the diminished role of the state and trade unions in economic strategy.

As we have seen, Kanter (1991) distinguished an Anglo-Saxon, a Northern and a Latin model, whilst Sparrow et al. (1994) differentiated France from Italy in their approaches to SHRM. These authors are sensitive to internal diversity within Europe, but still see a 'European model' emerging at a certain level of abstraction. On the basis of their interviews, they first distinguish the UK from the rest of Europe, and then 'the North' from 'the South'. The 'South', seen as presenting more state intervention, protectionism, hierarchy and intuitive/chaotic management, is differentiated between France and the other Mediterranean countries. The North, seen as presenting less state intervention, more liberalism, more participation and more organization, is differentiated into the Nordic/Scandinavian countries (more relationship oriented, more egalitarian and more people oriented), the Germanic countries and the Benelux countries. The small countries are seen as exhibiting diverse cultural influences (the Dutch from the British, the Belgians from the French and all from the Germans) and as having a generally 'more international' outlook.

The German model is of particular interest because it has often been taken to be *the* paradigm European model of SHRM (e.g. Thurow 1992). This is in part a reflection of the size and economic power of Germany within Europe, in part a reflection of its apparent economic success, and in part because its model offers a clear contrast to the American model of SHRM. Albert (1991), for example, differentiates 'capitalism Anglo-Saxon' from 'capitalisme Rhénan' – Rhenish capitalism is seen as closer to the Japanese model in some respects, with a common focus on organized competition rather than liberalism, a stakeholder rather than a shareholder orientation, a long-term orientation, an over-emphasis on high investment and stable capital structures, a high status given to production, a high sense of community and loyalty to the firm, and low geographical and inter-firm mobility of personnel.

However, just as Anglo-Saxon management in the UK differs from the US, German SHRM, of course, differs from Japanese. Its stress on individuals and on specialisms differentiates it from the Japanese emphasis on teams and generalists, and the German social market economy and its relationships with trade unions find no parallels in Japan.

In general, this German model of SHRM (box 3.6) with its procedural, legalistic and regulatory overtones contrasts sharply with the Anglo-American model of SHRM described in chapters 1 and 2. In particular, the functional personnel specialist plays a very different, more reactive, more technical and less strategic role. The role is seen in much more legal terms, with the traditional qualification

## BOX 3.6 NATIONAL MODELS OF SHRM: THE CASE OF GERMANY

This Germanic model of SHRM, with its strong links between banks and industry, its balance between the state and the regions, its well-developed systems of training and development, its system of co-determination and workers' representatives on the board, its collective orientation, and its long-term orientation and its in-house career systems, has been most fully analysed by Lawrence (1993). He stresses its formal (but not bureaucratic or authoritarian) management style, as manifested in titles, names, dress codes and reliance on official documents, regulations and committees (whereas Hofstede (1983) found Germans to score quite highly on uncertainty avoidance, they scored only modestly on power distance – no more than the UK). He also emphasizes the crucial and distinctive role of education and training in the German system – the abundance of graduates and managers with doctorates; the emphasis on engineering; the paucity of MBAs; the emphasis on in-company, specific, technical training; the under-emphasis on 'managerial' training; and the stress on 'Technik' (engineering knowledge and craft skills) – as both a means and an end, with a corresponding de-emphasis on marketing and finance compared to the USA and UK. Lawrence (1993) also draws attention to the social market economy, the role of *industrial* trade unions, the way wages are typically negotiated between the relevant trade union and employers' associations on an industry-wide basis and on a region (*Land*) by region basis, according to a well understood timetable of *Lander* and industries. He also crucially points to the role of the industrial democracy or co-determination system. Employee participation operates at three levels: representatives on the supervisory board, a labour director on the executive committee, and elected representatives on the works council. This whole system is legally based and of long-standing, and appears well accepted by employers. The works councils in particular have played a key role since 1952, having the legal power to decide on many practical issues such as working hours, holidays, breaks, canteen prices, appointments and transfers. Its economics committee has the right to receive information on the company's economic position.

being a doctorate in Law and the main role being to address the Labour Courts designed to settle labour disputes.

Such a model of SHRM is a salutary reminder that the Anglo-American model of SHRM, with its focus on employee autonomy, deregulation, mobility and enterprise-level strategies in terms of pay, recruitment and training is not the only path to economic success; nor does it seem, if we add Japan to Germany, that the economic prizes in recent years have gone to those countries valuing risk-taking and uncertainty or emphasizing free markets and an absence of state intervention. However, whilst both Albert (1991) and Lawrence (1993) are keen to stress their admiration for the German model and attribute German economic success to it, they also acknowledge downsides and limitations. Its high labour costs and relative downplaying of marketing may not help it in the future, whilst its technical, function-based system of management development and relative lack of interest in international management development or in globalizing its managerial labour force may not equip it to deal with the complexity and diversity of globalization.

However, Lane (1992) argues that the German system is internally consistent, integrated and stable with mutually supporting elements, in contrast to the British system, which is much looser. Recent ideologies of employee involvement and commitment in the UK are still fragile and unsupported by more prevalent contractually oriented institutional arrangements. Many studies have been content to interview a few selected multinational CEOs, or survey large company CEOs and HR directors, on a limited range of topics (e.g. Sparrow et al. 1994), or conduct more historical/cultural studies based on secondary sources (e.g. Albert 1991).

In contrast, the Price-Waterhouse–Cranfield study of HR practices across Europe has surveyed 14 countries and by 1995 had analysed 16,000 questionnaires (e.g. Brewster 1994; 1995). Brewster and his colleagues have also been interested in the notion of a 'European model' of SHRM, drawing attention to the lack of employer and managerial autonomy in many European countries, in contrast to the assumptions behind the US model of 'strategic SHRM'. The embeddedness of European organizations within cultural and legal limitations and within distinct patterns of ownership by the state, families, and banking and finance systems has also been noted. In addition, trade union involvement is seen as a further distinctive factor. All of these factors restrict organizational autonomy, make hiring and firing more difficult, restricting employee mobility, and giving a greater role to the social partners, in particular the trade unions, than is typical of the US model of SHRM. Collective bargaining at the national or regional level, greater state intervention, more comprehensive welfare systems and stronger links between educational experiences and career success also seem to characterize a European model. Brewster (1994: 328–9) argues that a European model of SHRM is required because current trends in Europe 'do not fit comfortably with the original US concepts of SHRM – what is happening in Europe is that there is a move towards the SHRM concept but one which, within a clearly established external environment, accepts the duality of people management. Thus, objectives include both organisational requirements and a concern for people; the focus on both costs and benefits means fitting organisational policies to external cultures and constraints; union and non-union channels are utilised; the relationship with line managers at all levels is interactive rather than driven by either specialists or the line.' This view of what is happening reinforces the need for an 'open' rather than 'closed' approach to HRS, and also demonstrates how European developments in HRS embrace both 'hard' and 'soft' approaches, to use the terminology developed in chapter 1. The approaches are seen to be 'open' in the sense that they accept and recognize different degrees of managerial independence, different ways of working with trade unions, different roles for government, and different routes to enhanced economic performance.

## *Towards a Common European SHRM practice?*

What are these trends in European SHRM practice? Brewster (1994) concentrates on five topics: pay and benefits; flexible working; equal opportunity; training; and employee relations – all key issues addressed in this text. His broad conclusion is that with regard to pay, flexibility and training, the US model fits, whereas with regard to trade union recognition and communications, it does not. Let us consider each of these areas in turn, and then address an area not considered by Brewster (1994), namely recruitment, assessment and selection practices.

With regard to pay, trends in this area (discussed in chapter 4) include the increasing decentralization of pay bargaining in both highly centralized systems, such as most Nordic systems, and in more decentralized systems, such as the UK and France, although national industry bargaining for manual workers remains common in much of UK industry.

Within the Nordic countries, commitment to multi-employer bargaining with trade unions remains high, with some shift to the industry level; less change is evident in Germany, where binding collective agreements remain in place. However, in general, variable pay, merit pay and performance-related pay initiatives have spread across Europe. These kind of initiatives seem least common in Scandinavia, with Denmark, the UK and the Southern companies making most use of them. Profit sharing and share options seem less widespread. Brewster (1994: 315) argues that 'in spite of some common trends towards more variable pay and pay decentralization, national and cultural differences remain strong'. In a similar vein, flexible working practices (defined here as atypical work patterns or contracts, a rather narrow definition) have become much more widespread, leaving Brewster (1994: 319) to conclude that 'all of the results – suggest that organizations across Europe are moving towards greater flexibility, even if they are starting from different positions'.

Practice around equal opportunity is much more divergent, with, for example, child-care facilities in France and Scandinavia being much more widespread and women participating in the labour force much more actively than in Greece or Spain. However, substantial vertical and occupational segregation based on gender is a feature of all European countries. With the exception of the UK and

**Table 3.3** Organizational dimensions of HRM by country (percentages)

| | *CH* | *D* | *DK* | *E* | *F* | *FN* | *I* | *IR* | *N* | *NL* | *P* | *S* | *UK* |
|---|---|---|---|---|---|---|---|---|---|---|---|---|---|
| 1 Head of Human Resources Function on Main Board | 58 | 30 | 49 | 73 | 84 | 61 | 18 | 44 | 71 | 42 | 46 | 84 | 49 |
| 2 Written HR strategy | 58 | 18 | 72 | 37 | 34 | 52 | 33 | 41 | 71 | 44 | 34 | 73 | 50 |
| 3 At least one-third of managers trained in performance appraisal | 69 | 34 | 19 | 31 | 47 | 42 | 45 | 43 | 64 | 51 | 32 | 77 | 71 |
| 4 Information on financial performance given to manual employees | 38 | 44 | 54 | 9 | 42 | 83 | 24 | 36 | 66 | 40 | 18 | 68 | 49 |
| 5 Change in union influence over previous three years (increase–decrease) | +5 | +14 | –23 | +19 | –33 | –6 | –30 | –13 | +16 | +11 | – | –18 | –50 |
| 6 Proportion spending more than 2% of annual wage bill on training | 37 | 43 | 25 | 23 | 80 | 36 | 24 | 40 | 36 | 40 | 39 | 60 | 26 |
| 7 Increase in line manager responsibility for training over last three years | – | 13 | 39 | 53 | 55 | 51 | – | 43 | 56 | 50 | 18 | 67 | 46 |

*Notes:* Country coding: CH – Switzerland; D – Germany; DK – Denmark; E – Spain; F – France; FN – Finland; I – Italy; IR – Ireland; N – Norway; NL – Netherlands; P – Portugal; S – Sweden; UK – Britain.

*Sources:* C. Brewster and A. Hegwisch (eds) (1994) *Policy and Practice in European Human Resource Management – The Price-Waterhouse–Cranfield Survey* (London: Routledge).

the Netherlands, the issue of racial discrimination has been much less of a concern than gender discrimination.

Again, training provision varies considerably between European countries, although there has been a general increase at all levels and especially for managerial staff. With the exception of France, where the law requires companies to spend at least 1.2 per cent of their pay bill on training, many organizations are unable to assess how much is spent on training. Relationships with trade unions remain a key issue for most European organizations, with union membership varying from 90 per cent in Norway to around 12 per cent in France. Grahl and Teague (1991) argue that in general, employee relations have moved from a Fordist trajectory to either one of competitive flexibility (the UK) or constructive flexibility (Germany and Scandinavia).

Table 3.3 shows some of the similarities and differences between countries in terms of HR practice revealed by the Price-Waterhouse–Cranfield survey. One interesting dimension not shown in table 3.3, but of interest to the general themes of the book, is the extent of 'HR integration' across Europe (in this instance, measured by such factors as having a written HR strategy and having the head of HR on the Main Board). The most integrated countries were France, Sweden and Norway; the least were Germany and Italy. Once again, the position of Germany shows that SHRM integration, often asserted as a key plank of any HR strategy, is not necessarily associated with economic success.

Another dimension brought out in the Cranfield studies, in addition to 'integration', is that of devolution or 'devolvement', associated with decentralization and the sharing or SHRM responsibility with line managers. Brewster and Larsen (1993) have plotted different countries against these two dimensions to generate an integration/devolvement matrix. The typical Swedish or Swiss organization is seen as exhibiting high levels of both integration and devolvement. These 'pivotal' types, with an orientation to facilitation and internal consulting by personnel managers, differ from the 'wild west' organizations found in Denmark and the Netherlands, where low integration and high devolvement leave line managers with considerable power and autonomy, running the risk of incoherence and inconsistency. German, British and Italian organizations typically score low on both dimensions, with their 'professional mechanic' personnel managers exercising specialist but limited (and strategically isolated) skills. Finally, the typical Norwegian, French or Spanish organization contains 'guarded strategists', highly integrated with senior managers but showing low levels of devolvement to the line.

Such an analysis is interesting, but perhaps obscures as much as it reveals. As we have seen, the German model of SHRM differs substantially from the typical British model, yet both are classified as 'professional mechanics'. The specialist expertise of personnel managers is exercised quite differently in the two business systems.

Before we leave the analysis of comparative SHRM, let us look at an area less fully explored by the Price-Waterhouse–Cranfield project – that of recruitment, selection and assessment practices. It is clear from many studies (see table 3.3) that in all countries studied, interviews, application forms/CVs and references are the most widely used methods, yet these are often regarded as amongst the least valid predictors of job performance. However, some interesting differences persist (see box 3.7).

What such surveys, including the Price-Waterhouse–Cranfield survey, often fail to explore are the *reasons* for such observed national and regional differences. Not only are such surveys typically limited to large organizations and frequently display a low response rate, but it is often unclear whether the terms used carry a common meaning for respondents. The term 'psychometric test' or 'assessment centre', for example, may mean very different things to respondents, who may not be in a position anyway to know what goes on in their organization at grass-roots levels. Brewster et al. (1995) note that respondents interpreted identical questions within specific cultural and legal contexts; for example, 'flexible working' in the UK and Germany was interpreted in terms of the participation of women in the labour force, whereas in France it was seen in terms of general changes in life-style. It is tempting to invoke post-hoc cultural, historical or institutional factors to 'explain' certain findings (for example, perhaps the professionalization of psychologists in the UK and the Netherlands 'explains' the greater use of psychometric tests and assessment centres; perhaps the French use of serial interviews is related to their higher uncertainty avoidance and power distance indices than is characteristic of Britain; perhaps the wide range of methods used in Belgium is also related to their culturally expressed need to reduce uncertainty), but such hypotheses are rarely tested for at the time, and *reasons* for using particular techniques are rarely probed (Iles 1994).

One reason for considering comparative differences in business systems, culture and HR practices across nations and regions is that such differences

## BOX 3.7 DIFFERENCES IN SELECTION PRACTICE ACROSS EUROPE

Shackleton and Newell (1994: 91) argue that 'harmonisation of selection practice in Europe is a long way off. Habit, tradition and culture determine the choice of selection method'. Belgian practice shows divisions between its Flemish and French-speaking regions, for example, especially in the use of graphology. This is a technique far more commonly used in France than in the Netherlands or the UK, where it is generally regarded as no better than astrology. The British seem wedded to the equally unreliable reference; Italian organizations seem least likely to use any other selection method than the interview; German organizations seem less convinced of the value of psychometric tests, and less likely to see the value of test training or training in giving feedback than British ones; French organizations seem less likely to use panel interviews and more likely to use a series of one-to-one interviews with progressively more senior line managers than British organizations.

contribute to the diversity and complexity of the global environment faced by international enterprises attempting to co-ordinate their activities across different locations and environments. It is to the role of international SHRM at this enterprise level that we consider in chapter 6.

## Conclusions and Summary

Interest in international SHRM differs considerably, in line with national differences in SHRM agendas, or organizational preoccupations. In this chapter two key issues have been addressed. First, we have explored the global context of multinational production, noting that key organizational decisions about, for example, the siting of production, administration or service activities can be seen as part of a grand (if often implicit) SHRM strategy, with respect to decisions about the attractiveness of local labour, the role of unions, host government attitudes etc. Furthermore, although these decisions are most conspicuous when western MNCs locate production in Third World countries – as happens frequently in the case of the two industries used as case studies in the chapter on electronics and the clothing industry – they are also apparent when corporations take advantages of nationally segmented labour markets, especially when lines of labour market segmentation coincide with gender and ethnic divisions.

However, this chapter has not focused solely on corporate exploitation of global or national labour market differentiation. It has also considered another sense of international SHRM – that SHRM practices and systems may differ along national or regional grounds. The second part of the chapter explored these possibilities, finding that certain important differences are certainly discernible. This finding raises interesting questions. One of the elements of much SHRM thinking and advice – as represented for example in those consultants who preach the virtues of the Japanese approach to organization and employment – is that western corporations can benefit from the practices of other societies (see box 3.3). But it is also possible that this idea in itself, or other key western SHRM notions like the primacy of the market as a paradigm for organizational structuring, is essential-ethnocentric and limited. Despite the claims to universality of most SHRM ideas, this chapter will have demonstrated that many of the ideas appear limited and parochial when one takes a broader, international perspective.

### Key Points

- The literature on international SHRM is often restricted to the analysis of expatriate recruitment and selection, training and development, and appraisal and reward systems. Occasionally, it also embraces the SHRM problems of strategic alliances of the largest MNCs. Key organizational decisions about the location of production need to be made within the context of power geometry: the relationship between industrial and less developed economies.
- At the global level earlier debates about modernization and dependency are

relevant to an understanding of the new international division of labour. While remaining sceptical of the more sweeping claims of the globalization theorists, this chapter supports the thesis of the new international division of labour, although recognizing that this requires a sensitive analysis of regional variations and regional cultures.

- At the regional and national levels there are important variations in SHRM systems, assumptions and practices that research has revealed. We have noted national diversity, particularly within Europe.

## Discussion Questions

1. How different is international SHRM from domestic SHRM?
2. What are the implications of the modernization and dependency theories of the relationship between the industrial West and the developing South, for the international management of human resources?
3. What are the implications of the new international division of labour, and the decisions of western corporations this perspective addresses, for the way staff are managed?
4. What key differences in national or regional SHRM principles and assumptions are apparent, and how do they matter?

## References

Albert, M. (1991) *Capitalisme Contre Capitalisme*, London: Seuil.
Amin, S. (1974) *Accumulation on a World Scale*, New York: Monthly Review Press.
—— (1976) *Uneven Development*, Brighton: Harvester Press.
Barnett, C. (1990) 'The Michigan global agenda: Research and teaching in the 1990s', *Human Resource Management*, Spring, vol. 29, no. 1, 5–26.
Bassett, P. (1995) 'No escape from the works councils', *The Times*, Thursday, March 2, 32.
Begin, J. P. (1992) 'Comparative human resource management (HRM): A systems perspective', *International Journal of Human Resource Management*, vol. 3, no. 3, 379–95.
Bloom, H., Calori, R., and de Woot, P. (1994) *Euromanagement: A New Style for the Global Market*, ERT/ESC, Lyon: Kogan-Page.
Braham, P. (1992) 'The division of labour and occupational change', in J. Allen, P. Braham and P. Lewis (eds) *Political and Economic Forms of Modernity*, Cambridge: Polity Press.
Brewster, C. (1991) *The Management of Expatriates*, London: Kogan Page.
—— (1993) 'Developing a "European" model of human resource management', *International Journal of Human Resource Management*, vol. 4, no. 4, December, 765–84.
—— (1993) 'European human resource management: Reflection of, or challenge to, the American concept', in P. Kirkbridge (ed.) *Human Resource Management in the New Europe of the 1990s*, London: Routledge.
—— and Larsen, H. H. (1993) 'Human resource management in Europe: Evidence from ten countries', *International Journal of Human Resource Management*, vol. 3, no. 3, 409–34.
—— (1994) 'The integration of human resource management and corporate strategy', in C. Brewster and A. Hegewisch (eds) *Policy and Practice in European Human Resource Management*, London: Routledge.

——, Hegewisch, A. and Mayne, L. (1994) 'Trends in European HRM: Signs of convergence' in P. Kirkbridge (ed.) *Human Resource Management in Europe*, London: Routledge.

—— (1995) 'HRM: The European Dimension', in J. Storey (ed.) *Human Resource Management: A critical text*, London: Routledge, 309–32.

Brewster et al. (1995) 'Trends in European HRM', in P. Kirkbridge (ed.) *Human Resource Management in Europe*, London: Routledge.

Crabb, S. (1995) 'Jobs for all in the global market?', *People Management*, 26th Jan., 22–7.

Dickens, P. (1995) 'Geography in The Open University', *B890 International Enterprise*, MBA, The Open University.

Elson, D. (1994) 'Capitalism and development in global perspective', in L. Sklair (ed.) 165–88.

Evans, P., Doz, Y., and Laurent, A. (eds) (1989) *Human Resource Management in International Firms*, London: Macmillan.

Frank, A. G. (1971) *Capitalism and Underdevelopment in Latin America*, London: Penguin.

Frank, G. (1996) 'The development of underdevelopment', *Monthly Review*, vol. 18, no. 4, 23–8.

Fröbel, F., Heinrichs, J., and Kreye, O. (1980) *The New International Division of Labour*, Cambridge: Cambridge University Press.

Giddens, A. (1990) *The Consequences of Modernity*, Cambridge: Polity Press.

—— (ed.) (1992) *Human Societies: A Reader*, Cambridge: Polity Press.

Grahl, J. and Teague, P. (1991) 'European level collective bargaining: A new phase?' *Relations Industrielles*, vol. 46, no. 1.

Guest, D. (1992) 'Right enough to be dangerously wrong', in G. Salaman et al. (eds) *Human Resource Strategies*, London: Sage, 5–19.

Hall, S. (1992) 'The question of cultural identity', in S. Hall, D. Held and A. McGrew (eds) *Modernity and its Future*, Cambridge: Open University/Polity Press, 273–326.

Henderson, J. (1994) 'Electronics Industries and the developing world: Uneven contribution and uncertain prospects', in L. Sklair (ed.) *Capitalism and Development*, London: Routledge, 252–88.

Hendry, C. (1993) *Human Resource Strategies for International Growth*, London: Routledge.

Hofstede, G. (1980) *Culture's Consequences: International Differences in Work-related Values*, Beverley Hills, CA: Sage [reprinted 1984].

—— (1983) 'The cultural relativity of organizational practices and theories', *Journal of International Business Studies*, vol. 14, no. 1, 75–89.

—— and Bond, M. (1988) 'The confucius connection: From cultural roots to economic growth', *Organizational Dynamics*, vol. 16, no. 4, 4–21.

—— (1991) *Cultures and Organizations: Softwares of the Mind*, London: McGraw-Hill.

—— (1993) 'Cultural constraints in management theories', *Academy of Management Executive*, vol. 7, no. 1, 81–91.

Hoogvelt, A. (1987) 'The new international division of labour' in R. Bush, G. Johnston and D. Contes (eds) *The World Order: Socialist Perspectives*, Cambridge: Polity Press.

Iles, P. A. (1994) 'Diversity in selection and assessment practice: Context, culture and congruence', *International Journal of Selection and Assessment*, vol. 2, no. 2, 111–14.

Jameson, F. (1991) *Postmodernism and the Cultural Logic of Late Capitalism*, London: Verso Press.

Kanter, R. M. (1991) 'Transcending business boundaries: 12,000 world managers view change', *Harvard Business Review*, vol. 69, no. 3, 151–64.

Kidger, P. (1991) 'The emergence of international human resource management', *International Journal of Human Resource Management*, vol. 2, no. 2, 149–63.

Laclau, E. (1971) 'Feudalism and capitalism in Latin America', *New Left Review*, vol. 64, May/June, 19–38.
Lane, C. (1992) 'European business systems: Britain and Germany compared', in R. Whitley (ed.) *European Business Systems: Firms and Markets in their National Contexts*, London: Sage.
Laurent, A. (1983) 'The cultural diversity of western conceptions of management', *International Studies of Management and Organization*, vol. 13, no. 102, 5–96.
—— (1986) 'The cross-cultural puzzle of international human resource management', *Human Resource Management*, vol. 25, no. 1, 91–102.
Lawrence, P. (1993) 'Management development in Europe: a study in cultural contrast', *Human Resource Management Journal*, vol. 3, no. 1, 11–23.
Levitt, T. (1983) 'The globalization of markets', *Harvard Business Review*, May/June, 92–102.
Massey, D. (1991) 'A global sense of place', *Marxism Today*, June.
McGrew, A. (1992) 'A global society?' in S. Hall, D. Held and A. McGrew (eds) *Modernity and its Future*, Cambridge: Polity Press.
Ohmae, K. (1985) *Triad Power: The Coming Shape of Global Competition*, New York: Free Press.
—— (1989) 'The global logic of strategic alliances', *Harvard Business Review*, March/April, 143–55.
—— (1990) *The Borderless World*, New York: Harper Business.
Pearson, R. (1988) 'Female workers in the first and third worlds: The "Greening" of women's labour', in R. E. Pahl (ed.) *On Work: Historical, Comparative and Theoretical Approaches*, Oxford: Blackwell.
—— (1994) 'Gender relations, capitalism and third world industrialization', in L. Sklair (ed.) *Capitalism and Development*, London: Routledge, 339–58.
Porter, M. E. (1980) *Competitive strategy*, New York: Free Press.
—— (1990) *The Competitive Advantage of Nations*, London: Macmillan.
Reich, R. (1991) 'Who is them?' *Harvard Business Review*, vol. 68, no. 1, 53–64.
Shackleton, V. and Newell, S. (1991) 'Management selection: A comparative survey of methods used in top British and French companies', *Journal of Occupational Psychology*, vol. 64, no. 1, 23–36.
—— and —— (1994) 'European management selection methods: A comparison and critique into market', *Journal of Selectional Assessment*, vol. 2, no. 2, 91–102.
Sklair, L. (1991) *Sociology of the Global System*, London: Harvester.
—— (1994) 'Capitalism and development in global perspective', in L. Sklair (ed.) *Capitalism and Development*, London: Routledge, 165–88.
Sparrow, P. and Hiltrop, J. M. (1994) *European Human Resource Management in Transition*, Hemel Hempstead: Prentice-Hall.
——, Schuler, R. S., and Jackson, S. E. (1994) 'Convergence or divergence: Human resource practices and policies for competitive advantage worldwide', *International Journal of Human Resource Management*, vol. 5, no. 2.
Thurley, K. and Wirdenius, H. (1989) *Towards European Management*, London: Pitman.
—— (1990) 'Towards a European approach to personnel management', *Personnel Management*, vol. 22, no. 9, 54–7.
—— and Wirdenius, H. (1991) 'Will management become "European"? Strategic choices for organizations', *European Management Journal*, vol. 9, no. 2, 127–34.
Thurow, L. (1992) *Head to Head*, London: Nicholas Brealey.
Towers Perrin (1992) *Priorities for Gaining Competitive Advantage: A Worldwide Human Resource Study*, London: Towers Perrin.
Trompenaars, F. (1993) *Riding the Waves of Culture*, London: Economist Books.

Wallerstein, I. (1974) *The Capitalist World Economy*, Cambridge: Cambridge University Press.
—— (1984) *The Politics of the World Economy: The States, The Movements and the Civilisations*, Cambridge: Cambridge University Press.
Warren, B. (1980) *Imperialism: Pioneer of Capitalism*, London: Verso.
Whitley, R. D. (ed.) (1992) *European Business Systems: Firms and Markets in their National Contexts*, London: Sage.

part 2

# Managing Performance

chapter 4

# Performance Management Strategies



CHAPTER OUTLINE

*This chapter was contributed by Greg Clark*

## Learning Objectives

After studying this chapter you should be able to:

- Define performance management, and say how it relates to business strategy.
- Model performance management as a cycle consisting of five elements: setting objectives, measuring outcomes, feeding back results, rewarding performance, and amending objectives and activities.
- Understand and be able to describe the theoretical frameworks which underpin performance management.
- Identify and assess the issues and problems which theory highlights for the design and implementation of performance management.
- Assess the results of empirical tests of performance management, using performance-related pay as a vehicle for exposing these results.
- Critically evaluate the concept of performance management, and its application.
- Know what factors to consider in assessing whether performance management can or should be introduced into your organization.

# Introduction

Essential to the notion of the *strategic* management of human resources is the requirement that the process of managing people is not an end in itself, but explicitly related to the wider goals of the organization. That is to say, SHRM must be a means to achieve strategy. Immediately this differentiates SHRM from functional human resource management, or personnel management, which is a more separable, self-referential administration of personnel issues in the organization.

The integration of human resource management and strategy implied by SHRM places policies and processes into a system whereby outcomes cannot be assessed without reference to a set of objectives and criteria supplied by other parts of the organization. The management of human resources therefore finds itself being judged on its contribution to wider goals, and, faced with this scrutiny, must develop its own procedures to report on its record. More generally it must provide a framework for internally auditing the means by which it delivers contributions to strategic goals, with a view to continuously improving them. *Performance management* is a means of addressing these requirements.

Performance management refers to a set of techniques and procedures which share the common features of:

- providing information on the contribution of human resources to the strategic objectives of the organization;

- forming a framework of techniques to secure maximum achievement of objectives for given inputs; and
- providing a means of inspecting the functioning of the process links which deliver performance against objectives.

It should be seen immediately that performance measurement is based on a particular set of assumptions and hypotheses about the nature of management and its feasibility. Performance management rests on an essentially rationalist, directive view of the organization. A number of implicit assumptions are made, of which the first is that strategy can be expressed in terms of objectives clear enough to be used in framing other policies of the organization; in this case, HR policy. The second assumption is that the outcomes of HR processes can be expressed in ways which allow an assessment to be made of whether they are contributing to the achievement of strategic objectives. A third assumption is that HR processes can be analysed as a set of interlinking cause-and-effect sequences whose links can be identified. A fourth assumption is made which is that the chain can be 'managed', in the sense that corrective action can be designed and implemented to repair poorly performing parts of the chain, this being carried out by people designated as 'managers' of the system. Each of these assumptions is the subject of debate, which will be addressed later in this chapter.

This chapter examines the concept of performance management as a process which managers of human resources may adopt to assist them in their ability to contribute to wider strategic objectives. Having defined performance management, and introduced the idea of a Performance Management Cycle, we argue that the essential features of performance management systems draw on two theories of social psychology: goal setting theory, and expectancy theory. Each theory highlights some key issues concerning the design, feasibility and desirability of performance management which practitioners must address if they are to succeed in their aims. The chapter makes a critical assessment of the underlying assumptions of performance management systems, and suggests that the models may not have the universal validity which their proponents claim for them since they ignore important contextual factors.

By looking in detail at one specific example of a performance management system, performance-related pay, we demonstrate that empirical evidence supports the observations we make. The lesson for managers is that only by following careful design and diagnosis can introducing a system of performance management be expected to produce the outcomes which it promises.

## A schematic model of performance management

There is no single, universally accepted model of performance management in use; rather, the management literature advances a number of separate contributions which fall under the umbrella term 'performance management' because they typically contain and *link* a common set of elements. These can be expressed as a 'performance measurement cycle' consisting of five elements.

- setting performance objectives;
- measuring outcomes;
- feedback of results;
- rewards linked to outcomes; and
- amendments to objectives and activities.

The Performance Management Cycle is depicted in figure 4.1. Performance management, as a cycle consisting of these elements, can be both a descriptive and a prescriptive device. Some writers use performance management as a convenient framework in which to analyse different aspects of strategic HR. Others argue that by distilling out the essential elements of the performance management process the cycle represents a model of how the process *should* be conducted by organizations wishing to take a rational and strategic approach to managing human resources.

The *level* at which a performance management system operates will vary according to how the organization chooses to apply the model, or the level at which the commentator analyses the process. That is to say that there is nothing in the model to indicate that the elements apply to the management of individual employees, or to groups and teams, or to divisions or strategic business units, or to the organization as a whole: in principle, the framework can be applied to any and all of these. However, the main focus of performance management is often taken to be the individual employee.

As a framework, the Performance Management Cycle refers to types of policies and systems – objective setting, measurement, rewards etc. – which must be linked if they are to constitute a practising system of performance management. The Cycle does not specify in detail what form these individual policies take. As we shall see, it is possible to operate a system of performance management in which people's performance is measured using automatically generated sales figures, or by individual annual appraisal interviews. Each approach will give rise

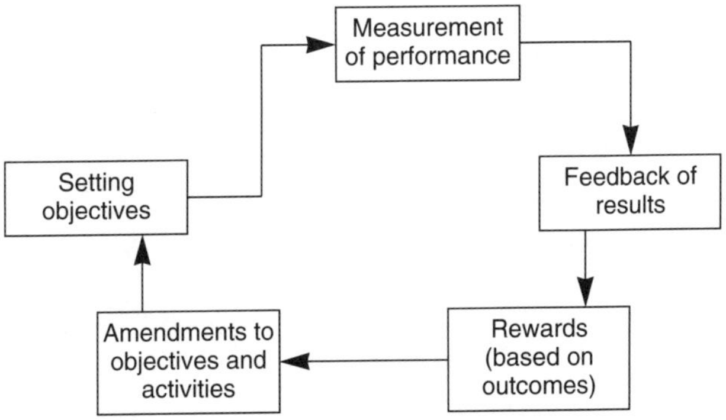


**Figure 4.1** The performance management cycle

to different problems of implementation, and may yield different results, but both are consistent with the model of performance management summarized in figure 4.1.

Sketches of human resource management policies at two organizations (box 4.1), the Scottish Development Agency and the National Westminster Bank, offer a taste of different applications of performance management.

## BOX 4.1 EXAMPLES OF PERFORMANCE MANAGEMENT

Target-based scheme: Scottish Development Agency

The performance measurement and appraisal scheme includes a system in which between three and six 'principle accountabilities' are identified for each job. These are the major job functions or purposes. At each appraisal, one or more 'goals' are agreed for each accountability target to be achieved during the next period. Each goal is given a percentage weighting, so that achievement of all goals would result in an overall score of 100 per cent. An 'achievement profile' is produced, in which actual achievement is scored against each goal. The total score is used to decide the performance payment. (Bowey et al. 1992)

Rewarding performance at National Westminster Bank

In common with other companies in this sector, NatWest has sought to change a culture rewarding predictability, security, long service and loyalty through a slow but steady incremental pay structure into a more dynamic and entrepreneurial one. It has attempted to enhance high performance by recognizing it financially through modifications to its salary structure and its performance appraisal and incremental systems. It has also introduced incentive-based annual bonus schemes related to key targets and incentive-based longer cycle bonus schemes. The aim was to enable all managers to improve their income through performance improvement and to focus attention on key areas of activity. Profit sharing as a percentage of basic annual salary continued, whilst senior managers gained access to an executive share option scheme designed to focus on long-term strategic goals. All of these changes were seen as contributing to 'management by leadership' rather than 'management by control', creating greater understanding of short and long-term strategic goals and focusing managers' attention on goals relating to corporate, divisional-unit and individual objectives. It also aimed to provide general rewards more clearly linked to personal performance and achievement. For the lowest four grades, the level of general increase applied to the published salary ranges continued to be negotiated with the Staff Association and the relevant trade union.
(Goodswen 1988)

# Performance Management: Underlying Theory

Performance management is not new, despite the fact that the use of the term has grown popular recently. Managers have always devised ways, formally or otherwise, to set tasks, see that they are carried out well, and make modifications designed to secure further improvements. Models of performance management may seem to be 'an apparently obvious invention' as Jevons (1883) described performance-related pay, one type of performance management system but nevertheless are founded on well developed theoretical foundations. Or rather it may be fairer to say, since the economist Alfred Marshall described the theoretical case for performance-related pay as 'a formalization of existing practice', that a substantial body of theory has grown up around models of performance management in use. All too often, however, the theory is forgotten in favour of searches for instant solutions to empirical problems, whereas referring to underlying theory provides a solid base for understanding and criticizing applications of performance measurement.

The essence of performance management is establishing a framework in which performance by human resources can be directed, monitored, motivated and refined; and that the links in the cycle can be audited. Unsurprisingly, given this, the principal theoretical foundation of performance management is social psychology, with its detailed consideration of the ways in which *people* are *motivated to perform*. Two theories are particularly pertinent to discussions of performance management: goal-setting theory (e.g. Locke et al. 1981), and expectancy theory (Vroom 1964).

## Goal-setting theory

Goal-setting theory was established by Edwin Locke in a paper published in 1968, in which he argued that goals pursued by employees can play an important role in motivating superior performance. In following these goals people examine the consequences of their behaviour. If they surmise that their goals will not be achieved by their current behaviour, they will either modify their behaviour, or choose more realizable goals.

We saw earlier that SHRM involves integrating the wider objectives of the organization with the behaviour of its employees. Accordingly, if managers can intervene to establish the organization's goals (or translations of them for the group or individual) as being worthwhile for employees to accept, they can harness a source of motivation to perform, and direct it to securing strategic outcomes.

Subsequent empirical research into goal-setting (cf. Mento et al. 1987) has specified more precisely the conditions necessary for organizational goals to be motivating to employees; these are that:

- goals should be specific, rather than vague or excessively general;

- goals should be demanding, but also attainable;
- feedback of performance information should be made; and
- goals need to be accepted by employees as desirable.

Goal-setting theory has been subject to a great deal of theoretical and empirical scrutiny since it was first advanced. The resulting body of evidence now provides a set of rigorously tested principles which offer clear guidance to designers of performance management systems. Later in the chapter we will be applying each of these lessons to performance management.

## Expectancy theory

A book published by Victor Vroom in 1964, *Work and Motivation*, stimulated a flurry of research interest in *expectancy theory* as a framework for understanding motivation at work. Expectancy theory hypothesizes that it is the anticipated satisfaction of valued goals which causes an individual to adjust his behaviour in a way which is most likely to lead to his attaining them.

In fact, while the popularity of expectancy theory is relatively recent, it draws on a tradition which can be traced back to the early Utilitarians. Mill and Bentham described an ethical system in which people determined their actions by a conscious calculation of the consequences which they expected the actions to bring about. In the twentieth century psychologists such as Tolman (1932) and Lewin (1938), as advocates of theories of performance by people which held that performance is governed by expectations concerning future events, turned a normative theory of how people *should* base their actions, into a positive theory of how people *do* behave.

The most immediate precursors of expectancy theory were Georgopoulos et al. (1957) with their 'path-goal' approach to productive performance at work. The path-goal hypothesis stated that 'if a worker sees high productivity as a path leading to the attainment of one or more of his personal goals, he will tend to be a high producer. Conversely, if he sees low productivity as a path to the achievement of his goals, he will tend to be a low producer' (1957: 346).

Expectancy theory has been developed from Vroom's early specifications to be expressed very clearly (e.g. Galbraith and Cummings 1967) as a combination of three factors:

- The person's own assessment of whether performing in a certain way will result in a measurable result. This factor is labelled the *expectancy*.
- The perceived likelihood that such a result will lead to attaining a given reward. This factor is known as *instrumentality*.
- The person's assessment of the likely satisfaction, or *valence*, associated with the reward.

These factors can be expressed in diagrammatic form as in figure 4.2. In

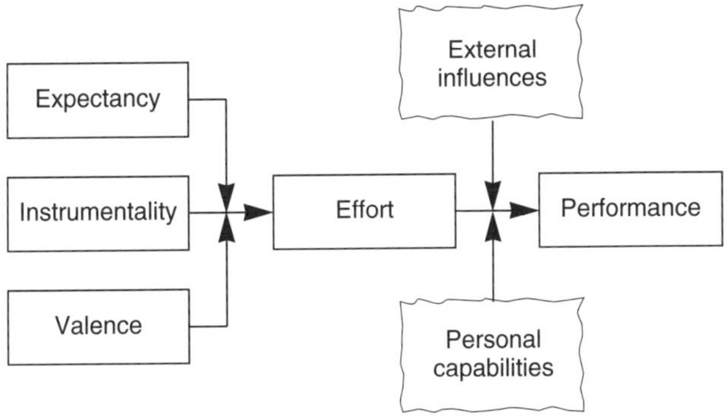


Figure 4.2 A simple expectancy model

practice, if a person sees it as being clear that performing in a certain way will bring about a reward which he or she values, then this individual is more likely to attempt to perform in that way than if the relationship between effort and measured performance, or measured performance and rewards, is slight or uncertain.

Like goal-setting theory, expectancy theory highlights some of the key design principles which practitioners face in establishing systems of performance management.

## Designing Performance Management Systems: Lessons from Theory

We have seen that both expectancy theory and goal-setting theory underpin the concept of a performance management system. In this section we will draw on the contributions of each of these models to add depth and complexity to the schematic model of performance management advanced at the beginning of this chapter.

Figure 4.3 summarizes a number of core issues, common, in varying degrees, to both expectancy theory and goal-setting theory. They represent the key factors which must be addressed in designing a system of performance management. We review the contribution of theory to each of these issues in turn.

### *Setting goals*

As an instrument of strategic human resource management, a system of performance management is predicated on the need to take the wide, strategic

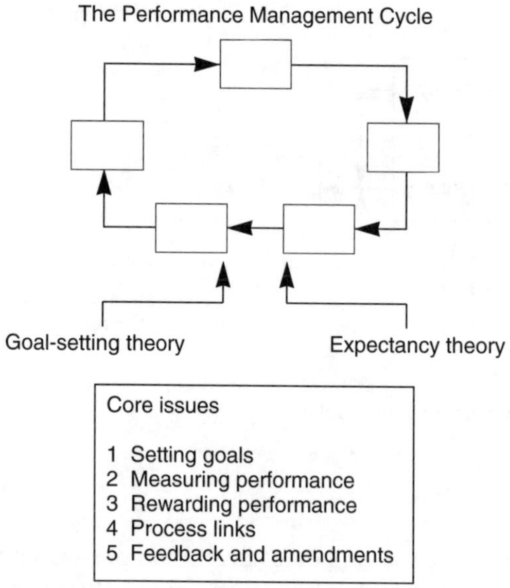


**Figure 4.3** Performance management: lessons from theory

goals of the organization, and translate them into goals for smaller groups and individuals.

Tests of both goal-setting theory and expectancy theory have demonstrated the importance of specifying, few, relatively concrete goals. Yet in practice, designing a performance management system which is in keeping with these principles may prove problematical, for three reasons: the organization may be unable to identify and articulate clear strategic objectives; objectives may be more diverse and numerous than are consistent with theory; and the strategic goals of the organization may be inherently unstable.

Identifying clear strategic objectives for itself is a precondition for an organization to be able to translate them into performance goals. You may be familiar, from studying business strategy (e.g. Mintzberg 1992), with the view that many organizations acquire and follow strategies not as a result of conscious, rational planning process but rather that strategies 'emerge' in response to time and events. Further, the organization may have a number of objectives at any one time, some of which may be potentially contradictory or competing (for example, a commitment to investing in people at the same time as a need to 'downsize'). If the organization is unable to set out explicitly its strategy (which is defined (Johnson and Scholes 1984) as summarizing its objectives and goals) it is unlikely to be able to carry out the next step from this, which is to identify particular dimensions of performance that are most likely to achieve its strategic goals. Case study research of the shifting psychological contract in three UK organizations, found that operationalizing the link between the strategy and values of companies concerned and the objective-setting process was problematic for three reasons: the short-term focus of the companies; the degree of change the companies were experiencing; the perception that objectives were imposed, not jointly negotiated (Stiles et al. 1997).

A second source of criticism is the exhortation of both expectancy and goal-setting models to choose a limited number of performance dimensions to measure and reward. People in organizations, whatever the terms of their written contract, can be said to have a 'psychological contract' with their employer, which is a rich and nuanced collection of shared understandings built up over time. Often, to choose and emphasize a limited number of performance dimensions is to fail to appreciate the subtlety of organizational life, and to risk shattering subtle structures of tacit but critical employee commitment by substituting a simplistic set of objectives. It carries the danger that if the system does 'work', in the sense that people focus on those elements of performance which have been selected and highlighted by the organization, the results may be not at all desirable: a pre-existing pride in skill and work may be replaced by a contractual focus on the rules. The following real-life example (box 4.2) illustrates this point.

A third problem concerns timing. Identifying desirable aspects of individual performance, which will be measured and rewarded, may be possible in an organization that enjoys a relatively stable internal and external environment, but where greater turbulence is experienced it is possible that objectives and hence performance dimensions targeted today may be inapplicable tomorrow. In the

## BOX 4.2 WHEN PERFORMANCE TARGETS BACKFIRE

A performance management system was introduced into a major continental European telecommunications utility in 1993. An overall corporate strategic objective of improved productivity was set, and cascaded down the organization. For the directory assistance division this objective was translated into a goal of reducing the time spent by operators in dealing with each enquiry. Performance against the goal was measured by a system-generated measure of the average length of call.

Managers scrutinizing the early results of the system found that the average length of each call had declined markedly, but operators seemed still to be continuously busy: apparently improved productivity did not seem to be translated into spare capacity. Closer investigation revealed that operators felt that the pressure to keep calls short conflicted with what they saw as an important personal desire to establish a rapport with callers, which they felt could not be done under time pressure. It turned out that operators had discovered that they could reduce the average time per call by immediately disconnecting one call in three, while continuing to spend the usual length of time in small-talk with the remainder of their callers.

early, rapid-growth phase of the UK telephone company Mercury Communications, for example, interviews with staff suggested that objectives set for them were typically overtaken by events within weeks, making any attempt to base a system of performance management on these objectives doomed to failure (Bradley 1992). Such a problem need not be fatal, but companies must be careful to diagnose the appropriateness of the *time interval* within which their objectives are set.

## *Measuring performance*

Assuming the organization has been able to identify which dimensions of performance it will choose to include in a performance management system, it faces another set of issues concerning how the dimensions will be measured. In practice, choosing objectives and setting performance measures is often linked, although not necessarily desirably: Fowler (1990) has suggested that performance dimensions are sometimes chosen not because they are most valued by the organization, but because they are the most easily measured.

### Quantitative measures

Most organizations will use at least some quantitative (i.e. numerical) indicators of their performance to assess whether they are achieving the goals they have set for themselves. For example, many organizations will have financial health as one of their objectives, explicit or otherwise, and so monitor their financial performance regularly, and are quite likely to cascade this objective down through the organization. In doing so they may monitor financial performance against budgets for groups and individuals. Moreover, organizations typically generate, or can access, a whole range of quantified data such as sales figures, output, productivity, absenteeism. Two types of problem can arise in choosing quantitative measures in a system of performance management. The first concerns their sufficiency, and the second their quality.

A performance management system which has genuinely distilled dimensions of performance to be applied to groups and individuals from its wider strategy, may find that some of the dimensions are not measured by existing indicators, and may not be available from the current management information system. It is possible, for example, that increasing customer satisfaction is identified as an outcome to be rewarded and encouraged, but that no adequate measure exists to report this. In this case the organization must do one of two things: either remove the objective from the set which a performance management system will concentrate on (which would undermine the rigour of the system), or develop a means to measure the dimension.

The second problem which must be addressed with quantitative measures is that of their quality. Although so-called quantitative measures often have an aura of robustness and objectivity surrounding them, a closer analysis reveals that they may be rather more arbitrary and subjective than supposed (cf. Walsh 1992).

Profitability would seem to be a tried and tested performance measure, for example, yet financial managers or accountants will confirm that profits are highly subject to decisions made by managers on how to treat costs and revenues, and when paper gains should be released onto the profit and loss account.

## Qualitative measures

Not all aspects of performance can be easily measured and quantified. You may be able to judge whether someone is competent or not, but find it difficult to put a precise figure on how competent they are. Many aspects of performance identified for inclusion in a performance management system may, if they are to be assessed at all, rely not on quantitative measures, but on qualitative judgements. Although quantitative measures have traditionally enjoyed a higher status, it is clear that many instances of hard data, such as accounting information, are actually more mutable than is commonly supposed. On the other hand, if qualitative assessments of performance are well designed, and thoroughly audited, their outcomes may be a more valid and accurate reflection of reality than many quantitative measures.

In general, the quality of any measure of performance or performance indicator will depend whether it is both valid and reliable. Validity refers to whether the indicator actually measures what it is supposed to measure. For example, profitability of a particular unit or group might be taken as an indicator of managerial effectiveness. However, it is possible that factors outside the manager's control could have a greater effect on profitability, and thus it is not a valid indicator of managerial effectiveness. Reliability is a simpler criterion. It means that similar results will be discovered if the measure is used on the same object or person by different people and/or at different times. So, reliability reflects repeatability, whereas validity describes whether you are measuring what you intend to measure. In addition, for practical reasons, a good measure needs to be straightforward to understand and inexpensive to collect. To the extent that these conditions are not met, a performance management system will include flaws which make it depart from the expectancy theory ideal.

Judgements about performance are made all the time in organizations. Most people will have a clear, and for that matter complex, picture of the ability and performance of a colleague with whom they work closely. Usually, this view will rely only in part on formal quantitative measures, but also on a variety of qualitative judgements. Inevitably, whatever measures are used there will be an element of subjective judgement. Promotions, for example – a possible element of a performance management system – are often made on the basis of subjective assessments of a person's performance and suitability for a new job. The challenge for a performance management system is that its procedures should be *auditable*, so that it can be verified that any measures are being used fairly and effectively. This tends to result in a move to formalize the process of subjective performance measurement. The most common way in which this is carried out is via a system of appraisal.

## Appraisal systems

Appraisal systems can take many forms, from annual verbal discussions between an employee and his superior, to systems which may include written reviews from peers and subordinates, as well as superiors and the use of various quantitative performance indicators. The common characteristic of each, however, is that on a regular basis a subjective assessment of an employee's performance is recorded.

Some question the extent to which appraisals can ever be an adequate means of assessing employees' performance because they inevitably involve subjective judgements. One school of thought emphasizes the social processes which underlie performance appraisals. It argues that because ratings are given by people to other people it is impossible to disentangle the social influences which are present: do the appraiser and appraisee enjoy a social rapport? Do non-relevant aspects of the appraisee influence the perception which the appraiser has of his performance? An example of this latter point is US research (e.g. Kraiger and Ford 1985), which demonstrates that employees receive significantly higher ratings from appraisers of their own race. Other studies have indicated that female success at traditionally male tasks is often ascribed to luck, ease of the task, or 'connections' rather than to superior performance. More generally, appraisers may feel socially uncomfortable about giving appraisal ratings which may be relatively poor. The reaction to this may be to cluster ratings artificially around the mean, or to give way to a general 'rating creep' by awarding more marks above a suggested mean than below.

An increasing number of organizations are using 360 degree feedback to support decisions about resourcing, appraisal and rewards (as against personal development); the concern here is that employees would be likely – in these circumstances – to manipulate the process for their own purposes.

Another perspective on appraisal comes from the analysis of power. Far from being a neutral exercise in seeking out the truth, appraisal may be a highly political process, with the parties involved pursuing their own power strategems through it. For example, appraisal may represent an ideal vehicle for a boss to consolidate his or her power over a subordinate by presenting an interpretation of performance consistent with a stance which he or she is trying to adopt (see, for example, Townley (1991)).

One type of solution which has been applied to overcome these problems with appraisal is to expand the number of appraisers who contribute to the subjective assessment of an employee. This would tend to even out any 'rater bias' in response that was related to particular appraisers, though of course it would not address the problem of group bias against racial or gender groups, for example. Increasing the number of contributors to an appraisal might also dilute the social pressure on the appraiser, resulting in allocating too high ratings. Another solution to this specific problem, which has been used by some organizations, is to 'force' appraisals to be non-neutral by specifying, for example, that a certain proportion of top grades must be allocated as well as a certain proportion of low grades. This can also be done statistically by forcing a certain desired distribution of ratings onto the actual ratings given by appraisers (box 4.3).

The solutions to the problems of bias in subjective appraisals can be one cause, however, of another problem frequently encountered by organizations making use of an appraisal system. This is that the process of appraisal becomes bureaucratic and unwieldy. This can lead to it consuming undesired resources in the organization, and being seen as an administrative nuisance and consequently not taken seriously by either appraisers or appraisees. More fundamentally, the practical implications of this aspect of performance management, in terms of bureaucracy and formalism, may be in direct opposition to other moves in the organization towards delegation, empowerment, team-work and devolution of previously centralized policies.

## Rewarding performance

A system of performance management will not succeed in bringing about high performance against objectives unless employees consciously act in ways seen as being most likely to achieve the objectives. Expectancy theory and goal-setting theory both emphasize the importance of ensuring that employees make this decision, but each takes a different route in describing what causes this to be made. Expectancy theory specifies the need to tie performance outcomes to *rewards* which are valued by employees. Goal-setting theory lays stress on the need for acceptance by employees of the goals *per se*, so that motivation is more intrinsically based.

### BOX 4.3 INCORPORATING PEER REVIEWS IN APPRAISALS

Performance management at the investment bank JP Morgan has at its heart an unusual appraisal system. Each employee of the rank of 'officer' (a term which covers the majority of employees) is required to ask up to five colleagues who have worked with him during the past year to submit confidential appraisals of his performance. In addition, anyone else in the company is entitled to submit an unsolicited appraisal on any other individual they have worked with, and it may be positive, negative or a mixture of both. Such unsolicited appraisals cannot be given anonymously: the person co-ordinating the assessment has the right to discuss their views further with them, but the identity of the unsolicited appraiser is not revealed to the subject of the appraisal. The manager of the appraisee's department collates the feedback, and summarizes it in a document which also contributes his own assessment. This document is discussed with the employee, and forms the basis of a performance ranking on which promotions, pay rises and bonuses will be made.

At one level, expectancy theory is almost tautological. It seems to suggest that people will perform in order to attain outcomes which they value, without specifying what it is that people value. This shortcoming has roots in the principles of hedonism, on which utilitarianism, and ultimately expectancy theory, is based. In claiming that all human actions are motivated by the desire to seek pleasure and avoid pain, the philosopher Hobbes proposed, in effect, a theory of psychological hedonism but failed to specify what *constitutes* pleasure and pain. If expectancy theory is to be applied usefully it requires a complementary theory of *what* motivates people; for the designer of a performance management system this carries the clear implication that a judgement must be made of what rewards will be valued by employees.

The concept of valence in expectancy theory establishes the notion that successful performance will only result to the extent that rewards on offer are valued by employees. There exists a myriad of rewards which firms can offer employees, of which money is just one. Others include power, autonomy, praise, status, and fringe benefits. A choice must be made by companies as to what rewards are to be granted in response to performance, and the choice must reflect the importance of that reward to individuals, as well as what the organization can feasibly offer.

Rewards which can be offered can be thought of as *intrinsic* or *extrinsic*. Intrinsic rewards arise from within the system itself. For example, the sense of achievement of meeting performance targets may be reward enough for some employees to cause them to strive for certain performance outcomes. Extrinsic rewards are added separately to the system and may be pecuniary (e.g. a cash bonus) or non-pecuniary (e.g. time off from work).

Pay is one possible means of rewarding employees in a system of performance management. Although performance-related pay is widespread, it need not be assumed that performance management is money driven. From early days, psychological research has argued consistently that pay is variable in its attractiveness to employees (e.g. Brayfield and Crockett 1955). In this regard, goal-setting theory is a useful complement to expectancy theory for designers of performance management systems. This is because goal-setting theory places particular emphasis on the *intrinsic* motivation associated with achieving performance goals which have been set. This becomes particularly important for organizations in the voluntary sector (see box 4.4).

The problem for practitioners is twofold. First, how to find out which goals or rewards will be valued by employees. A solution to this would seem to be preliminary research among employees to discover their preferences. A second problem arises from individual differences. Within an organization, different employees may have markedly different preferences for rewards, or views regarding which goals are valuable. While the ideal would be to tailor these to meet the preferences of individual employees, in practice this is likely to introduce excessive complexity into a performance management system, already subject to the risk of being overly bureaucratic. As a result companies should recognize they will be constrained to offer a 'second best' system.

All this assumes that, while preferences between people might vary, they are

## BOX 4.4 MANAGING THE PERFORMANCE OF VOLUNTEERS

'Many people working for voluntary organizations feel that they are not primarily in it for the money. Good senior managers recognize this and are aware of the desire of their staff to be recognized for their achievements. At the same time, the organization needs to make sure that poor performance is identified and corrected. The most positive aspects of performance management are (1) managers and supervisors are obliged to think through in detail what they expect of their staff or volunteers, who then have a clear framework for their work, and (2) it sends a clear message that performance matters, and allows the organization to set corporate goals and align individual personal objectives to those goals. The gains from the introduction of such a system can be considerable in terms of improved performance and morale.

On the down side, experience in both the private and voluntary sectors has shown that the personal biases of managers assessing performance can skew results. This is the fear most commonly voiced by opponents of such systems. To some extent, this can be corrected by training and by involving other managers in cross-checking their peers' performance appraisals.

The value system in voluntary organizations tends to emphasize personal worth, the development of the individual, and the removal of barriers to advancement. The reality of working in voluntary organizations can contrast sharply with this rhetoric, with the 'caring' values of the organization seeming to get lost under high work loads and inadequate people management skills. In this situation, providing support to individuals' personal development can be an important step in valuing individuals. People respond positively when they feel that their managers are taking a personal interest in their future, within and beyond their current job.'

Lawry-White (1997)

constant within a given person. That is to say, a person who values pay, or autonomy, highly will do so consistently, other factors being equal. There is, however a *marginal valence problem*. This problem is that the value (or valence) of a particular reward is likely to be subject to diminishing marginal returns, as is the case for most other valued goods and services. The value which a person places on autonomy, say, depends in part on how much autonomy he or she has currently. As more autonomy is granted, the value placed on further increase in autonomy is likely to fall (and may even become negative). Equally, goals which are committed to on one occasion, may be less motivating when repeated time after time. For managers designing a system of performance management the marginal valence problem means that it is not sufficient to choose and incorporate rewards, or goals, which are *currently* valued by employees. If the system is to be on-going, both must be reviewed regularly to assess whether they continue to be highly valued by employees, and if not, they should be replaced with others. This makes the point very clearly that a system of performance management may not be designed and left unchanged during its period of operation, but must be the subject of continuous review.

## Process links

Expectancy theory and goal-setting theory make it clear that for a performance management system to succeed in securing high performance, it is not sufficient to get the content issues (discussed above) right. Attention must be paid to the linkages within the system: in other words *how* the system works.

Expectancy theory in particular maintains that it is of crucial importance that employees perceive a close link between their efforts and what is measured as the chosen dimensions of performance. It is equally important that they perceive there to be strong ties between performance as measured and the rewards which may result. Goal-setting theory takes a different emphasis, which makes it not entirely commensurable with expectancy theory. Empirical tests of goal-setting theory have established that if they are to bring about high performance, goals should be demanding, but not unattainable. To this extent the theory shares expectancy theory's concern with the design of the links between objectives and the ability to attain them. However, whereas expectancy theory predicts that performance objectives which are easily met will prompt high performance (providing that they are closely associated with a valued reward), goal-setting theory contends that an easily met objective will fail to produce motivation to perform.

Two principal process links are to be found in models of performance management, the link between effort and measured performance, and the link between performance and rewards. We consider each of these links in turn.

### Linking effort and measured performance

Expectancy theory carries the clear implication that if a system is to promote effort leading to superior performance, people must feel confident that by adjusting their behaviour they will be able to affect the performance measures which have been established. Ensuring that this is the case will involve both design work and communication by the organization.

It is not automatically the case that an individual will be able to affect a given performance measure. Two reasons account for this. The first, as the expectancy model in figure 4.2 shows, is that individual effort and application are unlikely to be exclusive determinants of performance on a given dimension. The tools, either in the sense of physical equipment, or in the sense of skills and abilities, which someone is equipped with will play an important role in determining outcomes. If these are not supplied by the organization, the employee will justifiably feel a reduced ability to influence the performance measures, and, expectancy theory predicts, will not engage in an attempt to improve performance. It could also be the case that achieving performance standards which have been set is beyond the personal capabilities of the employee. Try as he or she might, a person may simply not have the interpersonal skills required, say, to meet an assessment criterion of being seen as a departmental leader by colleagues: such objectives, which appear unachievable, will neutralize any attempt to improve performance.

Another way in which people may feel that they are unable, through their own efforts, to influence performance measures significantly has to do with the size of groups whose performance is measured. An important debate in the economics literature (e.g. Jensen and Meckling 1979; Cable and Fitzroy 1980; Alchian and Demsetz 1972) concerns the question of 'shirking' or 'free-riding' by individuals in groups. This is the idea that if it is the performance of the whole team which is measured, and which determines rewards, then any individual worker can choose to work less hard than his colleagues, to 'take it easy', confident in the knowledge that he will benefit anyway from his team-mates' effort. But of course if everyone in the team thinks in a similar way, then no one will work hard with the result that the performance of the whole team will be poor. The expectancy theory interpretation of the problem is that any individual will see his or her own efforts as having sufficiently little individual effect on performance to justify supplying much.

Some writers (e.g. Alchian and Demsetz 1972) conclude that team-based performance management systems are flawed because of this problem. Others (e.g. Kanter 1989) suggest that the problem can be resolved internally by the social processes within groups and teams. Members of a team will monitor how well their colleagues are working, and exert 'peer pressure' on them not to let their performance fall, thereby letting the side down. It is easy to imagine such an atmosphere prevailing in a sports team, for example. Kanter reports that in a group-based performance management system at the Lincoln Electric Company in the USA 'peer pressure can be so high that the first two years of employment are called "purgatory"' (1989: 264).

The issue raises important questions for the design of performance measurement systems. In many circumstances it may not be feasible to separate out the contribution to performance of individual members of a group or team, and the performance of the group as a whole is measured as part of the system. On other cases it might be administratively more straightforward to measure team performance. Either way, this may be a weak link in the performance management cycle.

Expectancy theory emphasizes the link between effort and measured performance as *perceived* by the employee. To accept the argument that the organization is not so much a rational set of clear structures and policies as a socially determined environment is to allow the possibility that people's perceptions may not be objective pictures of actuality. People may be convinced that their efforts will not be noticed, even if the designers of a system of performance management have in fact addressed the potential problems with the links between effort and performance. It may therefore be necessary for a communications policy to be used to reinforce the message of the design of the system if perceptions are to be accurate. The type of communications policy that may prove effective could vary: in some organizations only seeing a performance management system piloted may be sufficient to persuade doubters of its validity.

## Linking measured performance and rewards

Expectancy theory, used as a framework for analysing performance management systems, also draws attention to the links which an employee perceives between measured performance and rewards, if the system is to succeed in encouraging maximum performance. As in the case of the links between effort and measured performance, it is the *perception* of the link which will determine the success of the system, although in an on-going system the most important determinant of this is likely to be the objective mechanisms in place.

There are two broad ways in which the measured performance-reward contingency can be structured: a formula-based determination, or a more informally determined approach. The advantage of the former is that it provides an objective basis for encouraging the perception that rewards are linked to performance, but suffers the drawback of inflexibility. A less rigidly determined contingency allows for a variety of unforeseen factors which may have affected performance (either positively or negatively) to be taken into account, but runs the risk of appearing arbitrary or political, thereby weakening the degree to which employees consider that rewards reflect actual performance.

Some organizations operating performance management systems, especially those which use financial rewards, rather than intrinsic factors, as motivators, specify precisely in advance the relationship which will prevail between achieved levels of measured performance and the rewards which they will trigger. This may be in the form of a policy which states, for example, that each grade above the average in an appraisal will earn the individual a financial bonus. Another form of this approach is to pay out to employees a proportion of the value of something allied to the stated performance objectives, such as increased sales. Gainsharing, a performance management system popular in the United States in recent years (cf. McKersie 1986), pays out to employees a pre-determined proportion of labour cost savings achieved during a specified period. The principal problem with such a mechanistic approach to linking performance and rewards stems from the problem of 'noise'. Performance measures even in a well-designed system may be unable to avoid being subject to the influence of factors other than employees' personal endeavours. External economic conditions, unforeseen incidents and other 'random' variation may still affect measures such as sales or production performance. At a time when these noise elements turn out to have been especially significant in determining measured performance, a closely defined system may distribute rewards unfairly. If an unexpected currency appreciation has severely affected export sales, for example, it may be unfair to penalize a salesforce which did relatively better than the competition, but whose rewards were tied to sales volume. Equally there are companies who reward their executives through bonuses related to their share price, who have found themselves paying out more than they intended following a general rise in the stockmarket, or after takeover interest in the company, unrelated to superior performance, has caused an increase in the share price. To some extent these problems could be overcome by better design of measures (using share price *relative* to comparable companies, for example, or sales *relative* to those of competitors), but in practice it may be impossible to specify the whole range of contingencies in a performance measure without overcomplicating the design and transparency of the system (box 4.5).

Links between performance and rewards which are not tied to a specific formula may avoid some of these difficulties. Rather than knowing precisely how much, in terms of reward, a given level of performance might bring, managers

## BOX 4.5 DIRECT LINE: A CASE OF EXCESSIVE PRP?

The question of the precise relationship between performance and rewards, it should be specified, is a perennial, and intractable one. The case of Direct Line, the motor insurer subsidiary of the Royal Bank of Scotland, illustrates the dilemma.

Peter Wood founded the Direct Line insurance company in 1985. As a new entrant to a UK insurance market dominated by large, household-name insurance groups, it was uncertain whether Direct Line's strategy of offering low-cost motor insurance by telephone would result in a viable business. Peter Wood sold his stake in the company to the Royal Bank of Scotland in 1988, agreeing to stay on to manage the business. In exchange for his shareholding, Wood negotiated an incentive pay package with RBS which would reward him through a fixed formula tied to the growth of assets of the insurance business.

As it turned out, Direct Line proved a phenomenal success, far exceeding expectations of its performance. Much of the success is certainly attributable to Wood, both for conceiving the strategy, and for proving a shrewd manager of the business. Direct Line's profits reached £50.2 million in the year ending 1993, and by 1994 the company had become Britain's biggest motor insurer. Peter Wood's performance related pay skyrocketed in line with the success. Wood earned £1.6 million in 1991, £6 million in 1992 and £18.2 million in the year to September 1993.

The Royal Bank of Scotland and Peter Wood became embarrassed by the remuneration figures, which were the subject of increasing public attention. In November 1993 the Royal Bank bought itself out of its contractual obligation by making a one-off payment to the Direct Line chief of £24 million.

The question which was exercising public opinion is unresolved today: is it appropriate for performance which is significantly better than envisaged to trigger rewards which are significantly more generous than envisaged?

may be granted discretion over a certain sum or other pool (e.g. a number of days of time off) which they can allocate to staff on the basis of performance against agreed objectives. For a large organization, this may be the only practical way to run a performance management system: it is likely to be difficult and complex enough to cascade the organization's strategic objectives down to the level of individuals' objectives, without having to specify in detail what the consequences of an individual attaining his or her goals will be. The obvious downside to this greater flexibility, however, is that it may weaken the *perceived* link between measured performance and rewards, and so undermine the system of performance measurement. The extent to which this does occur will be closely related to the level of trust within the organization, and experience of the system in practice. In a context of antagonistic relations within the company, the suspicion that the managers of the system could entice high performance through the promise of rewards which never materialize to the extent envisaged may be enough to prevent that performance from being made in the first place.

## ***Feedback and amendments***

Two aspects of feedback and amendment are relevant to the design of systems of performance management: the feedback, and discussion of individuals' performance, to assist them in continuous improvement; and the review of the functioning of the system as a whole.

### Reviewing individual goals and behaviour

Goal-setting theory places great emphasis on the need for the feedback of information on performance if employees are to be motivated to perform well, and most applications of the theory go further to specify the need for coaching on how performance can be improved. This reflects the role of performance management as a *communications process*, serving a number of information-flow functions from establishing strategic objectives in the minds of employees, to offering advice on how performance can be improved. It is obviously the case that, whatever the motivation of a person to perform, if they genuinely cannot see how their behaviour should be altered, then they will be unable to achieve any performance improvements. Performance management, and specifically the appraisal process, should therefore provide a platform for practical advice on ways in which behaviour should be changed to contribute the organization's strategic objectives.

The difficulty with this aspect of the performance management approach is that it brings together two aspects of communication between which there may be a tension. When an appraisal process determines rewards, expectancy theory itself would predict that employee behaviour within the process will be directed instrumentally towards securing the rewards on offer. This may conflict with the openness and candour needed for a sensitive discussion of ways to improve performance. For example, employees may feel the need to present a façade of confidence and competence to their appraiser which masks difficulties they are experiencing, and which could possibly be addressed if brought to the attention of the organization. Moreover, from a strategic point of view, the process could encourage a 'groupthink' by which employees feel the need to express commitment to the strategic objectives of the organization (since it is performance against these which is rewarded), with the result that no critical appraisal of the objectives themselves is made, or at least expressed. This carries the great risk that strategies which are proving unworkable, or damaging, persist without amendment thereby handicapping the organization.

### Reviewing the performance of the performance management systems

The second element of feedback and review concerns evaluation of the performance management process itself. Whereas we have characterized performance management as a cycle, expectancy theory is more often presented as a linear chain, without an internal feedback mechanism. To adapt the analysis of expectancy theory to the particular application of performance management we therefore need to build in a reflexivity into the process.

There are three reasons why continuous review of the operation of performance management needs to be conducted. First, the need for such reflexivity is fundamental to the strategic role of performance management. In the first section of this chapter we described one of purposes of performance management as being to provide a framework for internally auditing the means by which the organization delivers wider strategic goals, with a view to continuously improving them. Secondly, as we have already pointed out, strategic goals themselves may be far from fixed, but rather constantly evolving. The likelihood is that some unknown contingencies will reveal themselves only in application, so that the system must be capable of reforming itself to take account of lessons from practice.

Table 4.1 summarizes the elements of continuous scrutiny to which a performance management system should be subject. Performing the tasks implied is a mechanical process, but requires investigative, diagnostic and design skills on the part of those responsible for the system.

## Methodological Criticisms

In the first section we argued that the performance management approach rests on a set of essentially rationalist assumptions. Expectancy theory, and to some extent goal-setting theory, are themselves founded on the premise that people – managers (the designers and operators of performance management systems) and employees (the people to whom they are applied) – think in a way which is optimizing, calculative and individualistic. This set of assumptions has been labelled variously *rational economic man* (Hollis and Nell 1975), *neo-classical rationality* (Etzioni 1988), or simply as *rationality* (Leibenstein 1976).

These assumptions are rarely made explicit, still less criticized, with the result that often little thought is given to questions such as whether they are correct at

**Table 4.1** Feedback loops in performance management

| *Step* | *Review questions* | *Modifications* |
|---|---|---|
| 1 Identifying objectives | Are organizational objectives still appropriate? | Update objectives |
| | Are they adequately translated to group or individual level? | Amend cascade of objectives |
| 2 Choosing measures | To what extent were measures<br>• noise free?<br>• objective?<br>• simple to understand?<br>• inexpensive to collect?<br>• relevant to objectives? | Design and specify different sets of measures |
| 3 Defining links between effort and measured performance | Is training adequate for objectives to be met? | Provide appropriate training if justified |
| | Is equipment adequate for objectives to be met? | Provide appropriate equipment if justified |
| | Is support adequate for objectives to be met? (including time available) | Reconfigure support (time allocation, assistance, organization) |
| | Are persons' capabilities adequate for objectives to be met? | Consider substitution of person or less demanding objectives |
| | Does team size encourage perception of weak link between effort and performance? | Redesign link between measures and rewards |
| | Do employees perceive link between effort and measured performance? | Design and implement communications strategy |
| 4 Selecting rewards | Are rewards valued by employees? | Specify different rewards |
| 5 Defining links between performance and rewards | Do employees perceive link between performance and rewards? | Design and implement communications strategy |
| | Are extraneous factors affecting performance or rewards? | Redesign link between measures and rewards |

all times, and in all circumstances. Yet a growing body of theory and evidence suggests that human decision-making does not approximate to that assumed under this conception of rationality at all times and in all places. Mitchell (1980), for example, notes that the essential question is shifting from *does expectancy theory work?* to *where does it work?*

Take the question of national setting, for example. For many years researchers (such as Tonnies 1922) have identified important and consistent differences in the *values* of different national cultures. Hofstede (1980) has argued that the value of individualism forms an axis by which countries can be categorized: in the United States a strongly individualistic value system suggests that policies which rely on enlightened self-interest may succeed; whereas in Sweden, whose dominant value system emphasizes more collective interests, such policies may fail.

> An Eastern approach might call for holism and generalisation, while a Western approach calls for analysis and specialisation. Latins might emphasise intuition and flexibility, and the German cultures might prefer self-control and structure [. . .] To a Dutchman, whose heroes are quiet men, empowering is a perfectly normal practice; to a Frenchman it would mean abandonment (Hoecklin 1995: 132).

Etzioni (1975) found that individualism went hand in hand with a *calculative* decision-making process, such as that assumed under expectancy theory, and so the success of policies such as performance-related pay which are based on this way of thinking will be contingent on an appropriate national setting. It is significant that while performance-related pay is widespread in the United States, it is much less common in continental Europe. Yet this is too often ignored by those who peddle prescriptions: as Hofstede notes 'the silent assumption of universal validity of culturally restricted findings is frequent. The empirical basis for American management theories is American organizations, and we should not assume without proof that they apply elsewhere' (Hofstede 1980: 373).

It is not only nations which have values, governing ways of thinking and behaving, which may not be consistent with that assumed by expectancy theory and performance management. Particular organizations have their own traditions and cultures which may or may not be consistent with the successful use of performance management systems. For instance, research found that reactions to the introduction of performance-related pay were different across the 15 divisions of an Irish multi-divisional organization. The objectives of the HR Director who introduced the performance-related pay (PRP) scheme were often at variance with the managers involved, leading to difficulties with the scheme, as box 4.6 shows.

Another example might be companies with an entrenched culture of collective bargaining who find that the introduction of a performance-related pay system militates against the way employees think about their performance, and so prove unsuccessful. However, Guest (1993: 222) notes that 'attempts to use individualised PRP to drive a wedge through trade union membership have sometimes backfired.' At the very least, policies should diagnose at what level performance

## BOX 4.6 CONTRASTING VIEWS OF PRP IN AN IRISH MULTI-DIVISIONAL COMPANY

'The managers did not share the same set of perceptions of the scheme, nor did they share the same value system: for some the most important element in their jobs was pay and PRP did have a strong effect on performance, for others the reverse was the case. These differences could not be explained by factors such as age, length of service, trade union membership or gender, but had to be sought in the companies within which these managers worked.

This company comprised 15 subsidiaries, each with its own history and culture. Some were fairly new organizations, others were long established, yet the same PRP scheme had been implemented in each. From the HR Director's perspective, one of the objectives of the scheme was to reinforce and reward the changes involved in moving the company from a bureaucratic, public sector organization to one which would embrace a performance driven, enterprise way of thinking. However, given the diversity of companies operating within the group, it is not surprising to find that a uniform reward scheme was unable to achieve this purpose.'
Kelly and Monks (1998: 216)

management should be applied: in an organization with a strong teamwork culture, individual incentives may be resisted as incompatible (witness the hostile reaction to the attempt to introduce an individualized performance management system into the UK police force in 1993); equally, group bonuses applied to a salesforce may violate passionately-held attachment to individual autonomy.

The importance of contextual factors, such as culture, in the success of performance management systems highlight a potential hidden agenda behind some organizations' adoption of the approach. Clark (1995) has argued that while performance-related pay is often claimed to be introduced in order to create an incentive for improved performance, it is sometimes chosen by managers wishing to instigate *cultural change* rather than to achieve the vaunted improvements in individual performance. This may not be a misplaced strategy: Hofstede (1980) argues that changing first the behaviour of individuals, such as by forcing them to take part in a performance-related pay system, is one of the most effective ways of changing value systems, which are in turn (Schein 1984) a principal component of organizational culture. If cultural change is the real objective of introducing performance management systems, their success cannot be gauged on whether the systems improve individuals' performance, because they are quite likely to depress it initially if introduced into an 'inappropriate' context, but must be judged on whether they ultimately bring about changes in attitudes and values.

## Conclusions and Summary

Performance management is an approach to managing human resources which is designed to tie HR policies securely into a framework of achieving the strategic goals of the business. To do so it advocates the formation of a system for managing human resources which generates personal goals from wider strategic objectives, provides information on the extent to which contributions are being made to these objectives, and supplies a means of auditing the process links which deliver the contributions. Rather than comprising a blueprint set of policies, performance management is an approach which can be implemented through a variety of linked policies, including objective-setting, performance appraisal and performance related pay.

The performance management approach draws on a number of theoretical models, of which expectancy theory and goal-setting theory are the most prominent. Applying the models to performance management highlights a set of critical factors which the designers and practitioners of performance management systems must address. These are associated with the feasibility of setting goals, measuring performance, rewarding performance, the design of the process links within the system, and procedures for feedback and amendment. What emerges is a complexity of issues which a precipitous move to implement a performance management system may overlook. Empirical studies, including those applied to performance-related pay, tend to confirm the importance of getting these factors right. In many cases organizations fail to do so, with the result that the effect of performance management systems on performance has not been strong in practice, and is sometimes negative.

The performance management approach can be criticized for relying on a model of management which is more rational than is achievable in practice. In particular, prescriptions are often couched in universalist terms, which take no account of the contextual factors which play a large part in determining success. The contextual factors include cross-cultural differences between nations, as well as different corporate environments and traditions.

In addition, by contrast with the social systems which link people in the organization, performance management may imply a relatively simplistic model by which to achieve enhanced performance in line with strategic objectives. It carries the danger that it may substitute a crude set of mechanisms for a subtle psychological contract linking the organization and its employees.

The overwhelming lesson from theory and practice is that the complex, and sometimes contradictory, set of issues which performance management comprises requires a critical approach to the design of systems. A performance management system, if it is to succeed, must reflect an appreciation of the particular characteristics of the organization, and have included within it a strong element of continuous review. An off-the-shelf approach to choosing a performance management system is highly unlikely to achieve its aim of contributing to the achievement of strategic objectives.

## Key Points

- Performance management has become a popular vehicle for attempts to integrate the management of human resources with the organization's wider strategy.
- Performance management refers to an approach, rather than a particular package of policies. The approach involves linking five policy elements: setting objectives, measuring performance, feeding back results, setting rewards, and amending objectives and activities.
- Performance management is based on a rationalist conception of the organization and management, which may not reflect the subtlety, complexity and ambiguity of the actual world in which managers operate. In particular it has little to say about the social processes and power systems in which it will operate.
- Principles of goal-setting theory and expectancy theory underpin the performance management approach. They offer a set of lessons for the design and implementation of performance management systems.
- A host of crucial issues of design and implementation mean that operating a performance management system is a complex endeavour, requiring rigorous prior, and on-going analysis.
- Empirical studies confirm that performance management systems are successful in improving performance only where fundamental design principles are followed.
- The underlying assumptions of performance measurement tend to be universalist: they do not consider the importance of context. Yet the values of countries, organizations and people may depart from what is assumed, making models of performance management limited in their application.

## Discussion Questions

1. Which human resource policies does performance management potentially cover?
2. In what ways do modern performance management approaches draw upon traditional theories of social psychology? What assumptions do such models make, and are these justifiable?
3. How might expectancy theory help to identify the potential benefits and drawbacks of a reward system like performance related pay?
4. What are some of the contextual factors which might interfere with the more universalistic performance management systems?

## References

Alchian, A. A. and Demsetz, H. (1972) 'Production, information cost and economic organization', *American Economic Review*, vol. 62, 777.

Bowey, A., Fowler, A., and Iles, P. (1992) 'Reward management', Unit 10, *B884 Human Resource Strategies*, Milton Keynes: Open University Business School, 119 ff.

Bradley, K. (1992) *Phone Wars*, London: Business Books.

Brayfield, A. H. and Crocket, W. H. (1955) 'Employee attitudes and performance', *Psychological Bulletin*, vol. 52, 396–424.

Cable, J. and Fitzroy, F. (1980) 'Production efficiency, incentives and employee participation: Some preliminary results for West Germany', *Kylos*, vol. 33, 100–21.

Clark, G. (1995) *Performance Related Pay in the Public Sector*, London: Social Market Foundation.

Etzioni, A. (1975) *A Comparative Analysis of Complex Organisations*, New York: Free Press.

—— (1988) *The Moral Dimension*, New York: Free Press.

Fowler, A. (1990) 'Performance management: The MBO of the 1990s', *Personnel Management*, vol. 22, 75–80.

Galbraith, J. and Cummings, L. L. (1967) 'An empirical investigation of the motivational determination of task performance', *Organizational Behaviour and Human Performance*, vol. 2, 237–57.

Georgopoulos, B. S., Mahoney, G. M., and Jones, N. W. (1957) 'A path-goal approach to productivity', *Journal of Applied Psychology*, vol. 41, 345–53.

Goodswen, M. (1988) 'Retention and reward of the high achiever', *Personnel Management*, October, 61–4.

Guest, D. (1993) 'Current perspectives on human resource management in the United Kingdom', In A. Hegewisch and C. Brewster (eds) *European Developments in Human Resource Management*, London: Kogan Page.

Hoecklin, L. (1995) *Managing Cultural Differences: Strategies for competitive advantage*, Wokingham: Addison-Wesley.

Hofstede, G. (1980) *Culture's Consequences*, Beverley Hills, CA: Sage.

Hollis, M. and Nell, E. J. (1975) *Rational Economic Man: A philosophical critique of neo-classical economics*, London: Cambridge University Press.

Jensen, M. C. and Meckling, W. H. (1979) 'Rights and production functions: An application to labour-managed firms and co-determination', *Journal of Business*, vol. 52, 469–506.

Jevons, W. S. (1883) *Methods of Social Reform*, London: Macmillan.

Johnson, G. and Scholes, K. (1984) *Exploring Corporate Strategy*, London: Prentice-Hall.

Kanter, R. M. (1989) *When Giants Learn to Dance*, London: Unwin.

Kelly, A. and Monks, K. (1998) 'A view from the bridge and life on deck: Contrasts and contradictions in performance related pay', in C. Mabey, D. Skinner and T. Clark (eds) *Experiencing Human Resource Management*, London: Sage.

Kraiger, K. and Ford, J. (1985) 'A meta-analysis of rat race effects in performance ratings, *Journal of Applied Psychology*, vol. 70, 56–65.

Lawry-White, S. (1997) 'Management issues facing voluntary organisations', Briefing Paper, Swindon: Vine Management Consulting.

Leibenstein, H. (1976) *Beyond Economic Man*, Cambridge, MA: Harvard University Press.

Lewin, K. (1938) *Conceptual Representation*, Durham, NC: Duke University Press.

Locke, E. A., Shaw, K. N., Saari, L. M,. and Latham, G. P. (1981) 'Goal setting and task performance 1969–1980', *Psychological Bulletin*, vol. 90, 125–52.

McKersie, R. B. (1986) 'The promise of gain-sharing', *ILR Report*, 7–11.

Mento, A. J., Steel, R. P., and Karren, R. J. (1987) 'A meta-analytic study of task performance: 1966–1984', *Organizational Behavior and Human Decision Processes*, vol. 39, 52–83.

Mintzberg, H. (1992) 'Five Ps for strategy' in H. Mintzberg and J. Quinn (eds) *The Strategy Process*, Englewood Hills, NJ: Prentice-Hall.

Mitchell, T. (1980) 'Motivation: New directions for theory and practice', *Academy of Management Review*, vol. 7, 80–8.
Schein, E. (1984) 'Coming to a new awareness of organizational culture', *Sloan Management Review*, Winter, 3–16.
Stiles, P., Gratton, L., Truss, C., Hope-Hailey, V., and McGovern, P. (1997) 'Performance Management and the psychological contract', *Human Resource Management Journal*, vol. 7, no. 1, 57–66.
Tolman, E. C. (1932) *Purposive Behaviour in Animals and Men*, New York: Century.
Tonnies, F. (1922) *Gemeinschaft and Geselleschaft*, Berlin: Curtins.
Townley, B. (1991) 'The politics of appraisal: Lessons from the introduction of appraisal into UK universities', *Human Resource Management Journal*, vol. 1, no. 2, 27–34.
Vroom, V. (1964) *Work and Motivation*, New York: Wiley.
Walsh, E. (1992) 'Management accounting and the measurement of business performance: some dilemmas', in K. Bradley (ed.) *Human Resource Management: People and Performance*, Aldershot: Dartmouth.

chapter 5

# Training and Development Strategies

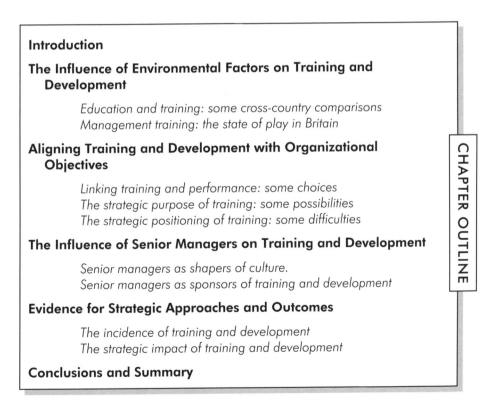

CHAPTER OUTLINE

## Learning Objectives

- To identify the features that elevate training and development approaches from the tactical and ad hoc to the concerted and strategic.
- To note some of the ways that an organization's investment in training and development activities can be influenced and triggered by its external environment.
- To analyse how strategic business imperatives come to be interpreted and addressed by a human resource development interventions.
- To explore whether training and development initiatives are becoming more extensive and influential as examples of strategic HR policy.
- To assess the strategic impact of training and development policies and practices.

# Introduction

The task of this chapter is to formulate a strategic approach to training and development – to attempt to identify the dynamics in an organization which demonstrate that development of self and others is being taken seriously at all levels and that such investment is having a positive impact on individual and corporate performance. Such a quest begs all sorts of questions. Does strategic training only incorporate that which has a quantifiable effect on business objectives, or does it include any development where individual learning is taking place? When we talk of, for instance, management development, whose strategic purpose is actually being served? (see box 5.1). What activities do we classify under the heading of training and development? Formal training programmes should obviously be included, but what about everyday learning opportunities? Where does learning stop and working begin? And can enchance expertise, creativity, productivity, even market share be reliably attributed to an organization's investment in training and development?

Despite the ambiguities that such conflicting agendas throw up, and the private misgivings about the purpose and value of much that is done in the name of training and development, organizations continue to commit resources to such activities. The internal contradiction of such policies is well illustrated in the findings of a survey seeking the views of chief executives and personnel managers in 91 UK companies with turnovers greater than £20 million (Parkinson 1990). Interviews uncovered that:

> Expenditure on the development and training of managers is highest in those companies where management development is part of the corporate plan. Senior managers need to believe that investment will allow them to respond more effectively to a changing environment. Companies in markets which have become increasingly turbulent in the last few years (e.g. retailing, leisure and brewing, and finance and property) demonstrate this, being amongst the largest spenders on management development and training . . . [yet] . . . Few

**BOX 5.1 THE MULTIPLE MEANINGS OF MANAGEMENT DEVELOPMENT**

'If management development is construed as the intersection of three variables – individual career, organizational succession and organizational performance – then much of the ambiguity can be interpreted as the difficulty of trying to manage some kind of accommodation between the variables. In idealized form, management development holds that all three variables can be integrated through compliance with its procedures and activities, offering the promise of a high level of optimization between individual expectations and organizational demands. In practice, each procedure and activity is subject to a range of interpretations and meanings by different parties, resulting in a multitude of assumptions and beliefs in any organization about how the variables are to be integrated. This is the socio-political domain of management – a complex dynamic of hopes and fears, ambitions and opportunities, threats and disillusionments, conflicts and contradictions.'
(Lees 1992: 91)

of the companies in the sample were able to quantify the benefits of management development programmes. (Parkinson 1990: 73)

So is it possible to meaningfully map out a strategic approach to training and development? Can learning activities be devised and implemented in such a way that they tangibly impact upon the capacity of a business to deliver its medium- to long-term objectives? Can the various actors, internal levers and political systems be galvanized around a concerted and effective human resource development strategy? Figure 5.1 draws together the key potential ingredients of a rational and strategic approach to training and development.

The logic of the model is that unless attention is paid to all six dimensions shown in the figure, then the quality of training and development will be impaired and their business impact will be flawed. While the actual training and development activities as experienced by trainees (perhaps a training course or a set of workshops, or on-the-job assignments or other developmental initiatives) are central to the model, they represent only one part of a cyclical process incorporating several other key players in the organization. The target represents the vision, mission or 'cause' of the organization, and assumes this is or can be articulated in some shape or form. From this starting point there are two flows: one into business strategy, where the mission will be broken down into medium- and long-term objectives and plans; the other flow is into human resource strategies where the competencies and performance criteria will be defined for the staff employed. This latter flow will hopefully inform each lever of HRM policy and procedure, providing continuity between recruitment and selection practices, appraisal and assessment, reward systems and career development processes. Critically, training and development provision needs to be mutually supported by each of these human resource levers.

Among those who scan the external environment and formulate business strategy for the organization as a whole, it is obviously advantageous to have a human resource specialist. Involvement in this early stage of business planning means that training and development can be set in motion to anticipate and meet likely knowledge, skill and attitude requirements of the work force in the future. Then there are those who represent the prevailing culture of the organization, usually senior managers and line managers, or some dominant coalition spanning different parts of, and levels within, the organization. While the model makes no assumptions about the *correctness* of their views and the value they jointly attach to training activities, their potential influence upon the nature and outcome of training and development cannot be underestimated. Certain line managers may be part of this dominant coalition, but whether they are or not, they play a separate and important role in the overseeing of training received and the development undertaken by their staff. Through setting up on-the-job development opportunities, pre- and post-course briefings/debriefings and on-going coaching, their participation in and ownership of training activities for their staff is essential.

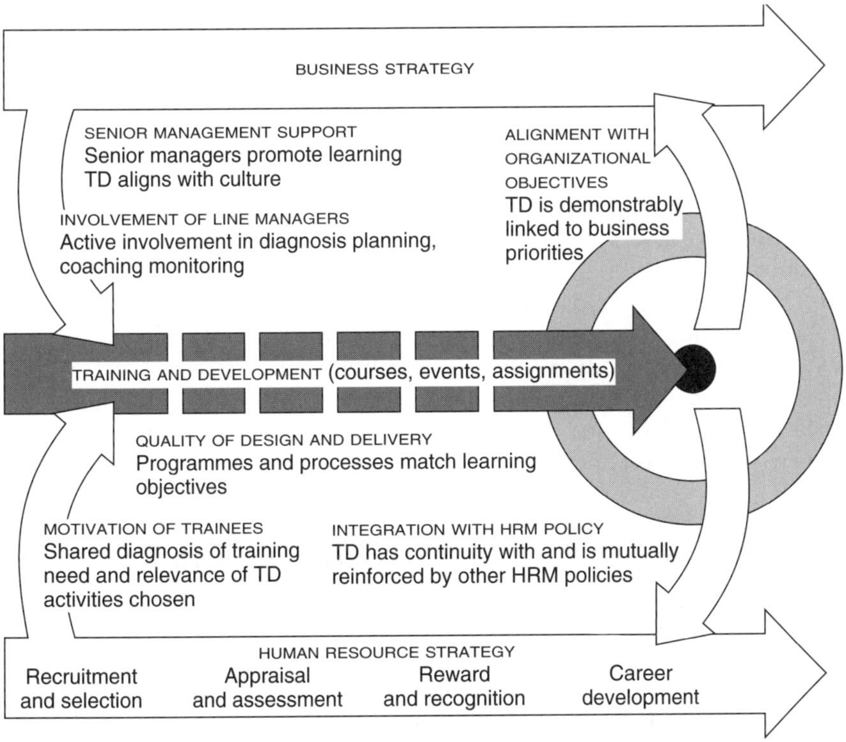


**Figure 5.1** Strategic training and development (TD)

Next are those participating in the development process. Naturally they need to be motivated and to perceive the training they receive as relevant to their jobs, careers and broader self-development. Finally, the training staff, who may include external consultants and training agencies, are crucial in the way they design and deliver training programmes and development activities. To do this effectively such staff may also assist with initial diagnosis and interpretation of training requirements, as well as subsequent evaluation which feed back into business objectives.

What the overall model highlights is the pivotal link that training and development activities *can* provide between business and human resource strategy. A strategic approach to training and development can be depicted as one where all those involved are engaged in a connected, explicit and developmental purpose which helps to simultaneously fulfil an individual's learning goals and the organization's mission. However, such a conception of training and development is probably both over-mechanistic and idealistic. In the same way that the three variables in box 5.1 (individual career, organizational succession and organizational performance) will rarely align perfectly, so the agendas and priorities of different interest groups within an organization will inevitably make the rationale for and the content of training activities contested terrain. All the more so, because more than most other HR initiatives, development activities touch upon the core purpose (personal, sectional, professional, cultural, occupational, organizational) and the raw nerves (who is developing whom, why, and to what ends?) of the negotiated psychological contract between employee and employer. In the rest of this chapter we explore the role of some of the stakeholders in the training process, in order to understand more fully the possibility and desirability of a truly strategic approach to training and development in organizations. Chapter 12 deals more fully with the internal processes by which training comes to be conceived and implemented in different organizational contexts.

There are, of course, groups external to the organization with a keen interest in an organizational training provision – like government departments, professional institutes, trade unions and employee associations, pressure groups and not least, shareholders and customers. Usually their power bases lie outside or in some cases traverse organization boundaries, but their influence upon internal decision-making can be immense. So we start with a consideration of the external environment, and the national training context in particular, within which an organization operates.

## The Influence of Environmental Factors on Training and Development

The effectiveness of an organization's training and development practices and policies cannot be divorced from extra-organizational influences, both national and international. These 'situational factors' (Beer et al. 1984) or the so-called 'outer context' (Sparrow and Pettigrew 1987) include such factors as technological investment, social and political attitudes, institutional practices, external labour markets, demographic pressures and changes in the regulatory context (e.g. privatization, deregulation). Each of these will combine to shape the assumptions and priorities of those responsible for training in a given organization.

## Education and training: some cross-country comparisons

Take, for example, some of the outer context factors which either inhibit or encourage the uptake of training in Britain. Lane's (1989) analysis of flexible specialization shows that Britain compares unfavourably with Germany and France on all five of the indicators chosen (table 5.1).

Attempts to adjust the organization of production to new and changing market demands have been hindered in Britain by traditionally adversarial industrial relations, the need to drastically reorientate worker training, and deployment which has a much weaker vocational base to start with (29% of British apprentices, technicians and foremen have formal qualifications compared with 61% in Germany), and the insufficient development of management technical skill. So it is that the inheritance of skills and capabilities, usually the produce of previous training and recruitment policies at a national and sector level, severely constrains what firms can attempt and how they go about it: 'Frequently underestimated in tracing such change . . . is the way manpower, training and job design policies over a period of time determine the skill structure of an organisation and the scope for adopting and benefiting from new technology' (Hendry and Pettigrew 1990: 28).

Detailed studies of matched industrial plants in Germany and Britain by the National Institute of Economic and Social Research (NIESR) attribute lower productivity, slower adoption and use of new technology, and frequency of downtime in the UK plants to the poorer level of training and technical competence. This and other examples, like the persistent use of subjective and discriminatory recruitment practices, illustrate the slow uptake of improved training and development in the UK (Keep 1989).

The degree to which the national education and training system supports in-firm training is obviously a key social-political factor and one that is closely linked to skills supply. During the 1980s and early 1990s in Britain the Conservative government was clearly of the belief that: 'the provision, content, finance and level of provision of training is largely the responsibility of employers, and that the role of government institutions is to provide guidance and research, as well as being directly involved in training the unemployed. During the last decade training institutions in Britain have consequently been reorganized to give a greater role to private sector employers' (Brewster et al. 1992: 570). The Confederation of British Industry (CBI) is in favour of this 'voluntarist' approach whereby employers train to meet business objectives, and market mechanisms operate to balance the supply and demand for training. Their view is that a training levy is unworkable, citing Australia and Sweden where the levy has been suspended on the grounds of excessive bureaucracy, ineffectiveness or incompatibility with the views of the governing political parties. In France the levy system is under review and in the Republic of Ireland proposals to introduce a levy have been dropped. Meanwhile the Trades Union Congress (TUC),

**Table 5.1** Factors supporting or inhibiting the move towards flexible specialization: a comparative perspective

| *Factor* | *Germany* | *UK* | *France* |
|---|---|---|---|
| Management | Actively committed to continuous technological innovation and competent to initiate and establish new technical systems. | Lack of confidence and, therefore, hesitancy about technological innovation; and a lack of competence to handle the more complex variety. | Technologically innovative management but less successful in adapting designs to the needs of production. |
| Labour-market supply | An ample supply of all-round skilled labour which can be broadly deployed and easily retrained. | A shortage of skilled labour and an absence of flexibility in existing skilled labour. | A shortage of highly skilled and polyvalent labour. |
| Training system | A well-established training system and a willingness by both management and labour to invest in further retraining. | A haphazard and underdeveloped system and a general reluctance by management to make the long-term investment required. | Recent state intervention to increase the supply of skilled production workers and a management strategy of creating a small, polyvalent worker elite. |
| Employment relationship | Relatively high degree of employment security and low degree of labour-market segmentation. | Relatively low degrees of employment security. Segmented internal labour market. | Relatively high degree of employment security for the core labour force but a notable increase in labour-market segmentation. |
| Industrial relations system | A co-operative system aiding worker identification with, and joint responsibility for, the efficient and competitive organization of production. Management no longer actively concerned with achieving domination. | An adversarial system based on a 'minimum interaction' employment relationship. Incompatibility with notion of worker responsibility for production flow and product quality. Management still struggling to re-establish control. | An adversarial system with an emphasis on hierarchy and close management control. Not conducive to the development of general worker responsibility and co-operation. |

*Source:* Adapted from Lane (1989).

concerned about the under-investment in training and skills shortages in the UK, argue strongly for a modern training levy collected centrally from all employers and to be disbursed by a national skills fund (Noble 1997).

The 'voluntarist' approach can be contrasted with countries where governments legislate and/or regulate the degree to which employers provide vocational and educational training (VET) for their staff. For instance, in Germany, employers are obliged to fund two-thirds of VET, but they also enjoy with the trade unions considerable influence over the system, along with central and local government (Beardwell and Holden 1994). One of the outcomes of this industry oriented and directed training culture is that Germany has three times more skilled workers than Britain, despite having a labour force of a similar size (Rose and Wignanek 1991). However the German functionalist model has been criticized as outmoded and failing to respond to workplace changes. In particular, it is noted that the system produces a surplus of skilled blue-collar workers, but fails to provide workers with more sophisticated computer knowledge and the flexibility to move from one job to another (*The Economist* 1994: 26, quoted in Noble 1997); namely, that it is export-oriented and ethnocentric in emphasis, and therefore ill-suited to the demands of globalization (Evans and Doz 1989), as well as being openly discriminatory against women and ethnic minorities. Since the introduction of successive legislation in the 1970s and 1980s, France can also be described as adopting a 'directive' training ethos. Laws requiring that employers spend 1.2 per cent of total gross salaries on training employees have had the twin longer-term benefits of encouraging employers to invest beyond the limit as they discovered the benefits of training and increasing accountability for the training budget. Table 5.2 shows that French organizations lead Europe in the amount spent on training. Interestingly, the training culture in Japan could be described as a mixture of directive and voluntarist. For the core workforce (primarily managerial and professional staff in large-scale companies):

> Lifetime employment allows for the long-term development of employees and enables the creation of a structured succession programme mutually beneficial to both the organization and the individual employee. Decision making is shared at all levels and there is a strong sense of collective reponsibility for the success of the organization, and co-operative rather than individual effort is emphasised, although achievement is encouraged. Training and development is part and parcel of company policy in helping to reinforce these working practices, as well as being used to improve skills in technology and other related working practices. Training and development is thus 'embedded' in Japanese companies, rather than extraneous, as in British organizations. (Beardwell and Holden 1994: 358)

Bournois (1992) notes that France – like Britain – has been less successful in alleviating long-term unemployment especially amongst its young people, possibly due to the poor perception of vocational training initiatives. Many commentators are doubtful that UK employers can in fact rise to the training challenge, posed

**Table 5.2** Organizations: training and development objectives/spending

| *Organizations with training and development as main objective* % | *Country ranking* | *Organizations spending more than 2% on training* *Country ranking* | % |
|---|---|---|---|
| 34 | D | F | 80 |
| 31 | N | S | 60 |
| 31 | DK | T | 47 |
| 30 | S | D | 43 |
| 26 | NL | NL | 40 |
| 25 | F | IRL | 40 |
| 25 | T | P | 39 |
| 24 | P | FIN | 36 |
| 22 | UK | N | 36 |
| 22 | IRL | UK | 26 |
| 19 | E | DK | 25 |
| 12 | FIN | E | 23 |

by the non-interventionist stance of their government due to a number of underlying structural factors that inhibit organizations investing in their employees, *particularly* in the area of training. In addition to those mentioned above Keep (1989) refers to four such factors: the shifting of productive capacity and investment overseas by British companies where they can buy new pre-trained workforces (and therefore obviate the need to reskill their UK workforces); the trend, among some large British companies (e.g. the food industry) toward takeovers and subsequent divestment which undermine the long-term commitment to their subsidiaries that is a pre-requisite to securing a reasonable return on investment in HRD (see also Naulleau and Harper 1993); the continued dominance of financial management and accounting systems in British board rooms which militates against people-centred development over the longer term (see also Tayeb 1993: 61); and the generally low adoption by British managers of systematic and coherent personnel practices. Actually, this last point is seen as typical of western Europe as a whole, where according to a survey of 5,450 organizations across ten European countries, 'in most countries and companies selection, appraisal, reward and development of human resources is neither strategically oriented enough nor integrated with each other, nor evaluated in an objective way' (Hilb 1992: 575).

## *Management training: the state of play in Britain*

In relation to management training in the UK, the evidence looks reasonably encouraging. A survey conducted among 2,051 members of the British Institute of Management, (BIM) to establish the quality and quantity of training undertaken (of all types, including own-time study) over a calendar year found that 82 per cent undertook some work-time training activities in 1991, and 49 per cent participated in training in their own time (Warr 1992). Even allowing for a sample skewed towards larger companies, and a definition of training broader than that of previous surveys, this still represents a significant improvement in the quantity of management training (Handy 1987; Mangham and Silver 1986). Another survey of 83 per cent BIM members found that managers averaged approximately eleven days of training per year, comprising 3.3 days off the job training in their own time, 5.3 in their employer's time, plus 2.2 days on the job training (Poole and Mansfield 1992: 212). It is worth noting from this survey that 60 per cent of managers report that the training they receive is at their own initiative, and a further 13 per cent report that it is also at their own expense. Increasing pressure for professionalism in management is undeniably a spur for such activity and a good goal, even though definitions of what this looks like remain problematic (see chapter 12 for a discussion of competencies). One index of this intent – though not necessarily the most accurate – is the growing number of organizations in public and private sectors which are signing up to support the Management Charter (1000 employers representing 25 per cent of the UK workforce in 1993 – Wills 1993). Such intentions *could* have a far-reaching impact on the quality of management and business performance in Britain providing the good practice and infrastructural support proclaimed by the Charter are translated into action.

Nevertheless, a number of questions remain about the growth and health of the UK management training context. One legitimate criticism levelled at many of the glowing reports cited to illustrate advances in management education is that they feature leading-edge companies, typically in the private sector and large enough to be able to afford the luxury of training investment and innovation. While it has always been the policy of the Council for Management Education and Development to foster such success stories, using them as exemplars for other organizations to follow, current progress (at least that which is published) does seem to be at the expense of smaller organizations (see, for instance, Vickerstaff 1991), not part of the Management Charter Initiative elite and not based in the South East (61 per cent of providers of management training and 71 per cent of training consultants are located there). Furthermore, little evidence is yet available on the extent to which traditionally disadvantaged groups are benefitting from this apparent growth in development opportunities. The Institute for Employment Research predicts that numbers employed will increase between 1987 and 1995 by 1.75 million and that 90 per cent of this increase will be women workers. The signs so far, however, are that women returners, to take one important source of labour supply, continue to experience downward occupational mobility and appear disproportionately in semi-skilled and unskilled work.

This brief review of the external training climate in a number of countries confirms that certain environmental factors are indeed important in shaping organizational training provisions, but it also highlights that the relationship between them is by no means one of simple manipulation, nor is it free of internal contradiction.

(1) Throughout this text we are careful to distinguish the rhetoric of what could and should be done, from the reality of what actually gets done. Drawing this distinction is especially necessary when assessing the influences of outer context factors upon the training and development plans and practice of individual firms (see box 5.2).

It is one thing to launch extensive training plans within an organization, and even to explicitly link these with strategic, business priorities – as was done at Lucas Industries – but, as the author goes on to state, this case illustrates 'the extreme difficulty of formulating and implementing an HRM approach – in part or in whole – in the context of traditional businesses in Britain which not only inherit whole congeries of expectations and past practices but which, at the same time, have also been facing harsh competitive pressures' (Storey 1992: 116).

(2) In the last decade, Britain's national training deficit has been exposed in very visible terms. While there is some evidence of gradual improvement, doubts remain about how the shortfall should be addressed and how any further improvement might be stimulated and measured. The government's approach has been in non-interventionist: that of providing support and infrastructure; but the apparent reluctance or tardiness of employees to take responsibility for their own training provision poses a dilemma. Government agencies could become more proactive by stipulating national targets of training days per year (Warr 1992), offering financial incentives to firms to invest in HRD, setting statutory requirements to publish details of investment in training and development in company annual reports and establishing training and development in committees based on the model of health and safety committees (Storey 1992: 175). The problem with all such enabling and/or penalizing approaches is that they shift the initiative *away* from the very place where real development takes place. Yet countries which have strong directives set by local and central government to enforce high quality training standards, like Japan (Dore and Sako, 1989), or the directed systems of Germany, France and Sweden, appear to be relatively successful in developing their employees at grass-roots level. From his international comparison of training policies in four OECD countries, Australia, Britain, France and Germany, Noble (1997) concludes that alternatives to levies need to be found to improve the effectiveness and efficiency of training. He suggests a combination of industry-specific programmes to support training and institutional arrangements to facilitate employer involvement in the longer term, with special attention given to the needs of small- and medium-sized organizations. This accords with other reflections on comparative training, and HRM systems more generally. 'The evidence from the most successful of the competitor nations suggests that what we regard as full-blown HRM requires a supportive institutional structure at a national level, so that employers' room for manoeuvre is restricted to investing in people. Simply relying on the market to provide fertile ground for

## BOX 5.2 THE ROLE OF TRAINING IN TURNAROUND

'In the period 1985–8, Lucas has spent around £40 million per annum on training which was equivalent to about 2.5–3 per cent of its total sales revenue. This expenditure was viewed as an 'investment' in that training and development was being called on to act as a major agent of change. The in-company consciousness of the key role of training was high. It was not seen as a poor-relation, peripheral activity, but as a potent source of change. The highlights of the contribution made by training in this company are:

- its link with the total strategy comprising marketing, product engineering, manufacturing systems engineering and business systems;
- the highly evident top management commitment to it;
- its role in developing and executing the competitive achievement plans (CAPs) which every business unit is required to have;
- the installation of business and engineering systems in to the SBUs;
- and the underpinning of business task forces through training on an essentially project-requirement basis.

The Lucas case provides an excellent example of a traditional mainstream company which, in seeking to turn itself around from a loss-making situation, has sought a radical strategic response – part of which has clearly involved a drive to enhance the capabilities and commitment of its human resources through the use of training.

And yet the Lucas case is, at the same time, instructive for another reason. Its training provision – especially its coherent, business-led analysis of the role of that provision – is distinctive for its singularity. Few companies – and this includes the rest of the cases involved in this project – could claim to match the emphasis upon human resource development, which has been shown by Lucas. But despite this lead position, it has to be said that only a little digging around is required to reveal that the impact, when viewed from the stance of the intended recipients of such provision, is, even in this lead case, often minimal. The approach looks coherent, sophisticated and integrated when presented by senior exponents, but it is often experienced rather differently by shop floor workers and indeed by many middle-level managers. Both groups relate how their own recent training experiences have been few and how the investment in-people theme is countermanded by more visible messages of cost cutting and pressure.'
(Storey 1992: 114, 155)

HRM will not produce the results' (Ashton and Felstead 1995: 250).

(3) Another way of stating the internal contradiction of externally inspired and monitored training activity is that training is not necessarily equivalent to learning. (It is for this reason that we devote a later chapter to individual and organizational learning.) Any extra-organizational attempts to catalyze training and development need to take account of (i) the quality of training – not simply the amount, (ii) the context of training – whether, for instance, it is linked to individuals' needs and organizational career paths, and (iii) the scope of learning – recognizing that learning is a lifetime activity, fed by all manner of personal experiences and not tethered to the post of one particular organization. It is encouraging to note that the framework of National Education and Training Targets in Britain appears to acknowledge these issues (Warr 1992).

(4) Any organizational training strategy based on prescriptions needs careful contextualization depending on the sector, product/service and workforce expectations of the organization concerned. Based on interviews carried out in 16 UK companies across several sectors, researchers reported that 'it was difficult to disentangle types of MTD (management training and development) from the strategies adopted by sectors and organizations. In fact, for a number of our larger respondents a major issue was that of locating a training process within a larger process of organizational development. That is, the emphasis was as much, if not more, on the *processual* aspects of implementation as on the content of MDT' (Brown et al. 1989: 80).

This last point leads us onto a detailed consideration of the intra-organizational features that shape the formulation and implementation of HRD at a firm level. Though undoubtedly influential, the external training climate of any given nation or regional bloc, no matter how favourable, does not automatically translate into effective training and learning for individuals and organizations. There are other sets of factors, historical and political, explicit and implicit, cultural and commercial that will shape and sustain such activity. It is to this 'inner context' (Sparrow and Pettigrew 1987) that we now turn in order to discover what choices are available and how they differentiate a strategic from a tactical approach to HRD.

## Aligning Training and Development with Organizational Objectives

Since the early 1980s there has been a growing recognition of the importance of linking training and development – and the practice of HRM generally – to the strategic intent of an organization (e.g. Tichy et al. 1982; Hendry and Pettigrew 1990; Schuler 1992). Indeed, it could be argued that: 'Instead of being activities peripheral to the achievement of corporate objects, the human resources of the organization are seen as a vital factor in corporate planning, and training and development as able to make an important contribution to the achievement of business objectives' (Keep 1989: 114). But how realistic is it to have training and development issues on the strategic agenda? What contribution can such discussions have in the process of business planning? If consideration of training *is* a strategic concern, can it be faithfully translated into VET and HRD activities which 'deliver' the required knowledge, skills and attitudes in a timely fashion? And, finally, can these business outputs be attributed to training initiatives in demonstrable terms? There is no doubting the internal logic of this classic training 'loop', but in this section we examine available evidence as to whether and how it happens.

## Linking training and performance: some choices

Based on in-depth case study analysis of why companies in the UK invested in training Pettigrew et al. (1988) found that whatever the source of pressure, the common feature of the triggers for strategic change was the highlighting of a skill performance gap. However, the researchers discovered that the particular pathways towards a heightened training and development culture varied from firm to firm. This casts doubt on the simplistic view 'that training leads to improved business performance (and that firms can therefore be expected to train more), or that improved business performance leads to increased (and more effective) training simply because firms can fund it more easily' (1988: 41).

There are in fact a range of possible responses that a firm *can* make when a skill gap has been identified (see figure 5.2). The exposure may prompt a concerted attempt to revise overall human resource management embracing such things as recruitment criteria, reward schemes, attempts to reduce attrition, enhanced accountability through appraisals, and increased or decreased use of flexible workers (response 1). A likely but not inevitable outcome of these changes in HRM policy is also a shift in the organization's approach to training (response 2). On the other hand, the performance skills gap may focus specific attention on the

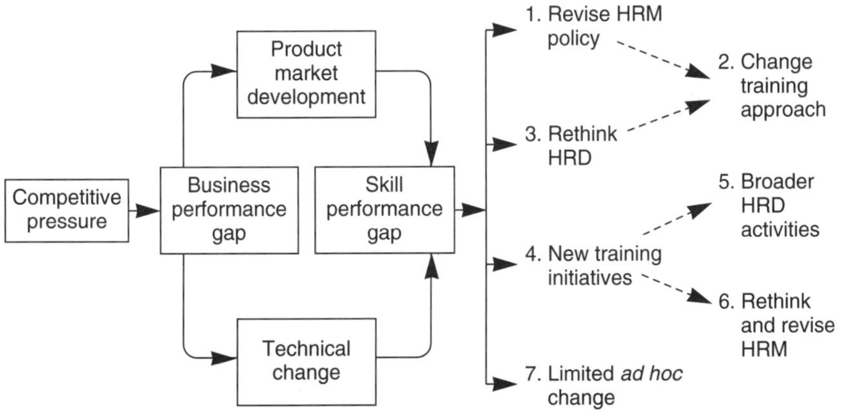


**Figure 5.2** Links between business performance and HR responses
*Source:* Adapted from Hendry, Pettigrew and Sparrow (1988: 41)

organization's human resource development (HRD) (response 3), with higher importance being placed on strategies like graduate recruitment, tiered recruitment or the appraisal process and assessment centres; it is likely that such activities would stimulate demand for off the job training as well as secondments, mentoring and self-development. In some cases the response may be direct and straightforward: the setting up of a one-off training course to plug the exposed skills gap (response 4). It is worth noting, however, that such training efforts *can* act as a spur to wider HRD or HRM activity which in turn begins to shape strategic decisions (responses 5 and 6). A case in point is the management at a car manufacturing plant who, having retrained their production operatives to handle new technology, finds this has repercussions on the career expectations and motivation of their newly skilled shop-floor staff; this, in turn, impacts upon the selection criteria when recruiting apprentices and ultimately influences supervisory and management style.

While this appears staightforward it should be remembered that the plurality of competing interests in a firm will affect its capacity to respond to external pressures and change itself, whether the change involves products, skills, culture or training systems. Strategic processes of change are multi-level activities which rarely accord with the 'commander' model of strategy management (e.g. Bourgeois and Brodwin 1984). Under these circumstances it is always possible that an organization's leadership will choose to ignore, will misperceive or will simply fail to detect the skills gap when it arises (response 7), or construct a case for one of the other responses that does not logically follow from the skills gap diagnosis.

## *The strategic purpose of training: some possibilities*

Many organizations have got to the point of recognizing that training and development is a strategic priority rather than a tactical or knee-jerk response, but choices still remain as to where to direct investment and to what ends. A common conception of strategic training and development. And the one considered as pivotal in figure 5.2 is to see it as a means to *assess and address skills deficiencies* in the organization. At shop floor level recent experience shows that this has frequently meant multi-skilling for craft workers and equipping production operatives with the knowledge and skills necessary to undertake routine maintenance. Upgrading the skills base of *managers* has also been a priority. A UK report on UK companies (Parkinson 1990) found improving managers' competences in core skills such as marketing, finance and production to be highest on the agenda, followed by training in skills and experience necessary to fit individuals for senior management roles. The notion of reducing managerial work to a set of generic competencies has some obvious shortcomings. Such 'narrow vocationalism' can all too easily crowd out any sustained concern with the 'social, moral, political and ideological ingredients of managerial work and the form of educational experience most appropriate to their enhancement and development' (Reed and

Anthony 1992: 601). Nevertheless some pinpointing of the capabilities necessary for staff to perform effectively in their future roles is an essential precursor to investment in training activity. More will be said about methods of diagnosis in chapter 12.

Another strategic purpose of training and development is to act as a *catalyst* for change (a purpose which frequently incorporates attempts to enhance skills as discussed above). This approach is frequently associated with organization leaders seeking to orchestrate cultural change amongst their workforce. Using such methods as participative workshops with vertical cross-sections of staff, quality improvement projects, team building, problem-solving groups, and so on, organizations seek to cultivate a fresh way of viewing themselves, their internal 'customers' and the market in which they compete. For instance, the establishment of the National Health Service Training Authority (NHSTA) in the UK was a classic example of using training and development to attempt a reorientation of the total organization so that customer relations became a key target. However, the introduction of catalytic processes in such complex organizations is by no means simple. In this case there were at least three stakeholder groups (the Management Education Division, the National Education Centres and the District General Managers) each having their own definitions and criteria of successful cultural change (Fox 1989).

The third and most strategic purpose of training and development is an attempt to give the organization *competitive edge*, both through the content of such activities and the way in which they are delivered. Indeed, it could be argued that this is the tacit intention of the first two purposes. More and more organizations are using human resource strategy, for example, as a way of integrating their business planning processes with organization-wide development and human resource activities, from recruitment through to succession planning. For example, because public enterprises cannot register success simply in terms of profit and market share, the way they acquire resources and deliver services is increasingly becoming a driver for competitive advantage. The crucial issue for such organizations and agencies therefore is the definition of their *raison d'être* in a way that is well understood and owned by their staff. Furthermore, the more an organization comes to have a reputation for progressive training and development, the greater its chances of attracting high calibre candidates when recruiting.

A fourth strategic purpose of training and development, and one with a different emphasis from the others, is that of encouraging a *learning climate* in the organization. The focus here is on the learning needs of individuals, guided by organizational goals and undergirded by the belief that within each member of staff is a latent talent waiting to be tapped. Accordingly, the trend is away from structured, taught courses and towards enhanced opportunities for self-development through such methods as on-the-job training, strategic secondments and temporary task forces, or computer-based open-learning systems where training material is provided which may but not necessarily relate to the individual's job. Chapters 10 and 11 explore further the tensions inherent within the concept of the learning organization.

The differing objectives described above are obviously not mutually exclusive; even something as apparently straightforward as implementing new policy guidelines can encompass a whole range of training objectives and methods (box 5.3).

## BOX 5.3 THE ROLE OF TRAINING IN SEXUAL HARASSMENT POLICY IMPLEMENTATION

Apart from removing unpleasantness and disruption in the workplace, sexual harassment policies also have a quantifiable impact, by reducing the likelihood of costly legal liability. Obviously, communication and training are important components of such a policy, and the messages are fairly complex and sophisticated in their reach: highlighting senior management's commitment to eliminating sexual harassment at work; publicising the policy so that staff know the procedures open to victims of harassment; their right to complain and to whom; and that their complaint will be dealt with quickly, fairly and without fear of embarrassment. Communication and training also need to address attitudes (and possibly core values) by challenging misconceptions and prejudice that many mangers have about the question of sexual harassment.

An IRS survey of 26 UK organizations (IRS 1996) found over 90 per cent of the sample had taken steps to publicize their sexual harassment policy, the most frequent methods being: issuing copies of the policy to all staff, publication of the policy in staff manuals, company handbooks and/or staff induction packs, distribution of leaflets and the display of posters and notices. While these media help to raise awareness, they are naturally inadequate – on their own – for dealing with the issue at a practical and attitudinal level. For this reason, a number of organizations, although fewer than might be anticipated, train their staff to help sexual harassment from taking place and to ensure complaints are dealt with effectively where they arise. This demonstrates the significance of training as an aspect of communication. In this instance, raising employees' awareness of sexual harassment as an issue, is likely to increase the volume of complaints; therefore impressing upon staff, especially line managers, the importance of the policy and then training them in how to implement it fairly is crucial. Furthermore, 'training also has legal implications, since the extent to which relevant employees receive training in sexual harassment issues is likely to be an important consideration in determining whether an organisation has taken "reasonably practicable" steps to avoid discrimination under the Sex Discrimination Act 1975' (IRS 1996: 10).

## The strategic positioning of training: some difficulties

Despite the intellectual appeal and the positive nature of many case-study accounts which celebrate the integration of training and development with business strategies and competitive performance, the approach is not unproblematic for a number of practical and conceptual reasons. First, we know that the formulation and implementation of strategy at any level is an uncertain and iterative process 'in which [the] additive accumulation of managerial decisions combined with the triggering effects of environmental disturbances can produce major transformations in the firm' (Whipp et al. 1988: 16). By implication the evolution of a training and development strategy is unlikely to be straightforward. At best, those responsible for deriving such strategies will be 'pattern recognisers . . . who manage a process in which strategies (and visions) can emerge as well as be deliberately conceived' (Mintzberg 1988: 85). Given the 'lead times' required for staging most types of training activity, together with the even longer timescales for organizational benefits to be felt, this poses a real challenge to most training departments reliant on providing institutionalized responses.

Setting in motion training and development activities that enhance collective capability as an instrument of policy, presumes that the organization's strategic intent can be clearly articulated. We know that for many organizations, particularly in the public and non-profit sectors, this is by no means an easy task.

> If agencies are to succeed, they will need a supporting management development strategy which includes techniques for managing careers within agencies for all civil servants. Agencies will also require clearer management objectives. However, given the doubtful utility of the value for money concept, as well as the inseparable link between policy formulation and the delivery of a service, it seems unlikely that the objectives will ever become clearer. An ideology of managerialism based on efficiency is not enough in motivational terms. There must also be a commitment to the public good, because unless there is a moral purpose to public policy, it has no intrinsic worth. (Tyson 1990: 30)

Secondly, even where organizational objectives are stated, there is often a gap between the espoused intentions and values voiced by those initiating and 'sponsoring' the development and the actual perceptions and motivations of those on the receiving end. Indeed, there may be all sorts of reasons why senior managers fund, and individuals participate in, development activities *other than those publicized*. Some of the differing 'agendas' for investing in management training are given in table 5.3, together with the assumptions underlying and the questions/issues prompted by each one (for further discussion, see Lees 1992 and Part IV, 'Managing Change'). Take the example of development centres, designed ostensibly to generate individually tailored career development plans (a functional-performance agenda). It becomes apparent that senior management are also using the opportunity provided by 'assessing' at the development centres to

**Table 5.3** The many agendas of management development (MD)

| *Type* | *Characteristic* | *Assumptions* | *Questions and problems* |
|---|---|---|---|
| Functional performance | Knowledge, skills or attitudes to improve performance, bring about change, increase national 'stock' of trained managers. | • Training needs can be objectively indentified and matched against training.<br>• Role performance can be precisely assessed.<br>• There is a tight 'means–end' link between MD and functional performance. | • Overlooks other factors influencing the the impact of MD on performance.<br>• Danger of a closed loop: corporate funding will only be given to successful MD interventions, therefore choose MD that can demonstrate success in corporate terms. |
| Political reinforcement | MD acts as an extension of the organization's political order.<br><br>Programmes (e.g. culture change) propagate the skills and attitudes believed by the top team as necessary to turn the company around. | • The top team's perception of how organizational performance is to be improved is correct.<br>• The 'recipe for success' can be translated into an MD programme and cascaded down the organization. | • The MD dogmas are frequently dependent on one or two key figures – what happens when they go?<br>• The approach leaves little opportunity to be questioned, and the career costs of doing so may be high. Such a climate defies genuine commitment. |

informally earmark high fliers (a political reinforcement agenda). Although these are not necessarily incompatible objectives of the one event, they constitute a dangerous tightrope to walk: once the hidden managerial agenda becomes known it is likely that candidates will seek to 'perform' rather than be open to reform.

Thirdly, there is as yet little empirical evidence to demonstrate that UK organizations are actually taking a strategic approach to training and developing their staff, despite all the good reasons for doing so (Keep 1989; Parkinson 1990; Storey 1992). Keep (1989) cites a small number of companies who are leaders in the HRM movement in Britain because they have successfully integrated their training and HRD systems into wider business planning and strategy. Yet a closer look at one of them, Lucas Industries, shows that even here, perceptions differ as to the real impact of training (see box 5.2).

Fourthly it may be that many organizations do not explicitly state the *strategic* intent of their training and development effort, and therefore, while a great deal

**Table 5.3** (Continued)

| *Type* | *Characteristic* | *Assumptions* | *Questions and problems* |
|---|---|---|---|
| Compensation | MD's activities are offered as compensation for the deprivations of employment e.g.:<br>• as a welfare substitute<br>• as an alternative focus to an alienating work place<br>• to promote self-development. | • Such activities encourage employees to acquire a habit of learning.<br>• Being sponsored on courses helps motivate managers and engenders commitment to the organization. | • This approach deflects attention from the causes of alienation – offering a palliative instead.<br>• It is deceptive – and morally dubious – to 'use' education in this manner. |
| Psychic defence | MD provides a safe situation in which to discharge anxieties by giving access to/ participation in more strategic matters. | • Managers need a social system to defend their psyche against persecutory anxiety arising from their competitive career drives.<br>• Apparently fair appraisal systems, target setting and ordered management succession help reduce the fear of disorder and chaos if latent competition were to break out. | • Would greater self-development and self-determination in the workplace necessarily lead to unbridled and selfish anarchy?<br>• Only a few MD activities would typically provide an opportunity for such displacement. |

*Source:* Adapted from Lees (1992: 89–105).

of such activity is perhaps being carried out, because it has little demonstrable reference to broader organizational goals it is disregarded by commentators as tactical and non-strategic. However, just because the links with organizational objectives are muffled or unstated it does not necessarily follow that valuable development is not taking place albeit outside the organization's frame of reference. Herein lies one of the key dilemmas of strategically orientated training and development: the typically unquestioned assumption that strategic equates to top-down.

Fifthly, there is the difficulty of closing the loop and demonstrating the value to the business of training and development. Attempts have been made to evaluate the cost benefits of training activity ranging from fairly sophisticated utility calculations (Smith 1992) to more broadbrush deductions: 'making some quite plausible assumptions some 20 years ago, I calculated that if a one-week residential training course increased a manager's performance by more than 0.5%, it was more profitable for the company to train than not to train' (Everard 1991: 26). But, in a sense such equations miss the point. 'Evaluation is about making value judgements as well as technical ones and it is about power, since action may involve, at the least, persuading others of the rightness of one's values first, through to imposing one's values onto them' (Fox 1989: 205). So it is that different stakeholders will have their own interpretation as to why the training evaluation is being undertaken, have competing views as to which evaluation criteria should be used, hold their own pet preferences as to which methods are best employed to fulfil these assessments and possibly have opposing opinions as to which methods are valid. Finally and unavoidably, various stakeholder groups will differ in the weight they place on various evaluation outcomes, depending largely on how they, and the constituent group(s) they represent, are affected by any ensuing changes as compared with other stakeholder groups.

In other words the way HR interventions are evaluated will be influenced by the perceived fairness of the new normative order (how has my access to rewards, status, authority and power bases been affected?) and social comparison with reference groups (how have reciprocity and exchange relations with significant others been altered?) (Carnall 1990). Given the complexities associated with such analysis it is perhaps not surprising that so few organizations carry out systematic evaluations of their training and development activities, and even when evaluation research is available it is often ignored (Legge 1984).

## The Influence of Senior Managers on Training and Development

Training is a political activity. This is because learning is about discovery of new knowledge (possibly privy to the organization) and concepts (potentially threatening to the uninitiated); it is about access to training courses (who gets selected and who does not); it is about career paths and plans (which secondments are developmental and which signify plateauing); and it is about enlightenment (being inspired by a fresh, corporate approach) or disillusionment (realizing that personal and corporate values do not match). In other words learning is as much about where the dominant cultural coalition of an organization is located as it is about the acquisition of new skills and techniques. Usually, but not always, this cultural coalition is synonymous with the senior management. In this section we examine the influence of senior managers from two perspectives: as shapers of prevailing culture and as sponsors of training and development initiatives.

## *Senior managers as shapers of culture*

We deal more fully with culture and its relationship to human resource strategies elsewhere (chapter 15), but the distinctive linking of prevailing culture and the development of human capabilities will be briefly examined here. In many ways culture is a central, all-pervasive reality of organizational life, encompassing the spectrum of attitudes, values, norms, style and cues – verbal, unspoken, visible, subtle, deliberate, unintended – that make up the distinctive feel of an enterprise. Culture has been aptly described as 'the predisposition to behave in a certain way'. Nowhere are people's cultural values more apparent than in the area of training and development. Few managers would argue with the logical implications of declining market share, most department heads would revise their operating plans in the light of budgetary analysis, but when it comes to changing the way others (or more importantly, we) behave the impelling logic seems to melt away! The point is well made by Brooks and Bate (1994). On the basis of an in-depth, ethnographic study of one of the newly-formed agencies in the UK civil service, they found any attempt to change from above was neutralized and frustrated by the cultural infrastructure at the local level (1994: 177). So when discussing 'prevailing' culture we should be careful not to assume that this is equivalent to the culture of senior management nor neglect the complicating objectives and vested interests of other *non*-prevailing works groups, and the impact these will have on internal development policies. This poses a problem for organizations pursuing HRM policies that are intended to integrate with their business strategies. Particularly for diversified corporations, it is likely that different policies will emerge for different divisions or subsidiaries which mutually reinforce their own business strategy, but possibly contradict HRM policies pursued in other business units or the overall policy priorities of the corporation. On this situation Legge comments:

> Strong unit sub-cultures, a claimed ingredient of competitive advantage, might well develop. A problem would only arise if there developed a perceived requirement to integrate two or more sub-units in a manner that required integration at operating level and, hence of personnel. Then not only would the difficulty of merging distinct sub-cultures be likely, but perceptions of potential inequalities and inconsistencies between erstwhile autonomous units' HRM policies might undermine the trust and commitment that is supposed to develop from perceptions of congruence. (Legge 1989: 31)

Furthermore cultures are not static; the prevailing culture may appear overbearing and feel relentless, particularly to temporarily disenfranchised groups, but shifting centres of cultural gravity are becoming increasingly commonplace. In some cases this is due to relatively 'aggressive' board level buy-outs and acquisitions; in other cases it follows decentralizing and/or devolving initiatives where responsibility and empowerment is deliberately pushed out to the further reaches, or down to the lower levels, of the organization.

Training and development is far from being a neutral process where the only resistance trainees have to absorbing new knowledge or acquiring new skills is their individual capacity or learning style. Invariably learning is 'a politicised process where new knowledge, systems and techniques are viewed suspiciously, even rejected because they are seen to represent the priorities of others whose priorities are distinct and possibly opposed, or to result in, a re-allocation of organizational resources, or a weakening of a section's traditional power-base' (Salaman and Butler 1990). The implications of this is discussed further in chapter 10.

Clearly, then, the notion that senior managers can be the shapers of culture, using training interventions to generate and reinforce their particular vision of the business is too simplistic. Undoubtedly senior individuals can be influential, and as a coherent top team (less common) their collective will can be yet more determining of organizational norms and values, but we have seen that this influence is neither one-way, nor inevitable. A better analogy might be to view senior managers as cultural conductors – giving a pivotal lead to the assembled 'players' while simultaneously being dependent on their assembled creativity and responsiveness; the interplay between conductor and 'orchestra' being a subtle amalgam of motivation, loyalty and expertise, some of which will be won and/or enhanced through training but much of it attributable to latent talents, predisposition, personal skill portfolio and the fickle chemistry of the moment.

## *Senior managers as sponsors of training and development*

Is the role of senior management more straightforward when it comes to discovering how an organization chooses and sustains its strategy for training and wider development activity? More specifically, how do dominant coalitions influence such decisions?

Again, the best evidence of policy and practice comes from the report produced for the Training Agency (Pettigrew et al. 1988). The researchers uncovered a number of factors present in the 20 companies they investigated that either work towards or against the adoption of fresh and sustained training approaches (figure 5.3). As we have already seen, technological or product market changes are driving forces for introducing a training strategy, unless the task skills identified relate to a small number of simple, standardized products or services requiring short learning time. In this instance a dose of 'top up' training may suffice, and mitigate against a concerted strategy. The non-availability of required skills in the external labour market, and the relative economic stability, will also promote training. The items listed in the 'external support for training' box we have already discussed, noting however that there are many historical, political and cultural factors that threaten to blunt training provision by organization in the UK, especially when compared with other European partners (e.g. Purcell 1989).

Among the features of the internal labour market that promote training are

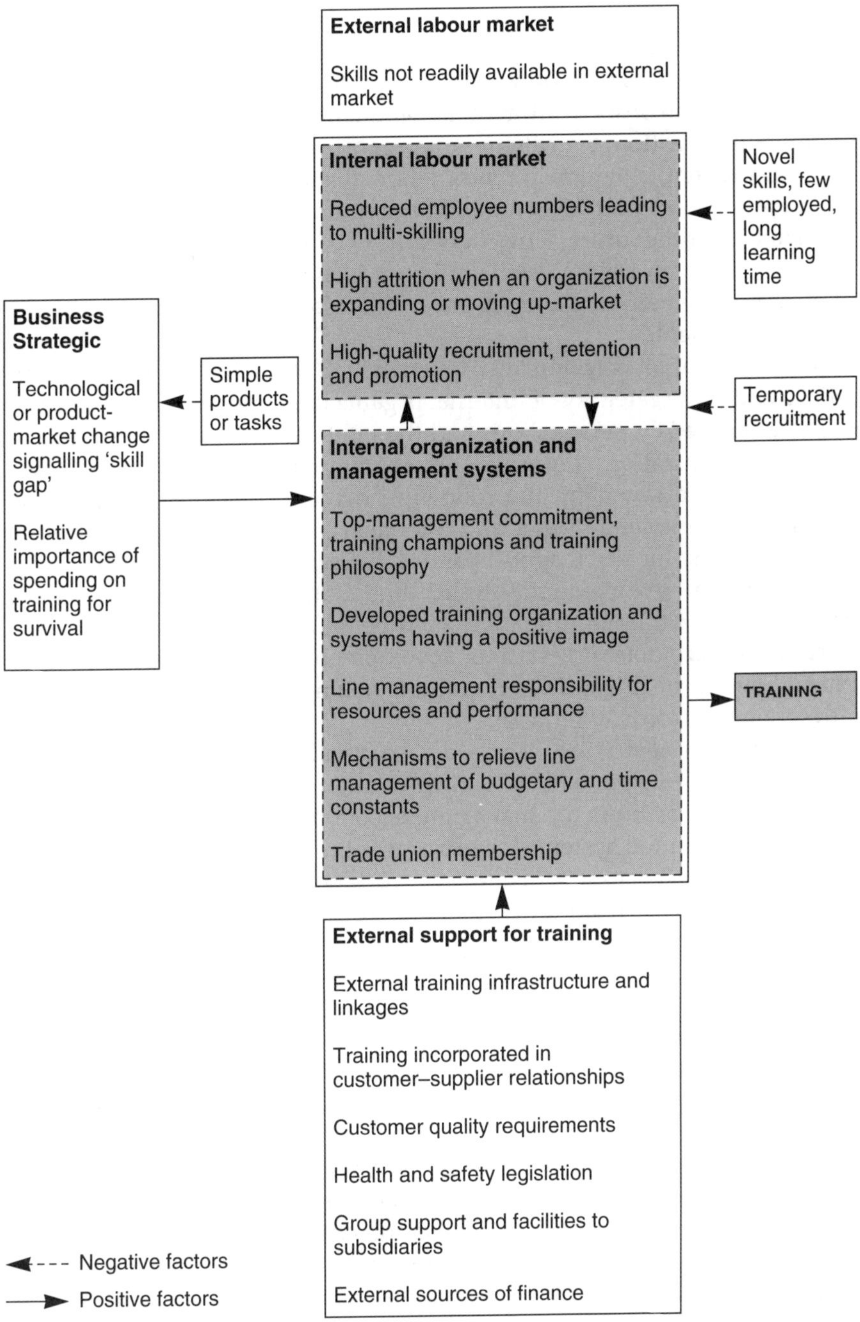
External labour market
Skills not readily available in external market
Internal labour market
Reduced employee numbers leading to multi-skilling
High attrition when an organization is expanding or moving up-market
High-quality recruitment, retention and promotion
Novel skills, few employed, long learning time
Business Strategic
Technological or product-market change signalling 'skill gap'
Relative importance of spending on training for survival
Simple products or tasks
Temporary recruitment
Internal organization and management systems
Top-management commitment, training champions and training philosophy
Developed training organization and systems having a positive image
Line management responsibility for resources and performance
Mechanisms to relieve line management of budgetary and time constants
Trade union membership
TRAINING
External support for training
External training infrastructure and linkages
Training incorporated in customer–supplier relationships
Customer quality requirements
Health and safety legislation
Group support and facilities to subsidiaries
External sources of finance
Negative factors
Positive factors

**Figure 5.3** Interaction of positive and negative factors on training
*Source:* Pettigrew, Hendry and Sparrow (1988)

moves towards the multi-skilling of production and maintenance staff, typically associated with reducing numbers of employees and expanding the tasks/skills of those that remain. Also an organization may adopt a positive policy of training and development in order to attract a higher quality staff, particularly if it has had problems with attrition. Thirdly, when organizations have a tradition of high quality recruitment, retention and promotion, the training of higher level skills is a viable option when preparing for and undergoing change because it represents an investment for the future. However, if the need is for specialist skills for a few and the lead time on training skills in-house is long, organizations are likely to opt for external recruitment and/or use contract labour, thus removing the need for HRD investment.

A further crucial set of factors instrumental in the triggering of training activity are those under the category of 'internal organization and management system'. These refer to the key personalities and the political decision-making processes within the organization concerned. A positive culture towards the value of training will be assisted by the following driving forces; first, the presence of 'training champions' especially amongst senior management; second, adequate systems for the diagnosis and delivery of training activities, and for these systems to have credibility; third, line managers being encouraged and supported in their training initiatives, and being relieved of the budgetary and opportunity costs of releasing staff for development; and fourth, internal pressure for such things as health and safety training (from trade unions) or equal opportunities training (from EO groups).

When Pettigrew et al. (1988) assessed the equivalent organizational triggers for human resource development, as against vocational education and training, the driving forces – apart from top management commitment to development – were found to be: integrated systems for recruitment, training and placement, awareness of multiple levels to secure effective work performance, the mentoring and monitoring of careers from an early stage, recognizing developmental opportunities within normal management process, and the provision of open learning facilities.

In both cultivating education and training, it can be seen that senior management (or the equivalent dominant coalition) influence a number of these driving forces. It is they who define the nature of training and development, and evidence from the National Health Service in the UK (box 5.4) shows how powerful such definitions can be.

However, no single factor of those depicted in figure 5.3 is sufficient by itself to create a positive training climate within an organization. It tends to be the case that those investing in training and development for their staff do so because a *number* of the driving forces described above are in place, and because they are relatively uninhibited by particular negative factors.

It goes without saying that organization leaders need to endorse training and development initiatives if only to release the resources and budget necessary to run them. But this is not enough. There needs to be a consistency between the outputs that development programmes teach and cultivate, and the observed actions and behaviour of the senior managers who 'sponsor' them. Unless indi-

**BOX 5.4 SENIOR PERCEPTIONS OF TRAINING IN THE NHS**

'Given the difficulty of evaluating management development, beliefs about the value of management development are shaped either by a strong organizational culture or by personal experience and that chief executives play a key role in shaping culture. Many United Kingdom executives have not been to university, most have not had extensive formal management development and most explain their career progress in terms of person factors rather than management development. They are therefore unlikely to shape a culture which emphasises management development. At best, they will pay lip service to the idea, but devolve responsibility for implementation to the personnel/management development function.

The managers in question can then be expected to formalise and bureaucratise management development as a means of ensuring control. The resulting formal systems will receive general support but will typically be seen as slightly detached from the mainstream of key organizational activity. Management development will be defined in terms of courses, which will be perceived as *a good thing*, but not the key to organizational and career success. Once such formal activities and beliefs have become established, even sophisticated management developers will find it difficult to change the system.'

Guest et al. (1992: 78–9)

viduals are convinced that senior management value and practice the skills and attitudes being advocated by such activities, they will exhibit instrumental commitment at best (Ogbonna and Wilkinson 1990). In addition, if senior management ignore or misread the cultural centre of gravity themselves, the training initiatives they launch are likely to avail little in the long term, and possibly indifference and cynicism in the short term.

## Evidence for Strategic Approaches and Outcomes

In this section we review the evidence, such as it is, for a more strategic approach to training and development. Is the macro climate now more conducive to training and development activities? Are organizations investing more in their training effort than they used to? Is there evidence that training interventions are more strategic in nature, and is it possible to say whether these result in organization-wide benefits?

## *The incidence of training and development*

There is reason to believe that more people are benefitting from training in organizations. A large-scale, nationally representative survey of 60,000 UK households and interviews with 157 employers asked respondents whether they had taken part in any education or training connected with their job in the previous four weeks: 'The figure derived for training incidence showed a marked increase in the number and proportion of workers receiving job-related training throughout the 1980s; the number almost doubled and the proportion rose from 9.25 in 1984 to 15.4% in 1990' (Ashton and Felstead 1995: 246). This figure was sustained, with a slight fall in training incidence, over the following three recessionary years to 1993. However, while the gap is closing, workers in professional occupations are still five times more likely to receive job-related training as their unskilled counterparts. As part of the same study, interviews with training managers in 1992 revealed that over the previous two-year period 43 per cent had increased their training activities, 27 per cent reported no change and 25 per cent reported cutbacks. The fact that the main determinants of training appeared to be 'push' factors such as BS5750, health and safety requirements, and occupational regulations leads the authors to conclude that such training is still fairly instrumental and is not consonent with a widespread adoption of HR strategies.

Investors in People (IiP) might be categorized as another push factor. It was launched by local Training and Enterprise Councils in the UK in 1990 as a stimulus to investment in more strategically focused and monitored training and development across all organizations. The initiative had a modest beginning: by June 1992 there were 63 companies who had been recognized as having achieved the National Standard, with a further 600 or so who had made an overt commitment to pursuing accreditation. At the time of writing these figures have mushroomed. The IiP organization report well over 8,000 company recognitions, with 21,350 commitments (*IiP Management Report, November 1997*). This means that nearly 40 per cent of the UK workforce are actively pursuing or have been successful in securing accreditation. Even if some of the motivation and somewhat mechanistic methodology associated with IiP has attracted criticism, it is noteworthy that so many organizations and employees are being prompted to consider and assess the strategic value of their development activities.

Britain's system of management development, both in its own context and in comparison to its main competitors, was found to have substantial weaknesses by a series of reports in 1987/8. In a part follow-up to one of these (Constable and McCormick 1987) a major study ten years later found a far more positive picture (Thompson et al. 1997). Compared to an average of about one day's training per year per manager a decade previously, this study revealed a very marked improvement in management training provision with an overall mean of 5.5 days across all organizations in 1996. Interestingly, the primary determinants of training activity were less structural factors (like size, ownership and sector of organization, or degree of centralization), and more internal processes (the priority given to MD, who takes responsibility for MD, and the formulation of training and development policy statements). These factors were also causally related to the perceived achievement of MD objectives and the perceived impact of MD on the organization. Vocational qualifications was the single most significant variable associated with reported amounts of training, and Investors in People was most strongly associated with the existence of a policy statement.

## BOX 5.5 MANAGEMENT TRAINING IN THE UK AND JAPAN

'The main contrast we found was between the relative robustness and stability of the Japanese management development systems and the relative vulnerability and instability of the British. This central divide had a number of aspects and consequences. The Japanese managers at all levels were able to describe the training and development systems in their companies; this was often simply not the case at all in the British companies. There were dramatic lurches in the British cases: elaborate suites of training courses were designed and refined for one period, only to be totally disbanded the next. Self-development would be the main emphasis at one time and then it would be more or less disregarded at another. As a consequence, line managers were confused and sometime cynical.

Management development specialists were anxious to stress that their cue was taken almost entirely from "the business strategy" or "needs of the business". When they drew their mental models of the place of management development in diagrammatic form they invariably placed business strategy or business needs at the centre or top of the figure. They tended to make a point of being rather dismissive of 'external' influences emanating from government, the civil service, the MCI and, to some extent, business schools as well as other vested interests whom they perceived as having wrong-headed or political agendas. Now, given this central focus on business need it is rather easier to understand that adaptability was equally prized. Hence, there was little compunction about making a clean sweep of a suite of training programmes or the closure of a management training college.

What was going on here was as a result of a deep-seated conceptualization of management development as necessarily a second-order, downstream, activity. The (turbulent) marketplace and the business strategy(ies) designed to engage with it were seen as unequestioningly paramount. In Japan, by contrast, there was less of a tendency to begin all conversations about the place of management development with a reaffirmation of the primacy of the market. There appeared to be a more securely based belief in the enduring value of *growing managers* in order to *meet* the changing character of market conditions.'

(Storey et al. 1997: 206–7)

How does management training now compare with competitor nations singled out by Handy (1987)? Research was undertaken to investigate at an in-depth level training provision in eight companies, comprising four matched UK–Japanese pairings (Lucas/Sumitomo Electric; NatWest Bank/Mitsui; Tesco/Jusco; British Telecom/NTT) (Storey et al. 1997). To the researchers' surprise, British managers reported more training and valued it more highly than their Japanese counterparts. But this finding disguised more fundamental differences, as box 5.5 shows.

The statement in box 5.5 suggests that, for all the encouraging signs of growing investment in, and incidence of, training, especially management training, its role as a *strategic* HR intervention is still dubious. This is because training is regarded, in the UK context at least, largely as a tool to achieve senior management ambitions; this is in contrast to viewing employees as a strategic resource whose development in the workplace will lead to the long-term sustainability and capability.

## The strategic impact of training and development

One of the hallmarks of SHRM, as against personnel management, is the link between human resource and business strategies. In recent years there has been a concerted attempt to demonstrate that investment in a given 'bundle' of HR policies, including training and development, leads to business benefits. The following are some examples.

- The most significant predictor of success in export performance among 388 US manufacturers was their human research strategy. For instance, if an organization gave substantial rewards to those who undertook international activities, emphasized this when recruiting and promoting managers, supported training and development in international business and included this as a dimension of any review of performance, then its exports were more likely to be successful (Gomez-Meija 1988).

- A research team examined the recruitment and selection, management development, performance appraisal, rewards and recognition, and career planning processes of 49 companies operating in the engineering and electronics sectors. The strongest relationships to emerge from the investigation was a clear positive relationship between financial performance and the degree of integration between corporate strategy and the human resource management functions in practice. In other words, the return on capital of a firm with a higher degree of integration between the human resource management function and corporate strategy is expected to be substantially above the average within its sector. There were also significant positive relationships between the return on capital and the degree of integration *between* human resource management systems when the human resource management focus was development, appraisal and career planning, and in proactive organizations (Fox and McLeay 1991).

- The HR strategies of 30 mills were compared and characterized as *commitment systems* where attempts were made to shape employee behaviours and attitudes by forging links between organizational and employee goals, or *control systems* where the goal of HR was to reduce direct labour costs, or improve efficiency by compliance with specified rules and procedures, and by basing employee rewards on measurable output criteria. The mills with higher commitment systems (including higher level of employee involvement in managerial decisions, formal participation programmes, training in group problem-solving etc.) had higher productivity, lower scrap rates and lower employee turnover than those with control systems (Arthur 1994).
- A study of nearly 1000 US firms from a broad range of industries and firm sizes examined the statistical impact of 13 HRM practices referred to as 'high-performance work practices' (e.g. a high percentage of the workforce participate in Quality Circles, have access to profit-sharing schemes, receive training, receive formal appraisals, are compensated on the basis of their appraisals, and so on). Firms employing these practices registered significantly lower staff turnover, higher staff productivity and better financial performance over both the short and long-term than those firms who did not adopt these practices (Huselid 1995).
- Across 590 firms in the US, progressive HRM practices, including selectivity in staffing, training and incentive compensation, are positively related to perceptual measures of organizational performance. These effects were similar in profit and not-for-profit organizations (Delaney and Huselid 1996).
- Competence-based management development had a quantifiable impact upon the business results of 16 UK organizations. Improvement in performance was found to be most significant where management development was linked to organizational strategy and where human resource development systems and processes adopted a management standards framework (Winterton and Winterton 1997).

Naturally, these examples are selective, and it is likely that a similar catalogue could be compiled where training policies (as a dimension of broader SHRM) were found to have no such demonstrable effects. However, three things are noteworthy about these and similar reports. First, they show that training and development activities are attracting high-profile attention as HR interventions. This serves to shift the focus from the somewhat sterile debates about methods for evaluating training courses to the more strategic issue of whether investment in training and development has an overall organizational impact. Secondly, the way the research is being conducted shows a great deal of sophistication. For instance, the Fox and McLeay team were careful to distinguish *intent* (HRM systems), *practice* (the reality of how staff are recruited, promoted, rewarded and developed) and the internal *coherence* of such activities; the Gomez–Mejia study assessed business results 30 months after initial measures of HR were gathered, so giving time for their impact to be felt; the research of the steel mills by Arthur was a deliberate attempt to distinguish *contingent* HR systems from universal, one-best-way approaches; and the Wintertons' in-depth case studies did not rely on senior management views alone – they also interviewed line managers and members of management work teams, triangulating all this with documentary evidence from the companies concerned. Such approaches compare favourably with, and the findings are likely to be more robust and generalizable than, single-organization case studies.

Thirdly, such studies are beginning to reveal, albeit in rather crude terms, quantifiable effects that can be readily understood and appreciated by non-HR specialists in the boardroom. A further boost to this trend comes from the 'balanced scorecard' framework. Popularized by Kaplan and Norton (1992), this approach elevates employees, alongside investors and customers, as a group of key stakeholders who have a need for the organization to be a healthy place to work as measured by employee and organizational outcomes. Viewing organizations in these terms prompts questions such as: do HR practices make a difference to business results? In what ways can HR practices add value to business performance? What are the most appropriate measures that drive business performance? (see Yeung and Berman 1997). When applied to the training and development domain, Ulrich (1997) summarizes some possible measures that organizations might adopt to audit this aspect of their balanced scorecard: number of training days/programmes per employee per year, cost per trainee hour, number of staff with development plans, percentage of payroll spent on training, payroll expense per employee, time for programme design and efficiency of training registration. It should be noted, however, that almost all of these concern 'input' measures or costs, and as such tell us very little about the quality of the training and even less about on-the-job, incidental, unprogrammed skill-formation activities. Such measures also fail to capture the impact of all this on the commitment and motivation of the staff involved.

## Conclusions and Summary

In this chapter we have sought to examine whether training and development can be seen as a truly strategic human resource intervention and, if it can, whether organizations are adopting this strategic approach in practice. Certainly the claim is that if the term 'human resource management' means anything then it should herald a radically different way in which organizations treat and develop their employees. It would appear that the macro climate is somewhat more conducive to investing in training and development than, say, a decade ago; although the socio-political drivers seem to be stronger in some countries than others. It was noted that because these drivers are so closely connected to their educational, institutional and cultural contexts, it is unwise to attempt to indiscriminately copy or transfer another country's training policies.

Research was reviewed which seems to demonstrate that where the business and training strategies of a given organization are aligned, there is more likelihood of positive performance outcomes. In contrast to the 'armchair' HR theorizing of recent years, there is now a growing body of empirical evidence to support this. The notion of alignment is problematic however. Just as the quality and extent of training provision at a national level is heavily influenced by the socio-political context, the same can be argued for training provision at an organizational level:

> By treating training provision in basically value neutral terms, the social dimension of skill and skill formation is neglected [. . .] The essential significance of training under HRM is not that workers should be provided with cognitive and non-cognitive capabilities, but that the knowledge they acquire should be at *management's disposal*, that it should be used in the pursuit of management's defined goals [. . .] the treatment of training and development within the HRM literature implies a 'positive-sum-game' in which employers benefit from a more committed, motivated and flexible workforce while employees experience psychological rewards from more interesting, varied and challenging work. There is a risk, however, of oversimplifying the causal connections between training provision and performance outcomes. (Heyes 1998: 99, italics in original)

More training is happening. This training is undoubtedly less tactical and piecemeal in many instances than it used to be. The impact of this training as a strategic HR intervention is being talked about. Some studies go further and claim quantifiable benefits derived from investment in training. Nevertheless, the *causal* relationship between training and development and business benefits remains elusive. Indeed, as Mueller (1996) notes, the ability to do this may well prove to be one of the rare, inimitable HR capabilities that allows a firm to remain competitive:

> Human resource policies or practices are unlikely to be truly scarce and inimitable resources, but rather what constitutes a strategic asset is a higher-order capability of evaluating their contributions to performance. This could be rephrased as managerial knowledge about causal relationships which typically would reside in the senior management echelons. (Mueller 1996: 763)

## Key Points

- Strategic training and development can be conceived as different things by different organizations, sometimes as an ad hoc activity, sometimes as a response to a complex and changing environment, sometimes even as a strategic device for attempting to change that environment.
- The value of training will be defined differently by the various stakeholders *within* an organization. Whether these respective agendas and rationales for training and development are primarily functional, political, legitimatory, symbolic or defensive (Lees 1992) will determine the design, meaning and outputs sought for any particular training activity.
- What distinguishes a strategic approach to training is that it can rarely be divorced from the wider competitive and cultural context of the organization. The prevailing

coalition will be especially influential upon the perceived value of, and funding for, training in an organization.

- There is growing evidence that training and development is enjoying a higher profile in organizations, and some assertions that strategic training interventions (especially when part of an HR 'package') can bring business benefits.
- Two concepts remain problematic: the possibility of aligning corporate and individual goals within a given training intervention, and then connecting this causally with organizational outcomes.

## Discussion Questions

1. Which factors, external to an organization, are most influential in determining its training policy and provision?
2. What are some of the reasons that organizations invest in management training? What assumptions lie behind these reasons about how people learn, and what they should learn?
3. Explain why training is a political activity.
4. How important is the role of senior management in the effective implementation of training activities?
5. What are the difficulties with attributing business outcomes to training and development?

## References

Arthur, J. (1994) 'Effects of human resource systems on manufacturing performance', *Academy of Management Journal*, vol. 37, 670–87.

Ashton, D. and Felstead, A. (1995) 'Training and development', in J. Storey (ed.) *Human Resource Management: A critical text*, London: Routledge.

Beardwell, I. and Holden, L. (1994) *Human Resource Management: A contemporary perspective*, London: Pitman.

Beer, M., Spector, B., Lawrence, P. R., Mills, D. Q. and Walton, R. (1984) *Managing Human Assets: the Ground Breaking Harvard Business School Program*, London: Macmillan.

Benjamin, G. and Mabey, C. (1990, 2nd edn) 'Facilitating radical change', in C. Mabey and B. Mayon-White (eds) *Managing Change*, London: Paul Chapman Publishing.

Bougeois, L. and Brodwin, D. (1984) 'Strategic implementation: Five approaches to an elusive phenomenon', *Strategic Management Journal*, vol. 5, 241–64.

Bournois, F. (1992) 'France', in C. Brewster, A. Hegewisch, L. Holden and T. Lockhart (eds) *The European HRM Guide*, London: Academic Press.

Brewster, C., Hegewisch, A., Holden, L., and Lockhart, T. (eds) (1992), *The European HRM Guide*, London: Academic Press.

Brooks, I. and Bate, P. (1994) 'The problems of effecting change within the British Civil Service: A cultural perspective', *British Journal of Management*, vol. 5, 177–90.

Brown, H., Peccei, R., Sandberg, S., and Welchman, R. (1989) 'Management training and development: In search of an integrated approach', *Journal of General Management*, vol. 15, no. 1, 69–82.

Carnall, C. (1990) *Managing Change*, London: Routledge.

Constable, J. and McCormick, R. (1987) *The Making of British Managers*, London: B.I.M.

Delaney, J. and Huselid, M. (1996) 'The impact of human resource management practices on perceptions of organisational performance', *Academy of Management Journal*, vol. 39, no. 4, 949–69.

Dore, R. and Sako, M. (1989) *How the Japanese Learn to Work*, London: Routledge.

Evans, P. and Doz, Y. (1989) 'The dualistic organisation', in P. Evans, Y. Doz and P. Laurent (eds) *Human Resource Management in International Firms*, London: Macmillan.

Everard, B. (1991) 'The costs and benefits of training', *Training and Development*, December, 26–8.

Fox, S. (1989) 'The politics of evaluating management development', *Management Education and Development*, vol. 20, no. 3, 191–207.

—— and McLeay, S. (1991) 'An approach to researching managerial labour markets: HRM, corporate strategy and financial performance in UK manufacturing', Paper presented to the British Academy of Management Conference, September, Bath University.

Gomez-Meija, L. (1988) 'The role of human resource strategy in export performance: A longitudinal study', *Strategic Management*, vol. 9, 493–505.

Guest, D., Peccei, R., and Rosenthal, P. (1992) 'Management development and career success' in K. Bradley (ed.) *Human Resource Management: people and success*. Aldershot: Dartmouth.

Handy, C. (1987) 'The making of managers: A report on management education, training and development in the US, West Germany, France, Japan and the UK', National Economic Development Office.

Hendry, C. and Pettigrew, A. (1990) 'Human resource management: An agenda for the 1990s', *The International Journal of Human Resource Management*, vol. 1, no. 1, 17–43.

——, —— and Sparrow, P. (1990) 'Linking strategic change, competitive performance and human resource management: Results of an empirical study', in R. Mansfield (ed.) *Frontiers of Management*, London: Routledge.

Heyes, J. (1998) 'Training and development at an agro-chemical plant', in C. Mabey, D. Skinner and T. Clark (eds) *Experiencing Human Resource Management*, London: Sage.

Hilb, M. (1992) 'The challenge of management development in Western Europe in the 1990s', *The International Journal of Human Resource Management*, vol. 3, no. 3, 575–83.

Huselid, M. (1995) 'The impact of human resource management practices on turnover, productivity and corporate financial performance', *Academy of Management Journal*, vol. 38, no. 3, 635–72.

IRS (1996) 'Assessing employee involvement strategies', *Employment Trends*, vol. 614, London: Industrial Relations Service, 4–12.

Jackson, L. (1992) 'Achieving change in business culture', *Management Decision*, vol. 30, no. 6, 149–55.

Kaplan R. and Norton, D. (1992) 'The balanced scorecard – measures that drive performance', *Harvard Business Review*, Jan./Feb., 71–9.

Keep, E. (1989) 'Corporate training strategies: The vital component?' in J. Storey (ed.) *New Perspectives on Human Resource Management*, London: Routledge.

Lane, C. (1989) 'New technology and changes in work organization' in C. Lane (ed.) *Management and Labour in Europe*, Aldershot: Edward Elgar, 163–95.

Larsen, H. (1994) 'Key issues in training and development', in C. Brewster and A. Hegewisch (eds) *Policy and Practice in European Human Resource Management*, London: Routledge.

Lees, S. (1992) 'Ten faces of management development', *Management Education and Development*, vol. 23, no. 2, 89–105.

Legge, K. (1984) *The Evaluation of Planned Organizational Change*, London: Academic Press.
—— (1989) 'Human resource management: A critical analysis', in J. Storey (ed.) *New Perspectives in Human Resource Management*, London: Routledge, 19–40.
Mangham, I. and Silver, D. (1986) 'Management training: Context and practice', ESRC/DTI Report, School of Management, University of Bath.
Mintzberg, H. (1988) 'Crafting strategy', *McKinsey Quarterly*, Summer, 71–89.
Mueller, F. (1996) 'Human resources as strategic assets: an evolutionary resource-based theory', *Journal of Management Studies*, vol. 33, no. 6, 757–85.
Naulleau, G. and Harper, J. (1993) 'A comparison of British and French management cultures: Some implications for management development in each country', *Management Education and Development*, vol. 24, no. 1, 14–25.
Noble, C. (1997) 'International comparisons of training policies', *Human Resource Management Journal*, vol. 7, no. 1, 5–18.
Ogbonna, E. and Wilkinson, B. (1990) 'Corporate strategy and corporate culture: The view from the checkout', *Personnel Review*, vol. 19, no. 4, 9–15.
Parkinson, S. (1990) 'Management development's strategic role', *Journal of General Management*, vol. 16, no. 2, 63–75.
Pettigrew, A., Hendry, C., Sparrow, P. (1988) 'The role of vocational education and training in employers skills supply strategies', Training Agency report in conjunction with Coopers and Lybrand, Sheffield.
Poole, M. and Mansfield, R. (1992) 'Managers' attitudes to human resource management: Rhetoric and reality', in P. Blyton and P. Turnbull (eds) *Reassessing Human Resource Management*, London: Sage.
Purcell, J. (1989) 'The impact of corporate strategies on human resource management', in J. Storey (ed.) *New Perspectives on Human Resource Management*, London: Routledge.
Reed, M. and Anthony, P. (1992) 'Professionalising management and managing professionalisation: British management in the 1980s', *Journal of Management Studies*, vol. 29, no. 5, September, 591–613.
Rose, R. and Wignanek, G. (1991) *Training Without Trainers? How Germany Avoids Britain's Supply Side Bottleneck*, Anglo-German Foundation.
Salaman, G. and Butler, J. (1990) 'Why managers won't learn', *Management Education and Development*, vol. 21, no. 3, 183–91.
Schuler, R. (1992) 'Strategic HRM: Linking the people with the strategic needs of the business', *Organisational Dynamics*, Summer, 18–32.
Smith, M. (1992) 'Utility and human resource management', *Supplementary Readings 2, B884 Human Resource Strategies*, Open University, Walton Hall.
Sparrow, P. and Pettigrew, A. (1987) 'Britain's training problems: The search for a strategic human resources management approach', *Human Resource Manager*, vol. 26, no. 1, 109–27.
Storey, J. (1992) *Developments in the Management of Human Resources*, Oxford: Blackwell.
——, Edwards, P., and Sisson, K. (1997) *Managers in the Making: Careers, Development and Control in Britain and Japan*, London: Sage.
Tayeb, M. (1993) 'English culture and business organizations' in D. Hickson (ed.) *Management in Western Europe: Society, Culture and Organization in Twelve Nations*, Berlin: DeGruyter.
Tichy, N., Fombrun, C., and Devanna, M. (1982) 'Strategic human resource management', *Sloan Management Review*, vol. 23, no. 2, Winter.
Thomson, A., Storey, J., Mabey, C., Gray, C., Farmer, E., and Thomson, R. (1997) *A Portrait of Management Development*, London: Institute of Management.

Tyson, S. (1990) 'Training civil servants into managers', *Money and Management*, Spring, 27–30.

Ulrich, D. (1997) 'Measuring human resources: An overview of practice and a prescription for results', *Human Resource Management*, vol. 36, no. 3, 303–20.

Warr, P. (1992) *Training for Managers,* A report for the Institute of Managers, sponsored by the Economics and Social Research Council, MRC/ESRC Social and Applied Psychology Unit, Sheffield.

Whipp, R., Rosenfield, R., and Pettigrew, A. (1988) 'Understanding strategic change processes: Some preliminary British findings', in A. Pettigrew (ed.) *The Management of Strategic Change,* Oxford: Blackwell, 14–55.

Wills, S. (1993) 'MCI and the competency movement: The case so far', *Journal of European Training*, vol. 17, no. 1, 9–11.

Winterton, J. and Winterton, R. (1997) 'Does management development add value?', *British Journal of Management*, vol. 8, June, S65–S76.

Vickerstaff, S. A. (1991) 'The management of training in the smaller firm', Paper presented to the British Academy of Management Annual Conference, September.

Yeung, A. and Berman, B. (1997) 'Adding value through human resources: Reorienting human resource measurement to drive business performance', *Human Resource Management*, vol. 36, no. 3, 321–35.

chapter 6

# International Human Resource Strategies

CHAPTER OUTLINE



*This chapter was contributed by Paul Iles*

## Learning Objectives

After reading this chapter you will be able to:

- Recognize the different stages of the staged movement of key SHRM systems towards a global configuration.
- Understand the ways in which managerial mind-sets or mental schema may impact on managers' recognition of the need for, and their capability to, design and implement an ISHRM architecture.
- Appreciate the significance of differences in continental origin, administrative heritage, managerial orientations, life-cycle phase and corporate strategy for international HRS.
- Evaluate the significance of different types of organizational configuration in international enterprise.
- Evaluate the significance of geographical dispersion and cultural diversity for HR policies in the areas of international recruitment and selection, training and development, performance management and the management of international diversity.

# Introduction

The field of international human resource strategy is still relatively underdeveloped; yet its potential for international and multinational organizations is considerable. This chapter looks at the ways in which international organizations can use SHRM to achieve strategic benefit. It acknowledges that designing international SHRM architectures may well require significantly different and complex models and mind sets – which may be different from, and require modification to, conventional managerial attitudes to SHRM system design. For this reason the issue of managerial orientation towards SHRM receives here considerable attention. Alert readers will recognize connections between this theme and the discussions of the same issue of managers' mind sets in chapter 17.

This chapter considers some of the key human resource strategies and tactics employed by organizations attempting to manage their international and global structures and systems. It does this through a framework for analysing the relationships between strategies and products, and four phases of the staged process of movement towards a truly global existence. In simple terms this structure encourages (but does not complete or close down) discussion about the relationships between dimensions of SHRM systems – structures, culture and elements of personnel systems – and stages of the process of globalization.

The chapter argues that a mixture of structural, cultural and HRD initiatives are relevant to an understanding of national diversity, and to the management of operations across international boundaries. The second half of the chapter considers a number of critical discrete elements of international SHRM systems:

recruitment and selection, training and development, performance appraisal, and reward management, in an international context.

# International SHRM at the Enterprise Level

This section will explore ways in which organizations are using human resource strategies (HRS) to create more strategically coherent, competitive international enterprises, using cases drawn from Asian, US and in particular European organizations in the light of changes in the international business environment.

It is frequently asserted that the increasingly global nature of business activities has placed new demands on organizational and managerial performance and has called for new responses. International assignments, for example, are being increasingly used not only for staffing, control and representational purposes, but as vehicles to develop managers' skills and knowledge, and as ways of enhancing organizational learning and capabilities. More managers are now involved in managing transnational joint ventures, mergers and acquisitions, and are operating in increasingly diverse environments with multicultural teams. Senior managers are often called upon to manage geographically and culturally diverse businesses, balancing the demands of global integration and centralization with those of local sensitivity and responsiveness. The geographical dispersion of operating units and the multicultural nature of international enterprise are often seen as posing new challenges for international HRS, including:

- How to ensure that organizational structures and systems enhance global effectiveness and enable organizations to achieve both global integration and local responsiveness.
- How to foster organizational cultures which value diversity and difference whilst simultaneously creating a sense of unified mission and acting as the 'corporate glue'.
- How to install effective personnel systems that attract, place, retain and develop managers and other key employees with the knowledge, skills and attitudes required to perform effectively in a global business environment.

This section will develop a framework for analysing international HR strategies, outlining the policy options and choices available in developing appropriate international HRS strategies in international enterprise. In order to develop such a framework, we will need to go beyond our earlier description of the external environment facing international enterprises as characterized by complexity, diversity and geographic dispersion.

## *Strategy, structure and international SHRM in a global environment*

One helpful framework for analysing the global environment faced by international enterprises is provided by Bartlett and Ghoshal (1989). They see the early phase of MNC activity, primarily dominated by European MNCs, as 'multinational'. Since this term is also often used to describe any kind of transnational corporation, we shall follow Harzing and van Ruysseveldt (1995) and use the term 'multidomestic', since up to the end of the Second World War MNCs emphasized foreign production for local domestic markets with decentralized decision-making and local autonomy. With a decline in protectionist policies, a reduction in tariff barriers and improved transportation, communication and logistics, American MNCs in particular entered international markets and initiated significant foreign direct investment. In this 'international' phase, as high-tech products produced in the US became more standardized, they were exported and then produced overseas. As the product became completely standardized economies of scale and mass production made low-cost production in less-developed countries possible, giving rise to the 'new international division of labour'.

Japanese companies in particular began to move beyond this phase in the 1970s as declining communication and transport barriers, new technologies and a greater homogenization of consumer tastes rendered centralized, standardized production and exporting activities profitable. Bartlett and Ghoshal (1989) term this the 'global' era; it describes the kind of environment Levitt's (1983) globalization thesis was designed to address. However, the rise of trade barriers, increased national regulation and the growth of flexible technologies in the 1980s have reinforced the importance of local responsiveness, stimulating not the re-appearance of 'multidomestic' environments, since the worldwide innovation and global efficiency demands of the international and global eras remain important, but the rise of what is termed the 'transnational' era (Bartlett and Ghoshal 1989; Harling and van Ruysseveldt 1995).

If we move from the global level to the industry level, we can see links between the competitive environments faced by MNCs and the demands of particular industries. Some industries remain multidomestic (e.g. branded packaged goods, like detergents and food). International strategy here essentially consists of a set of independent domestic strategies, and cultural, social and other national differences remain powerful influences. European companies are important players in this industry.

Other industries have become global, with standardized needs and efficiencies of scale, putting an emphasis on centralization and integration. The global industry does not consist of separate domestic industries, as the competitive position of the company in one country is linked to its position in other countries. The consumer electronics industry explored in chapter 3 is the classic example, dominated by Japanese and other Asian corporations.

In international industries, the ability to transfer knowledge and technology evolved in the home market to foreign affiliates is the key to success, as in telecommunications switching. It is a competence which has been particularly well developed by US companies. In the developing transnational industries, companies need to respond to the complex and often contradictory demands of other factors: the global efficiency demanded by global industries, the national responsiveness demanded by multidomestic industries, and the rapid transfer of learning, knowledge and innovation demanded by international industries (Bartlett and Ghoshal 1989).

This brief excursion into the realms of international competitive strategy has several implications for international HRS, particularly for organizational structure. First, we will note its relationship to the continental origin of the leading MNCs, as this seems to have influenced their 'administrative heritage' (Bartlett and Ghoshal 1992).

## People and structure in international SHRM

The driving organizational perspectives or bases that shape the distribution of power, influence and control in international enterprise are primarily function, product and geography. These three bases may compete with, conflict with or complement each other. Japanese multinationals like Nissan and Hitachi have typically divided their global operations along functional lines (e.g. production, marketing) and can be said to be functionally-driven. American multinationals have tended to stress a product perspective, whereas European multinationals such as Shell, ICI and BP have tended to be area-driven or geographically-driven. Only in the last few years have such organizations moved towards a more product-driven strategy (Humes 1993).

Some multinationals have sought to combine or mix approaches, creating a variety of 'hybrids', perhaps with some parts of the corporation stressing one approach and other parts another (e.g. Exxon). Other companies, like Philips, have developed 'matrix' or 'titled matrix' approaches, attempting to balance product and geography, often in transition to a product-driven strategy. Other companies, especially American ones like Procter and Gamble, have tended to continue to use an international division to manage their overseas operations, whilst their domestic operations remain product-driven.

On all three major 'Triad' continents, international enterprises have tended to place greater stress on either product perspectives (e.g. Bayer, Philips, BP, ICI) or area perspectives (e.g. Sony). According to Humes (1993), Japanese multinationals have typically combined functional perspectives with a managerial emphasis on shared values; American multinationals, a product emphasis with a focus on structures and systems; and European multinationals, an emphasis on area alongside the use of staffing practices to bring about co-ordination and control. However, multinationals from all three continents have attempted to utilize all three sets of dynamics in recent years.

Each of the phases has tended to be associated with MNCs from different continents. The typical American multinational company, for example, has tended to rely on an international division to co-ordinate all its international activities, often managed by a senior executive group at headquarters. Such a form tends to rely on formal structures and control systems, to adopt an ethnocentric orientation, and to use PCNs for control and co-ordination purposes. European multinationals, in contrast, have taken a different path, often moving directly from a classic '*mother–daughter*' structure characteristic of the multidomestic phase, to a divisionalized global structure employing transcontinental product or area divisions and polycentric staffing, without adopting the transitional stage of the international division. Japanese multinationals have tended to rely on trading companies to manage their international activities, with only slow movements towards other phases of internationalization and with the adoption of basically an 'ethnocentric' orientation. However, by the 1990s there has been some convergence among the leading multinationals from all three continents towards reliance of global operating divisions and towards the adoption of a geocentric or transnational perspective (Humes 1993).

The increasingly complex international environment encountered by an MNC may push it towards global integration, whereas host government pressure and the need for responsiveness to local markets and cultures may push it towards local responsiveness. To address this dilemma, international companies have often sought to go beyond a divisional structure towards other structures, such as mixed, matrix and network structures.

However, matrix forms in many international organizations have proved hard to manage, due to dual reporting leading to conflict and confusion, a proliferation of channels leading to log-jams, overlapping responsibilities producing a loss of accountability and battles over turf, and barriers of distance, language, time and culture – all combining to make conflict very difficult to resolve.

According to Bartlett and Ghoshal (1989) the most successful international organizations are now less likely to be searching for an ideal structure and more likely to be attempting to develop managerial abilities to operate 'a matrix in the mind', putting the emphasis on finding and developing managers with good interpersonal skills and tolerance of ambiguity. Whilst European multinationals, with their strong local presence, have tended to maximize responsiveness, Japanese organizations with their global scale efficiencies have focused on global integration. Other organizations (often American) like General Electric or Procter and Gamble have seemed very good at facilitating innovation. However, the challenge facing international organizations in the future may be to *simultaneously* build multiple strategic competencies. As Bartlett and Ghoshal (1989: 16) put it, 'to compete effectively, a company had to develop global competitiveness, multinational flexibility and world-wide learning capability *simultaneously*'. This requirement is seen as stimulating a new organizational model, the transnational, able to build on the advantages of the other organizational forms.

Bartlett and Ghoshal (1989: 61) use the term 'integrated network' to emphasize 'the very significant flow of components, products, resources, people, and information that must be managed in the transnational. Beyond the rationalisation of physical facilities, the company must integrate tasks and perspectives; rich and complex communication linkages, work interdependencies, and formal and informal systems are the true hallmark of the transnational.'

Such an orientation seems more characteristic of multinationals with roots in smaller European countries like Sweden (e.g. Electrolux, Ericsson), Switzerland (e.g. Nestlé) and to some extent Holland (e.g. Philips, Unilever) than of American, British or Japanese multinationals, perhaps because such countries experienced an earlier and greater need to move beyond very limited national boundaries. Box 6.1 shows one such example.

Where the analysis of Bartlett and Ghoshal (1989) is helpful is in pointing to the differentiated nature of MNC strategies and their links on the one hand to particular eras and industries, and on the other to organizational structure and SHRM policies. In contrast to the globalization thesis of Levitt (1983) and the assertions of the NIDL thesis, MNCs do not just pursue globally integrated strategies of 'efficiency, low-cost production and standardization, though such strategies did appear to have predominated in certain eras (the 1970s), certain industries (electronics) and amongst certain corporations (especially Japanese ones). Some MNCs may pursue multi-domestic strategies emphasizing national responsiveness, especially European MNCs operations in the packaged goods sector. Other MNCs may pursue international strategies emphasizing the transfer of learning, especially US companies in high-tech industries. Other MNCs from all three parts of the Triad recognize they face simultaneous demands for local differentiation, and global efficiency and world-wide innovation, and attempt to pursue 'transnational strategies'. These are especially important given the rapid changes experienced by different industries – for example, the use of synthetics and washing machines has put the emphasis on standardization in the multi-domestic detergents industry; political pressures for local production, trade barriers and renewed differences in customer taste have made responsiveness more important in the global consumer electronics industry; and whilst deregulation and new technology have placed greater importance on global efficiency in the 'international' telecommunications industry, government recognition of its strategic importance has also emphasized the importance of local responsiveness (Bartlett and Ghoshal 1989). It is also worth emphasizing that this analysis is at a high level of generality; different units, locations, tasks and functions may have considerable room for choice within these broad parameters.

Another valuable implication of the Bartlett and Ghoshal (1989) framework is

### BOX 6.1 COACHING FROM THE HQ TOUCHLINE

Electrolux, for example, makes over 80 per cent of its sales abroad and whilst in some respects it has sought to maintain a centralised approach with its global 'white goods' strategies and use of common components world-wide, in other respects it has sought to push central functions out to the subsidiaries, with headquarters acting as coach and co-ordinator. National units have global responsibility for developing and manufacturing specific products: for example Italy for washing machines, the UK for microwaves. Multi-disciplinary task forces are drawn from different units to facilitate design and development. (Barham and Oates 1991) its rejection of the notion that there should be a 'fit' between strategy and structure in favour of the recognition of organizational and strategic flexibility in the face of dynamic, complex environments. This ties in with our earlier analysis of the notion of integration and our emphasis on 'open' rather than 'closed' conceptions of HRS. Similar considerations apply to international HRS, as one of the benefits of the Bartlett and Ghoshal (1989) framework is that it points to the importance of management processes as the key to the successful implementation of strategy. However, the authors themselves, being corporate strategists, do not follow their argument through in detail to a consideration of human resource strategies. To do so requires us to pay closer attention to another model of international SHRM, one that focuses on managerial choice and management orientations to international enterprise, and to the ways in which HR strategies at the functional level may differ in international, as opposed to domestic, enterprise.

## The importance of managerial orientations of international SHRM

Successful implementation of international SHRM is often seen as requiring a shift in managerial orientations or 'mind sets'. For example Laurent (1986) argues that a truly international conception of SHRM requires explicit recognition that:

- particular ways of managing human resources reflect particular values and assumptions.
- these ways are different, not universally superior or inferior.
- foreign subsidiaries and affiliates may have different ways of managing people, perhaps more effective locally.
- such differences need to be accepted and discussed so as to make them usable as resources and assets.
- more creative and effective ways of managing people can be developed as a result of cross-cultural learning.

If an organization or its senior management has a weak global orientation, the importance and distinctiveness of international enterprise may be underemphasized or ignored. But as Bartlett and Ghoshal (1989: x) state, 'even companies that were not seeking to expand abroad were confronted by the emerging challenges as the forces of internationalisation reached out to embrace them'. Companies may adopt a *'parochial'* stance, ignoring what is happening elsewhere. Or they may adopt an *'ethnocentric'* stance believing that 'their way is better' and that domestic SHRM practices are easily transferable to operations in other countries, despite the evidence of substantial cultural differences and difference in business systems.

One of the most influential approaches to international SHRM, emphasizing the importance of managerial orientations, is that of Perlmutter (1969). He distinguishes between four basic orientations to international enterprize: the ethnocentric, the polycentric, the geocentric, and the regiocentric.

An ethnocentric attitude is associated with the view that home-country managers, management style and appraisal criteria are superior to the host country, implying that only parent country nationals (PCNs) are suitable for senior management at home and abroad. A polycentric attitude is associated with the recognition that national differences and the need for local responsiveness demand the use of local managers (HCNs – host country nationals) in host countries, but home-country managers remain dominant in headquarters. A regiocentric orientation also recognizes the importance of national and cultural differences, but perceives these as most important at the regional level. So a US company may adopt a 'Eurocentric' strategy within the EU, seeing European managers as suitable for movement anywhere within the EU, but seeing Asian affiliates as best run by Asian managers (HCNs) whilst using American expatriate PCNs to run affiliates in Africa. In contrast a geocentric attitude is associated with a global view, with managers drawn from any region of the world and appointed to positions at headquarters or subsidiaries regardless of nationality.

Many European companies, for example, in order to maximize local responsiveness, have attempted to staff local operations with HCNs rather than with expatriates. such staff are deemed to know their own cultures, work ethics and markets best (a polycentric strategy). Local subsidiaries often may then operate almost independently, the major controls being financial (e.g. Unilever and Lever Brothers in the US). However, locals may then find that they are barred from executive positions at headquarters because of their perceived 'over local' perspective! The local responsiveness emphasized in the polycentric orientation may push organizations towards decentralized structures, giving maximum autonomy, flexibility, and independence to local enterprises. The global perspective of the geocentric orientation may simultaneously call for greater centralization, co-ordination and integration.

The ethnocentric orientation seems to be particularly characteristic of domestic companies and export-oriented companies as well as those displaying a 'global' strategy. The polycentric orientation seems particularly characteristic of the classic multi-domestic/multinational strategy, whereas 'international' companies may be more inclined to display region-centric orientations. The geocentric orientation seems particularly characteristic of the transnational company.

If we extend Perlmutter's (1969) analysis of managerial orientations to the analysis of HR strategies, we can develop a framework which can guide the choice of recruitment and selection, training and development, performance management and other HR strategies in an international context. Before we do this, we need to consider two other useful approaches to international HRS, the 'stages' approach of Adler (1991), and the 'dual logics' of Evans and Lorange (1989).

Our discussion of the structural options open to MNCs is helped by analysing the 'two logics' facing international enterprise presented by Evans and Lorange (1989). We have already characterized the environment faced by MNCs as both more complex and more diverse than that faced by domestic organizations, primarily due to geographical dispersion and cultural diversity. Evans and Lorange (1989: 144) ask themselves 'how can a corporation operating in different product markets and diverse social-cultural environments effectively establish human resource policies?' and propose two logics that shape international HRS: a product-market logic related to the product life-cycle (thus introducing the notion of phase or stage) and a social-cultural logic related to the diverse legal, social, political and cultural environments faced by MNCs and the cultural diversity of their workforces. How MNCs respond to the question of diversity can be analysed in terms of Perlmutter's (1969) 'managerial orientations', or the 'administrative heritage' of the organization (Bartlett and Ghoshal 1989). By this term the authors are referring to the dominant management styles, values, patterns, assets and capabilities built up over generations (and themselves related to imperial (?) origins, as we have seen). These two related dimensions mediate the response of the organization to the strategic pressures it faces, affecting how it structures itself, according to such criteria as: whether to emphasize the global or the local, whether to pursue decentralization or centralization, whether to focus on differentiation or on integration, and whether to emphasize cultural logic or product logic (this list is taken from a much longer list of 'dualities' presented by Evans and Doz 1989). These design choices in turn are related to the bases of co-ordination and control selected by the organization as to whether to structure by area, product or function, or whether to use some kind of matrix structure employing two or more dimensions, or whether to use an international division to co-ordinate and control international activities. Finally, such choices influence the kind of configuration adopted, to use the terminology adopted by Bartlett and Ghoshal (1989).

## *Stage approaches to international SHRM*

A particularly useful framework for understanding the process of engaging in international HRS is presented by Adler (1991). This approach is based on a 'stage' or 'evolutionary' approach to internationalization, proposing that firms typically pass through several phases of organizational development as they internationalize: such as, moving from exporting, to establishing a sales subsidiary, to establishing foreign production, to creating an international division. What Adler tries to do is relate these evolutionary stages to HR policies and emphases, and it is this feature of her model that will be developed here. She argues that organizations have typically moved in their international activities through four phases or stages – from purely *domestic* organizations to what she calls '*international*' (or multi-domestic) organizations, and then from international organizations to *multinational* organizations. She identifies a fourth, emerging phase of development in international enterprise – the '*global*' organization. Each of these phases is characterized by differences in orientation, strategy, technology, and product or service. Each phase is also characterized by the increasing importance of international enterprise to their overall business activities. Table 6.1 shows how this 'stage' perspective may be applied to the issues of how to manage people in international enterprise. Unfortunately Adler (1991) uses the terms differently to Bartlett and Ghoshal (1989), causing some confusion. The 'domestic' organization is typically characterized by a centralized structure and a focus on functional divisions. The 'international' organization, on the other hand, typically operates with a more decentralized structure and tends to concentrate its activities in an international division. 'International' affairs may then be isolated from the mainstream of business, which is seen as primarily 'domestic' in focus. Consequently there may be little interchange or communication between the international division and the rest of the business, whether of ideas, people or practices, and little mutual learning or development.

The multinational organization attempts to move beyond this, perhaps by decentralizing and creating multinational business lines. As it evolves, it may increasingly enter into global alliances, and attempt to exercise a variety of measures such as: the creation and communication of a common, though shared, mission; the development of a shared sense of purpose and corporate culture; the use of management development practices to create a cadre of 'corporate resources'; and the use of financial controls.

Of particular interest to international HRS is that the issue of *culture* is seen as assuming increasing importance at each stage of internationalization. Using the Perlmutter (1969) framework, it can be seen that the domestic organization typically assumes an 'ethno-centric' perspective to HRS. Cultural sensitivity is regarded as of little importance, and the organization assumes there is only 'one way' (or at least 'one best way') to manage and organize. The international organization is held to take a more regiocentric perspective. Cultural sensitivity therefore becomes of critical importance, especially in managing employees of different backgrounds and dealing with clients, customers and suppliers of varying cultural backgrounds. It may seek to prioritize responsiveness and sensitivity to local labour and product markets.

Paradoxically, the *multinational* organization in Adler's analysis places somewhat less importance on culture, recognizing its importance primarily in dealing with its own employees and managers. Its focus is primarily on 'one least cost way'. The *global* organization, on the other hand, is regarded as taking a more fully developed geocentric or multi-centric perspective towards its operations. Culture becomes of critical importance, whether dealing with employees, executives, customers or suppliers, as it is held to take the view that there are simultaneously 'many good ways' to manage and organize.

Adler's framework is clearly open to the criticism that it is somewhat deterministic, implying that it is best to locate oneself on the right-hand side of table 6.1. Of most value to our analysis of international HRS is that it is possible to extend Adler's analysis to look at the specific HR implications of different stages of internationalization. The advantage of Adler's analysis is that it tries to bring together the 'product-market' and 'social cultural' logics identified by Evans and Lorange (1989), linking the product life-cycle emphases of Vernon (1966), and Bartlett and Ghoshal's (1989) concern, with strategy and structure, to issues of culture and SHRM. Table 6.1 shows this framework, much modified to give greater emphasis to HRS issues.

Organizations at the domestic or 'export' stage may only require low-level global training, mainly emphasizing the local culture of the export target and its consumer values and behaviour, and the interpersonal skills necessary to negotiate, sell and market to that culture. There is a need to carry out some training of HCNs, mainly in helping them understand home-country products and policies. At the *international* stage more extensive training is needed, with more emphasis on technology transfer, stress management and local business practices and law. At the *multinational* stage, the emphasis now shifts to two-way technology transfer, corporate values, and international strategy; more emphasis is placed on the training of HCNs in both technical and cultural issues. The *global* stage requires more rigorous, extensive training of HCNs and of all employees, including senior executives, in such areas as global operations, global strategy, multiple cultural values, and socialization into the corporate culture. Managing international diversity thus becomes of critical importance.

Shortly we will use the framework presented in table 6.1 to review strategies in four HR policy areas of great significance to IHRS: recruitment and selection, training and development, performance management, and managing international diversity. But first we need to note a few caveats (in addition to the suggestion that we should not read such a table in an overly deterministic, evolutionary way, nor read it as suggesting that HR strategies can somehow be 'read off' for each phase in an overly prescriptive way). The first caveat is that the Perlmutter, and Bartlett and Ghoshal, phases do not perfectly match or lock in to Adler's phase model; note that we have collapsed Bartlett and Ghoshal's multidomestic and international phases (with their very different orientations to responsiveness and learning) into one phase equivalent to Alder's 'international' phase. Also note that not all analysts see the 'geocentric' strategy as most effective in all cases – some prefer a 'regiocentric' strategy, with a regional strategy seen as a stepping stone to more effective international competition. As Morrison et al. (1991: 24) put it, 'under a regional strategy, companies extend home and country loyalties to the entire region. Managers are given the opportunity to solve regional challenges regionally'.

For example, Hilb (1992) argues that a 'Eurocentric' HR strategy is the most appropriate response for a European company. Such a strategy can exploit European-wide human resources instead of concentrating only on PCNs or HCNs, a consequence of following an ethnocentric or polycentric HR strategy, and can help identify subsidiary employees with corporate pan-European strategies.

In addition it can help create a pan-European company culture able to derive benefit from the advantages of all the specific national cultures in which the company operates, and offer career opportunities across a more integrated Europe by avoiding some of the staffing, communication and motivation problems inherent in a geocentric policy. However, some disadvantages of such a regiocentric policy are that it neglects human resources outside Europe, can close off career paths outside Europe and career paths for non-European TCNs, and its focus on Europe may neglect other markets of great importance, especially in the Asia-Pacific region.

**Table 6.1** Globalization and IHRS

| | *Phase One* | *Phase Two* | *Phase Three* | *Phase Four* |
|---|---|---|---|---|
| Adler (1991) | Domestic | International | Multi-national | Global |
| Bartlett and Ghoshal (1989) | Domestic | Multi-national | Global | Transnational |
| Permutter (1969) | Ethnocentric | Polycentric | Regiocentric | Geocentric |
| *Strategy and structure:* | Export | Foreign direct investment, technology transfer | International sourcing, production, marketing | Global strategic advantage |
| | Product/function centralized | Decentralized/co-ordinated federation, international division | Centralized hub, multi-national business lines | Integrated network, alliances |
| *Importance of cultural diversity:* | 'Marginal; one-way/one best way' | Important, esp. customers, clients, suppliers; 'many good ways' | Moderate, for managers and employees; 'one least-cost way' | Critically important for all staff; 'many good ways simultaneously' |
| *Recruitment and selection:* | | | | |
| expatriates | Very few | Many | Some, esp. top performers | Many, all levels |
| purpose | Reward | Fill position, complete project, transfer technology | Control, complete project career development | Co-ordination, integration, career and organization development |
| career impact | Neutral, negative | Negative, except locally | Important | Essential |
| repatriation | Difficult | Very difficult | Less difficult | Easy |
| origins of executives | Home country PCNs | Home country PCNs and token TCNs | Home country PCNs and token TCNs, HCNs | HCNs, PCNs and TCNs |
| career track | Domestic | Domestic | Token international | Global |
| identification | Home country HQ | Host country | Home and host | Global |

| | *Phase One* | *Phase Two* | *Phase Three* | *Phase Four* |
|---|---|---|---|---|
| *Training and development* | | | | |
| extent | Little | Limited | More extensive | High, continuous |
| rigour | Low | Moderate | High | High |
| target | Few | Expatriates, few HCNs | Expatriates, some HCNs | |
| skills | Technical, managerial | Plus cultural adaptation | Plus cultural diversity | Plus cultural synergy |
| content | Local cultural awareness | Plus interpersonal skills, technology transfer | Plus two-way transfer, global strategy | Plus global systems, multiple values |
| communications | Little | Little | One-way | Two-way, all ways |
| *Performance management:* | | | | |
| criteria | Corporate HQ | Local subsidiary | Corporate HQ | Global, universalized and local |
| motivation | Financial | Financial, adventure | Challenge, opportunity | Challenge, opportunity, advancement |
| reward package | Compensation | Compensation | Global | Global |

*Notes:* HCN = host country national; PCN = parent country national; TCN = third country national.

If we look at BPs evolution over the last 50 years (box 6.2) we can see that though there appears to be some relationship to the phases outlined in table 6.1 (e.g. the move from ethnocentric to polycentric to regiocentric orientations, the move from international to multinational to transnational strategies), the 'fit' is by no means perfect. For example, BP in the 1980s re-centralized and re-emphasized an ethnocentric orientation, and it has stopped short of utilizing a fully 'geocentric' model in favour of more 'regiocentric' models. In the 1990s, re-centralization again appeared to be on the agenda. This example shows how international enterprises can move backwards and forwards along the path suggested in table 6.1. Figure 6.1, shows some of these shifts.

**Table 6.2** Shifts in strategy, structure and HRS at BP

| *Era* | *Structure* | *Orientation* | *Aims* | *Focus* |
|---|---|---|---|---|
| 1940–73 | Integrated | Ethnocentric (international) | Skill transfer | Expatriate terms and conditions |
| 1973–80 | Conglomerate; matrix | Polycentric multi-national | Skill transfer | Expatriate terms and conditions |
| 1980–90 | Centralized | Ethnocentric | Common corporate culture | Expatriate career management |
| 1990– | Horizontal; network | Regiocentric/ geocentric (global?) | Learning 2-way; transfers; teams | Expatriate career management; team culture |

*Source:* Hendry (1993: 87).

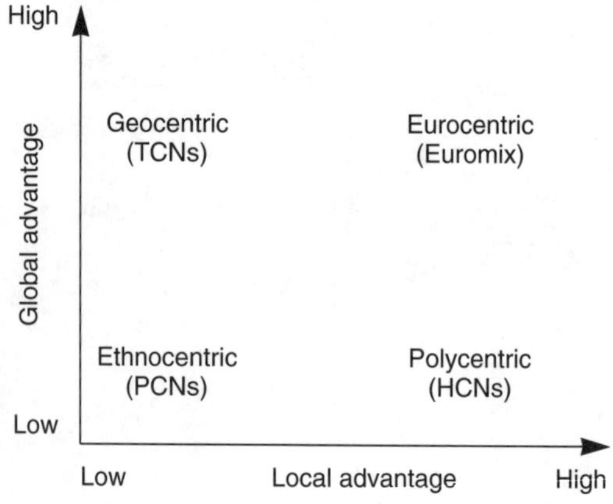


**Figure 6.1** Stages of European SHRM
*Source:* Adapted from Hilb (1992: 580)

## BOX 6.2 SHIFTS IN STRATEGY, STRUCTURE, ORIENTATION AND HUMAN RESOURCES AT BP

'BP is the UK's largest company in terms of sales, responding to increasing complexity and diversity by developing a changing portfolio of products and markets and revamping its HR strategies. Like Exxon, it has always tended towards greater centralization than Shell, and has moved away from its "imperial" sphere of influence in the Middle East. Between World War Two and the oil crisis of 1973, it primarily emphasized integration and strong central control of overseas plants and businesses through an "ethnocentric" HR strategy focused on transferring skills through a large cadre of primarily British career expatriates on long-term assignments. Expatriate terms and conditions were a major HR focus. After the rise in oil prices due to the actions of OPEC, BP used its oil revenues to open up reserves in Alaska and the North Sea and to diversify through acquisition into chemicals, animal feeds and coal. In this "conglomerate" phase, a more "polycentric" HR strategy was followed with a continuing focus on skill transfer and expatriate terms and conditions. A strong matrix organization focused around 11 business streams and 70 national affiliates was developed to manage this complexity.

However, this structure seemed not to facilitate decentralization, but to increase complexity. In the 1980s, following privatization, BP re-focused on its core oil business, acquiring both Britoil and Standard Oil of Ohio to provide marketing expertise and Alaskan outlets. This more centralized phase both increased the number of employees and brought in superior skills and expertise in some areas. A renewed "ethnocentric" HR strategy attempted to integrate these businesses within an overall BP culture, using short-term expatriate assignments by senior managers, marketing and technical staff to exercise greater control from London. Career management therefore became a major issue for international HRS. However, with the growth of non-oil businesses as alternative sources of power and influence (e.g. nutrition in the Netherlands), BP in the 1990s has begun to pursue a more regiocentric philosophy, with moves towards a "global" or "transnational" strategy. This has manifested itself in the use of two-way secondments, a more fluid, less British, less geographically focused expatriate cadre, and the encouragement of career management, teamwork and organizational learning. Such a focus requires not direction by a centralized personnel function but more fluid negotiation between individuals, businesses and functions, managed primarily through regional structures. Training and development activities are used to foster teamworking and an awareness of cultural diversity, whilst INSEAD and Harvard are increasingly used for top management education instead of British universities. However, 1992 witnessed the departure of the chairman, a growing awareness of over-indebtedness, scrutiny of such under-performing businesses as chemicals and nutrients, and greater emphasis on cost-cutting, redundancies, disposals and central controls.' (Hendry 1993)

## The Human Resource Implications of Internationalization

The analysis above presented a framework for analysing the environment, industry, strategy, structure and HRS options associated with international enterprise. It suggested that organizations in a multi-domestic industry should follow a multi-domestic strategy and adopt a multi-domestic/multinational structure, and that similar principles should apply for international, global and transnational industries (Harzing and van Ruysseveldt (1995). The HRS options associated with such a framework are perhaps best represented by using the integration/responsiveness matrix presented by Prahalad and Doz (1987), allied to the Perlmutter (1969) framework. Figure 6.2 shows the framework with the vertical axis representing the level of global integration or central co-ordination and the horizontal axis representing the level of national responsiveness or differentiation. Note that these two dimensions attempt to capture the importance of both cultural diversity and geographical dispersion previously cited as key dimensions of the complexity and diversity of international environments. As we have also stressed, our 'open' model of international HRS allows corporations to select a strategy and structure that does not 'fit' its industry exactly, perhaps in accordance with internal capabilities or as part of a move to transform its industry characteristics (Hamel and Prahalad 1995).

As we have noted throughout this chapter, different emphases may be appropriate for different situations, businesses, functions and industries. For example, packaged goods may put a greater emphasis on responsiveness than chemicals, the sales function may focus more on responsiveness than R&D, and product

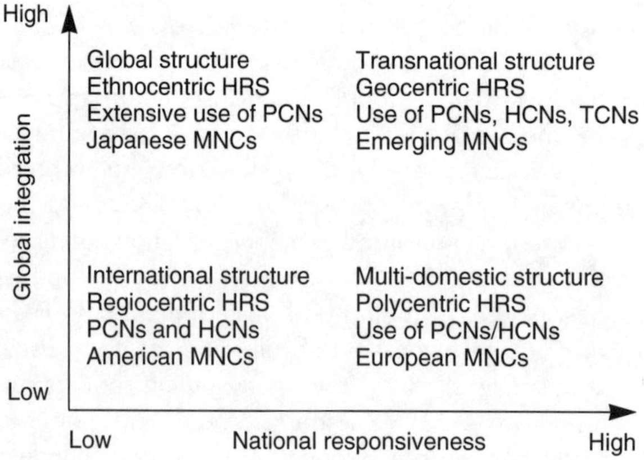


**Figure 6.2** A framework for international SHRM
*Source:* Adapted from Harzing and van Ruysseveldt (1995: 47)

policy may be more conducive to global integration than promotion or distribution (Bartlett and Ghoshal 1989). So we do not intend that figure 6.2 is used in a deterministic 'matching process' – it merely suggests ideal types. It does seem, however, as though certain organizational configurations have historically been associated with certain HRS orientations, mix of employees and continent of origin. Figure 6.2 also does not fully capture the position of the 'international' company. Though this company has some degree of concern with both national responsiveness and global integration, its major emphasis is on world-wide learning and innovation – a dimension not captured in the model presented in figure 6.2. It also suggests that certain organizational configuration has historically been associated with certain HRS orientations, mix of employees and continent of origin.

We now need to look briefly at four functional areas important in IHRS, namely:

- managing international diversity and multicultural teams.
- recruitment and selection.
- training and development.
- performance management.

Figure 6.3 shows how these four policy areas can be seen as part of an international HRS 'cycle', each contributing to more effective international performance and learning at both the individual and organizational levels of analysis. These areas are treated extensively in most textbooks of international SHRM (e.g. Torrington 1994; Hendry 1993; Dowling et al. 1994). Since our focus is on the strategic aspects, our discussion will be brief. We will begin with an area highlighted earlier in the discussion of the regional and national level of analysis and also highlighted in table 6.1 – that is the relevance of cultural diversity and the need to manage it successfully.

## *Managing international diversity*

In chapter 3 we saw that international enterprise is characterized by geographic dispersion, greater complexity and cultural diversity. Much attention has been given to the need for MNCs to be 'locally responsive', but the issue of cultural diversity goes much wider than this.

The workforce of all organizations is growing even more culturally diverse. In many countries extensive migration has meant that workforces often consist of people from a variety of ethnic, racial and cultural backgrounds. Internationalization has stimulated the exchange and transfer of human resources across borders and across continents. Managing this multicultural workforce poses a number of new challenges for HRS. Many organizations have sought to incorporate cultural diversity into their products and services in order to meet diverse customer needs and to recruit, retain and motivate a culturally diverse workforce.

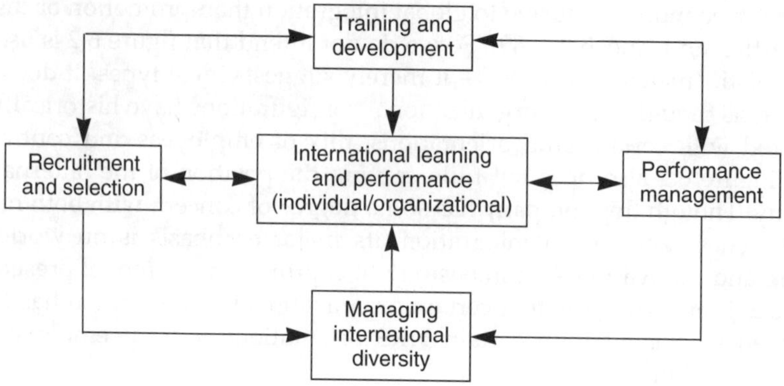


**Figure 6.3** The international SHRM cycle

A particular focus of interest in this area has been to develop multicultural teams which can use their diversity as a resource so as to achieve synergy (seen as a characteristic of the transnational/global organization in table 6.1). For example, some European-based multinationals like Exxon have begun to introduce diversity training as part of their attempts to manage international diversity, as box 6.3 shows.

The management of multicultural teams is likely to be of growing importance to international enterprises. These include not only teams that may be formed to work on specific projects like technology transfer, strategic alliances, joint ventures and headquarters–subsidiary relations or cross-unit integration, but also global cross-functional and task teams to work on issues of product development and service delivery. Indeed, some claim that 'the central operating mode for a *global* enterprise is the creation, organization and management of multicultural teams-groups that represent diversity in functional capabilities, experience levels and cultural backgrounds – effective efficient multicultural teams are the key to future global competitiveness' (Rhinesmith 1993: 106–7).

Many organizations, especially *parochial* and *ethnocentric* ones, have attempted to either *ignore* or *suppress* the cultural differences presented by multicultural teams. It is true that, initially at least, such teams may present difficulties of communication, comfort and comprehension, perhaps leading to tension, conflict and confusion. However, if actively managed, cultural differences can be an *asset* and a *resource*, especially where the organization needs to devise new ideas, entertain new perspectives and expand on existing plans. Diversity in teams can lead to greater flexibility and openness, and the avoidance of 'group think' (e.g. Janis 1977), whereby homogenous, cohesive teams come to suppress new or challenging ideas through self-censorship or through self-appointed 'mindguards' labelling any challenge as disloyalty or treachery. If cultural differences are recognized, valued and used to the organization's advantage, then greater *synergy* can result. But for this is to be realized, team-members will need to display both *cultural self-awareness* and *cross-cultural awareness*.

## BOX 6.3 DIVERSITY TRAINING AT EXXON CHEMICALS, EUROPE

Exxon Chemicals, part of the Exxon Corporation, has 'valuing diversity' in terms of culture and nationality as one of its core values. Given the changing demographics of its workforce and its belief that enhancing the effectiveness of diverse teams could be a source of competitive advantage, it conducted a pan-European employee attitude survey to serve as the basis for action. Employees felt that Exxon was monocultural, stressed conformity, tended to label and stereotype on the basis of gender and nationality, was male dominated, and US-dominated. These characteristics were felt to limit the job satisfaction and contribution of women and minority nationalities in particular, resulting in problems of communication and demotivation. Recommendations emerging included strengthening minority recruitment and career goals, removing artificial barriers and introducing more flexible contracts and conditions. Existing training was reviewed to reflect diversity issues, and experiential, outdoor development focused on awareness training for top management ('Quest') and middle managers ('Choices'). A multinational group with multilingual facilities worked on team-building and outdoor-development activities focuses on such issues as leadership, diversity, teamwork and partnership. A personal action plan and a team project based on course members and 'back home' teams followed this programme. (Phillips 1992)

Adler (1991) suggests that culturally diverse groups can perform either extremely well or extremely poorly. She also suggests that diversity may well be an asset in the creative, divergent-thinking phase of a task, but a source of friction and misunderstanding in the convergent-thinking, decision-making phases. It may, because of the potential for tension, misunderstanding and friction in diversity, be less of an asset in routine performance tasks (e.g. implementing strategy and evaluating options, as opposed to developing new products or services). If the potential synergies available from cultural diversity are to be realized, then members will need to be interculturally competent. They will need not only to understand their differences, but also continue to communicate effectively across these differences through empathy, negotiation and the ability to create a shared reality through collective participation, the open resolution of conflicts and the ability to use cultural differences as a resource. For instance, cultural diversity at all levels of an international organization can lead to greater understanding of diverse markets and customer preferences, as well as greater understanding of employees and supplier values, aspirations and preferences. It may also result in more culturally aligned human resource practices, especially in the areas of leadership style, communications, training, appraisal and recruitment. This implies that *intercultural competence* should be a selection criterion in the recruitment and selection policy area, which we explore next.

## International recruitment and selection

In most accounts of international SHRM, the issue of international recruitment and selection is seen primarily as an issue of *expatriate* selection. However, internationalization affects many other types of role. Bartlett and Ghoshal (1992), for example, identify four types of international manager, each of which requires a different mix of competencies.

1 *Business managers* or product-division managers, 'strategists plus architects plus co-ordinators'.
2 *Country managers*, 'sensors plus builders plus contributors', conveying to others the importance of collecting and evaluating information and responding to local sensitivities.
3 *Functional managers*, 'scanners plus cross-pollinators plus champions', extremely important for organizational learning in scanning globally for specialized information and promoting the transfer of best practice and information between different parts of the organization.
4 *Corporate managers*, 'leaders plus talent scouts plus developers', who play the initial role of co-ordinators and developers of new talent.

However, such a full range of roles applies only to the few fully developed 'transnationals', and only focuses on top managers. International responsibilities, skills and mind sets need to be developed much deeper within the organization and at other managerial levels.

This point can be illustrated by reference to table 6.1, which shows that different international strategies require different kinds of manager and different requirements for cultural sensitivity. In a phase one, *domestic* ethnocentric organization, little in the way of international experience or orientation, is valued. In the phase two, *international* organization, cultural diversity and an international orientation becomes very important for a variety of functional managers – sales representatives, technical experts and, managing directors amongst others.

When organizations do attempt to recruit across borders, they may find that the selection systems they use are ineffective. National differences within Europe, for example, may put barriers in the way of harmonizing recruitment practices and developing pan-European recruitment policies. British graduates may find it insulting to be told that they have been rejected by a French company over their handwriting. French graduates from prestigious *grands écoles* may find it equally insulting to be put through a battery of psychometric tests and group exercises in an assessment centre ('Haven't I proved my intellectual ability already?') An Italian graduate may find both practices equally bizarre ('Why don't they just look at my record and ask me about it at the interview?')

## BOX 6.4 DIVERSITY IN RECRUITMENT PRACTICE AT L'ORÉAL

'L'Oréal, having diversified into publishing and television, sees the need for a broadly educated management group with flexibility, technical expertise, and interpersonal skills. It has consciously sought to recruit from different disciplines and sources and to expand its recruitment based beyond France in order to reflect a wider mix of nationalities and cultures. The most important recruitment criterion is willingness to work in a team, with the recruitment decision made with participation from all levels of the organization. Personal skills and ability to live within the L'Oréal culture are emphasized; recruitment policies are not dictated from above or written down. Most cadres are recruited young, with experienced people only rarely brought in.'
(Sadler 1994)

If we move from graduate recruitment to the recruitment of more experienced managers, it appears shortages of such managers are hampering the globalization efforts of many British and Irish companies in particular (Scullion 1992a; 1994). The failure to recruit, retain and develop host country nationals (HCNs) is of course one factor. Such firms often appear to lack knowledge of local labour markets, show ignorance of the local education, training and qualifications system, ignore language and cultural problems, and attempt to export 'domestic' recruitment practices to foreign countries. One response to the shortage of international managers has been to use *external* recruitment more often to fill international management positions. Broadening recruitment activities to include a more internationally diverse pool in which to fish, especially in developing 'Euromanagers', is also, as we have seen, a step many firms have taken. However, restrictions on international mobility remain, and the pace of internationalization may outstrip the supply of appropriate international managers. One area is the *reward package* offered, an especially acute problem for British firms in particular. Another is the growing *resistance to international mobility* exhibited by many managers, stemming from a variety of sources. These include perceived political and security instability, a concern with the home economy in a recession and its impact on 're-entry', an unwillingness to disrupt children's education, a concern with 'quality of life' issues and dual-career family issues in particular, and the increasing reluctance of partners to leave their own job or career. In the face of such recruitment difficulties, it seems bizarre of many European MNCs to rarely consider *women* for international positions (though American financial services companies in particular are increasingly using women in these roles). There is some concern that women may not be politically, socially or culturally acceptable in many countries where women in management in particular are a rarity. However, it seems that women expatriate managers in Japan for example are perceived and treated more like foreign expatriate managers than like Japanese women. MNCs operating in Japan may well find Japanese women a highly-educated, but relatively under-employed, recruitment source who may well prefer to work in a European or North American environment than in the more restrictive, male-dominated environments of much of corporate Japan (Adler and Izraeli 1994).

Many organizations have engaged in more international recruitment, selection, development and career-planning activities in the 1980s and 1990s (for example: Brewster 1991: Scullian 1992). Some have attempted to manage labour shortages, others have tried to meet the staffing needs of foreign subsidiaries or joint ventures. For others, it is important to ensure national representation in the host country for political or status reasons, whilst to control the activities of foreign subsidiaries is often cited as a major reason for using expatriates. More recently, companies have sought to use international assignments to develop high potential individuals by giving them experience of a 'bigger' job and/or giving them international experience, and to assess and test potential through such assignments. As table 6.1 shows, a further motive behind international assignments is to develop the organization by encouraging the learning and sharing of new perspectives, and the fostering of organizational learning.

Traditionally, many multinationals as well as governments and aid agencies have used *career expatriates* to meet staffing needs, ensure national representation and exercise control. This is true of organizations displaying an ethnocentric orientation, not trusting local expertise and wishing to retain control from the home country. However, such a strategy is now less common. Political problems, the resentments and frustrations of local employees, the need to be more locally responsive, and the expense and decline in the numbers of such career expatriates, including dual-career family pressures, have all contributed to other strategies being adopted.

## International training and development

As the above discussions of multicultural team-building suggests, intercultural competence is often seen as a necessary attribute for an international manager or other employee. What might we mean by this term?

A review of Danish practice by Gertsen (1990) argues that what she calls 'intercultural competence' consists of three dimensions: not only 'affective competence', but also 'behaviour' (or communicative) competence (the ability to communicate effectively both verbally and non-verbally with HCNs) and 'cognitive competence'. By this she is referring to the ability of successful managers to be 'cognitively complex', not using crude stereotypes or narrow categorizations but dividing up the world in more subtle ways. This capacity seems to echo Ratiu's (1983) research on the ways in which successful international managers use tentative, provisional 'private stereotypes' rather than using the fixed, inflexible 'public stereotypes' typical of the less successful international managers.

The development of the global or transnational organization requires senior managers who are not only internationally mobile but who 'in their minds can also travel across boundaries by understanding the international implications of their work' (Barham and Antal 1994). How can such competencies best be developed? Many more organizations now seek to use international assignments for *individual and organizational development*, often with the assistance of a centralized human resource function which can plan and track the career of staff on a global basis. For example, Unilever's top Special Committee tracks as many as two hundred managers moving through developmental assignments all over the world as an essential part of its succession planning procedures. However, not all companies may adopt this formal, centralized solution. Electrolux, for example, prefers more informal dialogues between managers and units. Grand Metropolitan's subsidiary company IDV has instituted a 'cadre' programme which sends young high potential managers on international assignments where they can experience the full range of activities within a function, gain early experience of responsibility, and prepare for senior positions in the home country (Barham and Oates 1991). Other organizations have broadened their use of international assignments to include technical staff, senior managers and mid-career or 'plateaued' managers.

Some organizations, such as Shell, have sought to include specific intercultural training workshops for new graduates. Others, such as GE or Unilever, have sought to internationalize all courses. A common aim has been to include a mix of nationalities as trainers and participants. Training is often held in different countries alongside international action learning programmes to facilitate both formal and informal interaction. For example, Philips has developed a programme whereby teams of young, high-potential managers work in multinational teams on real problems outside their area of expertise. Such programmes are integrated with the appraisal of performance and potential, and also make use of human resource data-banks for succession planning, allowing the board to coordinate, track and monitor international development (Van Houten 1989).

A particular focus in this area has been the training and development of expatriates, especially in terms of pre-departure training. However, the strategic use of training and development is less common at other stages of the 'international career development cycle' (figure 6.1), which is surprising, since the culture shock of repatriation is often as great or greater than expatriation, since both the expatriate and the job to be filled (if there is one) will have changed, mentors and colleagues will have moved on, and strategic priorities will have shifted. Some Japanese companies seem to make more extensive use of training and development, and in particular better use of repatriates, as box 6.5 shows.

However, much 'training' is restricted to rather limited orientation sessions and cultural briefings, often imparted via lectures, handouts or case studies and supplemented by further reading. The analysis of inter-cultural competence (e.g. Gertsen 1991) notes that cognitive awareness and understanding, whilst important, are not the only important attributes of a successful international manager or expatriate. Black et al. (1992) suggest that the more novel the international assignment is, the more extensive interaction with HCNs will be, and the more culturally distant or culturally tough the host country will be from the home

**BOX 6.5 INTERNATIONAL SHRM AT NEC JAPAN**

'NEC is one of the world's largest manufacturing companies, with c.25,000 non-Japanese employees out of a total workforce of c.100,000. Its guiding vision is "C and C", the convergence of computers and communications. It has evolved sophisticated SHRM systems to "internationalize" its personnel and, like many Japanese companies, sees continuous learning and education, especially English language learning and on-the-job training, as keys to its success. In 1974, it began an international education programme and began to abolish distinctions between domestic and international careers for promotion decisions, so as to encourage international assignments. Employees are rigorously appraised for their suitability for overseas assignments, so as to match people with opportunities. The overall aim is to develop "global business people" who are technically competent, skilled at communication and adaptable. Ten development programmes target a wide range of staff, providing business, area and orientation knowledge and skills. Distance-learning is used for overseas staff, including HCNs, whilst returnee programmes are used to reintegrate repatriates. Repatriates' experiences are used to generate case-studies for the cross-cultural training of future expatriates. Secondments overseas are used to internationalize perspectives and HCNs are trained both locally and in Japan. All SHRM initiatives have a strategic focus, seeking to reach all employees, and overseas careers are positioned as attractive career moves.' (Holden 1994)

country. For example, an individualistic, low power-distance, task-oriented, tolerant of uncertainty Anglo-Saxon manager taking up an assignment in a collectivist, high power-distance, relationship-oriented, uncertainty-avoiding Asian culture, to use the Hofstede (1980) framework. In such cases training and development need to be 'rigorous' and extensive although the authors do not fully define rigour, except in terms of social learning theory. However, it is likely to be the case that intercultural competence in general, and competence in dealing with novel jobs involving extensive interaction with 'culturally distant' locals in particular, is best developed through more 'experiential' methods. Figure 6.4 develops and applies the framework to be introduced in chapters 10 and 11. This suggests that self-development, especially awareness of oneself, one's culture and how it impacts on one's beliefs, values and behaviour – an essential part of intercultural competence – is best developed through more methods such as cross-cultural sensitivity workshops, outdoor development with multi-cultural teams, field trips, action learning with a multicultural set, job rotation involving international assignments, and multicultural team-building exercises.

We close this section with an example of how Deutsche Aerospace (DASA) has

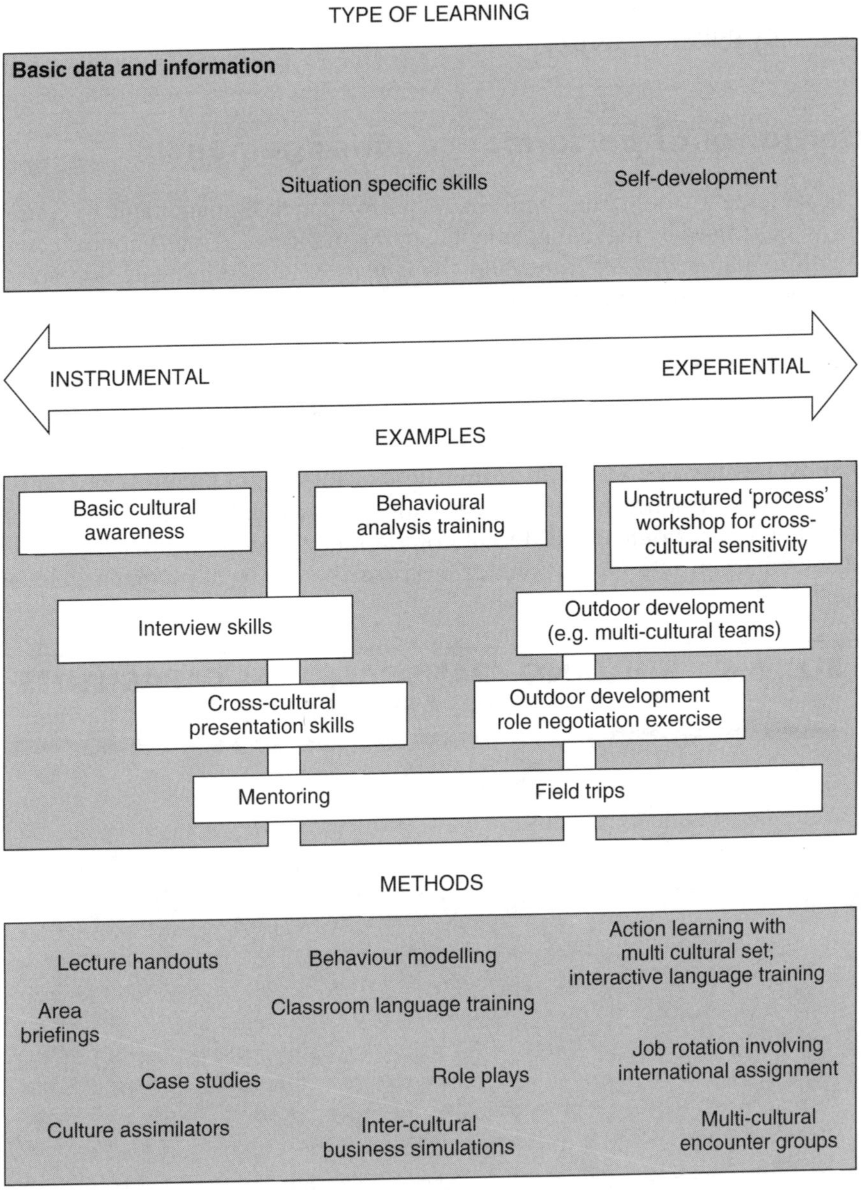


**Figure 6.4** Matching cross-cultural programmes and processes to the qualities being developed in diversity training

sought to use a variety of SHRM methodologies to build what it terms 'transnational capabilities' (box 6.6).

## International performance management

Here, we extend the earlier analysis of performance management to consider some issues raised by the management of performance in an international context. We will focus on the *differences* and the *options* available in designing suitable international performance management strategies.

### Performance appraisal

Successful performance in international assignments requires not only technical competence, but also (as we have seen) cross-cultural skills, interpersonal skills, empathy, sensitivity and adaptability. These factors might therefore be incorporated into performance evaluation systems at a strategic level. Differences in international roles demand different criteria and a different mix of head-office and subsidiary inputs. Operational criteria are likely to be of particular relevance

**BOX 6.6 BUILDING TRANSNATIONAL CAPABILITIES AT DEUTSCHE AEROSPACE AG**

DASA sees cross-cultural SHRM as a 'core skill' and has developed a variety of development programmes, learning alliances and transnational management, team and organizational development programmes to develop it. A corporate unit of Daimler-Benz, with wide-ranging aerospace and other interests, it has participated in an intercultural research project with universities and other companies to develop expertise in intercultural training and consultancy. It has developed a range of initiatives, including an international board, recruiting and developing high-potential international managers, exchange programmes, conferences, meetings, specific cultural awareness and intercultural skills training, and preparation for international assignments. Specialist staff are educated at the European Consortium for Advanced Training in Aeronautics. Systems integrators receive training in the Network for Aerospace Management in Europe. Project and Programme Managers receive training at the European School for Aeronautical Sales, whilst potential general managers receive an MBA education through the European Executive MBA Consortium. In general, the company eschews generic cross-cultural training in favour of tying learning to business strategy and integrating it into planned, ongoing business activities using a cross-cultural team of facilitators working in a cross-cultural learning environment.
(Sattleberger 1994)

to technical experts; strategic criteria are relevant to senior managers and subsidiary chief executives. Such criteria are likely to include adherence to *long-term* plans and goals, recognizing the complexity and flexibility involved in these areas. The overall performance of the subsidiary and the evaluations of, for example, the regional general manager (e.g. Europe, Asia Pacific) may be used to help ensure comparability and relative objectivity in promotion or transfer decisions.

However, appraisal in such contexts is affected by a number of factors, including: separation by time and distance; differing levels of market maturity; problems in collecting comparable, relevant statistics; environmental volatility; and the desired mix between global and unit performance (Dowling et al. 1994). In addition, expatriate performance is clearly affected by the national environment and its potential for facilitating successful performance. Jobs which demand a considerable degree of interaction with HCNs, perhaps particularly with government officials, are likely to be more dependent on social, interpersonal and cultural skills than more technical jobs. Jobs which differ in content and novelty from jobs previously held are also likely to be more demanding.

The framework for international SHRM, shown in figure 6.2, can help to devise a policy framework for options in this particular area because the international enterprise's *general approach* will also affect who sets what performance standards for whom. For example, *ethnocentric* enterprises are likely to use PCN and HQ standards, whilst *polycentric* enterprises are more likely to use local and HCN standards. As the business matures and changes its focus (e.g. from technology transfer to global performance), the priority and weighting given to various criteria are also likely to change. The accounting and financial strategies adopted by the international enterprise will also affect the meaningfulness of using financial data as appraisal criteria.

Some MNCs such as ICI are beginning to incorporate environmental performance (in the 'green' sense) into their appraisal and reward systems, whilst some US MNCs (e.g. Digital, Avon) incorporate the achievement of equal opportunity, diversity and positive action goals into managerial evaluations. Others use behaviour or process-oriented criteria (*how* things are done) instead of results-oriented criteria (*what* is achieved), or use them to complement such criteria (a hybrid or mixed approach). For example, concern over corrupt practices, perhaps embodied in specific legislation such as the US Foreign Corrupt Practices Act, may direct attention to the process used in obtaining results, not merely whether goals and targets are met. The issue of *who conducts* the appraisal and *how much weight* they carry – whether it be the subsidiary CEO, the immediate supervisor, the home-country manager, the SHRM function – is also managed differently by different companies (Dowling et al. 1994).

Other issues arise in appraisal such as the cultural acceptability of appraisal itself in group-oriented or collectivist countries like Japan, where *indirect* criticism and a focus on team or company performance seem to be emphasized. It is notable that many Japanese-owned or Japanese-influenced manufacturing plants pursuing quality enhancement strategies use more process, long-term and team-based criteria. Many western MNCs, attempting to introduce more team-based structures have also experimented with team appraisal and upward appraisal (where the boss's performance is appraised by direct reports). Such US-inspired 360 degree feedback systems may not be acceptable in high 'power-distance' cultures such as many Asian countries (or even France!). Some degree of cultural sensitivity will therefore be required, as well as consultation with HCNs about local suitability. Other organizations are attempting to use a flexible 'competency architecture' to co-ordinate recruitment, selection, assessment, appraisal, and development and reward activities. And broadly defined behaviour criteria may help comparability and give managers a common performance language. One example is Pepsi-Cola International (PCI) (see box 6.7).

## Managing rewards

Reward management in an international context requires that organizations are familiar with a range of issues not normally considered in a domestic context. One set of issues concerns industrial or employee relations; others include foreign country legal and employment practices, inflation, currency fluctuations, and the application of particular allowances in particular countries. The reason for the importance of these issues is that expatriates are usually costly employees – a main reason for US companies in particular to reduce their number and rely increasingly on HCNs. As with reward management generally, international reward management needs to serve a variety of objectives. These include supporting overall corporate strategy, contributing to cost-effectiveness, attracting, retaining and motivating needed employees, facilitating employee

### BOX 6.7 PERFORMANCE MANAGEMENT AT PEPSI-COLA

PCI has devised a common appraisal system designed to enhance individual performance whilst achieving administrative consistency. Factors associated with high performance in diverse markets and nations were identified so as to generate a common performance vocabulary. The dimensions emerging were: handling business complexity, results orientation, leadership, executive excellence, organizational savvy, composure under pressure, maturity, technical knowledge, positive people skills, effective communication and impact. Each dimension might be interpreted flexibly in different environments, but with the same overall goal of generating results. A five-step feedback mechanism is used to drive high performance and balance cultural diversity and global co-ordination: Instant feedback, coaching, accountability-based appraisals, development feedback, and human resource planning. *How* instant feedback is given is of less importance than *what* is given; successful delivery requires cross-cultural adjustment.
(Schuler et al. 1993)

transfers and ensuring perceived equity among employees.

Clearly there may well be tensions and conflicts between these various objectives. Using Perlmutter's (1969) framework different policy options, especially for PCNs, can be determined:

*home-based policies* linking base salaries to the salary structure of the relevant home country: an ethnocentric strategy.

*host-based policies* linking salaries to that of the host country but with significant international supplements (such as cost of living adjustments, housing, schooling and other allowances) related to home-country salary structures: a polycentric strategy.

*region-based policies* to reward expatriates in their home regions (e.g. Europe) at lower levels than in distance regions (e.g. the Gulf).

Companies typically differ in the kinds of reward systems they install, such as the reward mix (cash vs. non-cash elements) and the basis of reward (seniority vs.

### BOX 6.8 FERRANTI-THOMSON SONAR SYSTEMS: INTERNATIONAL HRS IN AN ANGLO-FRENCH JOINT VENTURE

In 1990, the large French-based multinational Thomson, the world's largest non-American electronics company, bought a 50 per cent stake in the sonar systems division of Ferranti Computer Systems Ltd, based in Stockport, UK. Initially, all employees were ex-Ferranti, and the strong Ferranti culture persisted. Cultural differences encountered were a greater French requirement for detailed, written information within a formal hierarchical framework, a greater French preference for unstructured agendas, and a French preference for making important decisions outside formal meetings. Despite the official company language, tuition is provided at Stockport and bilingual secretaries and other staff are now preferred. The prospect of international experience is seen as an important factor in recruitment, and awareness of the European and global picture has become more important. The Thomson international training programme of residentials, conventions and seminars is now available to Ferranti, though few personnel exchanges had occurred by 1994, partly due to the problems of security in the defence industry. Payment structures, pensions and salaries have continued to be determined locally. British managers had noticed that their French counterparts had fewer company cars, but generally higher salaries.
(Moran 1994)

individual performance vs. group or unit or company performance). An obvious difference arises in relation to the 'company car' – much more common at all levels of management in Britain (usually exquisitely tied to hierarchical position!) than in most of mainland Europe or the United States. Box 6.8 shows some of the differences encountered in an Anglo-French joint venture, and some of the organizational responses.

In general most analysts argue that a company's performance management strategy should be aligned with its overall corporate strategy. Companies stressing technology transfer and short-term assignments for example (e.g. hi-tech companies) may wish to use reward systems to encourage easy expatriation and rapid reintegration to the domestic reward structure. Companies using longer-term assignments (e.g. banks) may wish to encourage inter-country mobility and team-working, so may wish to discourage nationality discrimination and use some kind of 'international' reward structure. Finally, a company with an articulated global strategy and a desire to build up an 'international' management team with a global orientation may place greater emphasis on international experience in appraisal, reward and career development, and use its reward structure to attract people oriented to such a career and to facilitate international transfers (Dowling et al. 1994).

## Conclusions and Summary

The field of international HRS is relatively immature. Based on the little that has currently been written on the subject and drawing upon ideas and models from related fields, this chapter has identified some of the key human resource strategies and tactics employed by organizations who are attempting to bolster their international and global presence. Supplemented by observations of several case-study organizations, we have discovered a mixture of structural, cultural and SHRM initiatives being used to heighten understanding of national diversity, to facilitate operating across international boundaries, to optimize the advantages of employing an increasingly multicultural workforce, and to create transitions into a more global marketplace. Much of the evidence is as yet normative and uncritical, but what there is suggests that some organizations are achieving success in these areas, although – as noted – the effort and investment to support international human resource strategic change is high and not without continuing instances of cultural insensitivity. The chapter also illustrates some important lessons concerning managing diversity: for example, intercultural experiential workshops and sensitivity training may prove particularly powerful means of creating positive working relationships and customer perceptions.

Inevitably, many questions still remain. For instance, research on 'domestic diversity' demonstrates that valuing minorities helps them achieve better job satisfaction, job involvement, career achievement and lower turnover due to greater cultural value congruence. However, are such findings applicable to internationally diverse organizations? The evidence in this chapter suggests this is the case for attracting and retaining staff, enhancing creativity and problem-solving, and responding to customer needs through developing new products and services, but more work is needed to test such linkages between the HR approaches and performance outcomes.

## Key Points

- At the enterprise level, there are differences between international and domestic SHRM in terms of scope, country and employee national origin. This prompts the need for framework for international HRS based on cultural diversity, managerial orientations and product life-cycle.
- Designing and implementing an international SHRM system requires a distinctive mind-set of the part of managers – a mind-set that may require them to think outside of the parochial values and assumptions implicit in their own national approach to SHRM.
- This framework can be applied to different functional SHRM areas (e.g. managing international diversity, recruitment and selection, training and development and performance management). This highlights the diversity and complexity of the environment faced by international enterprises, the structure and configuration adopted, and the need to react both to local responsiveness and to global integration pressures.

## Discussion Questions

1. How are international managers best recruited, selected, trained, developed, appraised and rewarded?
2. What is the stage approach to international SHRM and how useful is it?
3. Taking a particular organization – e.g. BP from this chapter – how does the stage model apply to this organization's changing international SHRM systems and architectures?
4. Are there different types of international manager? If so what different competencies do they require, and with what key variables of strategy of international SHRM dimensions do they vary?

### References

Adler, N. J. and Ghader, F. (1989) 'International business research for the twenty-first century: Canada's new research agenda', in A. Rogosan (ed.) *Research in Global Strategic Management: A Canadian perspective*, Greenwich, CT: JAI Press.

—— (1991) *International Dimensions of Organizational Behaviour*, Boston, MA: Kent Publishers.

Barham, K. and Oakes, D. (1991) *Developing the International Manager*, London: Business Books.

—— and Antal, A. B. (1994) 'Competencies for the Pan-European manager', in P. S. Kirkbride (ed.) *Human Resource Management in Europe: Perspectives for the 1990s*, London: Routledge.

Bartlett, C. A. and Ghoshal, S. (1989) *Managing Across Borders*, London: Hutchinson.

—— and —— (1990) 'Matrix management: Not a structure, a frame of mind', *Harvard Business Review*, July/August, 138–45.

—— and —— (1992) 'What is a global manager?', *Harvard Business Review*, vol. 70, no. 5, 124–32.

Black, J. and Mendenhall, M. (1990) 'Cross-cultural training effectiveness: A review and theoretical framework for future research', *Academy of Management Review*, vol. 15, no. 1, 113–36.

Black, J. S., Gregerson, H. B., and Mendenhall, M. (1992) *Global Assignment*, San Francisco, CA: Jossey-Bass.

Brewster, C. (1991) *The Management of Expatriates*, London: Kogan Page.

Dowling, P. J., Schuler, R. S., and Welch, D. (1994) *International Dimensions of Human Resource Management*, Belmond, CA: Wadsworth.

Evans, P. and Doz, Y. (1989) 'The dualistic organization', in P. Evans, Y. Doz and A. Laurent (eds) *Human Resource Management in International Firms*, London: Macmillan.

—— and Lorange, P. (1989) 'The two logics behind human resource management', in P. Evans, Y. Doz and A. S. Laurent (eds) *Human Resource Management in International Firms: Change, Globalization, Innovation*, London: Macmillan, 144–61.

Gertsen, M. C. (1990) 'Intercultural competence and expatriates', *International Journal of Human Resource Management*, vol. 1, no. 3, 341–62.

—— (1991) *Intercultural Competence and Expatriates, International Division of Labour*, Cambridge: Cambridge University Press.

Hamel, G. and Prahalad, K. K. (1989) 'Strategic intent', *Harvard Business Review*, vol. 89, no. 3, 63–76.

—— and —— (1995) *Competing for the Future: Breakthrough strategies for seizing control of your industry and creating the markets of tomorrow*, Boston, MA: Harvard Business School Press.

Harzing and van Ruysseveldt (1995) *International Human Resource Management*, University Heerlen: Sage.

Hendry, C. (1993) *Human Resource Strategies for International Growth*, London: Routledge.

Hilb, M. (1992) 'The challenge of management development in Western Europe in the 1990s', *International Journal of Human Resource Management*, vol. 3, no. 3, 575–84.

Hofstede, G. (1980) *Culture's Consequences: International Differences in Work-related Values*, Beverley Hills, CA: Sage [reprinted 1984].

Holden, L. (1991) 'European trends in training and development', *International Journal of Human Resource Management*, vol. 2, no. 2, 113–31.

—— (1994) 'NEC: International HRM with vision', in D. Torrington (ed.) *International Human Resource Management*, vol. 2, no. 2, 113–31.

Humes, S. (1993) *Managing the Multinational: Confronting the Global-Local Dilemma*, Hemel Hempstead: Prentice-Hall.

Iles, P. A. (1994b) 'Diversity in selection and assessment practice: Context, culture and congruence', *International Journal of Selection and Assessment*, vol. 2, no. 2, 111–14.

—— and Mabey, C. (1994) 'Developing global capabilities through management and organization development strategies', Paper presented to British Academy of Management Conference, September, Lancaster University.

Janis, I. (1977) *Groupthink*, Boston, MA: Houghton Mifflin.

Kanter, R. M. (1991) 'Transcending business boundaries: 12,000 world managers view

change', *Harvard Business Review*, vol. 69, no. 3, 151–64.
Laurent, A. (1986) 'The cross-cultural puzzle of international human resource management', *Human Resource Management*, vol. 25, no. 1, 91–102.
Levitt, T. (1983) 'The globalization of markets', *Harvard Business Review*, May/June, 92–102.
Moran, A. P. (1994) 'Ferranti-Thomson sonar systems: An Anglo-French venture in hi-tech collaboration', in D. Torrington (ed.) *International Human Resource Management: Think Globally, Act Locally*, New York: Prentice-Hall, 111–21.
Morrison, A. J., Ricks, P. A., and Roth, K. (1991) 'Globalization versus regionalization: Which way for the multinational?' *Organizational Dynamics*, Winter, 17–29.
Perlmutter, H. V. (1969) 'The tortuous evolution of the multinational corporation', *Columbia Journal of World Business*, January/February, vol. 4, no. 1, 9–18.
Philips, N. (1992) *Managing International Teams*, London: Financial Times, Pitman.
Prahalad, C. K. and Doz, Y. (1987) *The Multinational Mission*, New York: Free Press.
Ratiu, I. (1983) 'Thinking internationally: A comparison of how international executives learn', *International Studies of Management and Organisation*, vol. 13, nos 1–2, 139–50.
Rhinesmith, S. M. (1993) *A Manager's Guide to Globalisation*, ASTD Irwin.
Sadler, P. (1994) *Managing Talent*, London: Financial Times, Pitman.
Sattleberger, T. (1994) 'Building transnational capabilities', presentation to American Society for Training and Development International Conference, May, Anatein, CA.
Schuler, R. S., Dowling, P. J., and de Cieri, H. (1993) 'An integrative framework of strategic international human resource management', *International Journal of Human Resource Management*, vol. 4, no. 4, December, 717–64.
Scullion, H. (1992a) 'Attracting management globetrotters', *Personnel Management*, January, 28–34.
—— (1992b) 'Strategic recruitment and development of the "international manager": some European considerations', *Human Resource Management Journal*, vol. 3, no. 1, 57–69.
Torrington, D. (1994) *International Human Resource Management: Think Globally, Act Locally*, Hemel Hempstead: Prentice-Hall.
Van Houten, G. (1989) 'The implications of globalism: New management realities at Philips' in P. Evans et al. (eds) *Human Resource Management in International Firms: Change, Globalization, Innovation*, London: Macmillan, 101–12.
Vernon, R. G. (1966) 'International investment and international training in the product cycle', *Quarterly Journal of Economics*, May, 190–207.

part

# 3

# Managing Structures

chapter 7

# Organizational Structuring and Restructuring

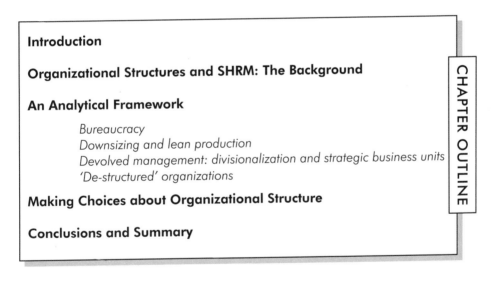

CHAPTER OUTLINE

## Learning Objectives

After reading this chapter you will be able to:

- Define organization structure and identify its purposes.
- Specify organizational dimensions which are amenable to design.
- Understand both the strengths and weaknesses of the basic bureaucratic model.
- Identify and describe ways in which the classic model may be redrawn in order to meet the changed demands of the contemporary competitive environment.
- Understand and describe the relative merits and demerits of the new structural forms.
- Appreciate the human resource dimensions of structuring and restructuring.

# Introduction

Organizational structuring and re-structuring are fundamental to the idea of a strategic approach to managing human resources. It can credibly be suggested that the shifts towards Strategic Business Units, the break-up of large internal labour markets, privatization, outsourcing and delayering have done more to fundamentally redraw the contours of relations at work than any number of new selection, training, payment or appraisal devices.

And yet, ironically, while rather extensive attention has been paid to new forms of organizations (including such examples as re-engineered, flexible and process-based forms) relatively little analysis has been devoted to the human resource management dimensions and implications of these organizational changes. The main aim of this chapter (and indeed the next) is to correct this neglect by exploring how organizational structuring and re-structuring impact upon strategic human resource management. In pursuit of this aim, these chapters will examine the potential for organizational re-structuring; the dimensions of structure which are amenable to change; the types of structure which have been designed; the principles underlying design and re-design attempts; and we will also explain the key developments by presenting a new classification of organizational designs.

Recent years have been witness to a bewildering array of examples of extensive drives to re-structure. For much of the twentieth century there seemed to be an inexorable concentration of power in large corporations. Huge conglomerates were created which embraced diverse and even unrelated businesses. Examples included Hanson Trust, Trafalgar House, Unilever, GKN and BTR in the UK and, in the United States, companies such as General Electric with turnovers larger than the gross national products of many nation states. Such industrial behemoths developed HRM strategies based around internal labour markets with job ladders, seniority rules, internal training and development systems and similar devices (see Edwards 1979 for more a more detailed account). In the public sector too, huge bureaucracies were created with the nationalization of the utilities in the late 1940s and also the creation of the National Health Service in 1948 which had many of the features of a classic bureaucracy.

In order to help manage the large organizations, multi-divisional structures were created. Such structures were designed to allow whole-company strategic issues to be handled at the central 'corporate' level while devolving other major business decisions relating to marketing, business positioning and the like to the divisional level (for more details on the growth of the multi-divisional (M-form) firm see the classic work by Chandler 1962). Tall structures were created with as many as 20 plus levels between the chief executive and the shopfloor operative. Managerial control of employees at all the multiple levels was based on a mixture of direct command and budgetary accountability. Hierarchy, command and control were the governing principles of employee management.

More recently, much of this trend would seem to have been thrown into reverse. We have seen many large multi-business organizations broken up. Examples include Hanson, Coates-Viyella and ICI. At the same time, the growth of larger and larger firms and larger work establishments have halted as the large bureaucracies have 'downsized'. Along with the smaller scale have been ushered-in a whole battery of 'new' managerial methods. Flexible organizations, responsive organizations, lean organizations, process organizations, re-engineered organizations, delayered, 'flatter' organizations; empowered, cross-functional teams – these are just a few of the more significant attempts in recent times to *restructure* the organization of work. Changes of these kinds constitute a key element in human resource strategies and also, in turn, they carry important additional human resource implications.

In this chapter, and the next, we seek to put some much-needed conceptual order on this array of measures and to explore the relationships with SHRM.

## Organizational Structures and SHRM: The Background

Central to the very idea of HRM are the ideas of flexibility, responsiveness, 'ownership' of organizational problems by as many employees as possible, empowerment and the winning of commitment. On the surface at least, each one of these appears to be the objective of contemporary restructuring attempts. Organizations in recent years have sought to enhance business and customer-oriented behaviours and priorities through the creation of Strategic Business Units (SBUs). They have sought to induce flexibility through cross-functional teams. Cost competitiveness has been pursued through slimmed corporate centres, the cutting away of 'overhead' and a cut-back in service functions by requiring production units to embrace a much wider range of functions and responsibilities. The tendency throughout much of the twentieth century for corporations to become larger and larger seems to have been halted, and in many countries to have been reversed. A veritable 'war' has been waged against bureaucracy – in Moss Kanter's words, giant's have had to 'learn to dance' (see for example, the case of Semco in Brazil as described by Semler 1994). In numerous cases they have first deemed it necessary to slim. But the restructuring that has excited attention in recent years goes well beyond mere adjustments in size and tinkering with the classical form. The logic impelling many of the restructuring movements we have witnessed in the past decade or so has been little less than the attempt to subvert the bureaucratic form.

Kanter (1991) showed just how pervasive organizational re-structuring has been throughout the world. Nearly 12,000 managers from twenty-five countries were surveyed and the results revealed widespread experience of downsizing, re-organizations, mergers and acquisitions and divestitures. The prevalence of re-structuring extended across national boundaries. Notably however, re-structuring based on downsizing and redundancy was especially associated with Anglo-Saxon countries and Eastern Europe.

To a large extent the aspirations and principles underlying the recent structural changes seem to reflect those which also underpin the ideas of HRM. There are

## BOX 7.1 HAVE THE MAJOR RE-STRUCTURINGS BEEN COMPLETED?

Re-structuring is by no means completed, according to a study by the Economist Intelligence Unit and Andersen Consulting. Managers are expecting corporate change to be more far-reaching in the future and many admitted that they are ill-prepared for the challenge. Nearly 80 per cent of executives said they expected more radical changes by 2010, even though half of them had already experienced big changes in their business in the past five years. The study, which questioned 350 senior managers from around the world, found that they were expecting competition from new directions, such as small, fast-moving knowledge-based companies. An executive at Canon, the Japanese equipment manufacturer, called this 'mega-competition'. Only the most flexible organizational structures would be able to withstand the stress of these changes, the executives said. The research also looked at attitudes to more loosely structured businesses, some of which rely on third parties to run large parts of their operations. This trend towards 'virtual' businesses was reflected in forecasts of more joint ventures, outsourcing, alliances and greater cross-sectoral-operations. Executives in larger companies demonstrated the greatest interest in improving flexibility and embracing the concept of the virtual organization. Managers from smaller companies tended to be more concerned about their ability to attract and retain people and how best to keep pace with technology. Almost 40 per cent of respondents named 'soft issues' such as cultural fit, effective people management and clear and frequent communication as the biggest challenges for the future. (*Financial Times*, May 1997) even the same hard and soft logics at play. From an organizational re-structuring point of view the 'hard' aspects are to be found in the drastic cuts in 'head-counts', the 'downsizing' and the 'outsourcing'. The soft side of the rationale is to be found in the ideas of 'empowerment', the 'learning' that is required to cope with multiple demanding tasks, and the 'teamworking' that is invoked. Both sets of facets appear to constitute, above all, a critique and escape from bureaucracy.

Organizational structuring and re-structuring are intimately intertwined with many aspects of human resource management. Different structures carry implications for career opportunities, for job design and job satisfaction, for learning and development opportunities, for power distance, work content and skill levels.

The interconnections between organizational structures and human resource management strategies are however complex. Integral to the logic of the large organizations, which grew after the end of the Second World War, was the method of what Edwards (1979: 26) described as the 'bureaucratic control' system. This strategy was based around internal labour markets and the winning of employee commitment through the prospect of long-term career advancement, job security, welfare packages and seniority pay systems. The elaborate job ladders were underpinned by company-provided training and development. Where they existed, trade unions also supported these firm internal labour markets. Such arrangements were, in many ways, also well suited to the principles of human resource management. The material elements were in place to encourage a psychological contract based on commitment; extensive investment in training and development made sense; the system ought to have encouraged careful recruitment and selection, systematic appraisal and elaborate performance management systems. To this extent the fit between this organizational model and human resource management was rather promising. But there were limitations. The bureaucratic form tended to foster complacency and the link with customers became tenuous. As competitive conditions changed these systems found it hard to adapt. Bureaucracy was used to command and control. Initiative was stifled. Hence, in these ways the *departure* from the bureaucratic control system could be interpreted as actually rather more in tune with the principles of human resource management than would its preservation. But, as we will see in the next chapter, this has to be heavily qualified because the nature of the departures made have often been such that the resulting employment systems have been in some tension with HRM.

## An Analytical Framework

We have already noted the almost bewildering array of forms which organizational re-structuring has taken in recent years. Mergers and take-overs are reported alongside de-mergers and corporate break-ups. Decentralization seems to be a perpetual process: a phenomenon surely only made possible by a series of moves which amount to increased centralization. More dramatically, in recent times there seem to have been some radical departures in the direction of

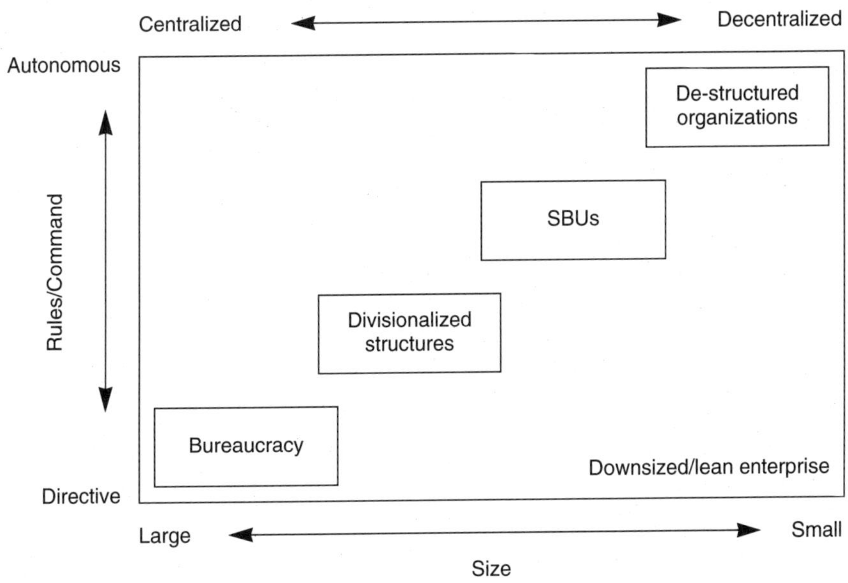


**Figure 7.1** Types of restructuring within organizational boundaries

networking and outsourcing – and even a good deal of talk about 'virtual organizations'. How is it possible to make sense of this apparent chaos? It can be fairly observed that not only has the field lacked a thorough exploration of the linkages between structuring and SHRM but, in addition, there has also been a notable failure in conceptual and analytical thinking in keeping pace with, and helping to explain, these myriad experiments.

To assist the analysis in this and the ensuing chapter a conceptual framework can be suggested, which arises out of the juxtaposition of different dimensions which appear to have been critical in recent re-structuring attempts. These are shown in figures 7.1 and 7.2. For the purposes of locating the various types of re-structuring which have taken place within conventional organizational boundaries it is necessary to refer to figure 7.1.

Figure 7.1 uses three cross-cutting dimensions. On the top horizontal axis is the dimension of centralized to decentralized; on the vertical axis is the dimension from 'directive' to 'autonomous'; and on the horizontal axis at the base of the figure is the dimension relating to size. For illustrative purposes, a selection of different organizational arrangements are shown. At the bottom left, the bureaucratic form is located to suggest a centralized, directive mode. Ascending the ladder and moving to the right, one progressively moves to divisionalized arrangements, to the use of strategic business units (SBUs) and then to autonomous, empowered teams.

So far, we have referred to forms of re-structuring which have occurred within

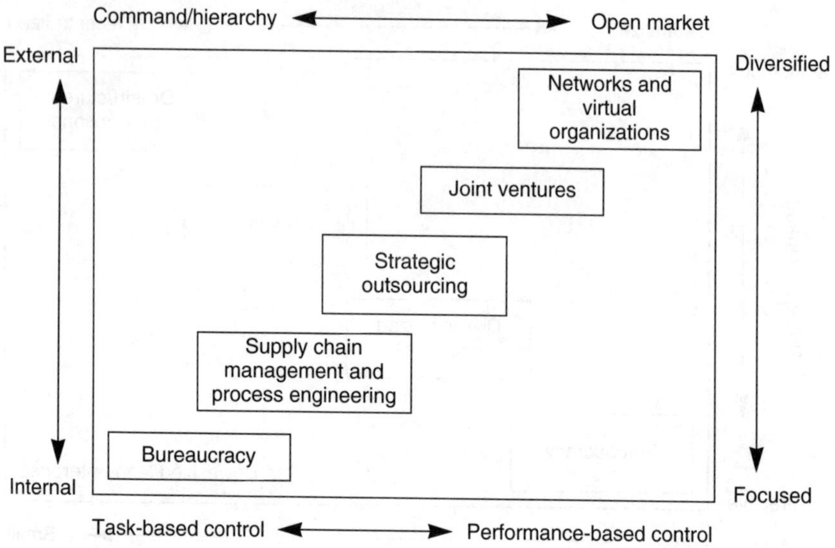


**Figure 7.2** A spectrum of relationship structures beyond conventional organizational boundaries

the confines of conventional organizational boundaries. But many of the recent experiments have transgressed and even broken free of these boundaries. These types of re-structuring are located on a separate figure (see figure 7.2). This uses four dimensions. The first, running along the top of the figure, illustrates the spectrum from internal hierarchical command relations at one end, to open market relations at the other. The second dimension, located at the bottom of the figure depicts the contrast between task-based control and performance based control. The third dimension is located on the left hand-side vertical axis and it shows the spectrum from internal relationships to external. And the fourth, on the right hand-side of the figure contrasts diversified forms with more focused forms.

Using these cross-cutting dimensions it is possible to reveal a patterned ordering in the variety of organizational types which have proliferated in recent years. Thus, for example, starting at the bottom left of the figure, the bureaucratic form of organization can be seen as characterized by an emphasis on internal relationships, a hierarchical command structure and a mainly task-based set of control criteria. Progressing up the ladder, supply chain management and process engineering, strategic outsourcing, joint ventures, and networks are shown to represent, and result from, varying degrees of shift along each of the dimensions.

Other types of initiatives in re-structuring can also be located on such a framework. For example, the experiments with the idea of the 'internal market' in the British National Health Service where previous hierarchical arrangements were displaced by purchaser and supplier relations, can be located part way along the bottom and right of this figure.

These frameworks are useful in mapping the conceptual possibilities. It is also hoped that they help clarify where the many and varied forms 'locate', when considered in relation to each other and in relation to certain key dimensions. The figures do not suggest that any type of form is 'better' than another; they are not prescriptive. Nor do these figures suggest any historical 'progression'. In order to assess 'appropriateness' and to interpret possible 'trends' it is necessary to examine more closely the various design principles. This is what we will do when we have reviewed the different types of structure shown in the figures. In this chapter we focus on the various re-structuring methods that have been attempted within organizational boundaries (as shown in figure 7.1). In the next chapter we turn to examine the re-structurings which extend beyond conventional organizational boundaries (as shown in figure 7.2).

## *Bureaucracy*

The contours of 'bureaucracy' (from the French word 'bureau', broadly translatable as 'rule by office') were drawn and analysed by Max Weber, around the end of the nineteenth century and the early years of the twentieth century. He was interested in describing and assessing the historic shifts in Europe from traditional authority regimes to the (then) new principles of formal rationality rather than in prescribing paths to 'efficiency' per se. While there is considerable doubt about whether Weber himself was endorsing the model, there were plenty of others who did (and who also assumed that Weber did too). At the same time, while many (particularly American scholars of complex organizations) have used the term in a positive, prescriptive sense, the popular everyday usage has been of a contrary nature – i.e. bureaucracy has a pejorative tone. In this usage it symbolizes unnecessary delay, red tape, ritual, and the stifling of individuality. However, the accelerated growth of large formal organizations throughout most of the twentieth century prompted social scientists to attempt a more dispassionate analysis of its characteristics and consequences (for example, Crozier 1964).

The key attributes of bureaucracy in the descriptive, social science, sense can be summarized as follows:

1 A clear division of work with stipulated boundaries to responsibilities; officials are given authority to carry out their assigned functions.

2 Referral by role occupants to formal (written) rules and procedures which ensure predictability and routinization of decisions.

3 A well-defined hierarchy of authority.

4 Appointment to posts arranged not through patronage or bribery but on the basis of technical competence.

5 A system of rules with formal (written) documentation of actions and decisions.

The model in its totality gave rise to impersonality – this was one of its intended characteristics. It had the advantage of overcoming nepotism, favouritism and arbitrary decision making. The principles seemed well suited to the administrative needs of the new democratic states and the emerging large industrial enterprises. This apparatus of legal rule stands in contrast to that which operated under patrimonial rule where custom, personal recruitment and obligation were the governing principles. In place of arrangements whereby posts could be appropriated and reward could derive from the revenue of the office, the typical alternative under bureaucracy is to reward the official by monthly salary based on a full time position and then by a pension following a lifetime career.

Three sets of 'unanticipated consequences' and 'dysfunctions' of bureaucracy have been pointed out by various organizational analysts (March and Simon 1958; Selznick 1949; Gouldner 1954; Merton 1957). The first derives from the emphasis on control. This can prompt rigidity of behaviour and defensive routines. The second focuses on the implications for the behaviour of subunits. Division of task and responsibility can elevate departmental goals above whole system goals – that is, lead to suboptimizing behaviour. And thirdly, as a result of the impersonality of rules the minimal acceptable standards can become transformed into targets and behavioural norms. Rules and procedures can also become ends in themselves.

Gouldner's study of an industrial bureaucracy illustrates some of these points very graphically. His case study revealed how formal controls triggered a vicious circle of increasing dysfunctionality. The working to rule routine led to apathy and minimization of performance. The supervisory response of increased direct control served to make power relations more starkly visible and in turn prompted conflict. This led to a vicious spiral of control and resistance.

## Bureaucracy in perspective

However, despite this catalogue of problems and dysfunctions it has been frequently pointed out (for example, Robbins 1990) that throughout the world the largest organizations are essentially still bureaucracies. They remain so despite the competing ideas because they meet their goals through this type of structure. In the light of this it is evident that the phenomenon of bureaucracy cannot be easily dismissed or written off. On the contrary it demands close attention. Despite the chronicling of problems and dysfunctions, and despite the oft-heralded death of bureaucracy, this form of organization has proved to be remarkably resilient. Inroads have undoubtedly been made: delayering has sometimes reduced the number of hierarchical levels, flexible job designs have replaced narrow job specifications, teamwork has displaced clear individual accountability, empowerment has substituted lengthy specifications of formal rules. And yet, in the face of these numerous experiments, initiatives and change programmes, big and small, many of the features of the classic bureaucratic form reassert themselves and await treatment by the next initiative. One reason for this resilience may be the inherent 'stickiness' and inertia in organizations. Another possibility could be that bureaucracy actually carries certain advantages and therefore, even when assailed, organizational members find reason enough to re-install or at least defend its existence.

One important strand in the drive against bureaucracy has been the ideological shift which urged the primacy of the market. This logic led to extensive deregulation and the consequent pressure on large organizations which had previously enjoyed oligopolistic conditions. It also manifested itself in the pressure to depart drastically from internal transactions and management in favour of actual or near-market 'contracts'. This type of market-based contractual relationship inevitably removed the need, the cause, and the opportunity to persist with each of the characteristic elements of bureaucracy described above. An associated development has been the relative decline of internal labour markets as the basis for managing employees be they managers or non-managers. In turn, the consequence of this shift from internal labour market techniques to an increasing reliance on external labour market methods has been a shift in the nature of human resource management methods deemed to be appropriate under these new circumstances. Thus, career planning and career management may not be required for large numbers of staff. Direct supervision, induction, training and development, socialization, appraisal, and even reward problems can potentially all be avoided by the primary contracting organization.

One of the functions of bureaucratic rules is to ameliorate the tensions which stem from differences in values and interests between different groups constituting an organization. As Gouldner sees it there are limits to the extent to which norms and values can be elaborated satisfactorily to everyone in the organization (1954: 240). Relatedly, the impersonality of bureaucracy is a response to the problem of succession – compliance is not contingent upon the persuasive influence of any individual boss. He further shows how rules can be used by supervisors and subordinates alike. Gouldner's study of an industrial bureaucracy explores the problems of control and the reactions to control. Impersonal rules he observes arise because they alleviate the tensions caused by subordination. But at the same time they create other tensions – in particular, they can reinforce the low morale of workers and thus provoke behaviour which stimulates close supervision. Both managers and workers use them selectively as bargaining tools, sometimes suspending the rule, at other times insisting on application.

Each of these American sociologists – Merton, Selznick and Gouldner take the Weberian model into new realms based largely on a human relations perspective. Crozier from a French political science perspective adds a power dimension to the analysis. He studied in great detail two French organizations which he termed the Clerical Agency and the Industrial Bureaucracy. Using the characteristic traits which he educed in these cases he sought to build a more dynamic model of bureaucracy than had been achieved by Weber or the American sociologists described above. For him the central problem of an organization's government is to achieve an acceptable level of conformity. Modern organizations deal with people who 'because of their education have already internalized a number of basic conformities' (Crozier 1964: 184). In addition, organizations use devices such as multiple communications, work flow, technical settings of jobs and economic incentives.

Organizational structures represent attempts to shape the relationships between the individual and the organization, and indeed between groups and the organization. As Crozier (1964: 175) puts it 'the world of power is one aspect of the complex relationship . . . The world of consensus and the world of the co-operative game are other aspects of this basic relationship.' The rationalistic ideal-type bureaucracy imposes a substantial amount of standardization on employees.

Crozier (1964: 185) also observed how, in practice, 'subordinates will bargain with their own conformity and use it as a tool with which to bind management. This is just another aspect of the fight for control. Subordinates tacitly agree to play the management game, but they try to turn it to their own advantage and to prevent management from interfering with their independence.' Hence, a clerk sticking rigidly to a ritual does so partly because of 'trained incapacity' but also for purposes of protection against punitive treatment in case of error. He found in a French clerical agency supervisors taking routine inadequate decisions in preference to having to face hostile relationships and risk of failure. Thus, Crozier's analysis is more dynamic and is built on close empirical observation. Predictability is in tension, with the need for adjustment and flexibility. These are two conflicting aims for organizations. Crozier actually defines a 'bureaucratic system of organization' as any system 'where the feedback process, error-information-correction, does not function well and where consequently there cannot be any quick adjustment of the programs of action in view of the errors committed. In other words, a bureaucratic organization is an organization that cannot correct its behaviour by learning from its errors' (1964: 187). In contemporary parlance such organizations are not responsive to customer demands. Crozier found that all decisions that had not been eliminated by the system of rules were taken at a central level – i.e. away from a point where personal pressures might be felt from those affected by the decision. Centralization was thus a means of eliminating personal power.

It was the kinds of problems with bureaucracy identified by Crozier and others that have led in recent years to extensive attempts to undertake radical organizational redesign as market changes made such features less tolerable. One of the most evident and dramatic of these changes was the reversal of the previous trend towards larger organizations. The large corporations began to cut back in a big way.

## Downsizing and lean production

Faced with rapidly changing environments many employers have responded by downsizing and in the process have also retreated from long term commitments to employees, which the internal labour market model allowed and facilitated. Kodak, IBM and General Motors are examples of the kind of large blue-chip corporations which formerly exemplified the bureaucratic model but which, in restructuring, have dismantled many of the elements of that model. In the United States it is estimated that over one million middle managers lost their jobs as organizations flattened organizational structures. The strategy of many companies over the past few years has been to reduce their size; 'take costs out of the business'; increase productivity by having fewer people undertake the same or even more work; and re-focus activity on the core business. Senior executives were rewarded for so doing: share prices tended to rise when these steps were taken and top management salaries increased. Table 7.1 shows some of the key changes in organizational size.

The compilation of accurate data about firm size distribution is notoriously difficult and some heroic assumptions are often made by those who make such calculations. Recognizing these uncertainties, the broad trend between 1979–1991 as shown in Table 7.1 reveals a significant increase in the share of employment accounted for by the smaller firms and a decrease in the share of employment accounted for by the larger ones. Thus, micro-businesses (with between 1–10 employees) increased their employment share from 20 per cent in 1979 to 28 per cent in 1991. Meanwhile, businesses in the 1,000 plus employment category experienced a decrease in their share – falling from 35 per cent in 1979 to 27 per cent in 1991. It would, however, be dangerous to extrapolate this trend into the future. More recent data from the Department of Trade and Industry (DTI 1997: 32) reveals that during the period 1995–96 the share of employment of all the size bands between 1–99 fell, while the size bands with more than 100 employees all increased their share of employment. Overall, the fact remains, however, that when compared with the bulk of the post-1945 period when employment policies were generally predicated on the assumption that the larger firm was the dominant model, recent years have seen a shift to an employment pattern in which small and medium sized environments have become far more important.

It has been suggested that when properly implemented, the 'lean organization' concept should involve a phased journey from cutting back on non

**Table 7.1** Trends in organizational size measured by numbers of employees in the United Kingdom

| | *1979* | *1986* | *1991* |
|---|---|---|---|
| 1–2 | 7 | 11 | 11 |
| 3–10 | 13 | 17 | 17 |
| 11–19 | 8 | 6 | 6 |
| 20–99 | 12 | 14 | 16 |
| 100–499 | 18 | 17 | 17 |
| 500–999 | 8 | 7 | 6 |
| 1000 + | 35 | 29 | 27 |
| Totals per cent | 101 | 101 | 100 |

*Source:* Adapted from D. J. Storey (1994: 21).

value-added activities and downsizing to a reformed stage where activities smoothly interconnect in a more efficient manner. However, Purcell and Hutchinson (1996) found that most organizations which embarked on this process remained at the first stage – i.e. simply downsizing rather than 'maturing' into a state that could allow proper use of just-in-time and total quality management (TQM).

One especially famous study claimed that lean production can *improve* work satisfaction for employees (Womack et al. 1992). Purcell, however, found it hard to locate evidence of this. The trauma experienced by the 15,000 job losses at Lloyds Bank are cited as an example. Middle managers, however, have been shown by some studies to feel less frustration in smaller hierarchies, following lean production, while others seem to be demotivated and demoralized. They work longer hours and feel insecure.

The backlash was perhaps bound to occur. People have asked at what point does the downsizing and externalizing have to stop and what impact has there been on other corporate strategies such as TQM? Stephen Roach the 'downsizing guru' has reportedly 'recanted' and has argued that corporations have taken this strategy too far. How compatible is the numerical flexibility with teamwork? How will training and development occur? Where insecurity prevails, people may be less inclined to train others, and where people have been encouraged to behave as independent competitive operators they too may be less inclined to share knowledge, information and ways of working. This may all trigger a vicious circle: lack of trust by employer and worker, disallowing long term commitment and trust, and therefore promoting reliance on further externalization.

## Devolved management: divisionalization and strategic business units

Perhaps the most obvious way to respond to the catalogue of problems associated with bureaucracy is to seek in one way or another to 'decentralize'. This is a well trodden path. Indeed, it seems to have occurred so frequently that one can only suspect that there is some cycle of decentralization and (re)centralization at play. Be that as it may, for the past 20 years or so the cycle would seem to have been very much on the downswing – that is, in favour of decentralized units. The tendency began with a wholesale switch to divisionalized structures, first in the United States and then more widely – especially in Britain. Later, by the 1980s, the mood swung further and 'strategic business units' became the fashion. Business units became pronounced in companies such as ABB and GE.

So far did this go, that as Hamel and Prahalad noted, 'In many companies, one cannot speak meaningfully of a "corporate strategy" because the corporate strategy is little more than the aggregation of the independent strategies of stand alone business units. Where the corporate role has been largely devolved, corporate officers have no particular responsibilities other than investor relations, acquisitions and disposals, and resource allocation across independent business units' (Hamel and Prahalad 1994: 288). Naturally, there are drawbacks to this arrangement – synergies and the advantages of the big company are lost. Opportunities remain unexploited and the potential to use core competencies across units is undermined. Hamel and Prahalad argue that senior managers should 'seek to identify and exploit the interlinkages across units that could potentially add value to the corporation as a whole' (1994: 289). Aspiring to this however is one thing, achieving it is another. It will require special measures to ensure that corporate effort, rather than business unit goal achievement, is rewarded.

Meanwhile, delayering has continued, at least in some companies. General Electric, a company with over 200,000 employees, has delayered and now has businesses with as few as three or four layers of management between front line workers and the chief executive. A corollary of such delayering is often the devolution of more HR responsibility to lower levels of line management.

Research by Hall and Torrington (1998) on the issue of 'devolving' HR to line managers suggests that unless line managers also secure the incentive of budgetary responsibility for HR interventions, then the realization of the aspiration will remain problematic. On the other hand, if line managers do get this responsibility there is the danger that they will manage human resources with short-term priorities and that the achievement of strategic HRM will be even further away. 'It is paradoxical that devolution has been seen as part of a move to enable personnel practitioners to play a greater strategic role and yet the logical consequence of devolution is to make the implementation of the strategy extremely difficult' (1998: 52).

## 'De-structured' organizations

By this term we mean to cover the collection of types of structural innovations variously described as high performance organizations, knowledge creating companies, empowered teams, ad hoc, boundaryless, and process-based organizations – among other similar terms. Despite the range of titles, the underlying ideas are similar: they point to a departure from traditional bureaucratic forms with their formal rules, hierarchy of office and vertical communication, and circumscribed role responsibilities, and celebrate instead the breaking down of internal barriers and formal structures. The new watchwords are teams (preferably cross-functional), lateral communications, the minimization (if not outright removal) of hierarchy, and the sparse use of rules. Informality and the exploitation of expertise, wherever it may lie in the corporation, is the essential idea. With some variance in emphasis, the same basic tenets can be found underpinning the so-called 'high performance work systems' and the 'knowledge creating companies'.

Ashkenas et al. (1995) title their influential book, *The Boundaryless Organization* and sub-title it *Breaking the Chains of Organizational Structure*. This book presages a new order for organizations as they shift from rigid to permeable organizational structures and processes. For example, Motorola is reported to have 'taken years out of its new product development cycle by replacing its traditional functional processes with fully accountable cross-functional teams composed of engineers, marketers, manufacturing experts, financial analysts and others (1995: 2). According to Ashkenas et al. the 'emerging organization' of the twenty-first century will act differently. Specifically, 'behaviour patterns that are highly conditioned by boundaries between levels, functions, and other constructs will be replaced by patterns of free movement across those same boundaries. No longer will organizations use boundaries to separate people, tasks, processes and places; instead, they will focus on how to permeate those boundaries – to move ideas, information, decisions, talent, rewards and actions where they are most needed' (1995: 2–3). This amounts to a 'paradigm shift' towards boundaryless structures.

Even these authors accept however that *some* boundaries are necessary. Boundaries help to give focus. They do not want to imply, they maintain, a total free-for-all. Rather, the permeability of boundaries will increase. Information, resources, ideas and energy must pass through the 'membranes'. The analogy is the living organism. They claim that already 'almost all organizations have experimented with some type of change process aimed at creating more permeable boundaries' (1995: 5). Sometimes this is impelled as a result of a crisis: for example at General Motors, IBM, Sony, Volkswagen, Lloyds of London, Citicorp and many others. These once great and seemingly unassailable institutions did not 'stumble' because of lack of planning, lack of investment or lack of technology. (General Motors probably invested more in automation than any other company in the world while IBM research investment was above the industry norm.) The general explanation was that they were faced with a rate of change that was beyond their capacity to respond. This is because they found, too late, that they lacked the flexibility and agility; their structures were too rigid.

The lessons here are said to point to a new paradigm. The organizational attributes which formerly conferred advantage can, under the new conditions, constitute disabling impediments. In summary form the contrast can be depicted in the two lists below.

| Old Success Factors | New Success Factors |
|---|---|
| ■ size | ■ speed |
| ■ role clarity | ■ flexibility |
| ■ specialization | ■ integration |
| ■ control | ■ innovation |

Source: Ashkenas et al. 1995: 7.

A rather similar narrative is presented by proponents of the idea of the 'knowledge-based' company. For example, according to Nonaka and Takeuchi (1995), the source of corporate success under contemporary conditions resides in the ability of a company to create new knowledge, disseminate it throughout the organization, and embody it in new services and products. Japanese companies such as Canon, Matsushita, NEC, Kao and Sharp have been identified as special in their use of knowledge management to create new markets and develop many new products.

As with Ashkenas et al., Nonaka and Takeuchi contend that the knowledge creating company is 'not a machine but a living organism'. Its competitive edge comes not so much from processing objective information, as from tapping the tacit and highly subjective insights of large numbers of employees. It draws out their insights, hunches and intuitions. The foundation stone for this type of company is one which is resonant with the fundamentals of HRM: 'The key to the process is personal commitment, the employees' sense of identity with the enterprise and its mission'. The managerial role in this new type of structure is far distant from the command and control activity of old. It is in many respects the antithesis of bureaucracy and of the classical administrative principles. The managers role is also very different: managers need to project ideals as much as ideas; they need to articulate a vision of where the organization ought to be; they need to handle images and symbols. There are other diametric departures from classical principles. The value of a person's contribution is determined not by their location in the hierarchy but by the significance of the information which he or she provides to the knowledge creating system.

The knowledge creating company does not only entail shifts in managerial roles. The rest of the structure needs to alter too. Everyone has, to some extent, become a knowledge worker. Personal knowledge needs to become available to others – this indeed becomes a central activity of the knowledge creating company. Here Nonaka refers to the idea of a spiral of knowledge – essentially from tacit to explicit and as this is disseminated and internalized by employees, to further growth in tacit knowledge and so on. To convert tacit knowledge into explicit knowledge requires finding a way to express notions that are not amenable to conventional, explicit, clearly-defined instructions. On the contrary, it requires the use of figurative language, metaphors, analogy and symbols. These can permit project teams and others to grasp something intuitively and then to find their own interpretations of what it could mean in practice for new products and technologies.

A further organizational characteristic is what Nonaka refers to as the 'principle of redundancy.' This is manifested in the sharing of overlapping information across different activities in order to enable them to find their own implications. It is expressed also in the way Canon organizes its product development using competing groups which develop different approaches to the same product idea and then debate the relative advantages and disadvantages. Yet another device is strategic rotation of managers and other personnel across different functions, products, and technologies. The intent is to make the organization's vast repository of knowledge more fluid, rather than see it locked up in distinct units. At Kao, reports Nonaka, all employees are expected to hold at least three different jobs in any ten year period. A further device to exploit 'redundancy' is the free access to company information. This allows different interpretations to emerge of the new knowledge.

So much for the range of structural types and the restructuring examples. Having gained some appreciation of these the next step is to reflect more fully on the dimensions which are amenable to design and also the kind of factors which govern the exercise of choice in one direction rather than another.

## Making Choices about Organizational Structure

This final section of the chapter examines the basis on which choices are made about organizational structuring. By the same token, we seek explanations for the different forms. As we have seen, there are numerous structural forms which are in co-existence. Moreover, development can move in opposite directions: for example, there can be centralization and decentralization, mergers and de-mergers can occur, companies can acquire and divest. Why do these things occur? What principles, if any, are brought to bear?

'Structure' sounds rather static. It might be thought that senior managers would only contemplate a change in structure if and when they were faced with a crisis. Yet in many cases organizations must continually (and do) rethink and redesign structure in order to achieve their strategic goals. Competitive conditions are changing at an accelerated rate and organizations need to make appropriate responses, or even more ideally be one of the drivers of these wider changes. Companies such as IBM, ICI, Unilever, have all recently reorganized in order to achieve new objectives. Redesigning organizational structure is one of the ways (arguably one of the more strategic and far-reaching) in which managers can intervene in order to mobilize behaviour to attain desired goals. 'Structure' then might be seen as not only a pattern of relationships between roles and sub-units and as a means of co-ordination but may also be regarded as a framework for planning, organizing, directing and controlling.

In simple terms it can be said that while strategy describes *what* to do organizing defines *how* to do it. The constituent elements of organizational structure include the set of formal tasks assigned to individuals and departments; formal reporting relationships, including lines of authority, decision responsibility, number of hierarchical levels, and span of managers' control; and the design of systems to ensure effective co-ordination of employees across departments. However, the factors influencing choice are many and varied. As we will see the emergence of particular structures may not always be explained so easily, as if it were the exercise of 'choice' in the sense of a free, calculated rational weighing of alternatives.

First, we can note the factors which could be said to constitute 'rational' considerations. These include the desire to hold individuals and sub-units accountable for the use of resources and the achievement of targets. Lines of reporting and the use of job descriptions are the kind of devices used for this purpose. Another criterion is usually to ensure the flow of communication. Senior managers will usually want structures which enable a clear and direct flow of communication from top to bottom and possibly may also want to facilitate upward communication as well. Yet while wanting to issue instructions which are received and understood and be able to hold named individuals as accountable, senior managers will also usually not want the structures they create to stifle all sense of initiative and motivation. Hence, many instances of organizational design will include some measure of autonomy in order to elicit these desired behaviours and attitudes. In the possibly more sophisticated companies structures may also be adjusted in order to facilitate learning and the buildings of future organizational capability. Thus, for example, boundary-breaking or at least boundary-spanning measures such as cross-functional and cross-unit teams may be established so that parts of the organization can learn from other parts.

Second, it has to be realized that particular structural forms can also arise for reasons other than the technical reasons suggested above. Top managers may judge it safest simply to follow the 'industry recipe' – i.e. the normal pattern for their sector. In a similar vein, some changes in structure may come about because of prevailing fashion. Sometimes this fashion is further fuelled by the work of management consultants and gurus. Thus there are waves of 'merger mania'; periods when downsizing is the norm and is expected of incoming chief executives. Then there are political reasons why structural changes may take place. Powerful 'barons' who head-up important territories or who are responsible for particular products may need to be appeased and to that end organizational design may be moulded around that need. Power struggles can occur between SBUs which seek to use optimal supply chain rationalities, and divisions which have assets to protect, such as sales or capital investment or jobs.

Third, various contingent factors such as technology have been argued as exerting an influence on organizational structure. Rarely, if ever, is this a determining factor, but the scale required in technological investment, in say an oil refinery, is likely to have some influence on the nature of the organization which is formed in order to exploit those technological assets profitably. In recent years new technologies have began to influence organizational structures and to a large extent, open them up: the mobile phone, PCs, lap top computers, modems and networked databases. Such technology has allowed teleworking and homeworking for some. For those remaining in offices the causal influence of the technology-structure link has often been reversed: i.e. the new demands for project teams has prompted a reshaping of office technology. Open plan office space, removal or reduction in hierarchical space standards and the private 'ownership' of space has declined in favour of 'temporarily occupied' space.

Similarly, in a global marketplace, the need to 'act local' (be responsive to local conditions) and yet take advantage of the benefits of a transnational organizational resource is also likely to influence organizational structure. Organizational 'size' as a possible contingent factor has long been a topic of contention. One would expect that, other things being equal, larger organizations would have more complex and formal structures. Nonetheless, even size is not a determining factor: some large organizations have managed to create informal arrangements while some smaller organizations have created more formal systems. In part, the variations are related to different contingencies faced in different industries. For example, in pharmaceutical industries, regulatory requirements ensure that 'good manufacturing practices' are followed and this in turn impels a certain measure of routine, formal procedure, accountability and record keeping. Also, in retail banking the duplication of routine activities in multiple small and dispersed locations tends to produce broadly similar structures across each of the main clearing banks.

In practice, managers are usually faced with a need to balance a series of diverse and sometimes conflicting considerations. Centrally, there is a need for balance between *differentiation* and *integration*. Formal organizations are notable for the way in which they divide-up tasks and responsibilities (differentiation) and yet also require some mechanisms for co-ordinating and controlling in order to pull these separate activities together (integration). Also, structures need to ensure some congruence between policies and priorities. If, for example, the organization is seeking to foster 'high commitment' this is unlikely to be attained by a tight command and control structure or with structures which limit discretion and autonomy (see box 7.2).

A classic dilemma is between structuring on the basis of management function or on the basis of products (see figure 7.3). Under the former, each function such as production, marketing, finance, and sales has its own hierarchy. It is particularly favoured by small and medium sized enterprises. The emphasis is upon technical quality and cost control. On the positive side it is the least complex of structures; it allows economies of scale; enables in depth skill development, achievement of functional goals and clear accountability. On the negative side it is slow to respond to environmental change, is poor at encouraging horizontal co-ordination and communication and is not conducive to innovation. It also tends to encourage a restricted view of organizational overall goals. Product-based structures are more likely to be found in large organizations and in environments of moderate to high uncertainty. They are more able to respond to unstable environments, and the units should be better able also to tailor themselves to clients' needs. On the other hand, such structures tend to involve some duplication of resources, they fail to fully exploit economies of scale in functional departments and, if fully deployed in a pure form may sacrifice in-depth technical competence.

Matrix structures are supposed to allow some balance between these types.

| | | Structure: Mechanistic | Structure: Organic |
|---|---|---|---|
| Environment | (Unstable) | Poor fit ✘ | Good fit ✔ |
| | (Stable) | Good fit ✔ | Poor fit ✘ |

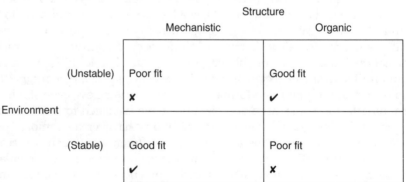

**Figure 7.3** Fitting structure to environment

## BOX 7.2 TO DIVEST OR CREATE A COHERENT, GLOBAL BUSINESS? THE CASE OF GEC

Lord Weinstock was the long-standing and highly influential chief executive of GEC. His successor, George Simpson, chief executive of GEC since September 1996, inherited a complex structural form. Weinstock's decisions reflected the pressures faced by companies of GEC's type in many European countries, as they lose their role as national champions under the pressures of globalization. Lord Weinstock's solution was to play for time, and for scale. As a result, many of the company's most important assets are locked away in joint ventures in power engineering, transport and telecoms equipment. These have a scale and scope they would lack had they remained purely British. But GEC directly manages none of them, greatly limiting its ability to shape its own future. Like any incoming chief executive, Mr Simpson must cope with his predecessor's decisions. But he must also cope with the difficult circumstances which gave rise to them. In the short run, he seems likely to take some obvious steps: seeking to free himself on acceptable terms from both big joint ventures; focusing the group on activities it directly manages; and building up the most promising of these. In the medium term, he must solve the intractable puzzle of the European defence industry, balancing the appeal of cross-border European link-ups against the possibility of creating a single strong British defence company, in a merger with British Aerospace.

In the long run, the task is harder still: to create a coherent, centrally managed business of global scale, drawing on shared resources of technology and skills. Many of the ingredients of such a company exist within GEC. But combining them fruitfully will require a commitment to patient, long-term daily management, without a guarantee of success. It would not be surprising if GEC's shareholders were to press instead for a rapid programme of divestment. But it would be a pity if the desire for certain gains prevailed over the opportunity to create a coherent world-class industrial group. Mr Simpson must sketch out such a vision, then persuade his colleagues and shareholders that he can achieve it. (Financial Times, Leader, 8 July 1997)

They should allow a focus on both economies of scale and product development, permit a balance between the demands of customer focus and functional specialization; and should be suited to complex decision situations. The weaknesses of matrix structures are that participants experience dual authority and this can lead to frustration and confusion. There is usually a higher degree of political behaviour with time-consuming and frequent meetings. Decision making may be slow with large coalitions entering the fray. It has been suggested that to help ameliorate these conditions one dimension of the matrix should normally take the lead and that senior management levels should be staffed with persons with collaborative styles and a high tolerance for uncertainty and ambiguity (Johnson and Scholes, 1993).

Another factor shaping the way in which 'choices' are made about structure is the prevailing set of images which key actors hold about the nature of organizations. We have noted above how both Ashkenas and Nonaka were keen to cast aside the idea of organizations as machines in favour of organizations as living 'organisms'. The power of such images has been explored in some depth by Morgan (1986). He extends the range of ideas or 'metaphors' we tend to hold in our attempts to make sense of organizations. The importance of these images is that they frame and shape not only the way managers think about organizations but also, in consequence, the options perceived as available for redesign. New design possibilities emerge he suggests if conventional thought patterns are broken. For example: given the globalization of business, the increase in international travel, the spread of the multinational and even transnational enterprise and, not least, the international exposure of major consultants and gurus, it might be expected that organizational structures in different countries will become increasingly alike. This argument, the so-called 'convergence thesis', has been advanced by many commentators – most notably by Bartlett and Ghoshall (1992), Humes (1993) and Ulrich and Lake (1990). However, important differences in structural forms have been found to persist between different countries.

## Conclusions and Summary

In this chapter we have examined the importance of organization structure and explored a number of the main types of structure. These types were located on an analytical framework using the three cross-cutting dimensions of centralized/decentralized; large/small; and autonomous/directive. Using this framework four main types of structures were identified and discussed: bureaucracy, divisionalized structures, strategic business units, and 'de-structured' forms. The characteristic features of the main types and their human resource management aspects were explored.

The chapter then moved on to a closer examination of the kind of factors which senior managers might bear in mind when making decisions about structuring and re-structuring. At the same time, we drew attention to the fact that organization structures were often emergent phenomena and that rational, technically-based weighing of alternative forms and their relative merits were often not the source of the structures which exist. Accordingly, various contingencies were identified and the influence of industry trends and organizational politics were also brought into the explanation.

This chapter has focused primarily on aspects of structuring which take place within the confines of conventional organizational boundaries. However, as we noted in the course of the chapter there are also instances of important re-structuring initiatives which cut across organizational boundaries and it is to a consideration of these types that we turn in chapter 8.

## Key Points

- Although talk about the end of bureaucracy is not new there does seem to have been rather more evidence of late suggesting that some fundamental and far-reaching changes are taking place in the way organizations are structured.
- Re-structuring has occurred under many different names but certain essential common themes re-occur in most of these instances: such as a shift from hierarchical command and control methods and structures and an emphasis on greater responsibility at front-line levels.
- But these changes do not mean the removal of control. In some instances the efficacy of the control is increased because outcomes of effort are made more transparent than before; targets are more stretching. Different devices – often budgetary in nature – are used to effect control.

## Discussion Questions

1 What are the key features of the bureaucratic form of organization?
2 What are (or were) the main advantages of this form and what are the disadvantages?
3 Which are the most important innovations in re-structuring and how enduring do you think they will be?
4 How much similarity (and dissimilarity) is there between the new organizational forms?

## References

Ashkenas, R., Ulrich D., Jick, T., and Kerr, S. (1995) *The Boundaryless Organization: Breaking the chains of organizational structure*. San Francisco, CA: Jossey-Bass.
Bartlett, C. and Ghoshall, S. (1992) *Managing Across Borders: the transnational corporation* Cambridge, MA: Harvard Business School Press.
Cascio, W. F. (1993) 'Downsizing: What do we know? What have we learned?', *Academy of Management Executive*, vol. 7, no. 1, 95–103
Chandler, A. (1962) *Strategy and Structure*, Cambridge, MA: MIT Press.
Collins, J. C. and Porras, J. I. (1995) *Built to Last: Successful Habits of Visionary Companies*, New York: Randon House.
Crozier, M. (1964) *The Bureaucratic Phenomenon*, London: Tavistock.
Daft, R. (1994) *Management* (3rd edn), London: The Dryden Press.
Drucker, P. (1989) *The Practice of Management*, London: Heinemann.
DTI (1997) *Small and Medium Sized Enterprise (SME) Statistics for the United Kingdom*, London: Department of Trade and Industry.
Edwards, R. C. (1979) *Contested Terrain: The transformation of the workplace in the twentieth century*, London: Heinemann.
Evans, P. and Doz, Y. (1989) 'The dualistic organization', in P. Evans, Y. Doz and A. Laurent (eds) *Human Resource Management in International Firms*, London: Macmillan.
Galbraith, J. (1977) *Organizational Design*, Reading, MA: Addison-Wesley.

Gouldner, A. (1954) *Patterns of Industrial Bureaucracy*, New York: The Free Press.
Hall, L. and Torrington, D. (1998) 'Letting go or holding on – the devolution of operational personnel activities', *Human Resource Management Journal*, vol. 8, no. 1, 41–55.
Hamel, G. and Prahalad, C. K. (1994). *Competing for the Future*. Boston, MA: Harvard Business School Press.
Humes, S. (1993) *Managing the Multinational: Confronting the global-local dilemma*, Hemel Hempstead: Prentice-Hall.
Johnson, G. and Scholes, K. (1993) *Exploring Corporate Strategy*, Hemel Hempstead: Prentice-Hall.
Kanter, R. M. (1991) 'Transcending businesses boundaries: 12,000 world managers view change', *Harvard Business Review*, vol. 63, no. 3, 151–64
Lawrence, P. R. and Lorsch J. W. (1967) *Organization and Environment*, Boston, MA: Harvard University Press.
March, J. G. and Simon H. A. (1958) *Organizations*, New York: Wiley.
Merton, R. (1957) *Social Theory and Social Structure*, Chicago, IL: Free Press.
Mintzberg H. (1983) *Structure in Fives: Designing Effective Organizations*, Englewood Cliffs, NJ: Prentice-Hall.
Morgan, G. (1986) *Images of Organizations*, London: Sage.
Nonaka, I. and Takeuchi, H. (1995) *The Knowledge Creating Company*, Oxford: Oxford University Press.
Purcell, J. and Hutchinson S. (1996) 'Lean and mean?' *People Management*, vol. 10, October 1996.
Quinn, J. B. (1992) *Intelligent Enterprise*, New York: Free Press.
Robbins, S. J. (1990) *Organization Theory*, New Jersey: Prentice-Hall.
Selznick, P. (1949). *TVA and the Grass Roots*. Berkerley, CA: University of California Press.
Semler, R. (1994) *Maverick!* London: Arrow.
Storey, D. J. (1994) *Understanding the Small Business Sector*, London: Routledge.
Ulrich, D. and Lake, D. (1990) *Organizational Capability: Competing from the Inside-Out*, New York: John Wiley.
Weber, M. (1947) *The Theory of Social and Economic Organization*, New York: Oxford University Press.
Womack, J. P., Jones, D. J., and Roos, D. (1992) *The Machine that Changed the World*, New York: Rawson Associates.

chapter 8

# Beyond Organizational Structure: The End of Classical Forms?

CHAPTER OUTLINE

## Learning Objectives

After studying this chapter you will be able to:

- Identify the distinctive features of the main new organizational forms and the extent to which they are emerging.
- Assess the degree of commonality and the extent of the differences between the various new types of organizations.
- Understand and explain how the various new forms map on to human resource management policies and practices.
- Explain their significance from a strategic human resource management perspective.

# Introduction

In the previous chapter we focused on the structuring and re-structuring initiatives which have occurred within conventional organizational boundaries. In this chapter we now turn to examine those forms of organizational restructuring which cross organizational boundaries as conventionally understood. In recent years there would seem to have been a quite remarkable degree of interest in forming new sorts of structures which reach out to engage associates, partners and even competitors in the wider marketplace. These new arrangements have taken various forms but most prominent seem to have been joint ventures, strategic alliances, networks and outsourcing arrangement. Mirroring these developments have been those writings which reflect upon the 'breaking' of organizational boundaries (see for example, Quinn 1992; and Ashkenas et al., 1995).

The focus in conventional organizational analysis was overwhelmingly upon internal organizational structures. Organizations were seen as systems with fairly distinct boundaries. However, increasingly, attention is being paid to the connections made across organizational boundaries. Alliances, federations and networks are seen as increasingly important. Information and communication technologies carry the capacity to transcend organizational boundaries and allow work to be done in new ways on a distributed basis. The past identity of an organization, resting as it did on a physical place and associated perhaps with distinct products, is becoming less important and even less valid.

Much of the work on the extra-organizational forms has been undertaken by economists. The human resource dimensions of these developments have been very much under-explored. It is intended that this chapter should help to illuminate this hitherto underdeveloped agenda. We will identify the human resource management dimensions of each major structural initiative as we proceed through each section; then, in the final section, we address the implications for the *strategic* potential in HRM presented by these structural developments.

# An Analytical Framework

Part of the problem to date has been the lack of an adequate conceptual mapping of the myriad developments. In this chapter we will use the framework first presented in the previous chapter and reproduced below (see figure 8.1). It should be emphasized that the main purpose of figure 8.1 is to locate the diverse initiatives on a conceptual map. Hence, the various forms which are creating so much new interest are located in reference to four key dimensions. They indicate a progression towards increasing externalization of relations; to diversified activities; to performance based control; and to an open-market mode of regulation (see the dimensions on all four sides of figure 8.1). Although many observers would, and many indeed do, assert a definite *trend* in the direction of the top-right of the figure, the evidence does not entirely point in one direction. Moreover, a historically-informed perspective on organizational studies would caution that apparent 'trends' are often more like 'cycles'. In this chapter we reserve judgement therefore on this point. As we will report on the body of the chapter, there are some instances where decisions are being made which indicate that at least some companies are re-internalizing rather than externalizing. Nonetheless, for the past few years it would be fair to say that the general thrust (possibly as much expressed in sentiment and aspiration as in concrete action) has been in the direction away from the conventional bureaucratic mode in the bottom-left and more towards the various forms in the upper-right direction.

We will start at the bottom left of figure 8.1 and work up the ladder to the top-

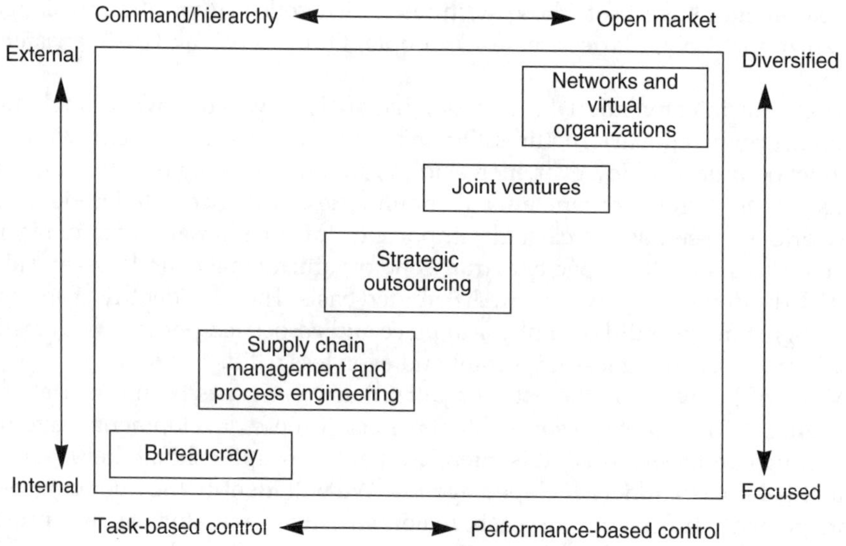


**Figure 8.1** A spectrum of relationship structures beyond conventional organizational boundaries

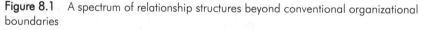

right. The phenomenon of bureaucracy was discussed in the previous chapter and it is not necessary to revisit it here. It is, however, useful to place it in the figure as a compass point. In this chapter we begin the analysis therefore with the second step – supply chain management and process re-engineering.

## Supply Chain Management and Process Re-engineering

A radical innovation in the way in which companies regard their structural arrangements has been the rise in popularity of the idea of dismissing function and products as structural principles in favour of a rigorous focus on supply chains and processes. A supply chain and process analysis can extend through, and beyond, organizational boundaries. The starting point is an analysis of the value-adding activities. Following this an attempt is made to identify and eliminate the non value-adding components.

Such a zero-based analysis is claimed to be very far-reaching in its implications for organizational structures and human resource management. Thus, 'everything that has been learned in the twentieth century about enterprises applies only to task-oriented organizations, everything must be rethought' (Hammer and Champy 1992). In this statement the originators of the business process re-engineering concept make clear their radical intent. They prescribe and foresee nothing less than the total displacement of classical structures. The central idea of re-engineering is that in order to survive under the new competitive conditions, companies must re-orient themselves around their core processes – the start to finish sequence of activities which create customer value. The human resource management implications are extensive. Re-engineering, it is claimed, means the end of narrow jobs, the end of supervisory management, of traditional career paths and much more. Above all, it represents an outright challenge to practically all of the classical principles of organization developed throughout the twentieth century and as described in the preceding chapter.

Many commentators have reacted to these dramatic claims with the counter-charge that it is really nothing more than a managerial 'fad'. They see it as an example of successful marketing by clever consultants and gurus. It may, however, be something rather more substantial. Arguably it represents a critical response to fundamental changes in the nature of competition and changes in information technology. Supply chain and process re-engineering, in this view, is one of the more crucial and revealing reactions to these historic changes in the wider environment of business. The label itself may indeed become less fashionable but the underlying ideas are, nonetheless, likely to be sustained – albeit in some repackaged form. Accordingly, it is worth examining the central ideas and propositions of Business Process Re-engineering (BPR) as illustrative of contemporary concerns about organizational structuring.

We can describe the key elements of process re-engineering as expressed by the most notable original exponents: Hammer and Champy (1992), Hammer (1996) and Davenport (1993). These expositions of re-engineering struck a resounding chord with managers in many countries. The triggers for it are increasing affluence, more discriminating consumers, competition from the Far East, and developments in information technology which have generated the capability for firms to meet the market challenges in more flexible and sophisticated ways. Davenport (1993) in fact subtitles his book 'Re-engineering Work through Information Technology'.

Thomas Davenport, was a consultant with Ernst & Young. In his book *Process Innovation* he writes:

> In the face of intense competition and other business pressures on large organizations in the 1990s, quality initiatives and continuous, incremental process improvement, though still essential, will no longer be sufficient. Objectives of 5% or 10% improvement in all business processes each year must give way to efforts to achieve 50%, 100% or even higher improvement levels in a few key processes. Today, firms must seek not fractional, but multiplicative levels of improvement – 10× rather 10%. Such radical levels of change require powerful new tools that will facilitate the fundamental redesign of work. (Davenport 1993: 1)

How are these things to be done? Process innovation combines the adoption of a process view of the business with the 'application of innovation' to the key processes. The objectives are drastic cost reductions, and major improvements in quality, flexibility and service levels.

The key elements of process innovations are said to be:

- a 'fresh start', 'blank sheet' review.
- a process rather than functional view of the whole organization.
- cross-functional solutions.
- step change.
- the exploitation of information technology.
- attention to work activities on and off the shop floor.
- adoption of a customer's view of the organization/producing value for customers.
- processes must have owners.

Hammer (1996) in *Beyond Re-engineering* explains how the 'process-centred organization' differs from traditional functional structures. The origins are traced to the late 1980s when a few advanced companies such as Ford, Taco Bell and Texas Instruments began programmes of business improvements which differed in kind from the usual run of the mill variety. They engaged in radical changes and redesigned their processes from a clean sheet of paper basis. The changes which they initiated have allegedly 'transformed American industry beyond recognition' (1996: xi). By bringing processes centre stage, re-engineering rendered redundant the accumulated wisdom of a hundred years of management thought.

> Virtually everything that has been learned in the twentieth century about enterprises applies only to task-centred enterprises, the hitherto dominant form of organisational life. For a world of process-centred organisations everything must be rethought: the kinds of work that people do, the jobs they hold, the skills they need, the ways in which their performance is measured and rewarded, the careers they follow, the roles managers play, the principles of strategy that enterprises follow. Process-centred organisations demand the complete reinvention of the systems and disciplines of management. (1996: xiii)

This scenario is not, he maintains, mere speculation: the concepts and techniques are already in use today. The take-up of re-engineering world-wide has been very extensive. In Britain, for example, it has been reported that a remarkable 70 per cent of large organizations have embarked on what their own managers say was a BPR programme. In America the transition to process-centred organizations began slowly in the early 1990s with organizations such as Xerox and Texas Instruments, but in a short time the trickle became 'a flood': Ingersoll-Rand, Shell, Levi Strauss, Ford, GTE, Chrysler 'are all concentrating on their processes' (1996: 8).

The will to undertake radical departures stemmed from the immensity of the problems faced by the traditional corporations. GTE, the telecommunications company, found that its customer service unit was able to resolve customer problems on first call in less than 2 per cent of occasions; Pepsi found that 44 per cent of invoices it sent to retailers contained errors; Texas Instruments discovered that its Semiconductor Group took 180 days to meet an order for an integrated circuit which a competitor could complete in just 30 days; Aetna Life & Casualty took 28 days to process an application for homeowners insurance of which only 26 minutes were real productive time. Radical remedies were required and achieved, and the key was a switch in focus from task improvement to a focus on process.

But what is a 'process' and how does it differ from a task? A task is said to be 'a unit of work, a business activity normally performed by one person. A process, in contrast, is a related group of tasks that together create a result of value to the customer' (Davenport 1993: 5). A process, on the other hand, is 'a structured, measured set of activities designed to produce a specified output for a particular customer or market. It implies a strong emphasis on *how* work is done within an organization, in contrast to a product focus's emphasis on *what* . . . a process is thus a specific ordering of work activities across time and place with a beginning, an end, and clearly identified inputs and outputs: a structure for action' (1993: 5).

Most companies, even large ones, are said to be able, if they try, to reduce their generic processes to less than 20 – for example Xerox has 14, Dow Chemicals has nine. These major processes, include produce development, customer order fulfilment and financial asset management. Business organizations for the past two hundred years have been based on tasks and the basic building block of organizational structures has been functional departments constituted by similar tasks.

## Human resource management considerations

Under these circumstances the first human resource management task is to ensure that everyone in the organization and across its wider reaches is aware of these processes. Shifting from a traditional mode of operating to a process-based one is no easy task. Employees fear that a process re-engineering initiative means job losses and extensive change. They are usually correct on both counts. Even years after the introduction of such a change employees may harbour resentment and blame the consultancy firm that was used. The implications for future commitment-winning measures can be problematical. Second, HR needs to help in the changing of mind-sets and behaviours which are required under such a radically different organizational form. One such crucial change is the abandonment of the task specialization we discussed in the previous chapter as a hallmark of bureaucracy.

In a process organization, workers engaged in operating a machine will need to see themselves, maintains Davenport, as there not merely to run the machine but to contribute to the 'order fulfilment process'. Hence, if production-flow backs-up, these operatives will be expected to investigate and then seek to resolve the problem. Such behaviour will simply be part of the new job. Indeed, language is so important to process re-engineering, say the gurus, that 'worker' should really be replaced by the term 'process performer'.

An additional step from an HRM point of view is that process measures are important in order to track performance and for planning improvements. This is allied to process management which entails a continual focus on process improvement and process redesign. A process centred organization entails and requires 'a fundamental reconceptualisation of what organisations are all about. It permeats every aspect of the business: how people see themselves and their jobs, how they are assessed and paid, what managers do and the definition and hence strategy and positioning of the business' (Hammer 1996).

New roles are required. 'Process performer' roles have already been noted; in addition, there is a need for 'process leaders', 'process owners' and 'process managers' whose jobs are to engage in process design and redesign, coaching and advocacy. This last means it is the process owner's job to obtain the necessary financial and other resources to meet the process needs; and to occupy a seat on the 'process council' (which is a forum of process owners and heads of remaining support services to discuss the business as a whole). Such a body is seen as necessary to avoid functional silos being replaced by 'process tunnels' or process protectorates.

This kind of process focus implies jobs that are much enlarged: jobs which require understanding, insight, autonomy, responsibility and decision making. Supervision is not supposed to be required. Hammer (1996) talks bluntly about 'the end of the organisation chart'. There are no departments or departmental managers, and very little hierarchy. Significant instead are 'centres of excellence'. These are to be thought of as in-house versions of professional associations. They are supposed to enable skill formation and continual development. In addition, they are intended to provide channels of communication which enable the sharing of knowledge and expertise. Because there are no managers, the best performers in a process organization do not become diverted into watching over others; they are freed-up to do what they do best. Corporations he says must adjust their reward systems accordingly. The old deal (or psychological contract) was based on obedience, loyalty and diligence in exchange for long-term security. The new deal exchanges initiative for opportunity.

These new entities are not only more co-operative internally, they are also inclined to be co-operatively interactive with external organizations too. Internal and external walls are broken down. Partnership here is not driven by goodwill as such but rather by 'enlightened self interest. The goal is not to change the way companies feel about their trading partners but the way they interact with them. Better interaction may well serve to modify feelings as a later consequence of mutual benefit received. But the tangible things, the underlying hard systems of operations, must be changed first' (1996: 173). It goes beyond outsourcing; it entails a co-operative endeavour where the partners excel together or sink together. Compartmentalism ultimately is not even possible at the level of the firm.

A more fundamental concern is that the model is based on a unitary view of the firm. In a telling section Hammer criticizes those corporate heads who so readily nowadays mouth the mantra of the primacy of 'shareholder value'. This is not what business enterprises are about he maintains, rather they are there for 'customer value'. While his main justification for this is couched in terms of the lack of guidance afforded by the former and the comparative clarity of needed behaviours under the latter, the underlying issue is never properly addressed: how does the worker/process performer come to identify so strongly with this enterprise? While it may be the case that a customer focus could be more persuasive than a sole concentration of shareholder value, it hardly seems sufficient to sweep away centuries of labour–employer conflict.

The role of coach, Hammer suggests, is critical for the organization's success. 'No matter how well designed a process is, it's the people who make it work' (1996: 117). And so in one sentence we arrive at the heart of the matter. The process alone cannot deliver. 'In the long run the equality of an organisation's coaching is a key determinant of whether it succeeds or fails. Process design alone is not enough. As more companies learn how to create state of the art processes, the advantage will belong to those with an institutionalised capacity for staffing these processes with well-selected and well-trained people' (1996: 118). In the end it all comes down to the skill of the coach to train and to readjust mind-sets so that process performers are willing to focus on 'customer value'. And thus it is that some rather deep-seated issues and conflicts are conjured away in the mysteries of the learning organization, the persuasive power of the coach and the unitary intent of the team.

# Strategic Outsourcing

'Outsourcing' refers to the situation when a company subcontracts to another supplier work that it was previously performing in-house. Strictly speaking, therefore, it does not denote all forms of purchasing from suppliers, though the distinction between being a former producer of the service or product and simply being a purchaser is in a practice very blurred. Essentially, however, outsourcing entails the externalizing of production and services. It is a manifestation of the classic 'make or buy' decision. The phenomenon has, as yet, generally found little recognition in the human resource management textbooks. In recent times it has been one of the more popular ways to cut costs and to refocus on core competencies. One graphic sign of the trend was that by the mid-1990s the labour agency Manpower Inc. had displaced General Motors as the largest employer in the United States. And a study of businesses and government agencies in the US showed that 44 per cent of the executives surveyed said they are doing more outsourcing than they did five years ago and 47 per cent said they expect to increase the amount of work they outsource in the future (Kelly 1995). Likewise, IT-related outsourcing revenues are estimated to be growing at 14.4 per cent annually (Bruno 1995).

In practice, there are many different types of outsourcing activity and usage. Some of the instances are piecemeal and opportunistic with little strategic character. Office cleaning is an example in most circumstances. The commissioning client has low vulnerability in relation to this kind of service, and likewise the contribution to competitive advantage is not likely to be high. But for other services the outsourcing decision might arise from a very close analysis of the value chain and this can permit strategic use of outsourcing. An example would be the link between certain Marks & Spencer suppliers where the reliable level of quality provides competitive advantage, and where the service is at the high end of the vulnerability scale. Determining just what is core can, however, be problematical. For example, Nike outsources all of its manufacturing; Apple Computers outsources 70 per cent of its components; while GM has outsourced its car-body painting activities.

The reasons for the growth of outsourcing are many. In a complex, fast-moving market it is a speedy way to gain access to specialist services. Alternatively, it can be a means to reduce costs by sourcing from low-cost producers, many of whom are likely to be non-unionized. In this regard, advances in information and communication technologies have played a part in that companies headquartered in high-wage cosmopolitan areas can outsource routine billing etc. to remote stations almost anywhere in the world.

Problems of scrap can be drastically reduced or even eliminated as defective components can simply be rejected. Outsourcing also enables flexibility in that supply can be more readily turned on or off – at least in theory. In some instances it is merely, however, a device to respond to pressures of 'headcount control' – i.e. a means, on paper at least, to show that the critical measure of direct employee numbers is being kept under control. But, according to the more cutting-edge theories of 'winning' companies, the outsourcing phenomenon is, above all, a manifestation of enterprises clearing-out peripheral, distracting activities, in order to focus on core functions and core competencies. Quinn (1992) argues that companies should concentrate on those 'core competencies' (these, he says are usually intellectual or service activities) in which they can be best in the world. The other activities should be outsourced.

## Human resource management considerations

In addition to the commonly outsourced services such as catering, security, IT services and the like, various HR functions can themselves be outsourced. To date, the most popular candidates have been training, retirement planning, outplacement services, relocation, counselling and various forms of consultancy. American Express, for example, has outsourced its retirement plan and benefits system. IBM created a spin-off company called Workforce Solutions in 1992. It outsourced its own HR staff functions to this company and Workforce Solutions can sell its services also to other customers.

There are consequences for organizational structures and human resource management, though it seems likely that the full consequences have not as yet been fully grasped or even researched. Organizational hierarchies are much flatter, there is reduced scope for inter-functional activity and therefore a lower need for co-ordination. The priority management task becomes not the handling of physical and capital assets but the management of intellectual processes and the management of staff who are not direct employees of the company. Negotiation of contracts with the providers becomes critical. There are issues of confidentiality, risk sharing, continual improvement and so on. Even where there are clear opt-out clauses for non-compliance the management of the actual occurrences may prove difficult.

A critical strategic human resource management issue is the potential loss of expertise in certain areas which may be difficult to recover. There is a danger of a serious 'hollowing-out' of the organization. The modern tenets of organizational learning, corporate culture and shared visions may all be put in some jeopardy if this occurs. Likewise, the sources of innovation needed in order to keep pace with rapidly changing markets may be put in jeopardy if a company is heavily reliant on strictly delineated services from a host of outside suppliers. Arranging the wherewithal to forestall this problem is an important HR challenge under conditions of extensive outsourcing.

The HR function could potentially assume a key role when outsourcing occurs. In fact HR departments reportedly already play a role in some 65 per cent of all company outsourcing cases in the United States (up from about 35 per cent in the past five years). So while the search and selection team ideally involves a top executive, the respective department manager and a legal expert, human resources often plays a critical role as facilitators and co-ordinators of the entire process. 'It is a natural role for human resource professionals to play because of their communication and administrative expertise' (Sunoo and Laab 1994: 70). A recent study of six UK building societies found, however, that five of them did not even have a formal policy towards outsourcing, only the Derbyshire had such a policy which enabled it to make plans for the identification and protection of core competencies (Jennings 1996).

Part of the human resource management function is to attract and retain people who have the appropriate skill sets required under the new conditions. A series of decisions to buy rather than to make, taken individually, may make economic sense, but collectively they may undermine the ability of a firm to compete. Using research conducted in North America, Europe and Asia, Bettis (1992) describes and illustrates how inappropriate outsourcing is promoting the continuing decline of many western firms. He extends the argument on a larger scale to the industry and country level.

While not all contracted staff are in the vulnerable, low-pay category, there has been some widening of inequalities as the remaining few permanent staff enjoy higher earnings, fringe benefits and better access to skill acquisition. This presents a further challenge to the maintenance of an organization which is low on formal control structures but is supposed to score high on shared values.

Drucker (1993) argues that companies will eventually outsource all functions that do not have a career ladder up to senior management. He contends that corporations, once built to last like pyramids, will be more 'like tents'. In this new world, managers he maintains, must take responsibility for their own career development by exploring their own competencies and making good competency deficiencies. Moreover, he suggests that information will replace authority as the executive's primary tool.

## Joint Ventures, Mergers and Alliances

Joint ventures and strategic alliances have become a common feature of the US business horizon. In the UK also, joint ventures and alliances have been very popular. For example, BT alone has more than 70 joint ventures and overseas distribution arrangements. Some pharmaceutical companies form as many as 20 to 30 new alliances per annum.

Through joint ventures, organizations are able to achieve a number of objectives. Large companies using their marketing expertise and systems can bring new products developed by smaller companies to market rather faster than a small company acting alone. For example, the joint venture between Hoechst and Schering to acquire a majority stake in Plant Genetic Systems, a small genetic research enterprise. Additionally, large companies may seek a joint venture in order to gain a foothold in new product areas and to acquire new expertise rapidly. This has been the case with large agrochemical companies which have allied with small- and medium-sized biotechnology companies. A third reason for joint ventures is to enable the partners to reduce their cost base by pooling resources. Companies have often cut their staffing levels and reduced their distribution costs. A fourth factor is that certain developing countries such as India and China may disallow inward investment which is not tied to some form of joint venture with a domestic concern. Salomon Brothers, the American investment bank, and Dresdner Bank of Germany, have both entered into joint ventures with Chinese financial companies as a result. Likewise, Royal Dutch/Shell invested in a power-generation plant in India in a joint venture with Essar Group, an Indian industrial company.

Despite these attractions and the frequency of occurrence, failure is high. In the United States approximately half of all alliances forged in the early 1990s were considered failures. In Europe too, a high failure rate of companies involved in international joint ventures has been noted (Harper, 1995). One of the most frequently-cited causes of such failures has been that the organizational and HRM issues were not adequately addressed.

## Human resource management considerations

The human resource management aspects have usually been neglected by companies embarking on new alliances and joint ventures. There are, however, a few exceptions. Merck, for example, in the US, has a high reputation for the way it uses the HR role in managing joint ventures. Numerous joint ventures, both national and international in character have been entered into by Merck and in each case the HR staff have been involved from the outset. Staffing solutions are devised, procedures and policies drawn up. Communication and education are given an especially high priority in order to ensure that the partners not only understand each other but can learn from each other. The overall HRM challenge involves blending corporate cultures, compensation schemes and overcoming staffing problems.

A variant on the joint venture is an arrangement whereby companies enter into co-operative arrangements to invest in and share common services – such as a local training facility. In a more formal way this is exemplified by the Shared Service Centre (SSC) established for the BBC by a joint-venture company formed by Coopers & Lybrand and EDS, the US systems group. A 10-year contract has been signed under which staff will eventually work for the joint-venture company – but on BBC premises. The shared service centre has allowed the finance function the opportunity to offer career development to two quite different groups of staff. 'High quality finance staff are not going to spend a lifetime pushing debits and credits. We want to build skills in the value-added areas,' claimed the Finance Director. In time other companies may use the SSC as it effectively becomes an outsourcing centre. For the present time it is located inside the BBC. Shared service arrangements have also been launched by General Electric, Seagram, Bristol Myers Squib and Whirlpool. Essentially an SSC does all those tasks that do not need to be kept close to the heart of a business. Placing an order with a supplier is a decision that must be taken at the centre – but the payment of the bill and recording of the transaction can be done at the SSC.

Meanwhile, the staff working on processing transactions find themselves in a larger single organization with greater career opportunities. There has also been a need to put in place management structures to ensure the main customer/contractor is able to keep a measure of strategic control (Jim Kelly, *Financial Times*, July 1997).

# Networks and Virtual Organizations

An organization such as Benetton is characterized by its organized network of market relations based on complex forms of contracting. It operates a retail system based entirely on franchising. On the other hand, its sourcing for garments is based on a putting-out system which has a long history. Nowadays, information and communication technology allows the total complex system to operate with rapid feedback system enabling it to operate with the absolute minimum of stock. In this system it is the wider network rather than the organization which is the interesting unit of analysis – indeed arguably Benetton, as such, is not an 'organization' at all in the conventional sense (Clegg 1990). Organizations such as Coca Cola and Visa, despite their strong world-wide presence, are likewise not traditional organizations of the kind described in the previous chapter. It is very hard to pin down the 'ownership' of these forms as some of them have no fixed assets. Some commentators maintain that they really are 'virtual organizations'.

A 'network organization' has been defined as an economic entity that operates through a cluster of compact business units, driven by the market, with few levels of decision making and a willingness to outsource whatever can be better done elsewhere (Snow 1992). It can be expected that new management functions will be needed – for example, brokers, architects, lead-operators, and caretakers.

This free-flow across organizational boundaries can reach a stage when the organization per se becomes undefinable and unrecognizable – what Davidow and Malone (1992) have described as the 'virtual organization'. They ask:

> What will the virtual corporation look like? There is no single answer. To the outside observer it will appear almost edgeless, with permeable and continuously changing interfaces between company, supplier and customers. From inside the firm the view will be no less amorphous, with traditional offices, departments and operating divisions constantly reforming according to need. Job responsibilities will constantly shift, as will lines of authority – even the very definition of employee will change as some customers and suppliers begin to spend more time in the company than will some of the firms' own workers. (Davidow and Malone 1992: 5–6)

## Human resource management considerations

The underlying logic of network organizations as presented by their advocates and practitioners is that 'know-how' and resource capability are now critical factors, and these are increasingly difficult to locate within the boundaries of a single organization. Know-how and capability are increasingly distributed across a network of different business and contractors. But if this is so, the human resource management challenge to identify, retain, develop and appropriate such scarce resources are immense.

Part of the know-how resides in the identification of the parties and the capability to bring them together. In the 'the boundaryless organization' there are huge uncertainties about who, if anyone, is managing these processes. External boundaries are barriers between firms and the outside world, including customers and suppliers, but also government agencies, special interest groups and the community at large. In traditional organizations there are clear demarcation lines separating 'insiders' from 'outsiders'. Role expectations were relatively clear. Management dealt with the former group and had mechanisms and techniques to help them do this. But these traditional methods are of doubtful validity in the network situation.

Under the network arrangement, there are contracts of a more commercial nature. Equally, there are connecting lines based on repeat business, trust and reputation. Mind-sets and attitudes have to change considerably. Traditional methods of negotiation, competition, win–lose, information withholding, power plays and the like, may cause difficulties.

Increasingly, boundary maintenance behaviour is seen as having dysfunctional consequences. When the boundaries are dissolved or drastically reduced, customers and suppliers may be treated as joint partners. Employees, as such, may be hard to identify. A range of parties may be expected to help the firm solve problems and to innovate. Effective network organizations need to make permeable the external boundaries that divide them from their customers and suppliers. The key concept here is that of the value chain. This is the set of linkages which create services and products of value to the end user. In the traditional view each company is supposed to maximize its own success with disregard for that of others. The overriding idea is that of competition. Under the new value chain concept the idea is to loosen external boundaries so as to create a win–win situation across the whole value chain.

Under the network concept co-operative relations between organizations are given high priority. As the cost of innovation increases, as complexity increases and everything changes so much faster, many companies have come to the conclusion that they simply cannot work alone. Business partners, customers and suppliers are urged to work together to co-produce value. This entails reconfiguring roles and relationships. The use of co-operative arrangements of a network kind has long been well developed in Japan. The *keitsu* consists of cross-locking companies often straddling very different sectors. They have shares in each others' equity but there is no governing holding company.

The successful value chain companies co-operate in both strategic and operational business planning. Network organizations require managers and staff to change their assumptions and behaviours. Instead of developing plans and strategies independently, planning needs to be co-ordinated and even shared with other participants in the network. Information therefore must not be hoarded and protected, but shared to allow joint problem solving. Moreover, measurement and auditing systems need to be co-ordinated.

Organizational members therefore need to adjust their mind-sets so that the well-being of the whole value chain is kept in mind and enhanced. For example, GE Appliances collaborated with key suppliers. Together they can plan for and respond more quickly to changes in the production schedules. Production, inventory, sales, specification and scheduling data can be co-ordinated. A monthly data package is shared with 25 main suppliers. An organization may be considered well linked into its value chain if it scores high on a set of measures of joint development in marketing plans, product development planning, production and inventory planning, distribution planning and information systems planning. And for the management of resources and capabilities the indicators would be shared resources as opposed to separate resources in the areas of technical expertise, financial expertise, management skills, information systems and training, and development.

How and why does a company become a core organization in a network's value chain? The main identifying feature of a core organization is that it 'manages the network' – a role that is not, however, legally recognized. The actual process of managing such a network is a difficult one and it requires skills for which, as yet, little or no formal training is usually offered. Boyle (1993) examines the role of the core as a user organization, as the provider and/or user of goods and services, and as the link organization. He sees the possibility of the role of the core organization changing over time as exemplified by Esso's shift away from being a petrol station franchiser to becoming a link organization by moving into forecourt convenience stores.

It is argued that the capacity to command and co-ordinate service activities, supplier networks and contract relations has become an important strategic weapon and scale economy for many successful enterprises (Quinn 1990). Because the role of service technology in providing added value is becoming predominant, strategies are increasingly being built around core service skills, rather than products. Examples of success achieved by such 'integrated' companies, according to Quinn, include Toys 'R' Us, Apple Computer and Honda.

According to these and other proponents of networks, the human resource management implications include the involvement of as many employees as possible so that they become familiar with customer and supplier needs. This can be done through inviting customers and suppliers to meetings where outlines of plans, goals and problems can be explained; by sending employees on customer and supplier field trips to encounter the detailed operations of day-to-day work; collecting and collating customer and supplier information. An additional stage can involve experiments with collaboration through, for example, organizing cross-value-chain task forces and sharing technical services. And a more ambitious step involves companies integrating their information systems and reconfiguring roles and responsibilities in the light of the collaboration achieved across the networks.

The immensity of these challenges has led some corporate chiefs to revert to old-fashioned command and control solutions. Thus, Lord Weinstock's successor at GEC has said that he wants to move away from 'the joint venture culture' and towards direct investment and control by GEC managers. In the late 1980s and early 1990s, partnership with rivals and others had been one of the central pillars of GEC's strategy. Now, it appears, this strategy is being largely abandoned in favour of attempts by the group to build global businesses on its own. Likewise, BA's chief executive has said he expects to employ as many people in the future as he does now. And Microsoft's business might seem more suited to virtual operation, yet it has 20,000 employees focused on developing its own software products. It is reported that Bill Gates is determined to maintain direct control. Where gaps appear in his company's expertise, he prefers to buy a specialist company and the people in it (*Financial Times*, June 1997).

## Implications for Strategic Human Resource Management

The host of structural developments reviewed in this chapter, such as strategic outsourcing and joint ventures, have sometimes been argued as offering a major opportunity for human resource management to raise its strategic profile. This case rests partly on the observation that the many failures in initiatives of this kind have been traced to the shortcomings in human resource management and therefore this presents a strategic opportunity. It also rests in part on the point that many of the challenges thrown up by such initiatives put a premium on strategic thinking about human resource issues.

There is, however, an altogether different case that can be made: this suggests that these structural developments are highly inimical to a strategic approach to human resource management and that they rather express and impel the short-term financial denominator management approach in place of the sustained, numerator approaches extolled, for example, by Hamel and Prahalad.

There are a number of reasons why these developments might impede a firm's strategic potential. Outsourcing and other moves to market-based contractual arrangements are likely to reduce the investment by the organization in long-term skill formation activities. This is likely to apply as much to management development as it is to employee development and training more generally. There are still uncertainties about the possible loss of intellectual capital when extensive outsourcing occurs. An organization which contracts for services other than peripheral matters such as cleaning, catering and security may, even though it initially gains a cheaper and perhaps more specialized service in the short-term, lose the capability to undertake an activity close to its core.

This set of reservations is of course not an argument for simply retaining the large bureaucracy and its internal labour market solutions. What seems to be required is a new type of strategic management within the context of the new form of 'boundaryless' or extended 'organization'.

## Conclusions and Summary

This chapter has traced the extent to which the traditional model of organizational structuring has come under attack. A proliferation of new organizational forms has signalled a revolution in the management of organizations. The old organizational model was also associated with particular sets of human resource practices. But the relationship between the two does not translate into a simple mapping of one onto the other. The bureaucratic structure was associated on the one hand with command and control, hierarchy and rigid job boundaries – all things which in large measure the human resource management movement was trying to overturn. Classical organization principles and Tayloristic job design with high division of labour and low trust were diametrically opposite to the high commitment intent of HRM. And yet, on the other hand the bureaucratic form and HRM can be interpreted as sitting together rather well. In so far as the large bureaucracies such as British Telecom and the major clearing banks offered life-time employment, career ladders, extensive training and development, career planning, above average pay and benefits and other appurtenances of the internal labour market, the correspondence between many of the features of HRM and this organizational type was rather propitious. Indeed, it was when some organizations began to dismantle the internal labour market model and abandoned lifetime careers, made large numbers redundant, cut back on training and development and outsourced or subcontracted significant parts of their activities that the real threat to HRM became rather clearer.

Thus it can be seen that classic bureaucracies harbour a *dual potential*. They can emphasize the rigid rules, multiple hierarchical levels and impede horizontal communication along with a command and control approach to worker management. Or, they may emphasize the psychological contract of security for long-term commitment and loyalty along with an infrastructure of training and development and corporate identity. In so far as the classic form has not been entirely abandoned these dualities remain.

But, as we have seen in this chapter, there have also been many very significant departures from this classic form. The alternatives have been numerous. Descriptions and prescriptions of these have proliferated. And, to a large extent, the alternatives are still unfolding. No one has a firm fix on the emergent form. Various key attributes have been championed: prominent front runners have been the process-oriented company, the network, joint-ventures and strategic alliances, the boundary-less organization and the virtual organization. We have argued in this chapter that there are some significant overlaps in these conceptualizations. For example, Ashkenas et al.'s (1995) concept of 'boundarylessness' both within and between enterprises shares very many features with Davidow and Malone's (1992) 'virtual organisation'. Likewise, Nonaka and Takeuchi's (1995) description and proselytizing of the features of 'the knowledge creating company' shares a great deal in common with Senge (1990) on 'the learning organisation', Quinn (1992) on 'the intelligent enterprise', and even Hamel and Prahalad (1994) on the vital strategic importance of building core competencies.

Thus, similarities and overlaps abound. Each management consultant and would-be guru is seeking to crystallize a complex set of developments into a central idea which can be made appealing, be packaged and sold. The variations around certain underlying themes should not therefore be too surprising. This is not to say, however, that the whole set can simply be dismissed as manipulated 'fads'. The numerous accounts of the nature of 'the new organization' are capturing, albeit it in a selective and partial way, critical features of important trends in organizational (re)-formation. They detect, record and chronicle initiatives in a select group of leading-edge firms. This knowledge they formalize into frameworks and concepts. They go on to project the beginning of a new trend based on their limited data. And beyond that they prescribe these frameworks and devise audit tools which indicate the gap between where client organizations currently are, and where they 'need' to go. The new forms are finally packaged into practical step-by-step action points to help managerial clients enact the new organizational form. But behind all this, and in a sense clouded by all of the prescriptive packages, are certainly the signs of actual change. Corporate restructuring has been the norm in large organizations at least.

But, as we have seen, there is no inevitability about the drive to more and more outsourcing or to the creation of virtual organizations. GEC, BA, Microsoft and Benetton have all shown signs of bucking the trend. Benetton, with 6,000 direct employees, has recently made a massive investment in one of the most advanced manufacturing complexes in the world. The processes which it does outsource tend to be those which do not suit centralized textile production – a practice of very long standing.

Moreover, there are significant variations in the use of these new forms across different countries. For example, despite the availability of the same telecommunications technology the use of teleworking in Japan is only one-quarter of its use in the UK. Similarly, according to a study conducted by the Centre for Economic Performance at the LSE, there are marked differences in the degree to which German and British companies have undertaken restructuring. Downsizing and delayering has been far more prominent in the UK than in Germany. Over the past ten years over three-quarters of British companies have reversed their diversification; in contrast German companies have been reluctant to pursue refocusing strategies. Joint-ventures and strategic alliances though have been a common feature strongly favoured by 47 per cent of companies in both countries.

The nature and character of these changes are, however, still somewhat uncertain. We may doubt whether they are in fact expressive of any single trend. At least two very different tendencies can be detected. On the one hand, there are indeed some instances of firms restructuring in a manner which allows them to locate and exploit knowledge and intellect far more effectively than in the past and to utilize it as a strategic resource. But on the other hand, a great deal of the restructuring which has taken place has been more to do with simple cost-cutting and the externalizing of costs and risks. In the latter instances, it might even be said that far from being 'new' developments in organizational structuring they reflect the outsourcing patterns of nineteenth-century capitalism (Edwards 1979; Littler 1982).

It seems likely that neither of these 'models' will entirely capture the future. Market segmentation will continue to find reflection in markedly different organizational forms. Nor are they perhaps quite so starkly opposite as they are usually depicted. Even 'knowledge-centred' organizations are likely to want to externalize as many costs and risks as possible. Thus, it would be too simplistic to categorize the two 'new' forms as 'good' or 'bad'. Consultants selling their favoured packages have a clear interest in so doing, but a more objective analysis suggests that the emerging organizational forms are not to be quite so easily pigeon-holed in value terms. Nonetheless, there will continue to be different emphases and mixes of positives and negatives. Some organizational forms will be more attractive than others. Hence, awareness-raising of the range of possibilities and of the ways to achieve the more enlightened outcomes are worthwhile missions for the organizational analyst.

## Key Points

- There are numerous indications that very significant departures have been made from the classical bureaucratic form. New organizational structures have been the clearest manifest sign of radical change in human resource and business strategies.
- Despite the proliferation of labels such as cluster organizations, network organizations, knowledge-centred organizations, and the like, there are many common elements in the various models which have been advanced. The underlying ideas and principles which have been most frequently catalogued as expressive of the New Organization include the stress on responsiveness, speed and flexibility; the primacy of knowledge, intellectual capital and hence learning; and the boundary-breaking character of these new forms – including vertical barriers, internal horizontal barriers between functions, and external horizontal barriers between the 'organization' and suppliers and customers.
- While developments of these kinds are invariably described in highly positive terms by the consultants and gurus, not all instances of the new flexible organizations can be quite so easily judged as good. In the real world, many of the initiatives to break down traditional bureaucracies have focused almost exclusively on cost-cutting of various kinds. These have included massive job cuts, outsourcing, and the creation of lean and mean organizations. Internal labour markets have been dismantled and replaced with part-time, casual and other contingent workers.
- The future of organizational structures is therefore likely to be characterized by multiple forms. It seems unlikely that bureaucracies will entirely disappear – indeed there may even be some reversal of outsourcing for example. Equally, the new network forms will vary between those trading on specialized knowledge and those trading on least cost deriving merely from near-nil commitment. The long-term sustainability of many of the enterprises in the latter category is open to question.

## Discussion Questions

1 What are the main ways in which the new organizational forms differ from the principles of classical bureaucracies?
2 What have been the main driving forces which help to explain the emergence of these new organizational structures?
3 To what extent and in what ways do the new organizations express the principles of the Human Resource Management model?
4 Describe two main competing variants of the new model organization.

## References

Ashkenas, R., Ulrich, D., Jick, T., and Kerr, S. (1995) *The Boundaryless Organisation*, San Francisco, CA: Jossey-Bass.
Bettis, R. A. (1992) 'Outsourcing and industrial decline', *The Academy of Management Executive*, vol. 6, no. 1.
Boyle, E. (1993) 'Managing organizational networks', *Management Decision*, vol. 31, no. 7, 23.
Bruno, C. (1995) 'Outsourcing mania', *Network World*, vol. 12, no. 51, 1–42.
Chesbrough, H. W., and Teece, D. J. (1996). 'When is virtual virtuous? Organizing for innovation', *Harvard Business Review*, vol. 74, no. 1.
Clegg, S. R. (1990) *Modern Organisations: Organisation Studies in the Postmodern World*, London: Sage.
Davenport, T. (1993) *Process Innovation: Reengineering work through information technology*, Boston, MA: Harvard Business School Press.
Davidow, W. H. and Malone, M. S. (1992) *The Virtual Corporation: Structuring and Revitalising the Corporation for the 21st Century*, New York: HarperCollins.
Drucker, P. (1993) 'The post-capitalist executive', *Harvard Business Review*, vol. 71, no. 3, May–June.
Edwards, R. (1979) *Contested Terrain: The Transformation of the Workplace in the Twentieth Century*, London: Heinemann.
Hamel, G. and Prahalad, P. K. (1994) *Competing for the Future*, Boston, MA: Harvard Business School Press.
Hammer, M. and Champy, J. (1992) *Reengineering the Corporation*, London: HarperCollins.
—— (1996) *Beyond Reengineering*, London: HarperCollins.
Harkins, P. J. (1996) *Outsourcing and Human Resources: trends, models and guidelines*, Lexington, MA: LER Press.
Harper, J. (1995) 'Mergers, marriages and after: how can training help?' *Journal of European Industrial Training*, vol. 19, no. 1, 24–9.
Harrison, S. (1996) *Outsourcing and the 'New' Human Resource Management*, Kingston, Ont.: IRC Press.
Hendry, J. (1995) 'Culture, community and networks: the hidden cost of outsourcing', *European Management Journal*, vol. 13, no. 2.
Jennings, D. (1996) 'Outsourcing opportunities for financial services', *Long Range Planning*, vol. 29, no. 3, 393–8
Kalleberg, A., Knoke, D., Marsden, P., and Spaeth, J. (1996) *Organizations in America: Analysing Their Structures and Human Resource Practices*, London: Sage.

Kelly, B. (1995) 'Outsourcing marches on', *Journal of Business Strategy*, vol. 16, no. 4, 38–42.
Littler, C. R. (1982) *The Development of the Labour Process in Capitalist Societies*, London: Heinemann.
Miles, R. and Snow, C. (1986) 'Network organisations: new forms', *California Management Review*, vol. 28, no. 3, 62–73.
Mullin, R. (1996). 'Managing the outsourced enterprise; you've finally cut to your core but can you hold the pieces together?', *Journal of Business Strategy*, vol. 17.
Nonaka, I. (1991) 'The knowledge creating company', *Harvard Business Review*, Nov./Dec.
—— and Takeuchi, H. (1995) *The Knowledge Creating Company*, Oxford: Oxford University Press.
Quinn, J. B. (1990). 'Beyond products: Service-based strategy' *Harvard Business Review*, vol. 68, no. 2, 58–64
—— (1992) *Intelligent Enterprise: A knowledge and service based paradigm for industry*, New York: The Free Press.
—— and Hilmer, F. G. (1994) 'Strategic outsourcing', *Sloan Management Review*, vol. 35, no. 4, 45–55.
Reilly, P. and Tamkin, P. (1996) *Outsourcing: A flexible option for the future*? Brighton: Institute for Employment Studies.
Senge, P. (1990) *The Fifth Discipline: The Art and Practice of the Learning Organisation*, London: Century Business.
Snow, C. C. (1992) 'Managing 21st century network organizations', *Organizational Strategy*, vol. 16, no. 4, 38–42.
Sunoo, B. P. and Laab, J. J. (1994) 'Winning strategies for outsourcing contracts', *Personnel Journal*, vol. 73, no. 3, 69–78.
Zeffane, R. (1995) 'The widening scope of inter-organizational networking: Economic, sectoral and social dimensions', *Leadership and Organization Development Journal*, vol. 16, no. 4.

chapter 9

# Employment Relations

## Learning Objectives

- To understand the nature, significance and dimensions of the employment relationship.
- To recognize the ways in which economic, political and social changes are impacting on the contours of that relationship.
- To understand the interests and behaviours of the various parties to the relationship.
- To be able to describe the key processes and the key current issues in employment relations.
- To be able to evaluate and make choices about the relative merits of the emerging models of employment relations.

# Introduction

This chapter examines the employment relationship, the parties who have a stake in it, the institutions which have been designed to govern it, the processes which constitute it and the key issues which make it vital and contentious.

Employment relations are in a state of flux. Trade unions in many countries have endured a period of marked decline, employers have been on the ascendancy, and the state in many countries has been engaged in a project of deregulation and the rolling-back of workers' rights. Yet at the same time we have witnessed the rise of European social legislation, we have seen the idea of social partnership enjoying some considerable success, and even in the United States where union density has declined to an overall figure of only about 14 per cent, the influence of the unions in shaping the direction of many large businesses has perhaps in some circumstances never been higher.

Important also is the fact that many of the profound changes to production processes, working methods and, as we saw in the previous chapter, to organizational restructuring, are inextricably interweaved with changes in employment relations. Thus, the shift to cellular organizational forms, to teams and lean production, the shortening of hierarchy, the changes in organizational cultures, the changes to working patterns such as the increase in part-time working, the introduction of various forms of flexibility, the reduction in the size of work establishments – all these, and many other similar changes, carry crucial implications for employment relations. Thus, for example, the numerous attempts to 'individualize' the employment relationship – by increasing the diversity and intensity of direct communications with employees, by shifting from collective contracts to individual contracts, and by the introduction of individualized performance pay – are all measures which carry the potential to reshape quite radically the traditional contours of employment relations. But, as we shall see in this chapter, there are a number of forces at play and a number of divergent developments which undermine any simple attempt to describe a single trajectory for employment relations. At the millennium, the state of employment relations is truly varied, is beset by conflicting tendencies and pulled in different directions by conflicting principles.

There are three main sections to this chapter. The first sets out the key concepts, frameworks and theories of employment relations. The second examines the critical features of the changing context which are reshaping the patterns of employment relations across many countries. The third examines in some detail the changing patterns and the new trajectories, focusing in particular upon the attempts by certain firms to forge new deals. It also assesses the distinctive features of employment relations in non-union settings and in small firms.

## The Employment Relationship

### *Concepts*

There are a range of terms which are variously used to cover the multiple aspects of relations at work. For example, among the more common are: industrial relations, human relations, employee relations and employment relations. Each of these has its own connotations. Arguably none of them succeeds entirely in capturing the essence of the numerous unfolding types of relations associated with work. For example, 'industrial relations' has been associated with the rather specific issues of collective bargaining and trade unions. Academics have usually regarded industrial relations as covering a wider remit, for example, Bain and Clegg, (1974: 98) defined industrial relations as 'the study of the rules governing employment and the ways in which the rules are changed, interpreted and administered'. The essential heart of the practice and study of industrial relations is therefore the 'making and administering of rules', and 'the study of rules governing employment and the way rules are changed, interpreted and administered'. These observations imply a wide remit, but in the public mind there is also an assumption that industrial relations are confined to particular sectors such as heavy manufacturing, coal and transport. As a consequence, some managers and commentators prefer the term 'employee relations', which has more neutral connotations and is less likely to be perceived as industry specific. It is, however, more likely to denote relations with individual employees to the neglect of collective relations.

In this chapter we recognize that these boundaries are permeable and, moreover, that some of the more interesting and profound changes cut across them. For these reasons we here use the general term 'employment relations' to encompass all of these levels. We will therefore be examining individual and collective relations, and relations in services and the voluntary sector, as well as in manufacturing. The focus of analysis is the employment contract in its various forms. Hence, in this chapter the term employment relations is used to cover areas which traditionally have been regarded as part of industrial relations, employee relations, workplace relations and work relations of all kinds.

## *Theory, frameworks and perspectives*

Understandings and insights into employment relations are not derived solely from data. They are influenced and shaped also by perspectives and different theoretical frameworks. In this section the main theories, frameworks and perspectives are described and explored.

Employment relations can be viewed from many different angles including, for example, the economic, sociological, psychological, political or legal. Participants as well as observers may well approach an event with one of these perspectives to the fore. For example, when a plant closure is being forced through, economic arguments may be given primacy by the drivers of the change while those resisting the closure and associated job losses may be giving priority to social arguments. Or, when pay differentials are being hotly debated, defenders of high executive rewards may draw upon free labour market rationales while critics might refer to the psychological demerits of excessive gaps between top and bottom levels of pay.

Perspectives also influence the very nature of what is deemed to be 'fair', 'best practice' or 'good practice'. From a managerial perspective, it is important to realize that the *expectations* upon management practitioners concerning 'best practice' or even just 'acceptable behaviour' in employee relations shifts around from time to time. What represents commendable behaviour and desired goals at one point in time becomes outmoded and even discouraged some short time later. Thus, for example, in the 1970s managers and employers were strongly encouraged to recognize and work with trade unions, and were expected to amplify and clarify procedures of all kinds. However, merely a decade later many of the good practice guidelines were turned on their head. Political and legal forces impelled employers to eschew 'compromise' and instead to reassert control. Formal, elaborate, comprehensive procedures became regarded as unhelpful; open, 'flexible' arrangements were instead encouraged. Job evaluation and clear job descriptions became passé; market-led behaviour and open-ended job scope took their place. Above all, collective bargaining and joint regulation was no longer officially promulgated as the skilled accomplishment of the competent manager; on the contrary, a winding-down or even withdrawal from collective bargaining altogether became the new touchstone.

### Conflict and co-operation

Industrial relations are characterized by both conflict and co-operation. The former stems from the divergent imperatives of the buyers and suppliers of labour. At its most fundamental, employers are likely to want to purchase labour at a lower price than employees would wish to sell it. Moreover, employers often want to purchase 'more' for the given price – i.e. more in temporal terms: extended hours, evening, night and weekend working; and more also in absolute terms based on higher productivity and 'intensification' of work in any given set of hours. Thus, employers seek to reduce 'headcounts' so that fewer workers fulfil the work formerly undertaken by the full complement, whereas employees have an interest in more workers being employed so that the work can be apportioned more comfortably. The inherent conflict of interest which arguably is often merely hidden beneath the surface was seen in sharp profile with the instance of the 'zero hours' contract imposed by Burger King on some of its staff. These employees were only paid during the hours when customer demand triggered the need for their activity. In slack periods they were 'stood-down' without pay. In fact, it was to a large extent this aspect of staff waiting around on the premises which provoked the outraged publicity for, as we will see later in the chapter, zero hours contracts are not so very unusual. These instances also highlight the importance of power – another key concept in employment relations. The parties with conflicting interests are by no means necessarily in a balanced power relationship. For a range of reasons, including for example, the easy mobility of capital (within and across international borders), the comparative immobility of labour, the vulnerability of many workers to job loss, and the fragmentation of labour, the power disparity normally tends to favour the employer. To a large extent, the very raison d'être of trade unionism is to seek to even-up the power balance by collectivizing and by presenting a united front on vital issues. The employment relations and industrial relations perspective is therefore often a highly valuable corrective to much HR and organizational development theory, which is frequently neglectful of the differences in both power and interests.

While there are sources of conflict and disparities of power there are also some common interests and signs of co-operation. Both purchasers and suppliers of labour can gain from the continued existence of an enterprise (profits and wages respectively). In pursuit of these ends there are numerous forms of collaboration: information sharing, joint consultation, and even co-operation in devising ways to resolve the occasional outbreaks of manifest conflict. For example, when Blue Circle Cement and trade union representatives from the TGWU, AEEU and GMB sat down in 1996 and drew up lists of their objectives and wants, it was found that the two resulting lists had much in common. Both emphasized the desire for a secure future, a thriving enterprise, stability and so on. Hence, in recent years employers and employees have grown used to the simultaneous handling of both co-operation and conflict. For example, Quality Circles and joint problem-solving teams may continue even during the period of a protracted pay settlement period or may be temporarily suspended until a pay dispute has been resolved. During such periods both sides are acutely aware of the conflictual *and* collaborative aspects of their relationship.

Of course, in practice the Industrial Relations system is more complicated than this. There are conflicts to be resolved within the manager/employer camp and also within the employee/union side. For example, different sections of the workforce may have different objectives – the higher paid will benefit from percentage pay rises while the lowest paid might benefit more from an absolute amount paid across all tiers. Managers may seek to exploit such divisions.

A major issue has been the extent to which trade unions or even sub-sections may vigorously pursue their own 'sectional interests' with perhaps little regard for wider trade union (still less, class) interests. The very concept of a trade union or labour 'movement' suggests a sense or possibility of solidarity which extends beyond direct personal interest and gain. However, there are often tensions and conflicts between and even within unions. Different trade unions compete for membership and in consequence the level of co-operation between them is sometimes rather low. And within the same union there can be outbreaks of conflict, as in the case of the TGWU where different segments of its membership at Ford become embroiled in a dispute over the allocation, or alleged misallocation, of staff to coveted and well-paid drivers jobs. This case reflects a wider criticism of traditional trade unions – that they largely represented the particular interests of white males with rather less concern for women, ethnic minorities or even the unemployed more generally.

## Frames of reference

Delineation and clarification of predominant perspectives or 'frames of reference' in employment relations was undertaken by Alan Fox as part of the background research support for the Royal Commission on Trades Unions and Employers Associations (Donovan, 1968). In what became a classic formulation, which has influenced analysis for some thirty years, Fox helped to distil three main frames of reference held by various participants and observers of the overall work relations system. The three were:

- the unitary perspective.
- the pluralistic perspective.
- the radical perspective.

Perspectives of these kinds are deeply and often subconsciously held by participants and it can be useful to surface them for a closer examination of their constituent assumptions.

## The unitary perspective

From this perspective, a work organization is rather like a team or a family. There is essentially only space for one source of legitimacy and there is or ought to be a single, shared, set of objectives. From within this perspective there is no legitimate place for trade unions because they represent an alternative, competing, source of legitimacy and crystallize alternative objectives. Likewise, there really ought not to be a place for conflict either. If it manifestly does appear then something has 'gone wrong', such as a failure to understand the commonality of interests. This in turn may have been brought about because of poor communications or poor managerial leadership. If conflict persists despite effective managerial action then the search may commence for 'trouble-makers' who simply do not want the system to work smoothly.

The unitary perspective underpins managerial prerogative. It sees managers as the rightful agents of owners and while communication of plans and consultation about plans with employees can easily be accommodated, there is no rightful scope for negotiation. There is no place for 'two sides' – only one.

## The pluralist perspective

Negotiation implies both concessions on the one hand, but also the legitimacy of different positions on the other. Thus, from a pluralist perspective conflict is accepted as a normal part of the order of things. The objective and the task is to bring about workable compromises. Within such a perspective then, trade unions, far from being vilified and excluded as if they were the sources of conflict, are accepted and even valued for their representational role. They are viewed as useful institutions helping to regulate and put some order on the potentially disparate (and therefore less manageable) expressions of diverse interests and wants.

As we shall see below, there are different stances within the pluralistic frame of reference. One wing perceives the immensity of the conflicts of interest and looks to hard bargaining and the hammering out of a series of 'temporary truces' as the realistic way forward. The other wing gives rather greater weight to the co-operation and commonality of interests which exist alongside the differences, and as a consequence proponents may urge and place greater faith in various forms of longer-term 'partnership' arrangements.

## The radical perspective

This third perspective places a far stronger emphasis upon the extent and irreconcilability of conflict in the employment relationship and indeed in society in general. In broad terms the radical perspective expresses the Marxist view. This framework of reference is posited on a view that modern society is, in its fundamentals, capitalist in nature. Such a society is further seen as constituted by two conflicting classes: one which owns the means of production and the other which has to sell its labour in order to survive. Thus, conflict in industry, from this perspective, can be viewed as a direct representation, and extension, of class conflict in the wider society.

From within such an analysis a number of important practical consequences for industrial relations follow. The institutions of collective bargaining, arbitration and so on are viewed sceptically. They are products of the fundamental inequalities of power and wealth and therefore cannot be regarded as 'fair' or permanent resolutions of the problem. Likewise, trade unions and their leaders may be viewed with some suspicion. They may be regarded as 'institutionalizing' conflict and thereby blunting the edge of class aspirations. Idealogical struggles within trade unions have often turned on this division between, on the one hand, those wanting to 'radicalize' the membership and to expose the inherent tensions within the system, and on the other those seeking to forge a role for trade unions in the pluralist mould as described above. There have been many bitter struggles along this fracture.

## The three perspectives considered

It is notable, though perhaps hardly surprising, that from each perspective proponents see their stance as the most 'realistic'. This term was indeed used by Alan Fox in his original exposition of the perspectives. He argued the point that the 'unitary' view, while much favoured by managers because it served their perceived needs and flattered their egos, was essentially idealogical in nature. On the other hand, Fox regarded 'pluralism' as more in tune with the reality of affairs. Whilst it might be less palatable for the busy manager to have his/her authority and decisions challenged, Fox argued that because it was more 'realistic' to accept the reality of the situation this would also enable a more competent handling of affairs. However, the claim to be able to see things 'as they really are' is open to persons operating from any of the perspectives. It is a very moot point as to whether one could demonstrate empirically that any of the positions accorded 'better' with reality than any of the others. It is notable that these 'frames of reference' do fluctuate in their predominance over time. Thus, broadly speaking, pluralism gained ground in the 1970s and holders of the unitary perspective seemed to be in retreat. Government practice, legislation and professional practice moved together in helping to establish pluralism as the conventional wisdom. Then, in the 1980s, as part of the Thatcher regime, the fundamental tenets of pluralism were subjected to sustained assault. Compromise, bargaining, trade unions, the 'going rate', arbitration and similar aspects were derided and pushed out. There was a resurgence of the unitary perspective and this was reflected in legislation, in political discourse and in industrial practice. The 1990s saw some further movement. 'Partnership' as a key concept in Europe came more to the fore in the UK and especially so in the Republic of Ireland. Trade unions have arguably gained greater public acceptance as one of the social partners.

# The Changing Context

The nature of employment relations are shaped profoundly not only by individual employer strategies and choices but by wider socio-economic forces. In the United States there has been speculation that a generation of union decline could have reached its watershed with the success of the strike against UPS, the parcel delivery service, in 1997. This took place against a background of major change in public attitudes towards organized labour. Having been regarded as 'the confrontational villains in the story of decline in US industry, polls suggest that they are now increasingly looked to as the working man and woman's bulwark against rapacious managers, downsizing and restructuring' (*Financial Times,* 29 September 1997). (The connection between employment relations issues and the themes discussed in the previous two chapters is here made evident.)

Although public attitudes may be switching, there remain some deep-seated structural features to bear in mind. Thus, for example, the shift in the economy of most western countries from heavy manufacturing to service industries, and the associated shifts in occupational composition, play an important part in patterns of employment relations. Additionally, the notion of the 'two sides of industry' becomes clouded if not entirely removed in the face of the growth in employment in the voluntary and not for profit sector. (The TGWU alone has some 50,000 members who are employed in the voluntary sector.)

## Changes to employment contracts

In recent years there have been extensive changes to the nature of what came to be regarded as the 'conventional' or 'standard' employment contract, which developed post-1945 in the form of full-time, 'permanent' employment. There has been an increase in so-called 'non-standard' contracts such as part-time working, temporary and short-term contracts, 'core hours contracts', 'personal contracts' and even 'zero hours' contracts (see box 9.1).

It is notable that the growth in these new forms of contract have occurred not only in the private sector but to a very considerable extent in the public sector also. Indeed in some regards the public sector has experienced the greatest change in contractual arrangements. This has been partly driven by the decentralization of bargaining and the dismantling of the traditional central machinery and partly as a consequence of compulsory competitive tendering.

### BOX 9.1 THE GROWTH OF TEMPORARY WORKING UK

Temporary work has been growing at a faster rate than the growth in full-time jobs – that is, where new jobs have been created the larger proportion of these have been of a part time nature. The Labour Force Survey reveals that between 1992 and 1996 the overall growth in employment was 2.5 per cent (including the growth in self-employment) but during this period temporary work increased by 30 per cent, fixed-term contracts went up by 39 per cent, agency work by 148 per cent and casual work by 21 per cent. This differential growth has led to the overall proportion of temporary workers in the labour force rising from 5.5 per cent of the total in 1992 to 7 per cent in 1996. The overall proportion of fixed-term contracts increased from 2.8 per cent to 3.6 per cent, and agency work from 0.4 per cent to 0.9 per cent. Thus, while the growth curve has been steep in recent years it is important to note that, overall, these much-discussed new forms of contract still constitute a relatively small part of overall employment.

## Flexibility and post-Fordism

At a fundamental level it could be argued that the changes to political and industrial policies are not simply the outcomes of 'perspectives' or ideology but reflect deep-seated material forces. Thus it has been theorized that it is possible to trace links between the nature of markets and the nature of regulation within firms. For example, the middle decades of this century were characterized by 'Fordism'. This entailed a complete, complementary, 'system' of production and consumption. The production process was based on assembly-line technology, standardized, mass-produced products employing large numbers of semi-skilled workers. Employment relations 'fitted' this system in that standardized contracts were negotiated which embraced these vast, relatively undifferentiated, groupings. The market was itself part of the system – mass produced products for mass markets with consumers who were not especially discriminating – (the apotheosis was Henry Ford's famous phrase, 'You can have any colour motor vehicle providing it is black'). The accompanying mode of regulation outside the firm involved state-managed macro-economic intervention and planning with comprehensive, universal and standardized welfare provision.

According to Piore and Sabel (1984) this 'mass production paradigm' is no longer the universal recipe for success because it has been displaced by a new and very different set of logics. Markets have become more discriminating, differentiated and quality conscious; production systems have become more flexible as they have been able to exploit the adaptability inherent in microelectronic-controlled equipment and manufacturing planning systems. Small, flexible, customer-tailored batches have become more common as products must change rapidly to capture fleeting consumer demand. Instead of the mass production paradigm, Piore and Sabel (1984) advance the thesis of the primacy of 'flexible specialization'. There has been a shift from narrowly defined jobs and dedicated machines to more flexible jobs and dedicated machines, and on again to more flexible jobs, using adaptable technologies to produce a range of specialized products.

Likewise, advances in manufacturing resources planning (MRP), which enable planned yet flexible production schedules based on decentralized data to small units, allow team-based production. The industrial relations implications of flexible specialization appear favourable from a range of viewpoints. Employers are able to devise a new system of production suited to commercial success in a post-Fordist era while workers break free from the constraints of mass production short-cycle assembly line work and enjoy the benefits of more varied and interesting tasks.

## The importance of the social and economic context

The cultures, legal systems and labour market characteristics of each country can make a profound difference to the conduct of employment relations. For example, in Britain, many of the changes to the profile of work and employment have resulted from government policy over an 18-year period to 'de-regulate' the labour market (see box 9.2). The official policy was to 'remove barriers' in order to 'create an economic climate in which business can flourish and create more jobs'. Measures included:

- promoting decentralized and flexible pay arrangements.
- compulsory competitive tendering in public services.
- industrial relations legislation which restricted trade union activity.
- an opt-out from the Social Chapter of the Maastricht Treaty with the aim of avoiding European regulations on employment.

A further change in the contours of employment has been in the area of occupational shifts. There has been a move away from manual occupations to non-manual occupations. The latter now account for 60 per cent of employees. Similarly, there has been a marked shift from jobs in the manufacturing sector towards the service sector. In the last 40 years the proportion engaged in service industries has doubled to nearly 76 per cent (16.5 million people). The largest increases have occurred in distribution, business services, hotels and restaurants and social work, while employment in public administration has declined.

## *The parties to the employment relationship*

The parties most central to the relationship are employers on the one hand, with managers acting as their agents; and employees on the other hand, with trade unions sometimes acting as their agents. Other parties can and do get involved. Among these are the state itself, along with its various agencies and associated agencies such the National Labor Relations Board in the USA and the Industrial Tribunals in Britain.

### The trade union role

In the post-Second World War period unions in the UK grew to a peak membership of over 12.6 million in 1979 from a figure of 9 million in 1950. Then, from 1979, membership declined every year. It fell back to around the 9 million mark again by 1990 and then decline continued thereafter to approximately 7.2 million in 1997. The erosion in trade union density has been by no means confined to the UK (see table 9.1).

As the statistics in table 9.1 show, while there has been a general international pattern of union decline, the fall has not been universal. In fact in some countries, such as Canada and Sweden, there was even an increase in trade union density. Overall, however, the decline has been extensive and of long-standing. Thus, in Australia, the density figure was as high as 48 per cent in 1980, before falling back to 40 per cent in 1990 and 35 per cent in 1995. France had a density of 17.5 per cent in 1980, Germany 35.6 per cent and Japan 31.1 per cent. The comparable figures

## BOX 9.2 WORKING PATTERNS IN BRITAIN

Britain has a higher proportion of the adult population in work than other major European economy. Some 70 per cent of the population are classified as 'in work'. The total 'workforce' in 1996 was 28 million – the workforce in employment totalled 26 million of whom 22 million were classed as 'employees in employment'. The long-term trend has shown a move from full-time towards part-time employment. In the ten-year period 1986–1996 part-time employment rose by 26 per cent to 6.5 million (5.2 million of these were female). Another notable feature has been the increase in the proportion of women in employment. Women now account for just over half of all employment. Approximately 45 per cent of women in employment are working part-time compared with 8 per cent of men. Nearly 1.3 million people had two or more jobs. Some 1.6 million people were in temporary jobs and half of these were classed as fixed-term contracts. Contracting out or 'outsourcing' by organizations of their non-core functions has increased.

The British case has also been somewhat unusual and distinctive because, over a long period of time, there was a relative lack of direct state regulation of employment relations when compared to most other industrial economies. There have been two broad contrasting views about the implications of this 'voluntaristic' tradition. The first view stems from a free-market perspective. This argues that freedom from constraint upon employers has a positive economic value and that it enables the flexible utilisation of labour, helps curb unrealistic and artificial levels of labour costs and as a consequence, attracts inward investment into the UK. The alternative argument holds that the lack of a regulative framework incentivises employers to pursue a least-cost strategy which ultimately leads to underinvestment in training, low skills, low pay and fierce competition at the low premium end of various product markets. (Streeck 1992)

for union density in the UK were 50 per cent in 1980 and 39 per cent in 1990 (OECD 1994). By 1996, union density in the UK had declined further to 31.3 per cent – the lowest it has been for 60 years (Labour Market Trends 1997). Notably, because of the decline in manual trade unionism the comparative density rates between manual and non-manual workers are now pretty much on a par. Professional workers are now far more likely to be union members than say sales staff. Public sector workers are more unionized than hotel and catering workers; employees in larger firms are more unionized than those in small companies.

Despite these changes it is far too soon to write off the unions – as the historical record of wax and wane attests. Unions have tried a number of not very successful recruitment campaigns and have taken other measures, including the

**Table 9.1** Trade union density in various countries

| *Country* | *Union density 1995 (percentages)* | *change in density 1985–1995 (percentages)* |
|---|---|---|
| Argentina | 38.7 | –42.6 |
| Australia | 35.2 | –29.6 |
| Canada | 43.5 | +1.8 |
| France | 9.1 | –37.2 |
| Germany | 28.9 | –17.6 |
| Italy | 44.1 | –7.4 |
| Japan | 24.0 | –16.7 |
| Korea, Rep. | 12.7 | +2.4 |
| Sweden | 91.1 | +8.7 |
| United Kingdom | 32.9 | –27.7 |
| United States | 14.2 | –21.2 |

*Source:* ILO (1997).

promotion of various financial and other services, without notable impact. But they continue to seek a way to reverse their fortunes as well as adjusting to new circumstances. At the current time, trade union merger activity remains strong.

## The management role in employment relations

The management role is now regarded as especially interesting and important. This was not always thought to be the case. Early textbooks tended to neglect the management role. Trade unions, shop stewards and the state were regarded as the prime movers and managers simply reacted. Today things are very different: indeed the conventional wisdom now is almost the precise reverse. As most of the other chapters in this book (and other comparable texts) reveal, managers are now regarded as the key players, the ones who launch 'initiatives' and the ones with the more influential 'strategies' which affect the whole spectrum of work experience and modes of engagement for employees.

There are two critical issues concerning the management role in employment relations and in a sense these issues are closely related. The first concerns the *degree of discretion* which managers have in making choices about employment relations. The second issue concerns the results of the exercise of that discretion, i.e. the *patterns of relations*.

The first issue is wrapped-up in the diverse ways in which the management role can be conceptualized. Three main theoretical conceptualizations have been influential: (i) managers as actors in a system; (ii) managers as strategic players and (iii) managers as simple agents of capital (Sisson and Marginson 1995). In the first model the societal context is given special weight and managers in consequence are regarded as only one of a multitude of competing actors; in the second, managers are treated as having a relatively free hand to mould the employment relationship as they choose; and in the third model they in a sense have relatively little real discretion because the underlying driving force is seen to be the paramount interests of capital which, by implication, would push aside any manager who failed to privilege those interests. In weighting each of these three models Sisson and Marginson (1995: 97) observe: 'each has valuable insights but none is sufficient in itself'. They note that the constant drive for efficiency is fundamental to many of the actions of management but that 'institutions contribute to and shape this search for efficiency and that management as a group of people cannot be abstracted from the wider context in which they operate'. These contexts are extremely diverse and there is at first sight bewildering variety and complexity. But equally, there are patterns, and to a considerable extent these patterns can be explained. Thus, by implication, the management role is best understood as the exercise of some choice within contexts of diverse institutions, processes and rules which make up national employment relations systems. The voluntary system in the UK, for example, is indicative of one form of pattern and it contrasts with the more regulated Continental system.

The second issue which we referred to above, that is the variety of management styles, has also been a fruitful avenue of enquiry. For example, Sisson (1989) used a two by two matrix based on the cross-cutting dimensions of 'individualism' and 'collectivism'. Sisson shows that it is impossible for managers to combine elements of both and this results in four different ideal type styles. The 'traditional' style scores low on both individualism and collectivism because labour is treated as a mere factor of production, and so little if any investment is made in training or other such measures. Likewise, managers take an oppositional stance to unions and refuse recognition. Under the 'constitutional' style, however, while low emphasis is still given to developing or dealing with employees as individuals, great attention is paid to regulating employment conditions through negotiation with trade unions. Employment policies centre on the need for stability, control and the institutionalization of conflict. Under the consultative style, a judicious mix of individualism and collectivism is chosen. Unions are recognized and negotiations over terms and conditions take place, but managers also engage in consultation with union and employee representatives on the wider business agenda and seek to draw employees in to an identification with and commitment to the enterprise. Finally, in the fourth quadrant there is an approach labelled 'sophisticated human relations'. Under this strategy managers give high priority to individual relations while excluding collective relations. Managers adopting this style seek to use internal labour market strategies, promotion and career ladders, employee appraisal, extensive communication and other such devices to inculcate employee loyalty.

Subsequent frameworks such as Guest (1995) have re-drawn attention to the continued significance of the 'traditional' style – one where low priority accorded to both industrial relations and HRM. This, paradoxically, may be one of the most interesting contemporary patterns from an analyst's point of view. It reflects a view that advantage can be gained by eschewing both trade unions and HRM. It represents what Guest terms a 'black hole' and is similar to what Sisson (1995) elsewhere terms a Bleak House option. There would seem to be some partial evidence at least in the third Workplace (WIRS3) Industrial Relations Survey (Millward et al. 1992; Millward 1994; and Marginson et al. 1993) that some sections of employment can be characterized in this way. If this is correct it clearly challenges many of the alternative analyses and prescriptions from many of the gurus featured elsewhere in this book.

## Patterns and Trajectories

### *Towards a new model?*

The term 'new industrial relations' actually goes back some way. In America, it was popularized in a *Newsweek* magazine article in the early 1980s which suggested that the phenomenon had emerged practically unnoticed and, until then, unproclaimed. The claim was that the old adversarial industrial relations system was being displaced by a more collaborative one and that this had come not from Japan but had been home-grown in America. A thorough academic treatment and review of the idea had to await the seminal work of Kochan et al. (1986) which highlighted the very positive contribution made by new forms of collaborative union-management relations. Kochan et al. argued that the traditional collective bargaining model, which had dominated the American scene since the 1930s, was giving way to an entirely new paradigm under which unions and management were collaborating at very high company policy levels to work towards jointly-sponsored new business plans.

This new industrial relations attitude in the UK was usually associated with greenfield sites and often indeed with inward-investing Japanese electronic companies. The electrical union the EETPU was one of the more active union partners and its activities ultimately led to its expulsion from the TUC. In practice, many other unions were also involved in the so-called 'beauty contests' at which management selected the single union to be recognized as having the right to seek to recruit right across the workforce.

This version of the new industrial thesis was investigated by Millward (1994) who used the WIRS3 data. In brief, it can be stated fairly clearly that he found little evidence that this 'alternative' model had made any substantial headway in transforming the broad sweep of employment practices. For example, he found that new-style agreements with no-strike clauses were extremely rare in practice. 'A mere 1 per cent of workplaces with a recognised trade union had pendulum arbitration and in workplaces with a sole union agreement the figure was less than half of one percent' (Millward, 1994: 123). Likewise, the incidence of company advisory boards or councils, was also less common than was often assumed. Where single union deals existed, only 17 per cent of workplaces also had a company board. The one area where extensive practice was recorded by the WIRS

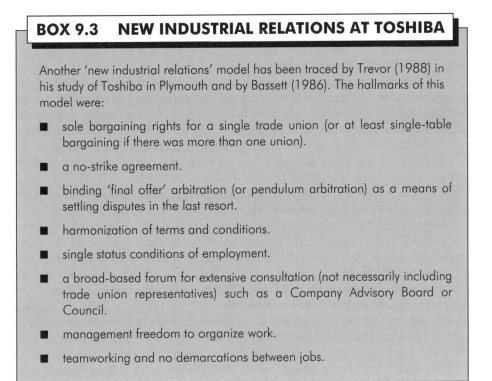

## BOX 9.3 NEW INDUSTRIAL RELATIONS AT TOSHIBA

Another 'new industrial relations' model has been traced by Trevor (1988) in his study of Toshiba in Plymouth and by Bassett (1986). The hallmarks of this model were:

- sole bargaining rights for a single trade union (or at least single-table bargaining if there was more than one union).
- a no-strike agreement.
- binding 'final offer' arbitration (or pendulum arbitration) as a means of settling disputes in the last resort.
- harmonization of terms and conditions.
- single status conditions of employment.
- a broad-based forum for extensive consultation (not necessarily including trade union representatives) such as a Company Advisory Board or Council.
- management freedom to organize work.
- teamworking and no demarcations between jobs.

data was in management freedom to flexibly organize work arrangements. But, as Millward's analysis confirmed, this was not a feature confined to the new-style workplaces with single-union deals.

The early version of the 'new' industrial relations appeared therefore to be restricted to a handful of cases which happened to enjoy a high media profile such as Toshiba and Nissan (see box 9.3). There are indications, however, that it would be premature and short-sighted to entirely write-off the concept of a new emergent model of employment relations. Thus, in the late 1990s a whole string of new agreements are emerging which resonate around a few common themes. For example, Castle Cement, the UK's second largest cement producer, signed a new deal with its trade unions after a detailed 18-month process of joint working. The key features of the new deal include: the replacement of job demarcations with multi-skilled work teams; the removal of supervisors and their replacement by teamleaders who work alongside their teams; abolition of overtime and its replacement by an annualized hours contract; a pay structure built on a single annual salary for each grade; harmonization of sick pay, redundancy and other benefits. At BP Chemicals at Hull, manufacturing changes and employment relations changes have proceeded hand in glove. The company aimed for world-class manufacturing status and as part of this initiative introduced single-status working so that all process, maintenance and craft workers became 'manufacturing technicians' with staff status. A new employee council has been given a role in running the site; individuals can retain membership of a union but collective bargaining recognition has been removed; a new employees–management representative forum has been established.

If we look beyond process industries to the engineering sector, we also find extensive change to employment relations. A survey by Industrial Relations Services (IRS 1997: no. 628, p. 5) reveals that 60 per cent of engineering companies had undertaken major restructuring in the past five years and these included cellular manufacturing, teamworking, TQM programmes and new pay systems to reflect the new ways of working. Moreover, 80 per cent of these companies recognized trade unions and nearly two-thirds of these companies said that the trade unions had been receptive to the changes the company had made. These sorts of changes have not been confined to the manufacturing sector or indeed to the private sector. In local government a 1997 agreement led to the merger of the manual and white-collar bargaining groups; common terms of employment were introduced and harmonized, such as working hours set at 37 hours per week for all categories of employee.

A key part of the new deals of the 1990s has been the attempt to arrive at 'employment security' policies and agreements (see box 9.4). A recent survey found such policies across a variety of sectors including construction, privatized utilities, financial services and local government (IRS 1997: no. 621). Invariably they were employment security statements rather than job security guarantees, and the norm is to state the means for handling any needed headcount reductions as in the manner of Scottish Power Generation, which stipulates the use of natural wastage, reviewing outside contracting work if circumstances demand, and activating similar measures to attempt to avoid compulsory redundancies. Similar deals have been signed at Sheffield City Council, United Distillers and Tate & Lyle.

## Employment relations in non-union workplaces

Non-union workplaces have become more prevalent. By 1990 just over half of workplaces were ones where the employer recognized one or more unions for collective bargaining over basic pay for some of the employees present. Even this figure of 53 per cent overall is pulled upwards by the preponderance of union recognition in the public sector. In the private sector there is now a minority of workplaces with union recognition. As table 9.2 shows, only 44 per cent of workplaces in private manufacturing recognize any trade union and only 36 per cent of workplaces in private services recognize a union.

Views about non-union firms and workplaces vary dramatically. On the one hand, they have been viewed as progressive harbingers of innovative, modern, human resource practice. This positive side has usually been associated with high-tech electronic companies. The high-profile cases of IBM and Marks & Spencer have also been held up as examples of far-sighted quality employers. The inward-investing foreign companies were also often regarded as indicative of a

## BOX 9.4 A NEW DEAL AT HONEYWELL

Honeywell Control Systems in Scotland have gone a stage further and claim to have replaced a traditional collective bargaining system with a modern four-year deal. As part of this they 're-engineered' the collective bargaining process itself so that instead of the company and the union planning in isolation there would be more joint work using a common data source (IRS 1997: no. 635, p. 12). The aim is reported to be to make negotiations less time-consuming and less confrontational. The agreement itself underscored the role of TQM, cellular manufacturing, teamworking, harmonization of terms and conditions and improved communications. A stability of employment understanding is also part of the package. There is a flatter structure and pay grades have been reduced from 17 to just one. Many similar deals are frequently reported in the late 1990s. The basic ingredients are to be found in case after case. This pattern, while widespread, may not of course be statistically representative. Confirmation of the extent of these new deals will need to await the analysis of results from the fourth workplace industrial relations survey. There are, however, sufficient indications to suggest that there is at the very least an emerging model of what 'good practice' in employment relations might look like as we approach the millennium.

necessary departure from outmoded brownfield site practices and traditions. On the other hand, non-union firms have been shown by Millward (1994) to portray a very different face. Drawing on the third Workplace Industrial Relations Survey data, Millward draws a comparison which reveals non-union establishments as providing fewer rights and benefits for workers, lower pay, higher rates of accidents and absenteeism, poorer employee communication. Perhaps in consequence, these establishments are shown also to display higher labour turnover and more dismissals. As Guest and Hoque (1994: 1) observe: 'what was thought to be potentially good, the ideal of the HRM-oriented non-union establishment where the interests of the staff were taken seriously, has now become bad, or to the extent that it is a deliberate exploitation of a weak, non-union workforce, even ugly'.

There was greater use of temporary contract workers and of freelance workers. Workforce reductions were no more common than they were in the unionized settings but when they did occur, compulsory redundancy was more likely. Dismissals were twice as likely. And although employees in non-union settings lacked trade union support for taking cases to industrial tribunals, the incidence of such action was just as common.

As Millward et al. (1994: 365) note, non-union industrial and commercial workplaces offered 'few formal mechanisms through which employees could contribute to the operation of their workplace in a broader context than that of

**Table 9.2** Trade union recognition (percentages)

| | 1980 | 1984 | 1990 |
|---|---|---|---|
| Establishments with recognized trade union for any workers (as percentage of all establishments) | 64 | 66 | 53 |
| Establishments with recognized trade union for manual workers (as percentage of all establishments) | 55 | 62 | 48 |
| Establishments with recognized trade union for non manual | 47 | 54 | 43 |
| Establishments with recognized trade union for private manufacturing (for any workers) | 65 | 56 | 44 |
| Establishments with recognized trade union for private services | 41 | 44 | 36 |

*Source:* Adapted from Millward et al. (1992: 71).

their specific job. Nor were they as likely to have opportunities to air grievances or to resolve problems in ways that were systematic and designed to ensure fairness of treatment. Broadly, speaking, no alternative models of employee representation – let alone a single alternative model – had emerged as a substitute for trade union representation'.

Non-union workplaces are unlikely as a category to be either all good or all bad. In order to tease out the range of practices, Guest and Hoque (1994) drew upon a survey of 156 new ('greenfield') establishments set up since 1980; 122 of these were non-union and 34 were unionized. The overall conclusion on non-union workplaces is that, when aggregated and compared with the unionized 'sector' the overall pattern of industrial relations is inferior. When disaggregrated, non-union workplaces evidently fragment across a range of standards; in Guest and Hoque's graphic phrase they cover the spectrum of the good, the bad and the ugly. The worry is that, as Sisson (1995) and McLoughlin and Gourlay (1994) suggest, the general tendency is towards an overall deterioration of standards rather than any forward progressive move towards a new model of sophisticated employee relations.

Other things being equal, as the WIRS3 team themselves point out (Millward et al. 1992: 363), one might have expected that the most likely workplaces in which evidence of HRM would be found would be those that are union-free. This is where many of the practices originated in the USA (Foulkes 1980; Kochan et al. 1986). It is also where commentators have suggested HRM might be found in its most developed state in the UK (Sisson 1989). In the event, the position is the exact opposite. It is the union rather than the non-union workplaces which exhibit the HRM initiatives that are to be found.

## Employment relations in small firms

Small firms in Europe (i.e. with fewer than ten employees) account for about one-third of all employment. This is equivalent (again in broad terms) to the proportion of employment accounted for by larger firms, i.e. those with over 500 employees each (Eurostat 1993; Scase 1995: 570). There is a widely-held view that relations in small firms are likely to be more harmonious and informal than in larger firms. By way of contrast, the larger firm is said to intrude formalization, proceduralization and conflict into the relationship. These contracts have prompted many observers to advocate the advantages of the smaller firm and prompted the departure from large concentrations of labour.

The Bolton Committee (1971) report on small firms made the following observations about job satisfaction and employment relations in small firms:

> In many aspects a small firm provides a better environment for the employee than is possible in most large firms. Although physical working conditions can sometimes be inferior in small firms most people prefer to work in a small group where communication presents fewer problems; the employee in a small firm can more easily see the relation between what he is doing and the objectives and performance of the firm as a whole. Where management is more direct and flexible, working rules can be varied to suit the individual. Each employee is also likely to have a more varied role with a chance to participate in several kinds of work . . . no doubt mainly as a result turnover of staff in small firms is very low and strikes and other kinds of industrial dispute are relatively infrequent. (Bolton Committee 1971: 21)

The report went on to observe: 'We are not suggesting that the present problems of industrial relations in this country would be solved if the role of small firms in the economy were greater, but perhaps they would be less acute' (1971: 21).

The report found that only 8 per cent of small firms were completely unionized, almost two-thirds had no union members at all, and only 1.5 per cent had been affected by strikes in the preceding two years. Commenting on these observations, David Storey (1994: 186) says that 'there is probably no dimension in which the Bolton Committee report was so seriously in methodological error'. Virtually all subsequent researchers who have examined the issue have 'referred with incredulity' to these comments from the Bolton committee. The Committee conducted no direct research among employees and it is inferred that these summations were derived from discussions with employers. Goss and other researches who have conducted empirical research among employees have reached very different conclusions. Curran, however, suggests that the bulk of small enterprises fall in the 'benevolent autocracy' category. In his work in the service sector he suggests that here at least social relations can be of reasonably high quality and that while Bolton's methodology can be critiqued the generalized conclusions are not necessarily so wide off the mark *in certain sections* of small business (Curran 1991; Curran et al. 1993). The problem is of course that small firms are tremendously heterogeneous.

There have been only a few studies of work relations in small firms (Rainne 1989; Goss 1988, 1991; Scase 1995; Bacon et al. 1996). Goss (1988), in a study of two types of printing firm (traditional, with craft, unionized, national rates) and 'instant' printing, (employing young unskilled workers, utilizing electronic-computerized typesetting), showed how vastly different employment relations could be in the small-firm sector. The emphasis on variety was also present in the work of Scase and Goffee (1982; 1987). They used a typology based on nature of proprietorial roles (for example, self-employed, owner-controllers and owner-directors). Across these types, small-firm employment relations are likely to be generally less institutionalized, formal and more particularistic. As firms grow, conflict is likely to emerge around the ambiguity between salience of *interpersonal* relations and *impersonal* means of control.

Curran and Stanworth (1979a, 1979b, 1981a, 1981b) argued that the working population in small firms had not necessarily made a positive choice to be in small firms; that there was a pattern of high labour turnover; and that social relations were often poor. Bacon et al. (1996) drew on a survey of employers across all size bands and industrial classifications in order to focus on small organizations. The most notable finding from the survey was the degree of take-up of new management practices among the small and medium-sized employing organizations. Initiatives such as culture change programmes, devolved management, team-working and performance appraisal were by no means confined to large firms.

In sum, while there is evidently no single form of 'small firm employment relations', and while much more research in the various types of small firms is needed, it is clear enough that there is no general model that can be easily pursued here as a way of dealing with employment relations tensions. In this section we have reviewed three sets of trajectories: the 'new model' relations attempted by a number of large, sophisticated firms, the non-union situation, and small firms. While none of them can be simply written-off, equally none of them offer any easy answers.

## Conclusions and Summary

Employment relations have persisted throughout the century as a contentious and yet critical part of organizational management. The idea as to what might constitute 'good practice' or even 'wise practice' in employment relations has fluctuated markedly. There have been periods when employers have been emphatically anti-union, likewise there have been other periods when the conventional wisdom has suggested that a 'realistic' stance is to seek a working accommodation with trade unions. On yet other occasions and in other places this view has even gone a step further and some managements have sought to engage unions as full partners in the running of the business. In very recent times we have witnessed the exercise of all three of these stances. This variety makes the predication of any single 'trend' not only risky but almost certainly misguided.

What we seem to be observing is a complex playing-out of a number of different 'formulae'. One of these is the 'high commitment model', which appeals to the American Dream of personal development, the opportunity for the fulfilment of human potential, and measures to engage enthusiastic cooperation so that the end result is 'growth' for the individual, the firm and society at large. And yet, while this formula is naturally proselytized widely on public platforms, we also witness a very different and altogether harsher reality. In the research data we can find considerable incidence of declining real wages, low levels of training provision, declining morale, an emergent secondary labour market with contingent labour, sub-contracting and temporary contracts. Far from the wider adoption of the high commitment employment strategies as predicted in the 1980s, this has been the strategy selected for the few and has existed alongside a growing trend for the many in the opposite direction.

Also, as we have shown in this chapter, there has been the persistence and even the embellishment of a third position – this one based around a negotiated order where trade union representatives are co-opted into an extensive process of constructive engagement leading to 'new deals'. These replace an adversarial stance with one where unions and management can hope to gain a win–win outcome built essentially around planned growth or stability through the flexible use of labour and other resources enabled in turn by single status, harmonized terms and conditions, and an effective representational voice.

In other words, there are many different employment strategies in evidence at the moment. A number of crucial questions remain unanswered: first, why managers opt for one strategy rather than another; second, the extent to which appropriate strategies are selected; third, with what outcomes? Finally, what processes and skills are required in order to implement the different strategic patterns? The answer to these questions await more detailed future research.

## Key Points

- The employment relationship has remained as a critical business, political, ethical, economic and social issue throughout the whole of the twentieth century and seems likely to continue as an area of concern.
- The perspectives and frameworks which inform thinking and action about employment relations are contentious and conflicting; as different interests are at stake and as power relations are also a factor these different 'ways of seeing' are likely to remain in play. At different times, however, the opportunity seems to arise for the parties to manage meanings in such a conjoint way that win–win outcomes can be achieved – at least for finite periods.
- While the chapter has argued that there is some scope for the parties to exercise strategic choice it also emphasized the importance of context in shaping and constraining those choices. Those contexts have been changing quite rapidly and markedly. In particular, the structures of the European economies and the structure of their labour markets have undergone extensive change and these changes have massive implications for the conduct of employment relations. A particular element has been the decline in organized labour and the associated rise in the possibilities for a more 'individualized' approach to managing employment. It was emphasized, however, that this needs to be kept very much in perspective because there is also evidence of situations where employers fail to give priority to either an individualized human resource management strategy or to an industrial relations strategy. The results of this (possibly intentional) neglect can be deleterious both for employment conditions and for economic growth.

- Employment relations in small firms have often been lauded as a model to emulate. The research evidence available to date does not support this belief or contention. The same points apply in large measure to the phenomenon of the non-union firm, although it should be recognized that there are different types of non-union firm and that there is hardly a coherent category to be analysed here.
- As for emergent 'new models', it was pointed out that the publicity accorded to the idea of 'the new industrial relations' as conceived in the mid-1980s far exceeded its significance on the ground. Nonetheless, it was also argued that there can be little doubt that traditional industrial relations have been extensively dismantled in many instances and at least in the weak sense, something 'new' is emerging. We went further, however, and pointed out that there are numerous instances of 'new deals' being negotiated over extensive time periods, and that for the unionized sectors at least these could herald the form which employment relations will increasingly take.

## Discussion Questions

1. Compare and contrast two different perspectives or frames of reference which have been used to understand the operation and nature of employment relations.
2. What have been the most important contextual changes which have radically reshaped the patterns of employment relations in the advanced economies?
3. In what different ways is the concept of 'flexibility' of significance in understanding recent changes to employment relations?
4. What contributions, if any, can trade unions make and what must they do to survive and prosper?
5. What evidence is there that managers can and do exercise 'choice' in the area of employment relations?
6. What, if anything, is new about the 'new deals' in recent employment relations?

## References

Bacon, N., Ackers, P., Storey, J., and Coates, D. (1996) 'Its a small world: Managing human resources in small businesses', *The International Journal of Human Resource Management*, vol. 7, no. 1, 82–100

Bain, G. and Clegg, H. (1974) 'A strategy for industrial relations research in Great Britain', *British Journal of Industrial Relations*, vol. xii, no. 1, 91–113.

Bassett, P. (1986) *Strike Free*, London: Macmillan.

Beardwell, I. (ed.) (1996) *Contemporary Industrial Relations: A critical analysis*, Oxford: Oxford University Press.

Beaumont, P. B. (1995) *The Future of Employment Relations*, London: Sage.

Bolton Committee Report (1971) *Report*, Royal Commission of Inquiry on Small Firms, CMN 4811, London: HMSO.

Brown, C., Hamilton, J., and Medoff, J. (1990) *Employers Large and Small*, Cambridge, MA: Harvard University Press.

Cave, K. (1997) *Zero Hours Contracts: a report into the incidence and implications of such contracts*, University of Huddersfield.

Claydon, T. (1996) 'Union derecognition: A re-examination', in I. Beardwell (ed.) *Contemporary Industrial Relations: A critical analysis*, Oxford: Oxford University Press.

Curran, J. and Stanworth J. (1979a) 'Self selection and the small firm worker – an alternative view', *Sociology*, vol. 13, no. 3, 427–44.

—— and —— (1979b) 'Worker involvement and sound relations in the small firm', *Sociological Review*, vol. 27, no. 2, 317–42.

—— and —— (1981a) 'Size of workplace and attitudes to industrial relations in the printing and electronics industries', *British Journal of Industrial Relations*, vol. 19, no. 1, 14–25.

—— and —— (1981b) 'A new look at job satisfaction in the small firm', *Human Relations*, vol. 34, no. 5, 343–65.

—— (1991) 'Employment and employment relations' in J. Stanworth and C. Gray (eds) *Bolton 20 years On: The Small Firm in the 1990s*, London: Paul Chapman Publishing.

——, Kitching, J., Abbot, B., and Mills, V. (1993) *Employment and Employment Relations in the Small Service Sector Enterprise: A report*, Kingston: ESRC Centre for Small Service Sector Enterprises.

Donovan, Lord (1968) *Report*, Royal Commission on Trade Unions and Employers' Association, London: HMSO.

Edwards, P. K. et al. (1992) 'Great Britain: Still muddling through', in A. Ferner and R. Hyman (eds), *Industrial Relations in the New Europe*, Oxford: Blackwell.

Eurostat (1993) *Enterprises in Europe: Third Report*, Luxembourg: European Commission.

Foulkes, F. (1980) *Personnel Practices in Large Non-union Companies*, Englewood Cliffs, NJ: Prentice-Hall

Goss, D. (1988) 'Social harmony and the small firm: a reappraisal', *Sociological Review*, vol. 32, no. 1, 114–32.

—— (1991) *Small Business and Society*, London: Routledge.

Guest, D. and Hoque, K. (1994) 'The good, the bad and the ugly: Employment relations in new non-union workplaces', *Human Resource Management Journal*, vol. 5, no. 1, 1–14.

—— (1995) 'Human resource management, trade unions and industrial relations', in J. Storey (ed.) *Human Resource Management: a critical text*, London: Routledge.

—— and Hoque, K. (1996) 'Human resource management and the new industrial relations' in I. Beardwell (ed.) *Contemporary Industrial Relations*, Oxford: Oxford University Press.

Huws, U. (1993) *Teleworking in Britain*, Employment Department, report no. 18, Sheffield.

IDS (1987) 'Single union deals and no strike clauses', *Report 509*, November, 28–30.

ILO (1996) *Yearbook of Statistics*, London: International Labour Office.

—— (1997) *World Labour Report 1997–98: Industrial relations, democracy and social stability*, London International Labour Office.

IM (1997) *Flexibility and Fairness – a survey of managers attitudes to part-time employment and part-time employees*, London: Institute of Management.

IS (1997) *Culture Change: Managing work practice*, Birmingham: Industrial Society.

ISR (1997) *Transition and Transformation: Employee satisfaction in the 1990s*, London: International Survey Research.

IRS (1997) *Employment Trends*, London: Industrial Relations Services.

Kochan, T., Katz, H., and McKersie, R. (1986) *The Transformation of American Industrial Relations*, New York: Basic Books.

—— and Osterman, P. (1994) *The Mutual Gains Enterprise*, Cambridge, MA: Harvard Business School Press.

Labour Market Trends (1997) *Trade Union Membership and Recognition*, London: Stationery Office.

LFS (1997) *Labour Force Survey*, London: HMSO.

Marginson, P., et al. (1993) *The Control of Industrial Relations in Large Companies: An initial analysis of the second company level industrial relations survey*, Warwick Papers in Industrial Relations, 45, Coventry: Industrial Relations Research Unit.

McLoughlin, I. and Gourlay, S. (1994) *Enterprise Without Unions: Industrial Relations in the non-union firm*, Buckingham: Open University Press.

Millward, N. et al. (1992) *Workplace Industrial Relations in Transition*, Aldershot: Gower.

Millward, N. (1994) *The New Industrial Relations*, London: Policy Studies Institute.

National Statistical Office (1997) *National Statistics on Manufacturing*, PA1002, London.

OECD (1991), *OECD Economic Outlook*, Paris: OECD.

—— (1994) *Historical Statistics*, Paris: OECD.

Piore, M. and Sabel, C. (1984) *The Second Industrial Divide*, New York: Basic Books.

Purcell, J. and Sisson, K. (1983) 'Strategies and practice in the management of industrial relations' in G. Bain (ed.) *Industrial Relations in Britain*, Oxford: Blackwell.

—— and Ahlstrand, B. (1993) *Strategy and Style in Employee Relations*, Oxford: Oxford University Press.

Rainne, A. and Scott, M. (1986) 'Industrial Relations in the small firm' in J. Curran, J. Stanworth and D. Watkins (eds) *The Survival of the Small Firm, Employment, Growth, Technology and Politics*, vol. 2, Aldershot: Gower.

—— (1989) *Industrial Relations in Small Firms*, London: Routledge.

Sabel, C. (1982) *Work and Politics*, Cambridge: Cambridge University Press.

Scase, R. and Goffee, R. (1982) *The Enterpreneurial Middle Class*, London: Croom Helm.

—— and —— (1987) *The Real World of the Small Business Owner*, 2nd edn, London: Croom Helm.

—— (1995) 'Employment relations in small firms', in P. Edwards (ed.) *Industrial Relations: Theory and Practise*, Oxford: Blackwell.

Sisson, K. (1989) *Personnel Management*, Oxford: Blackwell.

—— (1995) 'Human resource management and the personnel function', in J. Storey (ed.) *Human Resource Management: A Critical Text*, London: Routledge.

—— and Marginson, P. (1995) 'Management systems, structures and strategies', in P. K. Edwards (ed.) *Industrial Relations*, Oxford: Blackwell.

Smith, P. and Morton, G. (1994) 'Union exclusion: The next steps', *Industrial Relations Journal*, vol. 25, 3–14.

Stanworth, J. and Gray, C. (1991) *Bolton 20 Years On: the small firm in the 1990s*, London: Paul Chapman Publishing.

Storey, D. J. (1994) *Understanding the Small Business Sector*, London: Routledge.

Streeck, W. (1992) *Social Institutions and Economic Performance: Studies of industrial relations in advanced industrial countries*, London: Sage.

Trevor, M. (1988) *Toshiba's New British Company: Competitiveness Through Innovation in Industry*, London: Policy Studies Institute.

part 4

# Managing Learning

chapter 10

# Learning Organizations

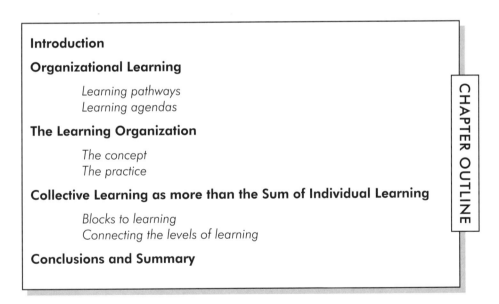

**Introduction**

**Organizational Learning**

*Learning pathways*
*Learning agendas*

**The Learning Organization**

*The concept*
*The practice*

**Collective Learning as more than the Sum of Individual Learning**

*Blocks to learning*
*Connecting the levels of learning*

**Conclusions and Summary**

CHAPTER OUTLINE

## Learning Objectives

- To appreciate the importance of learning for the commercial viability of organizations in 1990s and beyond.
- To differentiate the learning organization from an organization that learns.
- To analyse some of the factors which facilitate and impede learning in organizations.
- To identify the processes by which individual learning can enhance organizational learning.

# Introduction

The idea of 'the learning organization' has flourished in recent years as one way of summing up the sorts of organizational qualities called for and valued in today's changing environment. Senior management are recognizing that the way an organization learns is a key (and possibly determining) index to the way it innovates and remains a profitable enterprise: 'the rate at which individuals and organizations learn may become the only sustainable competitive advantage, especially in knowledge-intensive industries' (Stata 1989: 64). Competitive advantage will accrue, it is argued, to organizations which develop human resource policies that promote continuous learning, teamwork, participation and flexibility (Dertouzos et al. 1989). Such statements have received empirical support. On the basis of their in-depth case-study research across four UK sectors, Pettigrew and Whipp (1991) concluded: 'What becomes critical is the extent to which a company's knowledge base matches changing competitive conditions through learning. Learning here is seen as not just the acquisition of new knowledge. It also relates to how those within a firm collectively change their values and share mental models of their company and markets (shown graphically in Kleinwort Benson). Indeed it is the ability to shed outmoded knowledge, techniques and beliefs, as well as to learn and deploy new ones, which enables firms to carry out given strategies' Pettigrew and Whipp (1991: 238).

Much recent management literature and thinking stresses such values as flexibility and responsiveness, constant adaptation and change. 'The learning organization' is often a piece of shorthand for referring to an organization which tries to make a working reality of such desirable attributes. But beyond that, what does it mean in practice? According to Mills and Friesen (1992): 'Just as firms were required to create a particular business model (a combination of organization structure, management practices and internal support systems) to utilise mass production techniques, so will they need to build a business model to effectively encourage learning and utilise the outputs of innovation in their operations' (1992: 147). What might such 'business models' look like and what prescriptions should an organization follow if it is to turn itself into a learning organization? This brings us to the central conundrum of the learning organization: if management can be learned, can learning be managed? How can we relax control over the learning process while at the same time channelling the benefits from it? (Jones and Hendry 1994). Swieringa and Wierdsma (1992) are insistent that: 'one has to be prescriptive on the meta-level in order to keep the organization a learning one, especially where the handling of learning principles is concerned' (1992: 77). They go on to contrast the effort required to sustain learning with the incipient temptation to sink into the calm and security of the prescriptive organization, and because of this they advise that the desire to remain a learning organization should be non-negotiable. Is this a management paradox or a fatal internal contradiction in the concept of the learning organization? In this chapter we assemble some of the evidence to suggest that the notion of the learning organization is not only meaningful and definable, but also attainable. We also note, however, some of the pitfalls along the way and some of the presumptions that are currently obscuring the pursuit of an ethos where energized individuals and innovative organization processes work in creative tension together.

## Organizational Learning

### *Learning pathways*

Economists tend to view learning in terms of quantifiable improvements and some business writers equate learning with sustaining competitive edge or innovative efficiency. However, the concern of organization theorists and psychologists is to go beyond this to examine the process of learning as well as its outcomes, how things are learnt as well as what is learnt. It is usually assumed that learning generally has positive consequences, that organizations have the capacity to learn collectively and that such learning occurs at different speeds and levels within firms. For instance, R&D contracts with partners, joint ventures, strategic alliances, benchmarking successful competitors, tapping into professional/institutional networks, learning from customers and users, hiring key individuals, reverse engineering, exporting and investing abroad, are all sources of direct and vicarious learning.

But it is employees within organizations rather than organizations themselves that learn. Dodgson notes that 'individuals are the primary learning entity in firms, and it is individuals which create organizational forms that enables learning in ways which facilitate organizational transformation' (1993: 377–8). It is here that human resource strategies can play an important role by creating the structures and culture that will purposefully facilitate progress beyond mere adaptive, natural learning to develop and coordinate 'generative' (Senge 1990) learning in organizations necessitated by rapidly changing and conflicting circumstances. For instance, Schein (1985) regards culture as the basic assumptions and beliefs that are shared by members of an organization, which operate unconsciously and constitute '*Learned* responses to a group's problems of *survival* in its external environment and its problems of *internal integration*' (1985: 6). According to Hedberg (1981) such collective cultural learning actually becomes independent of individuals: 'organizations do not have brains, but they have cognitive systems and memories . . . Members come and go, and leadership changes, but organizations' memories preserve certain behaviours, mental maps, norms and values over time' (1981: 3).

We might ask how such 'memories' come to be built up and what, in practical terms, a cognitive system looks like. At least three aspects of an organization's structural capability are relevant here: first, its 'knowledge base' which refers to how a firm acquires articulates and enhances the unique knowledge which it controls; second, its 'firm-specific competencies', namely the mechanisms it employs to accumulate and dissipate distinctive skills and capabilities; and third, its 'routines' for using the skills and knowledge it possesses in an effective and competitive manner. These routines will include both its formal rules, procedures, technologies and strategies as well as its less formal – and sometimes contradictory – informal structure of beliefs, frameworks, paradigms, codes and cultures (Levitt and March 1988). However, as Dodgson (1993) points out, such approaches tend to underestimate the complexity and problems involved in learning and assume uniformity in learning capabilities within firms; they also take too little account of the importance of individual human agency. It is, after all, individuals who choose to build up a particular knowledge base or adopt a given routine, albeit influenced by the socializing context of the organization concerned. Furthermore individual learning theory tells as that learning can be conflictual (new knowledge and its exploitation may undermine the 'status quo'), conservative (it may alternatively serve to sustain existing outmoded structures) and/or unreliable (learning is shaped by new ideas often adopted more for their topicality, availability or political convenience than for their intrinsic worth).

## Learning agendas

Argyris and Schon (1978, 1981) have drawn attention to how individual learning in organizations can be harnessed positively to produce collective learning. Drawing upon the work of Bateson (1972) they describe the value of moving beyond 'single-loop' learning where errors are detected and corrected – which is effective for day-to-day operational matters but may lead to a rigid, unquestioning culture – to double-loop learning which challenges and examines these taken-for-granted internalized assumptions, and results in a deeper level of collective knowledge and understanding and reassessment of values. The cyclical and mechanistic nature of such feedback loops is called into question, however, by research on organizational capabilities by Pettigrew and Whipp (1991). They found that the way organizations learnt was in fact a highly intricate and complex process, with vital skills and knowledge often being acquired in hidden and unnoticed ways: 'In general terms the research shows that it is insufficient for companies to regard the creation of knowledge and judgements of their external competitive world as simply a technical exercise. Rather the need is for organizations to become open learning systems. In other words, the assessment of the competitive environment does not remain the preserve of a single function nor the sole responsibility of one senior manager. Nor does it occur via isolated acts. Instead strategy creation is seen as emerging from the way a company, at various levels, acquires, interprets and processes information about the environment' (Pettigrew and Whipp 1991: 30).

According to Jones and Hendry (1994) all the approaches discussed above (even the more sophisticated analysis of Pettigrew and Whipp) characterize organizational learning rather than the learning organization. This is because the learning under discussion is invariably framed within the current purposes of the organization. Thus, links are drawn between training, development and wider human resource management, and company performance and competitiveness. Even learning on the job and self-development, apparently enfranchising for the individuals concerned, is described as learning *harnessed primarily for organizational ends*. So, for example, in their critique of Total Quality Programmes, Kerfoot and Knights (1994) note some inherent and inadvertent contradictions:

> However, while at this level quality management reflects a concern to collapse or 'flatten' organizational hierarchies, it is also a motive force in their reconstitution and retrenchment. This occurs through processes or claims to empower workers. Suffice to say here that work empowerment and autonomy under quality programmes is heavily circumscribed by the demands for continuous improvement and error free standardization of products. Through a range of what are themselves perhaps bureaucratic procedures for identifying obstacles to efficient production and quality service, norms of quality are established and internalised. Partly out of a fear of the consequences of non-conformance and partly because of reward incentives, these procedures generate the kind of self-discipline that 'secures as it obscures' (Burawoy 1979) hierarchical forms, thus giving a renewed legitimacy to the authority of bureaucratic structures. (Kerfoot and Knights 1994: 8)

So long as the assumption remains that learning is essentially to support organizational structures and prescribe how people should behave within them; so long as organizational capability refers exclusively to the 'sum total of the organization working in unison' without reference to 'expanding and building on that which remains undeveloped' (Jones and Hendry 1994: 155) – then the point of the learning organization concept is being missed. Indeed descriptions which purport to profile the characteristics of a learning organization may, for these reasons, confuse rather than clarify the concept (see box 10.1).

While the elements elaborated in box 10.1 refer to the encouragement of taking risks, giving feedback and learning lessons – the 'softer', consensual side of human resource management – the manifest message behind each of these mechanisms or 'levers' is to 'support the change strategies and the values held by top management'. Clearly, for many in the organization, subscribing to and helping to further such values would not coincide with their own interests. In such circumstances, learning may well occur but not necessarily in a way which furthers the strategic goals of the enterprise.

## BOX 10.1 A LEARNING ORGANIZATION PROFILE – BUT ON WHOSE TERMS?

'A learning organization that is functioning well has several elements in place:

- A clear picture of how the organization should operate; employees at all levels understand the importance of both learning and doing.
- Rewards that encourage people to follow these norms. Employees are encouraged and rewarded for asking questions and challenging ways of work, with ideas coming from anywhere. Systems exist that encourage entrepreneurial behaviour.
- Performance reviews and career development that look at both what you do and what you have learned; organizations offer compensation systems that support the stated values and bonuses and incentives that are balanced between current performance, innovation, courage and risk.
- Feedback systems that guarantee ongoing information, not only about what has been done but about what has been learned that affects future actions. Improvement is valued as much as results. Personal feedback on performance, both positive and negative, is given frequently, up, down and sideways in the organization.
- Information systems that are designed and managed to support this balance between performing and doing. Information on "lessons" as well as on results should be widely available.
- Training and education programs that are designed to support the change strategies and the values held by top management. If learning is a priority, educational programs should be designed to maximize the balance between learning and doing.
- A communication strategy and program that keeps learning in the forefront of everyone's consciousness.
- A strategic planning process that is thought of as a learning as well as a doing process. More often strategic planning is regarded solely as a way of producing plans to fit the planning cycle. It can, in addition, be a most powerful lever for helping key people to learn, to change their mind-sets, and to develop a future focus.
- Strategic objectives that are defined to include the learning that must take place in order to achieve them.'

(Beckhard and Pritchard 1992: 22–3)

# The Learning Organization

## *The concept*

So, if what we have so far discussed misses the point of what the *learning organization* constitutes, what is it and what aspects of learning does the learning organization concept distinctively represent? Probably the most influential spokesperson in the US for replacing 'old models' of learning is Peter Senge.

In his book *The Fifth Discipline: the art and practice of the learning organization*, Senge (1990) takes a refreshing look at the new roles and skills required of leaders in organizations and the 'new' tools at their disposal, drawing for inspiration upon seminal work on personal and corporate learning (e.g. Argyris and Schon 1978; Mintzberg and Waters 1985). For instance, the need for systematic diagnosis as against event-driven reactivity; the provocative conception of leader as servant; the need to recognize, challenge and defuse defensive routines that inhibit learning; the return to simple skills like active listening ('balancing inquiry and advocacy'); avoiding premature conclusions ('seeing leaps of abstraction'); and discerning the gap between 'exposed theory and theory in use'. In particular, he notes that learning:

1 Can serve a variety of purposes and take a variety of forms. *Adaptive* learning is concerned with developing the understanding and capacity to cope with new situations. It entails reflecting on and analysing what one has done in the past with a view to making improvements and amendments to meet specific new needs and demands. 'What did I do?' 'What aspects went well?' 'What could have gone better?' 'How can we solve this problem?' *Generative* learning is concerned with developing new ways of looking at the world – and one's work and organization in particular. It is directed towards the future and involves speculation, creating possibilities and options, re-defining one's performance. 'What might we do?' 'What is the problem?' 'What possible ways could we approach it?' 'What would happen and what would it look like if . . . ?' (see box 10.2).

2 Learning can result from the creative tension between developing a shared vision and making a fuller analysis of current realities and practices. This is a standard tenet of the organization development approach to change interventions (see chapter 13).

3 Learning should involve attention to contexts and processes as well as tasks and outcomes. As 'designers' managers can facilitate learning and development, not simply by acting as charismatic leaders or competent role models, but by changing the circumstances which influence and shape their own and their staff's performance – the governing values, the policies and strategies and so forth. Effective learning involves the creation of a sense of shared ownership; the nurturing of strategic thinking is as valuable as the dissemination of the right or correct strategy.

## BOX 10.2 HOW JAPANESE COMPANIES LEARN

'No single Japanese company ever dominated a business the way IBM once ruled the computer business or the way General Motors and Sears once dominated the automobile and retailing industries, respectively. As rulers of their own fiefdoms, these companies sat comfortably on their laurels, becoming increasingly numb and blind to changes taking place around them. Certainty not uncertainty, became the norm. [ . . . ]

How do Japanese companies bring about continuous innovation? One way is to look outside and into the future, anticipating changes in the market, technology, competition, or product. [ . . . ] living in a world of uncertainty worked in favor of Japanese companies, since they were constantly forced to make their existing advantages obsolete. In fact, this trait – the willingness to abandon what has long been successful – is found in all successful companies, not only those in Japan. To these companies, change is an everyday event and a positive force. Contrast this mindset to that of the three monarchs mentioned earlier, who became preoccupied with defending their advantages and treated change with the fear that there was much to lose. They became insular, seeking predictability and stability.

Times of uncertainty often force companies to seek knowledge held by those outside the organization. Japanese companies have continually turned to their suppliers, customers, distributors, government agencies, and even competitors for any new insights or clues they may have to offer. Just as the proverbial "drowning man will catch at a straw", these companies accumulate knowledge from the outside almost in desperation during times of uncertainty. What is unique about the way Japanese companies bring about continuous innovation is the linkage between the outside and the inside. Knowledge that is accumulated from the outside is shared widely within the organization, stored as part of the company's knowledge base, and utilized by those engaged in developing new technologies and products. A conversion of some sort takes place; it is this conversion process – from outside to inside and back outside again in the form of new products, services, or systems – that is the key to understanding why Japanese companies have become successful. It is precisely this dual internal and external activity that fuels continuous innovation within Japanese companies. Continuous innovation, in turn, leads to competitive advantage.'

(Nonaka and Takeuchi 1995: 4–6)

4 Learning should involve developing insightful views of current practice and realities. As 'teachers' managers need to foster and support the capacity to identify and critically evaluate their own 'mental models' – i.e. the underlying repertoire of beliefs, assumptions, values and theories they possess about how the world works. This helps to distinguish espoused theory from theory in use, enabling people to

> have the confidence and ability to think analytically and self-critically, identifying inter-relationships, systems and processes rather than discrete events, probing behind surface symptoms and immediate causes. All this assists the process of learning.

It should be noted that Senge's view of organizations is primarily an optimistic one. His creative tension principle tends to assume that individual employees will be motivated by a given organizational vision once it has been clearly articulated and the current reality has been accurately portrayed. And his statement that 'negative visions carry a subtle message of powerlessness' may be true, but possibly neglects the incipient plurality of many organizations today in which powerless people cannot (or find it difficult to) create or subscribe to positive visions! (Mabey and Iles 1994).

The most frequently cited definition of the learning organization in the European literature is that of Pedler et al. (1991: 1): 'The Learning Company is an organization which facilitates the learning of all of its members *and* continuously transforms itself.' There are some important notions captured within this description – the authors refer to it as a 'dream' rather than a definition. First, there are aspects of the way the organization operates that actively facilitates and encourages individual learning: that is, it is insufficient for all members to have a self-development, or learning orientation, for the organization to be a learning organization. This is partly why they prefer the term 'company' to organization, because its convivial connotation suggests people engaged in a joint enterprise. Second, the emphasis is upon 'all members' of the organization. It is insufficient to be focused on selected groups, at whatever level of the organization. The notion is that individuals learn together in a collective 'system', where the learning of one individual, or sub-group, is likely to have knock-on effects on the learning of another. Where the organization attempts to restrict this transfer of learning, it is unlikely to be acting in the spirit of the learning organization.

Third, the definition implies that the organization is undergoing a process of continuous change and adaption; and focusing upon learning about the change process itself, while at the same time enabling individuals' learning.

Fourth, it seems clear from this description that the organization does *not* have all the 'right answers' in terms of how to direct individuals' learning. At times it is likely that individual learning initiatives will provide the leading-edge of organization change; while at other times a major breakthrough at the organization systems level of understanding will cause a 'reframing' of individual learning projects and approaches. Finally, there is no single success formula – each organization needs to discover its own learning pathways.

## The practice

As Pedler et al. (1991) emphasize, the evolution of the learning organization concept is long and varied and its precise form is yet to be (and perhaps will never be) defined. Drawing upon the literature on learning, organizations, training and development, and management of quality they propose 11 dimensions which characterize a learning organization (see figure 10.1).

The enabling *structures* represent the central pivot of the learning organization since they are designed to create opportunities for business and individual development. For instance, rules and procedures are frequently reviewed and changed if necessary; appraisals are geared to learning and development rather than to reward and punishment. The two clusters above structures are mirrored by the two below. *Strategy* consists of (1) a learning approach whereby company policy and strategy formation, together with implementation, evaluation and improvement are consciously structured as a learning process enabling continuous improvement through flexibility; and (2) participative policy-making which involves all stakeholders (including customers, supplying owner negotiations) in the strategy-forming processes with a commitment to air and work through conflicts. *Looking in* covers four dimensions: (3) informating, which means

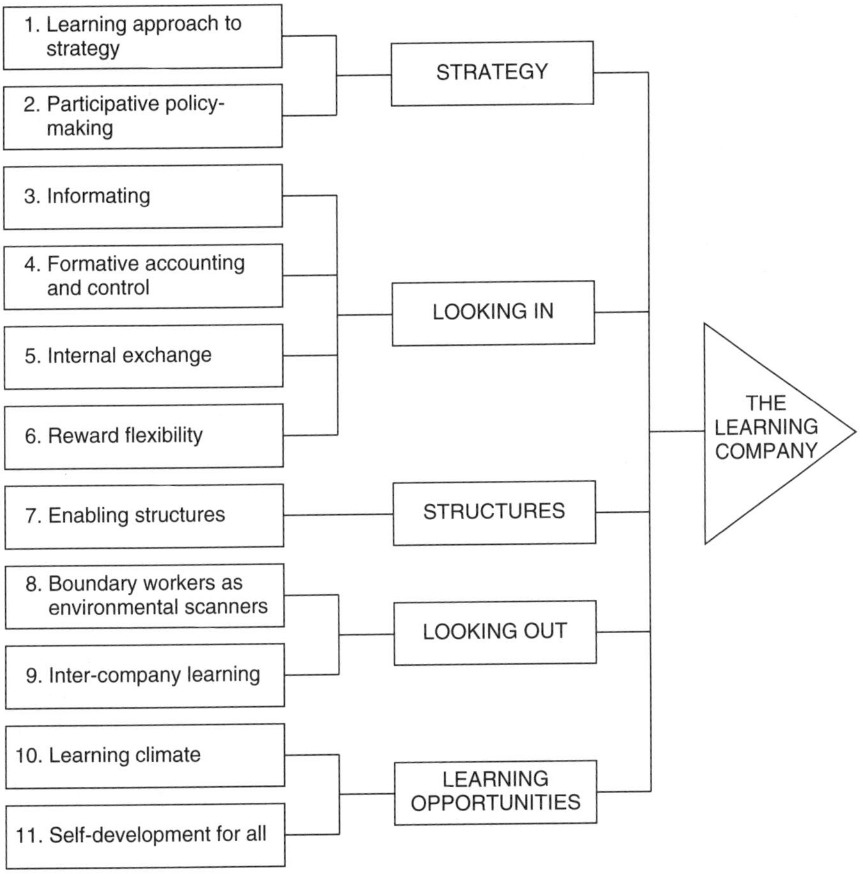


**Figure 10.1** The learning company 'blueprint'
*Source:* Pedler, Burgoyne and Boydell (1991: 25).

information technologies are used to inform and empower people, encouraging wide access to information and more 'open' systems; (4) formative accounting and control, comprising systems that are structured to assist learning and add value, encouraging individuals and units to act as small businesses and to think about who their customers are; (5) internal exchange between units and departments as suppliers and customers of each other, encouraging wide sharing of expectations and information, negotiations, contracting and providing feedback on goods/services received – (a) fostering an environment and (b) rewarding flexibility of collaboration rather than competition). The *looking out* cluster embraces (7) enabling structures, (8) boundary workers as environmental scanners, asking for, respecting and using the experiences of all members who interact with external customers to feed back information on customer needs; and (9) tutor-company learning whereby mutually advantageous learning activities are initiated, such as joint-trading, sharing in investment and job-exchanges. Finally *learning opportunities* imply the fostering of (10) a learning climate, a general attitude of continuous improvement, the positive valuing of difference (age, gender, colour and so on), learning lessons from mistakes; and (11) self-development for all, whereby facilities and resources are made available to all members, employees at all levels and external stakeholders. While many of these 'learning organization' nostrums smack of common sense, there are few examples of organizations consistently practising such principles.

In a deliberate attempt to discover the reality behind the rhetoric of learning organizations in the UK, Raper et al. (1997) concluded that there was little to suggest that the concept of the learning organization was acting as a major trigger for change in contemporary training practice, despite the greater incidence of on-the-job training, and some evidence of lower-level line managers taking more ownership of employee development. Part of the explanation was resistance amongst groups of staff and distrust of the new 'open' management, used by the organization they studied, to shift the culture. Against a backcloth of delayering and deskilling associated with new technology, they reported insecurity among the staff involved and a fear that they were being asked to deliver more for less.

The difference between the two concepts seems to be that organizational learning is a descriptive or heuristic device to explain and quantify learning activities and events, and as such can be subsumed under the wider concept of the learning organization which refers to the less tangible but real philosophical purpose and direction of an organization and its staff. However, as we come to delineate the pathways such learning organizations might take and, particularly in the context of this book, seek to map out the HRS ramifications of such a 'direction', further imponderables arise. Why is it that so many activities under the broad organizational label of training and development patently do not lead to learning – either at an individual or institutional level? Is collective learning more than the sum of individual learning, and if so how and at what point do the two connect and synergise? If learning truly is open and unprescribed whose needs are being met – who is to determine whether learning is acceptable or unacceptable, helpful or unhelpful? Can and should learning be managed? Is the ultimate custodian and benefactor of new skills, knowledge and attitudes the organization or the individual? As Jones and Hendry note, 'The paradox and dilemma for organizations is how to relax their control over the learning process while channelling the benefits from it' (1994: 160). If the benefits of learning *can* be established – and this is a moot point given the unorganized and hidden nature of much insightful experience – can lessons from one organizational context be passed onto another? And if they cannot, what is the value of studying learning organizations? Finally, if it is natural, spontaneous and habitual, why are individuals and organizations so successful at blocking and inhibiting learning?

At first glance, the learning organization appears to be both a timely (Pedler et al. 1991: ch. 2) and attractive (e.g. Drucker 1992; Senge 1990) estuary of many promising streams of thought and reflective action that have been sporadically evident through recent decades (organization development, action learning, self-development, pursuing excellence, total quality and continuous improvement, amongst others). On closer scrutiny the structural and behavioural manifestations of the concept, even at the metaphorical level, are more elusive and – at times – self-contradictory. In the remainder of this chapter, and in the following chapter, we seek to address some of the problematic issues prompted by the pursuit of the learning organization.

## Collective Learning as more than the Sum of Individual Learning

One critical distinction between an organization that learns and the learning organization seems to be that in the latter individual learning activities feed and integrate with broader and deeper learning processes in the organization; breadth being associated with the scope of learning transfer and depth being concerned with levels of meaning (e.g. being prepared to question the processes of learning themselves). Here we consider some of the hindrances to this kind of learning and its transfer, and some of the ways these hindrances might be overcome.

### *Blocks to learning*

Not all blocks to learning concern preferred style and not all hindrances to learning transfer can be attributed to the individual. Take the case of off-the-job training courses. An employee's previous learning experience may well have been the latter stages of formal education or attendance on a less than satisfactory training event elsewhere and this will probably conjure up unhelpful memories. 'Unlearning' may need to take place – emotional and educational – before new learning can commence; in other words successful development may be as much about the learning environment as the individual's learning style. Note the equivalence here with Lewin's (1951) model of organizational unfreezing, which is seen as a necessary percursor to cultural change. This initial willingness to learn will also be influenced by the diagnosis and selection process leading up to the training event: whether the individual's manager is involved in, and supportive of, the training activity. Whether personal learning needs have been identified, and so on.

Equally important is the reinforcement of new concepts, skills and attitudes in the work place *after* the training event or learning activities; again, the trainee's line manager plays a key role here in debriefing and overseeing any implementation plans. The less uncoupled the work place and off-the-job training activities the better – which is why on-the-job learning has many inherent advantages. At a wider level, unless the prevailing value system from which the course participant comes actively supports and rewards the new skills and behaviours being acquired, little personal learning is likely to be sustained or consolidated. For example, a 'skills workshop' may stimulate an increased awareness of customer requirements and may cultivate the accompanying listening and problem-solving skills. The trainee returns to his/her workplace eager and equipped, only to find that divisional performance targets specify an increased number of queries and complaints to be handled in a given time period – an organizational constraint which not only dampens but actually discourages the application of the newly acquired skills!

A far more subtle and potent source of learning disruption comes from the social context of learning itself. Learning usually implies change and work organizations are particularly adept at obstructing individuals' learning when major change is required: "Natural" learning processes within organizations seem to engage managers not only in analysing technical data and problems but also in efforts to avoid addressing fundamental issues and questions which may distress, embarrass or threaten themselves or others' (Butler 1992: 40). When new knowledge and new ideas are regarded as dangerous, disloyal or troublesome within the organization, managers learn not to learn, to avoid real issues and moreover to skilfully cover up that they are doing so (see box 10.3). They become guilty of skilled incompetence (Argyris 1987: 8), clever at 'not learning what they "must" learn (in order to make real change and progress) and almost certainly unaware of their own responsibility for the resulting maintenance of status quo' (Butler 1992: 40).

## Connecting the levels of learning

Individual learning is a necessary but not a sufficient condition for organizational learning. As we have seen above, individuals do not always learn that which is genuinely helpful for organizational progress and organizations do not automatically learn when individuals within it have learned something; there has to be a mutual behavioural change. There has to be an enhancement of collective competence among the members of an organization if organizational learning is to mean anything at all. This, in turn, usually means that the learning – at whatever level – is conscious, that there is a collective and explicit review, and possible rejection and renewal of the way things are done.

## BOX 10.3 ORGANIZATIONAL DEFENSIVE ROUTINES

'One of the most powerful ways people deal with potential embarrassment is to create organizational defensive routines. I define these as any action or policy that prevents human beings from experiencing negative surprises, embarrassment, or threat, and simultaneously prevents the organization from reducing or eliminating the causes of the surprises, embarrassment, and threat. Organizational defensive routines are anti-learning and overprotective.

These defensive routines are organizational in the sense that individuals with different personalities behave in the same way; and people leave and new ones come into the organization, yet the defensive routines remain intact.

Now to the example: Built into genuine decentralization is the age-old tug between autonomy and control. Subordinates want to be left alone while their superiors want no surprises. The subordinates push for autonomy, asserting that by letting them alone, top management will show its trust. They want management to trust them at a distance. The superiors, on the other hand, wanting no surprises, use information systems as controls. The subordinates see the control device as confirming mistrust.

Many executives I observed deal with this dilemma by acting in a way that they believe will lead to productive consequences. They send mixed messages. They keep communicating, "We mean it – you are running the show". The division heads concur that the message is credible up to the point that a very important issue is at stake and they want to prove their mettle; then headquarters begins to interfere. In the eyes of top management, they intervene precisely when they can be of most help, that is, when the issue "requires a corporate perspective".

In order to design and send an intentionally ambiguous message and have it look at if this is not the case requires skill. The sender has to follow four rules about designing and delivering mixed messages.

1 *Design a message that is ambiguous and clearly so; that is imprecise and precisely so*. For example, "Be innovative and take risks, but be careful about upsetting others" is a message that says in effect, "Don't get into trouble". But the designer is careful not to specify exactly what will and will not upset others. The ambiguity and imprecision are necessary to cover the designer. It is also necessary because it is difficult for the designer to be precise ahead of time.

   The ambiguity and imprecision, on the other hand, are clearly and precisely understood by the receiver. Indeed, a request for more precision would likely be interpreted as a sign of immaturity or inexperience. Moreover, the receivers may some day want to use the imprecision and ambiguity to their advantage.

2 *Act as if the message is not inconsistent*. When individuals communicate mixed messages, they usually do it spontaneously and with no sign that

the message is mixed. Indeed, if they did appear to be hesitant because of the mixedness in the message, that could be seen as a weakness.

3 *Make the ambiguity and inconsistency in the message undiscussable*. It is rare indeed for an executive to design and state a mixed message and then ask "Do you find my message inconsistent and ambiguous?" The message is made undiscussable by the very natural way it is carried out and by the absence of any inquiry.

4 *Make the undiscussability of the undiscussable also undiscussable*.'

(Argyris 1978: 6, 7)

**Table 10.1** Examples of collective learning and organization change

| *Single-loop learning* | *Double-loop learning* | *Triple-loop learning* |
|---|---|---|
| *An insurance company is confronted with complaints from agents about co-ordination and communication difficulties.* | | |
| • A quality action is instigated, computer programs are improved, policies are checked three times instead of twice and consultations between inspectors and head office are intensified. | • The insurance company begins to wonder whether perhaps different marketing strategies (such as segmentation) should be considered, and to what extent the complaints might have been caused by collective attitudes among the staff. | • The insurance company begins to wonder whether it ought really to operate with agents at all, whether or not it wishes to give itself a high profile as a market leader and whether it is primarily an insurance company or an institutional investor. |
| *An energy company decides to implement a series of major radical investment projects over the coming five years.* | | |
| • The management team proposes a plan with details of the consequences of the investments for the functions and responsibilities of operators, supervisors and maintenance teams. | • The management team of the energy company decides to run the project with a matrix structure, with as much involvement as possible from the processing and maintenance departments, in order to ease the transition of the new organization and give personnel the opportunity to learn on the job. | • The energy company, in consultation with the works council, decides not to adopt the blueprint model which would involve considerable opposition and political manipulation, but to opt for a programme of gradual development. |

**Table 10.1** (continued)

| *Single-loop learning* | *Double-loop learning* | *Triple-loop learning* |
|---|---|---|
| *The atmosphere has sunk below zero in a personnel department; other departments have begun to complain bitterly.* | | |
| • Two of the suspected instigators have been dismissed, other members of staff take two two-day periods off to talk the matter through and develop new rules of behaviour. | • The personnel department begins a discussion about how personnel matters could be investigated in a professional way. | • The personnel department begins discussions with the Board on whether a controlling or a supporting staff department should be developed. |
| *In one year, complaints in a small technical services company double.* | | |
| • After an investigation, improvements are implemented in transport routes, schemes of work, telephone messages, etc. | • When complaints in the technical service company remain at an undesirably high level, discussion of working methods is introduced into this previously very autocratically managed company. | • Two years later, the founder-director of the service company decides to step down and give his son a change to introduce a new style of leadership into the company. |
| *A college of higher education witnesses a gradual decline in applications from new students.* | | |
| • It is decided to intensify publicity, to produce a new prospectus, to hold open days and to mount extra-mural activities. | • The college begins to wonder about the curriculum it offers, and the atmosphere at the college. | • Teachers in the college develop a plan to transfer, within five years, from a discipline-based to a problem-based method of education. |
| *The work of the head of an employers' association is subjected to more and more criticism.* | | |
| • He is sent on courses by the management, division of responsibilities between him and his staff is adjusted, and the frequency of reporting is increased, etc. | • Members of the employers' association begin to discuss the structure of the association and the distribution of responsibilities of the office. | • The employers' association calls together its members to coincide in a strategic orientation round of talks the mission and goals of the association for the 1990s. |

*Source:* Adapted from Swieringa and Wierdsma (1992).

Following Argyris and Schon (1978), Swieringa and Wierdsma (1992) differentiate three levels of collective learning. Single-loop learning occurs when changes are made to existing 'rules', or the way they are interpreted. This does not necessarily equate with single, easy and trouble-free learning, but it is concerned with improving *how* things are done rather than questioning the underlying purpose.

Double-loop learning they equate to learning at a higher level of right, questioning *why* things are done. It is called for when external signals indicate that mere adjustment of the 'rules' is inadequate, or internal signals suggest there is confusion or conflict over the organization's 'rules'. Occasionally – indeed rarely – triple-loop learning occurs when the essential principles on which the organization is founded came under discussion: for instance, its place in the market, its role as an enterprise, its cultural identity.

Again it poses 'why' questions, but this time at the level of collective will and being. Organizational responses to similar circumstances will look very different depending on which level the learning is taking place (see table 10.1)

Swieringa and Wiersdma maintain that many organizations do not progress beyond single-loop learning because managers are fearful of putting basic principles up for discussion. Too often organizations turn to third parties to manage radical transitions instead of mobilizing internal knowledge and expertise, or start up new learning processes before previous ones have reached the point of concrete and visible behavioural change.

## The role of catalysts

This still leaves the question of how the different levels or loops of learning connect. For Garratt (1987, 1990) the vital link between level one and level two is the 'business brain' of the enterprise, not the directors but the people who straddle the domains of strategy and operations, who need to be effective at educating upwards as well as translating new vision and direction into operational reality. Pedler et al. (1991) see the learning company as a number of energy flows (figure 10.2). On the vertical axis there are two crucial 'connections' which are mutually beneficial: 'Individual purpose comes about through shared identity, which, in turn, fires our collective purpose. Equally, collective purpose gives meaning to our lives and our place in the company' (1991: 31). On the horizontal axis, there presumably is nothing to stop individual ideas and action feeding each other in a manner which is entirely discrete from the policy – operation loops. What begins to distinguish the learning company, however, is where inner searching and visioning leads to organizational policy, realized in collective operations and expressed through the learning and development of individual members. The authors point out that it is entirely possible for the organization to get stuck in one of the four cycles: perhaps all operations with little policy development, or a great deal of searching which does not realize the company's full potential. In these circumstances 'the effective intervention is one which helps the organization move out of the impasse which is holding it in unconscious patterns of repetitive behaviour' (Critchley and Casey 1989: 8).

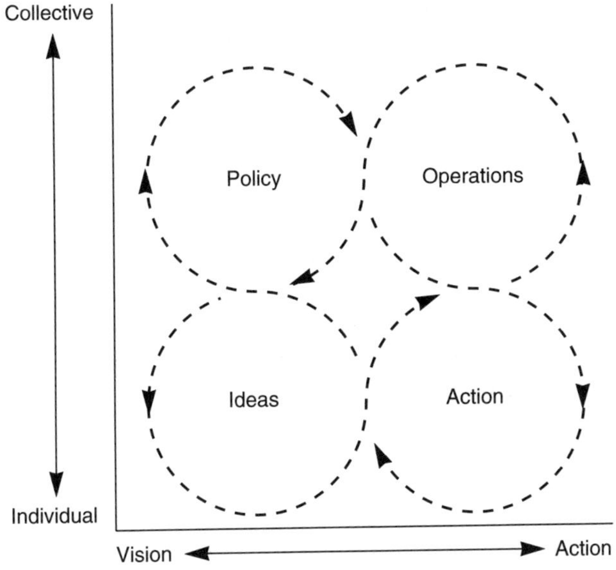


**Figure 10.2** The energy-flow model
*Source:* Pedler, Burgoyne and Boydell (1991: 32)

Many organizations have – in recent years – spawned a host of special project teams, cross-functional clusters, quality improvement groups and the like for the specific purpose of preventing this 'stuckness' and stimulating this interchange. However, Hawkins (1991) notes that there needs to be a structure for these strategy groups to dialogue and co-create the new organization together, and some kind of overarching vision to cohere their diverse endeavours. 'The greatest danger lies not in the lack of integration within the operational learning or strategic learning loops, but in the lack of the "business brain" that integrates the two cycles. Without this linkage, the most likely outcome is that there will be single-loop learning within both domains' (1991: 176).

The other possibility, of course, is that the top team won't listen to or 'hear' the messages coming from elsewhere in the organization, so reducing the value of generated and collected information (Garratt 1990) or filtering out its key, provocative insights (Argyris 1987). As Torbert (1994: 68) points out, 'only double-loop feedback adjusted for local coloring, and developmental timing specific to this unique occasion' is likely to accomplish the impact and spur the level of learning desired.

## The role of leaders

Who or what creates the link between double-loop learning (which helps to move an organization from efficiency thinking to effectiveness thinking) and triple-loop learning, which generates the capacity to address the fundamental question: effective for what, or to what end? For Hawkins (1991), the answer is to have at least some key members in the organization who can 'act like "salt to the soup" to draw out the awareness of the deeper purpose which contains and informs the strategic thinking and the operational realities' (1991: 183). They should be capable of recognizing the mind-sets that are locking the organization into dysfunctional patterns of behaviour and be able to lead an exploration of new purpose and core values, remembering that 'real learning only begins when the leaders of the company change not what they preach, but what they do. Here, there is a change not just in "espoused theory" but in "theory in action"' (Argyris and Schon, 1981). While formal leaders do not necessarily equate with opinion leaders, they do nevertheless carry a special responsibility, especially during periods of disruptive organizational change (see box 10.4).

## The role of teams

So far, we have been primarily considering how individuals can catalyze the learning of larger systems, but as Marsick (1994) reminds us: 'Managers can involve social units in collective learning – aggregates of people who are united by the pursuit of common concerns. Most obviously this may involve teams, but at the wider organizational levels, vertical or horizontal business networks, multinational business divisions, or customer–supplier partnerships may be involved.' (1994: 16).

The team can be a key to the learning organization because it provides minimum critical mass for the cross-fertilizing of ideas and for setting learning norms for itself (Senge 1990). A team can also achieve what none of the individuals within can do alone; with the right dynamic, a collection of ordinary individuals can achieve extraordinary feats. But the converse can also occur: a team can fail to achieve what any of its members could easily accomplish. For 'working groups' and 'pseudo-teams' this is not untypical (Katzenbach and Smith 1993), even when they are comprised of individually 'bright' members (Belbin 1993). This is because how a group learns is not exactly the same as how individuals learn: new skills and sensitivities are required. Collective competence is to a large degree determined by the interactional expertise of individuals. When applied to the running of learning events for groups of staff from a given organization, this results in some further paradoxes:

Participants of an organizational course must individually unlearn what they have learned together as a collective. In an organizational course collectively developed rules, insights and principles will be subjected to discussion. It is this collective agreement on what is permitted and what is obligatory which dictates the knowledge and understanding, the courage, the will and the ability of a collective. In an organizational course it is precisely this collective agreement that is the subject under discussion, and with it the ability and knowledge of each individual.

An organization which seeks to change its collective behaviour must be ready to discuss what has determined its collective behaviour. This is a paradox which

## BOX 10.4 RADICAL CHANGE AT BILLITON, ROYAL DUTCH SHELL

'The basis upon which an organization acts, adapts and implements changes is coming to interact more and more closely with personal values. As all employees play a more vital part in the organization's life so their learning – conscious and unconscious, explicit and implicit – becomes of greater consequence; and as learning in itself becomes more valued in organizations, and therefore more visible as an activity, questions about organizational purpose become more urgent and necessary to address.

A successful example of radical change occurred in the central office of Billiton International medals in The Hague. Billiton is the metals industry division of the Royal Dutch Shell Group. After seven years of fundamental over-supply in the metals market the company, with a turnover at the time of around $1.5 billion, had accumulated losses of $750 million. The parent company was considering disposal as an option when a new President was appointed in 1986. He advised that the business had to be put in better shape, even to sell it. Every operation in Billiton, world-wide, was reviewed "to determine what businesses we were in and why we were in them". A survival plan resulted, whereby product-oriented divisions were to be scrapped in favour of four core business segments. The management organization needed to be changed from a typical metals industry structure, heavily centralized to permit significant authority and responsibility to be transferred into the operating companies. Consequently, the role of central office had to change from command and control to a dual role which was very different, being more subtle and complex. The roles embraced first monitoring and auditing on behalf of the shareholder (Shell) and a second provision of advice to operating companies on request, and at market competitive rates. The radical change in attitude required could be described as being from "we're in charge" to "no one owes us a living". The change in role also required a reduction by half of staff numbers in central office, with some transferring to the operating companies and some taking redundancy, mainly on a voluntary basis.

In review, the management team, which has retained the same personnel throughout the period, have by their own open admission significantly changed the way they individually and collectively behave in business over this period of time. Every member of the central office has attested to a significant rethinking of who they are, where they are leading people, and how this related with the business. Most say that the process of radical change, and the ultimate survival of the business, was significantly affected by the close attention to vision, direction and strategy, alongside the implications for the values, expectations and assumptions of each person involved.'
(Benjamin and Mabey 1993: 181–6)

becomes more awkward the higher the level of learning involved. 'With triple-loop learning, at the level of principles, the paradox implies that you should discuss what it has been agreed not to discuss' (Swieringa and Wierdsma 1992: 125–6).

So it is possible to identify linkages that integrate much learning at individual level through groups and teams to learning at the organizational level. However, while the processes and dynamics that connect individual and group learning are relatively easy to observe these become more elusive as the scale and the complexity of the social unit grow, and certainly examples of triple-loop organizational learning are few and far between. Perhaps we should follow Marsick in interpreting 'organizational learning as subsystem learning that occurs across functional lines and takes place on a relatively large scale, for example, a business unit' (1994: 16), rather than confining the definition to wholescale organization transformation.

## Conclusions and Summary

Perhaps the greatest value of the learning organization debate is the attention it has focused on three areas of learning. First, the emphasis on regenerative or transformational learning begs the question of what an organization is being transformed into and why. Examples of organizations becoming 'learning laboratories' combined with, at a more mundane level, flatter and more open organizations, may well create tensions within organizations which result in employees asking searching questions of a social, ethical, moral and personal kind related to the purpose of work and the nature of society – a theme, incidentally, that has underpinned the self-development work of Pedler et al. (1991) for almost a decade. In the past, the workplace has been a major focus for social and personal development, and for fulfilling a wide range of needs through personal interaction. As old values and ways of doing things disappear, new activities challenge such deep-rooted assumptions and organizational structures, and create what people will at first perceive as a disruptive tension.

'The idea of "disruptive tension" provides the bridge between the developmental and mechanical description of the learning organization on the one hand, and the more philosophical definition provided by Pedler et al. (1988) on the other' (Jones and Hendry 1994: 156).

Secondly, previous discussion of organizational learning has tended to concentrate on formalized and prescriptive development and training needs, generic sets of competencies and the adoption of universalistic assessment, whereas the learning organization switches attention to the *process* of learning, the individuality of learning styles and creating the right environment for experiential learning to occur. It has been noted by Edmundson and Moingeon (1996) that: 'organisations can develop both capabilities – learning how *and* learning why – as potential sources of competitive advantage. Learning how is required for the many situations in which speed and quality matter; learning why is required for diagnosis and relationship building . . . the meta-source of competitive advantage is knowing when to use which resource' (1996: 34).

Thirdly, the debate has prompted the realization that much learning is as much acquired through emotion, attitudes, communication and habit mediated through imitation of role models, the forging of meaningful relationships, experience and memory, and developing a sense of self and values. Jones and Hendry (1994) contrast this 'soft learning' with the hard, pragmatic formal training typically undertaken by organizations. Whereas 'soft learning is often unintended, indirect, not controlled by the organization . . . it is at the heart of what the organization stands for while providing added value in adult learning' (1994: 160).

However, it must be said that some commentators are more sceptical that the notion of the learning organization can divorce itself so neatly from issues of control. For example, Coopey (1996) fears that:

> The learning organisation, like the notion of Organisational Culture . . . might well be destined to be transformed from a root metaphor, helping to explain the nature of organisational activities and performance, to a mechanism through which managerial control is improved under dramatically changed external circumstances. If this were so, employees could be expected to resist managerial pressures to conform. (Coopey 1996: 355)

## Key Points

- All organizations are learning, most of the time. The question is, to what extent is this learning repetitive and unconscious, or co-ordinated and channelled in a synergistic and progressive manner?
- Even when organizations *are* adopting reflexive learning processes, interpreting new data intelligently, discerning the lessons from past mistakes, experimenting with new ways of working, such activities are invariably designed to support organizational structures and prescribe how people should behave in them.
- The learning organization is a term that has been used to characterize an enterprise where learning is open-ended, takes place at all levels and is self-questioning. Here there is an energizing interplay between individual ideals and action, and company policy and collective operations.
- So far, the literature has been more successful at describing the learning organization and how it might be experienced, than providing examples of it happening; although by definition, there is no blueprint that can be transposed from one organization to another.

## Discussion Questions

1 What is the difference between organizational learning and the learning organization?
2 What are some of the blocks to learning in organizations?
3 How might an organization effectively engage in double-loop learning?

## References


Argyris, C. and Schon, D. (1978) *Organizational Learning: A theory-action perspective.* Reading, MA: Addison-Wesley.

—— and —— (1981) *Organizational Learning*, Reading, MA: Addison-Wesley.

—— (1987) 'The leadership dilemma: Skilled incompetence', *Business and Economic Review*, vol. 1, 4–11.

Bateson, G. (1972) *Steps Toward an Ecology of Mind*, New York: Ballantyne.

Beckhard, R. and Pritchard, W. (1992) *Changing the Essence: The art of creating and leading fundamental change in organizations*, San Francisco, CA: Jossey-Bass.

Belbin, M. (1993) *Team Roles at Work*, Oxford: Butterworth-Heinemann.

Benjamin, G. and Mabey, C. (1993) 'Facilitating radical change' in C. Mabey and B. Mayon-White (eds) *Managing Change*, London: Chapman.

Burawoy, M. (1979) *Manufacturing Consent*, Chicago: Chicago University Press.

Butler, J. (1992) 'Learning skills for strategic change', *Journal of Strategic Change*, vol. 1, 39–50.

Coopey, J. (1996) 'Crucial gaps in "the learning organisation": power, politics and ideology', in E. Starkey (ed.) *How Organisations Learn*, London: Thomson Business Press.

Critchley, B. and Casey, D. (1989) 'Organizations get stuck too', *Leadership and Organizational Development Journal*, vol. 10, no. 4, 3–12.

Dertouzos, M., Lester, R., and Solow, R. (1989) *Made in America: Regaining the competitive edge*, Cambridge, MA: MIT Press.

Dodgson, M. (1993) 'Organizational learning: A review of some literatures', *Organization Studies*, vol. 14, no. 3, 375–94.

Drucker, P. F. (1992) 'The new society of organizations', *Harvard Business Review*, vol. 70, no. 5, 95–104.

Edmundson, A. and Moingeon, B. (1996) 'When to learn and when to learn why: appropriate organizational learning processes as a source of competitive advantage', in B. Moingeon and A. Edmundson (eds) *Organizational learning and Competitive Advantage*, London: Sage.

Garratt, R. (1987) *The Learning Organization*, London: Fontana.

—— (1990) *Creating a Learning Organization*, Cambridge: Director Books.

Hawkins, P. (1991) 'The spiritual dimension of the learning organization', *Management Education and Development*, vol. 22, no. 3, 166–81.

Hedberg, B. (1981) 'How organizations learn and unlearn', in P. Nystorom and W. Starbuck (eds) *Handbook of Organizational Design*, vol. 1.

Jones, A. M. and Hendry, C. (1994) 'The learning organization: Adult learning and organizational transformation', *British Journal of Management*, vol. 5, 153–62.

Katzenbach, J. and Smith, D. (1993) *The Wisdom of Teams*, Cambridge, MA: Harvard Business School Press.

Kerfoot, D. and Knights, D. (1994) 'Empowering the quality worker? The seduction and contradiction of the Total Quality phenomenon', in A. Wilkinson and H. Willmott (eds) *Quality and the Labour Process*, London: Routledge.
Levitt, B. and March, J. (1988) 'Organizational learning', *Annual Review of Sociology*, vol. 14, 319–40.
Lewin, K. (1951) *Field Theory in Social Science*, New York: Harper and Row.
Mabey, C. and Iles, P. A. (eds) (1994) *Managing Learning*, London: Routledge.
Marsick, V. J. (1994) 'Trends in managerial reinvention: Creating a learning map', *Managerial Learning*, vol. 25, no. 1, 11–34.
Mills, D. Q. and Friesen, B. (1992) 'The Learning Organization', *European Management Journal*, vol. 10, no. 2, 146–62.
Mintzberg, H. and Waters, A. (1985) 'Strategies deliberate and emergent,' *Strategic Management Journal*, vol. 6, 257–72.
Nonaka, I. and Takeuchi, H. (1995) *The Knowledge-Creating Company*, New York: Oxford University Press.
Pedler, M., Boydell, T., and Burgoyne, J. (1988) 'Learning company project: A report on work undertaken Oct 1987 to April 1988', The Training Agency, Sheffield.
——, Burgoyne, J., and Boydell, T. (1991) *The Learning Company*, London: McGraw-Hill.
Pettigrew, A. and Whipp, R. (1991) *Managing Change for Competitive Success*, Oxford: Blackwell.
Raper, P., Ashton, D., Felstead, A., and Storey, J. (1997) 'Toward a learning organization? Explaining current trends in training practice in the UK', *International Journal of Training and Development*, vol. 1, no. 1, 9–21.
Schein, E. (1985) *Organizational Culture and Leadership*, San Francisco, CA: Jossey-Bass.
Senge, P. (1990) *The Fifth Discipline: The art and practice of the learning organization*, London: Century Business/Doubleday.
Stata, R. (1989) 'Organizational learning – the key to management innovation', *Sloan Management Review*, Spring, 63–74.
Swieringa, G. and Wierdsma, A. (1992) *Becoming a Learning Organization*, Reading, MA: Addison-Wesley.
Torbet, W. R. (1994) 'Managerial learning, organizational learning: A potentially powerful redundancy', *Management Learning*, vol. 25, no. 1, 57–70.

chapter 11

# Promoting Learning in Organizations

CHAPTER OUTLINE

## Learning Objectives

- To understand the conditions most conducive to adult learning.
- To apply the principles of effective individual learning to the design of an organization's learning and development environment.
- To appreciate that different learning orientations are appropriate for different organizations, depending on their core business and prevailing environmental conditions.
- To identify the experiential hallmarks of a learning organization.
- To describe some of the structural and cultural initiatives that can help to facilitate a learning ethos in an organization.

# Introduction

Pettigrew and Whipp (1991), in a study of the ability of a number of British firms to 'manage' strategic change and to assess the outcome for competitive performance, conclude that a common pattern emerges from the ways the firms handled strategic and operational change, and that there was an observable difference between the ways higher performing firms manage change and their less successful counterparts. They identify five key variables: environmental assessment, leading change, linking strategic and operational change, seeing human resources as assets and liabilities, and achieving coherence. All of these are essentially processes and qualities by which organizations learn.

The ability of an organization to understand the environment, for example, is related to the capacity of members of the organization to gather and act on pertinent data:

> The starting point in the process of competition derives from the understanding a firm develops of its environment. In general terms the research shows that it is insufficient for companies to regard the creation of knowledge and judgements of their external competitive world as simply a technical exercise. Rather the need is for organizations to become open learning systems. In other words, the assessment of the competitive environment does not remain the preserve of a single function nor the sole responsibility of one senior manager. Nor does it occur via isolated acts. Instead strategy creation is seen as emerging from the way a company, at various levels, acquires, interprets and processes information about its environment. (Pettigrew and Whipp 1991: 135)

It could well be argued that the achievement of all five of Pettigrew and Whipp's conditions requires what we might call a problem-solving approach. They all require the generation of good quality data, good analysis, open discussion, and so on. Indeed, the authors argue precisely this point in their summary:

> The ability of a company to learn should be under regular scrutiny. In other words, the ability of the organization to reconstruct and adapt its knowledge base (made up of skills, structure and values) should be a key task for managers. They should also be able to apply the 'unlearning' test. In other words, is the organization capable of mounting the creative destruction necessary to breaking down outmoded attitudes and practices, while at the same time building up new, more appropriate competencies. If in the wake of globalization, marketing, financial and manufacturing techniques become ever more capable of imitation, then their competitive advantage is correspondingly diminished . . . in this sort of world the ability to learn faster than competitors may be the sustainable advantage. (1991: 135)

In this chapter we explore more fully what this knowledge base – consisting of skills, structures and values – might look like and how an organization might go about creating this key capability. We start with the individual, and the ingredients that produce effective learning for employees, whether formal training or more informal development opportunities. Understanding these ingredients helps appropriate design features and methods to be considered. However, no matter how well designed, individual learning has to be connected to the organizational routines and be embedded in the cultural context if the cumulative and collective benefits of learning are to be realized. The latter part of the chapter analyses what helps to create and what hinders these synergies.

## How do Individuals Learn in Organizations?

In chapter 5, 'Training and Development Strategies', we noted that the trigger for training activity was invariably some awareness of a skills performance gap, which was then addressed in a purposeful and developmental way by the organization. However, the assumption that training and development delivered is equivalent to personal and corporate learning gained is obviously misplaced. In this section we determine what conditions make for a successful learning event or experience. Successful for the individual in that they develop their competence in a given area, and successful for the organization in that this newly-won expertise is then effectively deployed to achieve business objectives.

### *The goals of learning*

Over the years many people have endeavoured to categorize learning into different levels in order better to understand the way people assimilate new information and ideas, and the connection between this and changed behaviour and attitudes (e.g. Bloom 1956; Bateson 1972). One method of categorization for managers, at least, that has obtained popular currency (Burgoyne and Stuart 1976) is to break down learning into three classes:

*Basic data and information* representing those facts which appertain to the specific work environment and relevant professional knowledge understanding. This would include training in such things as industrial legislation, production processes and sources of finance.

*Situation-specific skills and response tendencies*, as well as skills associated with sensitivity to events (perceptiveness, data-getting skills), include the following: analytical, problem-solving, decisions/judgement-making skills; social skills and abilities (leadership, influencing communicating, using and responding to leadership); emotional resilience and proactivity – the inclination to respond purposeful to events.

*Qualities for self-development* including creativity, mental agility, balanced learning habits and self knowledge.

Rather than seeing these skills and qualities as discrete areas of learning they can be depicted as three non-hierarchical circles, each of which intersects the other two at some point, indicating that overlap exists between all categories, as shown in figure 11.1. The degree of overlap depends on specific situations. For instance, a junior manager may be learning to use a new accounting software package for a particular data analysis job; the learning curve is steep in terms of assimilating the numerous computer instructions (circle 1) and his/her keyboard and data interpretation skills may also be quickly enhanced (circle 2). However, because time is short, interfacing the completed analysis with the corporate and external databases is left to an analyst, thus limiting the possibilities for self-development (circle 3). If the manager had been led a step further, learning how to access, interrogate and file data from the central network, this would have opened up an infinitely greater range of self-development opportunities for the future and the potential for creative learning would have been increased. Likewise, the model should be viewed as dynamic, with the qualities of circle 3, for example, being continually achieved in our daily lives and permeating the qualities of the other two circles. When designing learning and development activities it is essential to know which qualities – or mix of qualities – are being sought in order to choose the appropriate learning methods and approaches.

## The openness of learning

Alongside the goals of learning we also need to consider the degree of learner autonomy, a subject which has been a major area for researchers in individual learning (e.g. Simpson 1980; Schon 1983; Knowles 1984a, 1984b). The various philosophies of education, and learning might usefully be depicted along a continuum. At one extreme there is a body of knowledge to be taught: practice is deduced from theory and then applied with an emphasis on formal learning methods. In human resource development terms this would result in fairly *instrumental* learning processes; subject matter will be covered in a predetermined syllabus where duration of study and quantity of earnings are important outputs.

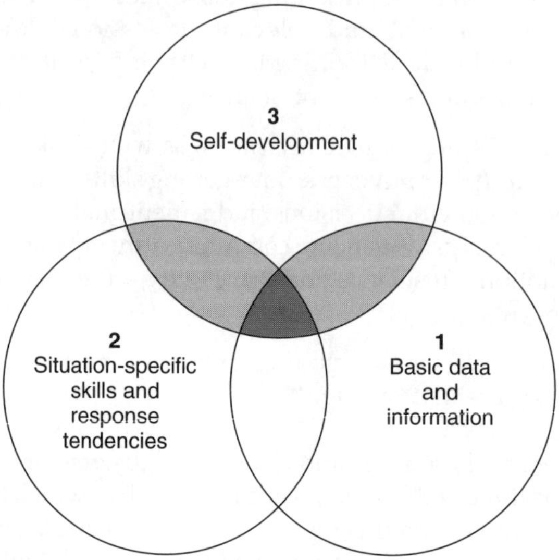


**Figure 11.1** The three-circle categorization of learning

Tutors are seen as teachers and experts, they will set and mark/give feedback on assignments and success/or completion of the training is often signified by formal qualifications or membership of an elite.

At the other extreme there are what might be called *experimental* learning contexts, which are based on the view that an individual's talent, ideas and views are to be drawn out, since knowledge evolves as we learn more about ourselves and the unbounded world we inhabit. This would lead an organization to arrange its training and development activities such that they are much more 'open-ended' and informal, with tutors acting as facilitators to help the learners discover their talents and realize their potential in order to achieve their own learning goals. This discussion about philosophy is an important one because from such presuppositions flow very different conceptions of how learning is deemed to occur, what learning system is appropriate to address given training objectives and in what role the trainer, tutor or mentor should be cast. The messages are pertinent to business schools and in-house training departments alike.

In the field of training and development, the notion of closed and open learning has been a particular focus, which can be likened to Handy's instrumental and experimental philosophies of education (Handy 1974). Thus closed and instrumental processes are likely to be concerned with the subjects covered in a predetermined syllabus where duration of study and amount of learning are seen as important and the tutor is seen as the teacher and expert. The open or experiential processes, on the other hand, are more likely to be concerned with the learner as an individual who is allowed to choose personal learning goals, with

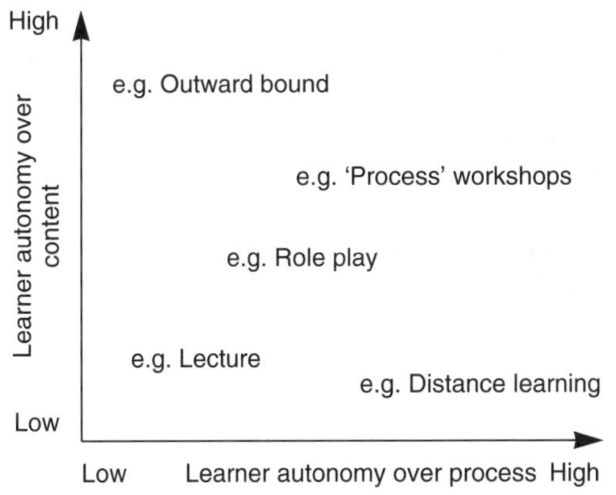


**Figure 11.2** Locating training methods against learner autonomy

the tutor acting as a facilitator to help the learner perfect his/her own skills and talents in order to achieve them.

So openness correlates with learner autonomy: that is the freedom of choice exercised by learners over the content of what they want to learn and the process by which they wish to learn it, within the process implemented by the tutor. The graph in figure 11.2 shows the amount of autonomy given to the learner for determining the process (the way the training activities are organized) on the vertical axis, and the amount of autonomy given to the learner for determining the content (the precepts, principles, skills covered) on the horizontal axis. Such a representation is useful when evaluating the most appropriate training methods for the trainees and the subject matter in question; for instance, this framework has been used to assess the most appropriate computer-based courseware for accounting and finance training (Mabey et al. 1998).

In the bottom-left corner we would place methods like lecture, and any kind of programmed learning case-studies which allow relatively little or no learner autonomy over either content or process. For example, the learner attends a lecture the content of which is transmitted in the way the lecturer chooses, following a curriculum with set readings, and so on. Even a case study, which may appear less constrained, usually conforms to a predetermined pattern of exploration, analysis and 'discovery'. One of the features of well-designed programmed learning techniques is the increased discretion they give to the learner. But there is a limited number of pathways through a given programme, so that while autonomy is greater than with a lecture, it can be still prescriptive.

Around the middle of the graph we would include such diverse activities as role play, management simulations and business games, projects and small-group work, which provide relatively more learner autonomy in terms of both content and process. For instance, during a role play learners have some choice in the way they portray the given role (content) but do so within a perspective normally set by the rules (process), and sometimes in behaviour modelled by the tutor or on a video. However, it is possible to use experiential behaviour modelling, thus allowing the learner some autonomy over the process as well as the content.

In the top-right corner appear such methods as encounter groups, counselling and unstructured process workshops which traditionally have the highest levels of learner autonomy both in terms of content and process. At this level it is usual for the learner(s) to identify the content they wish to work on themselves. The process is facilitated by a tutor although in such a way as to avoid constraining the learners; this encourages them to use and/or experiment with processes that feel right for them at that particular time. An example here might be an assertiveness training course where, following tuition and tutor controlled role play, learners are given the freedom and space to experiment with different behaviours without inhibition. Even here, of course, environmental parameters are still imposed by the 'staff' although the learner always has the ultimate recourse of exercising autonomy by leaving the learning event via the nearest door or window!

These three groups of methods align themselves with the three circles of learning discussed earlier and shown in figure 11.1: the first group with the circle associated with basic data and information, the second with situation-specific skills and response tendencies and the third with self-development. Less easy to categorize are such methods as outward bound and secondments. In cases where the nature of learning is relatively predictable but the way in which an individual goes about it may be idiosyncratic, these would be located at the top-left corner. As the content of learning becomes more open-ended, however, so these approaches would move towards the top-right.

## Designing Effective Learning

By way of summary we can now set out the different variables we have discussed, each of which has a significant bearing on the structuring of learning activities in organizations along a horizontal continuum (see figure 11.3). The left-hand pole represents the instrumental approach, which also corresponds with low learner autonomy over both content and process and a relatively closed strategy of training delivery. At the opposite extreme, which we term 'experiential', learning is open, with learners exercising free choice over the way they develop.

### *Learning methods*

We started with a consideration of the goals of *learning* and the qualities being sought in a given learner target group. Figure 11.3 rearranges the three intersecting circles along this bipolar continuum. It shows that when addressing basic

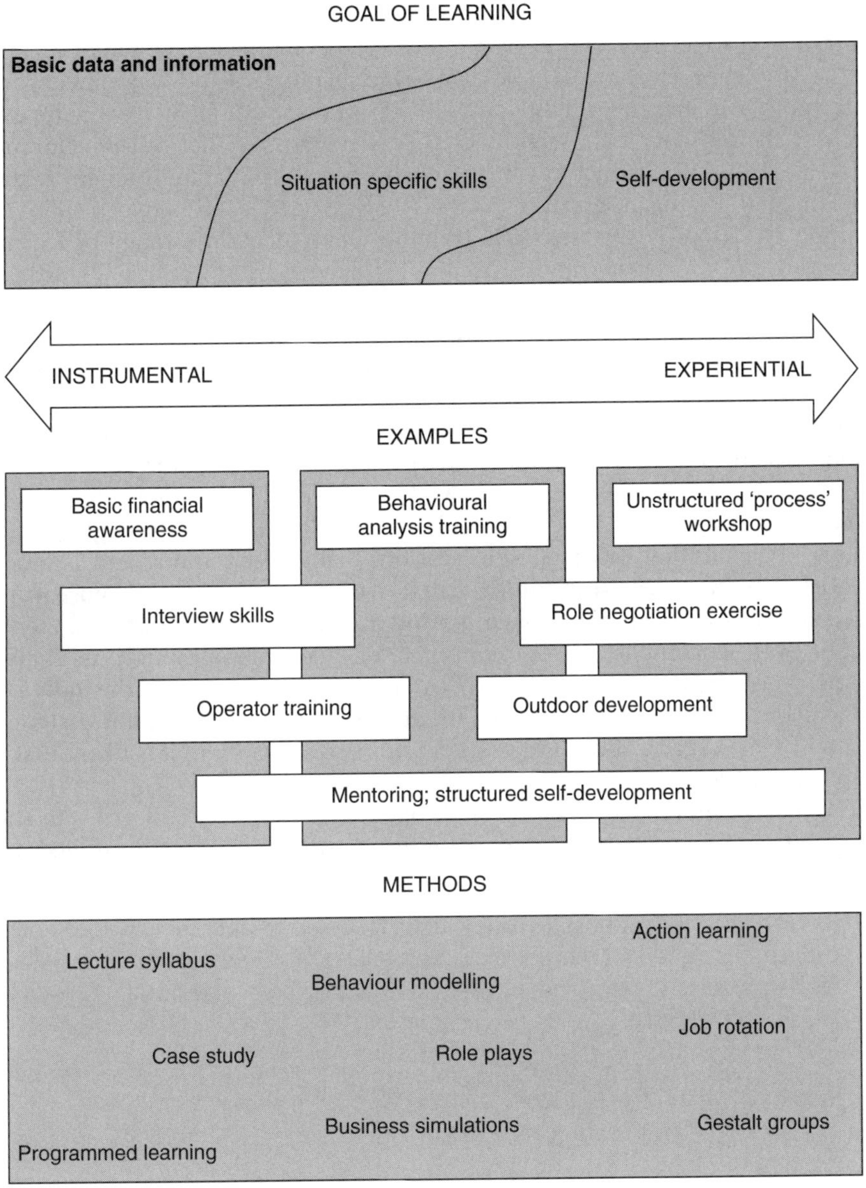


**Figure 11.3** Matching the processes of learning to the goals of learning

information and data-handling, the educational process is likely to be highly controlled with little learner flexibility, although it *is* possible to introduce greater discretion and openness of learning as with a self-paced instance teaching approach. Conversely, when attempting to facilitate self-development, the most congruent process would be one that allows a greater amount of learner autonomy in an open-learning environment. An example here would be a voluntary organization working in child care, which arranges self-development for its staff in order to empower them so that they, in turn, can facilitate the development of their clients – the children. This is not to say that self-development objectives could not be met in a more constrained learning environment with an instrumental approach, but it is far less likely. Sandwiched between these two training processes is specific skills training where a middle range of learning processes are appropriate, with decreasing trainer/tutor control towards the right-hand pole. Immediately beneath the three stages of learning contained in the box we have given some of training/learning activities *examples*. The third layer of the figure depicts a number of learning methods or *processes* ranging across the continuum.

In reality, most training activities combine two or more types of learning. Training staff in appraisal or interviewing skills will require tutor input on the organization's HRM procedures, as well as the legal and equal opportunities dimensions of the interview process; but it would be hard to imagine such a course not including practical skill sessions with observations and feedback. Hence this training would straddle the first two types in the box. Likewise, supervised self-development, perhaps under the watchful eye of an informal mentor, would well encompass all three types of learning, although its natural 'home' would be the 'high autonomy' end of the continuum since the individual is the primary driver of the process. Interestingly, if an individual is assigned a mentor by the organization (rather than finding his/her own) it is likely that the emphasis of learning activities will shift to the left.

The three layers have been depicted together in figure 11.3 in order to show how all training and development activities are based on certain implicit principles of learning (see Burgoyne 1977):

1 Lectures and syllabus-based programmes, including most case-study approaches, assume people learn by organizing, sequencing and relating new information to existing bodies of knowledge. They are appropriate methods for *information transfer* but little else.

2 Programmed learning, as employed by computer-based training, language laboratories and other rote-learning bases on the premise of *conditioning*: sufficient practice, feedback and reinforcement will change the habitual behaviour of learners.

3 Behaviour modelling and most role-play learning processes aim to provide trainees with certain predetermined learnable attributes. The learning premise here is one of *trait modification*.

4 Business simulations rely on learning via *trial, error and feedback*. The learners operate in a designed environment where they learn to cope with relationships which result from their own real interactions, rather than those built into the 'game' by the designer.

5 Action learning and out-door development programmes switch attention from the learners' behaviour to their *cognition map* of the world: the conscious or unconscious knowledge which steers their action. Through shared experience, reflection and insight are encouraged via heightened self-awareness and reinterpreting experiences in new ways.

6 Relatively unstructured activities like Gestalt groups are based on *experiential learning* theory, involving the total person (feelings, motives and emotions as well as cognition and behaviours): the principles of learning are autonomy and accommodation, and the removal of barriers to allow the natural growth process.

Understanding these derivations is important in matching the appropriate training/learning process to the learning goals being addressed. It is all too easy for a human resource specialist to pick a pre-packaged course on project management in the hope that it will help middle managers work more collaboratively on matrix-managed jobs. While the package may impart some excellent planning techniques and even give limited scope for learning and practising team leadership and problem-solving skills, the sponsor may be disappointed to find that, following the training, representatives of different departments still do not co-operate despite being on the same project teams. There may be many reasons for this: scarcity of resources, jealously guarded expertise, ignorance of each others' potential contribution, cultural stereotypes, and more. It is clear that even if these other organizational factors are supportive (and this is a big assumption!) real cross-functional collaboration will only come about when *attitudes* are changed. Methods rooted in behavioural approaches are not intended to – and are unlikely to – change people's predispositions towards others. It would take developmental activities involving sustained interaction with ample room for reflection, revision of perspectives and further experimentation derived from cognitive or experiential learning to shift attitudes in any significant manner; this could take a very long time.

Nevertheless, techniques which persistently encourage new ways of working in trainees may – through repetition and positive feedback – condition them to think differently also. In other words, repeated actions (particularly when public and freely chosen) may lead to attitude formation. This brings us back to a recurrent theme in this text as to whether staff adopt new attitudes genuinely or expediently as a result of structural, cultural – or in this case – training interventions (Ogbonna 1994; Mabey and Mallory 1995). It is not always easy to tell. The important point for training specialists and individuals developing themselves is that, having ascertained development needs, they then select learning activities and methods that are capable of delivering against the objectives chosen.

The discussion so far tends to take for granted that individual development needs can be – and typically are – addressed by the organization setting up some kind of training programme or learning activity for the individuals concerned. At one level this assumption is fine because although a great deal of on-the-job coaching and unstructured personal development does take place on a daily basis in all organizations, it is the case that these learning opportunities are rarely exploited to the full because they remain random, unreviewed and invariably dislocated from wider strategic HRM policies and plans (Mumford et al. 1987). It is also problematic at two other levels. First, because it assumes individual learning takes place to exclusively serve the current purposes of the organization, which by definition remains in control of the learning processes that have been 'constructed'. Secondly and related, it underestimates the amount of learning that results from situations which *lack* certainty, and controllability. Indeed, it is in this domain that truly innovative learning is likely to occur, as box 11.1 illustrates in relation to total quality management (TQM).

If learning, like management, is an active, purposive activity then it faces all the moral and ethical issues raised by the taking of responsibility for purposive action (Burgoyne 1994: 43). In other words, no matter how well matched the goals, methods and educational principles of a given training activity, unless the participant subscribes to its value, timing and personal pertinence, learning is unlikely to ensue. This leads us to consider learning and its outcomes from a less paternalistic view.

## Learning orientations

Drawing on the broad experience of adult education and training, Rogers (1986) suggests that, irrespective of wider questions and choices arising from different theories of learning, an awareness of the following general characteristics of adult learners can provide a well-grounded focus to the facilitation of learning in organizations:

*First*, to be effective, any programme of learning needs to coincide with the processes of maturation, self-fulfilment, perspective and self-determination of the individual learner. All those involved in the process of learning need to affirm that common adulthood in their relationships. Contrary to some assumptions, adults have not stopped growing and developing. The pace and direction of learning and change may vary from individual to individual, but all are actively engaged in a dynamic process of change. Effective learning needs to relate to that process.

*Second*, everyone brings a range of experience, knowledge and emotional investment to the learning they are embarking on. To be effective, learning has to relate to and build on what adults bring to their learning. Conversely and equally importantly, even when adults are engaged in learning wholly new abilities, devaluing or ignoring what they bring to their learning undermines and rejects their whole identity, not just particular experiences and values.

*Third*, learning is not simply the satisfaction of needs. It also involves an acknowledgement of the goals, intentions, motivations and aspirations – however diverse, contradictory or confused – that inform someone's decision to learn. The meaning and significance of their learning is shaped by those intentions.

*Fourth*, on basis of past experience, adults bring to their learning expectations about both the way in which learning occurs and their own capabilities to learn. Effective learning has to take account of people's initial expectations of the

## BOX 11.1 MANAGING THE PARADOX OF LEARNING AND CONTROL

'Our contention that TQM comprises two fundamentally different goals (control and learning) should not be taken to imply that organizations or their managers have the luxury of pursuing one or the other in blissful isolation. To the contrary, because organizational survival in today's highly competitive and rapidly changing world depends on both reliable performance and adaptability, organizational effectiveness hinges on the capacity to balance the conflicting goals of stability and reliability with those of exploration and innovation. Managers can gain competitive advantage from this apparent paradox if they are able to recognize that the everyday situations they confront almost inevitably involve both the exercise of control and the capacity to learn. [ . . . ] A second-order definition of learning in the TQM context would highlight increasing an organization's ability to explore the unknown and to identify and pursue novel solutions. For example, instead of maintaining a continued focus on enhanced reliability with current production, the strategic focus of a firm may swing toward discovering new product domains for which novelty rather than reliability is the key to competitiveness. Rather than relying on customers to articulate needs for products or services that they cannot yet imagine, a firm's strategy might emphasize improving the firm's ability to educate customers. To illustrate, in the computer industry, the product life cycle is so short that production techniques frequently become outmoded before they have had the chance to settle into a well-understood routine that would be amenable to the use of routine-oriented TQM practices. In settings in which the task is poorly understood, it may not only be impossible to specify appropriate measures, but it also may be impossible to conduct the necessary exploratory, high-risk work without making an irreducibly large number of errors [ . . . ]

In these *fundamentally* uncertain contexts, continuous improvement should focus on enhancing experimentation rather than on decreasing error rates. For example, pharmaceutical research on "new chemical entities" that are the basis for proprietary drug patents are unavoidably uncertain – and highly successful pharmaceutical firms like Merck, or Johnson & Johnson, have been described as places where "a mistake can be a badge of honor" (*Business Week*, 1998) to reflect that a focus on the elimination of errors is as essential in the *manufacturing* of drugs as it is a seductive delusion in the *development* of fundamentally new drugs.'

(from Sitkin et al. 1994: 540–5)

learning process and an individual's sense of the limits and possibilities of what they are capable of achieving.

*Fifth*, whatever the circumstances or occasion of learning, all adults come to their learning from a complete social environment. They bring to their learning demands and needs which arise from the full range of their relationships – parents, friends, neighbours and so forth, as well as working colleagues. Specific learning tasks and programmes are set against the demands and concerns of that wider background.

*Sixth*, all adults have already developed, implicitly if not consciously, their own particular ways of pursuing and coping with the demands of their learning and development. To be effective new learning needs to build on their preferred learning styles and patterns.

In the same way that individuals tend to have preferred learning styles (Kolb, 1984), it has been suggested that organizations have preferred learning orientations; these comprise the values and attitudes that determine where learning is likely to take place and the nature of what is learned (see table 11.1).

The authors of table 11.1 propose that understanding an organization's learning orientations provides a basic for designing change plans to increase learning capabilities. For instance, organizations may choose to change their orientation (and hence their culture); the example is given of organization learning at Direzione Technica in Fiat Auto (Dibella et al. 1996b), where efforts were made to change the paternalistic, religious and militaristic style of management to one which focused on flexibility, cooperation and integration. Alternatively, organizations may choose to enhance learning by improving what they already do well,

**Table 11.1** Organizational learning orientations

| | | |
|---|---|---|
| 1 | Knowledge source | Preference for developing knowledge internally versus seeking inspiration in ideas developed externally. |
| 2 | Product-process focus | Emphasize accumulation of product knowledge versus expanding competencies in basic processes. |
| 3 | Documentation mode | Knowledge seen in personal, tacit terms, as something possessed by individuals versus being seen as explicit statements of publicly available know-how. |
| 4 | Dissemination mode | Emphasize informal methods of sharing learning, such as role modelling and communities of practice, versus formal, prescribed organization-wide programs. |
| 5 | Learning focus | Emphasize incremental, single loop learning versus transformational, double loop learning. |
| 6 | Value-chain focus | Centre learning investments on 'design and make' side of the value chain versus the 'deliver' side. |
| 7 | Skill development | Stress development of individuals versus development of teams or groups. Emphasize indvidual skills versus skills in learning and working collectively. |

*Source:* Dibella et al. (1996a: 47).

as was appropriate for the safety conscious Electricite de France (EDF), the world's leading producer of electricity using nuclear fuel. EDF generates knowledge through the analysis of critical incidents, resulting in changes to fully publicized bureaucratic procedures. Understanding individual and corporate learning orientations helps those responsible for designing and supporting programmes, and processes of learning, in organizations. Such programmes and processes are more likely to be effective if they build on the routine ways in which individual adults learn, and the current learning capabilities of the organizations concerned.

## How can Learning Synergies be Created?

Our analysis of learning organizations so far has shown that pursuing the concept in terms of specific structures and cultures, normative models of good practice or grandiose schemes for sweeping change is probably less helpful than identifying the sorts of processes and values found in organizations that are adopting a learning-based approach to their management and development. This means focusing not on what learning organizations do, but on how they do it. It means considering what it is appropriate and feasible for an individual manager or team; recognizing what issues and choices are associated with effective and enduring learning in organizations.

### *The hallmarks of a learning organization*

There is no 'right model' of a learning organization. As we discovered in the previous chapter, developing a learning organization is not a matter of adopting policies and procedures used successfully elsewhere, because such 'copying' inevitably runs contrary to the spirit of path-breaking learning and change. For all its elusiveness, the learning organization is more than a metaphor or an ideal-type. But is it practically attainable? What can be said is that it has a recognizable and distinctive 'feel'. The experience of working in such an environment is well captured by Dale (1993). For her a learning organization:

- will work to create values, practices and procedures in which 'learning' and 'working' are synonymous throughout the organization.
- is inextricably bound up with organizational change and will seek to move beyond the learning associated with 'first-order change' (that is, learning to improve current performance and do the same things differently and more effectively) to the learning associated with 'second-order change' (learning how to learn and develop the capacity to continuously generate new ideas and insights in order to do different things).
- will involve the discomfort of living with the uncertainties and ambiguities associated with iterative processes of change. It also involves acknowledging the risk

associated with dynamic conservatism and consensus and working through – rather than just overcoming – the positive value of the conflicts arising from multiple agendas and diverging perceptions (see box 11.2).

- will require its managers to redefine their own roles and responsibilities. Rather than being essentially isolated individuals, they are members of a professional community of co-learners.
- will provide a safe environment for the risks and openness required for reflective practice in which questioning and self-doubt are as important as certainty and control.

Many of the issues and choices raised by the idea of the learning organization relate to broad questions of structure and culture. Individual managers can often feel relatively powerless to do anything about such aspects of their organization. The sorts of changes required to support learning throughout an organization appear to lie beyond the scope and influence of any individual. If real progress is to be made in the area of learning, therefore, it is important to identify the enabling structures, cultures and systems which are needed at organizational and individual levels.

With this goal in mind, Jones and Hendry (1992) have developed a five-phase model of learning in organizations (see figure 11.4). The lower three circles in this figure represent initial phases of individual/organizational learning – not necessarily in sequence, though it is likely that there is a progression from left to right, with the possibility of getting stuck at an early stage. The Foundation phase concerns basic skills development and equipping learners with the habits and enthusiasm to learn more. An organization, in one way or another, must take responsibility for ensuring that these basic 'social survival skills' are acquired, as well as developing HRD strategies to motivate and build confidence for further learning. Jones and Hendry refer to this as a learning organization in embryonic state. The Formation phase encourages and develops skills for self-learning and self-development: here the individual learner begins to learn about the organization as a whole, its meaning and purpose and their own place within it. The

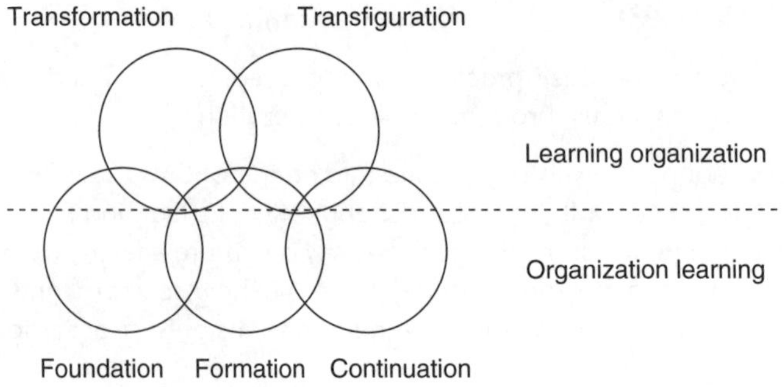


**Figure 11.4** Five development phases of the learning organization
*Source:* Adapted from Jones and Hendry (1992: 32)

### BOX 11.2 TOP TEAMS: A EUROPEAN STUDY

'A survey of several thousand top executives in seven European countries (Ireland, Spain, France, Germany, Austria, UK and Sweden) sought to establish which competencies – if any – among "top management teams" influenced organizational performance. They measured this by asking senior managers to rate such things as satisfaction, stress, confidence, ability to meet challenges and structural issues, and ease of managing long-term issues. Six competence areas were found to have a significantly positive bearing on these indices. If the top team

- had good interpersonal relationships with understanding of each other's values and management style;
- were able to discuss issues openly without arousing undue sensitivity or tension;
- had a high level of trust in each other;
- were approachable, and willing to receive feedback and criticism, implying the ability to give and receive feedback in an impersonal and objective manner;
- had sufficient discipline and cohesion to implement decisions upon which they agreed, without the need to follow-up decisions very closely;
- had the capacity to discuss and understand both long- and short-term issues.

The researchers conclude that "there is concrete evidence that the quality of interaction within the top management team can either enhance or damage business", and they add that management development should put emphasis on "examining interpersonal relationships, management styles, attitudes and values, openness, trust and communication within the team".'
(Alderson 1993)

challenge here is for the organization to make available opportunities and resources for training and development as the learner makes demands for new learning.

In the Continuation phase the learner and the organization are becoming more independent, innovatory, self-motivated and confident. HRD systems need to be sensitive to the differential pace of learning both on and off the job, and include counselling in skill development and a range of support measures for stressed, turned-off and plateaud individuals.

The two upper phases are evidence of a transition from organizational learning to the learning organization. Transformation is concerned with making a complete change in the form, appearance and character of the organization. This will involve change in structures and systems through the influence of technology, social change, and global factors; experimentation with alternative and more flexible work practices; and adapting to newly emerging social and human values, by actively implementing HRM policies and strategies which are not discriminatory in terms of race, sex, religion or disability. Attention is paid to how business is acquired and how its assets are managed, so that corruption does not occur. It develops strategies which actively support community initiatives for the enhancement of people at large. The social and ethical dimension underpins all organizational activity, with an emphasis on corporate responsibility; and learning focuses on managing personal change and self-assessment.

Finally comes the Transfiguration phase of the learning organization where the language description becomes noticeably less concrete and more idealistic. For example, such an organization will be concerned with transformation plus elevation leading to idealization; people coming first and a concern for society's general welfare and betterment; asking crucial questions about why the organization exists in the forms that it does, representing a way of life to be cherished because of its values; and developing to accommodate and understand global cultures, tolerance, integration and co-operation.

This five-phase depiction of individual/organizational learning – and the authors are careful to point out the dangers of deterministic modelling – highlights a number of issues. First, it suggests (but no more than this) that organizations can develop in a progressive manner towards becoming learning organizations. Secondly, it poses the possibility that 'an organization, which establishes itself as a learning organization from the very beginning, can transform and transfigure itself without all the trappings of traditional structures and systems' (Jones and Hendry 1992: 33). It also allows for discrete parts of an organization to develop and change at different rates and times. Thirdly, a fairly detailed picture of the practical implications of each of the first three phases can be discerned; for instance, the activities described can readily be subdivided into those which are structural, cultural and HRD issues, each with their own set of implied HR policy initiatives to be hammered out idiosyncratically by a given organization. However, this is less true of the transformation and transfiguration phases, which are necessarily less determinate and less tangible, while still giving an experiential flavour of what it might be like to work in such an organization. Jones and Hendry (1992) quote Illich in this regard:

> Learning is the human activity which least needs manipulating by others. Most learning is not the result of instruction. It is rather the result of unhampered participation in a meaningful setting. (Illich 1971: 399)

We now explore how such 'meaningful settings' might be constructed, looking first at organizational structure, and then at culture.

## Restructuring to promote learning

The learning organization refers not just to desired actions but also to ways of designing organizations in order to produce these actions. So working towards the learning organization necessitates structural and cultural change – often radical, uncomfortable change.

### Rewards, roles and responsibilities

People will be recognized and rewarded not just for achieving the obvious measures of performance (as was discussed in detail in chapter 4: Performance Management Strategies), but also for their ability to help others. The practices and values which are necessary for learning will be encouraged – for example openness, questioning, confrontation. Too often, organization structures inhibit learning rather than facilitating it, for example by denial, deference and defensiveness which stifles debate and self-questioning (Argyris 1987). An example of how hierarchical structures can obstruct learning is given by Roberts (1992):

> Potential problems of learning are often . . . compounded by the routine processes of operational control. Hierarchies typically reinforce the values of conformity; to contradict a superior can be seen as a challenge to their authority, and it can seem wiser and safer to discount one's own experience and defer. This is just one of the ways in which vital knowledge is censored out of the organization. In times of rapid change these processes are often intensified, with insecurity serving to heighten individual and group defensiveness, thereby further restricting the flow of information within the company. If at this stage the hierarchy is used to impose an ill-informed strategic change, then one has created a recipe for disaster. (Roberts 1992: 19)

Achieving a learning organization requires activity on a wide range of fronts. It demands serious, far-reaching and probably uncomfortable commitments and changes from senior managers, penetrating to the very basis of the organization (for example the way the Board define their role, and their relationship with the rest of the organization). The necessary structural changes require new work arrangements, a thorough break with traditional managerial elitism, sincere efforts to attract the commitment of the workforce, genuine reliance on worker initiative and creativity, and consequent reduction in managers' traditional conception of their 'right to manage' (which often means the right to make decisions in ways which are unaccountable and undiscussable). As long as the desire to become a learning organization remains at the level of exhortation via team briefings and quality circles (useful as these may be) and as long as residual patterns and structures of power, privilege and secrecy persist, which reflect differences of interest and commitment between senior management and the rest of the organization, the learning organization will not develop. This is well illustrated in box 11.3, which summarizes some of the key findings of research conducted into the health of quality circles in the UK.

## Teams and teamworking

A related approach to achieving synergistic learning in organizations is to extend autonomy through team working and to devolve decision making to non-hierarchical work groups. In general terms, what characterizes this approach is the fact that the wider employing organization specifies the required outcomes from different teams and the resources at their disposal; within that framework, teams have varying degrees of freedom to determine for themselves how to allocate tasks and responsibilities. In some ways, a production environment lends itself readily to push an approach to teamworking, but the practice is being explored across all industries and sectors at the present time. The process of decentralization within many departments of both central and local government, and the creation of 'internal markets' and systems of contracting within former state bureaucracies, are all rooted in such an approach to team learning and individual 'empowerment'.

'Releasing' leadership and learning in this way clearly opens up quite radically new ways of learning and working for all staff – and significantly reshapes the role of managers. Notwithstanding the rhetoric of what is potentially achievable

### BOX 11.3 WHY QUALITY CIRCLES FAILED BUT TQM MIGHT SUCCEED

'The dominant impression, conveyed by companies with and without circles alike, was of fragility. Every programme needed constant stimulus to keep it alive [ . . . ] all the evidence points to the widespread failure of circles to become institutionalized. The rhetoric of the early days of the boom, that circles would become a normal way of doing business was hollow. Circles never really took hold in the great majority of these firms, remaining both experimental and marginal throughout their lives [ . . . ].

The evidence [ . . . ] shows that top management did not take an active role in improvement, that responsibility for quality was not joined with the requisite authority, that middle managers were excluded by the dual structure, and that the issue of cultural change was only partly addressed. The ultimate absurdity was to train rank-and-file employees to use modern techniques of quality management while their managers remained largely in ignorance of these. Quality circles were in any case not, on their own, the appropriate vehicles to realize the objectives that senior management had for them. The bulk of quality improvement issues and all the really important ones are beyond the competence of circles, because they transcend the workplace or exceed the authority of workers and foremen. And poor management is the prime cause of lack of competitiveness. Outside the framework of TQM, circles continually run up against the problem that organizations are not structured to respond to bottom-up initiatives and that all levels of management fail to understand the nature of the improvement process, with the result that, even in the limited area where circles have competence, managers may obstruct improvement.

Under TQM, middle managers in each company reported that they had become more involved in quality management than before. The integration of the improvement process into the existing organization and as part of normal working practices meant that managers could now direct their subordinates to work on specific issues and approve initiatives from below. In every case, improvement activity was seen as more focused, coherent and relevant, less-time consuming, and delivering quicker and more substantial benefits, in comparison with circles and other schemes. In the British office automation company where TQM was introduced alongside circles, these continued to operate as before but managers could now assign all employees including circle members to quality improvement groups and corrective action teams. Indeed, quality circles achieved a new lease of life, and, far from withering away as they were doing prior to TQM, new circles were formed and their numbers grew, although they were few in number in comparison with the other group activities. Managers found circles easier to live with under TQM and dualism was less of an issue. The addition of managerially directed groups allowed them to meet their own immediate improvement objectives; the broader understanding they now had of quality improvement made them more appreciative of the value of voluntary commitment to quality; and they suggested that circle activities themselves were now more tightly focused on issues relevant to the quality of objectives of the company.'

(Hill 1991: 551, 6, 9)

in these ways, greater team autonomy and self-direction also have drawbacks.

For instance, in his assessment of 'teamworking' in the context of job design Marchington (1992) notes that it can lead to a more stressful factory environment when adopted as a managerial technique to intensify the work process and stretch the production system as far as it will go. It can also lead to a reduction in the number of management levels, with supervisory jobs being particularly at risk, thus undermining workplace union solidarity. Naturally, such patent disparities in rewards and security perceived or real, will militate against learning for many in the workplace. Salaman (1996) notes that attempts to introduce teamworking in two factories based in the Indian sub-continent were largely thwarted by deep-seated attitudes and practices that were incompatible with the proposed change. This emphasized the need for the local context to be supportive of teamworking for its potential benefits to be realized. Even *within* a team, despite an appearance of equality, team members can be frustrated by others who use their seniority to dominate others by lack of access to information or resources, and by group dynamics or covert political conflicts which inhibit contribution (Kanter 1994).

## Cultivating a learning culture

A learning culture is easier to experience than to describe. Cultures are significant because they define and encourage established skills, habits, taken-for-granted ways of thinking and behaving. A way of considering the cultural factors which impinge upon the development of learning in a particular work setting is to ask: What kinds of factors are operating which militate against change? What beliefs, habits, actions are perceived as good and what are seen as unacceptable? How is learning achieved, problems solved and performance analysed, reviewed and reported? Resistance to learning is often encountered from those who may have most to lose from, or feel most threatened by, intended changes – namely, senior management. Paul Bate, in his analysis of what impeded and finally foiled British Rail's (BR) attempt to introduce the Advanced Passenger Train (APT), suggests the reasons were not only technological, but also related to inappropriate and inflexible human resource strategies – with senior managers being among the most obstructive by imposing limits on innovation:

> the more radical change endeavours, like the APT, were 'paralyzed' by BR's organization culture – to be more specific, by its senior management culture. Structural and attitudinal problems were certainly encountered during the study, but many of these were found to be symptoms of the cultural problems affecting the senior management process at the time. The management culture was putting a straitjacket on innovation, restricting its growth and development. In Kanter's terms it was offering an extremely thin topsoil for the nourishment and growth of the APT project, laying down a whole set of inflexible norms governing what was acceptable and unacceptable, thinkable and unthinkable, possible and impossible in the organization situation. (Bate 1990: 7)

This is an example of how organizational defence routines are both anti-learning and overprotective (Argyris 1987). Such patterns of behaviour become so embedded in the culture that they are rarely questioned, and are so entwined in the unequal distribution of power that they are rarely challenged. The resultant unproductive cycle *can* be broken as follows: senior managers can be fed with information that they need, rather than what they want to hear. This is initially risk and countercultural but may help to challenge any entrenched ideas they might hold; it promotes open testing of ideas and hence people become less cynical and defensive, and more willing to provide accurate information. In turn, the senior managers become less anxious about being out of touch and respond by granting even more discretion to their subordinates and the production of information.

## Conclusions and Summary

For all the undeniable virtue (and competitive value) of being a learning organization, why is it that so few organizations achieve this kind of learning ethos? This chapter has revealed a number of obstacles that impede good intent. At an individual level we have seen that even where careful consideration has been given to the construction of learning activities the performance outcomes are not always as predicted or promised. Even where personal learning is achieved there are many reasons why the wider workplace may not benefit, or indeed want to benefit. Where there are huge disparities in rewards and security, conditional access to positions of power, structural inequalities in the development of careers and inherently different perceptions of organizational goals and priorities, learning is bound to be hampered by careerism, anxiety, stress, deference and unresolved conflict. Even where such 'interference' to learning is minimal, mechanisms needs to be in place which link individual to collective learning.

Problems here include reluctance to pass on countercultural messages, failure to capture and learn from the lessons of past experience, defensiveness of decision-makers to 'fresh' information and ideas or – conversely – the exploitation of such for partisan ends.

Clearly the process of organizational learning calls for extensive changes in structure, mindset and outlook at all levels. Moving in the sorts of directions outlined above and overcoming the considerable attitudinal and historical barriers to learning discussed earlier cannot be seen as a one-off project. Furthermore to move from being an organization that learns to a 'learning organization' refers not just to desired actions, but also to ways of designing or changing organizations in order to produce these actions allowing for the multiple, and often conflicting, learning agendas of those within the organization.

If a 'learning organization' is one which successfully facilitates the learning of all its members and continuously transforms itself, then human resource development strategy becomes central to business policy and to the development of structures and cultures which encourage learning throughout the organization. Learning becomes a core part of all operations rather than a peripheral and intermittent activity under the custodianship of the training department or HR unit.

We have seen that there is no single model of a learning organization. Organizations which are moving from first-order change/learning to second-order change/learning are characterized more by *how* they do things, than *what* they do. Managing within a learning organization is not easy or comfortable. It entails living with change as a constant; being prepared to question; and acknowledging the value of positive conflict and diversity. Individual managers within an organization can work most effectively if they adopt the 'learning company philosophy' in which they approach their work and staff development responsibilities as a community of professionals with a common purpose, rather than as isolated careerist individuals. However, alongside such common purposes, especially if they constitute organizationally inspired 'programmes' designed to empower and increase autonomy, is the ever present danger that existing patterns of labour fragmentation and control can actually be intensified rather than relaxed. The result may be learning, but highly circumscribed learning.

The prevailing culture and its receptivity to learning is perhaps the most critical factor of all. Theories of organizational change argue that change occurs when certain preconditions are in place. These are: a recognized problem; a shared diagnosis of the issues involved; a determination to face and resolve them; and an understanding of various courses of action and their implications.

Bate notes that, even when these conditions are in place, change still does not always occur. So why are situations allowed to persist when they are accepted by the parties themselves as problematic and undesirable? Bate suggest that:

> The culture, once established, prescribes for its creators and inheritors certain ways of believing, thinking and acting which in some circumstances can prevent meaningful interaction and induce a situation of 'learned helplessness' – that is a psychological state in which people are unable to conceptualise their problems in such a way as to be able to resolve them. In short, attempts at problem-solving may become culture-bound. (Bates 1992: 214)

It falls to each organization to determine the best pathways in overcoming dysfunctional, uncreative ways of working and to find the necessary mechanisms by which individual learning can be synergized collectively and channelled for the benefit of all staff in the organization.

## Key Points

- All individuals in organizations are learning constantly. Designing effective learning and development activities and opportunities requires an understanding of the goals and openness of the learning in question.
- Particularly important is matching the learning processes and methods to the type of learning that is required.
- Learning in organizations can be more effective if account is taken of individual learning styles and organizational learning orientations.
- While actual examples remain elusive, helpful attempts have been made to identify the distinctive experiential hallmarks of learning organizations.
- There are approaches that will facilitate a more productive learning ethos in a given company. These concern the way individual learning can be connected to organizational learning; the way defensive routines can be challenged and unlearning can be achieved; the way training and development activities are designed; and the way learning can be cultivated through revised cultural norms and structural reconfiguration of the organization.

## Discussion Questions

1 How might the purposes and the processes of training/learning activities be matched?
2 Why does effective learning at an individual level often fail to translate into effective learning for the organization?
3 How can an ethos of learning be established in an organization?
4 What are some of the difficulties associated with 'creating' a learning organization?

## References

Alderson, S. (1993) 'Reframing management competence: Focusing on the top management team', *Personnel Review*, vol. 22, no. 6, 53–62.

Argyris, C. (1987) 'The leadership dilemma: Skilled incompetence', *Business and Economic Review*, vol. 1, 4–11.

Bate, P. (1990) 'The cultural paralysis of innovation', Paper presented to the 7th International Conference on Organization, Symbolism and Corporate Culture, June, Saarbrucken.

—— (1992) 'The impact of organizational culture on approaches to problem-solving', in G. Salaman, et al. (eds) *Human Resource Strategies*, London: Sage.

Bateson, G. (1972) *Steps Towards an Ecology of Mind*, New York: Ballantyne.

Bloom, B. S. (1956) *Taxonomy of Educational Objectives*, vol. 1, New York: McKaye.

Burgoyne, J. and Stuart, R. (1976) 'The nature, use and acquisition of managerial skills and other attributes', *Personnel Review*, vol. 15, no. 4.

—— (1977) 'Management learning developments', *BACIE Journal*, vol. 31, no. 9, 158–60.

—— (1994) 'Managing by learning', *Management Learning*, vol. 25, no. 1, 35–56.

Dale, M. (1993) *Developing Management Skills*, London: Kogan Page.

Dibella, A., Nevis, E., Gould, J., and Moingeon, B. (1996a) 'Organizational Learning as a care capability', in A. Edmonson (ed.) *Organisational Learning and Competitive Advantages*, London: Sage.

——, Nevis, E. and Gould, J. (1996b) 'Understanding organizational learning capabilities', *Journal of Management Studies*, vol. 33, no. 3, 361–79.

Handy, C. (1974) 'The contrasting philosophies of management education', Paper presented at the Annual Conference of the European Foundation for Management Development, May, Turin.

Hill, S. (1991) 'Why quality circles failed but total quality management might succeed', *British Journal of Industrial Relations*, vol. 29, no. 4, 541–68.

Illich, I. D. (1971) *Deschooling Society*, London: Calder and Boyars.

Jones, A. M. and Hendry, C. (1992) *The Learning Organization: A review of literature and practice*, London: HRD Partnership.

Kanter, R. M. (1994) 'Dilemmas of teamwork', in C. Mabey and P.A. Iles, (eds) *Managing Learning*, London: Routledge.

Knowles, M. S. (1984a) *The Adult Learner: A neglected species* (3rd edn), Houston: Gulf.

—— (1984b) *Andragogy in Action*, San Francisco, CA: Jossey-Bass.

Kolb, D. (1984) *Experimental Learning*, Englewood Cliffs, NJ: Prentice-Hall.

Mabey, C. and Mallory, G. (1995) 'Structure and culture change in two UK organizations:

A comparison of assumptions, approaches and outcomes', *Human Resource Management Journal*, vol. 5, no. 2, 28–45.

——, Topham, P. and Kaye, R. (1998) 'Computer-based courseware: A comparative review of the Learner's experience', *Accounting Education*, vol. 7, no. 1, 51–64.

Marchington, M. (1992) *Managing the Team*, Oxford: Blackwell.

Mumford, A., Robinson, G., and Stradling, D. (1987) *Developing Directors: The learning processes*, London: Manpower Service Commission.

Ogbonna, E. (1995) 'Integrating strategy, culture and human resource management: dilemmas and contradictions', in P. Blyton and P. Turnbull (eds) *Reassessing Human Resource Management*, London: Sage.

Pettigrew, A. and Whipp, R. (1991) *Managing Change for Competitive Success*, Oxford: Blackwell.

Roberts, J. (1992) 'Human resource strategies and the management of change', *B884 Human Resource Strategies, Supplementary Readings 1*, Open University, 18–38.

Rogers, A. (1986) *Teaching Adults*, Milton Keynes: Open University Press.

Salaman, G. (1996) 'Indian snacks: changing and continuity', in J. Storey (ed.) *Blackwell Cases in Human Resource and Change Management*, Oxford: Blackwell.

Schon, D. A. (1983) *The Reflective Practitioner: How professionals think in action*, London: Maurice Temple Smith.

Simpson, E. L. (1980) 'Adult learning theory: A state of the art', in H. Lasker, J. Moore and E. L. Simpson (eds) *Adult Development and Approaches to Learning*, Washington, D. C.: National Institute of Education.

Sitkin, S., Sutcliffe, K., and Schroeder, R. (1994) 'Distinguishing control from learning in total quality management: A contingency perspective', *Academy of Management Review*, vol. 19, no. 3, 537–64.

chapter

# 12

# Managing the Process of Training and Development

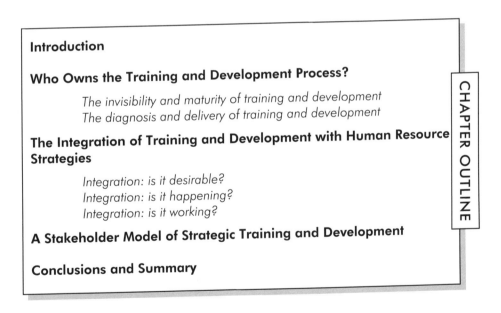

CHAPTER OUTLINE

## Learning Objectives

- To identify the factors that lead to training and development making a strategic impact.
- To explain some of the key decisions and choices influencing an organization's investment in training and development activities.
- To uncover some of the cultural inhibitors to training and the processes by which organizations get training and development 'into their bloodstream'.
- To explore whether training and development initiatives can be set up so that they are consistent with, and mutually supported by, other HR policies and processes.
- To describe a strategic approach to training and development which takes account of the political and sectional realities of organizational decision-making.

## Introduction

Training and development is the one dimension of SHRM that most people in organizations feel they have at least some expert knowledge. Few employees have not benefitted from training, secondments, mentoring, stretching experiences, learning from mistakes and watching role models. Many will have initiated training and development opportunities for others, been called upon to contribute to training events, and some even run training workshops or coached colleagues. Yet, for all the collective experience and tactical understanding of how we best learn, as individuals, teams and organizations, training and development strategies still have an immense capacity to disappoint. The two previous chapters in this book dealt with the issue of learning, and chapter 5 covered some of the more macro aspects of devising training and development strategies. Here, we are concerned with the internal decision-making in organizations that governs the effectiveness of training activities: how do training needs become apparent; what options present themselves for dealing with these needs; how do the chosen strategies dovetail with other dimensions of an organization's HR strategy and What are the factors which hinder and facilitate investment in training and development, such that it meets the desired objectives and contributes to the long-term sustainability of the enterprise? We conclude with a model of strategic training and development which begins to provide some answers to these questions.

## Who Owns the Training and Development Process?

In this section we address the question of who is responsible for the process of training and development and its outcomes? This takes us to the core issue of whether training is strategic and if it is, whose strategic purpose is actually being served? Is it the business planners, those who have recognized some kind of knowledge or skills gap that is jeopardizing organizational performance? Is it the sponsors of training, those who have commissioned and probably underwritten the training activity? Is it line management, who perhaps are the most immediately involved in the success or otherwise of training outcomes? A case could be made for each of these interest groups, and others, 'owning' training and development. Here we focus on line managers, trainees and developers themselves and – more briefly – those contracted to design and deliver the training events and learning activities. The individual is well placed to recognize his or her own strengths, weaknesses and development needs in relation to the realities and demands of the job, and given certain circumstances (timeliness, perceived relevance, infrastructural support and reinforcement) is likely to invest a great deal in the training process.

Unfortunately, such circumstances cannot be taken as given. In the case of off-the-job and external training much depends on the quality of the learning activity or training programme which will, in turn, be a function of the expertise of the designers, tutors and their support staff. Their motivation is slightly different, however; they will be concerned to construct an effective learning event or set of modules – but from a more detached perspective and with probably less credibility and power to influence outcomes. The respective benefits and drawbacks of relying on specialists, whether internal human resource advisers or external consultants, is summarized elsewhere (see chapter 14). Finally, much also depends on the line manager, project manager or supervisor of the individual trainee since it is they who are uniquely placed to assess both current *and future* skill requirements of the job, and they who can directly facilitate the development of the staff they manage. The linking of training and development to the required performance of the business unit or project for which they are responsible is the obvious advantage here.

Much play has been made in recent years of the difference between the normative models of HRM and personnel management. One purported distinction concerns the role of line managers:

> While both personnel management and HRM highlight the role of line management, the focus is different. In the personnel management models, line's role is very much an expression of the view that all managers manage people, so all managers in a sense carry out 'personnel management'. It also carried the recognition that most specialist personnel work still has to be implemented within line management's departments where the workforce is physically located. In the HRM models, HRM is vested in line management as business managers responsible for co-ordinating and directing *all* resources in the business unit in pursuit of bottom line results. Not only does the bottom line appear to be specified more precisely than in the personnel-management models, with much emphasis on quality of product or service, but a clear relationship is drawn between the achievement of these results and the line's appropriate and proactive use of the human resources in the business unit. Personnel policies are not passively integrated with business strategy, in the

> sense of flowing from it, but are an integral part of strategy in the sense that they underlie and facilitate the pursuit of a desired strategy. (Legge 1989: 27, 28)

In order to analyse the respective roles of line manager, trainee and trainer, we now look at training and development activity from two perspectives: the degree to which it is in the 'bloodstream' of an organization and how well it is diagnosed and delivered.

## The invisibility and maturity of training and development

The first thing to note is that appearances can be deceptive. A superficial observation of what development activities are taking place in an organization could be very misleading. Take a look at figure 12.1, which is based on an analysis of human resource development in diverse organizations. The first *intermittent* pattern represents a situation where there is little or no genuine commitment to HRD by most line managers. The second pattern could be called *institutionalized*: this is where activity and apparent commitment peak, perhaps because there has been a push from above to record training activity, or there is a need to use up development budgets, or the company compensation plan rewards active involvement by line managers. This may be true of an organization with its own HRD function offering well-established, off-the-job programmes to the rest of the business on a menu basis.

Whereas the activity level in pattern three appears to revert towards that of the first level, it actually depicts the more mature situation where training and development has become a natural and ongoing part of normal work relations: well *internalized* but less visible to the casual observer. This might represent a company where line managers are highly skilled in coaching and developing their staff, able to 'construct' everyday occurrences as learning opportunities for themselves and their staff, and where the prevailing ethos of people development militates against departmental talent-hoarding. In their report on how well 144 directors from 41 UK organizations were equipped for their responsibilities, Mumford et al. (1987) conclude that 'most directors have learned through a mixture of relatively accidental and unstructured experiences. Systems of management development have not been widely influential'. From this analysis Mumford puts forward three types of management development (1993: 35). The 'informal managerial type' comprises reactive training initiatives which are not only unstrategic but also likely to have minimal learning impact. The 'formal management development' type is equivalent to the institutionalized pattern, where training opportunities are more purposeful but learning is often limited because it is uncoupled from the trainees normal activities. The 'integrated managerial' type, as with the internalized pattern in figure 12.1, improves the individual and organizational relevance of the training and builds development opportunities around a more self-conscious use of everyday work experience,

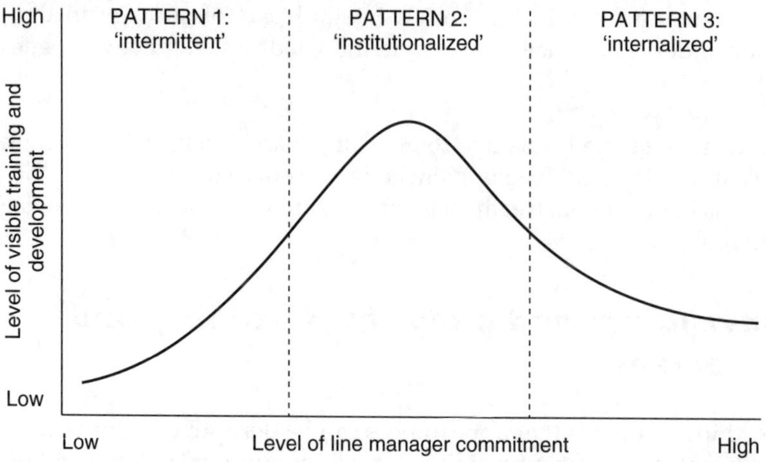


**Figure 12.1** Patterns of human resource development
*Source:* Adapted from Ashton et al. (1975: 6)

thus combining the virtues and eliminating the deficiencies of the other two approaches. In proposing a resource-based view of SHRM, Kamoche (1996) also notes the value of skill formation arising from tacit knowledge, action-centred learning, learning from mistakes, learning-by-doing and as a by-product of other activities. It is the very embeddedness of these activities into daily work routines (as compared with isolated, formalized training programmes) which makes them 'resource mobility barriers' because competitors will find them difficult to imitate:

> HR policies such as employee training and management development are unlikely to be the basis of the creation of SAs [strategic assets], unless they tie into subsequent or contemporaneous skill formation activities, including ongoing operational routines. Ongoing skill formation activities result in a 'reservoir' of skills, a certain part of which will not explicitly be recognised as such by management, i.e. in a 'hidden reservoir'. However, HRM policies can play a role as part of a process aimed at preventing obsolescence of skills by re-activating (part of) the reservoir. (Mueller 1996: 773)

Line managers also play a pivotal role in integrating the overarching strategic ojectives of their organization with its people development policies and practices. An index of this might be the extent to which all levels of staff are involved in knowledge, skills and self-enhancement in a way that mutually serves organizational purposes and their own growth as individuals. Based on research over many years at the Centre for the Study of Management Learning at Lancaster University, a six-step model describing organizations in ascending degrees of 'maturity' on these dimensions has been devised (Burgoyne 1988). From this analysis, the author draws three conclusions about strategic mature development activity. First, it has to be conscious and reflective. While a great deal of natural development takes place through the unplanned interpersonal and functional experiences encountered each day and careers frequently unfold in an uncontrived manner, these cannot be classed as *strategic* processes until they are explicitly linked to the implementation of corporate policy. This, of course, assumes that the corporate strategy is the one that matters! Secondly, the model infers incremental levels of maturity, such that an organization's approach to HRD is likely to grow in sophistication rather than suddenly become Level 5 or 6. It is not inconceivable that different aspects of the training strategy can vary in their connectedness to corporate policy within the same enterprise, and that training and development generally could slip downwards in maturity over time. The third, and perhaps most important, point from Burgoyne's analysis is the linking of training and development with what he calls the 'hard systems' of HRM on the one hand (which we take up in more detail later in the chapter) and collaborative career-planning on the other.

## *The diagnosis and delivery of training and development*

### Organizational strategies

From an organizational perspective a training needs analysis (TNA) is basically a process of collecting data which allows an organization to identify and compare its actual level with its desired level of performance. Performance here could be interpreted as meaning the competencies and attitudes necessary for staff to do the job effectively.

Typically the process involves collecting data on current levels of performance and comparing these with the current desired level of performance and the desired level over the long term. The shortfall in these comparisons reveals both immediate and longer-term training needs. However, organizations are not static: their view as to what constitutes effective performance will alter as they move into new business environments.

Sparrow and Bognanno (1993) identify four different categories of competency which help an organization attach a 'shelf-life' to a competency profile for the organization as a whole or to any given career stream or cluster of jobs: *emerging* competencies are those that will require greater emphasis as the organization pursues its particular strategic path; those that are *maturing* are those that are becoming less relevant – perhaps due to technology or work restructuring. *Transitional* competencies are those required of individuals during any change process (e.g. high tolerance of uncertainty and the ability to manage stress and conflict). Stable or *core* competencies are those that are central to an organization's performance and so have persistent relevance.

The double helix model in figure 12.2 shows how development action undertaken by individuals arising out of an organizationally driven review process can connect to the corporate objectives or mission of the organization (Shepherd

**Table 12.1** Linking individual development action to the organization's mission (adapted from Evans et al. 1989)

| | *Potential Identification* | • *Potential Development* |
|---|---|---|
| Dutch | *Unmanaged functional trial*<br>• Little elite recruitment<br>• Decentralized recruitment for technical or functional jobs<br>• 5–7 years' trial<br>• No corporate monitoring<br>• Problem of internal potential identification via assessments, assessment centres, indicators<br>• Possible complementary recruitment of high potentials | *Managed potential development*<br>• Careful Monitoring of high potentials by management review committees<br>• Review to match up performance and potential with short- and long-term job and development requirements<br>• Importance of management development staff |
| Germanic | *Apprenticeship*<br>• Annual recruitment from universities and technical schools<br>• 2-year 'apprenticeship' trial<br>– job rotation through most functions<br>– intensive training<br>– identification of person's functional potential and talents<br>• Some elitist recruitment, mostly of Ph.D.s | *Functional ladders*<br>• Functional careers, relationships and communication<br>• Expertise-based competition<br>• Multifunctional mobility limited to few elitist recruits, or non-existent<br>• Little multifunctional contact below level of division heads and *'vorstand'* (executive committee) |
| Japanese | *Managed elite trial*<br>• Elite pool or cohort recruitment<br>• Recruitment for long-term careers<br>• Job rotation, intensive training, mentoring<br>• Regular performance monitoring<br>• Equal opportunity | *Time-scheduled tournament*<br>• Unequal opportunity, good jobs to the best<br>• 4–5 years in a job, 7–8 years up-or-out<br>• Comparison with cohort peers<br>• Multifunctional mobility, technical-functional track for minority |
| Latin | *Elite entry, no trial*<br>• At entry<br>• Elite pool recruitment (non-cohort)<br>• Predictive qualities<br>• From schools specialized in selecting and preparing future top managers<br>– *'Grandes écoles'*<br>– MBAs<br>– Scientific Ph.D.s | *Political tournament*<br>• High fliers<br>• Competition and collaboration with peers<br>• Typically multifunctional<br>• Political process (visible achievement, get sponsors, coalitions, read signals)<br>• If stuck, move out and on<br>• The 'gamesman' |

1991). Each part of the double helix represents a separate circle of demand and supply but these are typically unconnected. Organizations frequently rely on some mystical process of communication to ensure that managers do the right thing and where the mission of the organization is well understood and shared, this may just work. Few organizations attempt to connect the systems that actually develop individuals to meet organizational need. They rely on a continuing turnover of people to ensure that individuals match job requirements. In an organization that has little turnover, skills quickly become outdated and the organization becomes less able to meet changing demands. Instant programmes of development are set in motion as solutions and often the training budget is too small to cope.

So how can training and development align with and contribute to the mission of a given organization, assuming such a statement exists and is meaningful (and we know this to be a major assumption)? There are four key elements all of which rely on the vision and skills of line management. The first is a manpower plan which usually contains details of the number of people at specific grades and tends to focus on broad requirements. It therefore lacks the refinement of a statement of skill need. The second element is some kind of skills audit. Failure to regularly review skills against needs results in emergency recruitment programmes to buy in scarce skills and/or redundancies or redeployment to cut out skills no longer required. A third element is performance appraisal. This

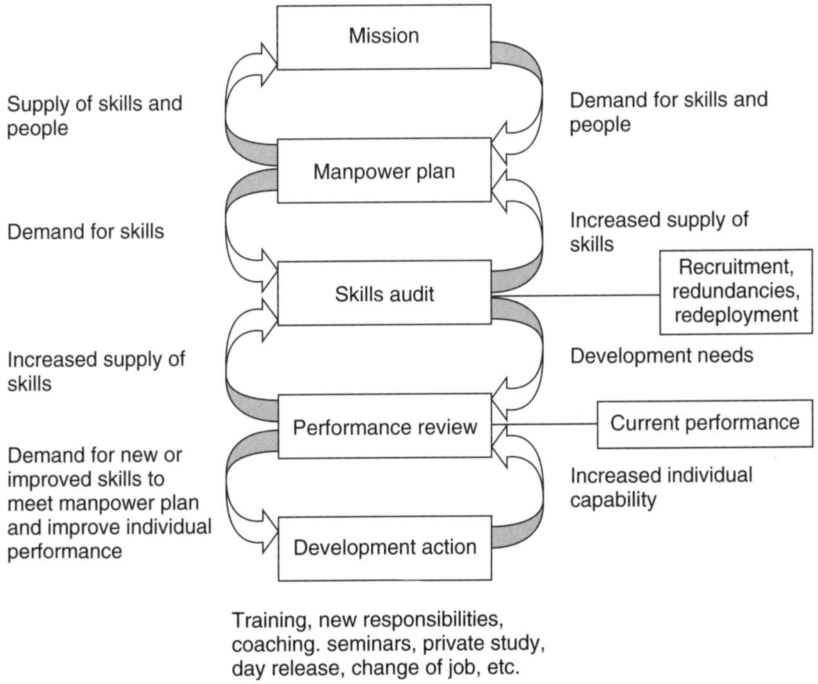


**Figure 12.2** Linking individual development action to the organization's mission.

usually concentrates on improving performance on the job but rarely reflects development for future needs of the organization. This probably happens because little is known by appraising managers about the strategic needs of the business outside their own areas. Finally, there is development action, frequently seen as something the trainers do. The intention of the double helix in figure 12.2 is to show that the overall process relies on both top-down and bottom-up communication and activity. When operated effectively training and development initiatives will reflect both the strategic priorities of the business as well as the personal aspirations of the individual trainees and developers, although it is usually assumed that the two correspond – at least potentially.

Naturally, culture influences the ways in which organizations interpret and carry out the various linkages. It is not surprising, therefore, that different career development models should gain currency in different countries. Table 12.1 summarizes some of the key elements in the way managers are initially identified as having potential, and then how they are typically developed in four country groupings. The influence of cultural values and preferences becomes evident, for example, in the choice of methods and criteria for progression for managers in respective countries. Thus, the more individualist, achievement-oriented Anglo-Dutch model relies more on assessment centres and review committees to identify potential and to determine the degree to which the individual is serving the goals of the organization. This is predicated on the following assumptions: that potential is 'objective' and measurable; that people must prove themselves in the tasks they were hired to perform; that almost anyone (within reason), regardless of age, background and family connections, can 'succeed' if they can achieve their capacity. This is in contrast to the more particularistic, ascriptive and diffuse Japanese and Latin models, where the career entry and progression is determined more by the elite institutions and right relationships (Hoecklin 1995).

## Individual strategies

How should training and career development needs, present or future, manifest or latent, be diagnosed? The organizational pros and cons of various methods like questionnaires, interviews, observations and work samples are well established (see, for instance, Olivas 1988). Less is known about how participants view such processes, which is strange given that it is their development that is being determined.

Research findings suggest line manager involvement in diagnostic and development activities is valued on two counts: their role in providing feedback on performance and the fact that such feedback and career planning advice is credible because it is coming from someone who is (usually) connected to the organizational power nexus and/or a carrier of important cultural information (Mabey and Iles 1993; Preston 1993). The usual forum for diagnosing training and development needs is the performance review or appraisal interview between the manager and his/her subordinate. However, such reviews are by definition evaluative and often linked to remuneration and promotion possibilities. In contrast, training needs assessment is a process of assessing an employee's mastery of certain skills in his/her present job for the purpose of general self-development rather than for a particular job or set of tasks.

The quality of this diagnostic approach tends to be enhanced when preparatory work is done by both parties; for instance, both could separately rate the skill elements required for the job and the job holder's current performance level against those respective skill areas. A comparison of the congruency or otherwise of these two skills audits will produce a basis for discussion about personal development and assist in the choice of learning opportunities to develop motivational, interpersonal, decision-making, supervisory or other skills. Interpreting the difference in perception of the same job behaviours can be extremely helpful in promoting self-awareness and there is no reason why peer feedback should not contribute to these insights too. Indeed, many in-house and externally run skills-building programmes incorporate 360 degree feedback (from subordinates, peers, senior colleagues and possibly customers) as a precursor to the training event because such feedback – when sensitively handled – can assist in the 'unfreezing' process, necessary before real learning can take place.

Whatever approach is used the diagnosis of training needs is as important for the individuals as it is for the organization. In its crudest sense this diagnosis involves each employee group exploring what they are trying to achieve, the barriers to achieving this and the suitability of training as a means to remove or counteract these barriers. The participation of individuals in this process is essential for two reasons. First, they will have personal strategies, some of which may align with those of the organization, but others which will reflect their career aspirations, their desire for qualifications, their family commitments and their out-of-work interests and commitments. Secondly, they are unlikely to invest much personal effort in training and development activities if they have played no part in identifying their relevance. There is an in-built resistance to development programmes or learning 'opportunities' which are not perceived to be personally, functionally or culturally appropriate. Such processes cannot be divorced from the macro-context of the organization concerned, and in particular the internal labour market. Research has shown that in-company education, training and development has acquired an even higher profile in Japan in recent years, as firms look to strengthen their competitive capability; in contrast, British firms were found to be moving away from structured internal labour markets towards individual activity and concepts such as employability, with 'development' becoming the property of the individual manager (Storey et al. 1997). Previously, organizations would provide development opportunities and long-term career paths, absorbing much of the anxiety that individuals might otherwise face. It seems that, in the UK at least, career development is now becoming the responsibility of employees who are expected to network and push themselves forward if they want promotion (McGovern et al. 1995). However, findings from a study of three major organizations undergoing large-scale change in the UK reveal a misalignment between the stated ambition of the companies concerned and the realized outcome and employees less than enchanted with these notions of employability:

> Because most of the organisations studied were involved in effecting significant numbers of redundancies, training largely centred on improving within-job performance. A large problem encountered was that, because of pressures on the businesses, allocating time for managers to attend courses was highly difficult. Further, those who did attend training were frequently unable to put their new skills to work, due to the demands of the business. What development opportunities there were seemed to be the preserve of knowledge workers, with the consequence that the majority of employees viewed the idea of employability with scepticism (e.g. 'it's a management cop-out'; 'it's a rationalisation of the fact they have no plan or processes'). In careers, the lack of promotion opportunities, and an unwillingness to accept that lateral moves were as important as vertical ones, brought great dissatisfaction with the career process. Employees also felt that they had little real influence in developing their own careers, and still wanted a clear steer from the organisation. (Stiles et al. 1997: 63)

One organization that has worked very hard at participative and culturally-sensitive management development is BP (see box 12.1).

## The Integration of Training and Development with Human Resource Strategies

A strategic approach to training and development would seem to imply the integration of these policies and plans with other, wider HRM strategies being pursued by the organization at the time. By definition such an approach is likely to involve several groups within an organization, including the top team, HRD managers and other personnel specialists apart from those participating in the training and development activities and their line managers. However, is such integration necessarily desirable? And what evidence is there to suggest that organizations are pursuing integrated HRM and that it is having positive outcomes?

### *Integration: is it desirable?*

A number of different HRM solutions can be detected amongst organizations since the mid-1980s as they grappled with major strategic change. In each case the intention was to 'add value to the organization by identifying, analysing and implementing a set of procedures and activities to solve the various people-related concerns' (Boam and Sparrow 1992: 7). Each of these 'strategic' reactions brought with it a particular focus to human resource activity. Three examples where these HRM policies incorporated particular training and development initiatives are illustrated in table 12.2.

The authors go on to advocate a resource development or competency-based

## BOX 12.1 ENSURING CROSS-CULTURALLY VALID COMPETENCIES AT BP

'BP chose to create a corporate-wide competency framework. It was appreciated that the process of decentralization and downsizing meant that implementation strategies would vary across businesses and countries. The performance criterion against which competencies were to be established, therefore, was the ability to enable change to happen (whatever that change might prove to be). A competency model was developed with consultants by comparing BP to other multinationals on their database and creating appropriate behavioural indicators that reinforced the culture and would enable Project 1990 to be implemented. It was essentially a desk-top exercise and the labels chosen to group the 67 identified essential behaviours were the same ones that had been used in relation to Project 1990, i.e. Open Thinking, Personal Impact, Empowering and Networking (OPEN).

Over a period of several months, the model was tested and validated internally and was then communicated throughout the business as awareness of the new competency model grew amongst senior managers. It then had to be devolved across all the national businesses. The challenge was that the OPEN competencies (and the 67 behaviours that evidenced them) had been designed to express BP's organizational culture, yet had to be adapted to suit a wide range of national cultures. The cross-cultural validity of the essential behaviours was challenged by non-British or non-American managers. They had been developed by a team of Anglo-Americans. Were they transferable to other countries?

BP conducted its investigation using a two-pronged approach: consultation of experts in the field of cultural diversity and the use of Focus Groups using non-Anglo-American employees. The expert reviews conducted by external academics and consultants sampled twelve countries. It was concluded that the competencies (i.e. the essential behaviours) were capable of cross-cultural implementations and represented a cogent statement of the shift in management behaviours required. However, the behavioural anchors used to describe specific competencies were, in some instances, unnecessarily directive and contained a culturally proactive bias. The greatest challenge came from competencies contained in the Personal Impact (Bias for Action, Knows What Makes Other Tick, Concern for Impact and Self-Confidence) and Empowering (Coaching and Developing, Building Team Success and Motivating) clusters. The recommendation was that BP step back from the behavioural detail of the proposed OPEN competencies and encourage people in different countries to offer their own illustrations of how they might change behaviours and culture. The process demonstrated that the OPEN competencies were capable of crossing cultural barriers in their essential meaning and purpose (reinforcing their use as a "corporate glue" to integrate human resource policies and practices), but also that their implementation and assessment would require greater effort in order to customize and translate the behavioural indicators to fit the culturally different groups involved. The customization process, however, had to fit the culturally different groups involved. The customization process, however, had to avoid any misinterpretations or fundamental change to the meaning of competencies.

BP ran a series of Focus Groups in France and Germany, in which it presented the intended objective of the behaviour contained within the competency and the intended meaning behind the English words. The Focus Groups each contained 10 to 12 national employees who spoke English as a second language. Meetings were held in the local language and were facilitated by consultants operating in the area of cross-cultural management and fluent in English, French and German. Each group was able to flex the behavioural indicators around each competency so that they were appropriate for their culture and organization. The feared barriers to cross-cultural implementation did not materialize.

Local business trainers and facilitators were then given instruction on how to present the OPEN competencies as part of change programmes being carried out in Europe and Asia-Pacific. It was found that it was better to instruct local trainers on the meaning and purpose behind the competencies and then let them fashion the actual training process used to introduce the competencies themselves.'

(Sparrow and Bognanno 1993: 54–5)

approach to HRM. According to this approach organizations generate what they call job models or performance models, which define in behavioural terms the criteria of competence at different levels and possibly in different functions of the enterprise. It then makes sense – they argue – to use this model to inform the person specification when recruiting, to provide a reference point for appraisal sessions, to guide the construction of career maps and, possibly, to feed into reward systems. This job or performance model can likewise be the spur for the diagnosis and delivery of training within an organization. Such models identify fairly precisely what a person needs to bring to a given role in order to perform well, and these competencies can be linked directly to business strategy (vertical integration). Once defined in this way, competencies provide the opportunity to create consistency, coherence and mutual reinforcement across and with HRM policies and practices (horizontal integration).

If all these levers of HRM are operating in concert there is at least the possibility of tracking their combined impact on the strategic objectives in a way that is far less likely when HR initiatives are piecemeal and uncoordinated. It also allays the fears of staff, especially those who are career minded, that the corporate goalposts are shifting. However, it is unlikely that even the most thoroughly researched job models will remain static for very long, so human resource

## BOX 12.2 COMPETENCIES: THE NEW CURRENCY AT CHASE MANHATTAN BANK

'Chase Manhattan has operations across the world, covering most geographic markets and product/industry categories. Throughout the 1960s, '70s and early '80s, customers were served according to their location or their business sector and the bank flourished. But, during the mid-1980s, something subtle began to happen; customers around the globe were transformed into global customers. Assumed boundaries such as the home base, local markets and market segment became less relevant as various recessions, crashes and booms forced hard thinking and tough competition for new markets and alliances.

The rapid expansion of international communications suddenly meant that domestic products and markets were no longer safe from the assault of "foreign" products supported by good marketing. The financial needs of customers around the globe metamorphosed into something beyond the grasp of cosy, locally focused relationships.

Chase, like many of its competitors, suffered during this phase and needed to find a way to focus its extensive resources on familiar terrain. Now it receives wide recognition for having attempted something different, and apparently doing it well. So what happened? For one thing, a much stronger emphasis on developing a clear, differentiated and customer-focused strategy emerged, prompted initially by an early internal paper which addressed the issues of "What are we good at?" and "What can we be competitive at?" It asked the question: "What are our corporate core competencies?" This strategic realignment led to a much clearer understanding of the customer base and a clear determination to focus on their needs.

On the global corporate finance side, a great deal of effort was put into determining what customers were demanding, and this ultimately led to a definition of the competencies required in each segment of the market, describing what skills, abilities, traits, behaviours, etc., individuals would need to deliver the business strategy.

At the same time, the HR function and senior line managers were taking this opportunity to jointly sponsor a co-ordinated global effort to define the "supply" side of the equation what the bank had to offer – and to establish who had what, to what degree they possessed it, where they were, what career history they had, and what degree of mobility they saw for themselves. This information on individual competencies could then be matched against the "demand" side of the equation – the data on which customers require what, where, to what degree and so on. Suddenly we were into the realm of marketing what individuals really had to offer against what customers demanded. The issue of jobs did not feature on either side of that equation; competencies became the new currency, and detailed analysis the new distribution mechanism.'

(Martin 1995: 20–4)

**Table 12.2** Training and development as part of a wider human resource management response to strategic issues

| *Reaction* | *Route* | *Main focus of attention* |
|---|---|---|
| 'We haven't got the right sort of attitudes or culture round here.' | Cultural/programmatic change | • Creation of a 'vision' for the business<br>• Reliance on charismatic leadership<br>• Large-scale change programmes<br>• Focus on global themes such as quality, customer satisfaction, market awareness<br>• Attention given to internal management processes<br>• Heavy use of internal communications<br>• Investment in training and education<br>• Emphasis on team building at local level |
| 'Better see what we've got and decide what we need before we do anything.' | Strategic/human resource planning | • Proactive data collection about what really happens<br>• Attempts to model what might happen<br>• Measuring the cost and benefits of the way people are recruited, retained and developed<br>• Deciding which areas to invest in<br>• Determining a critical path for the changes<br>• Sequencing and managing the implementation against a plan |
| 'We haven't got the right skills and we don't make the best of what we've got.' | Resource development (competency-based) | • Deciding what type of work needs to be done<br>• Analysing the way effective people do the work<br>• Communicating the model of effectiveness<br>• Making sure recruitment, development and performance management systems mutually reinforce the same behaviours<br>• Providing line managers with tools to assess and develop individual potential |

*Source:* Adapted from Boam and Sparrow (1992: 3, 9).

specialists need to be vigilant in reviewing the relevance and scarcity of skill mixes in their enterprises.

The emphasis on deriving behavioural repertoires that are organizationally meaningful and specific, rather than arriving at a set of generic knowledge, skills and attitudes for a given sector via functional analysis, is a desirable asset of this approach and would seem – at least, in part – to answer the criticism of competency definition levelled by Reed and Anthony (1992), among others:

> All too often, the educational community has retreated into a narrow vocationalism in which the overriding emphasis is given to functional and technical skills which crowds out any sustained concern with the social, moral, political and ideological ingredients of managerial work and the form of educational experience most appropriate to their enhancement and development . . . This would seem to be doubly inappropriate at a time when the nature of managerial work, and the constantly shifting environment in which it is practices, are likely to undermine and subvert the rigid application of technical skills or 'competencies', which are divorced from the social and organizational context in which they have to be applied. (1992: 60)

Arriving at a recognizable performance model or competency profile for a particular career path in a given organization has the potential for overcoming other problems too. Because behaviours are couched in terms of what people actually do (e.g. 'what differentiates an excellent performer from a mediocre performer in job X?') rather than what they say they do, the model has credibility where culture change programmes based on predetermined performance models often do not.

The example in box 12.2 of how Chase Manhattan attempted to link the bank's future supply of managerial competencies directly to anticipated customer demands, is fairly typical of competency-based HR approaches adopted by organizations in all sectors in the 1990s.

Although the precise definition of generic managerial competencies remains controversial, both in concept and content terms, there is general agreement that greater clarity about what observable criteria differentiate the excellent from the average performer is a valuable step forward toward strategic HR planning. Early indications are that competency-based approaches to both managerial assessment and development are gaining ground, with results being reported of more successful integration of HR policies (Mabey and Iles 1993), positive links being made with business performance (Shackleton 1992) and the use of competencies to articulate and even modify company cultures (Bognano 1992). Several difficulties remain however.

First, as in the Chase example in box 12.2, competencies are essentially part of a culture change process. They reflect a shift in definition of management: the traditional notion of management (seniority, privilege, status, as someone who was 'in charge'), has been replaced by the manager as entrepreneur, as responsible for commercial targets, budgets, costs. In short 'individuals who would deliver the business strategy'. As with other aspects of culture change this raises questions about the ethics of senior management seeking to manipulate the performance, values and attitudes of staff, through such techniques. Secondly, the competencies are often used not simply to redefine jobs in terms of new values, but also to assess current incumbents against these qualities, suggesting an inequality in power relations where 'the decision to accord the attribution of competence remains with the assessors' (Holmes 1996: 47).

Thirdly, responsibility for resolving the skills/attitude gaps surfaced by the process is clearly invested with the individual managers themselves. Although some support is available, it is clear that managers are expected to navigate their own development. This is exactly where the HR adjustment burden is frequently placed. Writing about equal opportunity and positive action programmes, Austin and Shapiro (1996) note that: 'the basic premise which underpins these policies is that specific employee groups require some additional training and development to ease their integration into the workforce, or "catch up" with "normal employees" . . . individuals are expected to surpress their differences and to assimilate into the prevailing organisational culture' (1996: 64). The same subtle idea of the individual gradually finding herself 'out of line' and deeming it necessary (because the alternatives are not practical or comfortable?) to accommodate to other corporately-inspired HR initiatives, is also true of such things as stress management workshops, culture change programmes and Total Quality Management.

Finally, at an operational level, involving representative groups of staff (if not all staff as individuals) in the derivation of the competencies for their level(s) in the organization is both intellectually taxing and time consuming. Resultant lists of competencies are likely to challenge traditional job definitions and promotion criteria as well as encroaching on the even more sacrosanct territory of reward strategies and employment contracts. This is not an argument against pursuing future orientated, strategic job models, rather a caution concerning the political and cultural consequences of doing so.

## Integration: is it happening?

Given these proposed benefits and associated difficulties, to what extent are organizations adopting an integrated approach whereby training and development coheres with other dimensions of the human resource strategy? From an employee perspective this would mean that the criteria encountered when joining the organization would have some internal consistency with those used in appraisal, performance review, promotion and reward discussions. Here we review briefly three sources for evidence of this type of internal integration: competency-based HRM, organization initiatives like quality management, and research which has sought to test HRM integration.

Although much is said about the virtues of competency-based HRM generally, and in particular, training and development, the number of reported examples is still, as yet, small (see table 12.3).

In an in-depth study of 16 UK organizations, four were found to be comprehensively adopting 'management standards' as part of their HRD systems and processes. A further three had partially adopted such frameworks and nine had not attempted this or had made little progress in this direction (Winterton and Winterton 1997). Those in the first category shared certain characteristics:

**Table 12.3** Examples of competency-based HRM in the UK

| *Organization* | *Key features* | *Reference* |
|---|---|---|
| BP | Efforts to link executive competencies to a cultural competency model | Bognanno (1990; 1992); Quinn, Mills and Friesen (1992) |
| Digital Equipment Europe (Ltd) | Creation of a business-oriented human resource strategy around competencies | Smith and Verran (1992) |
| Bass plc | Use of competencies to streamline, restructure and recruit in order to build a new company culture | Probert (1992) |
| Rank Xerox | Definition of boardroom competencies for development Directors, and for first-line management | Coulson-Thomas (1990); Mabey and Iles (1993) |
| National Westminster Bank plc | Use of competencies to accelerate changes in personnel practices and business performance | Francis (1992) |
| Medium-sized accountancy organization | Use of competencies to articulate a required performance in a changing business market | Shackleton (1992) |
| National & Provincial Building Society | Attempts to achieve internal and external integration of HR strategies through a career-focused, competency-based approach | Mabey and Iles (1993) |

management development and other training was competence based, and job profiles or job descriptions related to the competences outlined in the management standards (MCI) and appraisal systems were designed to support the attainment of management standards. A major benefit identified was the coherent structure which the standards provided for training, management development and personal development (although the standards were not extensively used for recruitment and selection, nor reward and remuneration systems). Gaps in competence, for example, were more readily spotted through appraisal, training needs were specified more precisely in relation to the competences required for individuals to meet the needs of the organization, and there were clear criteria for human resource planning and career succession. Also, management development was linked to a qualifications framework. Finally, and most impressive, the researchers found a statistically significant relationship between competence-based HRD systems, and both individual and business performance.

For all its rigour, this is a small-scale study, and it is not difficult to find other examples where such integration is missing. An analysis of Japanese training systems found them to be well embedded; usually training was part of a career development system which depended on and helped to reinforce a stable corporate environment. In contrast, training courses in British companies were well received but their purpose and connection with the wider managerial role were not well established (Storey et al. 1997). This concurs with the view that most training in the UK proceeds in isolation from an integrated strategy of HRM and that employers are still not taking a long-term systematic approach to training (Heyes and Stuart 1996); and that, despite the injection of funds from the Employment Department into training for small- and medium-sized enterprises (£1.47 billion in 1992/3) 'there appears to be little evidence that management training programmes clearly lead to better performance among participating SMEs' (Storey and Westhead 1994).

The second arena from which we can derive, at least inferential, evidence concerning the integrative nature of training and development activities is that of quality management. HR interventions, under such banners as Total Quality Management and Leadership through Quality, are characterized by thoroughly rehearsed and wide-scale training in quality techniques, problem-solving, innovation and team-working. It is not unusual for this training to be 'cascaded' through the organization and for it to be linked to other HR initiatives. So it could be argued that the enduring popularity of quality management, as well as examples of ensuing organizational benefits (e.g. Giles 1989; Hill 1991; Cruise O'Brien 1995), constitute validation of a strategically integrated approach to training and development. The integral role of training, both blue-collar and white-collar, in quality management programmes specifically, and change management interventions generally, is well-documented. Other commentators, mindful of the historical and current political context, are more sceptical. They note that TQM helps to fill the gap left open by the decline of earlier forms of collectivism, and that it chimes in well with the corporate need to concentrate on service quality, and it complements the wider social pressure to devolve responsibility to the individual (Kerfoot and Knights 1995). Part of the difficulty is that 'organisational effectiveness hinges on the capacity to balance the conflicting goals of stability and reliability with those of exploration and innovation' (Sitkin et al. 1994: 540). In reviewing practices associated with 'enlightened' HRM, including training in the context of teamworking, involvement and empowerment, Ezzamel et al. (1996) conclude that:

> HRM cannot free itself either from its own internal contradictions or, more fatefully, from the contradictory tensions that bedevil an employment relationship in which there is endemic conflict, as well as a coincidence of values and priorities between employers and employed. (Ezzamel et al. 1996: 78)

Such conclusions are less a comment of whether training and development is strategically integrated and happening on a wide scale (indeed, the fact that books have been devoted to case-study accounts suggest that the phenomenon is extensive (see, for example, Wilkinson and Willmott 1995). Rather they represent a criticism of the fundamental motives of management in implementing such schemes as TQM and a questioning of whether the promise of greater employee discretion, autonomy, flexibility and the like, is actually fulfilled.

A third source providing evidence of organizations adopting an integrated HRM approach – not necessarily based on a competency-based model – comes from a study of the UK National Health Service (Guest and Peccei 1994). Their study aimed to develop and compare four models of HRM (see box 12.4), each of which put different emphases on training and development, and to assess their respective effectiveness. Clear support was found for *'organizational integration'*:

> Where HR policy is 'owned' by top management, in the sense that they have formally agreed a written policy, then senior personnel and line managers give higher ratings of HRM effectiveness. Among personnel managers, this is reinforced if personnel management in the organization is judged to make an important contribution to key (non-personnel) organizational decisions. These results, it could be argued, reinforce the concept of integration in two respects. Firstly they appear to support the importance of an integration of line and personnel policy through a shared contribution to its formulation. Secondly, it implies line management ownership of the policy. Taking the political model a stage further, we might argue that this ownership is an important factor in ensuring the high ratings of effectiveness. (Guest and Peccei 1994: 237)

The research also found positive outcomes arising from the '*process* integration' model of HRM:

> The second clear predictor of HRM effectiveness is Process Integration. It appears that how personnel specialists operate matters more than who they are or how well the personnel department is staffed. If they are perceived to operate efficiently, this has an impact on ratings of administrative effectiveness and possibly on measures of labour turnover and absence. If they are perceived to display high quality and responsiveness, this predicts qualitative effectiveness, particularly among line mangers. (Guest and Peccei 1994: 238)

Empirical assessment of the effectiveness of HR strategies is, as yet, rare, so it is interesting to note from this study that the combined impact of board level and day-to-day level integration are indeed significant, and certainly more so than policy and functional integration. However, the conceptual and practical difficulties of achieving integration are considerable, and these will be discussed more fully in Part 6, Managing Meaning.

**BOX 12.3 FOUR MODELS OF HRM INTEGRATION**

1 Organizational Integration
A coherent HR strategy which is owned by the Board and readily accepted by line management. A willingness to incorporate an HR dimension in important strategic decisions.

2 Policy Integration
More concerned with the content of the strategy and the extent to which the resulting policies cohere. A clear and consistent priority for *one* of the following:

- the development and operation of routine, administrative personnel system;
- personnel seen as professionally competent and demonstrate the ability to carry out their mainstream activities very well; or
- a coherent set of policies designed to achieve a high quality, committed workforce.

3 Functional Integration
Emphasis upon a high-quality personnel department in terms of professionalism, ratio (of personnel to total staff) and representation on the executive board.

4 Process Integration
Concerned with the efficiency of personnel processes (e.g. value for money, goal achievement) and the quality of personnel processes (e.g. views of internal customers).

(from Guest and Peccei 1994)

## Integration: is it working?

Another way of assessing the degree to which training and development activities mutually reinforce other HRM initiatives and policies is to look at an organization's human resource development (HRD) plan. A survey of 90 Irish high technology companies (indigenous and multinational) contains some interesting insights into how organizations operate their strategic HRD (Garavan 1991). The results highlighted the following:

(1) *HRD policy*: 95 per cent of companies had an established HRD function, 81 per cent had a written HRD policy statement. The most important factors cited as shaping this statement were the organization's mission, goals and strategies, although prevailing culture, training needs, current state of technology, top management views and equality of opportunities were also mentioned.

(2) *Policy formulation*: it was typically drawn up by the HRD specialist, approved by the Personnel Director and subsequently by other members of the management team.

The recognized benefits of having a written policy statement (published as a policy manual or special brochure) were that it ensured consistency and equality of treatment, helping the managers to make more effective HRD decisions and facilitating the human resource planning process.

(3) *Implementation*: three key issues were identified. Publicity of the policy statement (through briefing sessions, induction programmes etc.) was necessary to ensure it was known, understood and accepted by those implementing it and affected by it. Simple, clear procedures, for instance, and yearly training plans were seen as key mechanisms for driving policy through the organization. Monitoring was seen as a vital safeguard against drift from original intentions and ensured continuous alignment with corporate strategy. In this respect, respondents saw HRD policies as flexible and open to modification, rather than static documents.

(4) *Priorities*: the HRD plans of the indigenous high-technology organizations tended to place considerable emphasis on technical training, management development, quality and the management of change. The multinationals gave more prominence to personal development and professional development activities. Garavan suggests this is because they were more likely to have their organization-centred HRD needs met, and could therefore focus on more personal/professional development activities (1991: 26).

(5) *Diagnosis and support*: 85 per cent of respondents had a formalized system for the identification of HRD needs (e.g. questionnaires, performance reviews, discussions with managers and employees, task groups and corporate assessments by the management team), usually done on an annual basis and fed into the HRD plan for that year; 95 per cent of responding organizations had training budgets to support their plan (54 per cent of these were centralized, 20 per cent departmental, the rest a mixture of both), which were up to 5 per cent of annual turnovers for 80 per cent of organizations.

(6) *Roles*: 41 per cent of respondents saw it as the sole responsibility of the HRD specialist to implement the HRD plan, 35 per cent indicated that it was the responsibility of the HRD specialist *and* the line manager, 8 per cent the line manager only, and 16 per cent the human resource specialist.

Evidence from ten European countries suggests that the responsibility for training and development by line management is increasing, both in identifying training needs and in making – or contributing to – policy decisions concerning HRD (see table 12.4).

This, once again underlines the pivotal role of line managers in the effective integration and implementation of human resource strategies. It is they who interpret and communicate the business plans and attempt to link – at an operational level – the human resource policies to strategic business goals; it is they who operate the procedures and monitor the performance; it is they who devote time and departmental resources to individual and team development; it is they who, in many ways, influence the subculture of their department or business unit. While this greater involvement is to be welcomed 'it puts considerable strain and responsibility on the line manager to perform the role with increasing

**Table 12.4** Line manager responsibility for training and development/increase in responsibility

| *Line manager responsibility for training and development* % | *Country ranking* | *Increase in line manager responsibility over the last 3 years* *Country ranking* | % |
|---|---|---|---|
| 21 | Turkey | Sweden | 67 |
| 19 | Denmark | Norway | 56 |
| 18 | Portugal | France | 55 |
| 16 | Sweden | Spain | 53 |
| 14 | Finland | Finland | 51 |
| 14 | Norway | Netherlands | 50 |
| 9 | Germany | UK | 46 |
| 9 | Spain | Ireland | 43 |
| 7 | Ireland | Denmark | 39 |
| 6 | Netherlands | Turkey | 20 |
| 4 | UK | Portugal | 18 |
| 2 | France | Germany | 13 |

*Source:* Larsen (1994: 119)

efficiency, not only in carrying out effective monitoring but ensuring the information is relayed back to the HR central function, which can act as a guide to overall HR policy within the organization in terms of being regionally, nationally and globally strategic in the formulation of HR plans and management succession and other strategic policies' (Holden 1992: 19).

Not all organizations will have or want a dedicated HR function or specialist. However, all but the most skilled line managers will probably need external help when it comes to integrating the diagnosis and delivery of training and development with complementary measures aimed at servicing various aspects of the employment relationship. This might involve, among other things:

- using recruitment as a training strategy. Holden (1992) found that in all ten European countries, with the exceptions of Germany and Sweden, training for new employees was cited as the most popular means used to aid recruitment out of 11 options.
- more systematic attempts to link training needs, analysing training delivery and performance appraisal systems. Brown et al. (1989) found a number of UK organizations were placing more emphasis on processual aspects of training (in this case, management training and development); locating training within the larger context of organization development, although another more extensive UK survey discovered more limited evidence of such perceptions (Parkinson 1990).
- ensuring that mechanisms are in place to positively reward and reinforce desired

## BOX 12.4 VALUING DIFFERENCE AT BRITISH AIRWAYS

BA admits it is 'essentially a very British company with its product being quite essentially British'. This provides the greatest challenge to its management and staff: how to act globally but retain its essential character. The chief challenges were 'how to generate an understanding and appreciation of cultural differences and: how to "Europeanise" management thinking (especially in a company where American business schools and management consultants have been revered): how to persuade people to learn foreign languages; . . . how to develop our understanding of the industrial relations implications of EC legislation to match that of our Trade Unions' (Lauermann 1992: 85). BA initially tackled multiculturalism from a training perspective by putting all senior managers through a training programme which included the Hofstede culture model to understand differences, problems and compatibility between different national groups. However, '18 months later it is quite hard to find people whose thinking was affected by it. A major reason would seem to be that although people understand the general need, they personally had no real hunger for the education or immediate requirement' (Lauermann 1992: 85). A more protracted, but perhaps ultimately more productive, approach is to use the dimensions of 'valuing difference' building on gender issues involved in equal opportunity work to include all forms of diversity with workshops held to explore the business imperatives involved, opening the door to valuing cultural differences. Instead of changing attitudes, the aim has been to encourage exploration of the advantages and risks to BA of equal opportunity and diversity, leading to practical initiatives, in recruitment, promotion and training such as the recruitment of more European graduates, mentoring schemes, the use of European Business schools, the use of flexible employment contracts, and attempting to influence EC legislation.

attitudes and behaviours (that have been targeted by training courses), recognizing that training typically achieves little more than behavioural compliance among participants while the 'underlying values and assumptions of the actors remain unchanged' (Ogbonna and Wilkinson 1990: 15).

- establishing feedback channels to communicate successes, correct problems and evaluate outcomes against original aims.
- setting up a range of career development systems which are deemed as fair and useful by individuals and tie-in with strategic priorities of the organization (Iles and Mabey 1993). Again, use of the on-the-job career development techniques varies from country to country. Hilb (1992) found, across the same ten European countries as in table 12.3, a wide use of planned techniques (formal career planning,

succession plans, job rotations and high flyer schemes) which appear to be strategic, but also a heavy reliance on the performance appraisal which often is not.

- the attempt to utilize a number of separate HRM policies in concert – including training and development – in order to achieve specific improvement in performance or shifts in mindset within an organization. Box 12.4 shows how a range of HR policies targeting the need to 'value difference' at British Airways, were more successful than more general attempts to 'act globally'.

## A Stakeholder Model of Strategic Training and Development

Chapter 5, Training and Development Strategies, began with a depiction of the way training and development could be designed and delivered in a strategic manner (figure 5.1). This model helps to highlight the pivotal link that training and development activities, both formal and informal, *can* provide between business and human resource strategies. It was noted, however, that the model is highly normative and not intended to be reflective of the way HRD actually takes place in organizations. Rather, the constituent elements of the model help to provide an agenda for examining training and development strategies. In chapter 5 we saw how the national socio-political context, those determining the strategic direction of an enterprise and those representing dominant cultural coalitions, all exerted important influences upon the uptake of training in an organization. The possibilities and difficulties of linking training and development policies to the strategic intent of the organization were also explored. This chapter has continued this exploration, focusing in more detail on the internal processes within organizations which either promote or inhibit training being regarded as a high priority. We have seen that those in key line management posts, those participating in training and development, the team who actually design and deliver training, and those responsible for integrating the different parts of HR policy, each have vested interests in how training and development is conceived, implemented and how its effects are measured in a given organization.

Collectively, the analysis in chapters 5 and 12 leads us to reconceptualize strategic training and development. It has shown that training and development strategies are better understood from a stakeholder perspective (see figure 12.3). So, while the six dimensions of the original model remain broadly intact, it is probably more helpful to represent them as specific stakeholder groups each with their own predispositions, priorities and degree of proactivity. The model thus intentionally becomes more fluid, and while the underlying sense of business direction remains (represented by the arrow), this is by no means taken as agreed upon or given. Each group of stakeholders will have a different interest in, influence over and ownership of, training and development strategies and outcomes, and examples of these are shown in the figure. The intersection of boundaries in the figure signifies that such sectional agendas will in some cases overlap and align, but

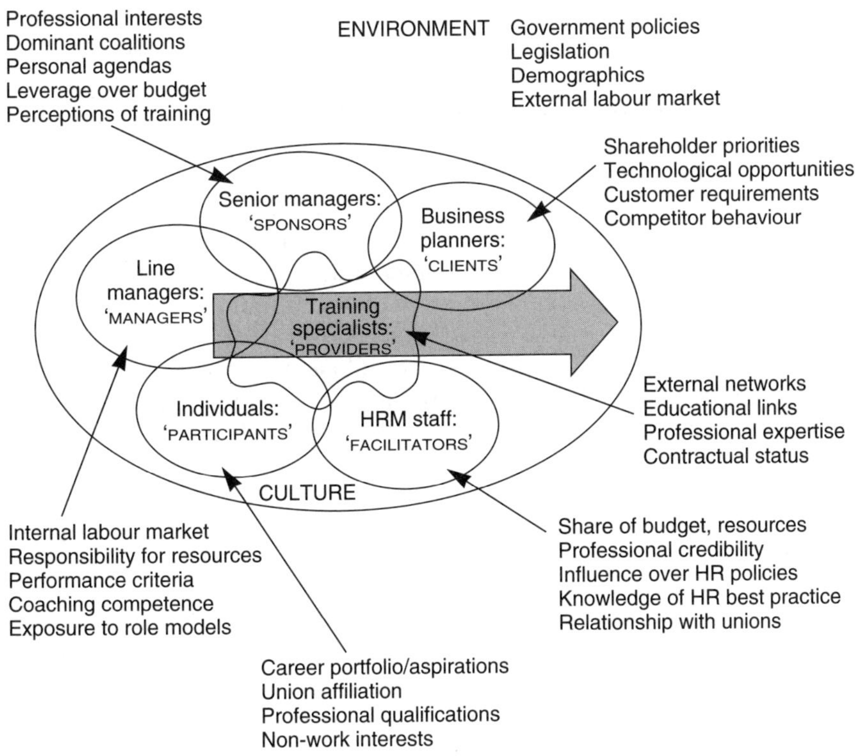


**Figure 12.3** Strategic training and development: a stakeholder approach

broadly speaking the nature of training and development can be seen as central, negotiated territory with the power of the providers of such activities ebbing and flowing between the client, sponsor, manager, participant and facilitator groupings within the organization, each influenced in turn by a host of factors – many of them beyond the boundary of the organization itself.

This interplay of competing and contested views, together with the influence of external, environmental forces, will shape the pathway of training strategies and implementation in a given organization. In other words, investment in training does not automatically translate into improved performance. Some examples of 'intersections' will serve to illustrate.

*The intersection of training with the pressures of line management.* Mintzberg (1990) has pointed out the relentless pace, fragmented, discontinuous and largely unreflective nature of much managerial work. It is not surprising that in these circumstances, managers frequently turn to training 'packages' advertised as the solution to a universally pre-existent problem: 'while managers might be well motivated towards providing training and development for their subordinates, time and attention are restricted to what is plausible rather than what is factually supportable . . .' (Mole 1996: 23). In describing the shortcomings of so-called 'genre training', which seeks a choice of solution from a limited range of prescribed options, the author quotes Katz and Kahn (1978: 658): 'Attempts to change organisations by changing individuals have a long history of theoretical inadequacy and practical failure. Both stem from a disregard of the systemic properties of organisations and from the confusion of individual changes with modification in organisational variables.' The result is a poor matching of training provision to trainee(s) requirements, a failure to understand the situational factors that shape behaviour and a misperception of the value of the training.

*The intersection of training with management conceptions of what is being achieved.* Closely connected to the point above is the collusion that often occurs between what the organization thinks it wants (in the way of training and development) and what external/internal agencies actually provide. It is a case of the 'performance' becoming as, if not more, important than the plot. This becomes particularly acute when sponsors of training in an organization hire the services of a culture change consultant or management guru, who can take on the guise of organizational witchdoctor:

> many guru performances are focused around programmes aimed at changing organisational cultures in order to change how employees feel about their work, their managers, employers and customers. Yet despite their highly doubtful claims to change *attitudes*, what these programmes actually change is *behaviours* rather than values. They achieve some degree of compliance, not surprisingly, but that they do any more than that is empirically unproven and theoretically unlikely. Yet the programmes persist and are highly popular. Behaviour is apparently enough. They are today's version of the rain-making ritual: focusing on *ideal* connections between events, not real ones – trying to produce causes by producing the results. It's like trying to make it rain by putting up umbrellas. (Clark and Salaman 1996: 101)

*The intersection between training and authority structures.* In a study of four UK organizations where quality management (QM) programmes had been introduced, including various training and development initiatives, Rees (1998) notes that the structure of authority in the respective companies was not radically altered by the panoply of HR policies ushered in under the banner of QM. While 'detailed control' at the point of production or service delivery, passed to employees, management increased their grip on 'general control'. He concludes that the introduction of QM led to a reorganization of control, whereby an organizationally-specific mix of contingent factors leads to a particular balance between control and consent. These findings could well be applied to many HR and training interventions, where despite the promise, a small step forward (rather than a radical overhaul) in the negotiated order takes place, due to the incipient resistance of existing authority structures.

*The intersection of training with social processes in the work unit.* Prevailing authority and power structures operate laterally in organizations, as well as vertically. These too can confound the best intentions of training. Heyes (1998) describes the introduction of new working practices and approaches to training in an agro-chemical plant where he conducted fieldwork as a non-participant observer. Here the intention was to extend management control through the formalization of practices which had previously been subject to informal negotiation. Understandably, the employees felt demoralized and devalued. But they reacted in a way that allowed them to regain a measure of control over the terms on which their skills were utilized, sometimes to the disadvantage of other shop-floor groups. They refused to passively accept a new order which, in their view, undermined the equity of the wage-effort bargain:

> the lateral tensions which were simultaneously reproduced on the shopfloor through the disruption of the internal labour market also encouraged the process workers to pursue other job controls (those surrounding the deployment of maintenance skills) at the expense of the former craft workers . . . This complex picture of solidaristic and sectional struggles and accommodations points to a difficulty in understanding the linkages between training provision and performance outcomes in isolation from social processes at the point of production. (Heyes 1998: 110)

Thus, albeit in a manner unanticipated by senior management who instigated the changes, a new order *was* established whereby shop-floor workers retained their 'choice' about when, how and with whom they would work flexibly.

*The intersection between training and formal procedures*. It is not unusual to find employees adapting, accommodating and improvising around organizational procedures. Research shows that participants in career development practices prefer the collaborative and overt philosophy of development centres, especially when the centre facilitated an honest discussion about career prospects with someone tuned into the nexus of organizational politics, than the more analytical, opaque and 'controlling' tenor of an assessment centre (Mabey and Iles, 1993). Beattie and McDougall (1998) found that in peer mentoring relationships in two Scottish voluntary sector organizations, mutual learning was more likely to occur where no formal structure existed. In other words, where such relationships are imposed on employees (i.e. chosen for them) and where the relationship is hierarchical (i.e. boss-subordinate) effective and supportive peer mentoring relationships tend not to develop. Interviewees revealed that, under these conditions, they found it difficult to develop communication, mutual support and collaboration essential for effective learning to take place.

*The intersection between training and wider political/economic agendas*. Training and development *can* have a very powerful influence on behaviour, if not attitudes, as part of an organization-wide initiative, especially when linked to mutually reinforcing HR policies. Sometimes, however, these effects are eclipsed by external factors which at best halt, and, at worst, undermine these impacts. This was true of an Executive Agency in the UK (see box 12.6), where significant headway had been made in changing staff behaviour (Mabey and Skinner 1998).

*The intersection of training and other strategic assets in the organization*. Strategic

## BOX 12.5 EMPOWERMENT IN AN EXECUTIVE AGENCY?

The majority of staff interviewed reported that some degree of responsibility and authority had moved away from the centre, creativity had been released and services had improved as a result. The staff clearly had ownership of performance targets and the need to provide value for money and the organization was generally perceived to have improved in both efficiency and effectiveness. While it is not possible to correlate precisely such perceptions with actual performance over the period of the so-called empowerment programme (1992–6), annual reports for this time-span reveal an impressive improvement against targets set by respective Secretaries of State: these include steady enhancement of service delivery, accuracy, financial and resource management and customer satisfaction.

For those reporting positively, the key appeared to be the perceived success of various training and development initiatives. While other business and economic pressures no doubt contributed to the attitudinal shifts apparent in the Agency, the cluster of communication, training, coaching, restructuring and job redesign initiatives that went under the general umbrella of 'empowerment' were undoubtedly an important catalyst, enabling individuals to genuinely address and resolve skill, job design and trust issues at a local level. In other words, Agency staff felt they had sufficient influence and discretion to be responsive to the demands of their client base (in this case, the general public).

However, there was cynicism concerning examples of 'backsliding' into hierarchical attitudes and doubts about *who* was actually benefiting from the management development initiatives which ushered in these changes. Also, it is clear that many of the business and *internal* customer benefits reaped as a result of the empowerment programme were, at the time of the study, in grave danger of being dissipated. Agency staff consistently remarked that the essential element of empowerment from their perspective was trust. This trust had been painstakingly established and a degree of common purpose, aligning with the organization's four 'core values', had been achieved over five years of the empowerment programme. However, in the climate of severe financial cutbacks faced by the Agency, it will be extremely demanding for the organization to maintain this degree of trust with staff who do not anticipate significant pay rises, who do not see performance pay as rewarding performance and who are uncertain about their long-term job security.

training and development activities may bring business benefits in the short term, but like other HR policies and practices, they are unlikely to yield sustained competitive advantage because such practices are easily copied and/or the training champions easily poached. According to the resource-based view of human resources: 'HR policies are likely to be effective . . . if undertaken in concert with (policies affecting) other SAs [Strategic Assets]. Thus, instead of espousing high expectations with regard to employee development and training policies, one would be well advised to devise development policies while keeping the principle of resource interdependence in mind' (Mueller 1996: 775). Because this more interdependent approach to developing human capabilities draws on the firm's broad array of material and intellectual resources, it is less imitable and thus represents a resource mobility barrier, which, in turn, enhances competitiveness.

This suggests that specifying how the investment in training links with such strategic assets as company and brand reputation, for example, is more likely to lead to sustained strategic benefits. This leads us back to the first intersection point above, namely that training interventions thoughtfully tailored for the organization will be more successful than 'off-the-shelf' solutions.

## Conclusions and Summary

This chapter has explored the internal processes and politics that determine whether training and development interventions make a strategic contribution to organizational performance. We noted at the outset that training is often invested with high expectations: perhaps a way to speedily prepare a sales team to launch a new product, perhaps a way of introducing flexible working on the shop-floor, perhaps the chosen means to improve relationships with customers or perhaps the cornerstone of a culture change programme? By examining the decisions concerning the diagnosis, choice and delivery of training options it has become clear that the connection between training and development effort and funding and desired organizational outcomes is by no means clear-cut. There is little doubt that training interventions have an impact, individually and corporately. What is more doubtful is that this impact is as strategic and as enduring as is often hoped for or claimed to be. The stakeholder model helps to explain why this is the case. In particular we briefly reviewed a number of ways in which training activity intersects with other interests, other agendas, other macro and micro variables, each of which have the capacity to distort (at best) and nullify (at worst) the best laid training plans.

As a way of illustrating this and closing the chapter we return to a company, encountered first in chapter 1, operating in the UK computer supplier sector in the mid-to-late-1980s. Figure 2.2 shows some of the competitive and business pressures facing this sector together with some typical strategic and HRM responses. An early trigger in this company's concern for and involvement in training activity was the need for new management competencies, or a 're-definition of the management task'. On the heels of necessary cost reductions there was an urgent requirement to cultivate marketing awareness to support an innovative product strategy instigated by a new top team.

However, all such changes have to be mediated through a firm's internal context. This will include the distinctive structure and culture of the organization, the style and processes of decision-making, the personalities and people, and the tasks and technologies traditionally employed. In this case the move toward a more aggressive marketing mentality in product design and increased profit accountability obviously ran counter to existing culture. The consequent restructuring around business units together with emphasis on customer service operations can thus be seen as internal precursors to investment in training.

Even though management education was used as a primary lever for engendering marketing skills and knowledge in the initial stages, it formed part of a wider *HRM strategy*, encapsulated in a five-year plan. This included a range of measures: a new tiered career structure, a realignment of graduate recruitment, the short-term use of specialist contract staff and the introduction of a performance system linked to appraisals. There were also implications for Vocational Education and Training (VET), notably the project managing of training throughout the company as a means of ensuring that line managers training needs were properly identified and met with each new training product having a senior line manager to personally 'sponsor' it.

Given that for this particular company the heavy investment in training and development 'paid off', what made these training activities successful at a strategic level? The answer to this question underlines many of the principles emerging in this chapter. The first and probably the most influential factor contributing to the effectiveness of training and development was the combined impact of a number of separate but connected triggers and levers: competitive necessity, CEO commitment and an HRM strategy that embraced a number of targeted training and career development activities.

Second, there was an explicit and regular attempt to match business plans and people management implications at all levels from business centre manager upwards. Education, training and development activities provided the vital linkage between corporate strategy and HRM policies.

Third, a quality education process was initiated in order to undergird this diagnostic and planning activity and the internal processes required to make it work. Attention was paid to the content of training but also the infrastructure to support it.

Fourth, the capability of the training function was enhanced with highly credible and skilled field managers who could 'internalize and integrate' the knowledge being provided by external trainers.

Fifth, the two-tiered training activity combined top-down cascaded modules with locally driven training initiated by line units. Each training product was 'sponsored' by a senior manager, so building in line management ownership and content relevance. An added stimulus for high quality training was attendance on courses of customers who demanded value for money.

A final small but not insignificant factor was the removal of budgetary constraints from line managers accompanied by block funding arrangements for departments into training projects a year in advance.

This case serves to illustrate some of the complex connections between internal and external stakeholders that help shape the ethos and practice of training and development in an organization. What is less evident is the messy, unfolding nature of events that look more rational in retrospect than they did at the time.

## Key Points

Strategic training and development:

- will be defined differently by the various stakeholders in an organization, each with their own vested interest in the success or failure of training interventions.
- requires perceptive diagnosis of training need, and 'delivery' (whatever form this might take) by people and methods that connote credibility and relevance to personal and business need.
- is bound up with, rather than separate from, other aspects of human resource strategies that this book covers: structure, culture, manpower planning, recruitment, reward and assessment strategies. Indeed, it could be argued that the skills, knowledge and attitudes engendered by a firm's training and development activities is pivotal to its human resource strategy.
- is likely to be part of an evolutionary process of organization change, with all the false starts, political repercussions, cultural mismatches and financial constraints that this implies.

## Discussion Questions

1 Why is it unreliable to gauge the effectiveness of an organization's training strategy only by reference to courses attended?
2 How important is the role of line managers in the effective implementation of training and development?
3 What evidence is there to suggest that training and development can be strategically integrated with other human resource strategies?
4 It has been asserted that training and development form the cornerstone of human resource strategy. Can such a view be sustained?

## References

Ashton, D., Easterby-Smith, M., and Irvine, C. (1975) *Management Development: Theory and practice*, Bradford: MCB.

Austin, S. and Shapiro, G. (1996) 'Equality-driven employee involvement', *Journal of General Management*, vol. 21, no. 4, Summer, 62–76.

Beattie, R. and McDougall, M. (1998) 'Inside or outside HRM? Lateral learning in two voluntary sector organisations', in C. Mabey, T. Clark, and D. Skinner, (eds) *Experiencing Human Resource Management*, London: Sage.

Boam, R. and Sparrow, P. (1992) *Designing and Achieving Competency*, Maidenhead: McGraw-Hill.

Bognanno, M. (1990) 'Facilitating cultural change by identifying the new competencies required and formulating a strategy to develop such competencies', Conference on

identifying and applying competencies within your organization, November 6, London: IIP Ltd.
—— (1992) 'Linking executive competences to a cultural competency model', Conference on the latest developments in identifying, measuring and applying competencies, January 28–29, London: IIR Ltd.
Brown, H., Peccei, R., Sandberg, S., and Welchman, R. (1989) 'Management training and development: In search of an integrated approach', *Journal of General Management*, vol. 15, no. 1, 69–82.
Burgoyne, J. (1988) 'Management development for the individual and the organization', *Personnel Management*, vol. 20, no. 6, 20–4.
Clark, T. and Salaman, G. (1996) 'The management guru as organisational witchdoctor', *Organization*, vol. 31, no. 1, 85–107.
Coulson-Thomas, C. (1990) 'Development directors', *European Management Journal*, vol. 8, no. 4, 488–99.
Cruise O'Brien, P. (1995) 'Employee involvement in performance improvement: a consideration of tacit knowledge, commitment and trust', *Employee Relations*, vol. 17, no. 3, 110–20.
Evans, P., Lank, E., and Farquar, A. (1989) 'The dualistic organisation', in P. Evans, Y. Doz and A. Laurent (eds) *Human Resource Management in International Firms: change, globalisation, innovation*, London: Macmillan.
Ezzamel, M., Lilley, S., Wilkinson, A., and Willmott, H. (1996) 'Practices and practicalities in human resource management', *Human Resource Management*, vol. 6, no. 1, 63–80.
Francis, K. (1992) 'Using a competency approach to achieve a higher business performance and the acceleration of change in personnel practices: A line manager's story', Conference on the latest developments in identifying, measuring and applying competencies, January 28–29, London: IIR Ltd.
Garavan, T. (1991) 'Strategic human resource development', *Journal of European Industrial Training*, vol. 15, no. 1, 17–30.
Giles, E. (1989) 'Is Xerox's human resource managment worth copying?', Paper presented to the British Academy of Management Annual Conference, September, Manchester Business School.
Guest, D. and Peccei, R. (1994) 'The nature and causes of effective human resource management', *British Journal of Industrial Relations*, vol. 31, no. 2, 219–62.
Heyes, J. and Stuart, M. (1996) 'Does training matter? Employees experiences and attitudes', *Human Resource Management Journal*, vol. 6, no. 3, 7–21.
—— (1998) 'Training and development in a agro-chemical plant', in C. Mabey, T. Clark and D. Skinner (eds) *Experiencing Human Resource Management*, London: Sage.
Hilb, M. (1992) 'The challenge of management development in Western Europe in the 1990s', *The International Journal of Human Resource Management*, vol. 3, no. 3, 575–83.
Hill, S. (1991) 'Why quality circles fail but total quality management might succeed', *British Journal of Industrial Relations*, vol. 29, no. 4, 541–68.
Hoecklin, L. (1995) *Managing Cultural Differences*, Wokingham: Addison-Wesley.
Holden, L. (1992) 'Does strategic training policy exist? Some evidence from ten European countries', *Personnel Review*, vol. 21, no. 1, 12–23.
Holmes, L. (1996) 'HRM and the irresistible rise of the discourse of competence', *Personnel Review*, vol. 24, no. 4, 34–49.
Iles, P. and Robertson, I. (1989) 'The impact of personnel selection techniques on candidates' in P. Herriot, et al. (eds) *Handbook of Assessment in Organizations*, Chichester: John Wiley.

——, —— and Rout, U. (1990) 'Assessment based development centres', *Journal of Managerial Psychology*, vol. 4, no. 3, 11–16.
—— and Mabey, C. (1993) 'Managerial career development programmes: effectiveness, availability and acceptability', *British Journal of Management*, vol. 4, no. 2, 103–18.
Kamoche, K. (1996) 'Human resources as a strategic assets: An evolutionary resource-based theory', *Journal of Management Studies*, vol. 33, no. 6, 757–85.
Katz, D. and Kahn, R. (1978) *The Social Psychology of Organisations*, New York. Wiley.
Kerfoot, D. and Knights, D. (1995) 'Empowering the "Quality Worker"?: The seduction and contradiction of the total quality phenomenon', in A. Wilkinson and H. Willmott (eds) *Making Quality Critical*, London: Routledge.
Kerr, S. (1989) 'AC or DC? The experience of development centres', Paper presented to the British Psychological Society annual conference, January, Windermere.
Larsen, H. (1994) 'Key issues in training and development', in C. Brewster and A. Hegewisch (eds) *Policy and Practice in European Human Resource Management*, London: Routledge, 107–21.
Lauermann, S. (1992) 'British Airways in Europe', *European Management Journal*, vol. 10, no. 1, 85–6.
Legge, K. (1989) 'Human resource management: A critical analysis', in J. Storey (ed.) *New Perspectives in Human Resource Management*, London: Routledge, 19–40.
Mabey, C. and Iles, P. (1993) 'The strategic integration of assessment and development practices', *Human Resource Management Journal*, vol. 3, no. 4, 16–34.
—— and —— (1994) 'Career development practices in the UK: A participant perspective,' in C. Mabey and P. Iles (eds) *Managing Learning*, London: Routledge.
—— and Skinner, D. (1998) 'Empowerment in an executive agency', Working paper, Centre for HR and Change Management, Open University Business School.
Martin, S. (1995) 'A futures market for competencies', *People Management*, March, 20–4.
McGovern, P., Stiles, P., and Hope, V. (1995) 'Career management in an era of insecurity', Proceedings of the Employment Research Unit Annual Conference, Cardiff Business School.
Mole, G. (1996) 'The management training industry in the UK: An HRD director's critique', *Human Resource Management Journal*, vol. 6, no. 1, 19–26.
Mueller, F. (1996) 'Human resources as strategic assets: An evolutionary resource-based view', *Journal of Management Studies*, vol. 33, no. 6, 757–85.
Mumford, A. (1993) *Management Development – Strategies for Action*, London: IPM.
——, Robinson, G., and Stradling, D. (1987) 'Developing directors: The learning processes', *MSC report*, London.
Ogbonna, E. and Wilkinson, B. (1990) 'Corporate strategy and corporate culture: The view from the checkout', *Personnel Review*, vol. 19, no. 4, 9–15.
Olivas, L. (1988) 'Designing and conducting training needs, analysis: Putting the cart before the horse', *Journal of Management Development*, vol. 2, no. 3, 19–41.
Parkinson, S. (1990) 'Management development's strategic role', *Journal of General Management*, vol. 16, no. 2, 63–75.
Preston, D. (1993) 'Learning the organisation: Confusions and contradictions for new managers', *Human Resource Management Journal*, vol. 4, no. 1, 24–33.
Probert, P. (1992) 'Using a competency model to streamline, restructure, recruit and build a new company culture with the aim of competitive advantage,' Conference on the latest developments in identifying, measuring and applying competences, January 28–29, London: IIR Ltd.
Quinn-Mills, D. and Friesen, B. (1992) 'The learning organization', *European Management Journal*, vol. 10, no. 2, 146–56.

Reed, M. and Anthony, P. (1992) 'Professionalising management and managing professionalisation: British management in the 1980s', *Journal of Management Studies*, vol. 29, no. 5, September, 591–613.

Rees, C. (1998) 'Empowerment through quality management? Employee accounts from inside a bank, a hotel and two factories', in C. Mabey, D. Skinner and T. Clark (eds) *Experiencing Human Resource Management*, London: Sage.

Shackleton, V. (1992) 'Using a competency approach in a business change setting', in R. Boam, and P. Sparrow (eds) *Designing and Achieving Competency: A competency-based approach to managing people and organizations*, London: McGraw-Hill.

Shepherd, D. (1991) personal communication, Shepherd Associates.

Sitkin, S., Sutcliffe, S., and Schroeder, R. (1994) 'Distinguishing control from learning in total quality management: A contingency perspective', *Academy of Management Review*, vol. 19, no. 3, 537–64.

Smith, B. and Verran, M. (1992) 'Business-oriented human resource development', Conference on the latest developments in identifying, measuring and applying competences, January 28–29, London: IIR Ltd.

Sparrow, P. and Bognanno, M. (1993) 'Competency requirement forecasting: Issues for selection and assessment', *International Journal of Selection and Assessment*, vol. 1, no. 1, 50–8.

Stiles, P., Gratton, L., Hope-Hailey, V., and McGovern, P. (1997) 'Performance management and the psychological contract', *Human Resource Management Journal*, vol. 7, no. 1, 57–66

Storey, D. and Westhead, P. (1994) 'Management training and small firm performance, working paper no. 18', The Centre for Small and Medium Sized Enterprises, Warwick Business School.

——, Edwards, P., and Sisson, K. (1997) *Managers in the Making: Careers, development and control in corporate Britain and Japan*, London: Sage.

Wilkinson, A. and Wilmott, H. (eds) (1995) *Making Quality Critical: New perspectives on organisational change*, London: Routledge.

Winterton, J. and Winterton, R. (1997) 'Does management development matter?', *British Journal of Management*, vol. 8, June, S65–S76.

part

# 5

# Managing Change

chapter 13

# Change Management Strategies and Assumptions

CHAPTER OUTLINE

## Learning Objectives

- To examine a range of assumptions that govern attempts to bring about strategic change in organizations and note the influence such assumptions have upon the change pathways chosen.
- To understand why many well conceived and well planned change interventions fail or result in unpredictable and unhelpful outcomes.
- To review a range of change management strategies, what premises they are built upon and what – potentially – they can achieve.
- To identify the most appropriate change management processes for the implementation of a given human resource strategy.

# Introduction

There will be occasions when business strategy, and by implication human resource strategies, will be aimed at steady-state scenarios. For example, the intention may be to reinforce existing priorities within the organization: perhaps, to modify the reward system so it reflects a greater performance-related element, or perhaps to extend an appraisal system which is working well at management grades to encompass supervisory staff and their teams as well. Such human resource initiatives will undoubtedly promote significant changes for certain groups of individuals but are unlikely to cause shock waves throughout the organization (although even minor revisions of policy like these can be delicate and their introduction requires sensitive handling!). However, in this text we have been dealing typically with human resource interventions which are advocated by, designed at and launched from a strategic level. While not *all* human resource initiatives necessarily imply change, most do and this is especially the case where they are linked to wider strategic intentions.

It is not unreasonable, then, to include in a text on human resource strategies an examination of change management. This apparently simple task takes us immediately to the heart of some very fraught questions. To what extent is it possible for organizations to initiate change in a proactive and purposeful manner? Can change be broken down into discrete chunks of activity? If it is possible to define a particular change strategy, how realistic is it to talk of that strategy being managed? Why do the 'simplest' of change interventions so quickly become problematical and unworkable? Why within the same organization do individuals often hold such emotively and radically different assessments of the same change initiative? Before enlisting the support of various change management approaches in our quest for strategically managed human resources we need to address some of the assumptions and paradigms that underlie them.

As table 13.1 shows, each aspect of change management – intention, implementation and interpretation – is governed by a set of assumptions which will, by implication, significantly alter the way organizational change is conceived and construed by those involved. Generally speaking, the left-hand column of assumptions represents the received wisdom on the subject of change management, particularly in the US literature (e.g. French and Bell 1984; Beckhard and Harris 1987; Buller 1988; Porras and Silvers 1991; Schuler 1992). Even if and when change comes to be seen as positive and pervasive, implementation can still be shaped by deterministic thinking. And, even if and when the less predictable, relational and multi-faceted dimensions of change implementation have been recognized it is still possible to interpret the outcomes in a way that downplays or ignores the differing versions, meanings and ideologies with which they are invested.

In this chapter we take a closer look at each set of assumptions in table 13.1 and discuss the implications of these for the way human resources are directed and developed in organizations.

**Table 13.1** Change management assumptions

| Assumptions about intentions of change | Implications |
|---|---|
| Is change | |
| *Exceptional* or endemic? | • Arrangements made for scanning, filtering and responding to signals for change |
| *Threatening* or desirable? | • Behavioural readiness to do things differently |
| *Deviant* or normal? | • Cultural responsiveness to do things differently |
| **Assumptions about implementing change** | **Implications** |
| Is change | |
| *Controllable* or controlling? | • Perceptions about the rightness, speed, scope and pace of change strategy |
| *Rational* or relational? | • Attention given to historical, cultural and political (internal and external) contexts |
| *Discrete* or multifaceted? | • Arrangements made to cater for systemic repercussions |
| **Assumptions about interpretation of change** | **Implications** |
| Is change | |
| *Directional* or reciprocal? | • Allowances made for differing versions of change process |
| *Managing people* or managing meaning? | • Credence given to different choices and evaluation of change outcomes |
| *Problem-solving* or pattern-seeking? | • Extent to which differing views, predispositions, ideologies explored and understood |

# Change Management Assumptions

## *Assumptions about intention*

It is often argued that the destiny of an organization is very much dependent on how well it attunes to and successfully confronts pressures to change. These pressures may be either internally generated such as attempts to innovate, new task and technological demands, resource scarcities, the expression of focused discontents and the like, or come externally from the environment in the form of demographic, economic, political, cultural, scientific, legislative or competitive influences.

> Within the literature, contingency theory has been widely adopted to explain organizational performance as a function of the fit between the organization's internal arrangements and environmental characteristics (Lawrence and Lorsch 1967). Volatile and uncertain environments require 'organic' management systems, threatening environments require centralised control, diverse environments require decentralised organizational forms, and stable, predictable contexts make bureaucratic forms effective. (Nicholson 1993: 208)

However, as the author points out, knowing the need for contingent relations does not necessarily mean an organization *can* adapt its design characteristics accordingly, nor integrate its sub-systems to consistently and collectively fit new or revised organizational goals. Furthermore the contingency approach tends to emphasize the need to adapt when change comes, rather than to assume change as a given. It also tends to treat as exceptional rather than endemic. Notice how this predisposition has important implications for the way boundaries are scanned, external/internal signals are interpreted, and how flexibly internal systems and structures are configured.

Another commonly held view is that individuals generally find change more threatening than desirable. Research by Dopson and Stewart (1993) found middle managers in the UK more resistant to change in the public than in the private sector. They linked this more negative stance: to seeing change as caused by a political decision rather than competitive threat; seeing change as abnormal, receiving little help to adapt to change, and seeing oneself as primarily a 'professional' than a manager. The inevitability of resistance to change through denial, inaction or action, which is a retreat to the familiar, has been challenged when it comes to managers:

> We propose an alternative interpretation, that managers respond to unfamiliarity by acting and therefore adding to it. They act in ways that convert exogenous into endogenous change. Ways of creating alternatives will perhaps be those that have produced previous success. Action in the face of unfamiliar

> change may be an attempt to recreate previous success or mastery; however, it is not a defensive denial of change, but rather a bid to better it. If action is the more common response to change among managers, then this implies a whole set of new problems and issues which are not anticipated in current change management models . . . Our research lends support to this view of change as a political process, in which managers obtain power by acting. By acting, seizing the initiative, the individual retrieves power over events. (Crouch et al. 1992: 42–4)

The lure of the HR or change strategy that promises to simultaneously improve productivity and resolve deep-seated pockets of resistance is difficult for any senior manager to resist, especially when he or she is attempting to manoeuvre herself or himself into a favourable political light prior to strategic alliance or a merger. But, even for the rank and file staff, the offer of greater discretion, more responsibility and the necessary training to support them in their new roles, is also seductive. As Martin et al. (1998) note in their analysis of attempts to change the culture of a Scottish Local Authority, 'Managers-as-consumers and consultants-as-producers of such programmes are frequently observed to consciously or unconsciously collude in applying packaged solutions to complex problems.' However, focus groups held with participants from the Housing Department revealed 'inconsistencies between espoused theory' concerning the attempted culture change and 'the theory in use': these included the counter-productive effect of increased workloads and the lack of consultation over business planning and target setting, poignantly contrasted with references to supervisors planning their own careers rather than concentrating on managing their own teams, and an announcement that the salary of the Director of Housing post was to be increased by a third!

This leads to a second related and implicit assumption, which is to regard change as something which happens to, or is perpetrated upon, a relatively passive organization. The usually unquestioned belief is that: 'change is manageable, its outcomes predictable and capable of being directed by those possessing organizational authority?' (Hosking and Anderson 1992: 7). Of course it is probably more realistic to see people and the individuals and the people who constitute the organization they work in, as 'co-constructing' each other; both acting, understanding and making sense of change as joint and dynamic players in the process. 'This perspective places the process of co-construction at the centre of person-organization relationships. This means that change is also centred, rather than being treated as a deviation from the stable norm' (Hosking and Anderson 1992: 11). Once again this placing of change at centre stage rather than as an aberration from the 'normal' smooth running of the system, makes a crucial difference to the way an organization operates, and in particular, the way change implementation is construed.

## *Assumptions about implementation*

Based on their study which examined the successful and the less effective management of strategic and organizational change in eight UK companies over more than 20 years up to 1989, Pettigrew and Whipp (1991) noted:

> Our research at firm level in four sectors of the UK economy confirms the findings of the critical school of writers – that in practice the development of HRM approach within a firm cannot be assumed. In the same way its positive contribution to competitive performance cannot be taken for granted. The dimensions which the vast majority of writers in the field minimise we see as paramount: the process by which human resources are developed such that they can contribute to the ability of the organization to accomplish strategic change and generate competitive bases. (1991: 210, 211)

Consistently, they found the difference between successful and unsuccessful change depended on the extent to which there had been a rising HRM consciousness in the organization, using situationally appropriate features to create a positive force for change, and demonstrating the need for business and people change. In short, successful organizations paid as much attention to the *process* of human resource change and its degree of progressive acceptance outside the HRM department as they did to the substance of the policies and procedures themselves.

Despite this essential highlighting of both the processual and contextual dimensions alongside the content strategic change (Whipp et al. 1989), there is nevertheless a tendency to focus on the outcomes of strategic decision-making whether in performance or quality terms. 'In this way, the underlying model is understood to have normative value for management – helping them to manipulate decision processes so they make "better" strategic decisions' (Hosking and Anderson 1992: 9).

Stacey (1996) points out that eight conditions need to be satisfied if managers are to control their organizations according to shared organizational setting (see table 13.2). This makes it clear that such control over long periods of time in an organizationally intended manner – using forecasting, planning and monitoring – is highly unlikely. 'This will be possible, on purely logical grounds, only if an organisation is simply building on old strengths and repeating and refining what it has already done. In all other circumstances the belief in intentional long-term control must be a fantasy defence to protect managers against the anxiety that uncertainty and ambiguity generate' (Stacey 1996: 140).

Box 13.1 describes how a medium-sized mutual life insurance company (under the pseudonym of Pensco) embarked on a programme of corporate change. One important plank in the change strategy was the reorganization of clerical work into team-based production groups.

This brief glimpse at the attempts to introduce new working arrangements in one organization illustrates well some of the conundrums and contradictions

**Table 13.2** Criteria for long-term organizational intention

| *Action* | *Conditions of strategic control* | *More likely scenario* |
|---|---|---|
| Set goals that remain stable over time. | The original organizational intent has been adhered to over, say, the last five years. | Managers alter their intended future state. The intention emerged, it was not predetermined. |
| Set goals that are specific and clear. | A single future state was spelled out clearly, so that achievement can be measured with precision. | The future state is articulated in sufficiently general, ambiguous or multifaceted, such that achievement can be rationalized with hindsight. |
| Set goals that are anchored to future reality. | The end state clearly defined such that organizational posture and position can be linked to financial performance. | Financial indicators plucked from thin air to demonstrate progress against strategic objectives. |
| Set goals that are overarching. | Managers have established a future state that covers the business as a whole within a consistent framework. | Managers intend many different and unconnected responses to many different changes. |
| Share the same goals. | A shared overarching future state resulting from organizational intention. | A future state emerging from the interaction of a number of individual and sub-unit intentions. |
| Set unique goals to differentiate themselves from the competition. | The intended future state is unique and specific enough to provide competitive advantage. | Future state defined in terms of 'return on capital' or 'delivering high quality' which are general rules of the game and therefore leave competitive advantage to some unspecified and therefore unintended factors. |
| Connect their goals to the action required to achieve them. | Managers deliberately use the intended future state to govern their actions, so that the connections between what they did and the state achieved can be demonstrated. | The achievement of the intended future state arises from a number of individual intentions and/or chance events. |
| Have foresight. | Managers can accurately forecast specific changes in the environment, then plan in advance the actions necessary to achieve the intended future state. | It is not possible to decide in advance what pattern of actions will yield the intended future state. It will emerge from the detail of what we do and be recognizable with hindsight. |

*Source:* Adapted from Stacey (1996: 138–9)

## BOX 13.1 WHICH COMES FIRST: THE POLICY OR THE PRACTICE?

'The team building programme can be summarised as an attempt to elicit employee commitment to the corporate objectives of profitability under the rubric of success and efficiency, and maintaining or increasing market share. In so doing, team building exposes employees to the competitive environment of the financial services market, personalising company goals and pushing responsibility for achieving corporate targets down to employees. What the team building programme aimed to achieve therefore, was the incorporation of employees into a managerially-led construction of the company-wide team, high levels of commitment to corporate/commercial objectives, motivation and self-discipline to achieve those objectives, personalising company goals, and "cascading" responsibility for achieving corporate targets down to employees.

Yet employees did not always accept the hype surrounding these management practices: the idealized notion adopted by Pensco of how "team spirit" would be advanced assumes a passivity on the part of the employees which is often contradicted. The identity of a worker cannot simply be erased and reconstructed at will by management – employees are clearly capable of some degree of distance from, resistance to, and criticism of what they regard as management manipulations . . .

There is little doubt that senior management in Pensco wanted to create a more self-disciplined clerical operative within an organizational culture transformed to reinforce and reward that discipline. However, insofar as this new form of management control was achieved it could not be directly linked with senior management decision-making. For despite management claims of success with team building, the improved working practices and self-discipline derived much more from slowly evolving and contingent changes in team working occurring in the lower reaches of the organization. Some of these improvements were enhanced as an unintended consequence of resolving recruitment shortages by employing "mature entrant" women; for it emerged almost accidentally that they could be employed as highly competent "matriarchal" leaders of teams. This was a fortuitous rather than planned strategy but once these older women were seen not only to resolve serious staffing problems but also [to have] a positive impact on team working, the "mature entrant scheme" was further institutionalized as a formal personnel policy. Otherwise team working, the publicly displayed league tables and the prizes awarded to departmental managers and section leaders responsible for specific team target success, was a line management issue.' (Kerfoot and Knights 1992: 660, 663–4) associated with change management. Invariably such initiatives start with ideal models of good practice and policy intentions in the heads of senior management. However, even if it were possible to control the methods and processes chosen to implement the changes (and this is doubtful), the full range of reactions, responses and countervailing forces are largely unpredictable. New factors emerge, unintended outcomes surface, latent support or opposition arrives from surprising corners of the organization, and external events frequently eclipse original intentions. In the case of Pensco, 'Changes in traditional working arrangements were stimulated by a number of coincidental factors, sustained by managers much lower down the hierarchy, but made possible by the encouragement of a Chief Executive who was routinely circumventing his AGM (Assistant General Manager) of Personnel in seeking to transform organizational practice' (Kerfoot and Knights 1992: 663). Organizational change, then, is inevitably iterative and cyclical in nature and contingent upon a diverse range of often unconnected and uncoordinated processes. It is also entirely possible for an organization to be experiencing discontinuous reorientations in different parts or all of its sub-systems. Such changes may be incremental, continuous and contradictory, yet when accumulated their net effect may result in radical change for the organization (Van de Ven 1988). Rarely can change be viewed as an isolated and discrete activity, without important systemic repercussions on other parts of the organization.

In his seminal work on sense-making in organizations, Weick (1995) astutely observes that 'Managers keep forgetting that it is what they do, not what they plan, that explains success. They keep giving credit to the wrong thing – namely, the plan – and having made this error; they spend more time planning and less time acting. They are astonished when more planning achieves simply nothing' (1995: 55).

## Assumptions about interpretation

This, in turn, makes the assessment of outcomes an equally imprecise art. It really depends on who you ask, what stake they have in the change process, the extent to which they have been consulted and involved, and whether they perceive their interests to have been furthered or damaged as a result. Such diverse interpretations and retrospective sense-making (Weick 1979) are not unimportant, because it is this 'history' which predisposes individuals to future change initiatives within the organization. Research by Crouch et al. (1992) suggests that:

> how managers interpret change is likely to be determined by a complex interplay of organizational and personal characteristics, such as perceived performance and perceived scope to influence outcomes, which may be partially a function of organizational seniority. Our embryonic understanding of these factors should provide an important qualification to our willingness to prescribe change management strategies, since a manager's capacity to 'manage meaning' for others is clearly dependent on her or his own

interpretations. Neither the perceptions, nor management, of change is free of a manager's interpretative framework, along with its biases and roots in past experience. (1992: 42)

We shall return to the role of SHRM on managing meaning in Part 5. Here we simply need to note that the outcomes of change processes are influenceable but ultimately beyond the control of any one actor or group of actors, and certainly not as easily orchestrated by management as some writers have led us to believe (e.g. Peters and Waterman 1982; Hammer and Champy 1993).

In some cases, human resource initiatives are applied to a 'steady-state' scenario or they are relatively small scale. However, for our purposes here we are assuming that the design and launch of new or revised human resource policies represents a fairly major strategic thrust for the organization, implying changes to personnel practices at least, and potentially having an impact on internal structures and cultures as well. In such cases the implementation of human resource strategies will resemble a change management process.

The 'inability to communicate', or capacity to bring about change in a determined manner, may be more to do with the underlying logics of change than the more tangible tactics of change being employed. Change is often presented as a matter of ideological or political choice, but the 'detailed consequences and inner logic of the alternative systems are rarely subjected to critical analysis' (Morgan 1986: 270) (see box 13.2).

# The Intentions of Change Management

## *Typical change responses*

In this section we assess some of the triggers which lead an organization to re-examine its utilization of human resources and some of the motives underlying the development of human resource strategies. Sometimes these are portrayed as calculated and well considered (e.g. Tichy et al. 1982), but in reality they are the product of iterative experimentation, trial and error, and shifting business priorities. Drawing on evidence gathered from a range of sectors in the UK (Pettigrew et al. 1988) and mainland Europe (Barham et al. 1988), a number of strategic human resource responses have been reported which organizations choose or are forced to take.

Some of these strategies were structural in emphasis, some were cultural and some focused on behavioural initiatives. Occasionally the human resource strategy encompassed all three and was an example of enlightened anticipation. At other times it was more piecemeal than coherent, more tactical than strategic, and came as a reluctant afterthought.

Invariably, however, the starting point for strategic human resource change is the impact of competitive forces which expose some kind of business performance

## BOX 13.2 MAKING SENSE OF ORGANIZATIONAL CHANGE: TELLING A GOOD STORY

'If accuracy is nice but not necessary in sensemaking, then what is necessary? The answer is, something that preserves plausibility and coherence, something that is reasonable and memorable, something that embodies past experience and expectations, something that resonates with other people, something that can be constructed retrospectively but also can be used prospectively, something that captures both feeling and thought, something that allows for embellishment to fit current oddities, something that is fun to construct. In short, what is necessary in sense-making is a good story.

A good story holds disparate elements together long enough to energize and guide action, plausibly enough to allow people to make retrospective sense of whatever happens, and engagingly enough that others will contribute their own inputs in the interest of sensemaking.

Sensemaking is about accounts that are socially acceptable and credible. Stated differently, "filtered information is less accurate but, if the filtering is effective, more understandable". It would be nice if these acceptable accounts were also accurate. But in an equivocal, postmodern world, infused with the politics of interpretation and conflicting interests and inhabited by people with multiple shifting identities, an obsession with accuracy seems fruitless, and not of much practical help, either. Of much more help are the symbolic trappings of sense-making, trappings such as myths, metaphors, platitudes, fables, epics, and paradigms. Each of these resources contains a good story. And a good story, like a workable cause map, shows patterns that may already exist in the puzzles an actor now faces, or patterns that could be created anew in the interest of more order and sense in the future. The stories are templates. They are products of previous efforts at sense-making. They explain. And they energize. And those are two important properties of sense-making that we remain attentive to when we look for plausibility instead of accuracy.'
(Weick 1995: 60–1)

gap. In response an organization reassesses its product market or makes technical changes to its operation. This may involve new concepts of service provision, different channels of distribution, restructuring and/or decentralizing business units (sometimes as part of a policy of internationalization, see chapter 6, International Human Resource Strategies), acquiring new business or engaging in cost-reduction activities. Each constitutes a strategic shift and usually implies the need for new competencies or skills and in some cases, values, amongst its staff.

In the short term, temporary advantage on costs, for example, can be achieved by the imposition of what some writers (Legge 1989) have termed 'hard' HR policies such as compulsory redundancy delayering, 'rightsizing' or other restructuring methods. However, to sustain a cost reduction/leadership strategy requires a deeper and significant change in the attitude and behaviour of the employees that remain. Similarly commitment to quality, another key competitive nostrum of the 1980s and 1990s, requires a long-term perspective. This linkage between business strategy and employee attitudes and behaviour has led to the notion of a 'soft' HR approach in which the employee is regarded as a valued asset to be developed and not just exploited as an expensive factor of production. But how can human resource policy priorities be formulated and matched appropriately to the stage of an organization's strategic development? In a paper which makes this linkage more explicit Schuler and Jackson (1987) use analysis of employee role behaviours and a typology of HRM practices in six key areas which are linked to notions of competitive strategy.

## *Claimed causal patterns of change*

This kind of analysis helps to demonstrate the likely linkage between an organization's product-market strategy and the desired, relevant human resource practices most likely to assist in 'delivering' that strategy. Such sensitivity to the demands of customers and the nature of competition is, after all, one of the key elements that differentiates human resource strategy from the traditional conception of personnel management. Another value of this contingency approach is that it highlights the possibility of multiple human resource strategies, for example, in different business units or functional areas of the same organization and/or the ability to change human resource policies over time to complement the changing requirements of evolving product or service life-cycles and business priorities. In short, the idea that there is 'one best way' to design and implement human resource strategies is scotched.

However, this attempt to 'fit' human resource strategy and business strategy has come to be viewed as somewhat prescriptive and not reflective of reality. An empirical study cited by Boxall (1991), suggests, for example, that while there is partial support for 'the proposition that organizations pursuing an innovation strategy seek to develop personnel practices for hourly paid workers broadly consistent with that thrust, it also demonstrated that personnel practices vary with manufacturing technology, industry sector, organizational structure and size and union presence. Most significantly, the research demonstrated that personnel practices were substantially different for managerial and hourly employees across the whole sample . . .' (Boxall 1991: 67). The 'fit' model is also underpinned, Boxall argues, by an overly-rationalistic conception of how strategy is formed, suggesting that strategy is always deliberate or formulated rather than emergent (Mintzberg and Waters 1985). Furthermore the empirical validity of simplistically mapping HRM practices to strategy has been questioned in a recent review by Ogbonna (1994). He notes that 'although researchers have articulated the links between strategy and culture on the one hand, and between strategy and human resource management on the other, there has been very little attempt to

**Table 13.3** Employee role behaviour and HRM policies associated with particular business strategies

| *Strategy* | *Employee role behaviour* | *HRM policies* |
|---|---|---|
| 1 Innovation | A high degree of creative behaviour | Jobs that require close interaction and co-ordination among groups of individuals. |
| | Longer-term focus | Performance appraisals that are more likely to reflect longer-term and group-based achievements. |
| | A relatively high level of co-operative, interdependent behaviour | Jobs that allow employees to develop skills that can be used in other positions in the firm; compensation systems that emphasize internal equity rather than external or market-based equity. |
| | A moderate degree of concern for quality | Pay rates that tend to be low, but that allow employees to be stockholders and have more freedom to choose the mix of components that make up their pay package. |
| | A moderate concern for quantity. An equal degree of concern for process and results. A greater degree of risk taking. A high tolerance of ambiguity and unpredictability. | Broad career paths to reinforce the development of a broad range of skills. |
| 2 Quality enhancement | Relative repetitive and predictable behaviours. A more long-term or intermediate focus | Relatively fixed and explicit job descriptions. High levels of employee participation in decisions relevant to immediate work conditions and the job itself. |
| | A moderate amount of co-operative, interdependent behaviour. | A mix of individual and group criteria for performance appraisal that is mostly short term and results oriented. |
| | A high concern for quality | A relatively egalitarian treatment of employees and some guarantees of employment security. |
| | A modest concern for quantity of output. High concern for process. Low risk-taking activity. Commitment to the goals of the organization. | Extensive and continuous training and development of employees. |

**Table 13.3** (continued)

| *Strategy* | *Employee role behaviour* | *HRM policies* |
|---|---|---|
| 3 Cost reduction | Relatively repetitive and predictable behaviour | Relatively fixed and explicit job descriptions that allow little room for ambiguity. |
| | A rather short-term focus | Narrowly designed jobs and narrowly defined career paths that encourage specialization, expertise and efficiency. |
| | Primarily autonomous or individual activity. Moderate concern for quality | Short-term results-oriented performance appraisals. Close monitoring of market pay levels for use in making compensation decisions. |
| | High concern for quantity of output. Primary concern for results. Low risk-taking activity. Relatively high degree of comfort with stability | Minimal levels of employee training and development. |

*Source:* Schuler and Jackson (1987: 213).

either develop the link between culture and human resource management or indeed link the three concepts' (1994: 1).

Another weakness of contingency conceptualizations is that they tend to underestimate the *way* change is introduced (see box 13.4). Human resource decisions, like any other area of strategic policy-making, may appear to have objective soundness, but in fact they are inevitably influenced by the cultural context of the organization and interpreted by those involved according to their personal frames of reference, their subjective motivations and the incomplete information they possess at the time. For example, one important interest group omitted from table 13.2 above is that of the unions and their view of what constitutes a safe, equitable and motivational working environment. Furthermore, fundamental change is only likely to occur when the prevailing paradigm of the organization has been challenged, discredited or devalued (Johnson, 1987). A number of factors can contribute to this erosion: the arrival of an 'outsider', the exposure of deficiencies in the current paradigm (via challenging and divergent views); the reconfiguration of power around a new axis, the activating and legitimizing of dissent and the overt advocacy of a new paradigm by those with power. It is noticeable, for instance, how many human resource interventions are ushered in by newly-appointed chief executives enjoying a brief honeymoon period in which to assert their particular brand of people management (see, for instance, Larson, 1996).

**BOX 13.3 STRATEGY FORMATION: RATIONAL OR RATIONALIZED**

In our view it is the limits to managerial action which are as telling in understanding the outcome of strategic changes rather than the assumed width of their discretion. Many views of strategy and competition emphasize the complexity of the firm's environment. We give equal emphasis to the intricacy not only of the environment but also of the firm itself. The processes by which strategic changes are made seldom move directly through neat, successive stages of analysis, choice and implementation. Given the powerful internal characteristics of the firm it would be unusual if they did not affect the process: more often they transform it – seldom is there an easily isolated logic to strategic change. Instead, that process may derive its motive force from an amalgam of economic, personal and political imperatives. Their interaction through time requires that those responsible for managing that process make continual assessments, repeated choices and multiple adjustments.
(From Pettigrew and Whipp 1991: 30–1)

## Change Management Strategies

So far we have examined the intentions behind attempts to manage change in organizations: the knee-jerk reactions and the more considered strategies, the explicit 'game plans' and the covert agendas, the public rationalizations and the private motives. To distinguish between intention and implementation is, of course, artificial for two reasons. First, how change strategies unfold depends very much on the mental maps inside the heads of decision-makers. Whether they are articulated or not, each of us possess different assumptions not only about *what* changes are required (in the workplace and out) but – even more crucially – about *how* they are to be enacted. Much of the conflict associated with change derives 'from the differences in the ways each of us constructs reality' (McWhinney 1992: 21); in other words, it is as much about personal values as the substance of the change itself. Secondly, intention does not precede implementation in quite the sequential way more linear, deterministic models of change would have us believe. With these important qualifications in mind this section assesses the choices available as an organization embarks upon change.

Invariably, the intent of a change strategy is to alter the way organizational members think, behave, interact, communicate, make decisions, reward, monitor, praise and coach. In short, the way they perform. Such changes may be sought at an individual or work group level or across the whole organization; they may require immediate action or be phased in over a period of years; they may be radical or incremental in nature; and the people involved may be receptive, indifferent or intransigent. Each of these conditions influences the unfolding of the change process. Subsequent chapters will explore more fully both the possibilities and difficulties associated with the claimed causality of specific change strategies. Here we note three broad approaches that have received support in the literature. The first argues that until the culture of an organization is reoriented little else will change, except at a cosmetic level and over a limited period of time. An alternative view is that behavioural change and enhanced organizational performances flows – primarily – from the way the organization is structured with regard to its strategy. Finally, a third view points to the importance of the *style* of change management, as against its intrinsic content.

## Cultural change

Culture change is often glibly prescribed but is more difficult to achieve in practice. It is relatively straightforward to change what Payne (1991) calls the explicit culture by making changes such as removal of clocking in/out, the phasing out of canteens for different seniority levels, the introduction of development centres, the restructuring of business units and so on. Underlying values or implicit cultures are somewhat harder to shift and usually require a heavy investment in education and training over a sustained period of time. What is significant about several of the cultural change interventions reported in recent years at organizations like British Telecom (Price and Murphy 1987), Billiton, Royal Dutch Shell (Benjamin and Mabey 1990), British Airways (Goodstein and Burke 1991), Manchester Airport (Jackson 1992), and Asea Brown Boveria (Richardson and Denton 1996), is the way multiple leverage points are used to initiate and support the changes and the way organization-wide human resource practices are deliberately aligned to reinforce desired cultural changes.

Another distinctive feature of many organization change programmes is the denunciation of previous principles of organization, management and structure. They are not offering a mere shift in direction. Rather they are going the whole way by suggesting that traditional organizational systems and processes are ill-suited to contemporary competitive conditions.

Kanter (1990: 356), for example, insists that organizations must 'either move away from bureaucratic guarantees to post-entrepreneurial flexibility or they stagnate'. Central to many of these ideas is the argument that traditional forms of organization and management, through their increasingly complicated structures, rules and regulation, have reached their limits and are inappropriate for newly current conditions. Dismantling and replacing them, however, may be more difficult than anticipated because they are supported and maintained by a cultural web of informal organizational processes and communication networks, rituals and routines and power structures (we discuss this further in chapters 15 and 16). Because all these factors are mutually reinforcing it is usually impossible to change one without changing them all.

Two favoured ways of going about a culture change process are described by Hendry and Hope:

> One is through a comprehensive programme of staff involvement, in which groups of staff are encouraged and assisted to retrace the steps by which top management first realised the need for change programme for themselves. The other is through the propagation of a corporate vision, in which the new culture is 'sold' to the company staff, through a combination of charismatic leadership, symbolic action and powerful advertising. Both methods depend heavily on effective communications, but the first relies mainly on rational argument, the second on emotive response. (Hendry and Hope 1994: 403)

However, as these authors admit, the 'jury is still out' on how effective these methods can be. Rajan (1997) carried out a study of 375 service organizations across ten different industries in the finance sector, to assess the success of culture change programmes in UK and mainland Europe. Seven years into their change programmes, most companies 'have proved strong on intentions and weak on deliverables'. He attributes this indifferent outcome to a combination of factors: the difficulty of empowering staff in the face of increased central, regulatory pressures (in the aftermath of City scandals) and increased competition leading to a 'zero-sum' game in which winners only lose because losers lose; the failure to ensure that senior management had the values, skills and behaviours consistent with the new internal realities; the lack of alignment between core values, business values and the artefacts and systems of the organization, leading to cynicism about the 'hype' of corporately-led culture change.

Partly, at least, this is due to the fact that there are few, empirically-based frameworks to guide the implementation of cultural change strategies. The closest we come to a thoroughly researched model is in the field of organization development (OD), which has been defined as 'an intervention strategy that uses group processes to focus on the whole culture of an organisation in order to bring about planned change' (Rowlandson 1984: 90).

Early criticisms of OD focused on the inability of experiential groupwork to achieve organizational goals, the over-reliance on personal changes in trust and openness (rather than taking on board the politics of the organization) and its ideological bias against strong management (Hollway 1993: 112). Somewhat ironically, more recent culture change programmes based around shared values have been criticized for being based upon managerialist, top-down assumptions (Beer et al. 1990); for overlooking the inherent contradictions of an organization striving for a 'strong culture' on the one hand and skills flexibility and devolved responsibility on the other (Legge 1989; Ogbonna 1992); and for underestimating the cynicism of professional knowledge workers in the 1990s who are increasingly more resistant to corporate cultural manipulation (Hendry and Hope 1994). More fundamental still is the presumption that culture can be changed in a deliberate and predetermined manner to implement strategic change.

It would be a mistake to regard culture-focused changes as synonymous with OD, however. Bate (1995) has outlined a number of cultural change approaches, and he argues that each have their appropriate place at different stages in the management of change (table 13.4). So it is likely that the disruptive style of the aggressive approach would prove useful when used positively as an unfreezing device at the start of a large-scale human resource initiative. This might involve restructuring responsibilities and lines of communication and introducing new performance review and reward systems. The collusive style of the conciliative approach might then be used to facilitate a period of consultation and ownership; more subtle human resource management levers could include career development activities and revised induction procedures. At this point the emerging ideas would need pulling together into a systematic consensus perhaps via the indoctrinative approach, although it would be better for the emphasis to be on learning rather than on teaching – especially where changes in norms and attitudes are being sought. Extensive training would also figure prominently, reinforced by well-defined succession planned and appraisal systems to reward newly-acquired skills and competencies. Once the parameters for the change have been established, the networking and alliance building typical of a corrosive approach could be harnessed to translate and implant the normative order. This would best be achieved by on-the-job human resource management in the shape of informal reward and recognition, role modelling and team briefing. At this stage conciliation might work well again to give enduring form and shape to the new order.

## Structural change

An alternative and very different change strategy is that which addresses the structure of the organization and the design of jobs and working arrangements as the key levers of change.

The linkage between strategy and structure is well established in the literature, stemming from Chandler (1962). He argued convincingly that structural change is triggered by an organization's inability to fully realize the strategy it is following due to administrative deficiencies caused by a mismatch between the new strategy and the existing structure. This argument that growth strategies result in different types of organizational structure has been taken further by Galbraith and Nathanson (1979), and Miller (1986).

At the workplace level, early organization analysis in the UK (e.g. Rice 1958; Trist et al. 1963) had an impact on programmes to restructure the workplace in the 1970s: specifically autonomous group working and initiatives under the 'Quality of Working Life' banner. More recent evidence (Fortune 1990) points to a QWL resurgence associated with a productivity breakthrough in the 1990s. Cameron, Francis and Storey (1992) report that despite some resistance from supervisors and middle managers the team concept is spreading rapidly in industries other than the motor industry, such as aerospace, electronics, food processing, steel and financial services. This has also found expression in the rush by western managers to attempt the introduction of Japanese work practices into their organizations. Gleave and Oliver (1990) reported that two-thirds of *The Times* 1000 were using or planning to use just-in-time production and 95 per cent were using or planning to use total quality control. This, they suggest, is due to the demonstrated capability of the major Japanese corporations to engineer a

**Table 13.4** Approaches to cultural change

| *Approach* | *Characteristics* | *It can:* | *But it usually:* |
|---|---|---|---|
| *Aggressive* | • Rapid change<br>• Dismantles traditional values<br>• New culture is non-complex<br>• Top-down monitored<br>• Detailed plans/ actions | • lead to a strong, integrated culture<br>• suit a situation where there is a simple source of authority | • mobilizes dissent<br>• is politically naïve<br>• lacks skills, breadth of support leads to crisis or change |
| *Conciliative* | • Reasonable, quiet<br>• Slow grafting onto new values<br>• Deals with means, not ends<br>• Collusion, not confrontation<br>• Continuous development<br>• Based on power and control | • lead to a 'common-sense' welcoming of the new culture<br>• disarm opposition | • loses sight of its radical intent<br>• gets seduced back to status quo |
| *Corrosive* | • Uses informal networks<br>• Unseen manipulation<br>• High participation<br>• Act first, legitimize later<br>• Planned programmed | • lead to genuine and large-scale change initiated by small scale network | • is used to defend existing order and oppose change initiators |
| *Indoctrinative* | • Explicit learning process<br>• Socializing<br>• Unified, logical framework<br>• Advocates one world view | • lead to wide-scale changes at an informational, technical level | • does not succeed in bringing about fundamental cultural change |

*Source:* Adapted from Bate (1990).

good 'fit' between their manufacturing strategy and their human resources strategy (1990; see also Oliver et al. 1992).

An example of this strategic approach is given in box 13.4. At Isuzu (renamed IBC) there was a determination to improve output at team level aided and abetted by appropriate training, job redefinition and a reworked labour agreement. Almost as a by-product this appears to have resulted in a change of attitudes and possibly even the culture at the plant.

Most organization change programmes begin by targetting the attitudes and values held by individuals, the assumption being that once the core culture is

## BOX 13.4 ISUZU: INDIGENIZATION OF IMPERIALISM?

By 1987, after 10 years of loss-making, the Bedford Commercial Vehicle part of the Vauxhall plant at Luton was facing closure by its owners General Motors. Poor labour relations and intense foreign competition had plagued the company such that it was now haemorrhaging £500,000 per week, adding up to total losses of £26 million per year (Wille 1990). Drastic action was called for to avert massive redundancies in Luton.

Such action came. In September 1987 General Motors entered a joint venture with Japan's Isuzu, which took a 40 per cent share in the business and appointed one of its Japanese executives as president of the new business. Together with four Japanese advisers and a British Vice-President he helped the new business, renamed IBC vehicles, return to profit. This took three years. On the face of it the unthinkable has happened. The best elements of Japanese working practices have been indigenized and grafted into the heartland of British car assembly; worker attitudes have shifted radically; and commercially the plant has been turned around. Another, more cynical interpretation is that at a time of economic crisis, foreign systems have been imposed, the unions have been railroaded into guarantees of co-operation, and a small number of employees are working harder to produce more with fewer defects.

The human resource strategy, conceived in order to bring about these radical changes in the company, consisted of four interrelated ingredients. The first three were structural and 'aggressive' (Bate 1995). A totally new employment agreement was drawn up, a radically revised inventory production system was introduced and the whole workforce was reconfigured into teams. Fourthly, in order to facilitate these changes the organization embarked upon comprehensive skills training.

The employee agreement hammered out by unions and management during 1987 was an essential springboard for a return to profitability; without it the joint venture could not and would not have been launched. In many ways it was an example of an attempt to minimize the extent to which employees and their representatives could interfere with the production efficiently as a desirable goal (Marsden et al. 1985: 118).

(Adapted from Mabey and Mallory 1995)

beginning to shift, then and only then, appropriate systems and procedures can be put into place in order to bring about the desired behaviour change. This in turn is believed to translate into enhanced quality of service and produce customer satisfaction and internal co-operation. At IBC the model of change was almost the reverse: the unspoken assumption here was that a radical redefinition of organization roles, systems and procedures would lead to a positive step-change in behaviour at an individual and team level. Apparently not anticipated was the fact that these new employee behaviour patterns would lead, over time, to a wholescale revision of workplace norms, beliefs and possibly even values, which collectively determine culture. The seeming success of targeting the level of relationships, roles and responsibilities as primary levers for renewal lends support to the argument put forward in an influential paper by Beer et al. (1990).

## Change management style

Attempts to trace a direct correspondence between the strategic intent of an organization and its human resource strategies, whether cultural or structural in their emphasis, can still neglect the vital role of the organizational change programme – or 'game plan' – that is being used to move the organization towards improved performance. According to Stace and Dunphy (1991): 'We can . . . predict more about which human resource strategies should be used from knowing the degree of change and type of change leadership being exercised than we can by knowing the corporate or business strategies being pursued by the management of the organization. It is the degree of internal change and repositioning required which makes the most powerful impact on which human resource strategies will be chosen. So change theory is the missing link in line business strategy/human resource management model' (1991: 271). This is not unlike the 'cement' in the model of HRM proposed by Guest (1992b: 129) which depicts leadership, culture and strategy as binding the human resource system together and ensuring that it is taken seriously within a given organization.

Stace and Dunphy (1991) put forward a situational approach to change management, challenging the view that incremental and collaborative approaches are the only, or even the best, way to implement change. Alongside 'developmental' HR strategy – which is compatible with much of the relatively recent HRM and cultural change models – they describe three other HR strategy types and the conditions for their use (see table 13.5). The two important dimensions for choice of change strategy appear to be first, the scale of change (from fine tuning through to corporate transformation), and second the style of change (collaborative through to coercive).

Based on extensive research they related this process model to how each aspect of change was managed in 13 Australian organizations. From this they discovered that:

- the dominant HR strategies were task focused and turnaround, reflecting the relative absence of stable or growth markets and the pressing need to produce greater business flexibility, more work unit autonomy and less centralism via radical change strategies (see figure 13.1).
- two organizations in the study were pursuing developmental HR strategies, and two were following paternalistic HR strategies due to their highly protected, nearly monopolistic position in their respective sectors.

**Table 13.5** HR strategy types and conditions

| *Type and features of HR strategy* | *Conditions for use* |
|---|---|
| **Task-focused** | |
| HR strategy is strongly focused on the business unit. | |
| • Strong bottom line orientation.<br>• Emphasis on workforce planning, job redesign and work-practice reviews.<br>• Focus on tangible reward structures.<br>• Internal or external recruitment.<br>• Functional skills training and formalized multi-skilling.<br>• Formalized industrial relations procedures.<br>• Strong business unit culture. | Use when markets/products/services are undergoing major change and 'niche' strategies are prevalent. HR strategies must deliver the capacity for rapid structural, systems, skill and cultural changes. Strong emphasis on business unit autonomy, maximum devolution, rightsizing (continues redeployment), outsourcing of labour. |
| **Developmental** | |
| HR strategy is jointly actioned by the corporate human resource unit and the business units.<br>• Emphasis on developing the individual, and the team.<br>• Internal recruitment, where possible.<br>• Extensive development programmes.<br>• Use of 'intrinsic' rewards.<br>• Corporate organizational development given high priority.<br>• Strong emphasis on corporate culture. | Use when markets are growing and product/market innovation is desired. HR strategies must create cross-organizational synergy, and a 'market leader' culture. Strong emphasis on individual development, corporate-culture management, developing a strong internal labour market (promotions/appointments) and team skills. |
| **Turnaround** | |
| HR strategy is driven for a short period by the executive leadership, characterized by challenging, restructuring or abolishing human resource systems, structures and methodologies.<br>• Major structural changes affecting the total organization and career structure.<br>• Downsizing, retrenchments.<br>• Lateral recruitment of key executives from outside.<br>• Executive team building, creating a new 'mindset'.<br>• Breaking with the 'old' culture. | Use when the business environment changes dramatically: when the organization is not in fit with its environment, and when the business strategy of the organization radically changes. HR strategies must break and abolish redundant HR practices, structures, and redefine a new culture. Strong emphasis on forced downsizing, lateral recruitment, new HR systems and radical work and job restructuring. |
| **Paternalistic** | |
| HR practice is centrally administered.<br>• Centralist personnel orientation.<br>• Emphasis on procedures, precedent and uniformity.<br>• Organization and methods studies.<br>• Inflexible internal appointments policy.<br>• Emphasis on operational and supervisory training.<br>• Industrial awards and agreements set the HR framework. | Use only in very limited mass-production situations where the organization has an absolute monopoly on stable markets/products, HR strategies are used as devices for 'control' and uniformity of procedure/ operations. Strong emphasis on formal, detailed job descriptions, formalistic employer–employee industrial relationships and industrial 'awards'. |

*Source:* Adapted from Stace and Dunphy (1991: 275, 279).

When the performance of the chosen companies was analysed according to their chosen organizational change strategies and HR strategies, the authors concluded that:

- task-focused and developmental HR strategies are associated with medium- to high-performing organizations.
- turnaround HR strategies are associated with organizations attempting to regain fit due to poor performance or a rapidly changing environment.
- paternalistic HR strategies are associated with lower performing organizations or monopolies.

As a result of his study of the way in which changes were being made in 15 UK organizations, Storey (1992) also rejects the notion of a universal change approach: 'some organizations . . . steer a major new approach to labour management in a step-by-step manner; others launched total programmes. Some of the changes were progressed in a top-down, cascade way, others were bottom-up in character. In some cases the human resource or personnel/IR specialists were intimately involved; in others the process was clearly driven from elsewhere and these specialists were either marginal or even acted in opposition. The overall lesson about managing change was that there is no set formula' (1992: 120). Storey also used two dimensions by which to analyse the 'types' of managed change processes: the degree to which change is unilaterally devised by management or negotiated by joint agreement, and the extent to which the path of change

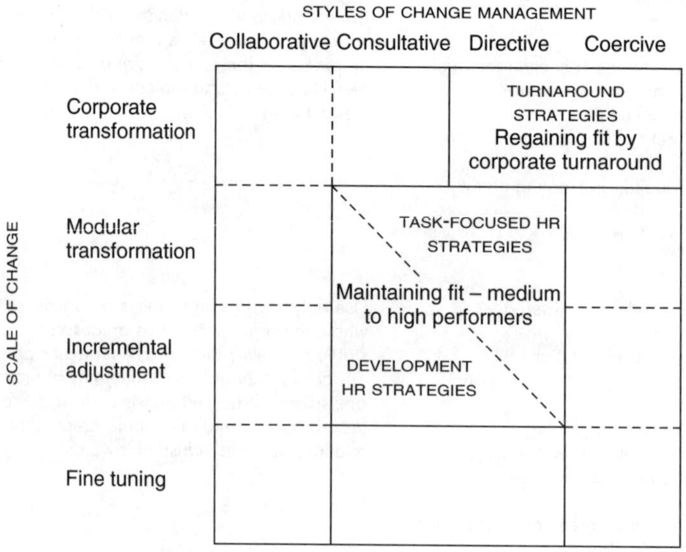


**Figure 13.1** The relationship between change strategy, HR strategy and performance
*Source:* Adapted from Stace and Dunphy (1991: 277, 281)

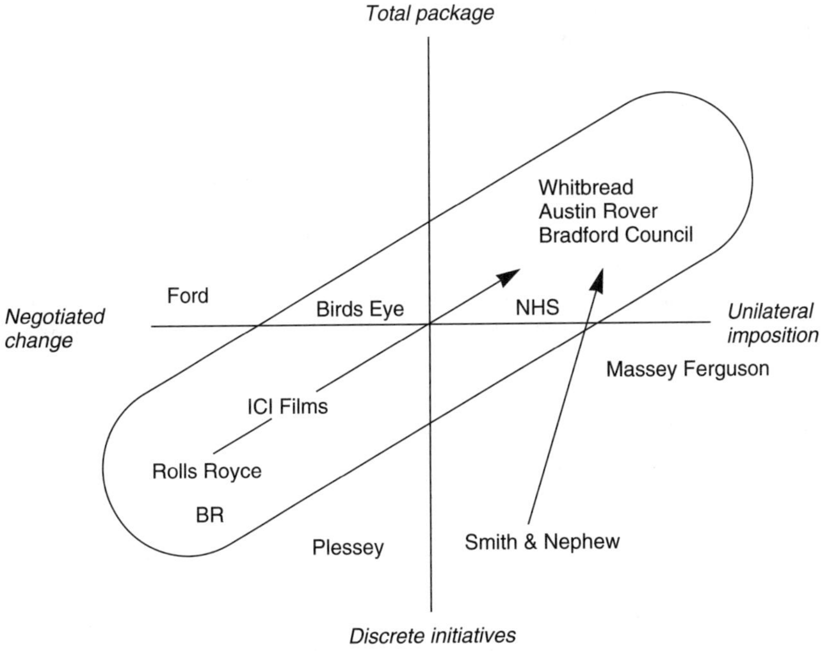

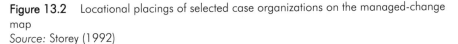

**Figure 13.2** Locational placings of selected case organizations on the managed-change map
*Source:* Storey (1992)

conforms to a total package or is characterized by a series of discrete initiatives. Each of the case study organizations were then located on the resulting 'managed-change map' (see figure 13.2). Given the similar typologies, it is interesting to note the resemblance between this map and that generated by Stace and Dunphy (figure 13.1). Storey notes a 'significant tendency' for the change process used by the organizations he studied in the UK to move toward the Type 1 (Topdown systemic), where there was a greater willingness by management to operate outside the negotiating machinery, a greater degree of careful planning and attempts to integrate different human resource initiatives rather than making changes in an opportunistic fashion. Although in both cases the samples are small, these two studies in Australia (Stace and Dunphy 1991) and the UK (Storey 1992) offer tentative, though consistent, support for the following notions: first, that organizations use a number and mixture of change management styles (with 'hard' and 'soft' approaches not necessarily being irreconcilable); second, that turnaround or task-focused HR strategies and top-down systemic change appears to predominate; third, that there is a discernible shift toward more strategically oriented, total change approaches; and fourth, that both task-focused and developmental HR strategies are associated with medium to high performing organizations.

# Conclusions and Summary

We have seen in this chapter that managing change in organization is by no means as straightforward as it seems. All too often the outcomes bear little resemblance to what was originally intended, and the ramifications rumble on – often counter-productively – long beyond intended timeframes.

It is amidst this confusion that those who launched the change intervention invest the organizational impact with new rhetoric – perhaps using selective 'success stories' to shape new ideas and images that will hopefully fuel increased effort, a new phase or a redirection. It is here that assumptions underpinning the change methodology might be revisited and, depending on whether the organization has the capacity for single- or double-loop learning (Argyris and Schon 1981) new objectives will be fashioned or commitment to traditional ones escalated (Staw 1980). It is at this stage that an official version of what has actually taken place will emerge: the 'reality' of organization change outcomes will be documented. Of course, this won't prevent other 'versions' from circulating. The extent and degree of diversion or damage caused by such parallel accounts will depend on the extent to which stakeholders on the receiving end feel their access to power and relative status has been enhanced and whether personal and collective goals have been furthered by the changes. In all these ways, then, the objective nature of the change process will be retrospectively reconstructed to form the historical – and even, in time, mythological – context of successive change interventions. Given that such interventions are never discrete – rather ebbing and flowing – it can be seen that the cultural context of change is ever complex and potent. Organizational decision-making rarely follows a rational problem-solving pathway: this is as true at the inception of change initiatives as it is during the implementation and evaluation stages. Such decisions, about the need to change or revise the way things are done, are frequently an organization's 'garbage can', into which various problems and the solutions of different participants will be dumped (Cohen et al. 1976). Thus the principal participants will be influenced by all sorts of things, such as prior commitments and alliances, the need to justify past actions, the wish to make scapegoats of certain individuals or departments, the desire to cement loyalties and the opportunity for recruiting, socializing and power-broking. None of which bears much resemblance to the highly rational models of strategic planning that have dominated the change literature for so long.

## Key Points

- Different change strategies are predicated upon different assumptions about the inevitability, costs, controllability and ultimate value of any 'package' of change proposals.
- The predispositions of those initiating and championing change will have as much influence on the outcomes as the intrinsic worth of the strategy itself.

- While conventional change strategies have some currency when managing human resource interventions, they typically underestimate the process issues associated with change management.
- Increasingly popular are change management programmes that encompass a wide range of HR policies and practices. Whether culture change or structural change is the priority, intentionality remains problematic.
- One arena where it appears choice *can* deliberately impact on outcomes is that of the approach, style or game plan governing the proposed changes.

## Discussion Questions

1. Can organization change be managed?
2. In what way are individuals co-creators of organizational change?
3. How helpful is Organization Development as an approach to managing strategic HR change?
4. Thinking of a current organizational change you are involved in, which approach or style would be most appropriate to adopt?

## References

Argyris, C. and Schon, D. (1981) *Organizational Learning*, Reading, MA: Addison-Wesley.

Barham, K., Fraser, J., and Heath, L. (1988) *Management for the Future*, Berkhamstead, Herts: Foundation for Management Education and Ashridge Management College.

Bate, S. P. (1990) 'A description, evaluation and integration of four approaches to the management of cultural change in organisations', Paper presented to The British Academy of Management Conference, Glasgow, September.

Bate, S. (1995) *Strategies for Cultural Change*, London: Butterworth Heinemann.

Beckhard, R. and Harris, R. (1987) *Organisation Transitions: Managing complex change* Reading, MA: Addison-Wesley.

—— and Pritchard, W. (1992) *Changing the Essence: The art of creating and leading fundamental change*, San Francisco, CA: Jossey-Bass.

Beer, M., Eisenstat, R. A., and Spector, B. (1990) 'Why change programmes don't produce change', *Harvard Business Review*, Nov./Dec., 158–66.

Benjamin, G. and Mabey, C. (1990) 'A case of organisation transformation', *Management Education and Development*, vol. 21, no. 5, 327–34.

Boxall, P. F. (1991) 'Strategic human resource management: Beginnings of a new theoretical sophistication?' *Human Resource Management Journal*, vol. 12, no. 3, 60–79.

Buller, P. F. (1988) 'For successful strategic change: Blend OD practice with strategic management', *Organization Dynamics*, vol. 16, 42–55.

Cameron, S., Francis A., and Storey, J. (1992) 'Structural Strategies', in *B884 Human Resource Strategies*, Open Business School, Milton Keynes: Open University.

Chandler, A. D. (1962) *Strategy and Structure: Chapters in the history of the American industrial enterprise*, Cambridge, MA: MIT Press.

Cohen, M. D., March, J. G., and Olsen, J. P. (1976) 'People, problems, solutions and the ambiguity of relevance' in J. G. March and J. Olsen (eds) *Ambiguity and Choice in Organizations*, Bergen: Universitetsforlaget.

Coopey, J. and Hartley, J. (1989) 'Tensions in organisation commitment', Paper presented to the British Psychological Society conference, Windermere, January.

Crouch, A., Sinclair, A., and Hintz, P. (1992) 'Myths of managing change' in D. M. Hosking and N. Anderson (eds) *Organizational Change and Innovation*, London: Routledge.

Dopson, S. and Stewart, R. (1993) 'What is happening to middle management?' In C. Mabey and B. Mayon-White (eds) *Managing Change*, London: Paul Chapman Publishing.

Fortune Magazine (1990) 'Who needs a boss?' *Fortune International*, 7 May.

French, W. and Bell, C. (1973; 1984, 3rd edition) *Organization Development: Behavioural science interventions for organization improvement*, Englewood Cliffs, NJ: Prentice-Hall.

—— (1978) *The Personnel Management Process*, Boston, MA: Houghton Mifflin.

Fullerton, H., Ironside, A., and Price, C. (1989) 'A picture of health in the 1990s', *The Health Service Journal*, June, 73–82.

Galbraith, J. R. and Nathanson, D. A. (1979) 'The role of organisational structure and process in strategy implementation', in D. E. Schendel and C. W. Hofer (eds) *Strategic Management: A new view of business policy and planning*. Boston, MA: Little Brown.

Gleave, S. and Oliver, N. (1990) 'Human resource management in Japanese manufacturing companies in the UK: 5 case studies', *Journal of General Management*, vol. 16, no. 1, 54–68.

Goodstein, L. and Burke, W. (1991) 'Creating successful organisation change', *Organisation Dynamics*, Spring, 5–17.

Guest, D. (1992) 'Employee commitment and control', in J. Hartley and G. M. Stephenson (eds) *Employee Relations*, Oxford: Blackwell.

Hammer, M. and Champy, J. (1993) *Reengineering the Corporation: A manifesto for business revolution*, London: Nicholas Brealey.

Hendry, J. and Hope, V. (1994) 'Cultural change and competitive performance', *European Management Journal*, vol. 12, no. 4, 401–6.

Hollway, W. (1993) *Work Psychology and Organizational Behaviour*, London: Sage.

Hosking, D. and Anderson, N. (1992) 'Organization change and innovation challenges for European work and organization psychology', in D. Hosking and N. Anderson (eds) *Organization Change and Innovation Psychological Perspectives and Practices in Europe*, London: Routledge.

Iles, P. A., Mabey, C., and Robertson, I. (1990) 'HRM practices and employee commitment: Possibilities, pitfalls and paradoxes', *British Journal of Management*, vol. 1, no. 3, 147–57.

Inns, D. (1996) 'Organisation development as a journey', in C. Oswick and D. Grant (eds) *Organisation Development: Metaphorical explorations*, London: Pitman.

Jackson, L. (1992) 'Achieving change in business culture', *Management Decision*, vol. 30, no. 6, 149–55.

Johnson, G. (1987) *Strategic Change and the Management Process*, Oxford: Blackwell.

Kanter, R. M. (1990) *When Giants Learn to Dance*, London: Unwin Hyman.

—— (1991) 'Championing change: An interview with Bell Atlantic's CEO Raymond Smith', *Harvard Business Review*, Jan./Feb., 119–30.

Keenoy, T. (1990) 'HRM: A case of the wolf in sheep's clothing?', *Personnel Review*, vol. 19, no. 2, 3–9.

Kerfoot, D. and Knights, D. (1992) 'Planning for personnel – human resource management reconsidered', *Journal of Management Studies*, vol. 29, no. 5, 651–68.

Kleiner, B. H. and Corrigan, W. A. (1989) 'Understanding organisational change', *Leadership and Organisation Development Journal*, vol. 10, no. 3, 25–31.

Larson, H. (1996) 'Oticon: Thinking the unthinkable: radical laws successful organisational change', in J. Storey (ed.) *Blackwell Cases in Human Resource Management*, Oxford: Blackwell.

Lawrence, P. R. and Lorsch, J. W. (1967) 'Differentation and integration in complex organizations', *Administrative Science Quarterly*, vol. 12, 1–47.

Legge, K. (1989) 'Human resource management: a critical analysis', in J. Storey (ed.) *New Perspectives on Human Resource Management*, London: Routledge, 19–40.

Mabey, C. and Mayon-White, W. (1993) *Managing Change*, London: Paul Chapman Publishing.

—— and Mallory, G. (1995) 'Structure and culture change in two UK organizations: A comparison of assumptions, approaches and outcomes', *Human Resource Management Journal*, vol. 4, no. 2, 1–18.

——, Skinner, D. and Clark, T. (1998) *Experiencing Human Resource Management*, London: Sage.

Marsden, D., Morris, T., Willman, P., and Wood, S. (1985) *The Car Industry*, London: Tavistock Publications.

Martin, G., Beaumont, P., and Staines, H. (1998) 'Changing corporate culture: paradoxes and tensions in a local authority', in C. Mabey, D. Skinner, and T. Clark (eds) *Experiencing Human Resource Management*, London: Sage.

McCalmon, J. and Paton, R. (1992) *Change Management*, London: Paul Chapman Publishing.

McWhinney, W. (1992) *Paths of Change*, London: Sage.

Miller, D. (1986) 'Configurations of strategy and structure: Towards a synthesis', *Strategic Management Journal*, vol. 7, 233–49.

Mintzberg, H. N. and Waters, A. (1985) 'Strategies deliberate and emergent', *Strategic Management Journal*, vol. 7, 233–49.

Morgan, G. (1986) *Images of Organization*, London: Sage.

Nicholson, N. (1993) 'Organisation change', in C. Mabey and B. Mayon-White (eds) *Managing Change*, London: Paul Chapman Publishing.

Ogbonna, E. (1992) 'Organisation culture and human resource management: dilemmas and contradictions', in P. Blyton and P. Turnbull (eds) *Reassessing Human Resource Management*, London: Sage.

—— (1994) 'Integrating strategy, culture and human resource management: a case study of the UK food retailing sector', Paper presented to the Ninth Workshop on Strategic Human Resource Management, St Gallen, Switzerland, March.

Oliver, N., Delbridge, R., Jones D., and Lowe, J. (1992) 'World class manufacturing: Further evidence in the lean production debate', Proceedings of the British Academy of Management Conference, Milton Keynes, 155–68.

Payne, R. (1991) 'Taking stock of corporate culture', *Personnel Management*, July, 26–9.

Peters, T. and Waterman, R. (1982) *In Search of Excellence*, New York: Harper and Row.

Pettigrew, A., Hendry, C., and Sparrow, P. (1988) 'The role of VET in employers' skill supply strategies: main report', Sheffield: The Training Agency in conjunction with Coopers and Lybrand Associates.

—— and Whipp, R. (1991) *Managing Change for Competitive Success*, Oxford: Blackwell.

Porras, T. J. and Silvers, R. C. (1991) 'Organization development and transformation', *Annual Review of Psychology*, vol. 42, 51–78.

Price, C. (1987) 'Culture change, the tricky bit', *Training and Development*, October, 20–4.

—— and Murphy, E. (1987) 'Organisational development at British Telecom', *Training and Development*, July, 45–8.

Pritchard, W. (1984) 'What's new in organization development?' *Personnel Management*, July, 30–3.

Rajan, A. (1997) 'How not to manage culture change: A case study of the European finance sector', *European Management Journal*, vol. 13, no. 4, 339–45.
Rice, A. K. (1958) *Productivity and Social Organisations*, London: Tavistock.
Richardson, P. and Denton, R. (1996) 'Communicating change', *Human Resource Management*, vol. 35, no. 2, 203–16.
Rowlandson, P. (1984) 'The oddity of OD', *Management Today*, Nov., 91–3.
Schuler, R. and Jackson, S. (1987) 'Linking competitive strategies with human resource management practices', *Academy of Management Executive*, vol. 1, no. 3, 207–19
—— (1992) 'Strategic human resources management: Linking the people with the strategic needs of the business', *Organization Dynamics*, Summer, 18–32.
Stace, D. and Dunphy, D. (1991) 'Beyond traditional paternalistic and developmental approaches to organizational change and human resource strategies', *The International Journal of Human Resource Management*, vol. 2, no. 3, Dec., 263–83.
Stacey, R. (1995) 'The science of complexity: An alternative perspective for strategic change processes', *Strategic Management Journal*, vol. 16, 477–95.
—— (1996) *Strategic Management and Organisational Dynamics*, London: Pitman.
Staw, B. (1980) 'Rationality and justification in organizational life', in B. Staw, and L. Cummings (eds) *Research in Organizational Behaviour*, Greenwich, CT: JAI Press.
Storey, J. (1989) *New Perspectives on Human Resource Management*, London: Routledge.
—— (1992) *Developments in the Management of Human Resources*, Oxford: Blackwell.
Thomson, R. and Mabey, C. (1994) *Developing Human Resources*, London: Butterworth Heinemann.
Tichy, N. M., Fombrun, C. J., and Devanna, M. A. (1982) 'Strategic Human Resource Management', *Sloan Management Review*, Winter, 47–61.
Trist, E. L., Higgin, G. W., Murray, H., and Pollock, A. B. (1963) *Organisational Choice*, London: Tavistock.
Van de Ven, A. H. (1988) 'Review essay: Four requirements for processual analysis', in A. Pettigrew (ed.) *The Management of Strategic Change*, London: Tavistock.
Walker, B. (1994) 'Valuing differences: the concept and a model', in C. Mabey and P. A. Iles (eds) *Managing Learning*, London: Routledge.
Weick, C. (1979) *The Social Psychology of Organizing*, London: Addison-Wesley.
—— (1995) *Sensemaking in Organisations*, London: Sage.
Whipp, R., Rosenfeld, R., and Pettigrew, A. (1989) 'Managing strategic change in a mature business', *Long Range Planning*, vol. 22, no. 6, 92–9.
Wille, E. (1990) 'Back from the brink', *Ashridge Management Review*, Summer, Berkhamstead.
Williams, A., Dobson, P., and Walters, M. (1989) *Changing Culture*, London: Institute of Personnel Management.

chapter 14

# Change Management Choices and Outcomes

CHAPTER OUTLINE

## Learning Objectives

- To examine some of the choices available when introducing strategic change within one organization.
- To specify some of the outcomes resulting from the adoption of different change strategies.
- To identify the aspects of change which are predictable and controllable, and those that are not.
- To provide a framework which helps those managing change to choose the most appropriate mode of decision making and control.
- To anticipate the likely sources of personal and institutional reaction and resistance to strategic change, and to take this into account in the way the change process is managed.

# Introduction

Although the implementation of human resource strategies is rarely as rational, purposeful and cohesive as depicted, it is helpful to at least start with the conscious intentions of such change efforts and then to track the iterative, trial and error activities that ensue.

In some cases, human resource initiatives are applied to a 'steady-state' scenario or they are relatively small-scale. However, for our purposes here, we are assuming that the design and launch of new or revised human resource policies represents a fairly major strategic thrust for the organization, implying changes to personnel practices at least, and potentially having an impact on internal structures and cultures as well. In such cases the implementation of human resource strategies will resemble a change management process.

In chapter 13 we discussed the assumptions and intentions governing change interventions and some of the strategies available for introducing organization change. Here, we move on to the issues associated with implementation, and in particular the choices, challenges and implications of different change management strategies. We then briefly sketch out how different change frameworks can inform and guide such interventions, with particular reference to the level depth, scope and direction of the proposed human resource changes. However, the situations which allow for well-planned, highly controlled change are limited to those where there is a high degree of both agreement and certainty. More typical are change scenarios with a number of competing interests at stake and many unpredictable elements in the environment. Here the management of change is less about planning, monitoring and control, and more about negotiating, agenda building and muddling through. Later, we focus on some of the factors that influence the perceived outcome of change in organizations. Introducing radical change will never be a problem-free process, but anticipating likely reactions and addressing possible objectives to change can improve the likelihood of success.

# The Management of Change

Having discussed some important issues concerning the context of change in the previous chapter, we now apply this analysis to the implementation of human resource strategies in particular. Other chapters in this book take up specific areas of human resource policy and practice in more detail; here it is our concern to examine the options available, and the likely outcomes, when introducing human resource changes.

## Level and depth of intervention

We have seen in the previous chapter that when formulating and implementing change strategies it is important to identify the *level* of analysis (Harrison 1987): whether the target for change is to be at a task/work group level, at an intergroup level or at an organizational level. It is also important to identify the *depth* of the change intervention required, which will depend on the basic nature of the organizational problem being addressed and whether it is concerned with current behavioural symptoms, with structural requirements or with the cultural context of the organization, or indeed a combination of these.

Taking first the level of analysis. A manufacturing organization might be concerned to radically improve its productivity, reliability and quality. To achieve this it may:

- give an assembly line worker responsibility for minor maintenance (individual level);
- set up teams to apply a new inventory production system to minimize waste (task and work group level);
- give these teams the freedom to collaborate with others in different departments to resolve the occurrence of defects (inter-division level);
- set up new delivery standards for their suppliers in order to cut down on inventory costs (organizational level).

The human resource policies and practices to facilitate these changes differ according to the level of analysis. Thus recruitment, training, job design, involvement in objective setting and incentive schemes, might be devised to differentially affect the organizational goals for various categories of staff. Although the very notion of human resource strategy would seem to imply a multifaceted set of policies and priorities embracing all levels and functions of an organization, it is not the coverage of human resource initiatives that makes them strategic. Rather it is how they are connected: that is, the degree to which they link in with each other and contribute to the achievement of business objectives.

It is important to recognize that by 'level' here we are talking about level of analytical focus, not hierarchical level in the organization. Thus 'poor job definition' for an individual might apply to any level in the organization hierarchy from shop-floor supervisor to main board executive.

Second, is the depth of intervention. Behavioural strategies lend themselves to the most direct and least radical human resource initiatives. For example, the sponsorship of managers on MBA and Diploma programmes might be intended to expose selected middle managers to a wider range of rigorous business analysis techniques. As such it could be regarded as an overdue remedy for deficiencies in the current management development system rather than an example of strategic HR change (a behavioural strategy at an individual level). Often, however, this degree of intervention may not be sufficient to achieve the required aims owing to the way jobs are configured, the way roles and responsibilities are assigned and the poor quality of systems support. In these cases the human resource strategy might involve an organization benchmarking its competitors' best human resource practices with a view to overhauling its own human resource planning policies (a behavioural strategy at an organizational level). Or it may involve restructuring so that cross-functional groups can operate with greater autonomy and improved communication flows, constituting a structural strategy at a divisional level. Alternatively, attitudes within the organization may prove to be so entrenched and resistant to change that a radical shift in leadership style around a new raison d'être for the organization might be necessary. This would take the human resource strategy into the cultural arena at an organizational or divisional level.

It can be seen that as the human resource strategies call for a greater degree of intervention they require deeper changes to the infrastructure, information flow and job design, and ultimately the context or culture of an organization. While cultural, and to some extent, structural strategies present possibilities of more deep-seated change, they also present the risk of more widespread systemic disruption if they backfire. Furthermore, this type of human resource change likened by some to a shift in paradigms or religious beliefs (Beech 1996), is likely to require considerable time, sensitivity and expenditure. Chapters 15 and 16 examine in more detail the desirability and feasibility of culture change in organizations.

## Speed and scope of HR changes

Consideration of the time it takes to bring about different types of change leads to another dimension of choice when launching human resource initiatives; that is, the required speed and scope of change. Three types of change can be usefully differentiated, each with their own human resource implications.

1 *Incremental* change is an improvement on the old way of doing things, with the aim of doing more things or doing things better. This kind of change, such as the introduction of a new career planning process, does not represent a major change in direction or policy and is therefore unlikely to disrupt the status quo. Such a measure could undoubtedly have strategic consequences in terms of preparing

for future skill requirements, but if it builds upon appraisal and developmental processes that are already in place, then it could be seen as a fairly minor, refining enhancement which can be implemented quickly.

2 *Transitional* change involves the implementation of new strategies and requires the rearranging or dismantling of old operating methods. A good example comes from the description by Hendry (see box 14.1) of how three large UK corporations (Pilkington, GKN and IMI) coped with decentralizing from functional structures to divisionalized business units and profit centres.

3 *Transformational* change is usually the most profound and traumatic and is so described because it implies comprehensive change at several levels. The associated features, according to Kleiner and Corrigan (1989), are:

- reformed mission and core values;
- an altered distribution of power;
- reorganization to support new roles and break the traditional business-as-usual structure;
- revised communication and decision-making patterns; and
- fresh leadership bringing the necessary drive, energy and commitment to overcome organizational inertia.

Kleiner and Corrigan also describe transformational change as being implemented rapidly in bursts. We question whether this always holds true. While the initial 'boardroom shuffle' may indeed be swift and mission statements rewritten overnight, the reality of organization change is far more protracted. This is because even transformational change is rarely the simple execution of an elaborate strategic plan. As Quinn (1989) reminds us from his research, strategy formulation and implementation are not separate, sequential processes:

> successful managers in the companies observed acted logically and incrementally to improve the quality of information used in key decisions; to overcome the personal and political pressures resisting change; to deal with the varying lead times and sequencing problems in critical decisions; and to build the organizational awareness, understanding, and psychological commitment essential to effective strategies. By the time the strategies began to crystallize, pieces of them were already being implemented. Through the very processes they used to formulate their strategies, these executives had built sufficient organizational momentum and identity with the strategies to make them flow toward flexible and successful implementation. (1989: 33)

If this is true for business strategy, it is doubly true for the implementation of human resource strategies, which are ideally set in motion to facilitate the information flow, overcome the resistance, and build the competences and commitment that Quinn refers to.

## BOX 14.1 THE HRM OF DECENTRALIZATION

'All three of the companies cited espouse a philosophy of decentralization to varying degrees, with Pilkington least far down this road. However, at some point, all face the question how far they intend to allow an internal labour market to operate to offset the incipient fragmentation of decentralization. This typically arises over ensuring top succession . . . and doubts over whether the company has adequate "strength in depth" in its management, as it enters a renewed growth phase. In the 1980s, such doubts have been triggered by the combination of decentralization and the demanning that resulted from recession. GKN, for example, lost two-thirds of its UK employees, and more than halved its worldwide complement. IMI and Pilkington both almost halved their UK numbers. Such outflows included a massive haemorrhage of management and technical skills. As a result, as these companies have moved into an era of more confident growth, and additionally as they diversified into new areas, they have been forced to review their whole range of human resource policies.

The challenge has been to develop corporately inspired (and, in many cases, corporately managed) solutions which do not negate the benefits of sharper management accountability and employee motivation, which are at the heart of the decentralization philosophy' (Hendry 1990: 98).

The author goes on to describe a range of human resource tactics that were employed to meet this challenge. These include a limited number of "group contracts" created to retain key managers and produce a pool from which top jobs could be filled.

'Difficulties in making appointments in these decentralized organizations also prompted them to review their succession planning and appraisal practices with information on shortfalls and excesses being consolidated into an annual management development register. With the demise of specialist central functions (such as engineering, R&D and management services) the companies used the newly created profit-responsible roles at relatively junior levels as "seedbeds" of basic learning and broadening experiences for up-and-coming managers.

Alongside this the three organizations – particularly Pilkington – assigned people to task-centred action learning teams outside their normal area of operation to help knowledge transfer, promote an organizational perspective and assist cohesion. Each of these shifts in human resource practice and policy represent strategic manoeuvring on the part of the three companies as they adjusted to the "known new state" of divisionalized business units.'

(Hendry 1990: 98)

From their ethnographic analysis of one of the newly-formed agencies in the UK civil service, Brooks and Bate (1994) conclude that the Next Steps initiative is failing to address the issue of the 'politics of acceptance'. On the one hand, the change has been imposed, eliminating ownership of the change process, and on the other hand, the incremental nature of its introduction had allowed local subcultures sufficient time to build their defences and strengthen their resistance to change.

## Direction of HR changes

A final set of choices confronting those planning and implementing human resource strategies concerns direction. Given that the human resource policies adopted are intended to assist in the delivery of strategic objectives, it might be assumed that the impetus for new or revised human resource strategies will always come from the top of the organization. While the conception of such strategies will usually happen at senior levels, the outworking of the human resource plans and tactics, the harnessing of energy and the mobilization of support can and do emanate from different points in an organization.

### Top-down

An example of top-down change is the human resource strategy adopted by Grampian Health Board in Scotland prior to them achieving Trust status. The intention of the programme was nothing less than to bring about a comprehensive change of culture (Mabey and Mallory 1995). This was deemed necessary by the Board for the following reasons: (1) In a labour intensive, service-based organization like the National Health Service, the co-operativeness, internal integration and anxiety-reducing friendliness of staff was reckoned to have a dramatic effect on organizational performance; (2) the previous bureaucratic system of fragmented accountability and indecision needed to be replaced by an attitude of responsible risk-taking whereby 'the huge amounts of human talent and energy could be released'; and (3) the introduction of general management principles heralded the need to break down the historical defensiveness between medical and administrative staff. It was recognized that a concerted change programme was needed. This, together with the restructuring into six health care and three support divisions, made it all but inevitable that the change process would be managerially driven, heavily programmed and organization-wide in scope. The strategic planning process, once devised, had to be fully publicized externally and internally. Senior managers were trained in strategy formulation and the first draft ten-year strategic plan was completed in December 1987 (Fullerton et al. 1989). Although many of the ensuing human resource actions (such as operational planning, team-building workshops and training in creative problem-solving) were designed to enhance grass-roots participation, the prevailing trajectory of this human resource strategy was top-down. Undoubtedly this has the benefit of providing clear, sustained direction which is well resourced and co-ordinated. It also runs a severe risk of not being owned by large numbers of staff leading to medium-term indifference, if not cynicism (see for instance, Brooks and Bate 1994; Martin et al. 1998.)

## Bottom-up

The human resource strategy at Isuzu (see box 13.4) also had elements that were imposed, planned and administered from the top. Indeed, one interpretation of the events at the Luton plant is to see them as a calculated business move on the part of Isuzu, opportunistically using the ailing assembly plant to enhance their order books in Europe. Likewise, the new contract of employment, the company joint council (with the five trade unions being required to elect a single spokesperson) and the just-in-time working practices were hardly introduced in a participative manner. And yet, having established these non-negotiable elements of the human resource strategy (not dissimilar to the temporary job guarantees at Volkswagen, as described by Garnjost and Blettner (1996)) much of what followed was, perhaps surprisingly, bottom-up. The manufacturing director, George Chalmers, described the change process in the early stages as like 'having a tiger by the tail!' Assembly-line workers clamoured to become team leaders, not only for the financial incentive, but also for the opportunity to be trained on and off the job (at a local college), for the enhanced career opportunities and for the new sense of kudos that went with the position. The new inventory production system gave teams the expertise and the opportunity to redesign their workstations in an effort to eliminate waste. Even more suggestive of bottom-up change was the obvious sense of pride in their work and work place evident in the IBC plant; team working had apparently succeeded in flattening the management pyramid, creating trust in what was previously a highly stratified company (Mabey and Mallory 1995).

Strictly speaking, bottom-up change would not only be implemented from lower levels of the organization, but initiated from there also. The point about this example is that although the broad business parameters concerning finished vehicle throughput, inventory levels and quality standards were set by senior management, and a new set of human resource 'ground rules' was established in the revised labour agreement, the subsequent human resource *tactics* took place at a grass-roots level, and took on a momentum of their own with new cultural norms being established by the workteams themselves at a shopfloor level.

## Sideways-in

Although the scale of product and capital investment is different, there are parallels between the business strategies adopted for the assembly of light commercial vehicles at Luton and the assembly of aeroplanes at British Aerospace's old Hatfield plant in the late 1980s. At both plants, in an attempt to cut costs, inventories were reduced, there was a move to cellular or team working with corresponding changes to management structure, and comprehensive training was set up to raise awareness of, and transfer skills to, quality working. The interesting feature of the human resource strategy at British Aerospace (BAe) was the use of one cell group (door assembly) as a pilot scheme. The advantages of implementing human resource strategy in this localized manner are clear. It provides a relatively low-risk opportunity to test new layout and operating techniques without wide-scale disruption (although once running effectively it poses supply and bottleneck problems for neighbouring sections of the assembly process). It facilitates team-building and accountability on a small and controllable scale. Equally important is the message projected to the rest of the business: the pilot scheme signals senior management's seriousness about human resource change, provides a demonstration of effective cellular working and is a showcase for the site being innovative. Beer et al. (1990) give two basic criteria for the selection of so-called 'developmental laboratories':

1 adequate resources (especially skilled managers); and
2 a high probability of success, especially if it can be measured in bottom-line terms.

In many ways, BAe's choice of the door assembly conforms to these conditions. It required minimum reorganization and investment costs – the complex mechanical assembly lent credibility to the pilot scheme. But, most importantly, it was a high-profile location with outcomes that could be easily measured. The stunning results appear to support the choice: by 1990, the thirty-week assembly cycle had been reduced to thirteen weeks; inventory was down by 43 per cent; modification to workflow and layout had resulted in a space reduction of 18 per cent; and a manual saving on labour costs of £9,000 and on transaction costs of £66,000 had been made (Salaman 1992). Despite these impressive performance figures the Hatfield plant was subsequently closed by BAe for broader political and commercial reasons which perhaps highlights the vulnerability of sideways-in change, even if it is successful.

Of course, to characterize human resource implementations in these directional terms alone is over-simplistic. As we have already noted, there are likely to be elements of all three 'thrusts' in any large-scale organizational intervention and there are many possible sub-systems of an organization which could be considered as a starting point for a change effort (Beckhard and Harris 1987):

1 top management;
2 a management group known to be ready for change;
3 'hurting' system (a group where current conditions have created acute discomfort);
4 new teams without a history and whose tasks require a departure from old ways of operating;
5 a staff group that will be required to assist in subsequent implementation of strategy; and
6 temporary project teams, specifically set up to carry through a change plan.

The intention in this section has been to discuss where the primary driving force for change is coming from and what human resource strategies are appropriate for the effects being sought. For this reason, we have also considered the levels of analysis, the scope of change and the type of change. All of these factors have a bearing on how effective the HR strategy will be for an organization in the longer term.

The implementation of a new or revised human resource strategy will probably need to use a range of change management methods. The higher the level of analysis (intergroup or organizational as opposed to individual) and the wider the scope of the human resource strategy (cultural and structural, as opposed to 'simply' behavioural) the more this assertion holds.

## The Complexity of Change

We have already noted in the previous chapter that assumptions concerning the linearity and causality of change management are spurious. So, although describing change interventions in terms of level, depth, scope and direction is useful for exploring the choices available for managing change, it can only be a starting point. In fact, all that we have said so far needs to be qualified by two considerations: the limits of control and the opportunities of complexity.

### *The limits of control*

In summarizing the literature on managing and controlling change, Stacey (1996) helpfully charts the different types of decision making associated with particular change contexts (see figure 14.1). The figure has two axes. One concerns the degree of certainty; this will be high only in situations where the time frames are short and the conditions, within and external to the organization, are relatively predictable. In such a scenario, steady-state management is appropriate. The further the situation is from certainty the more likely it is that individuals will experience anxiety when seeking to make decisions and exercise control. The other axis concerns the extent to which members and managers within the organization share an understanding of the change situation and are agreed upon the actions required. It is not unusual for joint action to be called for when there is a great deal of disagreement concerning the objectives and strategies.

Putting these two axes together helps to identify the contexts in which various modes of decision making and control might be deployed by those managing change in an organization. For instance, despite the ubiquitous tendency of managers, strategic planners as well as academics and consultants, to describe strategic outcomes as the consequence of conscious intentions, the opportunity to adopt technically rational decision-making and a monitoring form of control in organizations (area one in the figure) is relatively rare. This is because such actions are limited to short-term planning and to situations where forecasts are likely to be accurate. Where there is relative certainty but little agreement, political processes are the only ways in which both decision making and control over change can be exerted (area two); and in situations close to agreement but far from

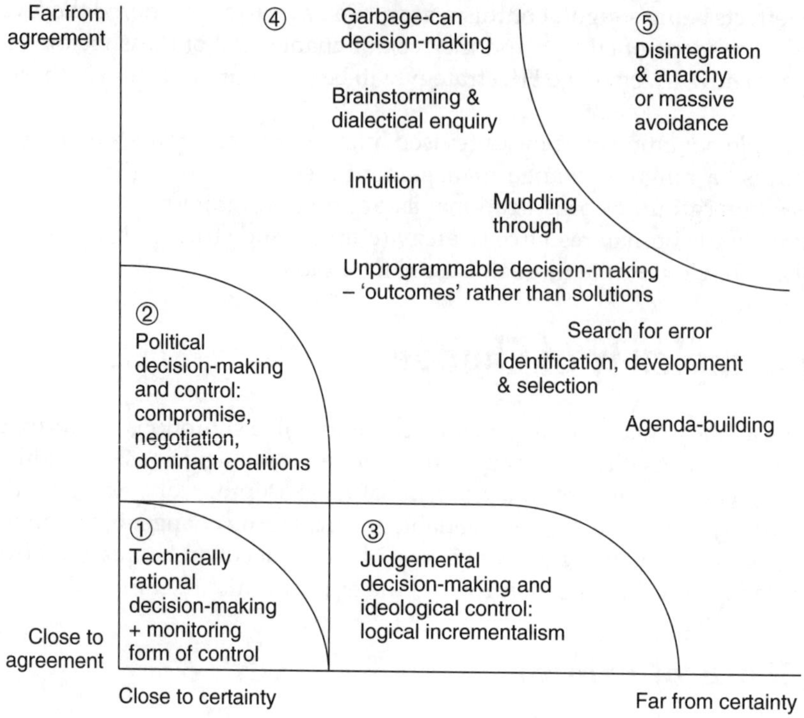

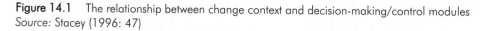

**Figure 14.1** The relationship between change context and decision-making/control modules
*Source*: Stacey (1996: 47)

certainty (area three), both decision making and control are likely to be ideologically driven, with decisions based on judgement and control based on conformity. Here, effective managers will have a clear sense of what they are trying to achieve, but maintain a 'trial-and-error' flexibility about the methods for reaching the organizational goals, recognizing that strategy emerges in small incremental, opportunistic steps (Quinn 1980).

If a group of people find themselves in a situation far from agreement (leading to high conflict) and far from certainty (leading to high anxiety) they may either avoid and abdicate and thus be at the mercy of change or, alternatively, they may disintegrate into full-scale anarchy, where the possibility of coherent, constructive joint action breaks down altogether (area five). The spectacular failure of certain mergers and takeovers suggests that the lack of operational and/or cultural common ground, whether pre-existent or negotiated, and the turbulence of the marketplace, brought about a situation where control of the change was impossible. Between the extremes (area four), the figure depicts a range of change management methods. As members of the organization move away from certainty and agreement, decision making tends to be rather intuitive and unprogrammed, and control tends to be based on group pressure. One example is 'muddling through' (Lindblom 1959), where it is impossible to identify all the change objectives of interested parties, so a policy is judged by its desirability and degree of widespread support, rather than how well it achieves a given goal. Another example is so called 'garbage-can' decision-making, where the flow of choices over time are erratic and haphazard. Cohen et al. (1972) found this to be true of large public-sector institutions with widely distributed power, complex, unclear hierarchies and no shared values. In these circumstances decisions and their outcomes occur largely by chance, depending heavily on the context that prevails at the time, and collective, progressive learning is hampered (see Simpson and Thorpe 1996).

### *The opportunities of complexity*

It is interesting to note that while area four in figure 14.1 probably describes the reality of most decision making and control modes in organizations, it is the arena of change management about which least is known. Stacey also observes that it represents an arena of great opportunity to organizations, since it is here (where ordinary management processes are impossible) that extraordinary management can be contemplated. This invites the use of feedback processes to challenge the status quo and allows new and, if necessary, radical strategic directions to emerge. He also describes this as double-loop learning, which we explore further in chapters 10 and 11. In other words, complexity *can* produce creativity and innovation rather than anxiety and avoidance (see box 14.2).

So the key to successful change management appears to lie in sustaining an organization at the edge of chaos, between the borders between stability and instability.

> In organizational terms this means that the formal systems operate in a stable way to secure efficient day to day operations while the informal system operates in a destabilising manner to promote change . . . For example, while some managers are operating in the formal organization using budgetary forms of control to keep the organization stable, others are simultaneously operating informal networks in order to get around these same budgetary controls and engaging in political activity designed to undermine the status quo. Other examples of chaos take the form of conflict, as when an organization experiences the clash of counter cultures, the tensions of political activity, the contention and dialogue through which managers handle ambiguous strategic issues. (Stacey 1995: 485)

## The Interpretation of Change

Up to this point we have been referring to change strategies from a reasonably objective viewpoint. We have discussed the merits and drawbacks of different

**BOX 14.2 APPLYING COMPLEXITY THEORY TO CHANGE MANAGEMENT**

'For me the key message coming from the science of complexity is this. It is possible, with much effort, for someone, or some small group of powerful people, to predict the outcomes of group, organizational and societal systems and, therefore, to remain "in control" of them. But this is possible only if such systems are held well within the stable zone of operation, far away from the edge of chaos. The result will be stability, perhaps for a long time, but it will be the death of creativity and innovation and hence, ultimately, the death of the system. If it is to survive, every human system must return to the edge of chaos, where outcomes are unknowable and no one can be "in control". So, the system cannot move according to some blueprint, but it will produce emergent new outcomes and it will be controlled through the process of spontaneous self-organization itself, unless we, in our desperate attempts to stay "in control", cause it to tip over into the unstable zone. For managers it is a message about having the courage to let go and let it happen, while vigilantly seeking to avoid tipping an organization into the unstable zone. It is a message for members of organizations to reflect publicly on their own processes while they act, in order better to understand the operation of their organization's shadow system. The key seems to lie, not in preparing blueprints, but in trying to understand how to contain the anxiety of operating at the edge of chaos. The true role of the leader of a creative system is not to foresee its future and take control of its journey, but to contain the anxiety of its members as they operate at the edge of chaos, where they are creating and discovering a new future that none could possibly foresee.'
(from Stacey 1996: 346)

change models, styles and methodologies, and we have noted the difficulties and opportunities associated with managing complexity. However, when we begin to explore the way in which such organizational changes are perceived, interpreted and ascribed meaning by those on the receiving end, we are no longer in the realm of single reality.

## Perceptions of change

Perceptions of change are inevitably coloured by a host of factors from whim to world view, and everything in between. Some of the more important include the following. *Thinking style,* which has been shown by research to be completely independent of thinking capacity and intelligence (Kirton 1987; Schroder 1989; Tefft 1990), means that two equally capable individuals could produce very

## BOX 14.3 'EXCELLENT' TIMING

'Another factor in the success of *In Search of Excellence* was undoubtedly its timing. The book appeared in the early years of the Reagan era when the United States was beginning to rebuild its self-confidence after several years of introspective self-doubt. In industry this has been reflected in uncertainty about how to cope with the increasing threat of Japanese competition. The success of Japan had kindled an interest in Japanese management for the American Market. The most successful illustration of this was Ouchi's (1981) *Theory Z*. The message from *In Search of Excellence* was rather different and fitted in well with Reaganite America. It was that to find the lessons for success in American industry you need to look no further than in your own back yard. The lessons were to be found by exploring the practices of the best American companies and not by looking overseas. Furthermore, what one found by looking at these companies was a return to a number of traditional American beliefs based on keeping things simple, building on what you know best and reinforcing essential values. There is also a careful blend of rugged individualism and reinforcement of the family based on the concept of the organizational family. It is understandable that this optimistic message should strike a chord in American industry.'
(Guest 1992: 14–15)

different solutions to the same change scenario. Jung's work on psychological types (1923), operationalized as the Myers–Briggs Type Indicator, reveals two very different *perceiving preferences*: 'The sensing types, by definition, depend on their five senses for perception. Whatever comes directly from the senses is part of the sensing types' own experience and is therefore trustworthy . . . The intuitives are comparatively uninterested in sensory reports of things as they are. Instead, intuitives listen for the intuitions that come up from their unconscious with enticing visions of possibilities' (Myers 1986: 57).

Research by Crouch et al. (1992) suggests that response to change amongst managers is very much dependent on the *power to act*: 'managers respond to unfamiliarity by acting and therefore adding to it. They act in ways that convert exogenous into endogenous change. Ways of creating alternatives will perhaps be there that have achieved previous success . . . This view of change [is] a political process, in which managers obtain power by acting. By acting, seizing the initiatives, the individual retrieves power over events' (1992: 43–4). We refer, in a moment, to the predicament of those who do not feel themselves to have such room for manoeuvre. Such perceptions are closely allied to feelings of *personal worth, power and difference* in the workplace – whether this be based on gender, ethnic origin, age, disability and so on. Walker (1994) notes that when 'locked into an either/or approach to life, people become threatened by any deviation from their perceptions of the norm. They fear that others' differences mean they must change. Therefore they close in and join ranks with people whom they believe to be most like themselves. They respond like victims. The difference between feeling and not feeling like a victim is one's sense of personal empowerment – one's ability to accept, move toward and even embrace different ideas and perspectives' (1994: 214). Organizations are getting better at acknowledging and valuing *cultural diversity*, in the way they introduce change, but insensitivities still persist (Iles and Mabey 1994).

Then there is something as trivial yet significant as *timing*. Receptivity to change can simply be reaping the rewards from launching the right ideas at the right time. Guest (1992) attributes the success of the 'excellence' brand of HRM in part to this factor (see box 14.3).

Another powerful determinant of how employees view and respond to change is ideology, or what Morgan (1986) calls *organizational frame of reference*. For instance, the radical view sees the organization as 'the battleground where rival forces (e.g. management and unions) strive for the achievement of largely incompatible ends' (1986: 188). This frame of reference is based on very different premises to the unitary perspective which emphasizes common goals and the possibility of achieving them by being a well-integrated team. The pluralist view – somewhere between these two extremes – regards the organization as a loose coalition of diverse individuals and stakeholder groups, which has only passing interest in the goals of the organization. Finally, and more global still is the *world view* to which individuals subscribe, which influences every area of their lives, including their attitude and response to organizational change: 'we do not have to go beyond differing beliefs about cause to find the sources of unavoidable conflict. We don't have to assume that either party is evil or even that they have opposing goals. Conflicts arise from constructions of their minds, from the beliefs and styles by which an individual or group makes a choice; only incidentally are they in the content of the issue . . . changes take place when boundaries between the logics of alternative realities are transgressed' (McWhinney 1992: 22–3).

Understanding the sources of these plural and subjective realities is important, because it is upon such rocks of heritage, enfranchisement, ideology and intransigence that organizations change efforts frequently run aground.

## Reactions to change

The implementation of organizational change usually implies personal disruption or discomfort; for example, acquiring new skills, working in a redesigned role or job, being paid and rewarded on a different basis, and having accountability for a larger (or smaller) budget. Sometimes the changes will affect a single department or business unit, but if the human resource initiatives are truly strategic they are more likely to have an impact on everybody in the organization.

Several authors have identified reasons why managers encounter resistance when implementing new ways of doing things, and have offered tactics for

## BOX 14.4 ORGANIZATIONAL BEREAVEMENT

The articulation of this conflict is therefore as crucial to assimilating social changes as mourning is to bereavement. Even if it were possible to foresee how interests might be balanced with the utmost fairness, everyone has still to work out in his or her own terms what it means to their particular attachments, gradually reorientating their essential purposes. No one can resolve the crisis of reintegration on behalf of another, any more than friends can tell the bereaved how to make the best of it. Every attempt to pre-empt conflict, argument, protest by rational planning can only be abortive: however reasonable the proposed changes, the process of implementing them must still allow the impulse of rejection to play itself out. When those who have power to manipulate changes act as if they have only to explain, and, when their explanations are not at once accepted, shrug off opposition as ignorance or prejudice, they express a profound contempt for the meaning of lives other than their own: for the reformers have already assimilated these changes to their purpose, and worked out a reformulation which makes sense to them, perhaps through months or years of analysis and debate. If they deny others the chance to do the same, they treat them as puppets dangling by the threads of their own conceptions. When liberal white people propose reforms on behalf of black, men on behalf of women, rich for poor, even the most honourable intentions can be profoundly alienating, if they assume the identity of those they seek to help and tell them what their lives should mean. The presumption is, I think, more intimately threatening than indifference or hostility, and is bitterly resented. To be told the meaning of your life by others, in terms which are not yours, implies that your existence does not matter to them, except as it is reflected in their own.
(Marris 1974: 155)

dealing with them (e.g. Hirschowitz 1975; Marris 1974; Kanter 1985; Kotter and Schlesinger 1989). In essence they revolve around three sources of loss. Perceived loss of control, loss of security and loss of face.

Change imposed by others feel threatening rather than exciting. The removal of choice leads to a sense of powerlessness resulting in stress and defensive behaviour; as Kanter (1985) notes: 'It is powerlessness that corrupts, not power'. Communicating as much information as possible about the proposed changes can help to alleviate these feelings. This may include creating channels for raising concerns, asking questions and giving feedback.

Commenting on loss of security Peter Marris makes an insightful comparison between bereavement on a personal level and the collective impact of disruptive organization change (box 14.4).

He goes on to suggest three principles for the management of change, each of which corresponds to aspects of grief, and represents a crisis of reintegration which cannot be escaped, hurried or resolved on behalf of another.

1 The process of reform should expect and even encourage conflict, because people need to be given the chance to react and voice their ambivalent feelings to help them make sense of what is going on.

2 The process should 'respect the autonomy of different kinds of experience so that groups of people can organise without the intrusion of alien conceptions' (Marris 1974: 156).

3 There must be time and patience, to allow people to digest and accommodate the implications of the proposed changes. In human resource terms this may mean providing a clear timetable of events, sharing the 'big picture' with details about the new state, breaking this down into smaller, more manageable and familiar actions, and letting people take the first step. It will also mean being honest about less palatable aspects of change: explaining the costs at an early stage and face-to-face if possible.

Strategic change initiatives usually imply that the previous procedures, policies or ways of working are inadequate. It is therefore not easy – especially for those who have invested much in these past practices – to suddenly switch allegiance and commitments without feeling *loss of face*. As the sociologist Erving Goffman (1959) has pointed out, people's reactions to events are largely a function of how others define and regard them (their 'social identity') and they will go to great lengths (even engage in actions contrary to their long-term interests) in order to avoid embarrassment. For the initiators of change, the task is one of putting past actions into perspective without unduly discrediting them, and depicting the new circumstances that require fresh strategies. This allows staff to portray flexibility and strength while still retaining a sense of continuity with the healthy aspects of past traditions.

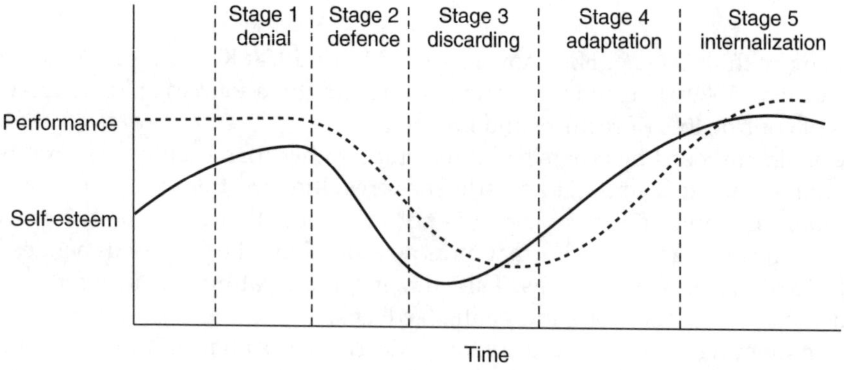


**Figure 14.2** How individuals typically cope with personal life changes
*Source:* Carnall (1991: 94)

Carnall (1991, building on earlier work by Adams et al. (1976), describes how individuals typically cope with personal life changes (figure 14.2).

Self-esteem during the early stage of *denial* may actually increase as the advantages of the present situation are magnified and work-group cohesion solidifies. Unless the change is sudden and traumatic, performance will not necessarily decline as individuals attempt to minimize the impact of changes. The reality of such changes dawn during the *defence* stage – leading to feelings of frustration, depression and defensive behaviours. *Discarding* is the phase when people let go of the past and begin to look forward to the future. From this trough of turmoil and disorientation individuals begin to re-establish their own identity and grow into the new situation. However, they need support and time for this to happen. Self-esteem begins to climb during the period of *adaptation*. As new routines are mastered and early successes are achieved, performance increases. Anger and frustration may still be present, but this is evidence of trying to make the changes work rather than opposition to them. Finally, *internalization* and a newly-established sense of integration occurs when those involved have tested, modified and accepted the new system, processes and organization. Carnall (1991) notes that the engine for rebuilding performance is the self-esteem of the people involved and suggests four categories of need required during this process: empathy, support, skills and intelligible information.

## Barriers to change

Change is not always perceived negatively. Casey (1993) notes that 'People are not by nature resistant to change and neither are organizations; on the contrary they are open to change and they continually change themselves. It is all a question of where the change comes from: if it comes from within, it feels good; if it is imposed from outside it can feel like a threat, because it is unknown and outside one's own control. It should be no surprise that people (and organizations) are defensive in the face of perceived threat – we are all absolutely right to be defensive when threatened, it is irresponsible not to defend against threat. But it is not the *change* which we resist, it is the *threat* which fills us with fear . . . Organizations are defined as resistant to change, only by those who are trying to change them' (Casey 1993: 89–90).

It is very clear that much depends on the way organizational change is introduced and managed. Box 14.5 shows eight key questions which identify how commitment to a change process might be gained.

Given the formidable array of forces that can get in the way of any change management intervention, how is a critical mass of support mobilized in order to effect lasting change? An early and essential step is the identification of key power groupings wherever they might be situated in the organizational hierarchy and adopting strategies appropriate for each in order to either win their commitment or neutralize their interference. For instance, the unions were cast as 'opposers' to the planned joint venture of General Motors and Isuzu in 1987, and a calculated risk was taken by the new management team to 'neutralize' their interference.

## BOX 14.5 HOW CAN CHANGE BE ENJOYED RATHER THAN ENDURED?

1 What *personal benefit* will be gained by individuals involved? Active participation in the change process depends on the extent to which the needs, attitudes and beliefs of individual employees are taken into account.

2 What is the view of the official or unofficial leader(s) of the workgroups involved? The *expectations and opinions* of those in prestige positions tend to carry more weight than the members of their work groups and/or the influence of staff 'trainers'.

3 What fresh, *objective information* is available about the need for change? Data centred on one's own organization or group is more meaningful and influential than more generalized information about attitudes and behaviour.

4 To what extent are facts pertinent to the change process generated from *within the workgroup*? The planning, gathering, analysis and interpretation of diagnostic data by the individuals and groups involved are more likely to be understood and accepted than those presented by outside experts.

5 To what degree can those involved in the change *influence the change process*. Complete participation by all the members of the affected workgroups is likely to be most effective. However, participation by representatives of the group and/or the supervisor only can reduce the amount of overt opposition.

6 How *attractive is the workgroup* to its members? When change is being proposed, group cohesiveness (which will be high if the group satisfies the needs of its members) will operate to reduce resistance to change if the group sees the changes as beneficial. This is because strong group membership tends to lead to greater individual conformity to group norms.

7 Does the change process involve bringing individuals from different groups together, *off the job* in temporary groups? Change programmes that involve individuals within the context of their immediate job situation are likely to be more successful because this group has more psychological meaning to an individual than does a group with only *temporary membership*.

8 How open are the *communication channels* relating to the need for, plans for and consequence of change? Change processes that provide specific knowledge on the progress to date and specify the criteria against which improvement is to be measured are most successful in establishing and maintaining change.

(Adapted from Huse 1980: 120–3)

First they were left out of the final negotiations leading to the formation of the new company. Then they were bound by the newly-formulated labour agreement which, among other things, instigated a Company Joint Council which required the five different trade unions to elect a single spokesperson. Finally, the implementation of team-working and the inventory production system largely circumvented the need for shop-steward representation of worker grievances. In power terms the unions were marginalized. This is not an untypical story of the 1980s. At its most pragmatic, using political power to shape change boils down to appealing to the better interests of key individuals: it is their interpretation of events and whether they perceive gain (ideological or personal) from the proposed changes that will ultimately determine their support or opposition.

Alongside this there are at least four other factors affecting the political terrain of an organization. One is the behaviour of key and powerful leaders whether they be hierarchically senior or leaders of opinion. In order to mobilize change in others leaders need to be personally open to change themselves (Benjamin and Mabey 1990). An account of successful organizational change at the Danish hearing aid manufacturer, Oticon (Larsen 1996), points to a number of symbolic acts made by the new CEO to support the change process. These included dispensing with his office and moving around when appropriate with his trolley-desk like all other staff, and taking a personally high financial stake in the company (and raising a bank loan to do this).

A second and related factor is the use of symbols and language to manage the meaning of, and create energy for, change. It could be argued that the effective management of change in organizations requires that explanation be removed beyond doubt and argumentation. 'Other devices for the symbolic construction of reality include the rhetorical construction of oral and written communications so as to outline a general framework, a world view, from which it is difficult to dissent and from which consequences intended to flow . . . so as to influence the receiver's framework of reference favourably' (Anthony 1992: 87).

One of the reasons for the occasional success of human resource strategies under the umbrella of Quality is not that the concepts, skills and measurement criteria are revolutionary in themselves (often they are old ideas repackaged), but rather that they have rapidly provided the workforce with a succinct and common language and an incontrovertible logic for describing and attaining high standards and a range of graphic methods for monitoring and improving it. Some manufacturing plants have taken this further by regularly involving staff in 'quality presentations' to customers visiting the plant. This active identification with the finished product provides a powerful cue for employees to attend to detail in their job. Empirical studies have shown that while the structure of authority and control remains largely unchanged in organizations adopting quality management approaches, nevertheless employees at the point of production can benefit from greater 'detailed control' and discretion (Rees 1998; Glover and Fitzgerald Moore 1998).

A third factor in the successful implementation of strategy is the formal or informal presence of a change agent, or change management team. Line managers, human resource specialists and external consultants each have unique vantage points when it comes to fulfilling this role. Shipton and McCauley (1993) put forward a strong argument for personal practitioners to take on the role of change consultant. However, each organization is different and the pros and cons of different change agents will vary accordingly (table 14.1).

A fourth factor concerns the readiness of the organization to learn from outcomes that were *not* planned. Frequently change initiatives bring about unintended consequences and these can provide valuable learning opportunities as box 14.6 shows, but only if the organization is alert to such outcomes and capable of consolidating the benefits.

In this section we have suggested that change is often resisted not because it lacks visionary value or commercial logic but because of the way it is construed

**Table 14.1** Choosing the change agent

| *Line manager* | *Human resource specialist* | *External human resource consultant* |
|---|---|---|
| Grassroots knowledge of what will work and what won't | Understand internal human resource systems and how they link | Wide, comparative knowledge of human resource strategies in other organizations |
| Credibility and successful role model (usually!) | Awareness of business plans and priorities | Can contribute an objective perspective |
| Vested interests in human resource because judged on people performance | Regular, wide-ranging contact with organization stake-holders | Can use 'expert status' to solicit views widely in the organization |
| Close relationship with staff promotes concern for their development | Access to human resource networks, internal and external | Knowledge of techniques, frameworks, models to help unlock *impasse* situations |
| Awareness of (and immersion in) local and organization culture | Author of human resource policies delineating roles and responsibilities; Specialist expertise in diagnosis and delivery of human resource strategies | Fresh insights, ideas can be catalytic |
| *But possibly . . .* | | |
| Over-cynical | Limited access to top team | Peddles ready-made solutions |
| Threatened by change themselves | Lacks credibility with line managers | Objectives coloured by chief client's wishes |
| Under-resourced | Confused role boundaries with personnel and line management | Poor on follow-through and evaluation |
| Too immersed to see the need for change | | Can leave before implementation and completion |
| Not being assessed on people performance | | |

## BOX 14.6 A FRENCH MAIL-ORDER FIRM: PLANNED AND UNPLANNED CHANGE

'The organization which provided the setting for this case study was a private mail-order firm in the north of France. About two-thirds of the company's 3,500 employees had barely completed primary school, and had clerical and manual jobs such as packing parcels or unloading trucks. Of 649 employees tested by a university educational institute, 52 per cent were found to have language abilities equivalent to that of eight-year-olds in the third year of primary school.

### The planned change

Convinced of the potential aptitudes and willingness of its employees and workers, the company decided to introduce general education courses in its training programmes. The objective was to upgrade the low academic levels of volunteer employees and workers, making them eligible for technical or commercial courses which would develop the skills and capacities required to hold jobs in the future.

Traditionally, the company's training programmes were concerned only with job-related matters, and most seminars were reserved for executives and supervisors. In September 1985, however, general education subjects such as spelling and grammar were introduced in the training programmes, and were made available to volunteer clerical employees and workers. Courses were held during working hours in company premises, at no cost to trainees. Eleven courses of four types were offered to volunteer employees: . . .

### Summary results

The first measure of the project's impact was the number of persons it affected directly. A total of 1,046 persons underwent training in one or more of the eleven courses. That 46 per cent of the target population manifested the expected behaviours in terms of their agreed personal development objectives may be interpreted as the first change in the organization.

The second measure of impact was the actual improvement in the qualifications and skills of the trainees. The upgrading of language and mathematical abilities of the trainees were clearly demonstrated by performance in tests before and after training. [ . . . ]

The changes observed in persons, groups, procedures and norms *not* directly involved with the project illustrate the interrelated dynamics in a human organization. The company is indeed a system wherein a change in one domain necessarily has repercussions through the whole system. A comprehensive evaluation of the impact of a planned change on the whole organization requires going beyond the sub-systems targeted by the planned change, and identifying, and if possible, quantifying the modification which took place in other components of the organization. The lack of appropriate instruments available to measure these unanticipated changes limited the author to the use of observations and verbal reports of the presence or absence of changes. [ . . . ]

**The non-anticipated changes**

Managers of the company were confronted with the conflict between strict norms of productivity and time "lost in unproductive training". They had to adjust their notions of production to a new notion of training as part of working hours. What was until then a vague notion of "human resources development" became more concrete, and had to be integrated in the existing management practices and rewards system.'
(Ernecq 1992: 279–83)

by those on the receiving end. If the change strategy – and almost as important – the way it is delivered, is interpreted negatively or suspiciously by stakeholders, then this collective judgement will impede even the best prepared plans.

## Conclusions and Summary

So how do those initiating organizational change decide which change management choices and strategies are appropriate? According to Harrison (1987) this depends on a number of factors:

- Does the organization need fundamental change, structural reorganization, process or technological innovation, a major overhaul of its internal communication systems and procedures; or does it need more minor system adjustments like tweaking the incentive scheme, adjusting the operating process or shifting the external recruitment target group?
- Is there readiness for change? Is there sufficient unease among members of the organization and external stakeholders (as a result of poor quality, declining sales, labour unrest, missed market opportunities etc.) to precipitate the adoption of new goals and strategies? If this dissatisfaction does not exist, is there evidence from diagnostic feedback that suggests that it should be?
- How might internal/external stakeholders react to proposed changes? Apart from creditors and shareholders themselves, these might include regulatory bodies (such as the Equal Opportunities Commission), community groups (such as 'green' pressure groups), managers (perhaps threatened by unfamiliar interventions) and unions and employees (perhaps resistant to new work practices and the consolidation of jobs and units).

- Does the organization have the capacity to change? Even if there is no active resistance to change, the organization may lack the resources, the structural capability, the technological expertise or the cultural willpower to facilitate and implement the proposed human resource strategies.
- Will the change strategy bring about undesirable consequences that will outweigh the positive outcomes?

Stacey (1995, 1996) reminds us that much change management takes place in an arena where there is little agreement and much uncertainty about goals and the means to achieve them. The insight provided by complexity theory is that organizations are being simultaneously pulled in opposite directions. The pull towards stability is fuelled by the forces of integration, maintenance controls and the human needs for security and stability. However, if taken to an extreme, this tendency will lead to failure because the organization becomes ossified and unable to change easily. The opposite pull is towards unstable equilibrium by the forces of division and decentralization, and by the human desires for excitement and innovation. If this drive takes over the organization will ultimately disintegrate. So while agents can apply step-by-step analytical reasoning and planned controls over the short term, such agents cannot control the long-term future of an organization. This will be a spontaneous, self-organizing process from which new strategic directions emerge. The challenge for change management is to cultivate sufficient informal social networks and learning communities as to generate self-questioning and radical solutions to problems, without tipping over into chaos.

Given that change strategies are often messy rather than well planned, intuitive rather than calculated, cyclical rather than linear, is there any merit in organizations attempting to unravel and analyse the different steps of planning, design and implementation?

We have argued in this chapter that through such analysis valuable lessons can be learned, weaknesses highlighted and cases built for further more enlightened investment of resources and effort in future change interventions. It is important, for instance, to disentangle the success or failure of the strategy *per se* from the success or failure of its implementation. A change strategy which is both poorly thought through (perhaps owing to inadequate diagnosis) and ineptly implemented (possibly because of poor change management) will obviously achieve nothing. However, the way an intervention is managed can be a success in its own terms, owing to opportunism and political favour, but still fail to contribute to a successful outcome in terms of organizational strategy. The planning of an intervention may be well timed and incorporate appropriate human resource activities, yet be subverted by widespread resistance because of the way the initiatives are introduced or simply overtaken by unanticipated and unforeseeable events. The most optimistic – and probably the most ambitious – scenario is where such resistance is anticipated and authentically addressed; where the tension between chaos and order, the radical and the status quo, is 'managed'; and the human resource initiatives have enduring organizational and individual benefits.

## Key Points

- Those managing change in organizations are faced with a number of strategic choices concerning the level, depth, scope and intended direction of the proposed intervention.
- Due to the fact that the majority of decision-making and control in organizations happens in situations of low agreement and high uncertainty, preconceived and preplanned change strategies are unlikely to be as effective as those which allow constructive tension between stability and chaos.
- Strategic change will be greeted with varying levels of enthusiasm, indifference and intransigence depending on a number of personal, occupational, cultural and political factors, as perceived by different interest groups in the organization.
- Change is constant rather than discrete, and iterative rather than sequential. Hence the meaning invested in current changes and their outcomes will provide the immediate context for any new changes being proposed.

## Discussion Questions

**1 What are some of the options available when planning strategic HR interventions?**
**2 What are the relative merits and drawbacks of top-down, bottom-up and sideways-in change?**
**3 What is 'extraordinary management', and why is it called for in many organization change situations?**
**4 Why might the same organization change be viewed and evaluated very differently depending on who you ask?**

### References


Adams, J., Hayes, J., and Hopson, B. (1976) 'Transitions', *Understanding and Managing Personal Change*, London: Martin Robertson.

Anthony, P. (1992) 'Cultural strategies', *Human Resource Strategies*, Milton Keynes: Open Business School, Unit 6.

Beckhard, R. and Harris, R. (1987) *Organisation Transitions: Managing complex change*, Reading, MA: Addison-Wesley.

Beech, N. (1996) 'Organization change interventions: a new set of beliefs?' In C. Oswick and D. Grant (eds) *Organization Development, Metaphorical Explorations*, London: Pitman Publishing.

Beer, M., Eisenstat, R. A. and Spector, B. (1990) 'Why change programmes don't produce change', *Harvard Business Review*, Nov./Dec., 158–66.

Benjamin, G. and Mabey, C. (1990) 'A case of organisation transformation', *Management Education and Development*, vol. 21, no. 5, 327–34.

Brooks, I. and Bate, P. (1994) 'The problems of effecting change within the British Civil Service: A cultural perspective', *British Journal of Management*, vol. 5, 177–90.

Carnall, C. (1991) *Managing Change*, London: Routledge.
Casey, D. (1993) *Managing Learning in Organizations*, Buckingham: Open University Press.
Cohen, M., March, J., and Olsen, J. (1972) 'People, problems, solutions and the ambiguity of relevance', in J. March and J. Olsen (eds) *Ambiguity and choice in organizations*, Bergen: Universitetsforlaget.
Crouch, A., Sinclair, A., and Hintz, P. (1992) 'Myths of managing change' in D. Hosking and N. Anderson (eds) *Organizational Change and Innovation*, London: Routledge.
Ernecq, J. (1992) 'Planned and unplanned organizational change' in D. Hosking and N. Anderson (eds) *Organizational Change and Innovation*, London: Routledge.
Fullerton, H., Ironside, A., and Price, C. (1989) 'A picture of health in the 1990s', *The Health Service Journal*, June, 73–82.
Garnjost, P. and Blettner, K. (1996) 'Cutting labour costs without redundancies', in J. Storey (ed) *Blackwell Cases in Human Resource and Change Management*, Oxford: Blackwell.
Glover L. and Fitzgerald Moore D. (1998) 'Total quality management: Shop floor perspectives', in C. Mabey, D. Skinner and T. Clark (eds) *Experiencing Human Resource Management*, London: Sage.
Goffman, E. (1959) *The Presentation of Self in Everyday LIfe*, London: Allen Lane/The Penguin Press.
Guest, D. (1992a) 'Right enough to be dangerously wrong: An analysis of the "In search of excellence" phenomenon' in G. Salaman et al. (eds) *Human Resource Strategy*, London: Sage, 5–19.
—— (1992b) 'Employee commitment and control', in J. Hartley and G. M. Stephenson (eds) *Employee Relations*, Oxford: Blackwell.
Harrison, M. (1987) *Diagnosing Organisations: Methods, models and practices*, Beverley Hills, CA: Sage.
Hendry, C. (1990) 'The corporate management of human resources and conditions of decentralization', *British Journal of Management*, vol. 1, 91–103.
Hirschowitz, R. (1975) 'The human aspects of managing transition', *AMA Personnel*, vol. 51, no. 3, 9–17.
Huse, E. (1980) *Organization Development and Change* (2nd edn), Minnesota: West Publishing Co.
Iles, P. and Mabey, C. (1994) 'Developing global capability through management and organizational strategies', Paper presented in the 9th Workshop on Strategic HRM, March, St Gallen, Switzerland.
Jung, C. (1923) *Psychological Types*, New York: Harcourt, Brace.
Kanter, R. (1985) 'Managing the human side of change', *Management Review*, April, 52–7.
Kirton, M. J. (1987) 'Adaptors and innovators: Cognitive style and personality', in S. G. Isaksen (ed.) *Frontiers of Creativity Research: Beyond the basics*, Buffalo, NY: Bearly Limited.
Kleiner, B. H. and Corrigan, W. A. (1989) 'Understanding organisational change', *Leadership and Organisation Development Journal*, vol. 10, no. 3, 25–31.
Kotter, R. and Schlesinger, L. (1989) 'Choosing strategies for change' in D. Asch and C. Bowman (eds) *Readings in Strategic Management*, Basingstoke: Macmillan, 294–306.
Larsen, H. (1996) 'Oticon: thinking the unthinkable: radical (and successful) organizational change', in J. Storey (ed.) *Blackwell Cases in Human Resource Management and Change*, Oxford: Blackwell.
Lindblom, L. (1959) 'The science of muddling through', *Public Administration Review*, vol. 19, 79–88.
Mabey, C. and Mallory, G. (1995) 'Structure and culture change in two UK organizations:

a comparison of assumptions, approaches and outcomes', *Human Resource Management Journal*, vol. 5, no. 2, 28–45.
Marris, P. (1974) *Loss and Change*, London: Routledge and Kegan Paul.
Martin, G., Beaumont, P., and Staines, H. (1998) 'Changing corporate culture: paradoxes and tensions in a Scottish Local Authority', in C. Mabey, D. Skinner, and T. Clark (eds) *Experiencing Human Resource Management*, London: Sage.
McWhinney, W. (1992) *Paths of Change*, London: Sage.
Morgan, G. (1986) *Images of Organization*, London: Sage.
Myers, I. B. (1986) *Gifts Differing*, Palo Alto, CA: Consulting Psychologists Press Inc.
Ouchi, W. (1981) *Theory Z: How American business can meet the Japanese challenge*, Reading, MA: Addison-Wesley.
Quinn, J. B. (1980) *Strategic Change: Logical incrementalism*, Homewood, IL: Richard D. Irwin.
—— (1989) 'Managing strategic change' in D. Asch, and C. Bowman (eds) *Readings in Strategic Management*, Basingstoke: Macmillan, 20–36.
Rees, C. (1998) 'Empowerment through quality management? Employee accounts from inside a bank, a hotel and two factories', in C. Mabey D. Skinner and T. Clark (eds) *Experiencing Human Resource Management*, London: Sage.
Salaman, G. (1992) *B884 Human Resource Strategies*, Milton Keynes: Open University.
Schroder, H. M. (1989) 'Managerial competence and style', in M. J. Kirton (ed.) *Adaptor and Innovators: Styles of creativity and problem-solving*. London: Routledge.
Shipton, J. and McCauley, J. (1993) 'Issues of power and marginality in personnel', *Human Resource Management Journal*, vol. 4, no. 1, 1–13.
Simpson, B. and Thorpe, R. (1996) 'Are universities learning organizations?', Paper presented to British Academy of Management, Annual Conference, Aston University, September.
Stacey, R. (1995) 'The Science of complexity an alternative perspective for strategic change processes', *Strategic Management Journal*, vol. 16, 477–95.
—— (1996) *Strategic Management and Organizational Dynamics*, London: Pitman Publishing.
Tefft, M. (1990) 'Creativity through the lenses of the TTCT, MBTI and KAI: The level-style issue examined once again', *Teorie Vedy* (Theory of Science), vol. 1, no. 2, 39–46.

chapter 15

# The Role of Culture in Organizational Performance

CHAPTER OUTLINE

## Learning Objectives

After reading this chapter you should be able to accomplish the following:

- Be fully aware of the variety of ways – some of them fundamentally conflicting – in which the concept of culture has been used in analysis of organization.
- Recognize the implications, assumptions, strengths and weaknesses of these approaches.
- Recognize the nature, origins and limitations of the corporate culture approach associated with the writings of Peters, Deal and Kennedy and others.

# Introduction

This chapter explores three interrelated issues:

- The role of culture in organizational analysis.
- The claimed *role* of organizational cultures in determining levels of organizational performance.
- The *nature* and components of organizational cultures – i.e. how can they be defined and measured?

One of the most striking and pervasive claims of the SHRM movement is that an organization's culture is the key to its performance, and that these organizational cultures can be manipulated to ensure that employees are enthusiastic, committed and compliant. This chapter focuses on these attempts to identify and manipulate organizational cultures – an approach which is here termed the corporate culture approach to organizational cultures.

This approach – corporate culture – is one of a number of ways in which the concept culture has been applied to organizations, and because of its importance it is given considerable attention here. Much of this attention is critical, and much of the criticism stems from the over-simple way in which this approach defines culture and organizations, and from the distorted, ideological nature of these analyses. This chapter sets out the corporate culture approach and identifies some of the major criticisms of it. But if corporate culture is vulnerable to such criticism, then how do we explain the continuing high levels of interest in culture change projects? This question is considered towards the end of the chapter. The chapter as a whole then ends on a slightly negative note – pointing out the weakness of the approach in question. This does not mean that overall our assessment is entirely negative however, and in the following chapter we continue our interest in this topic and conclude with some tentative suggestions for a definition of culture and an approach to cultural change that are defensible and useful, if relatively unambitious. However our purposes are as much to warn as to recommend.

The concept of culture (and the argument that culture is at the heart of organizational performance and effectiveness) is one of the key ideas of SHRM thinking and associated approaches to organizational restructuring which also see the management of culture as the central responsibility of modern managers (Legge 1989). The emphasis on culture change is a major reason for the strength and appeal of much SHRM thinking, for one of the qualities of the organizational culture literature is that it has a particular, and powerful, appeal, especially to managers and consultants. But equally if the emphasis on culture accounts for the appeal of SHRM literature to managers and consultants, it also represents, for some academic commentators, one of the major weaknesses of the SHRM approach. Few elements of SHRM thinking and consultancy have simultaneously attracted so much excitement and so much criticism.

## The Role of Culture in Organizational Analysis

Reference to the two brief cases in box 15.1 shows many of the common themes of recent writings on corporate culture.

Since the beginning of the industrial period, and certainly since the development of factories on a large scale, employers have faced a crucial dilemma: on the one hand, they had to have tight control over what their staff did and how they did it – to ensure that time wasn't wasted, the materials weren't misused or stolen, to ensure quality etc. But on the other hand, they always relied, to varying degrees (but always to some degree) on the goodwill, creativity, good sense, responsibility etc. of the workforce. No factory can be run by rules; for no set of rules entirely catches all that is required of the employees. Unfortunately these two priorities led to two conflicting systems of work organization or work control.

Efforts to achieve tight control – because they were frequently oppressive, intrusive, unpleasant, demanding, dominating – risked damage to workers' commitment on which their goodwill and common sense were dependent. Tight control alienated workers and had negative consequences for quality, industrial relations, absenteeism etc. It tended to breed the worker attitudes it assumed – low trust and low commitment. On the other hand, it worked – at least as far as the production of low cost, high volume products was concerned: the classic Fordist approach to work design. Allowing workers autonomy on the other hand, generated higher levels of commitment and participation but seemed dangerously risky, and might represent or lead to, reduced management control. It is possible to argue that the history of the changing philosophies of management, organization and work design systems is nothing more than the history of different management efforts to 'solve' this dilemma. And the final dilemma, arguably, is this: that any solution actually sets up new problems – or rather revives old problems in a new form or degree.

Ultimately all solutions fail because they simply involve the exchange of the difficulties associated with one solution for the difficulties associated with the other: tight control breeds resentment and poor commitment; empowerment results in greater commitment but risks the loss of management control and the introduction of objectives other than those of management. Thus, 'all forms of

## BOX 15.1 ORGANIZATIONAL PERFORMANCE AND CORPORATE CULTURES

This is a classic account of the nature and impact of culture change projects. Wickens, in his analysis of Nissan UK, takes time out to discuss the orientations of other companies. He describes the situation at Pratt and Whitney, USA. The traditional culture of the company is described as product-oriented, where quality was achieved through monitoring and inspection; people were regarded as an expendable resource, management was basically control, and communications were one-way. This situation has now changed; now the 'value-system' (i.e. culture) has changed to one where the 'customer is the centre of the universe, quality is built in and people are regarded as the single most important part of the organisation and its only appreciable asset' (Wickens 1987: 183). Wickens adds that in Pratt and Whitney 'The purpose of management is to facilitate and thus recognise that the largest single repository of ideas is the workforce, so "two way communication" is of paramount importance' (ibid.: 183).

Deal and Kennedy (1982) describe the corporate culture of The Tandem Corporation, and assess its implications. They attribute (albeit guardedly – 'Only time will tell whether Tandem can maintain its pattern of high performance . . .' (p. 8)) the success of Tandem to its strong culture. This has a number of elements: a widely shared philosophy, which stresses its commitment to the importance of people. This value is 'broadcast by T shirts, bulletin boards and word of mouth' (p. 10). Another element is the remarkable lack of formal structures, roles and rules which are replaced, argue Deal and Kennedy, by their far more effective functional equivalent: unwritten rules and shared understandings. Interestingly the authors note: 'Tandem seems to maintain a balance between autonomy and control without relying heavily on centralised or formalised procedures, or rigid status hierarchies' (p. 11).

Another feature of the culture is the emphasis on the heroic status of the company's CEO. These values are supported by and transmitted through a series of social events and activities 'These provide opportunities for employees to develop a spirit of oneness and symbolise that tandem cares about employees' (p. 12). The authors conclude: 'Tandem is a unique company. And much of its success appears as intimately tied to its culture as to its product and its market place position. The company has explicit values and beliefs which its employees share. It has heroes. It has storytellers and stories. It has rituals and ceremonies on key occasions. Tandem seems to have a strong culture which creates a bond between the company and the employees and inspires levels of productivity unlike most other corporations' (Deal and Kennedy 1989: 12).

control contain, in different degree, two dimensions of control: the specification of levels of performance (and this may vary from highly specified, to highly autonomous) and some effort to develop some level of consent or acceptance of the legitimacy of the employment relationship' (Littler and Salaman 1984: 57). This paradox lies behind management's need to ensure the most effective and efficient utilization of labour (maximum production for lowest cost) while at the same time trying to ensure that the arrangements that follow these priorities do not so oppress the workers that they damage their commitment, and their consent.

It seems, however, as if this perennial and depressing management dilemma might finally have been solved. Corporate culture writers claim that by developing strong corporate cultures managers can finally have it both ways: tight control over performance *and* high levels of commitment and enthusiasm. Employees now want to do what their managers want them to do: no need now for rules or rigidly defined roles. These are ambitious claims; no wonder managers take them so seriously. Maybe we should take them seriously too.

There has been an enormous level of interest in corporate cultures in recent years. One commentator notes: 'The concept of culture has been linked increasingly with the study of organization' (Smircich 1983: 339). Even as early as 1980, *Business Week* ran a cover story entitled: 'Corporate Culture: The hard to change values that spell success or failure'. The reason for this high level of interest is the claimed connection between the nature and strength of organizational cultures and levels of organizational performance and effectiveness.

Interest in organizational cultures, however, comes from two rather different directions, with rather different implications. Not all who write about organizational cultures are primarily concerned with issues of performance. On the one hand, there are academics and researchers who 'welcomed the topic of culture as a long overdue source of "fresh air", an antidote to sterile number crunching focused on easily measured variables'. On the other hand, there are those with a more practical agenda who, 'were attracted by the seductive promises of culture as a key to improved morale, loyalty, harmony, productivity and – ultimately – profitability' (Frost et al. 1991: 7).

## Practitioner and academic approaches to corporate cultures

The culture literature is not homogeneous: it consists of a literature which at one extreme is consultancy-based, popular, rather bland and prescriptive, aimed at managers; and at the other end more theoretical, descriptive studies aimed at scholars. A number of writers have distinguished these two approaches.

1 Barley et al. call these different literatures 'practitioner' and 'academic' approaches. Interestingly these authors note that over time the research focus of both groups, initially very different, began to converge markedly. By 1984, both groups were researching more or less the same issues: the economic values of

controlling culture, the scope and role of rationality, and the integrative value of culture (Barley et al. 1988).

However, not only has the concept of organizational culture been defined in a number of very different – even opposed – ways, it has also been used in different ways, in different content areas, to do different sorts of things.

Barley et al. note how early interest in culture arose from two separate sources. On the one hand there were those management authors who argued that an emphasis on rational strategies, on formal structures and systems, led to an underestimation of the role of values, symbols, beliefs in engaging loyalty and influencing behaviour. These authors argued that rational strategies had a limited effect on performance and productivity, and that the manipulation of values, norms, symbols and beliefs was a powerful but under-used source of managerial advantage.

On the other hand, but at very much the same time, a group of academic researchers began to conceptualize organizations in terms of structures of meaning – focusing on how people at work construct and negotiate the sense of their and others' behaviour in terms of values, myths, norms and beliefs. As Barley et al. note this second approach was essentially an alternative and radically different paradigm with which to study organizations: 'thus while the first group turned to culture as a way of improving organizational effectiveness, the second saw in culture the basis for paradigmatic revolution' (Barley et al. 1988: 32).

Our focus in this chapter is primarily on the first approach, because of the importance of its claims, and its central role in SHRM writings.

2 Knights and Willmott (1987) develop a similar classification: they argue that interest in the concept divides into 'practitioner-oriented' literature and literature which 'is heralded as a new direction in organisational analysis involving a movement away from quantification, prediction and structure toward studies of organisation that are more qualitative, appreciative, and processual' (Knights and Willmott 1987: 40).

3 Sackmann also distinguishes academic from practitioner applications and notes that the first is concerned with understanding, the second control and prediction. She also notes the role of what she calls the cultural anthropologists' tradition which refers to the academic area where the concept was originally developed. This is only relevant to organizational applications in that this original sense of the term supplies a degree of rigour, and of conceptual clarity which is largely missing from organizational applications. One of the main weaknesses of managerialist and consultancy applications ('practitioner') is that they fail to acknowledge the complexity of the concept and some of the fundamental criticisms, from within anthropology, to which their definition and usage of culture is vulnerable (Sackmann 1990). For example, to return to the cases presented earlier, Deal and Kennedy, in their description of the culture of Tandem seem, wittingly or unwittingly, to be trying to portray the culture of Tandem as if Tandem was a mini-society, as if this culture was essentially the same as that of a society, or a tribe. Employees 'share values . . . heroes, stories, storytellers, rituals and ceremonies strong bonds . . . unwritten rules . . .'. We probably accept the power of culture in societies, especially small stable societies; we know that members of such societies can be moved to great levels of commitment; heroism,

shame and sacrifice by such values. But can organizational cultures really be compared to societal cultures? Is a flag the same as a corporate T shirt? And is the role of culture, in a societal, tribal or corporate context, necessarily consensus building, commitment generating, 'positive' in its implications?

4 Smircich (1983) also distinguishes practitioner and academic applications of culture although she explores and develops the distinction more fully. She suggests five areas of the application of the concept culture. These five applications derive from different ways of seeing organizations and culture and focus on different objectives and carry different assumptions. They are worth our attention because aspects of these applications are apparent in the way those concerned with manipulating corporate cultures approach their subject and their work – even if they don't know i

Essentially the first two ways of using the concept are concerned with the identification and analysis of cultural variables that are related to variations in organizational performance, and so, broadly, fall within the 'practitioner' school, although work within these areas can vary considerably in its thoroughness and scholarship. The other three approaches ('academic') are concerned not with efficiency or performance, but with understanding what organizations are, and how they work. Her classification is useful for its thoroughness and also because she includes cross-cultural studies. These five areas are:

cross-cultural or comparative management;
corporate culture;
organizational cognition;
organizational symbolism;
unconscious process and organization.

## Cross-cultural or comparative management

This approach is concerned with identifying and analysing culturally-based variations in management practice and organizational process across countries. Such research is of obvious importance given, for example, the high level of interest in understanding the *Japanese* basis of Japanese economic performance. Broadly speaking this tradition of research defines culture as an independent variable which develops within the organization as a consequence of the organization's location within a host society. The cultural values, distinctive to the host society, are revealed in the behaviours of organizational members. This type of research seeks to map and classify differences in cultural variables and relate these countries.

Child has revived and synthesized this literature very usefully (Child 1981). He notes that this use of culture has three objectives: to identify the extent to which organizational characteristics vary in relation to their location within different countries; secondly, to isolate the national attributes associated with such differences, and thirdly, if there are national differences, to explain how organizations are coloured by national differences. He notes that research to date has argued that some organizational characteristics, particularly employees' attitudes and interpersonal styles, do vary between countries. For example, the work of Hofstede (1980), who on the basis of an enormous survey of 160,000 employees of IBM, argued that there are four discrete dimensions of culture: power distance (extent to which people accept the unequal distribution of power); uncertainty avoidance (the extent to which people dislike ambiguity and uncertainty); individualism (the extent to which people are oriented towards the well-being of themselves/families as against an orientation towards a wider social grouping); and masculinity (the extent to which material forms of success are prized over values such as caring and nurturing). On the basis of his research he argues that countries differ significantly in their 'score' on these dimensions.

Hofstede shows how these dimensions can be used to illustrate organizational cultures and practices. He argues, for example, that two dimensions – power distance and uncertainty – can be combined to form a matrix within which organizations can be located. Organizations low on power distance and low on uncertainty avoidance prefer a lack of overriding hierarchy, and a flexible approach to rules, while organizations with low power distance but high on uncertainty avoidance expect actions to comply with and to be directed by, rules and procedures.

However, in reviewing work on cultural differences, Child argues that there has been little thorough or persuasive work that explains why these attributes are intrinsic to the development of the host societies, or how they influence organizations within these societies. A major source of the problems in the use of national culture as an explanatory variable is a result of the way in which the frequently ill-defined concept of culture is simply used to account for identified differences in organizational behaviour or values. It is used as a rather indiscriminate, general explanation to account for differences otherwise unaccounted for. Studies of cross-national differences 'have managed to identify variations in organisational or member characteristic associated with nationality, but have ascribed these to culture without locating it in a relevant social context. Culture has thus been treated as a residual factor' (Child 1981: 306).

While aware of the weaknesses of this cross-cultural approach to analyses of organizations, Child is unwilling entirely to reject this approach. This is largely because his review of two other explanations for differences in organizational structures and functioning (these are known as arguments from contingency and from capitalism) suggests that neither of these is wholly satisfactory either. Child therefore seeks to rescue culturalist explanations. However this involves a number of elements.

1 Although noting the large number of definitions of culture Child emphasizes that the essence of culture is its concern with the normative and the relationship between norms and values and action. If, he argues, citizens of one country hold values in common then these will presumably influence how they behave, in specified context and in an observable manner.

2 Child then uses a framework for the classification of the elements of cultures. Like many other commentators he uses Kluckhohn and Strodtbeck's model of value dimensions (1961).

3 He argues that studies of cultural differences must be able to avoid the common danger of simply inferring culture as a national phenomenon to account for any contrasts which arise from a comparison of organizations located in different countries. 'Even if such contrasts are unambiguously national in scope, they could possibly be due to other non-cultural phenomena such as national wealth, level of industrialisation or even climate' (Child 1981: 328). This point is important, for many authors have accounted for national differences in organizational structure and functioning by references not to values per se, but to differences in the pattern of industrialization or modernization, or to the institutional structures of societies, or the underlying character of the economic system.

Child concludes his analysis by suggesting that despite the problems with the term culture in cross-national analyses, it is worth retaining as long as culture is (a) treated rigorously, and (b) is regarded as just one of a number of inter-related relevant variables.

## Corporate Culture

This application is particularly important for these chapters since it represents the major way in which the concept culture is employed within the SHRM literature. This is the approach that is apparent in the two short cases quoted earlier. Within this tradition culture is seen as an *attribute* of organization – something that organizations *have*. In general this application employs a systems approach to organizations, seeing them as collections of inter-related variables, the inter-relationships between which determine the nature of organizational process and effectiveness. Traditionally the key variables identified by such an approach would be the 'hard' variables of structure, technology etc., but recently (see below) 'soft' subjective variables such as culture have been emphasized.

The key argument of this application of culture is simply that the culture of an organization contributes to its performance. In this and the following chapter this argument, central to SHRM writing, will be thoroughly discussed and criticized.

Both the earlier two applications of the concept of culture to organizations see organizations as organism-like entities existing within environments which supply pressures for action and adjustment. In both cases attention is focused on the patterns of relationships within organizations or between organizations and their environments. Smircich notes that both approaches share the assumption that: 'The desired outcomes of research into these patterns are statements of contingent relationships that will have applicability for those trying to manage organisations. Underlying the interests in comparative management and corporate culture is the search for predictable means for organisational control and improved means for organisational management' (Smircich 1983: 347).

Thus both applications treated so far, in regarding organizations as organisms, see culture as an attribute *of*, or an element *of*, these organisms – something the organization *has*. However, an alternative view is to see organizations *as* cultures.

In this sense organizations are seen *as if they were* cultures, a metaphor which stresses the subjective, consciousness, expressive, symbolic aspects of organizations rather than seeing organizations in instrumental, material terms. Within this metaphor the focus of research activity is not performance in the sense of efficiency or effectiveness, or competitiveness or output, but performance as continuous theatre, as the management of, and construction of, meaning.

This approach to organizational culture: seeing it as something the organization *is*, differs fundamentally from the earlier approach (something an organization *has*) not only in its approach but also in its objectives. Here the focus is not on improving performance, supporting management, or strengthening (while disguising) management control, but on understanding organizational action in the terms in which participants themselves understand it.

This 'culture as metaphor' approach to organizational analysis has produced three constituent schools of research:

In one approach culture is defined in terms of the *structuring of cognitive processes* within organizations. This approach regards organizational cultures as a structure of ways of understanding and knowing the world, of rules that govern cognition. Such an approach, potentially of enormous value in analysing and revealing the taken-for-granted assumptions and convictions that lie behind organizational members' decisions and relationships, focuses on the structures of shared meanings and frameworks and recipes that determine members' analysis and perceptions.

Another variant is when the focus is on culture as *systems of shared symbols* within organizations. Here researchers seek to analyse, to 'read' the meaning of members' action, and on how members themselves read others' behaviour and learn to construct their own and to display their mastery of the informal, symbolic systems. This approach seeks to understand cultures in terms of the ways in which organizational members manage to understand and make sense for, each other.

Finally a third form of the metaphor approach to the use of the concept of culture is when organizational cultures are seen as the *expression of psychological processes* and needs.

We see then that there is general agreement that applications of the notion of culture to organization take two basic forms: one practitioner-focused, concerned with issues of efficiency and performance, the other more academic, concerned with issues of understanding and analysis. This in itself is not necessarily surprising; but what makes it highly important in this discussion is the suggestion, voiced by many writers, that the practitioners' analysis (and the prescriptions and promises built on these analyses) have overlooked some of the complexities of the concept of culture and of organization in their eagerness to discover, or pass on their seductive promises: that if cultures can be changed it is a lot harder, and a lot less certain in its outcome, than the enthusiasts recognize, or admit. This is why it is necessary to expose the corporate culture approach to a thorough critical analysis.

## The Role of Culture in Organizational Performance

As we have noted, the reason for so much recent managerial interest is because of the claim that culture plays a major part in determining organizational performance. If it was not for this claim – and the power and appeal of this claim – there would be little need to discuss organizational cultures. And there is enormous interest. 'Probably never before in organisational studies has an innovative area been given so much attention so rapidly' (Stablein and Nord 1985: 22).

What precisely is the argument of the corporate culture writers? In general they argue:

- That organizations have cultures.
- That they become more effective when they develop the right 'strong' cultures (which needs careful definition).
- That these cultures create consensus and unity and motivate staff.
- That cultures have an effect on corporate performance.
- That when necessary, cultures can be – and should be – changed.
- That it is the responsibility of senior managers to change them.

The corporate culture approach presumes that organizational cultures can be assessed, managed, constructed and manipulated in the pursuit of enhanced organizational effectiveness. Employees' norms, beliefs and values can (and when necessary should) be changed so that they contribute the appropriate behaviour, commit themselves to the organization, support management and strategy. This view holds that the norms and values shared by members of the organization create consensus, create unity and generate appropriate behaviour. Cultures integrate the organization (Meek 1992).

The corporate culture approach specifies the positive role of corporate cultures: 'Organisational culture' is considered 'the managerial formula for success' (Jaggi 1985) that determines an organization's 'success or failure' (Values 1983). Managers are promised a 'culture of "productivity"' (Akin and Hopelain 1986) if they understand the elements that all cultures of productivity have in common. The 'right' culture may 'reap a return on investment that averages nearly twice as high as those firms with less efficient cultures' (Denison 1984). 'Sustained competitive advantage' (Barney 1986) is expected from the 'right' culture, which is also characterized as 'strong' (Bleicher 1983: 495) 'rich' (Deal and Kennedy 1982: 14), 'healthy, blooming' (Ulrich 1984: 313), 'consistent' (Hinterhuber 1986) and 'participatory' (Denison 1984: 7; Sackmann 1990: 119).

This argument is probably most associated with (and is certainly well developed within) the writings of Tom Peters and the 'excellence' approach which he represents and articulates. Peters and Waterman (1982) argue that in 'excellent' companies employees are committed to their organization and to its goals, and that this is a firmer basis for achieving competitive excellence than the traditional determinants of behaviour – structures, procedures and rules. This argument is nicely caught in the summary of one commentator: 'There is a growing international consensus that, for the western countries, economic renaissance is dependent upon the cultural transformation of large-scale business and, in particular, on the extent to which decaying bureaucracies can be replaced with dynamic, organic cultures' (Sadler 1988: 127).

This view is not restricted to Peters. Deal and Kennedy, for example, argue that: 'Since organisational values can powerfully influence what people actually do, we think that values ought to be a matter of great concern to managers. In fact, shaping and enhancing values can become the most important job a manager can do. In our work and study we have found that successful companies place a great deal of emphasis on values. In general, these companies shared three characteristics:

- They stand for something – that is, they have a clear and explicit philosophy about how they aim to conduct their business.
- Management pays a great deal of attention to shaping and fine-tuning these values to conform to the economic and business environment of the company and to communicating them to the organization.
- These values are known and shared by all the people who work for the company – from the lowliest production worker right through to the ranks of senior management. (Deal and Kennedy 1991: 22)

Notice how 'strong' cultures are here regarded entirely positively. Deal and Kennedy argue, for example: 'Strong culture companies . . . communicate exactly how they want their people to behave. They spell out standards of acceptable decorum – so people who visit or work in any of their places of business can know what to expect. They call attention to the way in which procedures – for example strategic planning and budgeting – are to be carried out. The fault if the procedures fail is substantive not just a failure to follow prescribed process . . . In strong culture companies nothing is too trivial . . . These companies take pride in the way they do things and work hard to make sure that the way is right' (Deal and Kennedy 1991: 59–60).

If organizational cultures have consequences for employees' behaviour and attitudes, then the manipulation of such cultures and the symbols of which they consist, becomes a primary task for managers – possibly *the* primary task: 'If organizations are systems of shared meanings and beliefs, and if they are organized through the development of shared paradigms, then clearly one important administrative activity is the development of such understandings within the organization' (Pfeffer 1981: 21).

Peters supports this view of the manager's new role: 'symbols are the very stuff of management behaviour. Executives, after all, do not synthesise chemicals or operate fork lift trucks; they deal in symbols' (Peters 1978: 10). The potential benefit of such action for commitment and consensus is forcefully identified: 'Symbolic action may serve to motivate individuals within the organisation and to mobilise persons . . . to take action . . . Symbolic actions may serve to mollify groups that are dissatisfied with the organisation, thereby ensuring their continued support of the organisation and the lessening of opposition and conflict' (Pfeffer 1981: 34–5); see also Deal and Kennedy (1982) and Kilmann et al. (1986).

## The Nature and Components of Organizational Cultures

Within the organizational culture field issues of definition assume centre stage. If we are to assess the claims of the corporate culture advocates, we must know what they mean by culture and what assumptions they are making about the nature and origins of culture. The analysis of organizational culture is a focus of an enormous amount of activity, academic research, and consultancy. We have seen already that there are significant differences in the way in which the culture concept is applied and the usages to which it is put. So what is corporate or organizational culture? What are these authors talking about when they stress the importance of the management of culture?

It will be no surprise to find that the concept itself is defined in very different ways. Much of the confusion and conflict between writings (and recommendations) on corporate culture stem from major and fundamental differences in how culture is defined. And these differences are not haphazard: they are related directly to equally fundamental differences in assumptions about how organizations work. 'Organisational culture researchers do not agree about what culture is or why it should be studied. They do not study the same phenomena. They do not approach the phenomena they do study from the same theoretical, epistemological, or methodological points of view' (Frost et al. 1991: 7).

### *Definitions*

Our focus within these chapters is mainly on the managerialist, consultancy approach to organizational cultures – corporate culture. Therefore in this section we will focus mainly but not exclusively on definitions of culture from within the corporate culture tradition. However, other definitions will also be mentioned mainly in order to highlight and counterpoint the consultancy definitions.

Definitions of culture within the corporate culture approach have a number of common features.

First, the definitions are highly functionalistic, normative, prescriptive and instrumental. Cultures are defined in terms of their impact on performance and are regarded in terms of their positive contribution. For example, Kilmann et al. remark: 'A culture has a positive impact on an organisation when it points behaviour in the right direction . . . Alternatively a culture has negative impact when it points behaviour in the wrong direction' (Kilmann et al. 1986: 4, quoted in Alvesson 1989: 125). Another contributor to this managerialist tradition displays unashamedly a managerialist perspective: 'Good cultures are characterised by norms and values supportive of excellence, teamwork, profitability, honesty, a customer service orientation, pride in one's work, and commitment to the organisation. Most of all, they are supportive of adaptability – the capacity to thrive over the long run despite new competition, new regulations, new technological developments, and the strains of growth' (Baker 1980: 10, quoted in Alvesson 1989: 125).

Many of these definitions are overtly functionalist in the sense that they argue that existing cultures exist because they play a positive role in the maintenance and effectiveness of the organization: they have a survival role. Schein represents this view very clearly. According to him, 'Culture is:

1 A pattern of shared basic assumptions,
2 invented, discovered or developed by a given group, as it
3 learns to cope with its problems of external adaptation and internal integration.
4 That has worked well enough to be considered valid and therefore,
5 is taught to new members of the group as the
6 correct way to perceive, think and feel in relation to those problems.' (Schein 1992: 237)

Secondly, these definitions of culture commonly refer to the *integrative* role of culture: 'Culture . . . refers to a shared system of values, norms and symbols. The term culture conveys an entire image, *an integrated set of dimensions/characteristics and the whole behind the parts*' (Louis 1981; quoted in Alvesson 1987: 4, our emphasis).

They also insist that cultures are *shared* by members of the organization. 'Shared meaning, shared understanding, and shared sense-making are all different ways of describing culture. In talking about culture we are really talking about a process of reality construction that allows people to see and understand particular events, actions, objects, utterances, or situations in distinctive ways' (Morgan 1986; quoted in Alvesson 1987: 5).

Thirdly, these definitions argue that cultures consist of values, beliefs and cognitive assumptions.

A different, and contrasting approach is offered by Pettigrew (1979: 574). His definition does not assume that the values in question are shared by all members of an organization (which is empirically highly unlikely anyway). He focuses not on the organization but on the group. He notes that when people work together they develop a sense of what they are doing and why, of how they should relate to each: in short a system of meanings. But he does not assume that cultures are necessarily positive, or integrating, or shared. 'Culture is the system of such publicly and collectively accepted meanings operating for a given group at a given time.' Pettigrew sensibly objects to the assumption that cultures are unitary, consensual and consistent. He prefers to argue that culture is a source of a family of concepts, all of which have their use: symbol, language, ideology, ritual, belief.

## Differences underlying these definitions

A number of writers have attempted to categorize and organize the heterogeneous definitions of cultures into categories. The basis for these classifications is usually the purpose that is seen to lie behind the definitions and these purposes are often categorized in terms very similar to those discussed earlier – of whether the definition is intended to aid managerial objectives, academic understanding, or radical critique of organizations.

Frost et al. (1991) argue that it is possible to organize the different definitions of culture under three headings: integration, fragmentation and differentiation. The integration perspective sees cultures as consistent and consensual; the differentiation perspective stresses inconsistency, variation, even conflict between sub-cultures. And finally, the fragmentation perspective sees cultures as ambiguous, fluctuating, inconsistent, unclear.

Obviously the integration perspectives represents the classic consultancy approach of Peters, Deal and Kennedy etc. It asserts that a strong or desirable culture is characterized by consistency, organization-wide consensus and clarity, and that these result in commitment, and improved performance.

Other authors have used the work of Habermas to classify approaches to organizational cultures. Habermas's distinction between three types of cognitive interest in a subject is useful. Three such approaches are distinguished: the technical, the practical and the emancipatory. Habermas describes these as: 'information that expands our power of technical control; interpretations that make possible the orientation of action within common traditions; and analyses that free consciousness from its dependence on hypostatised powers' (Habermas 1971: 313; quoted in Stablein and Nord 1985: 14).

The first is aimed at achieving control over the subject; the second seeks to achieve understanding; the third focuses on the achievement of that which is liberating, that removes compulsion and reveals power and compulsion. While the first two approaches clearly work to sustain existing relationships and institutions and to legitimate them; the third critiques and questions such patterns. Very clearly, the majority of analyses of organizational cultures fall into the first category: they attempt to harness and direct the power of culture to further the manipulation and control of workers in pursuit of managerial purposes.

## Conclusions and Summary

Organizations are structures of symbols and meaning. Even talking about or researching organizations is symbolic and life within organizations cannot occur without the symbols and myths that make it meaningful and possible. Therefore as researchers, managers or consultants we must of course focus on these – on the 'cultural' aspects of organization. Yet while such a (hermeneutic) project is necessary and desirable we have argued in this chapter that much corporate culture literature is flawed and inadequate – a fad. So why is there so much interest? If definitions of cultures are complex and differentiated; if culture is applied in such different ways, if consensus and unity are rare, if culture occurs at different levels and most important of all if cultures are complex and difficult to change, then why has so much effort been spent on studying organizational cultures?

On one level of course the appeal is obvious: the corporate culture approach promises to support management control by winning the hearts and minds of employees (Willmott 1993: 516). But its appeal lies deeper than this.

We have noted that the rise of interest in corporate cultures should be seen in terms of two processes: the gradual historic emergence of a conviction of the importance of 'soft' aspects of organizational structure and process in contrast to rational, systems and structures; and the persuasive argument that the manipulation of organizational cultures offers a solution to the increasingly obvious limitations of traditional, oppressive forms of control. We have also noted the powerful appeal of culturalist writings and prescriptions. How can we account for this appeal? (There is something to explain here, because although the appeal of the corporate literature may lie in its promises it is important to recognize that there is little evidence that these promises have been fulfilled. The appeal of the literature lies in the nature of the message and the promise. Somehow these strike a chord with managers.)

A number of authors have tried to answer this question. There are three reasons for the appeal of corporate culture. First, that the explanation for the success of those organizations and economies that most threaten US and UK companies (Japanese and South-East Asia) lies in their superior cultures and their recognition of the role of culture as a source of commitment, focus and cohesion in the workforce. Secondly, concern about the declining competitiveness of US and UK corporations which is attributed to the inability of these corporations to understand and manage their corporate cultures. And finally, the claim that the organizations required by new competitive circumstances will be characterized by new forms of control and cohesion. (For a fuller exploration of these factors see Salaman 1997.)

An important part of the appeal of Corporate Culture writings lies in the complex and appealing ways in which the message – a mixture of aggressive attack and comforting reassurance – resonates with the values of its audience. It cleverly uses the threat of 'the other' – the Japanese for example – to reassert traditional homely values. 'The language . . . renders opaque developments clear, not by providing a more objective analysis and solution, but by providing a persuasive rendering of these. Moreover, part of the persuasive essence lies in the resonance that it "reveals" between American past glories and future conquests . . . American industry is weak now because rather than despite of the fact that it was so strong before; and American industry will be strong again because, rather than despite of, America culture' (Grint 1994: 194).

Thus, as Guest has remarked, corporate culture writings appeal because of their resonance with existing cultural values (Guest 1992). He draws connections between elements of the culture literature and some basic themes in the American Dream. And this attempt to identify resonances and affinities with the culture literature and other bodies of values currently powerful within the society has proved a fruitful line of analysis (Guest 1990; du Gay and Salaman 1992). Elsewhere, Guest (1992) refers to the fact that books such as *In Search of Excellence* are not only about the importance of values and feelings in organizations, they also cleverly tap into, and appeal to, the values and feelings of their manager readers. He quotes the analysis of Conrad that 'the appeal of a book like *Passion for Excellence* lies in its mythos, its capacity to transport readers symbolically from a world of everyday experience to a mythical realm' (Conrad 1985).

The dream that these books promise to realize has long been a dream of managers; their aspiration has always been to be able to manage staff without their knowing or resenting this control, to get workers to accept managerial goals and managerial authority and managerial decisions so that they don't need managing, or controlling; in fact so that they see the organization and their work as the managers see it. The corporate culture approach offers to managers the seductive promise that they can, on Wilmott's terms, 'colonize the affective domain . . . (by) . . . promoting employee commitment to a monolithic structure of feeling and thought' (Willmott 1993: 517). One of the distinctive features of this approach is that it claims that it is possible to achieve a situation where employees want, on their own, what managers want them to do. Control is now built-in; employees can safely be autonomous because they will 'own' responsibility for doing, to high standards, what they are required to do. Employees can be 'free' because they can be relied on to do what the organization wants them to do. This is the offer. No wonder the culture literature is powerful and popular. But is the Corporate Culture project feasible, is it realistic and credible?

## Key Points

- Many recent writers – academics and consultants – have argued seductively that the key to improved organizational performance and the answer to managers' old dilemma of how to attract the commitment and energy of employees, is to understand and manipulate the culture of the organization.
- This argument – which is most appealing to managers – is extremely important in its implications; but there is no point and no advantage in confusing the way we would like things to be with the way they actually are: we need to examine very carefully and very thoroughly the basis, inherent assumptions, and potential limitations of this

approach. Does the 'corporate culture' approach to organizational analysis bear closer scrutiny and rigorous testing?

- One important key point is just how different writers define culture and what fundamental assumptions they make about organizational cultures. These definitions and approaches require careful analysis for some definitions carry some very dubious and insecure assumptions.

## Discussion Questions

1. **Describe the different ways in which the concept culture has been used in organizational writings.**
2. **Describe the key elements of the Corporate Culture approach.**
3. **Discuss and contrast some of the main ways in which the concept organizational culture has been used in analyses of organizations.**
4. **Assess the strengths and weaknesses of the 'corporate culture' approach to organizational cultures.**

## References

Akin, G. and Hopelian, D. (1986) 'Finding the culture of productivity', *Organisational Dynamics*, vol. 15, 19–32.

Alvesson, M. (1987) 'Organisations, culture and ideology', *International Studies of Management and Organisation*, vol. 17, no. 3, 4–18.

—— (1989) 'The cultural perspective on organisations: Instrumental values and basic features of culture', *Scandinavian Journal of Management*, vol. 5, no. 2, 123–36.

Baker, E. (1980) 'Managing organisational culture', *Management Review*, June, 8–13.

Barley, S., Meyer, G., and Gash, D. (1988) 'Cultures of culture: academics, practitioners and the pragmatics of normative control', *Administrative Science Quarterly*, vol. 33, no. 1, 24–60.

Barney, J. B. (1986) 'Organisational culture: can it be a sustained source of competitive advantage?', *Academy of Management Review*, vol. 11, no. 3, 656–65.

Bleicher, K. (1983) 'Organisationskulturen and fuhrungsphilosophien in Bettewerb', *Zeitschrift furb Betriebswirtschaftliche Forschung*, vol. 35, 135–46.

Child, J. (1981) 'Culture, contingency and capitalism in the cross-national study of organisations,' in L. L. Cummings and B. Staw (eds) *Research in Organisational Behaviour*, Greenwich, CT: JAI Press.

Conrad, C. (1985) 'Review of *A Passion for Excellence*', *Administrative Science Quarterly*, vol. 30, no. 3, 426–8.

Deal, T. and Kennedy, A. (1982) *Corporate Cultures*, Harmondsworth: Penguin Books.

—— and —— (1991) *Corporate Cultures*, Harmondsworth: Penguin Books.

Denison, D. R. (1984) 'Bringing corporate culture to the bottom line', *Organisational Dynamics*, vol. 12, 5–22.

du Gay, P. and Salaman, G. (1992) 'The culture of the customer', *Journal of Management Studies*, vol. 29, no. 5, 45–61.

Frost, P., Moore, L., Louis, M. R., Lundberg, C., and Martin, J. (1991) 'Introduction', in P. Frost et al. (eds) *Reframing Organisational Culture*, Newbury Park, CA: Sage, 7–10.

Guest, D. (1990) 'Human resource management and the American dream', *Journal of Management Studies*, vol. 27, no. 4, 377–97.
—— (1992) 'Right enough to be dangerously wrong', in G. Salaman et al. (eds) *Human Resource Strategies*, London: Sage, 1–19.
Grint, K. (1994) 'Reengineering history', *Organisation*, vol. 1, no. 1, 179–202.
Habermas, J. (1971) *Knowledge and Human Interests*, Boston: Beacon Press.
Hofstede, G. (1980) *Culture's Consequences*, London: Sage.
Hinterhuber, H. H. (1986) 'Strategie, innovation and unternehmenskultur', *Blick Durch Die Wirtschaft*, vol. 20, no. 10.
Jaggi, D. (1985) 'Corporate identity als unternehmerische erfolgsformel', Paper presented at the Second WEMAR – Tagung.
Kieser, A. (1987) 'Zur funktion von werten, mythen, ritualen und symbolen', *Working Paper, Institut für Allgemeine Betriebswirtschaftslehre und Organisation*, University of Mannheim.
Kilmann, R., Saxton, M., and Serpa, R. (1986) 'Five Key issues in understanding and changing culture' in R. Kilmann, M. Saxton and R. Serpa et al. (eds) *Gaining Control of the Corporate Culture*, San Francisco, CA: Jossey-Bass, 1–16.
Kluckhohn, F. R. and Strodtbeck, F. L. (1961) *Variations in Value Orientations*, New York: Row, Peterson.
Knights, D. and Willmott, H. (1987) 'Organisational culture as a management strategy', *International Studies of Management and Organisation*, vol. XVII, no. 3.
Littler, C. and Salaman, G. (1984) *Class at Work*, London: Batsford.
Legge, K. (1989) 'HRM: A critical analysis', in J. Storey (ed.) *New Perspectives on Human Resource Management*, London: Routledge.
Louis, M. R. (1981) 'A cultural perspective on organisations', *Human Systems Management*, vol. 2, 246–58.
Meek, V. L. (1982) 'Organisational culture: origins and weaknesses', in G. Salaman et al. (eds) *Human Resource Strategies*, London: Sage, 192–212.
Morgan, G. (1986) *Images of Organisation*, Beverley Hills, CA: Sage.
Peters, T. (1978) 'Symbols, patterns and settings', *Organisational Dynamics*, vol. 9, no. 2, 3–23.
—— and Austin, N. (1985) *A Passion for Excellence*, New York: Random House.
—— and Waterman, R. (1982) *In Search of Excellence*, New York: Harper and Row.
Pettigrew, A. (1979) 'On studying organisational cultures', *Administrative Science Quarterly*, December, 570–81.
—— (1990) 'Is corporate culture manageable?' in D. Wilson and R. Rosenfeld (eds) *Managing Organisations*, 267–72.
Pfeffer, J. (1981) 'Management as symbolic action', in L. L. Cummings and B. M. Staw (eds) *Research in Organisational Behaviour*, vol. 4, Greenwich, CT: JAI Press.
Sackmann, S. (1990) 'Managing organisational culture: Dreams and possibilities' in J. Anderson (ed.) *Communication Yearbook*, vol. 13, Newbury Park, CA: 114–48.
—— (1991) 'Managing organisational culture: Dream and possibilities', in J. Anderson (ed.) *Communication Yearbook*, vol. 13, Newbury Park, CA: Sage, 114–48.
Sadler, P. (1988) *Managerial Leadership in the Post-Industrial Society*, Aldershot: Gowever.
Salaman, G. (1997) 'Culturing production', in P. du Gay (ed.) *Production of Culture/Cultures of Production*, London: Sage, 235–84.
Schein, E. (1992) 'Coming to a new awareness of organisational culture', in G. Salaman et al. (eds) *Human Resource Strategies*, London: Sage, 237–53.
Smircich, L. (1983) 'Concepts of culture and organisational analysis' *Administrative Science Quarterly*, vol. 28, 339–58.

Stablein, R. and Nord W. (1985) 'Practical and emancipatory interests in organisational symbolism', *Journal of Management*, vol. 11, no. 2, 13–28.
Ulrich, P. (1984) 'Systemsteuerung and kulturentwicklung', *Die Unternehmung*, vol. 38, 303–25.
Values (1983) 'The hard-to-change values that spell success or failure', *Business Week*, October 25, 148–59.
Wickens, P. (1987) *The Road To Nissan*, Basingstoke: Macmillan.
Willmott, H. (1993) 'Strength is ignorance: Slavery is freedom; managing culture in modern organisations', *Journal of Management Studies*, vol. 30, no. 4, 515–52.

chapter 16

# The Possibilities of Culture Change

CHAPTER OUTLINE

## Learning Objectives

After reading this chapter you should be able to accomplish the following:

- Be alert to the criticisms levelled at the Corporate Culture movement which draw attention to its inherent weaknesses and limitations, and to the possibility that the corporate culture approach has major ideological elements.
- Be able to identify the key dimensions of organizational cultures.
- Yet also recognize that, despite the difficulties associated with the concept and with the corporate culture approach, there is still good reason for us to be concerned with the nature and role of organizational cultures, and advantage in focusing attention on them.

# Introduction

The corporate culture approach to culture discussed in the previous chapter is potentially of enormous importance. After all, it promises a way, finally, to overcome the historic weakness of the large-scale employing organization – that organizational means of control and co-ordination inadvertently create and reproduce the very grounds for their existence, by damaging and reducing the commitment of the workforce. Management and organization (and all the subsystems these imply for payment, direction, monitoring etc.) are necessary in order to ensure that labour works as required. But when employees are subject to external control and discipline their internal commitment and enthusiasm can be damaged. As we saw, Corporate Culture promises a way out of this paradox: now employees can be made to want what their managers want them to want. Or can they?

Peters and Waterman, at least, are characteristically clear and forceful: 'The guiding aim and abiding concern of Corporate Culture . . . is to win the "hearts and minds" of employees, to define their purposes by managing what they think and feel, and not just how they behave.' The strengthening of Corporate Cultures, it is claimed, provides the key to securing 'unusual effort on the part of apparently ordinary employees' (Peters and Waterman 1982: xvii).

In this chapter we will consider some of the doubts and criticisms that have been levelled at the corporate culture movement. It has been criticized, for instance, for having major *ideological* elements: it is purposive and bland because its function is to support management goals, and the aspects of organization associated with these goals.

Academics are sometimes accused by practical, practising managers of being overly critical, as if they enjoyed critique for its own sake, or as if critique was somehow perverse, negative and unhelpful. But critique is necessary. If corporate culture is empirically unsuccessful or conceptually flawed or riddled with internal contradiction; if it confuses hope with experience, ignores the realities of everyday organizational life, then we might as well know this in order not to waste time on it, or to enable us to take whatever measures are necessary to reduce the possibilities of failure. After all, we often find that: 'reforms are easier to initiate than to decide on, and easier to decide on than to implement' (Brunsson and Olsen 1993: 6).

These criticisms do not apply to all applications of culture to organizations. When culture is used as an analytic tool it is less amenable to criticism. The weaknesses of the ideological application of culture writings do not apply to the 'culture as metaphor school': 'When culture is a root metaphor, the researcher's attention shifts from concerns about what organisations accomplish and how they may accomplish it more efficiently to how is organisation accomplished and what does it mean to be organised' (Smircich 1983: 353).

But when culture becomes part of an attempt to change the organization; when it becomes a management tool, then it can be seen to serve ideological purposes, in a number of ways.

The basic problem here is that corporate culture initiatives, while they are overtly aimed at *changing* the culture of the organization, paradoxically actually *reflect* the existing values and culture of senior management. Within organizations – all organizations – the thinking, planning and decision-making of senior managers are defined by a series of implicit rules and conventions which 'define legitimate participants and agendas, prescribe the rules of the game, and create sanctions against deviations, as well as establishing guidelines for how the institution may be changed . . . They influence and simplify the way we think and act, what we observe, how we interpret what we observe, our standards of evaluation and how we cope with conflicts' (Brunsson and Olsen 1993: 21). These rules can be seen as part of the organization's culture. And they strongly influence managers in their conviction that organizational cultures can be changed; that organizations are consensual and unitary phenomenon etc. This is what we mean when we describe corporate culture as ideological: that it reflects the views, mindsets, assumptions and purposes of managers. We shall explore this ideological aspect of corporate culture in more detail.

## The Ideology of Culture: Culture as Ideology

There are three important ways in which Corporate Culture writing can be seen as ideological. First, those who contribute to the Corporate Culture approach are clearly committed to the *enhancement of management control* and management goals, and to the improvement of organizational performance, by means of the manipulation of corporate culture – culture change programmes. These writers focus on the value of controlling organizational cultures and the benefits of so doing. 'The key assumption of authors writing on culture and symbolism proceeding from a technical cognitive interest, is that knowledge about the functioning of symbols and how intentionally to change and control significant symbols in organisations, provide potential means for the management and manipulation of symbols. Symbols are . . . viewed as aspects of organisations possessing the potential to be exploited and subordinated to the intentions of . . . top managers' (Alvesson 1991: 216).

Secondly, these writings are partial, *selective and discriminating* in the aspects of management culture on which they chose to focus.

Thirdly, Corporate Culture writing adopts a particular, and highly contentious conception of what organizations are like and how they function, stressing a *unitary, consensual and co-operative* view of organizations, and by stressing these desirable attributes, seeking to achieve them.

The focus on consensus, with its implication of mutuality, obstructs the role of power in underpinning existing organizational structures, and the ways they work. One of the curious features of the consultancy approach to organizational cultures is that despite the claim to be concerned with structures of values and beliefs, the actual focus is remarkably limited: Corporate Culture is usually concerned far more with the values of some groups within the organization – managers – than with others – lower level employees. Corporate Culture does not usually attend to 'the role of symbols and the expression of culture in the reproduction of labour processes through which the fundamentally exploitative character of production relations, involving the pumping out of surplus from employees, is routinely secured as it is concealed' (Knights and Wilmott 1987: 43).

The same point is made by Alvesson (1989), who argues that the concept of culture is excessively focused on instrumental preoccupations and values within the organization, while at the same time being insufficiently concerned with exploring (or even acknowledging) core aspects of western managerial culture which might (a) be inimical or damaging to consensus, and cultural unity, and (b) might undermine employee commitment and obedience – i.e. such values as hierarchy, control, instrumental values, racism etc.

However, while these approaches are directly concerned with the pursuit of management objectives they present themselves as exercises in neutral, academic/scientific research and analysis. In other words they deny their nature and origins. They support attempts to control the workforce while claiming that their interests are purely neutral and academic. They claim to represent objective scientific analyses of the way the world is – or organizations are – but in fact they represent the way managers see the world, and the interests they pursue. 'The questions formulated and answered, the perspective taken, the sectional interests supported etc. are grounded in a world view, a set of beliefs and values, which indicate that the top managers of corporations and other organizations are a highly important group, whose actions are normally supposed to support the social good . . . managerial actions . . . are worthy of support and it is the duty of management writers to provide it' (Alvesson 1991: 217).

The focus on 'culture change' for example, is often an attempt to impose a consensual, unitarist conception of the organization on all employees, and thus to gain their commitment. It is an attempt to deny and define away differences of view point, of experiences, of interests and values. It attempts to re-define – re-imagine – the organization and its employees. Organizational attempts to achieve homogeneous, unitary cultures contrast, and possibly conflict, with a view of the organization as an arena of conflicting and different groups and value systems.

The rhetoric is denied by reality. Even Wickens, an enthusiast for the corporate culture approach, acknowledges that 'We spend vast amounts of time talking and negotiating about employee involvement and very little time actually involving employees. As with many of these ideas – the flavour of the month that will be our managerial salvation – we construct en edifice which simply invites opposition' (Wickens 1987: 85).

## Conceptual Limitations

Although the concept of culture is obviously borrowed from cultural anthropology, those who have used it in analyses of organizations have drawn selectively from available definitions of culture and have failed to note, or address, the assumptions underlying the definitions they have employed, or criticisms of these assumptions.

Definitions of culture in the corporate-cultures approach have made a series of basic assumptions about the nature and role of cultures which are unsustainable. For example, they borrow heavily from a particular tradition within anthropology and sociology – structural functionalism – which has been roundly criticized. Yet these criticisms, which also apply to corporate applications, have been overlooked by recent culture writers. For example, one key assertion of the structural-functionalist approach is that, 'social order is created and maintained through individuals internalising dominant social norms and values' (Meek 1992: 195), a view which overlooks the role of power and coercion in social organization. The approach has also been critiqued for regarding people who hold alternative norms and values as socially deviant, which tends to assume a single and dominant conception of culture and to undermine or dismiss alternative culture(s). Finally this approach – like its Corporate counterpart – is vulnerable for its assumption that the parts of a society (or organization) 'exist in a natural state of equilibrium, functioning effectively so as to maintain the effectiveness of the total social structure' (Meek 1992: 195). This view ignores the realities of conflict and dissension, often centering around cultural differences or even different interpretations of shared cultural traditions.

Within the corporate culture literature therefore this structural-functionalist approach has a major, if implicit, influence. It is apparent in the argument that corporate cultures are a unifying force; that they reflect the collective will of the organization; that they are consistent with, or derive from, the wishes of senior management; that deviants must be dealt with. All these assumptions are questionable on conceptual and empirical grounds – as well as on the basis of experience.

As a result of the borrowing of structural-functional assumptions, managerialist approaches to corporate culture tend to ignore inherent systemic conflicts within the organization, ignore structures of power and interest, ignore structures of hierarchy and inequality and ignore difference and differentiation of groups and of cultures (Meek 1992: 195).

Knights and Willmott (1987) note, as have other authors – see, for example,

Peter Anthony – that recent research on organizational culture of the corporate-culture variety has tended to remove the study of organizations from the relations of power and conflict that co-exist around cultures. The material and political contexts within which organizational cultures develop and with which they engage, are ignored by many studies of organizational cultures. This removal of culture from conflict follows, as Meeks notes, the functionalist approach of this view of organizational culture. As a result culture is viewed 'as a product of consensus rather than as the precarious outcome of continuous processes of contestation and struggle' (Knights and Willmott 1987: 41).

### *Empirical problems*

There are two closely interrelated ideas here, both of which follow closely the conceptual issues explored above: first, that organizational cultures are not necessarily (or even usually) homogeneous and unitary but are differentiated; and secondly, that therefore not all employees are equally committed to a single organizational culture. For example, organizations may be (or have) a number of different, even competing cultures. Organizational subunits may have their distinctive ideologies and structures of meaning. These may compete with other, or more dominant cultures within the same organization (Pfeffer 1981).

Also it is probably more sensible to focus on organizational cultures not as systems of shared values and norms (see above) but as 'a common understanding among individuals about what they are expected to do and say, how to behave, mastery of the subtleties of their existence, which presupposes a certain cultural competence . . . Culture might thus, at least in rational bureaucratic organisations . . . be seen as a common instrumental set of attitudes towards the activities and the setting people are engaged in' (Alvesson 1987: 10). This may not be a very rich conceptualization of culture; but it may be a realistic one, and one that gets round some of the obvious flaws of the conceptualizations that promise too much but deliver less.

These different cultures may not simply differ, they may conflict. Different groups may hold views which directly oppose other sets of beliefs, and associated practices. These differences may occur on a vertical or a horizontal axis – between groups arranged hierarchically (managers/workers, or senior executives and other managers), or between regional, divisional, functional groups.

Organizations are usually the sites for considerable conflict and one of the arenas in which these conflicts occur is structured differences in values. Culture can *reflect* conflict, can be used *within* conflicts, and can be a *source* of conflict.

## Components of Culture

If organizational cultures are important, and if variations in organizational cultures have implications for different levels of organizational performance, then it becomes important to be able to describe these differences, and to identify the key differences. And this is a project which would interest many with a concern to study or to influence organizational structure and functioning. How do cultures differ? How can we talk sensibly and comparatively of corporate cultures? The consultancy literature offers various classifications, many of which involve categorizing organizations into simplistic over-general, monolithic cultural types. However, there are some points that can be made reasonably safely.

First, one aspect of cultures noted by many writers is that they consist of a variety of elements which themselves can be seen as occurring on different levels: such things as symbols, myths, ideologies and rituals. Symbols provide meaning and evoke emotions. Languages are collections of symbols. Cultures also consist of knowledge and assumption – cognitive systems, models and frameworks that structure what members know, and how they think, reason, argue, decide (Meek 1992; Pettigrew 1979).

Schein, like other commentators, differentiates a number of levels of organizational cultures: first, visible artefacts which consist of technology, art, visible and audible behaviour.

The second level which we refer to as 'values', focuses on why people behave as they do, and the nature and role of values in determining employees' action. Underlying these values are basic assumptions – the third level – which consists of the five dimensions derived from Kluckhohn and Strodtbeck. These, Schein argues, are 'typically unconscious but which actually determine how group members perceive, think and feel . . . taken-for-granted assumptions are so powerful because they are less debatable and confrontable' (Schein 1992: 239). He insists that the fact that these are non-debatable and taken-for-granted is powerful and important precisely because these assumptions are not obvious to those who hold them – they are 'typically unconscious but . . . actually determine how group members perceive, think and feel' (Schein 1992: 239).

Pettigrew has also noted the different levels of culture, and argued also that 'At the deepest level, culture is . . . the complex set of values, beliefs, and assumptions that define the ways in which a firm conducts its business. Such core beliefs and assumptions are, of course manifested in the structures, systems, symbols, myths and patterns of reward inside the organisation . . .' (Pettigrew 1990: 266). There are two implications to this: first, that Pettigrew sees such elements as structures and systems is at least partially cultural in the sense that they arise out of, and reflect, basic cultural values. He thus collapses the conventional distinction between so-called 'hard' and 'soft' variables. Secondly, if culture occurs on a number of levels, attempts to change culture will presumably be more effective (and less significant) at the more superficial levels, and will be more effective if those managing the change process recognize these levels.

Many of the more thoughtful commentators recommend, or use, the same basic classificatory framework for the analysis of organizational cultures and this can be an extremely useful analytical tool. Child (1981), for example, recommends a return to a framework for cultural analysis developed by Klukhohn and Strodtbeck (1961). This lists five key human dilemmas to which there is a limited range of 'answers'. Within a given society a dominant value system will be apparent (Child 1981: 325). All five values/orientations are potentially applicable to organizational structures and behaviour. In table 16.1 Child describes the five variables and suggests some ways in which particular positions on the five variables could relate to organizational issues.

A broadly similar approach has been adopted by both Bate (1992) and Schein (1992). Both frameworks are derived from the work of Kluckhohn and Strodtbeck (1961). These authors have other features in common. Both suggest that cultures are 'solutions' to, or overviews on, a limited number of basic issues or problems. However these authors differ fundamentally in their assessment of the adequacy of these 'solutions'.

Thirdly, many writers accept the possibility of a relationship between an organization's culture and the behaviour of its employees and therefore, ultimately, the performance of the organization. But this relationship is (a) attenuated and complex, and (b) is not necessarily positive, or negative.

We have, for example, earlier noted Schein's definition of culture. Remember that Schein argues that the constituent assumptions of a culture exist in order to 'cope' with the organization's problems of external adaptation and internal integration. He argues that 'Cultural elements are defined as learned solutions to problems' (Schein 1992: 243). He distinguishes five external problems (table 16.2), and six internal problems (table 16.3).

There is obviously considerable overlap between these lists and the list of cultural dimensions in Child's table quoted earlier. But note that Schein sees culture as supplying positive, constructive, efficiency-enhancing 'solutions' to these problems, whereas Child and the authors from whom he derives his classification simply note that these dimensions supply the key bases on which cultures *vary*; they say nothing about the *implications* of these variations.

However, although Schein is in general highly optimistic about the impact of cultural solutions for organizational effectiveness, he reveals some awareness of the possibility of complexity of the implications of these cultural solutions for organizational performance. He writes, for example, 'It is very important to recognize that cultural strength may or may not be correlated with effectiveness. Though some writers have argued that strength is desirable, it is clear to me that the relationship is far more complex.'

Nevertheless the general drift of Schein's analysis is clear: cultures supply solutions to problems groups face. Cultures are 'learned solutions' to problems. He offers what is essentially a form of social Darwinism to explain this. When faced with problems groups try out various situations until they find one that works. This is used and becomes habitual, and, ultimately, cultural. Similarly with the attempts to avoid anxiety-creating situations. Again, successful responses become normal and ultimately normative. As Meek has noted of this sort of writing, it assumes a biological metaphor and defines the organization as an organism which ultimately offers metaphysical explanation for organizational structures and processes (Meek 1992).

The work of Paul Bate is important in this discussion in two respects: for his classification of the component elements of cultures, and for his analysis of the impact of cultures on performance. With respect to the first, he defines the issues

**Table 16.1** Examples of relationships postulated between cultural value orientations and organizational characteristics

| *Value orientation (> = stronger than, or preferred)* | *General organizational characteristics* | *Examples of specific practices* |
|---|---|---|
| 1 Human nature: good > evil | Emphasis on subordinate autonomy and intrinsic motivation | Subordinate goal-setting: job enrichment |
| 2 Man to nature: mastery > subjugation | Policies of innovation, and of developing individual expertise | Support for venture management; positive exercise of strategic choice including active negotiation of boundary conditions with external groups |
| 3 Time orientation: future > past | Strategic emphasis on long-term planning; formal schemes for thorough organizational socialization and career planning | MBO approach rather than budgetary control; use of manpower planning and assessment centres |
| 4 Orientation toward activity: being > doing | Human relations philosophy; emphasis on interpersonal sensitivity; interest in social as well as economic and technological criteria in work organization | Management style high on consideration relative to initiating structure; organizational morale and climate included in performance monitoring |
| 5 Relationships: individual > hierarchical | Minimization of hierarchy; emphasis on delegation and participation; control through assessment of achievement rather than through insistence on conformity to rules | Amenities and fringe benefits not differentiated by status; employees deal directly with members of public (where relevant) without referral upwards |

*Source:* Child (1981: 327).

**Table 16.2** Problems of external adaptation and survival

| | |
|---|---|
| Strategy | Developing consensus on the *primary task, core mission, or manifest and latent functions of the group.* |
| Goals | Developing consensus on *goals*, such goals being the concrete reflection of the core mission. |
| Means for accomplishing goals | Developing consensus on the *means to be used* in accomplishing the goals – for example, division of labour, organization structure, reward system, and so forth. |
| Measuring performance | Developing consensus on the *criteria to be used in measuring how well the group is doing against its goals and targets* – for example, information and control systems. |
| Correction | Developing consensus on *remedial or repair strategies* as needed when the group is not accomplishing its goals. |

*Source:* Schein (1992: 245).

covered by organizational cultures in terms of six key dimensions (Bate 1992: 230). His dimensions do not replicate all of the dimensions listed by Child, but are a development of Kluckhohn's fifth variable: how people relate to each other. But as can be seen Bate develops and expands this into six constituent elements. These are described in table 16.4

This classification is useful. It is broadly consistent with other useful work which focuses on the ways in which organizational cultures provide norms and values that impact on the nature of interpersonal relationships, and styles, of various sorts (see Child 1981).

But Bate's second contribution lies in his view of the impact of cultures (measured according to his dimensions) on performance. Unlike Schein he does not argue that culturally supported patterns of behaviour are necessarily solutions to anything. He does not assume that cultural solutions or viewpoints are necessarily positive, or that they contribute to success. In fact they may contribute to failure.

In his study, Bate argues that the culture of the organization he studied was high on unemotionality, depersonalization, subordination, isolationism, antipathy, and medium on conservatism. The consequence of this profile was significant. He argues that 'culture can affect the type and quality of interpersonal relationships, which in turn affect the approach to joint problem-solving processes . . . certain shared cultural meanings . . . define what are acceptable, natural, desirable and effective ways of relating and acting' (Bate 1992: 228).

But the nature of this impact in the case studied by Bate was negative. It produced a strong sense of futility, pessimism, helplessness, withdrawal, alienation. The situation is one of 'socialised helplessness' where people know it is no use trying to achieve change, and therefore created a self-fulfilling prophecy whereby the resulting organizational inertia and lack of change confirms the cultural assumptions.

Bate's point surely fits better with our own experience than does Schein's

**Table 16.3** Problems of internal integration

| | |
|---|---|
| Language | *Common language and conceptual categories.* If members cannot communicate with and understand each other, a group is impossible by definition. |
| Boundaries | Consensus on *group boundaries and criteria for inclusion and exclusion.* One of the most important areas of culture is the shared consensus on who is in, who is out, and by what criteria one determines membership. |
| Power and status | Consensus on *criteria for the allocation of power and status.* Every organization must work out its pecking order and its rules for how one gets, maintains and loses power. This area of consensus is crucial in helping members manage their own feelings of aggression. |
| Intimacy | Consensus on *criteria for intimacy, friendship, and love.* Every organization must work out its rules of the game for peer relationships, for relationships between the sexes, and for the manner in which openness and intimacy are to be handled in the context of managing the organization's tasks. |
| Rewards and punishments | Consensus on *criteria for allocation of rewards and punishments.* Every group must know what its heroic and sinful behaviours are; what gets rewarded with property, status and power; and what gets punished through the withdrawal of rewards and, ultimately, excommunication. |
| Ideology | Consensus on *ideology and 'religion'.* Every organization, like every society, faces unexplainable events that must be given meaning so that members can respond to them and avoid the anxiety of dealing with the unexplainable and uncontrollable. |

*Source:* Schein (1992: 246).

optimism. One of the striking features of current organizational change is that organizations are currently trying desperately to change the ways their members think, act, relate, work. The historic 'normal' is no longer adequate. Yesterday's recipes are not suitable for today's problems. The evidence is all around us that organizational cultures are as likely to obstruct as much (if not more than) they are to facilitate, organizational effectiveness. Bate's work, and one's own experience, suggests that the bland optimism of the managerialist perspective – that strong cultures produces consensus, commitment and productivity – is theoretically naive and empirically inaccurate.

Other writers have contributed to the debate about the components of organizational cultures by suggesting that some writers on organizational culture may show a preference for some aspects (or levels, in Schein's terms) rather than others. Specifically it has been suggested that some approaches to organizational culture actually reveal the very cultures they study, and that they therefore take for granted some key elements in the culture.

For example, the Corporate Culture approach to organizational cultures displays a paradox. While very clearly focusing on the importance of managing cultures for success it actually ignores key and pervasive elements in many corporate cultures. This may be because: 'The tendency to view culture primarily as

**Table 16.4** Organization issues with cultural responses

| *Basic organization issues* | *Cultural responses* |
|---|---|
| 1 How emotionally bound up do people become with others in the work setting? (Affective orientation) | Unemotionality |
| 2 How far do people attribute responsibility for personal problems to others, or to the system? (Animate–inanimate orientation to causality) | Depersonalization |
| 3 How do people respond to differences in position, role, power and responsibility? (Hierarchical orientation) | Subordination |
| 4 How far are people willing to embark with others on new ventures? (Change orientation) | Conservatism |
| 5 How far do people choose to work alone or with and through others? (Individualist–collectivist orientation) | Isolationism |
| 6 How do people in different interest groups relate to each other? (Unitary–Pluralistic orientation) | Antipathy |

*Source:* Bate (1992: 232).

a "resource" or "instrument" to be exploited and manipulated by dominating groups means that attention is concentrated on the manageable dimensions, while the deeper layers of culture and the cultural context of organisations and managerial actions are taken for granted not only by corporate members but also by researchers' (Alvesson 1989: 128). By the 'deeper layers' Alvesson is referring to the fundamental features of western organizations such as: 'efficiency, rationalization, productivity, glorification of advanced technology, exploitation of nature, control, hierarchy, unequal distribution of rewards, dominance of typical male values, glorification of leadership, etc.' He notes dryly: 'For some reason these aspects are not perceived or at least not interpreted as part of organizational and business culture in the vast majority of current writings on the topic' (Alvesson 1989: 128).

In other words, the consultancy approach to organizational cultures, whatever its other deficiencies and partialities, is guilty of an advanced myopia. When insisting that it classifies and describes 'the way we do things around here', it conveniently ignores absolutely fundamental assumptions about organizational practice which could well be the basis for conflict, division, difference. Western managerial culture it seems is so 'taken-for-granted' by culture writers that they either don't notice it, or take it as given. This approach to organizational cultures in effect focuses only on what may be performance-related aspects of culture but ignores other systemic elements which may be seriously counter-productive to the achievement of commitment, loyalty, etc.

Some writers would prefer to shift the focus of enquiry from culture to ideology – while recognizing that the concept of culture usefully focuses on a very wide spread of variables and behaviour – 'a complex totality of connections' (Alvesson 1987: 14). He advocates attention to organizational ideologies which avoids many of the weaknesses identified above and has the merit of drawing attention to differences between ideologies, and to their location in, and relationship between, groups, power and interests.

## The Possibility of Culture Change

Central to any consideration of organizational cultures is the suggestion that it is possible and fruitful to change these cultures from less performance-enhancing types to positive, performance enhancing cultures (however these are defined – see above). However, *can* cultures be changed? *How* can cultures be changed?

Many contributors to this debate argue strongly that cultures cannot be changed, at least not fundamentally. Meek for example argues against the view that 'there exists in a real and tangible sense a collective organisational culture that can be created, measured and manipulated in order to enhance organisational effectiveness' (Meek 1982: 192). She notes that cultures are not created; they emerge through social interactions over a long period. Leaders do not create cultures; on the contrary, leaders reflect the cultures within which they occur.

Similarly Alvesson remarks: 'when the concept is defined in a theoretically precise way based on anthropological thought, the practical relevance and value of the concept is rather small. It is barely possible to create, or even affect culture in the former meaning. Here it signifies an historically emerged, persistent pattern of beliefs, values and attitudes to social reality, deeply ingrained in consciousness' (Alvesson 1990: 41).

Part of the difference between those writers who are sceptical about the possibility of culture change and those who insist on its possibility stems from the different ways in which they define, approach and use the concept Corporate Culture. But the disagreement is probably also partly about what would constitute evidence of culture change. As we shall see, some authors concede that culture change programmes have an impact but insist that it is at the behavioural not the normative levels. They argue that culture change programmes may achieve acquiescence or compliance but not commitment.

### *Some difficulties*

Any discussion of whether or not cultures can be changed must identify which aspects or levels of culture are being discussed. It is more difficult to change the beliefs and assumptions of employees than to change what Pettigrew calls the 'manifestations' of culture.

However, even Meek is prepared to agree that while culture as a whole cannot be changed, and the optimistic recommendations of the Corporate Culture approach are flawed because of their denial of conflict, differentiation and power. Also, organizational cultures are not static and they do change over time. While insisting on the variety and complexity of cultures, and their role in internal conflicts, Meek accepts that 'management does have more direct control than other organisational members over certain aspects of corporate cultures, such as control over logos and officially stated missions and ethos' (Meek 1992: 202).

The ways in which managers may try to influence some aspects of corporate cultures is relatively unstudied and not well understood. There is a great deal more prescription than description. To argue that it is important to assess how management may intervene in organizational cultures, and with what consequences, is very different from assuming that the primary role of management is to create the organizational culture or that management efforts to manage culture will succeed.

Ogbonna (1992) usefully reviews the literature on the management of culture. He raises the possibility that strategies to change organizational cultures 'are simply extending . . . behavioural strategies' (Ogbonna 1992: 74). That is, at best they change behaviour but not underlying values. They create obedience but not commitment. They achieve what Ogbonna and Wilkinson call 'resigned behavioural compliance' (1988).

Certainly from what has been said earlier in this and the previous chapters, about the different levels of culture, it would clearly be extremely difficult to surface, far less to change, deep-seated, taken-for-granted assumptions and frameworks. And ironically this is revealed by much of the Corporate Culture literature itself which clearly fails to address its own assumptions about management, organization, hierarchy etc.

With regard to attempts to manage the more accessible levels of culture, Ogbonna focuses attention on two key issues: the claimed role of leaders, and the role of communications. Many writers have commented on the crucial importance of the organization's leader in culture change projects. Ogbonna, however, notes that employees' values are as much determined by their membership of subgroups; that leaders frequently do not articulate, communicate or model themselves on the new values; they do not have the power, or the inclination, to project the new values but become absorbed by the original culture. Similarly Sackmann (1990) also sees the naive assertions about the role (and possibility) of leaders managing culture change as a source of serious problems.

She notes, for example, that cultures are influenced by members, not just by leaders, and remarks that this also suggests that cultures are unlikely to be stable and homogeneous. But the more fundamental point concerns the possibility of managing cultures at all. The idea of managing cultures is based in a metaphor from rational-mechanistic systems where instructions or directions have a direct and determined impact on what is desired – as in driving a car or switching on a lighting system. But cultures are more complex, and less amenable. Although of course cultures are obviously therefore likely to change, constantly, it will be very difficult to change them in a desired direction because of their very nature. She describes how efforts to change and manage organizational cultures ran into trouble precisely because cultures are not amenable to direct management; they are highly complex, and are reflexive with multiple reciprocal relationships. Cultures are not simple systems. For one thing, cultures determine how efforts to change culture are understood and reacted to.

Communications, too, are frequently stressed in culture change programmes. Again Ogbonna notes that communications are actually extremely difficult to manage.

Employees often hear information transmitted by management in terms of the cultural values they already hold about those transmitting the message. Culture change programmes are likely to be heard and interpreted by staff in terms of the pre-culture change culture(s) prevailing within the organization. Communication success in culture change assumes the very consensus and commitment it is trying to achieve.

In practice culture change programmes experience these and other difficulties. A common problem is that the message being transmitted actually contradicts the experiences of the employees. A good illustration of the ways the values exhorted in cultural change programmes might clash with experienced reality is the tension between 'hard' and 'soft' sense of SHRM – that employees may be told they are the organization's most valued resource, and soon afterwards find themselves in a redundancy programme. Or they may be exposed to various forms of participative management styles, team work, cellular working etc., and simultaneously exposed to aggressive anti-union policies. Indeed there may be contradictions within a single policy: work intensification within job enlargement, for example. Ogbonna noted other contradictions in the organization he studied: for example, between a focus on high trust and commitment, and the installation of surveillance equipment and other work monitoring systems.

Another possible contradiction lies at the heart of culture change programmes. Attempts to manipulate organizational cultures are effectively attempts to mobilize new, less overt and more covert forms of organizational control. As such in themselves they reflect the power resources of those who design the interventions. So managerial attempts to achieve consensus and commitment through culture change programmes actually reveal the inequality and differentiation of power and interests within the organization which the culture change programme are usually designed to deny.

Does this mean that the final message on the management of culture is entirely bleak; that it is impossible? One answer to this focuses on the approach to, and definition of, cultures. We must remember that answers to this will ultimately depend on the way in which culture is defined, and indeed on how organizations themselves are conceptualized. The definition of culture is a highly practical question: it impacts on whether or not you believe cultures can be changed. An approach to corporate cultures which is based on a foundation of a flawed conception of culture will itself be flawed. For this reason, in the final section, an approach to cultures which avoids the difficulties discussed but offers some (limited) insights into cultures and how they change (and possibly how they can be changed) is necessary.

But at a more practical level, there are some suggestions that are useful and well-founded.

Probably the most important is to forget the bland promises of the prescriptive literature and to recognize that any programme of culture change is going to be long and hard. It is also important to recognize the actual nature of such cultures, as frequently stated throughout this chapter; and to recognize the different levels on which cultures occur, that cultures will not be homogeneous, that there will not be total consensus, that cultures may conflict, that they may be negative as well as positive in their implications for performance etc.

In these chapters we have noted the difficulties in changing cultures. It is now time to turn the work of a researcher who has studied and worked with programmes of culture change and who has devised a sensible list of recommendations based on actual practice. It is worth quoting in full. Pettigrew distinguishes 'outer' from 'inner' context. 'Outer context refers to the social, economic, political and competitive environment in which the firm operates. Inner context refers to organisational context – the structure, corporate culture and political context within the firm through which ideas for change have to proceed' (Pettigrew 1990: 267). Note that in his analysis Pettigrew clearly outlines the complexity, and arduousness of any attempt to change cultures; and he also notes that such efforts are more likely to effect the surface levels of culture than the core assumptions.

Pettigrew argues that the following factors are important in facilitating changes in organizational cultures.

1 'A receptive outer context, together with managerial skill in mobilizing that context in order to create an overall climate for change to occur.

2 Leadership behaviour either from individuals recently brought into the organization from outside, or from individuals who have been pushing for change from a powerful internal position for some time. Most of the cases of change reveal a very clear and consistent drive from the top.

3 The existence of inarticulate and imprecise visions from the agents of change at the very top.

4 The use of discrepant action by key figures in the new guard in order to raise the level of tension in the organization for change.

5 Using deviants and heretics, both external and internal to the organization in order to say the unsayable and think the unthinkable. External and internal consultants are regularly used for this purpose.

6 Releasing avenues and energy for change by moving people and portfolios.

7 Creating new meetings and other arenas where problems can be articulated and shared and energy focused around the need for change.

8 Altering the management process at the very top. A key aspect of this seems to be the need to change top management processes from being highly divisive in character to being much more coherent and cohesive.

9 Reinforcing any embryonic cultural shifts through closely matched structural

changes, then strengthening such cultural and structural changes through the public use of organization's reward systems.

10 Finding and using 'role models' who can through their own public behaviour display key aspects of the new culture. The identification of people who can 'walk and talk' seems to be a key aspect of making concrete and public the desired cultural changes. These role models of the new era also help the continuing re-inforcement of change.

11 Carrying the message deep into the organization through the use of training and development strategies.

12 Transmitting the new beliefs and behaviour down into the organization by revamping employee communication mechanisms.

13 Finally there is the old-fashioned but critical need for persistence and patience.'

'All of the studies of strategic change we are looking at emphasize the complexity and difficulty of effecting such change, even where the change is eventually triggered by major environmental disturbances. Persistence and patience is critically important at the difficult stage of breaking down the core beliefs of the old guard, getting new problems senses and articulated in the organization, developing a sense of concern that these problems are worthy of analytical and political attention, and then articulating the new order often through highly inarticulate and impressive visions of the future' (Pettigrew 1990: 271–2).

## Conclusions and Summary

Alvesson (1990) notes the importance of the business context, of the obvious economic malaise the West, in the reception accorded the corporate culture approach but stresses also the attractions of what he describes ironically as 'the product' (organization culture theory): 'the organisation culture theory is often presented in a way that makes it appear to be of crucial importance for understanding what is going on in organisations and how to get control of it. The broad area of relevance and application of culture in organisations, concepts that are mystical and fantasy-provoking, are important features of this type of knowledge' (Alvesson 1990: 46). He notes too that an attraction of this material is its promise to allow managers to manage the meanings and values of employees and thus to enable managers access to powerful but internalized sources of control and commitment, a point stressed in the previous chapter.

We have noted earlier some of the problems with the use of the concept culture in organizational analysis – particularly those usages within the consultancy/practitioner approach. However, the weaknesses of this application should not imply that the concept should be abandoned altogether. Certainly this particular approach is seriously flawed – which means that we must consider why it continues to attract so much attention. But in other applications the concept is potentially very interesting and exciting. However, for the concept to be rescued from the hands of the consultancy writers it is necessary to attend to, and address the weaknesses identified earlier (i.e. the consensual, unitary conception of cultures); to acknowledge and attend to the nature and role of power and conflict within organizations as the context of organizational cultures; to recognize the ideological role of cultures (or the ideological components of cultures) and to widen the concept to include aspects of organizational culture that many writers prefer to regard as so 'normal', natural and given that they transcend cultural analysis.

One implication of this approach is that the consultancy approach (corporate culture) to management culture as described earlier, can now be seen less as an analysis of existing organizational cultures and more as an element of management's attempts to *construct* organizational cultures – to gain worker commitment through the management of meaning. 'Once it was deemed sufficient to redesign the organization so as to make it fit human capacity and understanding: now it is better to redesign human understanding to fit the organization's purpose' (Keenoy and Anthony 1992: 239).

We have earlier argued that despite the claims of the consultancy approach that culture is used to explore 'the way we do things around here', such analyses in fact studiously ignore certain key elements of organizational structure and process – the nature and role of power, of conflicts, or exploitation, of difference. Some of the basic assumptions and taken-for-granted 'realities' of organization are left unquestioned and unanalysed by cultural analyses. The very purpose of culture change programmes themselves are left unexplored and undiscussed, except in the bland terms of the proposed culture of consensus and commitment. MacIntyre makes the important point that management itself is not a neutral or objectively rational process: 'managers . . . conceive of themselves as morally neutral characters whose skills enable them to devise the most efficient means of achieving whatever end is proposed . . . Nonetheless there are strong grounds for rejecting the claim that effectiveness is a morally neutral value . . . I am suggesting that "managerial effectiveness" functions much as Carnap and Ayer supposed "God" to function. It is the name of a fictitious, but believed-in reality, appeal to which disguises certain other realities; interpretations of managerial effectiveness in the same way lack the appropriate kind of rational justification' (MacIntyre 1981: 71–3; quoted in Carter and Jackson 1987: 66–7).

Certainly if the concept of organizational culture is to be used to its full potential and to avoid the sectional and flawed definition criticized above, it must be deployed in a manner which moves beyond a focus on those dimensions which, if manipulated, could support managerial efforts to achieve control. Rather, it should focus on the 'overall cultural characteristics of organisations (which) are not taken for granted in a way that allows for the exclusive concentration on performance-related norms and behaviour patterns' (Alvesson 1989: 129).

Frequently studies of organizational culture reveal these cultures less in their analyses than in their (hidden) assumptions: they themselves reflect the key features of the managerialist culture by their focus on performance, their concern with commitment, their lack of interest in divisive exploitative hierarchical aspects of organization, all of which, from a managerial point of view are 'natural', neutral and necessary. In this respect the corporate culture approach shares many of the assumptions of earlier organizational analysis which accepted the inevitability and rationality of organizational structures (Salaman 1981).

The problems with the corporate culture approach stem from the largely unexplored and implicit theoretical assumptions about organizations and how they work, on which the approach depends. This is frequently derived from an unreflexive systems theory – an approach which looks at the organization from the point of senior management; which explains internal organizational patterns in terms of their contribution to the survival of the organization within its environment. As Silverman (1970), in an early and important critique of systems theory, remarked, such an approach is defective and would be better replaced by an analysis which looked at organizations in terms of the purposes of their members and of their capacities to impose these ends on others. In order to do this, it is necessary to understand the subjective purposes of each actor, or group of actors. And this of course means that the analysis of cultures within organizations is crucial to an understanding of structure and process, because such cultures inform members' actions. But the approach to cultural analysis must recognize the diversity of meanings, the variations in interests, the potential conflict between groups, and not wish these away with the bland descriptions of a consensus with which they try to create the very situation they fallaciously describe.

This point has interesting implications for the consultancy approach to corporate culture discussed and critiqued in this chapter and its predecessor. It may well be that the interesting and useful application of culture of organizations lies less in the pursuit of prescriptive (and probably abortive) interventions aimed to achieve commitment, acquiescence and obedience within the workforce, and more in attempts to uncover some of the deep, and typically undiscussed assumptions on which organizations and management rest. Carter and Jackson, for example, have argued that a valuable application of the culture approach ('root metaphor' or hermeneutic approach in terms of earlier classification) is to explore the cultural assumptions underlying management's model of the world, organizations and management: 'Management's model of the world it manages is not fact, but a particular myth . . . When management for example claims to pursue efficiency this means efficiency in one sense, among may possible senses' (Carter and Jackson 1987: 79). The value of the culture approach may lie not in its claimed contribution to organizational effectiveness but in its use in exposing and analysing the nature assumptions and truth claims of managerial discourse.

But such an approach may not totally rule out any concern to change organizational cultures, though it will severely limit these efforts and make them demanding and difficult. Sackmann's work is useful here. Noting the gap between academic (culture as metaphor) and practitioner applications she proposes an approach which uses a definition of culture that avoids the weaknesses of the practitioner approach discussed earlier, but does so in a form that addresses issues in the management of culture. She describes this approach as seeing organizational culture as a dynamic construct. She hopes this approach will combine the pragmatic side of the practitioner perspective (corporate-culture approach) with the rigour and honesty of the metaphor of organizations as cultures approach. She notes that the culture as metaphor approach is not interested in application, but her model of culture in this hybrid approach avoids the weaknesses of the corporate culture approach discussed above, while at the same time promising less, and insisting on the complexity and arduousness of any attempt to change cultures at any level. 'The problems associated with the variable perspective [corporate-culture approach] are overcome since the underlying assumptions are different and closer to the metaphor perspective. Organizations are seen as evolving, dynamic, complex systems with inconsistencies and paradoxes, and several cultural groupings or meaning systems. Within this perspective, the management of culture can only take the form of a culture-aware management that tries to create, interpret, negotiate, and communicate meanings in conscious efforts. The result of these efforts, however, cannot be determined in advance . . . A culture-aware management is aware of the existing meaning systems within the organisation, its cultural strengths and weaknesses. These are consciously cared for, or deliberately neglected' (Sackmann 1990: 138). However, she notes the difficulty – and rarity – of culture-aware management. This takes us back of course to the arguments of Carter and Jackson, and others above: that most writings about corporate culture take for granted the same values and assumptions that are embedded in the cultures they study, and therefore fail to notice or address them.

## Key Points

- Although Corporate Culture writers – and those managers who subscribe to their approach – define organizations in terms of their cultures and insist that these can and should be changed, there are a number of grounds for arguing that this position is ultimately an ideological one. And this chapter rehearses some of the ways in which the approach could be regarded as ideological because of its sectional and partisan focus and its emphasis on some culture(s) and values at the expense of others.
- Despite the ambitious claims of the Corporate Culture writers there are both conceptual and empirical grounds for questioning the feasibility and adequacy of their arguments and recommendations. Many of these hinge on the shaky assumptions inherent in the approach regarding the nature, role, and pervasiveness of values within the organization, the disregard of other means of achieving control, and the dismissal of the existence of structured differences of interest, values and priorities.
- If organizational cultures are important – and this chapter would certainly agree that they are highly significant although not necessarily in the sense promulgated by the Corporate Culture writers – then it is important to be able to describe, classify and

compare them. This requires some taxonomic system, and this chapter has considered a number of useful ways of describing the elements of such cultures.

- The Corporate Culture approach focuses vigorously on the need to change cultures and this raises questions of *how*, if at all, such cultures can be changed. This is clearly important.
- Part of the weakness of the corporate culture approach stems from its very qualities that appeal to managers – this approach relates closely to managers' view of the world and the organization. Possibly part of its appeal therefore is that this approach owes more to management ideology than it does to analytic rigour. This possibility needs investigation.
- If organizational cultures are important then we need a sensible and well-founded basis by which to distinguish the basic dimensions of cultures. Such a system exists and has been much used and is discussed in this chapter.
- Finally, if cultures can be changed it is necessary to think thoroughly and carefully about the ways in which they can be changed and this issue too is considered.

## Discussion Questions

1. In what ways can the Corporate Culture approach be described as 'ideological'?
2. What are the main conceptual and empirical vulnerabilities of the Corporate Culture approach?
3. How can corporate cultures be classified and described? What are the components of Corporate Cultures?
4. If cultures can be changed what does this require in terms of the way culture is defined, the various levels of culture and the necessary mechanisms of change?

## References

Alvesson, M. (1987) 'Organisations, culture and ideology', *International Studies of Management and Organisation*, vol. XVII, no. 3, 4–18.

—— (1989) 'The cultural perspective on organisations: Instrumental values and basic features of culture', *Scandinavian Journal of Management*, vol. 5, no. 2, 123–36.

—— (1990) 'On the popularity of organisational culture', *Acta Sociologica*, vol. 33, no. 1, 31–49.

—— (1991) 'Organisational symbolism and ideology', *Journal of Management Studies*, vol. 28, no. 3, 207–25.

Bate, P. (1992) 'The impact of organisational culture on approaches to organisational problem-solving' in G. Salaman et al. (eds) *Human Resource Strategies*, London: Sage, 219–34.

Brunsson, N. and Olsen, J. (1992) *The Reforming Organisation*, London: Routledge.

Carter, P. and Jackson, N. (1987) 'Management myth and metatheory, organisational culture and ideology', special issue of *International Studies of Management and Organisation*, vol. 17, no. 3, 64–90.

Child, J. (1981) 'Culture, contingency and capitalism in the cross-national study of organisations', in L. L. Cummings and B. Staw (eds) *Research in Organisational Behaviour*, Greenwich, CT: JAI Press.

Deal, T. and Kennedy, A. (1991) *Corporate Cultures*, Harmondsworth: Penguin Books.

Keenoy, T. and Anthony, P. (1992) 'HRM: Metaphor, meaning and morality', in P. Blyton and P. Turnbull (eds) *Reassessing Human Resource Management*, London: Sage, 233–55.

Kluckhohn, F. R. and Strodtbeck, F. L. (1961) *Variations in Value Orientations*, New York: Row, Peterson.

Knights, D. and Willmott, H. (1987) 'Organisational culture as a management strategy', *International Studies of Management and Organisation*, vol. XVII, no. 3.

MacIntyre, A. (1981) *After Virtue*, London: Duckworth.

Meek, V. L. (1982; 1992) 'Organisational culture: Origins and weaknesses', in G. Salaman et al. (eds) *Human Resource Strategies*, London: Sage, 192–212.

Ogbonna, E. and Wilkinson, B. (1988) 'Corporate strategy and corporate culture: The management of change in the UK supermarket industry', *Personnel Review*, vol. 18, no. 6, 10–14.

—— (1992) 'Organisational culture and human resource management: Dilemmas and contradictions' in P. Blyton and P. Turnbull (eds) *Reassessing Human Resource Management*, London: Sage, 74–96.

Peters, T. (1978) 'Symbols, patterns and settings', *Organisational Dynamics*, vol. 9, no. 2, 3–23.

—— and Waterman, R. (1982) *In Search of Excellence*, New York: Harper and Row.

Pettigrew, A. (1979) 'On studying organisational cultures', *Administrative Science Quarterly*, December, 570–81.

—— (1990) 'Is corporate culture manageable?' in D. Wilson and R. Rosenfeld (eds) *Managing Organisations*, 267–72.

Pfeffer, J. (1981) 'Management as symbolic action', in L. L. Cummings and B. M. Staw (eds) *Research in Organisational Behaviour*, vol. 4, Greenwich, CT: JAI Press.

Sackmann, S. (1990) 'Managing organisational culture: Dreams and possibilities' in J. Anderson (ed.) *Communication Yearbook*, vol. 13, Newbury Park, CA: Sage, 114–48.

Salaman, G. (1981) 'Towards a sociology of organisational structure' in M. Zey-Ferrell and M. Aiken (eds) *Complex Organisations, Critical Perspectives*, Glenview, IL: Scott Foresman, 22–46.

Schein, E. (1992) 'Coming to a new awareness of organisational culture', in G. Salaman et al. (eds) *Human Resource Strategies*, London: Sage, 237–53.

Silverman, D. (1970) *The Theory of Organisations*, London: Heinemann.

Smircich, L. (1983) 'Concepts of culture and organisational analysis', *Administrative Science Quarterly*, vol. 28, 339–58.

Ulrich, P. (1984) 'Systemsteuerung und kulturentwicklung', *Die Undernehmung*, vol. 38, 303–25.

Wickens, P. (1987) *The Road To Nissan*, Basingstoke: Macmillan.

part 6

# Managing Meaning

chapter 17

# Some Key Difficulties

CHAPTER OUTLINE

## Learning Objectives

When you have read this chapter you will:

- Be aware of the complexities and contradictions that underlie much strategic human resource management (SHRM) prescription and thinking.
- Be aware of the limitations – and strengths – of SHRM recommendations and thinking.
- Recognize the key ways in which the core concept of SHRM – various types of integration – may be problematic.
- Understand how the processes of decision making underlying the design and implementation of SHRM projects may be less rational and successful in reality than they appear in many SHRM writings.

# Introduction

The appealing and attractive simplicity of the SHRM approach to organizational change, which focuses and legitimates change programmes, masks a number of problems and complexities. This chapter and the one that follows it, are dedicated to a consideration of the realities of SHRM – the possibility and the consequences, of SHRM. Is it happening and, if it is, what effects is it having? To some degree these are empirical questions and answers to these questions will depend on available empirical research into what is happening. This is largely covered in the next chapter. But to some extent these are also conceptual questions – where the answer depends upon whether or not *in principle* we would expect SHRM to occur and to work – i.e. these questions engage with the feasibility of SHRM. These conceptual matters are the subject matter of this chapter. Our concern is, simply, this: from what we know of organizations and of the processes and dynamics upon which models of SHRM (implicitly) depend, would we expect SHRM to be likely, or possible, or easy to achieve?

It's useful to remind ourselves of some of the sorts of difficulties we have already raised in earlier discussions of SHRM initiatives. For example: Do the classic prescriptions of SHRM models fit together and support each other? To what extent do new styles of management with devolved autonomy clash with the need to achieve policies that operate throughout the company as a whole? Local arrangements between management and staff are vulnerable to company-wide developments stemming from financial exigencies, or difficulties with trade unions at national level. Do measures such as downsizing or hire-and-fire recruitment policies, or the use of out-sourced labour – all of which clearly communicate to staff that they should actively manage their own careers in an extra-organizational labour market – clash with the claimed concern to cherish and develop sustainable learning and the development of deeply embedded learning cultures?

These potential contradictions raise important questions:

(1) Is SHRM more significant as an ideology of change than as a set of change principles? Is SHRM essentially a way of legitimating and disguising programmes of change, which, by using the language of strategic focus (of restructuring, staff commitment, empowerment and 'ownership') and by claiming the value of 'human resources' all in the name of environmentally driven change, actually serve to justify and direct programmes of change whose main purpose is increased control over labour while reducing its cost? Is SHRM 'a meta-narrative: an image intensifier which presents us with a set of idealised action imperatives'? (Keenoy and Anthony 1992: 240).

One element of this is the insistence in much SHRM language of the key role of 'the market'. Not only is internal change now explained by and attributed to, developments in the market but within the organization itself, relations between organizational sub-units are reconceptualized and structured as if they too were market relations. The market rules. Chandler's (1977) dictum was that the development of the large-scale modern enterprise depended upon the development of an administrative component which was able to co-ordinate internally the activities of numerous business units and function. Is this notion of the 'visible hand of management' replacing the invisible hand of market forces now upturned? (see Hales 1994).

(2) If SHRM is concerned with substantial restructuring of the organization is this, as is sometimes claimed, to ensure that the organization allows and enables employees to commit themselves, to contribute to the establishment of organizational goals, and to contribute to decision making? Or is it essentially concerned with the manipulation of the symbols of consensus and commitment – the management of effects but not the transformation of reality?

A study of change programmes points to a disjunction between senior managers' words and organizational realities, not least because of the conflicting pressures and demands to which they are exposed. Brunsson and Olsen note that: 'it may be important or necessary to produce hypocrisy: to systematically satisfy certain demands and norms by talk and decisions to confront others through action . . . the ability to describe and explain actions to the rest of the world in order for them to be accepted or appreciated is often an important management task' (1993: 63–4).

For some critical students of SHRM, the ideas and prescriptions of SHRM constitute a sort of relay between societal and political projects, values and objectives, and internal organizational dynamics and changes. They do this by making available ways of understanding organizations and ways of recognizing weaknesses and how they can be corrected, by offering: 'images of the enterprise, techniques of management, forms of authority, and conceptions of the social vocation of industry which can align the government of the enterprise with prevailing cultural values, social expectations, political concerns and personal ambitions . . . [They] link together changing political rationalities and objectives, the ceaseless quest of business for profitability, and a basis for managerial authority, with interventions directed at the subjectivity of the worker' (Miller and Rose 1993).

So SHRM ideas have implications for the *subjectivity* of the employee – that is, they attempt to define what employees should be like, as people. One obvious aspect of this is that employees should be committed to the organization's values and objectives.

(3) Similarly, how neutral and satisfactory are the measures of performance and efficiency that are used in SHRM calculations and justifications? The ways in which business units' 'performance' is measured is not a neutral or technical matter. It assumes priorities and values. And it may have serious negative consequences for the organization overall. Treating each section of an organization 'as if' it were a separate business may be short-sighted and counter-productive. Defining internal organizational relationships as if they were market transactions may generate internal divisions, short-sightedness and discourage investment, and co-operation.

For example, the use of financial contribution as a measure of performance may encourage unhelpful behaviours by discouraging long-term planning, by encouraging conservatism and risk-avoidance. Use of financial returns to control profit centres may encourage managers to achieve results by lack of investment and reduced technological innovation. It has been argued with respect to the decline of manufacturing in the USA that: 'Analysts of manufacturing decline almost unanimously pinpoint the rise to prominence of (financial) calculations as the immediate cause of the sharp decline in expenditure on new process technologies, facilities and research and development' (Higgins and Clegg 1988: 80). Solutions to one problem can breed new problems; solutions are often introduced and imposed simply because, at the time, they seem right because they resonate with current values and convictions. 'General and ready-made norms about proper organisational forms free reformers from the need to find the most suitable forms for their specific organisations: they imitate rather than innovate . . . environment also create a supply of problems: there are widely held beliefs about what problems organisations have or should have; fashionable problems are suited to the solutions that are in fashion' (Brunsson and Olsen 1993: 38).

(4) Finally, are SHRM models based on firm and well-validated assumptions about how organizations operate, how groups work together, and how decisions are made? Or is SHRM naively over-rationalistic, underestimating the realities of politicized decision-making and culturally-limited problem-solving? These questions are complicated by the fact that organizations themselves, through their cultures and structures, establish shared ways of thinking which in themselves, influence and simplify the way senior managers – the people who make SHRM decisions – observe, think and act.

This chapter will address these issues: *can* SHRM 'work'? (the next chapter considers: *does* it work?) Is SHRM based on naive and simplistic notions of what organizations are, and how they work? The main focus here is the nature and feasibility of SHRM-style integration. Integration is the core idea behind SHRM. If there are difficulties, even contradictions, surrounding the possibility and practicality of achieving integration, these will severely limit the possibility of SHRM itself. What follows is an analysis of aspects of organizational structure and functioning which, by introducing an inevitable element of politics, conflict and irrationality into organizational processes, pose serious challenges to some key assumptions of the SHRM model. This is because they have the potential for seriously undermining the possibility of achieving integration.

## Integration in SHRM

The fundamental feature of SHRM as a set of ideas is that the design of human resource structures and systems, and indeed 'human resources' themselves – employees – are integrated into, and support, the organization's strategy. In SHRM thinking all aspects of the organization, including all human resource dimensions, and every aspect of employee behaviour and attitude, must support the achievement of competitive advantage or other strategy-based measures of organizational performance.

'The main dimensions of HRM [involve] the goal of integration, (i.e. if human resources can be integrated into strategic plans, if human resource policies cohere, if line managers have internalised the importance of human resources and this is reflected in their behaviour and if employees identify with the company, then the company's strategic plans are likely to be more successfully implemented), the goal of employee commitment, the goal of flexibility/adaptability (i.e. organic structures, functional flexibility) the goal of quality (i.e. quality of staff, performance, standards and public image)' (Guest 1987; quoted in Legge 1989: 24).

Integration takes four main forms.

(1) Reference to the definitions of SHRM in chapter 2 show the centrality of the idea that SHRM is integrated with, or supports, or fits, the organization's strategy. For example, Beer and Spector (1985) remark: 'a business enterprise has an external strategy . . . It also needs an internal strategy: a strategy for how its internal resources are to be developed, deployed, motivated and controlled . . . the external and internal strategies must be linked . . .' (1985: 5–6; quoted in Beaumont 1992: 23). Or, the, 'need to establish a close, two-way relationship between business strategy . . . and HRM planning' (Beaumont 1992: 4). This 'fit' between business and HR strategies can be called *vertical* integration.

(2) Also critical is the idea that the various elements of SHRM (personnel systems of various sorts, organizational structures, cultures,) 'fit' together. That is, they mutually support each other to generate appropriate behaviour. 'The very idea of an internal (SHRM) strategy implies that there is consistency among all the specific tactics or activities that affect human resources. Hence the need for practices to be guided by conscious policy choices to increase the likelihood that practices will reinforce each other and will be consistent over time' (Beer and Spector 1985: 6). This is *horizontal* integration.

(3) But there is more to the centrality of integration than these two forms. There is a third type of integration, that of the individual into the organization: 'high levels of individual employee and work group participation in task-related decisions' (Beaumont 1992: 27). As Sewell and Wilkinson (1992) have noted, one of the central claims of the SHRM literature is that it is possible – and profitable – with human resource practices, to close the gap between the interests of the organization and the employees. This is done through each and every dimension of the SHRM approach: selection, induction, training, reward, job design, culture change etc. Furthermore, the achievement of

this 'fit' of employee and organization ensures the valuable pay-off of a congruence between organizational and employee values and goals.

(4) A fourth form of integration is the integration of the various departments, disciplines and groups within the organization into one unified, normative, consensual system. 'The American models of HRM . . . assume a unitary frame of reference: that 'there is a long-run coincidence of interests between all the various stakeholders of the organisation' (Beer and Spector 1985: 283; Legge 1989: 25). This is either naive or deliberately manipulative. It is certainly wrong, empirically. In a study of British employee attitudes Gallie and White found that nearly two-thirds of those interviewed were positive about their work and nearly a third were positive about the job as a whole. But very few were committed to their employing organization (Gallie and White 1993). While SHRM proponents may *wish* that organizations were consensual and unitarist, and even try to achieve this through policies which reduce the power of unions and engage with employees on an individualistic basis, many of the policies which stem from SHRM initiatives actually display very clearly the potential opposition of interests between senior managers and other employees. These policies, it is claimed, are aimed at achieving the 'enterprising' and committed employees. But many have questioned the sincerity of these claims. Gorz, for example, argues that SHRM ideas claim that the organization becomes a place where employees achieve personal fulfilment in empowered roles in devolved structures, and this is essentially ideological. In reality SHRM conceals 'the real transformations that have taken place, namely that enterprises are replacing labour by machines, producing more and better with a decreasing percentage of the work-force previously employed, and offering privileges to a chosen elite of workers, which are accompanied by unemployment, precarious employment, deskilling and a lack of job security for the majority' (Gorz 1989: 66).

Coopey (1995) has noted that many years ago researchers identified the emphasis placed by senior managers on financial values to the exclusion of other considerations such as a sense of responsibility for employees. Twenty years later, when SHRM totally dominates, researchers have found that the modern equivalents of these managers, 'while still not interested in industrial relations questions are deeply concerned with symbolic aspects of HRM – of corporate culture, quality of service and so on – that help divert attention from internal issues of hegemony, control and potential conflict onto imperatives that are represented by management as externally imposed and on leaders' vision designed to deal with these imperatives' (Coopey 1995: 72).

There are, then, clearly grounds for questioning the possibility, in reality, of achieving integration. Are senior managers serious in their quest for integration? Is integration simply an ideological chimera? Is it at odds with organizational realities?

## Integration: the impossible dream

The starting point is the distinction noted earlier in the opening chapters between two types of definition of SHRM – one 'open', stressing the need for integration of SHRM and strategy but not specifying the nature of any particular SHRM programme, the other 'closed', specifying a particular combination of SHRM elements: flexibility, participation, commitment and so on. These two views offer incompatible conceptions of integration. SHRM cannot simultaneously be open to choice but also insist on just one set of answers in every case.

There is an inconsistency arising from these opposed notions of integration: 'at the surface level the value of integration that it (SHRM) promotes contains a logical contradiction, given the dual usage of the concept of "integration". "Integration" appears to have two meanings: integration or "fit" with business strategy and the integration or complementarity and consistency of "mutuality" employment policies aimed at generating employee commitment, flexibility, quality, and the like . . . The problem is that while "fit" with strategy would argue a contingent design of HRM policy, internal consistency (at least within the "soft" human resource values associated with "mutuality") would argue an absolutist approach to the design of employment policy' (Legge 1989: 29).

A similar distinction has been stressed by Bartlett and Ghoshal (1992), and Galbraith and Kazajian (1986), who identify a basic problem in the SHRM literature – the idea that as organizations achieve structural 'fit' they actually disable themselves for complex and inherently changeable environment. In other words, any SHRM 'fit' would soon become inappropriate – as new circumstances require new strategies and new arrangements. The solution to this is an emphasis on the flexible, or learning organization – a type of organization where the key characteristic is not the fit of SHRM and strategy, but the capacity of the senior managers to scan the environment, analyse data, think creatively, design and implement change – and then change it all before it's complete. This approach to SHRM stresses 'organisational and strategic flexibility rather than structural fit. To build the most viable strategic process, [these] models shift towards considering the management process that will make strategic decisions work . . . The role of management must therefore be to create an internally consistent and balanced design' (Paauwe and Dewe 1995: 57).

However, this focus on the role of management in designing and implementing constant processes of change is not specific to this approach: management plays a similar, if less emphasized role in all forms of SHRM. For this reason, the nature of, and limitations to, management thinking and decision-making constitutes a major theme of this chapter. For it is important to consider what factors might facilitate or obstruct the capacity of managements to behave, think, observe, analyse, in the way required.

Another flaw in the SHRM emphasis on integration arises from a contradiction that surrounds the soft human resource values associated with 'mutuality': commitment, flexibility and quality. Storey has noted that the term SHRM allows two interpretations, and that in fact both readings are apparent within the logics of SHRM programmes. On the one hand, SHRM can be viewed in terms of the priority and value of treating 'human resources' as valued assets to be developed and cherished and whose commitment and creativity are crucial. This is the 'soft' sense of SHRM: 'Which treats labour as a valued asset rather than a variable cost and which accordingly counsels investment in the labour resource through training and development and through measures designed to attract and retain a committed workforce' (Storey 1989: 8). Within the rhetoric of SHRM there is emphasis on the nature and importance of an approach to staff and to organization which 'empowers', liberates, develops the individual employee in order to develop and engage employees' commitment and creativity and energy.

On the other hand, SHRM also allows a view which stresses the importance of identifying and implementing whatever HR strategy is appropriate for the chosen business strategy. Moreover, the very notion of SHRM allows for, even encourages, a conception of organization and of employees as resources to be exploited like any other organizational resource. Some have seen this as a 'tension': between SHRM as a way of ensuring and justifying (or even disguising) attempts to maximize economic returns from 'human resources' by the efficient and consistent use of these resources (reducing numbers, cutting costs), and SHRM as a way of releasing resourcefulness.

What is at issue here is not simply managerial honesty or opportunism, important as these are. There are obviously going to be occasions when overt espousal of the 'soft' sense of SHRM is hypocritical or dishonest – mere PR. But there may also be cases when the commitment is real, but is overtaken by events. One writer, after reviewing the literature on the take-up of SHRM in practice, reports: 'The picture these studies present reveals a contradiction between the rhetoric of the "soft" HRM model and the realities of the "hard" model, and of tensions between the values embedded in the "soft" model' (Legge 1994: 45). She goes on to note that quality management techniques, with their emphasis on surveillance, could undermine employee commitment; the introduction of teams may not aid empowerment, but management control through peer pressure (1994: 46).

There is also an ambiguity in the notion of allying SHRM initiatives to market and strategic exigencies, when these may require measures which do not comply with, may even directly oppose, the welfare-humanist principles of some common conceptions of SHRM. In the 'open' view of SHRM, strategy and the environment may require a highly instrumental approach to 'human resources'. This view 'emphasises the quantitative, calculative and business strategic aspects of managing the headcounts resource in as "rational" a way as for any other economic factor. By contrast, the "soft" version traces its roots to the human-relations school; it emphasises communication, motivation and leadership' (Storey 1989: 8). However in practice, the 'hard' approach to SHRM type organizational changes is a very common one. In practice, whatever the good intentions of those who espouse or disseminate, the 'soft, welfare-humanist' conception of SHRM, they are likely to be overwhelmed by the exigencies of financial performance measures and requirements. For example, it is likely that, as Legge (1989) has noted, that there is no reason to believe or expect that senior managers will respond to external competitive pressures, or the dictates of corporate head office expectations of sub-unit contribution, by measures designed to generate employee commitment rather than by cutting costs, reducing head count, and other measures which treat labour as a variable cost rather than as a resource to be cherished and developed.

Under these conditions of competitive pressure many organizations may find it hard to pursue in practice the goals of classic SHRM: 'matching HRM policies to business strategy calls for minimising labour costs, rather than treating employees as a resource whose value they may be enhanced, in terms of Guest's model by increasing their commitment, functional flexibility and quality' (Legge 1989: 32).

There are, as noted, two main conceptions of integration in the SHRM literature: 'vertical' integration of SHRM into the corporate strategy and 'horizontal' integration of the various aspects of SHRM. Concerning the first it has been noted that if an organization is made up of a number of diverse businesses then logically, at least according to the 'open' conception of SHRM, different businesses within a conglomerate might sensibly wish to pursue different HR strategies. However, while this may certainly affect the degree of corporate-wide SHRM integration, arguably it would not affect the integrity of SHRM integration at the business unit level. It has also been noted that some of the classic prescriptions of the SHRM literature (closed model) might produce effects very different from those that are desired. For example, there may be a conflict between strong organizational cultures and employees' capacity to respond flexibly and quickly. Strong cultures can be conservative, limiting responses that fall outside of, or challenge, the shared core assumptions of the culture (Legge 1989: 36).

On a more prescriptive level, it has also been noted by Lengnick-Hall and Lengnick-Hall (1988) that much SHRM literature assumes a uni-directional model of vertical integration – the designing of human resource structures to fit strategies. They note: 'rarely are human resources seen as a strategic capacity from which competitive choices should be derived' (1988: 456). They argue for a multi-directional approach to both strategy and HR strategy – whereby both develop interactively: strategy should be developed in terms of HR capability, and HR strategies should be developed in terms of business strategies and their implementation requirements.

## Organizational Decision-Making and Organizational Politics

The SHRM literature underplays two key issues. These are: 'the inherent features of the employment relationship which structures employer–employee relations and . . . impact of organizational structures on behaviour. Both require reference to power-relations and the institutionalization of socio-economic conflict. . . . Differential competing interests are an inevitable feature of any social institution characterized by the division of labour and a hierarchy of authority' (Keenoy 1990: 380–1).

This issue is highly relevant to an analysis of integration within SHRM. Chapter 2 argued the importance and value of an SHRM approach: matching human resources and behaviour to organizational objectives. That chapter also identified a number of developments which *could be* evidence of SHRM. But if the achievement of integration is central to the achievement of SHRM, and if the processes of matching SHRM to business strategy (and furthermore, the processes of decision-making that lead to the development of organizational

## BOX 17.1 THE DIFFICULTIES WITH VERTICAL AND HORIZONTAL INTEGRATION

The main difficulty with 'vertical' integration arises from the possible naïveté of conceptions of strategy formulation which overestimate the clarity, and rationality of this process (for if there is no coherent or unified strategy, then no HR strategy can be integrated with business strategy); and from the nature of assumptions about relations between groups within organizations and between individuals and organizations that are fundamental to the achievement of vertical integration. The strength of SHRM as a movement, and as a body of 'theory' and rhetoric arises in part from its suppression of ugly and difficult organizational realities in the purveying of a rosy conception of possibilities which is problematic not simply because it is unrealistic, but precisely because it attempts to redefine reality whilst simultaneously denying and reproducing it.

There are also problems in achieving 'horizontal' integration. These difficulties arise with the 'closed' approach to SHRM – i.e. that approach which advocates a precise 'package' of SHRM measures. Simply, is it empirically likely that these measures are internally consistent? Keenoy has usefully mapped some major inconsistencies. He has noted that the individualistic focus of many of the 'packaged' prescriptions of the closed model to encourage staff are internally incompatible. They simultaneously encourage staff 'to compete with each other through the use of individual contracts, performance related pay and individual performance appraisal and to take individual responsibility for budgets while at the same time being expected to become team players through quality circles, team briefing and communication cascades. The imperatives of marginal cost must co-exist with the insistence on quality and customer care. Managers are exhorted to minimise unit and variable costs while at the same time being expected to develop and create loyalty and commitment from their valued human resources' (Keenoy 1990: 379).

strategy) are themselves influenced by politically-inspired decision-making, and by systemic and inherent irrationality, then integration is unlikely, and so is the achievement of SHRM.

Furthermore, if the integration of employees into the organization (commitment, involvement) is central to SHRM, and if the co-operation and agreement of different groups (consensus) is also critical, then the existence of political or sectarian issues will gravely threaten these forms of individual and group integration.

Does the SHRM literature assume naive, apolitical, consensual conception of organizational decision-making and of organizational life? It is important to distinguish between the realities of organizational conflicts and politics and the neat, consensual but unrealistic models purveyed in the literature. If this book is to be of practical value we must engage with the real, if muddled, world of actuality.

Lorenz's accounts of the process of decision-making at BP hints strongly at such messy realities: struggles between 'regional barons' or between them and the centre; individuals opposing or embracing change for reasons connected with their vigorous, but possibly sectarian view of what was valuable and necessary to BP (and conceivably to them). Individuals, we are told, behaved in ways which were aggressive to others such that a senior manager had to 'read the riot act'.

In reality organizational decision-making is characterized by two opposing tendencies. On the one hand, inherent conflicts between factions, departments, units and levels and individuals over scarce organizational resources breed conflict, opposition, careerism, negotiation, compromise. Thus conflict and competition may adversely affect problem-solving and strategy formulation. On the other hand, decision-making may be affected not by difference and disagreement but by consensus and similarity – by the fact that decision-makers share the same cognitive frames of reference and do not realise that they share these cognitive schema. The following section explores the role of difference in decision-making; the section after that explores the role of similarity.

Organizational conflicts and differences may not appear or be manifested in blatant form: they are more likely to appear in the form of arguments that deny their very existence, deny their origins in structured differences and internal struggles, and which lay claim to consensual, harmonious values and principles – for example about what is best for the company – and in claims about key organizational values. But underlying the rhetoric are struggles for resources, jobs and power; struggles about what the organization should be like and about individuals' roles in it. These political, sectional elements have an impact on decision-making.

Thus we find a crucial, if paradoxical, aspect of SHRM decision-making and implementation. Organization structures within which SHRM decisions are made, which include decisions about future structures and systems, are themselves structures of power and interests. This will affect the nature of decisions about SHRM. In other words, existing power structures will affect future (or planned) SHRM structures (see box 17.2).

This political dimension of SHRM has a number of implications. First, the SHRM approach itself frequently carries fundamental assumptions about the possibility and role of conflict and politics within organizations. These assumptions concern the possibility of achieving the 'integration' of the organization – the achievement of consensus, co-operation and commitment among a divided and differentiated workforce.

Secondly, it means that the implementation of human resource strategies and choices is dependent on the successful overwhelming of political fissures and forces. Those responsible for SHRM must consider carefully – strategically – how they are going to design, prepare, launch and implement their chosen package in order to build support, undermine resistance, persuade, and win over the

### BOX 17.2 THE INFLUENCE OF POWER STRUCTURES UPON SHRM

'Human resource policy choices are not taken in a vacuum. On the contrary, they depend on the strategic managerial group being sufficiently powerful to ensure that particular policy choices are taken along lines which are consistent with an overarching strategy, and are also reflected in actual practices within the firm itself. Power is also relevant for understanding the relationship between human resource policy choices and situational factors (the power of the various stakeholders being important here). Furthermore, it is especially consequential so far as the implementation of human resource policies and choices within the actual company is concerned. Thus, in organisations with plural power centres, implementation is problematic, frequently circumscribed and often subject to detailed negotiation with diverse interest groups. Moreover, to the extent that one of the key elements of human resource management (i.e. employee influence) is developed to its full potential, the more likely it is that diverse values will impact upon (and ultimately shape) human resource policy choices themselves.'
(Poole 1990: 8)

resisters, and the sceptical. The implementation of any SHRM programme must take cognizance of internal political structures and interests, and must recognize that any organizational change affects established interests and values (see chapter 2); but, more fundamentally, the processes of strategic design themselves will be significantly influenced by the existence of political structures and interests within the organization. Existing SHRM structures will influence the ways in which senior managers design new SHRM strategies.

## SHRM and the Unitarist Conception of the Organization

Organizations are structures of power: they only exist and survive because their members can be relied on to comply with orders. They are also domains of conflict: 'there are recurrent struggles over the question of whose purposes, or interests, work (production) is to serve – the owner, the manager, the producer, the consumer? . . . there are (also) struggles over how work is to be organized – autocratically, bureaucratically, democratically?' (Alvesson and Willmott 1992: 6).

Organizations are also systems for the highly unequal distribution of rewards and resources (including, of course power itself, but also many others: pay, security, fringe benefits, job discretion etc.). 'Organizations and environments should be conceived as arenas. Within these arenas differentially valued resources are competed for by differentially powerful agencies, exercising differential control of these resources, in complex games with indeterminate rules which each agency seeks to exploit to its advantage' (Clegg 1990: 85). It is because of variations in the distribution of power and resources that the possibility of conflict arises along lines of perceived differences of interest and control (typically on lines of subordination/super-ordination). One major line of horizontal fracture (but by no means the only one) along which such conflict commonly occurs is between shop-floor staff and management, and it is this sort of conflict which is expressed by, and underlies, structures of employee representation and trade unionism.

There are constant struggles within organizations over issues such as the direction in which the organization should move, the interests it should serve, how work is to be organized, which group or section should suffer or benefit. These struggles do not necessarily take explicit or obvious form. Nor need they be institutionalized in coherent, organizational form. But they exist. Analyses of organization – or suggestions for organizational structuring – that ignore such realities are misleading. Organizations systematically produce conflict (and of course co-operation) as a result of their hierarchical and inegalitarian structures. However, this always remains a possibility, never a certainty. Precisely how, in any particular organization at any historical moment, conflict arises (and it may or may not be expressed in an organized form) remains an empirical matter. Nevertheless, this model of organizational structures and processes has significant implications for a consideration of SHRM.

One implication of the political nature of organizations is that SHRM, and the changes associated with it, represents the views and goals of a particular political faction – senior management. In other words, SHRM is a form of senior management ideology. The view within SHRM thinking and writing of the organization as an organic unity, and the insistence that there exist no serious conflicts of interest within the organization (unless externally introduced), represent the view of one organizational group, and are of benefit to it. SHRM values are also highly individualistic – focusing on the importance of employees relating to the organization as individuals rather than members of representative bodies or groups.

Much SHRM writing clearly adopts such views: that the interests of all members of staff are the same, that the commitment of all staff to organizational (i.e. senior managers') objectives can be achieved; that systematic conflict can be removed, and is a thing of the past; that unions are unnecessary as a form of collective negotiation and can now be replaced by considerations of career and rewards on an individual basis; that all members of the organization are equally powerful. Hales, for example, in an analysis of internal marketing as an approach to SHRM notes the limitations of the view that employees and employers meet equally in market for labour. Within the organization, employees are not consumers of the employer, and lack the sorts of power normally associated with consumers. 'Therefore when the interests of employees and employers diverge . . . it is not the interests of employees which . . . generally prevail' (Hales 1994: 62).

Not only are these ideas in themselves clearly sectional – in that they represent the views and the interests of senior managers – they are also unrealistic. The reality of many SHRM changes, and the ways they are imposed on employees, may be surrounded by the rhetoric of SHRM but the nature of the impact of these changes on employees will indicate to them the extent to which senior management is really prepared to commit itself.

Most SHRM programmes involve management efforts to generate commitment, change culture and attitudes. Such efforts not only assume a unitarist view of the organization (see below) they also try to gain something for nothing: 'management appears to be adopting the vocabulary of commitment without recognising the two-way nature of commitment, and the need to support their call for higher employee commitment through improved job security, high quality terms and conditions of service, and prospects for career advancement' (Blyton and Morris 1992: 128).

SHRM has been seen to assume an anti-union stance, and Guest has noted that SHRM can threaten unions in three ways: by bypassing them and developing new channels of communication; by implementing management practices which are less likely to require traditional defensive reactions; and, in non-union organizations, by HR policies designed to ensure that there is no – or little – need for unions (Guest 1989: 44).

However, although the rhetoric of SHRM is either opposed to unions, or assumes (and tries to achieve) their irrelevance, the practice of SHRM, as noted above, is unlikely to encourage employees to agree with such view of unions. On the other hand, recent events have so weakened the power of unions that employees may well feel that they are unlikely to be able to support resistance to management programmes of change. In fact, as Story and Sisson have noted, the evidence suggests that SHRM programmes of change, or at least some of the elements of SHRM change, and the individualistic values associated with them, seem to co-exist with more collectivist values and practices: 'trade union recognition and union relations and bargaining co-exist with SHRM changes in work design and communication and pay systems' (Storey and Sisson 1993: 22).

It remains to be seen how far these assumptions of consensus can survive the pressures of competitive pressure, technological innovation, variations in demand, and other environmental threats. A major source of internal organizational conflict is experiences which are interpreted by staff as indicating a conflict of interest between management and staff, head office and the operating company, and so on. Employees' conceptions of the degree of coincidence of their interests and the organizations', and their preparedness to commit themselves to the organization, are developed primarily not by the rhetoric of management, not by slogans and logos, but by experience: how they are treated (Coopey 1995).

The focus on 'culture change', for example, is often an attempt to impose a consensual, unitarist conception of the organization on all employees, and thus to gain their commitment. The SHRM focus on seeking to achieve a homogeneous or consensual organizational culture and values is unrealistic in the fact of a view of organizations as pluralist entities. As was noted earlier, is it appropriate for the values of the managed to be decided by people other than themselves?

The application of SHRM principles, with their assumptions about what relations between categories of staff ought to be like, may well be threatened by the imperatives of external factors which then produce responses which threaten consensus. This point clearly relates to the distinction between 'hard' and 'soft' definitions of SHRM noted earlier. Also many SHRM developments are either intended to have an impact on existing industrial relations systems and patterns, or to take advantage of a period when trade unions are relatively weakened by numerous factors (labour markets, legislation, management initiatives, IT, a particular ideological climate). A concern to redefine industrial relations is particularly apparent in the North American SHRM literature. The possibility of either intention being achieved is significantly affected by specific historical conditions. By the time this book has been in use for a few years we may well witness changes in the role and power of organized labour. It is therefore unwise to assume that SHRM requires or can rely on a consensual organization. It is safer to assume that it needs to achieve a greater degree of compliance and consensus, whilst recognizing that this achievement will always be vulnerable.

## Organizational politics, organizational divisions and decision making

The achievement of integration – and thus of SHRM – assumes that managers are able to identify what needs to be done, and are able and willing to implement SHRM strategies that 'fit' with each other and with the business strategy (and indeed that they are able to develop appropriate business strategies). But are these assumptions about the processes of organizational decision-making realistic and sound? In this section we consider the nature of organizational decision-making, and the role of structured differences of power and interest in influencing management thinking on SHRM issues.

Organizations do not simply *respond* to clear, unambiguous environmental demands; strategies do not simply emerge; SHRM strategies have to be actively developed. In all aspects of SHRM thinking, and in the achievement of all types of SHRM integration, managerial intervention, thinking and rationality are critical. Sparrow reviews a number of studies of the nature, origins and implications of managers' mental models and identifies an important paradox. Managers cope better with potential information overload if they develop mental models – schema – which, built up through experience, enable them to identify key issues, to focus attention on them and to analyse them in terms of familiar organizing frameworks and processes. However, applying these schema also incurs costs: 'The economy of processing that generates useful schematic knowledge also makes the same knowledge vulnerable to errors' (Sparrow 1994: 165). These are what others have called 'success recipes'. They incur risk by increasing inflexibility, discouraging reflection and permitting excessive attention to selected environmental signals at the cost of less familiar and unexpected ones.

For example, how the 'environment' is defined and understood and scanned, and how 'responses' are framed and selected, are themselves consequences or prior conceptions, ideological convictions, and other limiting assumptions and values. If senior managers and others are now keenly aware that their existing systems, structures, cultures, job-design principles, etc., are inefficient, and even counter-productive, how then were these elements ever introduced and allowed to continue? How was it possible for organizations ostensibly concerned with efficiency to accept systems which were not efficient? Did those who designed or reproduced or worked within bureaucracies appreciate their negative effects? How can we be confident that the decision-making currently in progress towards achieving new systems and structures is any better than the thinking which for years tolerated, even supported, the now much maligned old methods?

There are a number of possible answers: that managers knew and were indifferent because in some ways the systems suited them, or their departments; that managers were unaware of the deficiencies of earlier forms of organization; that these structures fitted earlier, less competitive times; or that it was too difficult and dangerous to confront such issues.

These alternative explanations raise the possibility that organizations can be poor at identifying and correcting errors and incompetence; this incompetence is produced by structures and systems in which managers responsible for decisions and for evaluating decisions have positions, status, and some considerable investment. 'Individuals who identify with established organizations – because, for example, they have been in power for extended periods and are seen as the architects of current structures – are unlikely to propose and seek to introduce comprehensive reform programmes inconsistent with established institutional identities' (Brunsson and Olsen 1993: 22). Also, if managers are unaware of the unhelpful implications of the structures and systems in which they work, then ignorance or lack of awareness, not collusion and defensiveness, are significant.

All these possibilities demonstrate the complex relationship between structures and ways of thinking, seeing and deciding. Existing organizational structures both reflect ways of thinking (e.g. bureaucracy and the typical bureaucrat, the isolation of the holders of centralized power) and generate ways of thinking – which will have major implications on the view and possibility of fundamental organizational change. This raises questions about the complexity of designing structures and systems to produce desired behaviours, and the possibility that such structures, however well designed, might produce unforeseen and undesirable consequences (as the earlier forms, such as bureaucracy, clearly did).

The case of ELB (see box 17.3) is highly significant because of its unusual exploration not simply of the flawed strategy of the company but of the reasons for senior managers defective decision-making and problems-solving. The senior managers of ELB were intelligent, thoughtful people who genuinely wanted to do the best thing for their company. Yet the way they worked together, thought and analysed together, and developed corporate strategies together, were deeply flawed – by analytical inadequacies and cognitive weaknesses. Collectively, they couldn't think straight and they did not even realize that they couldn't think straight. This is why this is such an important case study: it reveals how much of the SHRM literature overlooks the powerful pressures within organizations, that encourage senior executives to mismanage their organizations futures.

There is an important issue here: the relationship between organizational structures and organizational decision-making. Differentiated and hierarchic structures are inherently likely to produce decision-making of a politicized (incremental and negotiated) sort, and to encourage defensive, politicized behaviour. Alvesson and Willmott remark: 'managers are obliged to justify their existence by demonstrating their value to the organization as a whole. Yet the demonstration of their value . . . barely conceals their sectional interests . . . in developing or sustaining arrangements that, they anticipate, will secure their position of . . . comparative privilege' (Alvesson, and Willmott 1992: 18).

Organizations have, by implication in SHRM texts, been defined as neutral, rational structures, which can with sufficient knowledge be adjusted by their employees to enable them to do their work more effectively. Not only does this raise questions about what efficient structures would look like, it also calls into question the relationship between structures and managers' actions and decisions, including their decisions about the structures themselves. The worrying possibility exists that, by virtue of their location within organizational structures, managers' decision-making might be affected in ways that reduce its rationality.

This possibility follows from two important aspects of organizational structuring: the vertical differentiation of power and privilege and horizontal differentiation into functional or discipline (or regional) departments and specialisms. The first can generate deference, careerism, arrogance and defensiveness; and the exercise of power and control, particularly when associated with differences in levels of reward, opportunity and privilege (as between management and shop floor) can generate sharply opposed conceptions of interest and hence conflict. Thus the vertical differentiation of organization can result in the development of a variety of conceptions of the nature and objectives of the organization, and to antagonistic internal organizational relations.

The horizontal differentiation into specialist areas and departments breeds politics: differences of perspective, priority and interest. Within structures of power individuals and groups seek to defend and advance their sectional interest by proclaiming that it is in the interests of the organization as a whole and its 'real' objectives. As individual members of organizations compete for scarce rewards, so departments, sections and specialists tend to defend their share of the budget, their resources, their conception of the organization's purpose, and their particular skill and information. One consequence of the inevitable sectionalism of large organizations is that information becomes a useful resource for protecting or advancing sectional interests: and change becomes potentially threatening to some (but attractive to others).

Each service, each division, indeed every sub-unit, becomes a guardian of its own mission, standards and skills; lines of organization become lines of loyalty and secrecy. In industry, the personnel department defends its control of selection and training; accounting, its standards of reporting; production, its schedules of output; sales, its interest in product design and customer service – each

## BOX 17.3 ORGANIZATIONS AND ENVIRONMENTS

ELB is a British company that started life in the early 1900s and early in this century developed its markets in Europe, Africa and the Near East. The 50s and 60s saw a huge growth in demand for its products. By the mid-1970s it had enjoyed 15 years of uninterrupted growth in sale and profits, had a turnover of over £100m and employed 9,000 people. However building new factories and developing new products drained considerable amounts of money from the business. Profits peaked in 1977 and in the following two years the company drew heavily on reserves. By 1980 the dividend had to be cut.

The problem was that the company could not learn. It was a victim of its own history of success – the immediate experience of 15 years of uninterrupted growth. Senior managers simply projected the company's past – their 'success recipes' – into the future. 'Not to believe in the company's traditional product strengths would have been to deny their experience. Success brings with it a confidence and trust in one's own judgement: a belief perhaps that success flows from one's own wisdom and experience rather than fortuitous changes in the market.' The world brand strategy that emerged explicitly in 1976 (and which contributed significantly to the company's misfortunes) was an affirmation of senior manager's experiences. The company's strengths became weakness: success recipes were applied when they were inappropriate; senior managers deluded themselves into feeling invulnerable; their confidence being based on the company's historic near monopoly in the UK; and their market strength allowed them to export their inefficiencies. Internally the company's performance made senior managers capable of resisting any calls for change. To question policies was seen as questioning the basis of managers' authority. The hierarchy obstructed key processes of environmental scanning, signal recognition, data analysis, identification and assessment of possible new strategies and goals. Hierarchy created silence and deference. Individuals began to believe that the 'system' was beyond change and control; that power was elsewhere; that they individually were not responsible for what many of them could see happening around them. It was always 'them'.

The causes of the company's demise lie not in the changing environment, but in senior managers' unwillingness to scan and understand this environment – in using lessons from the past to study the future. Their strategic myopia stemmed from their corporate isolation. 'It is to the routine effects of the working of the hierarchy one must look to explain how senior managers came to pursue a strategy that went so clearly against the experience of so many junior managers and which carefully excluded consideration of important changes emerging in ELB's market.'
(Roberts 1992: 18–38)

restricting information that might advance the competing interests of the others (Wilensky 1967: 48).

One obvious example of this is when, as increasingly happens, organizations are structured in terms of separate profit centres. This has advantages in terms of encouraging on-the-spot responsiveness and commercial and business responsibility; but it clearly also discourages relations and co-operation across the various business units.

When these phenomena result in conflict, manipulation of information, sectionalism, occasional distrust and politicking, the outcome may be a pattern of decision-making which varies considerably from the super-rationalist conception of decision-making that is frequently assumed by much SHRM literature – that is, a pattern of decision-making which is emergent as well as deliberate (Mintzberg and Waters 1989: 4), incremental, politicized, negotiated to some degree. Thus decision-making and the strategies it produces can best be seen as the product of the political, cognitive and cultural fabric of the organization. The expectation would be that strategic decisions could be explained better in terms of political processes than analytical procedures; that cognitive maps of managers are better explanations of their perceptions of the environment and their strategic responses than are analysed position statements and evaluative techniques; and that the legitimacy of these cognitive maps is likely to be reinforced through the myths and rituals of the organization (Johnson 1987).

Argyris has analysed the ways in which senior managers' thinking and analysis may be clouded by their location, specifically that it may suffer from defensive routines whereby issues of apparent threat or embarrassment are avoided, and so learning and analysis are also avoided. The way in which managers work together when developing organizational or human resource strategies – in teams – may encourage this tendency towards politically inspired decision-making, which seeks to support analyses and decisions that are felt to be acceptable to existing power groups and to existing cultural and group norms. A moment when this is particularly apparent is in organizational discussions of poor decisions. Such post-mortems offer a marvellous opportunity for organizational and individual learning, but all too often what takes place is a process which Argyris (1987) describes as 'skilled incompetence': being skilled at ensuring the analysis does not embarrass, threaten or even surprise one's colleagues. These techniques, which Argyris labels defensive routines, are organizational and collective.

Newcomers to the organization learn how to avoid learning and how to avoid threatening others. Furthermore, the very fact that this process is occurring becomes in itself something that cannot be talked about without risking disapproval or charges of betrayal.

Argyris describes this common situation as follows. Within an organization it has become clear that a major decision was a mistake. However, 'Questioning the original decision violated a set of nested organisational norms. The first norm was that policies and objectives, especially that top management was excited about, should not be confronted openly. The second norm was that bad news . . . had to be offset by good news . . . These two norms had to be camouflaged . . . When the participants camouflaged the norms, and camouflaged the camouflage, they did so because they knew that to hide information violated organisational policies . . . If they exposed the errors, they would call into question a set of nested norms that were supposed to be kept covert. If they did not expose the errors, they created and/or reinforced processes that inhibited organisational learning' (Argyris 1987: 3).

The description of 'group think' as analysed and conceptualized by Janis (1972) is also relevant to SHRM decision-making and incorporates similar processes to those described by Argyris. Group think refers to the phenomenon where ties of group loyalty, plus deference to senior figures, discourages radical questioning of assumptions, obstructs the critiquing of proposals, encourages the selective use of data to support popular solutions, and results ultimately in the achievement of a sort of collective fantasy where much thought is given to how to install and implement the strategy but far too little to evaluating its quality.

Schafer and Crichlow (1996) in an empirical study of 'group think' have given substantive support to Janis' suggestions. They found that three of the factors identified by Janis are empirically related to the incidence of problematic decision-making by senior management groups: leadership style; the existence of traditional group procedures and patterns of group behaviour. These factors introduce partial leadership, non-methodical decision-making processes and allow an overestimation of the group, closed-mindedness and pressure towards conformity.

## SHRM Decision-Making: An Over-Rationalist Approach?

The achievement of integration of SHRM elements, and of SHRM and corporate strategy, is central to the concept of SHRM. Yet are there organizational limitations on the capacity or willingness of senior members of organizations to embark on, design and implement, such integrated programmes of SHRM change?

Do models of SHRM assume a naive and over-rationalistic view of the processes of organizational strategic decision-making? Do these models assume that managers are omniscient, rational, willing and able to pick up relevant information, process it and act on its analyses? Managers are not functionaries; they are not cyphers, they will respond actively to perceived environmental challenge or plans for re-structuring in terms of their ideologies, cultures, interests, limitations. The social relations within which managers live and work will systematically 'foster and sustain very limited and often distorted forms of communication between' different groups within the organization (Alvesson and Willmott 1992: 7). Existing structures influence managers' role and reaction to change.

There are two possible ways of explaining limitations on the rationality of managers' decision-making.

(1) One approach would be to consider the wisdom and rationality of currently fashionable nostrums and to point out that senior managers who implemented such fashionable ideas were likely to produce effects they did not desire simply because they were blinded by, or misled by current fashions of organizational restructuring.

How 'rational' are the forms and principles of organizational restructuring that are fundamental to current approaches to SHRM change? As noted earlier in this chapter, this question may lead us to consider the relationships *between* dimensions of these change programmes – between processes of control, and processes designed to gain commitment, between the focus on the individual, and on the team. But we also need to consider the value, and effects of some key SHRM principles, for some commentators have argued that these principles are positively dangerous and damaging; that they are inherently flawed.

As Brunsson and Olsen remark of SHRM ideas and recommendations, their very simplicity is appealing, plus the fact that such ideas are attractive because of their fashionableness. SHRM ideas may appeal precisely because they appear so much more attractive than the existing organizational reality. 'It is not difficult to find . . . better solutions when designing reforms: current practice seldom appears as attractive as novel solutions; unlike current solutions, reforms promise to overcome both current and future problems. Simple principles can more easily attract enthusiasm and support than can complex descriptions of reality' (Brunsson and Olsen 1993: 36–7). Indeed through the activities of management writers, consultants, even academics, the profusion and pervasiveness of SHRM recommendations may be so great that it actually becomes more difficult not to change organizations than to change them. One consequence is that the actual ideas and principles of SHRM, although presented as correct solutions to organizational problems, may gain their strength and appeal from their pervasiveness rather than from their internal strength (see box 17.4).

(2) The second approach to SHRM irrationality looks not at the inherent value and rationality of SHRM elements and methods, but at the processes whereby human resource decisions are made. Interestingly, while the literature on strategic decision-making addresses the ways in which this decision-making process is likely to be emergent, negotiated and, politicized, conceptions of SHRM decision-making tend to be much more rationalist and in consequence unrealistic.

Much SHRM literature assumes a naive apolitical, over-rationalist view of organizational decision-making. Not only does it ignore political realities; as we have noted, it also ignores how senior managers' understanding, knowledge, analysis and decisions on SHRM matters (the challenges of the environment, the need for change, the possibilities for change), are themselves shaped by the organizational structures, cultures and personnel systems within which the managers operate. It is not an overstatement to say that managers' capacity to make SHRM decisions (by virtue of their senior location) is often precisely what makes the resultant decisions inadequate. This is not surprising: senior managers have developed within the organization, have absorbed it's culture, have risen because of their skills, have positions of seniority and power within the structure. They have a very real interest in the status quo. Indeed the very distinction between

## BOX 17.4 ROI – HELP OR HINDRANCE?

*Return On Investment* (ROI) is frequently used as a basis for the measurement of organizational performance, part of the current strategy of eliminating bureaucratic rules and requirements; it is said to be liberating, enabling, empowering – while insisting on the achievement of tightly defined performance targets. Clegg has argued, building on earlier work of Hayes and Abernathy, that such measures of performance, can encourage unhelpful long term behaviour and strategy. For one thing, ROI can be manipulated to appear more positive simply by reducing the 'Investment' side of the equation which immediately improves the level of return. 'A profit-centre manager can achieve quicker, surer and easier results by delaying replacement of old or worn out equipment, replacing equipment eventually with technologically dated or inferior substitutes, and skimping on maintenance, research and development and personnel development' (Clegg 1990: 197). Some commentators have argued that the prominence of such managerial values – and the skills required to enforce them – have produced managers who systematically mismanage: 'They regard plant as an embarrassing constraint on financial manoeuvrability and try to buy pre-packaged solutions, commonly on an inappropriate and grandiose scale. But what they do well is more damaging than what they do badly. "Managing by the numbers" collapses time frame: individual businesses have to show quick returns on minimal outlays or be deliberately run down and liquidated as "cash cows"; in conglomerates individual businesses are reduced to bargaining chips, quickly acquired and shed. A "successful" American manager doesn't plant or harvest' (Thurow 1984: 23; quoted in Clegg 1990: 199).

structures and cultures and individuals hardly holds. Senior mangers have often absorbed and internalized much of the organization. Therefore their thinking on the need for change, and their thinking about what change is needed will be coloured by their membership of the organization that needs to be changed. Johnson (1987) argues the importance not only of differentiating aspects of organizational structure, but also of shared values and ways of thinking. This so-called paradigm, can be seen to include strong cultural or ideological elements, for it covers not only taken-for-granted knowledge and ways of seeing, knowing and doing things, but also values and moralities: the ways things should be done around here.

This point is of great importance. The key element of organizational change is not any particular direction of change, but achieving the constant capacity to change. And this means that those responsible for change need to be able to break out of the paradigms, the ways of thinking and seeing, of the existing organization. Pettigrew and Whipp, in introducing their study, note that their central aim is to 'link the competitive performance of British firms to their ability to adapt to major changes in their environment' (Pettigrew and Whipp 1989: 26). Similarly Hamel and Prahalad (1989: 69) note that 'An organisation's capacity to improve existing skills and learn new ones is the most defensible competitive advantage of all'. Clearly, if the achievement of this capacity is crucial, it is also complex and difficult. A fundamental starting point is the realization that achieving the capacity for organizational learning will probably require unlearning; and this can be painful and worrying, not only because existing skills are frequently almost unconscious, but also because they are cherished and comforting.

Pettigrew and Whipp remark that: 'The ability of a company to learn should be under constant scrutiny. In other words, the ability of a company to reconstruct and adapt its knowledge base (made up of skills, structures and values . . .) should be a key test for managers. They should also be able to apply the "unlearning test". In other words, is the organization capable of mounting the creative destruction necessary to break down outmoded attitudes and practices while at the same time building up new, more appropriate competence?' (1991: 290).

Learning new skills and behaviours must start with unlearning old ones, now inappropriate. And just as existing skills and practices can hamper new behaviours, so the achievement of corporate strategies can be obstructed by tried and tested success formulas (see box 17.5). Brunsson and Olsen (1993) note the role of 'organizational forgetfulness' in facilitating organizational change programmes: those introducing fashionable packages of change have to forget about previous reforms often of a very similar sort, that failed to deliver. And they have to forget that buying promises is easier than achieving success. 'Forgetfulness ensures that experience will not interfere with reform: it prevents the past from disturbing the future' (Brunsson and Olsen 1993: 41).

The role of culture in structuring senior mangers' views and responses has been exemplified by Bate. He shows that in an organization he studied, even when the established 'preconditions' for successful organizational change were in place, change did not occur: 'Something . . . was enmeshing people in their problems in a persistent and repetitive way.' Bate (1992) argues that under certain conditions culturally valued practices and attitudes produce a 'learned helplessness' (Bate 1992: 214). He identifies the issue as follows: 'why were situations allowed to persist when they were accepted by the parties themselves as problematical and undesirable?' His answer: 'the parties were actively colluding in a process which effectively removed all possibility of a resolution to their problems . . . people in organisations evolve in their daily interactions with one another a system of shared perspectives of "collectively held and sanctioned definitions of the situation" which make up the culture of these organizations'. Furthermore, this culture offers to employees ways of thinking, seeing and knowing which prevent rational analysis and understanding.

**BOX 17.5 WHEN SUCCESS RECIPES BECOME FAIL RECIPES**

Hamel and Prahalad (1989) identify another aspect of organizational thinking that can interrupt decision-making. They note the role of success recipes – established ways of thinking and problem-solving which are usually implicit and taken-for-granted and which have earned widespread acceptance and credibility – if not symbolic value – because of their contribution to success. But these recipes are a source of vulnerability when times and competitors change. A competitor's commitment to a 'success formula' is possibly its greatest vulnerability, because strategy recipes limit opportunities for competitive innovation (1989: 72). They list a number of such common recipes: over-commitment to strategic business units with consequent business-unit deskilling, over-commitment to the use of financial ratios which can be improved, reductions in stock, investment, etc., rather than growth of revenues (1989: 73–4).

This point has also been noted by writers concerned with the nature and implications of corporate cultures. These cultures can generate a sort of strategic myopia. The beliefs that managers hold by virtue of their culturally-based values and mind-sets, determine not only what they see but how they analyse and understand what they see when they scan the environment or the structure and functioning of their organization.

## Conclusions and Summary

SHRM promises a great deal; its influence on recent and current programmes of organizational restructuring has been enormous. To a major degree SHRM supplies the agenda for programmes of organizational change – the introduction of internal markets within the UK National Health Service; the subcontracting and privatizing of public utilities; the delayering and devolving of many previously centralized businesses; the introduction of JIT, TQM, team-working, PRP and all the other current fashions, many of which have been considered in this volume.

But if it promises much, what does it deliver? We have reason to be wary of fashionable programmes of organizational restructuring; after all we have been here before, or somewhere very similar. There have been other philosophies of organizational restructuring: Scientific Management, Human Relations, Worker Participation, Management by Objectives, Organization Development, and so on. The fact that senior mangers seem to like SHRM, that politicians clearly approve of some of its central elements, does not make it true, or right.

There is therefore a need to consider SHRM in terms of its key ideas and assumptions and to assess its feasibility as a body of recommendations and assumptions. This analysis is conducted in this chapter. Such an analysis shows that SHRM is characterized by a number of basic problems, limitations and contradictions: it means a variety of different things ('open' versus 'closed', 'hard' versus 'soft'); it makes a set of recommendations which could well conflict; it claims high moral purposes but seems to be vulnerable to short-termism.

Central to SHRM is a concern for the integration of structures and strategies and for human resource systems with each other. Without these integrations, SHRM becomes meaningless. Yet as this chapter has shown, achieving these sorts of integration is far from assured. A major reason for this is that SHRM depends upon a highly rationalist notion of management decision-making – for the design and implementation of SHRM projects depends on the alertness and analysis of senior managers. Can we assume that senior managers will actually undertake SHRM in this way? In fact the chapter argues that from what we know of how other decisions are made in organizations, and from what we know of the role of existing structures, cultures, mind-sets and politics on managers' thinking, there are serious grounds for questioning the rationality of management decision-making.

Models of SHRM offer an enticing promise – they offer a number of ways in which the historic problems of organization and management can be overcome, performance improved, inefficiencies removed, animosities eliminated and irrationalities reduced. But, in a number of ways, models of SHRM themselves rely on potentially unrealistic assumptions about how organizations work, about the possibility of integration and consensus, and about strategic and HR decision-making. This chapter has explored these issues. The point of this chapter is not to suggest the impossibility of SHRM, but rather to point out the difficulties that surround attempts to achieve a strategic approach to the management of human resources. This chapter has explored the dark side of SHRM – it has addressed the empirical realities of organizational structures, processes, relationships and decision-making that can impinge upon the idealized pictures and assumptions of SHRM. We will only make progress towards the objectives of SHRM if these difficulties themselves are overcome. One of the tests of SHRM therefore is not the extent to which it assumes consensual, rational, integrated organization, but the extent to which it actively seeks to achieve these necessary circumstances. By the same token, SHRM initiatives which fail to address relationships between groups, building consensus, which fail to generate commitment from employees, which fail to address the rationality and learning of senior managers, but which concentrate instead on assuming all these conditions and impose codified SHRM packages, will not only fail to achieve the true possibilities of SHRM, they may actually make things worse – by damaging employee commitment and institutionalizing senior management's unwillingness to learn.

## Key Points

- While SHRM sounds great in theory – and obviously appeals to many managers and management consultants and writers, it is no help to anyone to gloss over what may be serious inherent problems in this approach. These problems are of various sorts and are considered in this chapter. Some arise from contradictions in the very idea of SHRM itself – for example, the conflict between 'open' and 'closed' models or between 'hard' and 'soft' approaches. Others tend to centre around the notion of integration, intrinsic to SHRM models, the approach to organizations, and organizational relationships intrinsic in SHRM thinking, and the view of management decision-making adopted within SHRM models. All these are arguably simplistic and unrealistic.
- There are four main kinds of integration that are assumed and promoted by SHRM thinking, and they are all significant as sources of problems in the achievement of SHRM. These types are explored in this chapter and their implications considered. This is important because if any or all of these types of integration is impossible or difficult to achieve it will have devastating implications for the possibility of SHRM in practice.
- Much SHRM thinking and prescription assumes a naive conception of the neutrality, objectivity, analytic competence, open-mindedness, and disinterestedness of senior management decision-makers whose responsibility it is to recognize that an SHRM decision is necessary, to gather the relevant data and analyse them, and to make a sensible decision. If these assumptions are infirm, the SHRM decisions will be flawed. The limitations on managers' decision-making are explored in this chapter. Perversely, they include the consequences of the prevailing SHRM situation, which will limit how managers see the situation and how they react to it.
- Given the apparent inherent problems surrounding SHRM it becomes all the more important to see to what extent SHRM is actually occurring – the empirical test of SHRM as distinct from the assessment of SHRM conceptually. Here the evidence – discussed in the next chapter – is ambiguous. Change is certainly occurring; but it is not certain that it is always or even frequently sufficiently strategic, or is more than ad hoc opportunism.
- For some commentators this gap between SHRM theory and empirical reality is not an incidental feature of SHRM but is actually central to SHRM: SHRM is significant more as rhetoric or ideology than reality – as a large-scale attempt to manage meaning for managers and employees.

## Discussion Questions

1 Discuss some of the inherent contradictions in, and limitations of, SHRM thinking.
2 Why is integration – of various types – central to SHRM?
3 Why is integration likely to prove difficult to achieve?
4 What are the in-built limitations to the rationality of senior managers' thinking and decision-making on SHRM issues?
5 Is SHRM more rhetoric and ideology than reality? And what are the implications of this?

## References


Abernathy, W., Clark, K. B., and Kantrow, A. M. (1981) 'The new industrial competition', *Harvard Business Review*, October, 69–77.

Alexander, L. D. (1989) 'Successfully implementing strategic decisions' in D. Asch and C. Bowman (eds) *Readings in Strategic Management*, Basingstoke: Macmillan Education, 388–96.

Alvesson, M. and Willmott, H. (1992) 'Critical theory and management studies: An introduction', in M. Alvesson and H. Willmott (eds) *Critical Management Studies*, London: Sage, 1–20.

Argyris, C. (1987) *Change and Defensive Routines*, Boston: Pitman.

Bartlett, C. A. and Ghoshal, S. (1992) *Transnational Management*, Homewood, IL: Irwin.

Bate, P. (1992) 'The impact of organisational culture on approaches to organisational problem-solving' in G. Salaman et al. (eds) *Human Resource Strategies*, London: Sage, 219–34.

Beaumont, P. (1992) 'The US human resource management literature', in G. Salaman et al. (eds) *Human Resource Strategies*, London: Sage, 20–38.

—— (1993) *Human Resource Management*, London: Sage.

Beer, M., Spector, B., Lawrence, P. R., Mills, Q. N. and Walton, R. E. (1984) *Managing Human Assets*, New York: Free Press.

——, ——, ——, Mills D., and Walton, R. (1985) *Human Resource Management: A general managers perspective*, New York: Free Press.

Blyton, P. and Morris, J. (1992) 'HRM and the limits of flexibility', in P. Blyton and P. Turnbull, (eds) *Reassessing Human Resource Management*, London: Sage, 116–30.

Brunsson, N. and Olsen, J. (1993) *The Reforming Organisation*, London: Routledge.

Chandler, A. D. (1977) *Strategy and Structure*, Cambridge, MA: MIT Press.

Clegg, S. (1990) *Modern Organisations*, London: Sage.

Coopey, J. (1995) 'Managerial culture and the stillbirth of organisational commitment', *Human Resource Management Journal*, vol. 5, no. 3, 56–76.

Galbraith, J. R. and Kazanjian, R. K. (1986) 'Organising to implement strategies of diversity and globalisation', *Human Resource Management*, vol. 25, no. 1, 37–54.

Gallie, D. and White, M. (1993) *Employee Commitment and the Skills Revolution*, London: Policy Studies Institute.

Gorz, A. (1989) *Critique of Economic Reason*, London: Verso.

Guest, D. E. (1987) 'Human resource management and industrial relations', *Journal of Management Studies*, vol. 24, no. 5, 503–21.

—— (1989) 'Human resource management: its implications for industrial relations and trade unions' in J. Storey (ed.) *New Perspectives on Human Resource Management*, London: Routledge, 41–55.

Hales, C. (1994) 'Internal marketing as an approach to human resource management', *Journal of Management Studies*, vol. 5, no. 1, 33–62.

Hamel, G. and Prahalad, C. K. (1989) 'Strategic intent', *Harvard Business Review*, May/June, 63–76.

Hayes R. H. and Abernathy W. (1980) 'Managing our way to economic decline', *Harvard Business Review*, vol. 58, no. 4, 66–77.

Higgins, W. and Clegg, S. R. (1988) 'Enterprise calculation and manufacturing decline', *Organization Studies*, vol. 9, no. 1, 69–89.

Janis, I. L. (1972) *Victims of Groupthink*, Boston, MA: Houghton Mifflin.

Johnson, G. (1987) *Strategic Change and the Management Process*, Oxford: Blackwell.

Keenoy, T. (1990) 'HRM: A case of the wolf in sheep's clothing?' *Personnel Review*, vol. 19 no. 2, 3–9.

—— and Anthony, P. (1992) 'HRM: Metaphor, meaning and morality', in T. Blyton and P. Turnbull, (eds) *Reassessing Human Resource Management*, London: Sage, 233–60.

Legge, K. (1989) 'Human Resource Management: A critical analysis', in J. Storey (ed.) *New Perspectives on Human Resource Management*, London: Routledge, 19–40.

—— (1994) 'Rhetoric, reality and hidden agendas', in J. Storey (ed.) *Human Resource Management: A Critical Text*, London: Routledge, 33–62.

Lengnick-Hall, C. and Lengnick-Hall, M. (1988) 'Strategic human resources management: a review of the literature and a proposed typology', *Academy of Management review*, vol. 13, no. 3, 454–70.

Miller, D. (1986) 'Configurations of strategy and structure: Towards a synthesis', *Strategic Management Journal*, vol. 7, 233–49.

Miller, P. and Rose, N. (1993) 'Governing economic life' in M. Gane and T. Johnson (eds) *Foucault's New Domains*, London: Routledge, 75–105.

Mintzberg, H. and Waters, J. A. (1989) 'Of strategies, deliberate and emergent', in D. Asch and C. Bowman (eds) *Readings in Strategic Management*, Basingstoke: Macmillan Education, 4–19.

Paauwe, J. and Dewe, P. (1995) 'Organisational structure of multinational corporations', in A. W. Harzing and J. V. Ruysseveldt (eds) *International Human Resource Management*, London: Sage, 51–76.

Pettigrew A. M. and Whipp, R. (1989) *The Management of Strategic Operational Change*, ESRC.

—— and —— (1991) *Managing Change for Competitive Success*, Oxford: Blackwell.

Poole, M. (1990) 'Editorial: Human resource management in an international perspective', *International Journal of Human Resource Management*, vol. 1, no. 1, 1–15.

Roberts, J. (1992) 'Human resource strategies and the management of change', in *B884 Human Resource Strategies, Supplementary readings Book 1*, Milton Keynes: Open University, 18–38.

Rose, N. (1989) 'Governing the enterprising self', Paper presented to University of Lancaster Conference on The Values of the Enterprise Culture.

Schafer, M. and Crichlow, S. (1996) 'Antecedents of groupthink: A quantitative study', *The Journal of Conflict Resolution*, vol. 40, no. 3, 415–35.

Sewell, G. and Atkinson B. (1992) 'Empowerment or emasculation? Shopfloor surveillance in a total quality organisation', in P. Blyton and P. Turnbull (eds) *Reassessing Human Resource Management*, London: Sage, 97–115.

—— and Wilkinson, B (1992) 'Empowerment or emasculation? Shopfloor surveillance in a total quality organisation', in P. Blyton and P. Turnbull (eds) *Reassessing Human Resource Management*, London: Sage, 97–115.

Sparrow, P. (1994) 'The psychology of strategic management: Emerging themes of diversity and cognition', in C. Cooper and I. Robertson, (eds) *International Review of Industrial and Organisational Psychology*, vol. 9, Chichester: Wiley, 147–81.

Storey, J. and Sisson, K. (1993) *Managing Human Resources and Industrial Relations*, Buckingham: Open University Press.

—— (1989) 'Introduction from personnel management to human resource management' in J. Storey (ed.) *New Perspectives on Human Resource Management*, London: Routledge, 1–18.

Thurow, L. (1984) 'Revitalising American industry: Managing in a competitive world economy', *Californian Management Review*, vol. 27, no. 1, 9–40.

Wilensky, H. (1967) *Organisational Intelligence*, New York: Basic Books.

chapter 18

# SHRM – The Redefining of People and Organizations

CHAPTER OUTLINE

## Learning Objectives

On completing this chapter you will:

- Be better acquainted with the currently available research material on the incidence and consequences of SHRM – as variously defined, and be aware of the strengths and limitations of this material.
- Be alert to the possibility that SHRM is as important as a powerful management rhetoric as it is as a guide to practice.
- Be able to come to your own, informed and balanced assessment of the value of SHRM.

# Introduction

This chapter is concerned with the following questions: do the current nostrums of SHRM actually work? And indeed, what does 'work' mean in this connection? If and when SHRM does support the achievement of organizational strategies is this because SHRM is essentially an approach to the effective management of cost cutting and decline, or because it is an approach which enables the full development and harnessing of the human potential of the organization? Are SHRM organizations lean and fit, or anorexic and debilitated? The previous chapter looked at the conceptual basis of SHRM promises. We considered the conceptual feasibility of SHRM by identifying and discussing some of the key assumptions implicit in SHRM approaches. We also noted that there are grounds for being sceptical about some SHRM promises, which tend to stress an idealized, consensual, integrated and over-rational organization. In this chapter we take this analysis of the possibility of SHRM further by reviewing the evidence for the occurrence of SHRM and data on its impact.

In the second part of the chapter we take a broader view, and consider the ways in which SHRM has for some writers been important not simply through its empirical applications and effects but through its impact on the ways we think about organizations and our relationship to them, and indeed for the way we are encouraged to think about ourselves as members of these organizations.

# SHRM and its Effects

'HRM is the repository of good intentions. Management of human resources is the area in which executives realise they ought to be doing more and to which they promise to turn their attention the day after tomorrow' (Guest 1990: 392). At the beginning of this book we promised that later in the volume we would address the question: does SHRM work? And while we also noted that to some extent the entire volume is concerned with this question, we recognize that it requires specific and focused attention. Now is the time to consider the question directly.

## What is SHRM?

We cannot address this question directly without first agreeing about what this thing – SHRM – actually is. So, once again, we must first consider what is meant by SHRM, and then analyse whether it is working (and of course consider what the expression 'working' means). Many writers have noted the complexity and difficulty of analysis of the effects, or effectiveness, of SHRM. And while we will seek to present the available research material clearly, there is no doubt that many of the research findings raise as many questions as they answer.

Is SHRM happening? Guest has noted that discussions of the impact of SHRM have three interrelated elements: '*if* an integrated set of HRM practices is applied *with* a view to achieving the normative goals of high commitment to the organisation plus quality and flexibility *then* higher worker performance will result' (Guest 1996: 5, our emphasis). Clearly, therefore, each element of this view (the empirical occurrence of HRM practices; the intentions of senior management; and the outcomes) will require separate attention.

The empirical occurrence of SHRM has already been aired throughout this volume. You will remember in Figure 1.1 that Storey and Sisson present material on the occurrence of the various elements of SHRM and their conclusion of the relative rarity of SHRM, if this is seen as a long-term, integrated and strategic approach to SHRM.

It is true that there is considerable case study and general media information available about claimed SHRM developments and their impact on performance – and we shall consider this material in due course. The case of BP, for example (referred to in chapters 2 and 12), is one of a number of well-known recent cases of what are claimed to be apparent heroic and successful attempts to adjust one or more of the key dimensions of SHRM (usually culture) in order to achieve some significant (often fundamental) change in employee behaviour. Within many British banks, to take another example, there is currently a concern to achieve a radical change in staff behaviour and attitudes as the banks move from a focus on performance as measured by compliance with bureaucratic procedures and rules, to a focus on business-getting and profit-making. But case studies are not a secure way of establishing the prevalence of SHRM, and the research evidence on the other hand is somewhat confusing. We have seen that there are a number of widespread changes occurring on a number of fronts. But do these constitute SHRM change? And do they have the sort of impact on organizational performance that SHRM change is desired to achieve? Guest (1989: 51) argues that the changes apparent to achieve flexibility, quality etc. 'are consistent with moves towards human resource management'. But other commentators are far less sure of this.

Guest has argued that SHRM consists of four 'policy goals' – high commitment, high quality, flexibility and strategic integration, and has asserted that 'Only when a coherent strategy, directed towards these four policy goals, fully integrated into business strategy and fully sponsored by line management at all levels is applied will the high productivity and related outcomes sought by industry be achieved' (Guest 1990: 378). With such a demanding set of criteria very few full cases of SHRM cases can be found, particularly when Guest's definition emphasizes a clear and direct causal connection between policy goals and productivity outcomes. Also by arguing the causal relationship between policy goals and performance, Guest excludes situations where other measures (cost-cutting, increased controls) are used to achieve performance.

An important test of the degree to which organizational change programmes are evidence of, or part of, SHRM, is the extent to which these initiatives are genuinely strategic. Here also problems arise. Many definitions of SHRM argue that for SHRM to be truly strategic senior management must be seen to play a major role in the development implementation and articulation of HR strategy: this is what strategy in this context means. This seems sensible. It requires that senior managers are explicitly committed to, and seeking to implement in SHRM terms, an overall approach to staff and organization (e.g. the four policy goals described by Guest). If SHRM decisions are not inspired by this sort of approach, then the initiatives would not be regarded as genuine SHRM.

This is the view taken by Mueller (1996), who argues that a key feature of SHRM is the proactive role of senior management in the strategic management of human resources. He reviews available research material in terms of this definition of SHRM – that senior management plays a major and active role in HR matters, articulating HR strategy and that HR policies are integrated. He concludes that overall there appears to be little evidence for stating a direct link between SHRM on the one hand and a firm's performance on the other hand. It is this which Purcell (1989: 73) terms the 'ambiguity in human resource management'. Demands for management to embrace SHRM therefore do not appear to be actually based on knowledge of the performance-enhancing effects of SHRM. This has led Dyer and Reeves (1995: 668) to speak of a 'strategic bandwagon' which is likely to continue to roll in spite of 'the rather fragile empirical undercarriage on which it currently rests' (Mueller 1996: 764).

## Is SHRM actually happening?

By these criteria, then, SHRM is clearly a relatively rare phenomenon, despite the much vaunted claims of the few well-known case studies. And researchers have concluded on the basis of empirical studies that certainly in the early 1980s, 'By and large British management does not have a strategic approach to the management of people: pragmatism or opportunism continue to be very much the order of the day' (Sisson and Sullivan 1987: 492). Similarly, Ahlstrand and Purcell argue that on the basis of their research into the relationship between corporate strategies and strategies concerning employee relations (a sub-set of SHRM), 'in the formulation of corporate strategies, management and employee relations issues are rarely taken into account unless the effect of a strategic decision has distinct industrial relations and personnel implications, seen for example in major redundancy and plant run down' (Ahlstrand and Purcell 1988: 9).

Secondly, these authors point out that some common corporate developments may themselves have limiting effects on SHRM progress. For example, the need to respond to market demands for reduced costs and increased efficiencies 'make it more difficult for the enterprise to adopt institutional strategies or management style statements which provide the basis for coherent, corporate-wide standards of employee relations management based on beliefs about the best way to manage people at work. Diversity and decentralisation are encouraged' (Ahlstrand and Purcell 1988: 29). This tendency could be exacerbated by processes of decentralization and delegation which 'push down' responsibility to semi-autonomous business units, exerting strong pressure to cut costs, limit investment, improve margins. These are examples of the contradictions recognized earlier and described by Guest as the conflict between the hard and soft versions of human resource management: one which regards human resources as a cost, the other as an asset to be developed. But development costs money and takes time.

On the other hand, there is evidence, as reported by Guest (in Storey 1989: 50), that 'at a significant proportion of foreign-owned green-field sites, management is pursuing some of the central features of HRM. These include flexible working, employee commitment and attention to high quality, which is partly reflected in the investment in careful selection and training.'

That certain elements of the SHRM approach are being used together is supported by Wood and Albanese, who refer to these elements as 'high commitment' SHRM or management practices. They list: career ladders and training, flexibility, reduced hierarchies, teams, jobs with upgraded skills, and job security, new forms of assessment and payment systems and a focus on quality (Wood and Albanese 1995: 222–3). They argue, and it is a point that finds considerable research support, that the extent of the use of these elements in the plants studied was extremely variable with little clustering at either extreme end, and that the majority of plants has some of these elements, and that there was therefore a limited and far from extensive use of these high commitment elements in UK organizations (Wood and Albanese 1995: 242).

Nevertheless, they also conclude that despite this it does make empirical sense to take a high commitment phenomenon – i.e. a package of SHRM elements which consists of selection for training and commitment, team working and group problem-solving. Of this bundle of elements they conclude: that HCM (high commitment management) – i.e. these elements listed – are found to occur together – 'HCM on the shop floor is an identifiable phenomenon. It is a form of high commitment management centred on a selection for trainability and commitment, team working and group problem-solving' (Wood and Albanese 1995: 242). The authors also note that HCM does not seem to be related to aspects of the firms' strategy or environment – 'does not appear to be a simple response to changes in the environment', and that there was no relationship between these elements and aspects of the firm's context (pp. 242–3). In other words, this study apparently supports a closed or universalistic view of SHRM – the occurrence of the non-occurrence of high commitment elements did not seem to be related to contingent circumstances.

Furthermore, other recent work, using a similar approach, has researched if certain packages or bundles of typical SHRM elements (a) co-exist together, and (b) have an impact on performance. These packages are defined somewhat differently by different authors. Purcell summarizes the bundle of SHRM elements that apparently have consequences for corporate performance as:

> careful recruitment and selection (with emphasis on competences);
>
> extensive use of systems of communication;
>
> teamworking with flexible job design;
>
> emphasis on training and learning;
>
> involvement in decision-making with responsibility; and
>
> performance appraisal with links to pay. (Purcell 1996: 4)

He summarizes research into the impact of these elements thus: 'What we have now is an emerging body of empirical evidence on both sides of the Atlantic which appears to point decisively in the direction of the best practice model. This is captured by the term "bundles" which, taken together are claimed to have a significant impact on firm performance. This bundle, providing the individual policies within it are mutually reinforcing (there is internal fit) is much more powerful than the individual practices on their own' (Purcell 1996: 2).

In summary, while there is a relative lack of evidence that SHRM systems in the fullest, richest sense are being installed, there *is* evidence that a less ambitious form of SHRM is taking place – the clustering or bundling of certain measures and dimensions of SHRM systems (see also box 18.1). We must now consider if these forms of SHRM have any impact on corporate performance.

## Are current organizational changes necessarily evidence of SHRM?

There is a growing body of research evidence that links this high commitment or best practice bundle of SHRM elements to performance. As Guest has noted, many studies (Huselid 1995; Huselid et al. 1995; Delaney and Huselid 1995; Arthur 1994; Ichniowski 1990) support the proposition that firms which install 'high performance' or 'best practice' SHRM elements (see above) perform better as measured by productivity, labour turnover and financial indicators. Once again, support for the 'closed' view of SHRM. Huselid remarks: 'All else being equal, the use of High Performance Work Practices and good internal fit should lead to positive outcomes for all types of firms' (Huselid 1995: 644).

Arthur for example distinguishes between 'high commitment' and the control SHRM systems. He hypothesized that 'high commitment' systems would be related to superior production performance, and his research supports this hypothesis: 'commitment is significantly related to both fewer labor hours per ton and lower scrap rates'. He also predicted that 'control' SHRM systems would be associated with negative personnel indicators and this too is confirmed: staff turnover was twice as high in control systems as compared to commitment systems (Arthur 1994: 679).

However the significance of these findings on the existence and effects of bundles of SHRM practices and of discrete aspects of SHRM (quality programmes, management competences) is not entirely unequivocal or uncontested.

There is no doubt that organizational change of various sorts is occurring, even apparently that bundles of SHRM elements are being installed; and there is no doubt that some of these changes are concerned either with classic SHRM 'levers' of change (culture, performance related pay, flexibility, high commitment management elements, etc.); also there is no doubt that some of this change is associated with the rhetoric of SHRM, and the claimed values of SHRM. And there is evidence that these SHRM type developments – when they occur – are associated with superior performance. But this is not necessarily to suggest that managers are taking a long-term strategic view of human resources, nor that their view of employees has been influenced by the arguments of the soft SHRM approach, nor that they are concerned with achieving a new form of organization with new partnership relationships between workforce and management. As Wood and Albanese remark drily, 'high commitment management is as yet at least, more about eliciting commitment from employees than the making of *mutual* obligations' (1995: 242, our emphasis). Little of the research into best practice SHRM bundles disproves the view that these initiatives demonstrate that managers are opportunistically and haphazardly applying some of the change initiatives associated with SHRM. They do not show that SHRM is occurring. Remember that even by Guest's own definition a key element is management's intention *to achieve higher commitment to the organization*. If the test of genuine SHRM is that the change programmes are concerned with the welfare-humanist conception of employees – the soft view of SHRM – then this is a test that many change programmes simply can not pass.

The evidence seems to support this conclusion. Armstrong has noted (1989) that decisions about organizational structures and process, and the treatment of employees are as much influenced by accountancy logic as by SHRM principles, such that 'the treatment of human resources (becomes an) instrument for the achievement of short run accounting targets' (1989: 164). Similar arguments – that organizational change programmes – in a variety of areas – frequently show a greater concern for cost reduction, increased control, improved surveillance, rather than for increased autonomy, participation, come from Storey's early collection (1989).

Work by researchers at Warwick studied the values underlying programmes of organizational change. They concluded: 'it is difficult to escape the conclusion that, although the great majority of our respondents claim that their organisations have an overall policy or approach to the management of employees, with the exception of a number of companies which are overseas owned, or financially centralised, or operating in the service sectors, it would be wrong to set very much store by this . . . the general weight of evidence would seem to confirm that most UK-owned enterprises remain pragmatic or oppor-

## BOX 18.1 TRACKING THE IMPACT OF SHRM

There is evidence that discrete elements of SHRM may have positive effects. Rosenthal et al. for example, in their exploration of a quality programme, found that it was associated with positive effects: staff were committed to it and displayed this commitment in their behaviour (Rosenthal et al. 1997). The authors conclude that: 'This investigation provides no support for the view that, if a company's objectives of improving service quality are realised, they are achieved through some combination of sham empowerment, work intensification and increased surveillance' (Rosenthal et al 1997: 497). On the contrary, the study found that a majority of employees endorsed the quality programme and half say that they engage in the sort of behaviours required by the programme. The quality initiative made sense to them and they were prepared to commit themselves to it in practice.

On the basis of a study of the application of management competences in a number of UK organizations du Gay and Salaman (1996) found that the installation of management competences, which was closely associated with programmes of far-reaching culture change, was a key element of organisational efforts to create a radically new sort of manager (or to develop a managerial rather than professional basis of organizational authority). These competence projects strongly appealed to senior managers who saw them as a way of representing in individualized form the qualities required by, or assumed in, the process of organizational change. This was hardly surprising. What is more surprising, at least to some sceptical observers, is that the competence programmes also appealed to the managers themselves. Like the respondents in Rosenthals et al.'s study, the managers regarded the initiative as sensible and rational. They welcomed the fact that their organization was attempting rationally and sensibly to identify what people should do and what qualities they needed to do their jobs and that people would be assessed in terms of the fit between role and skills/performance. This approach appealed because it resonated with employees' own view of how their organization should be managed. Although the project required constant improvement against behavioural standards (what some would call the 'intensification of effort') and assumed a high level of employee commitment to the organisation and its objectives (what some would call the 'management of meaning') employees rarely questioned either its content or its consequences. In fact they welcomed it as a 'common-sense' approach to organizational change.

tunistic in their approach' (Marginson et al. 1988: 120; quoted in Storey and Sisson 1993: 71)

Purcell directly addresses the relationship that exists between strategy and structures, specifically SHRM developments. He identifies different levels of strategic decision-making and attempts to relate these different levels to differences in SHRM planning. It starts with what he calls 'first-order strategic decision-making' at the level of decisions about cash generation or cash usage. This analysis is organized in terms of differences in product market life-cycle, as classified by the well-known Boston Consulting Group matrix.

He then focuses on 'second-order strategies' which affect the ways the organization is structured and business units are controlled. This level of strategic decision-making relates closely to the classification offered by Child (1987) in chapter 1. Purcell uses the classification of types of relationship between head office and business units identified by Goold and Campbell (1986). In this way he seeks to relate SHRM developments to high-level developments in business planning. In a sense he is asking: from what we know (or are told) about the higher-level strategic decisions concerning business planning and organizational structuring, is it likely that organizations will develop and maintain human resource strategies? His conclusion is, indeed, gloomy. Essentially, he argues that current pressures on organizations, which frequently lead to stronger financial controls, make it harder 'to develop integrated and meaningful institutional strategies or management style at the corporate level, and – to the degree that short-run rates of return on investment, emphasis on margin improvement, and tight financial controls are imposed on unit managers – harder at the unit level to develop and maintain long-run human resource policies' (Purcell 1989: 90). This should not be interpreted as arguing the impossibility of SHRM, but rather the difficulty of achieving it. He suggests that despite the powerful appeal of SHRM ideas, ideas which are strongly represented in chairmen's statements in annual reports (see Gowler and Legge 1986), in reality external pressures make the achievement and maintenance of SHRM difficult.

Similarly, Armstrong (1989: 156) notes that by insisting on a close and supportive relationship between SHRM practices and practitioners, 'personnel professionals will increasingly marginalise their independent contribution by subjecting their activities to the value criteria of budgetary planning and control' (Keenoy 1990: 365).

Support for this argument can be found in a number of studies. For example, Delbridge and Turnbull (1992) argue that JIT systems and quality controls actually represent a significant increase in control, surveillance, and the capacity to identify, and 'correct' worker mistakes and performance. 'Quality control is therefore used not simply to improve product quality, but to discipline the workforce. Quality charts in particular are part and parcel of a more extensive system of surveillance and monitoring which is used to ensure compliance' (Delbridge and Turnbull 1992: 65). Indeed these authors go further, and argue that the distinction between 'soft' and 'hard' conceptions of SHRM may ultimately be compatible – for many of the key principles of soft SHRM may really involve new forms of control: 'teamwork, quality consciousness and flexibility which characterise . . . HRM strategies are in essence the means by which the workforce is controlled, through a mixture of stress, peer pressure, surveillance and accountability (Delbridge and Turnbull 1992: 68).

Yet, Blyton and Morris (1992) in a review of flexibility initiatives, conclude that despite the long-term, apparently strategic focus of SHRM, in practice the enthusiasm for flexibility in the UK is largely short-term, cost-driven and ad hoc. Furthermore, as they note, the introduction of flexibility, far from being part of a general strategy to maximise employee potential and commitment, is more likely to undermine employee commitment (Blyton and Morris 1992: 127).

Recent research into change programmes within UK companies support the view that such change typically emphasizes short-term performance objectives achieved in the main by initiatives selected solely for their performance or cost control implications (i.e. not long-term strategy or concern with workforce commitment). A number of recent studies suggest significant improvement in the performance of UK firms. For example, the 1997 World Competitiveness Yearbook found that the UK has improved its position in world competitiveness (International Institute for Management Development 1997), and a Cranfield Management School comparative study of UK and German manufacturing performance found that the gap between the two countries has been steadily closing since the early 1980s. But to what extent is this the result of the application of classic SHRM measures and approaches, or is it simply a consequence of greater cost control? A recent study of UK manufacturing offers some sobering conclusions. 'It is characteristic of British arrangements for manufacture at plant level that they do not depend on high levels of skill or high levels of investment. The model of the new flexible firm . . . involves the idea that existing technology, labour and organisation have been reconfigured in a characteristic way. Profitable manufacture is not secured . . . through the acquisition of a highly trained "core" labour force, nor yet as others have claimed by investment in new technology. We suggest that output is achieved in part by some reorganisation of machinery, but more significantly by a heavy dependency on the flexible use of relatively unskilled labour plus a willingness to utilise external sources of production. The core of the arrangement for manufacture is the use of standard technology by means of self-regulating and formally and flexible unskilled workers. Production is organised into a number of semi-autonomous segments, which also feature as cost centres. Each of these is periodically and individually assessed in terms of its costs and benefits, and this feature shapes most aspects of management organisation and activity including the control of labour' (ESRC 1997).

## *Does SHRM work? A summary*

The evidence on the effects of SHRM is inconsistent and unclear. On the one hand, there is undeniable evidence from a variety of sources studied of discrete SHRM programmes as well as that on HR 'bundles', as described in chapter 5, that they are associated with positive outcomes in employee attitude and performance indicators. It is true that there are methodological doubts about some of the large survey studies, and single-case studies are always of limited value. But nevertheless it certainly does seem that some SHRM initiatives are achieving positive effects. On the other hand, as many authors have pointed out, there is relatively little evidence of the sort of management attitude towards employees of the sort encapsulated in many of the more ambitious definitions of SHRM – that senior management take a strategic view of the organization's human resources and establish structures and employment and work regimes which develop and engage employees' skills and commitment.

On the whole the picture depicted here is far from most conceptions of SHRM. This is often simply a new version of old practices and priorities: tight control of labour, minimal investment, short-term focus, control of labour through deskilling and the threat of downsizing or outsourcing. The study of recent changes in large British-owned manufacturing companies reports: 'There are many indications that contemporary factory regimes do not involve the continuation of some of the features of managerial control that traditionally have been important; but there is actually little to support the idea of the introduction radically new forms of management. The continued decline of payment of results and the long-term rise of group incentive payments, indicates only the removal of traditional, direct control of individual work activity' (ESRC 1997).

Furthermore, if the expression *strategic* is defined not by reference to a set of core SHRM values, but simply by reference to the degree of fit of SHRM initiatives to corporate strategy, the result is hardly more impressive. Here the issue is not that certain currently popular organizational changes have been initiated, but that the changes can be seen directly to support the organization's strategy. This is Miller's test: 'We can say that if managements manage their employees in ways which recognise their role in strategy implementation, it is behaving strategically. If, on the other hand, it makes decisions simply in order to avoid trade unions, or better to control employees, it is operating in a fashion which is separate from the business and (is) non-strategic' (Miller 1989: 51; quoted in Storey and Sisson 1993: 67).

This point is supported by Beaumont, and others. Beaumont notes that if the key to SHRM is the existence of a 'close, two-way relationship between business strategy or planning and HRM strategy or planning', research suggests that such a linkage rarely exists to any sizeable extent or depth across a wide range of organizations (Beaumont 1993: 4).

There is much support for these views of the reality of SHRM/strategy linkages, and for the role of non-strategic priorities and opportunism in SHRM thinking. Hendry and Pettigrew note that while much SHRM literature, especially the Excellence literature, makes a claim for the integrative role of corporate culture, the reality is that SHRM initiatives are 'simply pragmatic and or expedient – less reflective of a coherent set of management attitudes than it is of the economic environment in which that organisation operates' (Hendry and Pettigrew 1986: 5; Beer et al. 1984).

Some writers have argued that one cause for the limitations of SHRM in practice is that it draws too heavily on the values and priorities of senior management, to the exclusion of other organizational groups, and involves an over-rationalistic conception of organizational processes (see box 18.2).

Thus, apart from doubts about the internal consistency and possibility of SHRM (the tension between hard and soft, the possibility of achieving 'integration', the possible conflicts between aspects of SHRM etc.) there is evidence that many of

## BOX 18.2 SHRM – REDEFINING THE RULES OF THE GAME

McKinlay and Starkey (1988) consider SHRM develoments in three UK companies. Beginning with a useful summary of the background to SHRM, the authors point to the growing appreciation of the need for a 'broader change agenda' than that encompassed by the highly rationalistic' structural focus of earlier change programmes. A significant part of their argument can thus be seen to confirm the view that the behaviour of employees is a result of more factors than merely structural ones, and, more contentiously, that it may be simpler and easier to manipulate these non-structural factors. Furthermore, the authors maintain that complex, multi-layered organizations (sometimes called bureaucracies) generate 'inertia, slothful and adaptive change, and the chronic attachment to buried assumptions and routine behaviour'. They argue that increasingly change programmes are designed to attack these behaviours and the structures which generate them. This is an interesting suggestion because it suggests that one important role of SHRM thinking and the initiatives frequently associated with SHRM may be not their practical significance, but that they are important as legitimating ideas and symbols in management attempts to achieve tighter control, reduced costs, greater freedom for management action – that SHRM ideas enable management to redefine the 'rules of the game' within organization, to change the way they and employees in general, think about the organization, their work and their employment. One way, for example, in which SHRM achieves this is by offering a pivotal role to management as champions of change made necessary by external environmental change. This has the great merit of defining the consequent change as inevitable and inexorable and unchallengeable. (The fact that many of these changes are by managers' own admission unsuccessful does not threaten managers' right – indeed responsibility – to initiate further changes.)

the apparent SHRM changes are more to do with increased employee control and a focus on cost control and the 'bottom line', than on initiating a new form of, and approach to, the management of staff. When SHRM does occur it is usually in unusual and distinctive organizations. Despite the rhetoric of SHRM, the reality is that much SHRM-type change is concerned more with the hard 'utilitarian-instrumentalism' (Keenoy 1990b: 368) than with 'developmental-humanism', i.e. is hard rather than soft. As the following section will argue, SHRM is important for supplying a powerful rhetoric, a rhetoric which facilitates increasing control and management of employees, of structures and of meaning itself. Storey and Sisson argue, for example, that there is little evidence of a strategic approach to human resource management being adopted in most organizations (Storey and

Sisson 1993). Part of the problem here, as usual, lies in how SHRM is defined – what the nature of SHRM is seen to be, and specifically whether the various dimensions of SHRM occur together, and indeed are mutually compatible. The research does not show that firms that are introducing SHRM-type initiatives are doing so because of a commitment to Pettigrew and Whip's dimensions – to 'developmental-humanism', to the soft values of SHRM. On the contrary, Hendry et al. (1988) conclude that those firms which have made developments in their HRM have done so under the pressure of competitive forces. Their conclusion is supported by others: 'Evidence from other studies also supports the view that strategic HRM is primarily directed toward increasing organisational efficiency in the use and productivity of the labour resource in order to compete more effectively' (Keenoy 1900: 377).

Storey and Sisson (1993) have noted that, even in terms of efficiency, there is a 'massive gap' between rhetoric and reality. Despite the enormous public espousal of 'soft' SHRM values by senior managers, the evidence on levels of installation of such key elements of SHRM as training and development, and the integration of HR practices and business strategy, suggest that: 'Britain still has a long way to go . . . Senior managers are either not practising what they espouse or they are installing new initiatives in an incompetent and ineffective way' (Storey and Sisson 1993: 50–1).

Furthermore, if there are reasons to doubt that research evidence into putative SHRM bundles that apparently produce positive outcomes (albeit by narrow financial measures) demonstrates evidence for the success of SHRM as a whole, it is also relevant to note that many studies into the efficacy and impact of discrete SHRM measures record high levels of frustration and ineffectiveness. A recent study found that the effectiveness of 12 widely-accepted SHRM techniques – (including TQM, Just-in-Time, empowerment, BPR etc.) was rather disappointing. And in more than half the cases, HR practices were seen to have failed to meet their goals of improving quality, increasing responsiveness and cutting costs. The study also shows that even the most successful practices were seen as frequently prone to failure, and such pervasive practices as BPR were – despite the claims of its advocates that it represents an entirely new basis for organization – seen as mainly used for cost-cutting and as successful in barely half of its applications (ESRC 1997). Studies of the impact of downsizing in the United States report that although downsizing is intended to reduce overheads, and bureaucracy and increase earnings, more than 50 per cent of firms studies reported unchanged or reduced productivity (Henkoff 1990). Another study reported that around 30 per cent of firms found costs had actually increased after downsizing (Halstead 1996).

Also, the impact on survivors of such downsizing measures is often very traumatic and serious if largely undisplayed and therefore unnoticed by senior management. Studies in the USA and the UK report survivors experiencing shock, anger, stress, anxiety and insecurity (Doherty and Horsted 1995; Brockner et al. 1993).

Finally in this assessment of research into the impact of SHRM and associated practices ('bundles) it is worth remembering the warnings of Mueller. Mueller

(1996) has tried to assess the relationship between the conventional, strategy-based approach to SHRM and the resource-based approach. He argues that corporate success lies, as the resource-based theorists would maintain, in deeply embedded and hard to imitate competences. These so-called 'social architectures develop slowly over time and encourage valuable processes of co-operation, learning and 'appropriation'. It is these resource-based aspects of organization rather than the pervasive and fashionable codified SHRM practices that make a real difference to organizational performance and account for the success of the small number of high-performing organizations. There are two implications of this proposition that merit attention. On the one hand, it means that SHRM policies might contribute significantly to the maintenance and development of these embedded (but often implicit) social architectures. This means that the easily imitated fashionable practices will have little benefit since they are by definition, standard practices. On the other hand, it also means, potentially at least, that some of the more codified SHRM practices might be inadvertently damaging, precisely because they run counter to, and undermine, these crucial social architectures; for example, by damaging the historic capacity for appropriability, or by alienating key staff, or by damaging commitment.

One striking feature of this research into the impact and consequences of SHRM is the gap that appears to exist between the promises and the reality, between the words (of consultants, academics, CEOs, personnel professionals, even managers themselves), and the realities of current organizational developments. As a result of the promises, analyses, recommendations, the lectures, performance textbooks, seminars, it is as if we all expect SHRM to be 'real' and to be apparent in everyday organizational practice and to be having the consequences promised for it. Yet research paints a contrasting if differentiated picture: inconclusive findings, different interpretations. Does this mean that SHRM is merely rhetoric – mere words, pictures in the air – smoke and mirrors, created through the artistry and magic of SHRM consultants? And if SHRM is largely rhetoric, does this mean that it doesn't matter?

When responding to research initiatives into the efficacy of SHRM initiatives, senior managers tend to respond in terms of their particular ways of understanding and seeing the world, and in terms of the pressures under which they work. They may well respond in terms of the highly pervasive currently available SHRM approaches which have now established a powerful prism through which managers view their organizations and themselves. SHRM has become a way of knowing. More than this, SHRM offers managers two things. First, an attractive and powerful legitimating language whereby they can demonstrate to themselves and others that they are applying the very latest in organization technology. And secondly, a way to demonstrate the nature and importance of their contribution to the change process.

## SHRM as Rhetoric and Discourse: Its Values and Assumptions

There are major difficulties in the achievement of the types of integration fundamental to SHRM. These problems arise from the realities of organizational structures and processes. We have noted that, for many commentators, the achievement of SHRM is empirically uncertain. Yet this does not mean that SHRM is a delusion, or is unimportant; far from it. SHRM is powerful and important. Yet the importance of the strategic management of human resources is as much in SHRM as a body of ideas (with certain consequences) as it is in SHRM as a set of practices: 'what is significant about 'human resource management – and the factor that could explain the remarkable level of interest in it – is that it marks a departure from a largely prevailing orthodoxy, it promises an alternative (or more accurately and significantly) a set of alternatives to what might be described as the "Donovan" model' (Storey 1989: 8).

### *The instruments of SHRM*

The importance of SHRM is much more, and much wider than, the various practices which arguably reflect its operationalization. While there are undoubtedly many changes occurring in organizations that impact on the structure and processes of work and employment, these are less significant as indicators of a new SHRM approach to human resources, and more important because of their simultaneous appeal to powerful new values and assumptions and reliance on old forms of power and control. For some writers it is this combination of new rhetoric and old imperatives, of new solutions and old problems, that is the defining feature of SHRM.

The radical critique of SHRM takes a number of forms, as Thompson and Ackroyd (1995) have noted. For some writers, SHRM is a new form of management control, with cultural forms of manipulation replacing traditional and more obvious forms of coercion. For these writers new SHRM practices like TQM and BPR seek to apply and enforce workforce commitment to management values and objectives: 'Within organisations, programmes of corporate culturism, HRM and TQM have sought to promote or strengthen a corporate ethos that demands loyalty from employees as it excludes, silences and punishes those who question' (Willmott 1993: 520). These writers regard such initiatives as the move to discrete profit centres, the imposition of best practice and other performance standards, and the move to internal customer relationships as implicitly imposing managerial values and priorities, which are embedded in the new processes. Such an approach would argue that the preoccupations of management remain the same as ever – to achieve control, ensure and increase productivity and profitability – yet at the same time to ensure that as far as possible, employees are willing to do what is required, are compliant, co-operative, creative. This is the essential paradox of management. If SHRM offers anything really new, it offers new techniques, and new language and constructions of meaning, with which management approaches this dilemma.

Furthermore, there may well be a connection between changes in work organization which require discretion on the part of workers, and an approach to management which entails organization, training and culture change. These strategic HR interventions seek to ensure compliance on the basis not of formal (rigid) rules, but on the basis of 'shared norms of understanding, a common grammar of interpretation . . . the internalisation of the organisation's "goals" or "norms" to ensure that the individual interprets the area of discretion correctly from the organisation's point of view' (Townley 1989: 103).

Other writers have stressed the direct, technical controls inherent in such practices. In particular they point out that computerized information is made available to management and can be used for surveillance and control purposes, connected to payment and performance management processes, and generally used to monitor and manipulate employee performance. It could be argued that computerized information systems supply and support a major dynamic of organization restructuring: they permit the disaggregation of organizations into small performance-centred units (SBUs, work teams, profit centres) while at the same time ensuring continued (indeed improved) management monitoring of the performance of these units. Management is thus able to 'empower,' and delegate to, apparently autonomous performance units (including individuals) and hold them responsible for their performance while ensuring a continuous monitoring of performance. Thus IT systems allow management to manage from a distance.

## The language of SHRM

Other writers have taken a broader view of the control implications of SHRM, preferring to collapse the distinction between words and actions employed by the earlier writers and stressing instead the importance and power of the words – or rhetoric – of SHRM. They see SHRM as a powerful and new form of managerial language, whose power lies not simply in its impact on performance, but in its capacity to reflect current societal values and political priorities, and to represent managerial conceptions of the organization, and of intra-organizational relationships. It is thus seen as a new form of managerial control, but not simply control through managerial practices and organization change and restructuring. Rather, it is control of the ways in which thinking about, understanding and knowing organizations, and organizational dynamics and purposes, and critically, organizational members, is conducted and framed. These writers would also stress the implications of SHRM as a way of thinking and talking about and knowing organizations and employees, for employees' identities. One of the key features of modern life is that institutional developments (such as new organizational forms, new personnel techniques of selection and assessment, the undercutting of traditional customs), have direct implications for individual life and therefore with the self. A distinctive feature of modern society is the increasing interconnection between wider social and political developments – including organizational developments – and personal dispositions and identities.

Many radical critics of SHRM have addressed the ways in which SHRM seeks to supply structures of value and meaning within which employees can – or should – make sense of themselves. This includes the way they plan their careers, become aware of themselves through feedback and counselling, become enterprising, market themselves, develop themselves to enhance their market value, network themselves to develop personal databases. All activities which result in them becoming the sort of people the organization wishes to employ.

This critique would see SHRM as a powerful and new form of managerial rhetoric, whose power lies not on its impact on performance, but in its capacity to reflect current societal values and political priorities, and to represent managerial conceptions of the organization, and of intra-organizational relationships. Such an approach argues that the preoccupations of management remain the same as ever (to achieve control, to increase productivity and profitability), yet at the same time to ensure that as far as possible, employees are willing to do what is required; to ensure that they are compliant, co-operative, creative. This is the essential paradox of management. If SHRM offers anything really new, it offers new techniques, and new language and constructions of meaning, with which management approaches this dilemma. As Keenoy and Anthony remark: 'to understand the HRM phenomenon in Britain it is necessary to treat it as a cultural construction comprised of a series of metaphors which constitute a "new reality". HRM reflects an attempt to redefine both the meaning of work and the way individual employees relate to their employers.' (Keenoy and Anthony, 1993: 234). Or as du Gay and Salaman have noted with respect to a key element of SHRM thinking (the focus on market forces and relationships, and thus on the value of enterprise): 'the discourse of enterprise within organizations, (and the practices and organisational technologies which are inspired by this focus) is essentially co-terminous with the political-economic-social project of Thatcherism'. (du Gay and Salaman 1992: 627.)

The important point here is not simply that SHRM ideas and practices carry 'ideological' implications and priorities, but that these ideas are realized and reproduced through a set of SHRM practices occurring at many levels – affecting structures, cultures and personnel practices – which display the power and reality of the rhetoric. Thus SHRM is about attempts to change behaviour and to transform values and norms, and at the same time, to seek to define this project of behaviour and value-change in terms of the values and principles of SHRM, regardless of its actual appropriateness. SHRM thinking argues that it is 'simply' the application of enterprise and market principles to organizations ('releasing initiative', 'empowering staff', 'replacing hierarchy by market principles,' 'establishing autonomous business units' etc.). Thus its own ideology is represented as neutral and innocent (and inevitable), indeed as pure realism.

Much of the SHRM literature displays a dual focus: partly on changed practices, and partly on the management of meaning – the assertion of the morality, or moral value of the restructuring principle. Frequently in this chapter, and earlier in this volume, we have referred to studies which have suggested that what changes are apparent may be defined in terms of, and legitimized by reference to, the values and assumptions of SHRM; but in fact, they bear little resemblance to the strategic, humanistic, values associated with the 'soft' conception of SHRM.

## *The resonance of SHRM*

The SHRM literature in general, and the Excellence literature in particular, is marked by its less than rigorous conceptual clarity and its cavalier use of evidence on which claims are based. But the point is not simply that much SHRM literature is conceptually ambiguous, or confused, or that it is ill-based, empirically. The critical point is rather that the rhetorical, symbolic power of the SHRM message is important in itself – important in masking, or distorting the literature, by creating undesirable and inconsistent views of reality.

For example, discussions of the flexible firm illustrate how an idea widely promoted by government agencies and frequently offered as a panacea for the ills of western capitalism in management literature is significant precisely because it resonates with key current values and is part of a powerful and attractive model of the organization of the future (Pollert 1988).

Pollert has noted that writing on flexibility, and the flexible firm, is characterized by 'a consistent style of global prophesying, sweeping generalisation from very limited evidence, economic or technical determinism and an assumption of radical break with the past' (1988: 229). Flexibility is frequently seen as a universal panacea for the ills that are associated with bureaucracy. Bureaucracy is regarded as equivalent to rigidity, and is therefore negative; flexibility is associated with responsiveness – to circumstances and to clients, and is therefore virtuous. This view overestimates the negative aspects of bureaucracy and ignores its many strengths (see du Gay 1994 and Part 3 of this volume). In other words, the 'flexible firm', is an idea, by combining aspects of organization and strategic response, which is particularly attractive to management writers and ideologies.

Furthermore, Pollert argues that part of the appeal of the concept flexibility is that it resonates with broader, societal and political values and purposes. She notes that part of any explanation of the power of the notion of flexibility during the 1980s certainly must require reference to environmental issues – Japanization, neo-classical economic policies. But these are not sufficient; there is also a need to understand the resonance between the nature and power of the concept of flexibility and an 'ideological level of explanation'. By this she refers to the linkages between flexibility and the theory of industrial society which focuses on the 'universal evolution of technological and economic rationality which led to the convergence of all societies towards industrial society', and which she claims, assumed considerable power in social, political and social science thinking and writing in the 1980s (Pollert 1988: 8).

She argues persuasively that the attractiveness of the idea – the background to its power and importance – is due less to its empirical existence or success, and more to its association with powerful political and ideological values: 'Its preoccupation with labour flexibility and market recovery swim with the stream of the neo-classical revival; at the same time its concern to find a new solution or "third way" for the future which is neither "Keynesian" nor "monetarist" and its obsession with fragmentation suggest that beneath the surface of certainty and assertiveness lie disorientation and a desperate search for panaceas . . . But its analytical weaknesses does not necessarily mean its downfall. While its political message remains strong, it may well survive into the 1990s' (Pollert 1988: 30).

Pollert's critique of flexibility is extremely useful, for this form and focus of

## BOX 18.3 SHRM, REAGAN AND THATCHER

How do we explain this phenomenon and wherein lies the power of these messages? These issues are explored by David Guest (1992). Guest notes that the appeal of these ideas lies not simply in the elements of the approach but also in its timeliness: 'It is American, optimistic, apparently humanistic and also superficially simple' (Guest 1992: 379). Guest charts the main elements of the 'Excellence' approach and offers an explanation for the power of these ideas. He then critiques it from two standpoints: those analyses which have addressed the empirical validity of the literature and, more significantly, the normative appeal of the literature. As he says, one possibility is that Peters and Waterman are right; another is that whatever its validity, 'managers and other readers believe the message to be correct. In one sense the medium is the message' (Guest 1992: 13). An important reason for the success of the book is the way in which its messages resonate with other, broader, socio-political values and assumptions among managers. (See Guest: 1992)

The same point has been argued with respect to the emphasis on customer relations as a blueprint for internal organizational relations by du Gay and Salaman (1992), who trace the connections between the success of this idea and aspects of political ideology under Thatcher. These authors argue that many programmes of organizational change are centred around the attempt to redefine internal organizational relations and structures as *if* they were market relations – between suppliers and customers. This in turn has significant consequences for the redefinition of key roles, and their constituent competences and for the identities of those who fill them (du Gay, Salaman and Rees 1996). More importantly the focus on, and value of, enterprise also demonstrates key resonances with external, socio-economic political values and assumptions: namely Thatcherism: 'the key feature of contemporary political rationalities and technologies of government has been the attempt to establish connections between the self-fulfilling desires of individuals and the achievement of social and economic objectives' (du Gay 1991: 58).

analysis can be applied more widely to the SHRM movement as a whole, as well as to its constituent ideas and practices.

For example, the Excellence literature is powerful and influential as a body of ideas rather than simply a set of practices. Like much SHRM writing, but to a greater degree, the Excellence literature represents the very process it advocates. It argues the importance of the managerial manipulation of meaning – the management of organizational culture – a focus which is fundamental to SHRM: 'Most HRM models emphasise the organisation's culture as the central activity for senior management' (Legge 1989: 26). Yet the Excellence literature itself, like all SHRM literature, represents a major attempt to manage meaning – to reflect and manipulate some critical current conceptions of organizations, management and employees.

Whatever the academic assessment of the Excellence literature itself, it should be taken very seriously indeed; for by now it is almost taken for granted, as unquestionably true, as beyond debate. It has become almost sacrosanct (see box 18.3).

It may well be that ultimately the distinction between rhetoric and reality becomes blurred and meaningless and loses its value. The rhetoric becomes real, and real in its consequences. The power of SHRM to redefine management, organization, and the employee, and to impose a conception of how managers and employees relate to each other and to the organization (and the customer) as liberated, autonomous, enterprising employees, supplies a conception which is unassailable. This is because of its resonance with, and dependence upon, wider societal/political conceptions of the market and the primacy of market forces and values, and conceptions of the individual. The rhetoric and language wherein SHRM is explained and developed and justified, the activities in which it results, are inextricably related to practices and systems which define, develop, reward and empower the individual. These SHRM rhetorics and practices in turn connect not only to the challenges of recession and the increased competitive threat, but also to the constant attempt to devise new strategies, cut costs, and improve margins. And in turn these views of managers, workers, and their relationships through structures and cultures, are embodied in expert systems of classification, payment systems and other technologies, in job design, assessment systems and criteria.

## The (re)defining power of SHRM

SHRM is a system of knowing and understanding the organization, the environment and the individual employee (and crucially the relationships between these three). It is therefore a basis for the redesign of organizations; it supplies assumptions, classification systems, technologies, and ways of talking and thinking about organization and employees, which reflect and support this knowledge, and which are important for their effects on individuals even when the actual patterns of organizational restructuring cannot – as so often – be seen as genuine examples of SHRM practice.

One view of this is to see the hidden hand of management, deliberately using the language of SHRM to mask its real purposes, and to seek to gain employees' commitment to, or resignation in the fact of, programmes of change. Keenoy remarks: 'far from indicating a new era of humane people-orientated employment management . . . the primary purpose of the rhetoric of HRM might be to provide a legitimatory managerial ideology to facilitate an intensification of work and an increase in the commodification of labour' (Keenoy 1990b: 375).

Others would see the emergence of contradictions that have been seen to characterize in some form every attempt to redesign the nature of work and employment; particularly the contradictory need for management to achieve, simultaneously, control over the workforce (a need which is even more important today with JIT, TQM, etc.) and the need to develop and attract the commitment and creativity of the workforce. The emergence of these dual but opposed needs may underlie the way SHRM is implemented. Legge for example notes: 'What evidence we have is of a patchy implementation of practices designed to achieve flexibility, quality and commitment, often constrained by the contradictions inherent in enacting these slippery concepts, and motivated more by the opportunities afforded by high levels of unemployment and the constraints of recession and enhanced competition, than by any long-term strategic considerations' (Legge 1994: 47).

Yet others, however, would stress the role of power in SHRM thinking and practice not in its role in serving the functions and interests of senior management but in terms of the overall *government* of the organization. The use of the term government draws attention to the fact that power 'traverses all practices – from the "macro" to the "micro" – through which persons are ruled, mastered, held in check, administered, steered, guided, by means of which they are led by others or have come to direct or regulate their own actions' (Rose 1990). Power is thus not seen as located simply or only in the actions of senior management; it is present in all knowledge and practice that regulates individuals.

One key idea in the SHRM literature is its analysis and treatment of causality and 'responsibility' – of the nature of relationships between key elements or levels of the approach: environment, organization, individual. SHRM locates organizational responsibility (for performance, quality, the 'implementation of change' etc.) with newly liberated, empowered, autonomous individual employees. The responsibility of managers is to ensure that the organizational environment and structure are 'enabling'. Once this is achieved, the employees must rely on their competence and, crucially, their enterprise, to ensure that individual performance meets the demands of the myriad of customers by whom employees are now surrounded and whom they supply. Thus the metaphor of the market becomes the organizational reality by which employees and their work are judged, and how they judge themselves. It thus 'deflects human responsibility to the hidden hand of the market in the justification of means for ultimate ends' (Keenoy and Anthony 1992: 249).

Possibly the most important feature of SHRM is not simply the many changes – most of them far-reaching and pervasive – which are taking place in organizations. Rather it is the manner in which SHRM supplies a new, authoritative, theory of how organizations work and how individuals must be managed, rewarded and directed, which (because of its strong links with associated notions of 'excellence' and the role of markets and of enterprise) seeks to redefine not just organizations, but individuals. It is this that is the greatest contribution of SHRM, and potentially the most ominous.

## Conclusions and Summary

In the previous chapter we rehearsed the reasons for being sceptical about the possibility of achieving the promises of SHRM. But this left an important question that required attention: what is the actual evidence on the occurrence and impact of SHRM? This question has been the subject matter of this chapter. The evidence is that considerable and widespread change is certainly taking place, but whether or not this constitutes SHRM is more questionable. For many writers the picture is less one of organizations becoming more flexible, building employee commitment, putting into practice the commonplace adage that their most precious resource is their staff, and more one of cutting costs, tightening control, delayering, installing quality monitoring systems, reducing inventories and, subcontracting peripheral activities.

We have seen that there is evidence that 'bundles' of SHRM packages are being installed and that these are having effects on organizational performance. However, the methodology of these studies is open to question in many cases since they rely heavily on the assessments of a few senior managers who may have interests in adopting a positive view of initiatives with which they were closely associated. We have seen too that although these activities are presented as if they were genuine SHRM, many researchers see them as little more than the pursuit of traditional managerial goals by new methods – and not involving a distinctively new approach to, or philosophy of, organization and management. And this co-existence of programmes of organizational change based on the 'hard' sense of SHRM but accompanied by the rhetoric of 'soft' SHRM, has caused some commentators to see this situation not as accidental or temporary or a result of overwhelming recessionary pressures, but as central to SHRM itself. For these writers SHRM becomes a sort of stage-management – a magical process which seeks to transform actions aimed at cutting costs and tightening controls into actions which are strategic, and people-focused aimed at building commitment. In this view SHRM becomes an exercise in the management of meaning, disguising real purposes, claiming the logic of disembodied natural forces ('the environment', 'the market', 'performance', 'the customer', quality and so on), and thus building the legitimacy of measures which are ultimately no less sectional than the more obviously oppressive measures of earlier generations of managers.

In this chapter we have focused on two issues which are ultimately two aspects of the same issue: what is the meaning of SHRM in practice? In the first part of the chapter we presented and discussed available research material on the occurrence and impact of SHRM but noted that this evidence is far from conclusive.

There is evidence that some aspects of SHRM are being installed and having effects; but there are also grounds for questioning the extent to which these initiatives could be regarded as evidence of SHRM in any meaningful sense, and there is also contrary evidence that much apparent SHRM activity involves old-fashioned cost-cutting through the reorganization and manipulation of labour – tactics which whatever there short term benefits are unlikely to lead to a new and more employee-focused form of organization.

But the impact of SHRM may not depend simply on the empirical occurrence and consequences of SHRM measures. In the second half of the chapter we widened the discussion to consider the consequences of SHRM not simply for organizational restructuring but for changing the ways in which we think about organizations, and managers and employees. And here there may be a paradox: that the most significant consequences of SHRM may lie less in the empirical application of SHRM packages and more in the impact of SHRM language and thinking on the meanings employees and managers attach to their organization, themselves, and their work.

## Key Points

- Is SHRM happening, and if it is, what are its consequences? This key question turns out, on close inspection, to be complex and multifaceted. A critical first consideration is to consider what we mean by SHRM? For this question of definition supplies with us the criteria to be used in assessing whether or not SHRM is occurring at all.
- Once these criteria have been developed, they can be used to ascertain whether or not the elements and programmes of SHRM are actually occurring.
- Research into the occurrence and impact of SHRM is concerned with the conventional classic view of SHRM – that structures and systems must be adjusted to 'fit' strategies. But this approach involves an 'open' and a 'closed' version. At first sight the research on the occurrence and impact of SHRM 'bundles' strongly supports the 'closed' approach. However, there are methodological and conceptual grounds for scepticism about these findings and there is also contrary evidence that much apparent SHRM change – for example, the development of flexibility within UK manufacturing – cannot be defined meaningfully as evidence of SHRM.
- Much apparent SHRM change is more associated with old-fashioned management concerns like the control and mobilization of labour and cost-cutting rather than with the values of consensus, partnership and commitment associated at least with soft versions of SHRM.
- For some writers, the installation of SHRM-type initiatives of the sort associated with the high-performance bundles might actually have negative effects unless they contribute to the maintenance or development of the sort of deep social architectures which are seen to underpin the organizational capabilities or competences associated with the resource-based approach to SHRM. It is at least possible that some SHRM initiatives – downsizing, the move to out-sourcing, PRP, BPR etc., might

actually threaten some of the historic sources of organizational appropriability, for example by undermining employees' commitment.

- The real importance of SHRM may lie less in the practical empirical application and impact of SHRM elements and more in the ways SHRM has redefined many critical aspects of the modern organization – including the nature and identity of the new manager and employee.

## Discussion Questions

1. How should we set about establishing if SHRM 'works'?
2. What are the main findings from available evidence on the occurrence and impact of SHRM?
3. What are the strengths and weaknesses of this evidence?
4. What is your opinion, in the light of the materials in this chapter and elsewhere in the book, about the impact of SHRM?
5. In what ways and with what consequences has SHRM offered a new way of thinking about and knowing the modern organization and the modern employee?

## References

Ahlstrand, B. and Purcell, J. (1988) 'Employee relations strategy in the multi-divisional company', *Personnel Review*, vol. 17, no. 3, 3–11.

Armstrong, P. (1989) 'Limits and possibilities for HRM in an age of management accountancy', in J. Storey (ed.) *New Perspectives on Human Resource Management*, London: Routledge, 154–66.

Arthur, J. B. (1994) 'The link between business strategy and industrial relations systems in American steel minimills', *Industrial and Labor Relations Review* 45, 488–506.

Beaumont, P. (1993) *Human Resource Management*, London: Sage.

Beer, M., Spector, B., Lawrence, P. R., Mills, Q. N., and Walton, R. E. (1984) *Managing Human Assets*, New York: Free Press.

Blyton, P. and Turnbull, P. (eds) (1992) *Reassessing Human Resource Management*, London: Sage.

Brockner, J., Grover, S., O'Malley, M., Reed, T. F., and Glynn, M. A. (1993) 'Threat of future layoffs, self esteem and survivors' reactions', *Strategic Management Journal* 14, 153–66.

Chandler, A. D. (1977) *Strategy and Structure*, Cambridge, MA: MIT Press.

Child, J. (1987) 'Information technology, organization and response to strategic challenges', *California Management Review*, vol. 30, no. 1, 33–50.

Delaney, J. T., and Huselid, M. A. (1995) 'The impact of human resource management practices on perceptions of performance in for-profit and non-profit organisations', Paper presented to the Academy of Management Conference, Vancouver, August 6–9.

Delbridge, R. and Turnbull, P. (1992) 'Human resource maximisation: The management of labour under just-in-time manufacturing systems', in T. Blyton and P. Turnbull (eds) *Reassessing Human Resource Management*, 56–73.

Doherty, N. and Horsted, J. (1995) 'Helping survivors to stay on board', *People Management*, January 12, 26–31.
du Gay, P. (1992) 'Enterprise culture and the ideology of excellence', *New Formations*, vol. 13, Spring, 45–62.
—— and Salaman, G. (1992) 'The culture of the customer', *Journal of Management Studies*, vol. 29, no. 5, 45–61.
—— (1994) 'Colossal immodesties and hopeful monsters: Pluralism and organisational conduct', *Organization*, vol. 1, no. 2, 125–48.
—— and Salaman, G. (1996) 'Making up managers: Contemporary managerial discourse and the constitution of the "competent" manager', Report to ESRC.
——, —— and Rees, B. (1996) 'The conduct of management and the management of conduct: Contemporary managerial discourse and the constitution of the "competent" manager', *Journal of Management Studies*, vol. 33, no. 3, 263–82.
——, —— and —— (forthcoming) 'Making Up managers', *Journal of Management Studies.*
Dyer, L. and Reeves T. (1995) 'Human resource strategies and firm performance: What do we know and where do we need to go?', *International Journal of Human Resources Management*, vol. 6, no. 3, 656–70.
ESRC Centre for Organisation and Innovation, Institute of Work Psychology, University of Sheffield (1997) *The Use and Effectiveness of Modern Manufacturing Techniques, in the UK.*
Goold, M. and Campbell, A. (1986) 'Strategic decision-making: The corporate role', *Strategic Management Styles*, vol. 1, London Business School: Centre for Business Strategy.
—— and —— (1987) *Strategies and Styles: The Role of the Centre in Managing Diversified Corporations*, Oxford: Blackwell.
Gowler, D. and Legge, K. (1986) 'Images of employees in company reports – Do company chairmen view their most valuable asset as valuable?', *Personnel Review*, vol. 15, no. 5, 9–18.
Guest, D. E. (1989) 'Human resource management: Its implications for industrial relations and trade unions', in J. Storey (ed.) *New Perspectives on Human Resource Management*, London: Routledge, 41–55.
—— (1990) 'Human resource management and the American dream', *Journal of Management Studies*, vol. 27, no. 4, 378–97.
—— (1992) 'Right enough to be dangerously wrong', in G. Salaman et al. (eds) *Human Resource Strategies*, London: Sage, 5–20.
—— (1996) 'Human resource management, fit and performance', Paper given as ESRC/BUIRA Seminar Series on the Contribution of HR Strategy to Business Performance.
Halstead, R. (1996) 'Revenge is sweet', *Business Age*, vol. 4, no. 68, 28–36.
Hamel, G. and Prahalad C. K. (1991) 'Strategic intent', *Harvard Business Review*, May/June, 63–76.
Hendry, C. and Pettigrew, A. (1986) 'The practice of strategic human resource management', *Personnel Review*, vol. 15, no. 5, 3–8.
——, —— and Sparrow, P. (1988) 'Changing patterns of human resource management', *Personnel Management*, November, 37–41.
Henkoff, R. (1990) 'Cost cutting: How to do it right', *Fortune*, vol. 121, no. 8, 40–9.
Huselid, M. (1995) 'The impact of human resource management practices on turnover, productivity and corporate financial performance', *Academy of Management Journal*, vol. 38, no. 3, 635–72.
——, Jackson, S. E., and Schuler, R. S. (1995) 'The significance of human resource manage-

ment implementation effectiveness for corporate financial performance, Paper presented to the Academy of Management Conference, Vancouver, August 6–9.

Ichniowski, C. (1990) 'Human resource management systems and the performance of US manufacturing businesses', NBER Working Paper series 3449, Cambridge, MA: National Bureau of Economic Research

——, Shaw, K., and Prennushi, G. (1994) 'The effects of human resource management practices on productivity', Working Paper, Columbia University.

International Institute for Management Development (1997) *World Competitiveness Yearbook*, Switzerland.

Keenoy, T. (1990a) 'HRM: A case of the wolf in sheep's clothing?', *Personnel Review*, vol. 19, no. 2, 3–9.

—— (1990b) 'HRM: Rhetoric, reality and contradiction', *International Journal of Human Resource Management*, vol. 1, no. 3, 363–84.

—— and Anthony, P. (1992) 'HRM: Metaphor, meaning and morality', in T. Blyton and P. Turnbull (eds) *Reassessing Human Resource Management*, London: Sage, 233–60.

Legge, K. (1989) 'Human resource management: A critical analysis', in J. Storey (ed.) *New Perspectives on Human Resource Management*, London: Routledge, 19–40.

—— (1994) 'Rhetoric, reality and hidden agendas', in J. Storey (ed.) *Human Resource Management: A Critical Text*, London: Routledge, 33–62.

Mabey, C., Skinner, D. and Clark, T. (1998) *Experiencing Human Resource Management*, Oxford, Blackwell.

MacDuffie, J. P. (1995) 'Human resource bundles and manufacturing performance: Flexible production systems in the world auto industry', *Industrial Relations and Labor Review*, vol. 48, 197–221.

Marginson, P., Edwards P. K., and Martin R. et al. (1988) *Beyond the Workplace: Managing Industrial Relations in Multi-Establishment Enterprises*, Oxford: Blackwell.

McKinlay, A. and Starkey, A. (1988) 'Competitive strategies and organisational change', *Organisation Studies*, vol. 9, no. 4, 555–71.

Miller, P. (1989) 'Strategic HRM: What it is and what it is not', *Personnel Management*, February, 46–51.

Mueller, F. (1996) 'Human resources as strategic assets: An evolutionary resource-based theory', *Journal of Management Studies*, vol. 33, no. 6, 757–85

New, C. (1997) 'British factories forge ahead', *Independent on Sunday*, August 17.

Pollert, A. (1988) 'The flexible firm: Fixation of fact', *Work Employment Society*, vol. 2, no. 3, 281–316.

Purcell, J. (1989) 'The impact of corporate strategy on human resource management', in J. Storey (ed.) *New Perspectives on Human Resource Management*, London: Routledge, 67–91.

—— (1996) 'Human resource bundles of best practice: A utopian cul-de-sac?', Paper given at ESRC/BUIRA Seminar Series on the Contribution of HR Strategy to business Performance, 1996.

Rose, N. (1990) 'Governing the soul', Paper presented at Conference on The Values of the Enterprise Culture, University of Lancaster, 1989.

Rosenthal, P., Hill, S., and Peccei R. (1997) 'Checking out service: Evaluating excellence, HRM and TQM in retailing', *Work, Employment and Society*, vol. 11, no. 3, 481–503.

Sewell, G. and Atkinson, B. (1992) 'Empowerment or emasculation? Shopfloor surveillance in a total quality organisation', in P. Blyton and P. Turnbull (eds) *Reassessing Human Resource Management*, London: Sage, 97–115.

Sisson, K. and Sullivan, T. (1987) 'Management strategy and industrial relations', *Journal of Management Studies*, vol. 24, no. 5.

Storey, J. (1989) 'Introduction: from personnel management to human resource management' in J. Storey (ed.) *New Perspectives on Human Resource Management*, London: Routledge, 1–18.

—— and Sisson, K. (1993) *Managing Human Resources and Industrial Relations*, Buckingham: Open University Press.

Thompson, P. and Ackroyd, S. (1995) 'All quiet on the workplace front? A critique of recent trends in British industrial sociology', *Sociology*, vol. 29, no. 4, 615–33.

Willmott, H. (1993) 'Strength is ignorance: Slavery is freedom: Managing culture in modern organisations', *Journal of Management Studies*, vol. 30, no. 4, 515–52.

# Index